THE VERDICT OF PEACE

Britain Between Her Yesterday and the Future

THE VERDICT OF PEACE

Britain Between Her Yesterday and the Future

CORRELLI BARNETT

MACMILLAN

First published 2001 by Macmillan
an imprint of Pan Macmillan Ltd
Pan Macmillan, 20 New Wharf Road, London N1 9RR
Basingstoke and Oxford
Associated companies throughout the world
www.panmacmillan.com

ISBN 0 333 67982 2

1 3 5 7 9 8 6 4 2

A CIP catalogue record for this book is available from
the British Library.

Typeset by SetSystems Ltd, Saffron Walden, Essex
Printed and bound in Great Britain by
Mackays of Chatham plc, Chatham, Kent

For Jude

And in Memory of Paul

The moral of the work:

'I wish to dissipate if I can the idle dreams of those who are always telling you that the strength of England depends, sometimes they say upon its prestige, sometimes they say upon extending its Empire, or upon what it possesses beyond these shores. Rely upon it, the strength of Great Britain . . . is within the United Kingdom.'

William Gladstone

Contents

Contents

Acknowledgements

First and foremost, I wish to thank my wife Ruth for acting yet again as a first-class quartermaster and one-woman general staff, and also for her critical reading of the first draft of this book, which saved me from many typing errors and infelicities of phrasing. It is the simple truth that I could not have completed five years' work on this book without her devoted and unstinted support.

I wish to express my gratitude to my publisher and editor, Mr Jeremy Trevathan, for his support and forbearance during what has inevitably proved a long gestation, and for all he has done to promote the book's success. I would like particularly to thank Mr Nicholas Blake, Senior Desk Editor at Macmillan, for his meticulously detailed scrutiny of the text, which has saved me from many errors and anomalies.

I wish to express my gratitude to Ms Suzanne Reeve, who, as the then Secretary of the Economic and Social Research Council, first encouraged me to undertake the research that led to the present book as well as to *The Lost Victory*. I would also once again like to thank my agent, Mr Bruce Hunter, for all his shrewd advice, as well as all members of his team at David Higham Associates for their willing and efficient help.

The present book being in part the product of a research contract awarded to me by the Economic and Social Research Council, I wish to thank the Council for commissioning the work and the Council's staff for their cordial collaboration.

I must yet again express my indebtedness to the professional knowledge, courtesy and willing help of the Search Room staff at the Public Record Office, where so much of the research was carried out; to Miss Mary Kendall, the Librarian of Churchill College; to Mr Allen Packwood and his colleagues in the Churchill Archives Centre; to Mrs Gillian Hughes; and to the staffs of the following institutions: the University of East Anglia Library; the London Library; the Library of the Royal United Services Institute for Defence Studies; and the *Statistisches Bundesamt*.

I would like to record my appreciation of Dr Martin Campbell-Kelly's kindness in reading the draft chapter on the British computer and business-systems industry, and of Dr Walter Eltis's kindness in reading the draft chapter on 'Operation ROBOT', and thereby saving me from many howlers, though not from those that remain. I am also grateful for the generous advice of Sir Michael Alexander, Dr John Charmley, Mr David Clement, Dr B. M. M. Hardisty, Mr Donald Hindson, Herr Jost Lemmerich, Dame Pauline Neville-Jones, Dr Michael Sanderson, Mr Alan Smith, and Dr Doron Swade. I have further benefited from discussions with Professor Michael Gregory, Dr David Edgerton, and Dr Terence Kealey.

Every effort has been made to contact copyright holders of material reproduced in this book. If any have been inadvertently overlooked, the publishers will be pleased to make restitution at the earliest opportunity. I am indebted to the following for permission to quote from works or documents in their copyright:

Mr Winston Churchill: excerpt from a speech by Winston Churchill. British Institute of Management. Charles Babbage Institute Archives. The International Institute for Strategic Studies. Mr David Clement: letter to me. Dr B. M. M. Hardisty: letter to me Cassell: *The Memoirs of the Rt. Hon. Sir Anthony Eden*, by Sir Anthony Eden. Davis-Poynter: *Aneurin Bevan; A Biography*, vol. two: *1945–1960*. Hasler Publishing: *LEO: The First Business Computer*, by P. Bird. HarperCollins: *Mountbatten: the Official Biography*, by P. Ziegler. Macmillan: *The British General Election of 1951*, by D. Butler; *Tides of Fortune*, and *Riding the Storm*, by H. Macmillan. Oxford University Press: *Labour in Power 1945–1951*, by K. O. Morgan; *The Commonwealth and Suez*, by J. Eayrs, copyright © Oxford University Press 1964. The Department of Trade and Industry: *The History of the British Coal Industry*, by W. Ashworth. The Clarendon Press: *ICL: A Business and Technical History*, by M. Campbell-Kelly, copyright © Martin Campbell-Kelly 1989.

Acknowledgements

W. H. Allan: *British Rail after Beeching*, by G. Freeman. Chartwell-Bratt: *The Origins and Growth of Action Learning*, by R. Revans. Hutchinson: *Iain Macleod*, by R. Shepherd. Weidenfeld & Nicolson: *Attlee*, by K. Harris. Allen and Unwin: *Nationalized Industry and Public Ownership*, by W. A. Robson. The author also wishes to thank the following newspapers and periodicals for permission to quote from their columns: *The Coventry Evening Telegraph*, *The Daily Express*, *The Financial Times*, *The Daily Mirror*, *The Daily Telegraph*, *The Daily Worker (the People's Press Printing Society)*, *The [Glasgow] Herald*, *The Guardian*, *The Morning Advertiser*, *The Observer*, *The Sunday Telegraph*, *The Autocar*, *The Economist* and News International for material from *The Sunday Times*, copyright © Times Newspapers Ltd 1956.

Extracts from Crown Copyright material are reproduced with the Permission of the Controller of Her Majesty's Stationery Office.

Author's Preface

The Verdict of Peace brings to a conclusion three decades of research and authorship, being the final volume of the 'Pride and Fall' quartet, which narrates Britain's descent as a power from triumph in 1918 over Imperial Germany to humiliation in 1956 at Suez. Like its predecessors, it is an operational study: its purpose is to explain how and why between the outbreak of the Korean conflict in 1950 and the Suez debacle the British squandered the last of an irrecoverable opportunity to reinvent and reposition themselves as an industrial nation before their commercial competitors fully recovered from defeat and occupation.

The book – again like its predecessors – is written from the standpoint of 'Total Strategy', a concept first defined in the preface to *The Collapse of British Power* in 1972 as 'strategy conceived as encompassing all the factors relevant to preserving or extending the power and prosperity of a human group in the face of rivalry from other human groups.' The fundamental factor in the total strategy of a nation lies in industrial and commercial performance, for it is this which determines power and wealth alike. Yet that performance is in turn governed by a nation's character: its skills, energy, ambition, discipline, adaptability, and enterprise; its beliefs and myths. Moreover, national character also governs other key factors making for total-strategic strength: cohesiveness and efficiency in social and political structures; dexterity, foresight and willpower in the conduct of foreign and domestic policies.

The verdict of peace, as returned by the historical record and documented in this book, is that the British people a decade after the Second World War were deficient in every one of these qualities

xv

and categories, whatever may have been their personal and civic virtues as citizens of a free and stable democracy. They were short of skills owing to a defective education and a training system long overdue for reconstruction. They lacked adaptability and ambition in comparison with the Americans: lacked energy, discipline and enterprise in comparison with the West Germans as well as with the Americans. Their industrial, social, educational and bureaucratic structures alike were disjointed, desperately slow in decision and action, and deeply resistant to change. Their beliefs and myths about themselves as a nation were the misleading products of romantic historical nostalgia and unshakeable self-satisfaction. And dexterity, foresight and willpower were qualities notably absent from politicians and bureaucrats of appeasing temper who muddled forward from one crisis to another, their minds still prisoners of Britain's recent past as a great imperial and industrial power.

It is the central theme of *The Verdict of Peace* that the psychological legacy of this recent past served in the 1950s as a general drag-chain holding back the process of national adaptation. The legacy explains why governments strove to perpetuate Britain's traditional world role with the resources of a now fragile economy; why they entangled Britain in the Korean War; why they embarked on a grandiose rearmament programme to the detriment of exports and industrial investment, and did so even when old trade rivals were again challenging Britain in world markets. It also explains the British people's complacent belief in their industrial excellence. For they still believed the boastful propaganda about their technological achievements during the Second World War; they still cherished an older, Victorian faith that in manufactures 'British Is Best'.

The book examines other manifestations of the psychological legacy from the past. People and governing elite alike remained in thrall to the myth of Commonwealth, that 1930s rebranding of a British Empire which itself represented a contrived late-Victorian packaging of a historical ragbag of colonies, white and black. The civil service, the managements of industry, and the trade unions still remained in the 1950s essentially Victorian in character, ethos and even operating methods; Victorian too in their mutual suspicions and antipathies. The intelligentsia and the educational establishment still lay under the spell of high-minded Victorian cultural values, with the result that academic proficiency continued to be prized above practical capability, the humanities above science, 'pure' science above technology, and technological pioneering per se above eventual market success.

The past even influenced the attitude of governments towards advanced technology, for they saw it primarily as a novel means of promoting a traditional end: Britain's status as a world power. In consequence, they misdirected scarce R&D resources into ambitious, costly but unprofitable and often abortive projects, both civil and military.

The Verdict of Peace therefore finds the British people and their leaders guilty of failing to confront total-strategic reality, and instead finally confirming Britain in a fateful pattern of national overambition coupled with industrial underperformance. The consequences still reverberate in the twenty-first century.

Correlli Barnett
East Carleton, Norfolk and
Churchill College, Cambridge
August 2000

Note to the Reader

For most topics the 'real-time' narrative of this book spans the period from the outbreak of the Korean War in 1950 to the 1957 aftermath of the Suez adventure. In the case of industrial relations, management, business systems and computers, and education-and-training, the 'real-time' narrative spans the period 1944–1957, with brief glances forward at later developments. For the root causes of contemporary problems the book searches back through the nineteenth century, and, in the case of industrial relations, to the late eighteenth century.

Although *The Verdict of Peace* is the fourth book in the 'Pride and Fall' quartet, it is written as a free-standing narrative, with subjects that were dealt with in detail in earlier books being here summarized.

PART ONE

The Turning Point

There was no evidence that this adventure [the North Korean invasion of South Korea] contained the seeds of a major war and it was important to cope with it in such a manner as to restrict it to minor proportions.

(Report of briefing given by George Kennan,
US Under-Secretary of State, 26 June 1950)

We should emerge from the rearmament period with inadequate reserves, with no assurance of further U.S. aid, with our export markets reduced, with a continuous and possibly increased claim on our resources for defence, with German and Japanese competition at full blast and finally, with industrial efficiency in a relatively worse position compared with the United States than it is now.

(R. A. Butler, Chancellor of the Exchequer,
30 November 1951)

Even new industries like motor vehicles shrank from competing abroad for exports, and preferred to swaddle themselves in the eiderdown of the home market. And so throughout the 1920s, while other nations were enjoying a boom, Britain remained in chronic depression, with unemployment never falling below one and a quarter million.[9]

Like the elderly in retirement she relied more than ever on the income from investments (in her case, overseas) made in a happier past. But between 1929 and 1932 the world slump more than halved that income and the return from 'invisibles'.[10] When sterling came off the gold standard in 1931, it signified the final snuffing-out of the post-war hope that Britain might be restored to her old dominating place at the centre of a world network of finance and trade.

Economic stagnation meant stagnant revenues and hence tight national budgets. The resulting desire to hold down defence expenditure had fitted in all too conveniently with the naive belief prevailing in the 1920s among politicians and public alike that disarmament and the League of Nations could together ensure the peace of the world. By 1931 the armed forces, especially the Royal Navy, had been emasculated: impotent, as the Chiefs of Staff repeatedly warned, either to protect the global sprawl of the British Empire or to fulfil Britain's altruistic new obligation under the Covenant of the League to halt aggression anywhere in the world, by force if need be.[11]

And so for the National Government in 1931 there could be no question of resorting to a 1914-style ultimatum as a solution to the dilemma created by the Japanese occupation of Manchuria. Instead Britain fell back on moralizing at Japan from the pulpit of the League of Nations.[12]

Caught in similar dilemmas in 1935, when Fascist Italy invaded Abyssinia in defiance of the League, and 1936, when Nazi Germany openly breached the Versailles and Locarno Treaties by sending a terrifying advance guard of three battalions across the Rhine bridges into the Rhineland demilitarized zone, Britain simply took refuge in diplomatic fudging.[13] For the contradiction between the facade of British world power and the reality of vulnerable overstretch was sharpening year by year. In 1937 the Chiefs of Staff tersely summed

7

up the predicament in which Britain was now trapped:

> we are in the position of having threats at both ends of the Empire
> from strong military powers, i.e., Germany and Japan, while in the
> centre we have lost our traditional security in the Mediterranean . . .
> So long as that position remains unresolved diplomatically, only very
> great military and financial strength can give the Empire security.[14]

Doubly vain hope! The rearmament programme launched in 1936 was as large as the British economy could bear, and yet even when complete would not provide armed forces powerful enough to protect the Empire from the worldwide triple threats defined by the Chiefs of Staff. Moreover, the rearmament programme itself constituted a fresh audit of British technological capability, exposing it as yet again deficient.[15] In consequence Britain had to turn to huge imports of sophisticated foreign equipment, from machine tools to weaponry. In this way, however, rearmament only locked Britain into an even deeper quandary, for the cost in foreign exchange of these imports ran her straight towards a balance of payments crisis. Far from there existing the 'very great' financial strength wistfully mentioned by the Chiefs of Staff, it had become doubtful by 1938 whether even the Royal Air Force peacetime programme could be financed beyond 1939–40.[16]

In the midst of such worries had erupted the first direct threat to the European balance of power since 1914, when Nazi Germany's invasion of Austria in spring 1938 was followed in the summer by ostentatious preparations for an attack on Czechoslovakia. The National (predominantly Conservative) Government now found itself pinioned in a dilemma comparable to that which had faced the Liberal Government on the eve of the Great War.[17]

But though the dilemmas were comparable, Britain's circumstances were not. In 1914 she had taken it for granted that the whole Empire would obediently accept her decision whether or not to go to war; in 1938 she was strongly pressed by the now independent Dominions to avoid conflict at all costs: hardly a moral reinforcement. In 1914 the Liberal Government had only to concern itself with Germany and the European crisis, for the British Empire lay under no threat from other powers. This meant that Britain could concentrate her naval strength against Germany. But in 1938 the National Government had also to bear in mind the looming Japanese threat to British possessions in the Far East and ultimately to Australia and New Zealand. There was also the menace of the Italian navy (Fascist Italy now being Nazi Germany's ally) to the imperial route through the Mediterranean. Yet to parry these triple threats Britain could only deploy sixteen capital ships, all but two of them at least twenty years old, compared with the twenty capital ships in the Grand Fleet at Scapa alone in 1914, all of them less than seven years old. And in 1914 Britain could mobilize a well-equipped, superbly trained expeditionary force for deployment alongside the French Army; in 1938 there existed no such thing.

How in this crisis could Britain's historic role of great European power be reconciled with her national weakness and her total-strategic overextension? The Prime Minister, Neville Chamberlain, had a ready answer to the dilemma: negotiate a permanent European peace settlement with Hitler at Czechoslovakia's expense, and with one bound John Bull would be free. This brilliant wheeze suffered from one flaw: it was totally unrealistic, given the well-known nature of Adolf Hitler – as was cruelly proved in March 1939 when Hitler, evidently not 'appeased' at Munich by being given the Sudetenland (containing the Czech defence system), occupied the hapless rump of Czechoslovakia.

Now it was accepted in London and even in Dominion capitals that the next time the German army marched across a frontier Britain would have to go to war. Yet this could only serve finally to call her bluff as a world and imperial power. In spring 1939 the Chiefs of Staff pointed out:

> We are considering a position in which we, allied to France, would be engaged in war with Germany and Italy simultaneously and when Japan would also be a potential enemy . . . The British Empire and France would thus be threatened at home, in the Mediterranean and in the Far East at the same time, and it would be hard to choose a worse geographical combination of enemies.[18]

The Chiefs warned that the Allies' only hope of victory lay in a war protracted over several years. But the Treasury had a contradictory warning to impart: 'if we were under the impression that we were as well able as in 1914 to conduct a long war we were burying our heads in the sand.'[19]

In other words, while Britain could only hope to win a long war, she could only afford a short one. Here was the worst dilemma of all, one from which there could be no escape. For once a war broke out, Britain's total-strategic bankruptcy must inevitably follow. And so it did.[20] The collapse of France, abandoned diplomatically by Britain throughout the 1920s and 1930s and to a large extent abandoned militarily in 1940, left Britain alone (except for the Empire's moral support and modest military succour) to wage a protracted and costly war against Germany and Italy. By March 1941 Britain's reserves of gold and dollars were utterly at an end. Henceforth it was only free American supplies of military and industrial technology, oil and food under the Lend-Lease Act that enabled Britain to fight on, or even nourish her people.

Back in the days of the grand European coalitions against Bonaparte, England in her swelling wealth had subsidized penurious allies. Now Britain was the client state with the outstretched hand.

The collapse of the actual structure of British power – more accurately the facade – swiftly followed in 1941–42, when the Japanese humiliatingly evicted imperial forces from all Britain's Far Eastern possessions up to the frontier of India, and the responsibility for defending Australia and New Zealand passed to America.

Yet from these twenty years of total-strategic overstretch and their catastrophic denouement the Labour Government which came to power after Germany's surrender in 1945 had learned nothing. Rather than make a start at winding up Britain's burdensome world and imperial role, they strove to renew it and perpetuate it – and this at a time when Britain, struggling to recover economically from the war, again relied on American loans and handouts.[21] To adapt Samuel Johnson on second marriages, it was a triumph of hope over experience.

In an imperially pink haze of nostalgia, the Government (and especially the Foreign Secretary, that working-class patriot Ernest Bevin) saw the Commonwealth and the Sterling Area as assets conferring top-table 'prestige' and 'influence' and 'status' (all favourite words) on Britain, rather than as the strainful obligations that they were in fact.

But then the Government was not alone in believing, in the euphoric aftermath of victory, that as a power Britain could have a future like her past. So also believed the Conservative Party in opposition; so also believed the British people. The mental chains of imperial history shackled them all.

Although the Labour Government did at least dump India in 1947, it tenaciously but indiscriminately preserved all the rest of Britain's traditional military and naval commitments in the Mediterranean, Middle East, and Far East — on the score that these were the essential buttresses of (in Bevin's words in 1948 about the Middle East) Britain's 'position as a great Power'.[22]

Moreover, unlike before 1914 and before 1939, Britain was also maintaining land and air forces on the continent of Europe, now the evident key to her own security. In 1950 the cost of bearing this double strategic burden of Europe and the world role amounted to 7.7 per cent of gross national product — and about half of this was accounted for by the world role.[23] Every year the Cabinet anxiously debated how maintaining global military commitments might be reconciled with economizing on the defence budget. The resulting fudges merely meant that as the Lord President of the Council, Herbert Morrison, astutely pointed out in 1949, Britain was in danger of 'paying more than we could afford for defences that are nevertheless inadequate, or even illusory.'[24]

In fact, the gulf between British pretensions and British resources was now far wider than even in the 1930s. For 1950 marked the tenth year that Britain had depended on American loans or handouts to keep her national life going.

When Lend-lease was ended in 1945 the Labour Government had successfully cadged a loan of $3.75 billion in Washington to tide Britain over the temporary pecuniary embarrassment caused by a ruinous war. This loan was supposed to last until 1951 but in fact had been mostly blued by 1948. However, in that year the Americans coughed up again in the form of the European Recovery Programme (Marshall Aid), of which Britain by 1950 was receiving the largest share of any European country.[25]

The truth was that even now, five years after the war, Britain's own economy could not carry unaided her self-imposed role as (to quote the Minister of Defence in 1949) 'a centre of world influence and power.'[26] For Britain's European trade competitors were now on their way to recovery from defeat and occupation, and fast eroding Britain's post-war head-start in world markets.[27] Barely five weeks before the North Korean invasion of South Korea the Chancellor of the Exchequer, Hugh Gaitskell, had warned his colleagues that prospects for exports were far from brilliant.[28] In the case of engineering goods, Gaitskell wrote, 'present assumptions are already optimistic on the basis of any previous experience, and in some sectors, notably that of motor vehicles, it seems extremely unlikely that even the present level can be maintained.'[29] And just three weeks after the Korean crisis broke, the Chancellor proved just as gloomy about the general prospects for the balance of payments, writing in regard to the Sterling Area as a whole that 'if Marshall Aid was ignored, the year 1950–51 was expected to show a dollar deficit of over $200 million.'[30]

The untimely march of the North Korean army into South Korea therefore shut Britain into the trickiest of all her twentieth-century total-strategic dilemmas. For whereas in 1914 she had in reality been a first-class power, and in 1938–39 at least the dominant voice in an alliance of near-equals, she was now hopelessly out-weighted by America's plenitude of wealth and power. The truth therefore was that in contrast to 1914 or even 1938–39 she enjoyed in 1950 little real independence of decision.

This was why the painfulness of the Labour Government's predicament in the hectic days and weeks following the telegram of 24 June 1950 from the Washington Embassy to the Foreign Office derived not so much from the onward march of the North Korean army in the field as from the onward march, tambourine in hand, of crusading anti-Communist zeal in Washington.

On 26 June the Prime Minister, Clement Attlee, and the Minister of State for Foreign Affairs, Kenneth Younger, consulted the Foreign Secretary, Ernest Bevin, in hospital where he was recovering from an operation. They agreed that Britain must back America in calling for action by the United Nations.[31] Next day a report came in from Sir Oliver Franks, British Ambassador in Washington, about an 'informal' briefing of North Atlantic Treaty ambassadors at the State Department. George Kennan, American Under-Secretary of State, read to the ambassadors a draft statement by President Truman announcing air and maritime support for the South Korean forces, and the dispatch of the US 7th Fleet to cover Formosa (where Chiang Kai-shek's Nationalist regime had taken refuge from the Communist victors in the Chinese civil war). More ominously, the statement attributed armed aggression anywhere in the Far East to 'centrally directed Communist Imperialism'.[32] Yet Kennan himself briefed his audience that

> the U.S. Administration did not consider that the Russians [sic] were preparing to enter the war. There were signs that they intended to leave themselves a way out and it was a reasonable assumption therefore that the Russians were merely making an important probing. There was no evidence that this adventure contained the seeds of a major war and it was important to cope with it in such a manner as to restrict it to minor proportions.[33]

And of course there could be no better way of so restricting it than for the US President to make a public accusation about 'centrally directed Communist Imperialism'. But, as telegraphed to London by Franks, Kennan had further inconsistencies to offer. On the one hand the US Government 'did not attach overwhelming importance to strategic position of South Korea.' But on the other:

> The symbolic significance of preservation of the Republic was however tremendous, for if the world should notice weakness in the handling of this problem, the repercussions would be great, first in Japan and then all over the Orient . . . if Korea went, Formosa would be next . . .[34]

When Franks asked him what was meant by air and sea support for South Korea, Kennan answered, according to Franks, that 'such help as could be given by MacArthur would be supplied from facilities within the Pacific Command. He added that he would like to make it clear that MacArthur would not allow U.S. action to be pressed north of the 38th Parallel [the dividing line between the two Koreas] . . .'

13

All this occasioned the British Cabinet much unease when it met that day. Was it expedient, they asked themselves, to attribute the aggression, as the US proposed to do, to 'centrally-directed Communist Imperialism?'[35] They recognized that by using such terms 'the U.S. Government was deliberately taking the major risk of making it clear to the Soviet Union that they were resolved to put a stop to armed aggression.' However, the Americans 'were doubtless influenced by the consideration that, as had been amply demonstrated by the events preceding the Second World War, it would be easier to make such a stand in the earlier, rather than the later, stages of imperialist expansion by a totalitarian State . . .'[36]

For it had now become a Western myth that if only the democracies and the League of Nations had 'stood up' to Japan's occupation of Manchuria in 1931 and Italy's invasion of Abyssinia in 1935, then Nazi Germany would not have tried to expand in Europe from 1936 onwards. This myth was and is strategic nonsense, for armed intervention – possibly even leading to protracted war – by France and Britain against Japan or Italy could only have left them critically weakened in the face of Germany, as the Chiefs of Staff warned at the time.[37] What general would divert forces to the defence of a peripheral front on the grounds that this would deter the enemy from attacking a strategically vital objective?

The Cabinet finally decided at this meeting on 27 June to support a new US resolution in the Security Council calling for members of the UN to come to the aid of the South Koreans, but at the same time to urge the US *not* to mention other 'Communist encroachments' in Asia, nor to refer explicitly to 'centrally directed Soviet aggression.'[38] However, President Truman simply took no notice of anxious British fingers plucking his sleeve, announcing that same day that the 7th Fleet would protect Formosa on the score that 'the attack upon Korea makes it plain beyond all doubt that Communism has passed beyond the bounds of subversion to conquer independent nations and will now use armed invasion and war . . .'[39]

On this busy day of 27 June the Head of the American Department of the Foreign Office, Robert Scott, met the Chiefs of Staff to brief them about the Cabinet's decisions and solicit their advice both about the military situation in Korea and about what measures

Britain should take, irrespective of whether or not the American resolution was passed by the Security Council.[40] The First Sea Lord, Admiral Sir Bruce Fraser, reported that the Royal Navy had one light fleet carrier, two cruisers, and four destroyers in Japanese waters. The Chief of Air Staff, Air Chief Marshal Sir John Slessor, said that the Royal Air Force had no squadrons in Japan, that it would be logistically impossible to send a fighter squadron to Japan from Hong Kong, and that in any case 'it would be wrong from a military point of view to reduce our forces in Hong Kong and Malaya.' The meeting moreover concurred that 'in view of the army's commitments elsewhere in South East Asia [meaning especially the campaign in Malaya, a valuable asset because of its dollar-earning tin and rubber, against Chinese Communist guerrillas] it would be very difficult for us to send land reinforcements.'

And so the Chiefs reckoned that 'the most the United Kingdom could do would be to send a naval force on the lines suggested by the First Sea Lord.' Next day the Cabinet Defence Committee, in endorsing this proposal, also recommended that Britain use her influence on the Commonwealth 'to persuade them to make similar *token* [added emphasis] contributions . . .'[41] This cautious commitment was signalled to Marshal of the Royal Air Force Lord Tedder (Chairman of the British Joint Services Mission in Washington), along with a key proviso: 'Important that no British forces should participate in operations relating to Formosa.'[42] For Whitehall was already anxious lest Britain, with Hong Kong at Communist China's military mercy, be drawn into any confrontation between America and China over Formosa.

Thus far Britain, both as a European state entangled in Asian affairs because of its colonies and military 'presences' and as a debtor state with a cash-flow problem, had made a sensibly minimum response to the UN/US call for aid to the South Koreans. The Foreign Office nonetheless thought that the response offered an opportunity to wheedle Washington into greater appreciation of Britain's standing as a 'world power'. After all, was it not because of this standing that Britain disdained to take part in closer European integration, as America would wish? On 30 June the Office's American Department expressed the hope to Franks that he would use the prompt British offer of naval forces 'to counteract U.S.

criticism of His Majesty's Government's policy in relation to Europe and the "foot dragging" issue generally':[43]

> There could not be a more useful demonstration of the United Kingdom's capacity to act as a world power with the support of the Commonwealth and of its quickness to move when actions rather than words are necessary. It would be both unjust and short-sighted if the U.S. Government in return were now, owing to certain pre-conceived and ill-founded notions about European integration, to reduce their assistance to us under E.R.P and so weaken our position and our ability to play a world part in defence of freedom.

By the first days of July, as MacArthur whipped American troops from the soft life of an occupation force in Japan into battle in Korea, the British Government was beginning to grapple with the much wider questions raised by the North Korean invasion. First and foremost, how far were the Soviet Union and/or China implicated? After all, judgement as to this would bear directly on the American belief that there existed a centrally directed Communist global strategy of aggression. Secondly, if in the grip of this belief the United States became involved in war with China in defence of Chiang Kai-shek's regime in Formosa, what would be the consequences for Britain and Hong Kong?

On 3 July a Foreign Office memorandum on US policy towards Formosa observed that 'it is not yet clear, on the present information available, whether the Central People's Government [of China] were fully consulted in advance [about the North Korean attack], or . . . whether they were possibly in complete ignorance of it or at any rate of its timing . . .'[44] As late as May, the memorandum pointed out, it had been the common British and American aim to prevent the alienation of [Communist] China from the West and prevent her falling under Soviet domination. But it was evident that the United States now considered China to be under such domination – hence the open US hostility.[45] Yet the Chinese had refrained from speaking of British 'imperialism' in regard to Hong Kong, Malaya or Korea. It was therefore in the British interest, argued the memorandum, to 'maintain some foothold in China . . . provided we can still do so without sacrificing our ability publicly to indicate our solidarity with the U.S. in the wider aspects of their Far Eastern policy . . .' This was clearly going to call for a feat of diplomatic agility that would test even the Oxbridge-honed mental athletes of the Foreign Office. But in any case, comfortingly reckoned the memorandum, a Chinese move against Hong Kong was unlikely.[46]

As for the Soviet Union, the Chiefs of Staff reported on 7 July that they had 'no intelligence at present of Soviet intentions to start a major war in the near future,' and that they therefore believed that 'Communist aggression . . . will conform to the "war by proxy" technique.'[47] The British Ambassador in Moscow, Sir David Kelly, equally guessed that the Soviet Union wished to keep its distance from the Korean conflict.[48] Even Kennan at his initial briefing of ambassadors at the State Department had acknowledged that 'there was no evidence that this adventure contained the seeds of a major war'.

But meanwhile MacArthur was deploying the US 24th Infantry Division in support of the already disintegrating South Korean army. On 5 and 6 July 1950 the North Koreans, in a renewal of their offensive, inflicted on two task forces of the division the kind of rout the British experienced at Japanese hands in Malaya in 1941–2.[49] As the American commitment to the campaign grew pell-mell, the United States looked to her allies for soldiers. As early as 3 July the British Minister of Defence was asking the Chiefs of Staff for their opinion of a suggestion (apparently from General Omar Bradley, the US Chairman of the Joint Chiefs of Staff) that Britain might supply a token land force.[50] The Chiefs proved far from enthusiastic. The Vice-Chief of the Imperial General Staff, Major-General C. D. Brownjohn, opined that no transfers could be made of air or land forces from Malaya or Hong Kong. As for the Middle East, British forces there had already been reduced. In Brownjohn's view, 'we could in fact be said to be holding the ring for the Americans in the Middle East just as we had been doing for some time in South East Asia.'[51] Nor was he keen on sending troops from the strategic reserve in the United Kingdom: 'He considered that to send such a force from the United Kingdom would be fundamentally unsound and would be playing into Russian hands by dispersing our forces . . .'

On 5 July the Chiefs repeated these points in a formal report to the Cabinet Defence Committee.[52] A briefing note for the Prime

Minister[53] drew his attention to the salient point of the report: 'The Chiefs of Staff reiterated the view that it would be militarily unsound to make available any land or air forces for the Korean campaign. They support this view with detailed Orders of Battle which are attached to this paper as appendices . . .'

It was now up to the politicians to make what they would of the Chiefs of Staff's clear-cut advice that 'it would be militarily unsound to make available any land or air forces for the Korean campaign.'

Next day, 6 July, in the forenoon, the Prime Minister presided over a meeting of the Cabinet Defence Committee, at which the Minister of Defence, Emmanuel Shinwell, was present and which was attended by the Vice-Chief of Naval Staff, the Vice-Chief of the Imperial General Staff and the Chief of Air Staff. In a thorough tour d'horizon of the situation in Korea, the military men had this to say about Britain's readiness for war:

> . . . our present defence policy was only acceptable on the assumption that there would be a period of warning of 18 months or more. It was clear from events in Korea that it was more than possible that there would be little, if any, warning. In these circumstances the peace-time forces maintained by the United Kingdom were hardly more than a bluff.[54]

A bluff! So this was the end-product of five years of defence budgets averaging twice the proportion of GNP any other NATO member, and equal to the proportion spent on defence at the peak of Britain's pre-war rearmament. How could this be? The orders of battle appended to the Chiefs of Staff's report to the Defence Committee give the answer. Money which might have produced a battle-ready field army plus a tactical air force for Europe and a fighting navy for the Atlantic sea-lanes had been spent instead on maintaining the garrisons, flag-showing squadrons and costly bases demanded by the world role.[55]

In the present circumstances, the Defence Committee could hardly do otherwise than accept the Chiefs' advice and decide 'that no land or air forces should be made available for Korea.'[56]

In the afternoon the Prime Minister reported this decision to the full Cabinet:

In view of the risks we were exposed to elsewhere in the Far East and South-East Asia, it was proposed that no further United Kingdom forces should be sent to Korea [beyond the limited naval force already committed] . . . It was specially important at the present time that preoccupation with Korea should not divert attention from other danger-spots in these areas; and also that we should not allow the situation in the East generally to blind us to the risks to which we were exposed in Europe.[57]

After the Cabinet had duly taken note of the Defence Committee's decision, the Prime Minister rounded off this full day of 6 July by sending a telegram, barren of immediate result, to the US President proposing detailed joint military and political discussions in order that the two countries could plan in concert.[58]

But already, on 10 July, the United States had shown the degree of its interest in consultation between allies by unilaterally hi-jacking total political and military command of what it itself had initiated as *United Nations* action in support of South Korea, and appointing MacArthur as Commander-in-Chief of the United Nations Command. At the same time it rejected a proposal by the UN Secretary-General that overall direction should be vested in a UN 'Committee on Coordination for the assistance of Korea'.[59]

With the United States now barging up the international field like a American football player monstrous in padded armour, it was time for even those welterweights who believed themselves still heavyweights to become alarmed as to the likely course of the game. On 12 July, Pierson Dixon, Deputy Under-Secretary at the Foreign Office, minuted Bevin after meeting the Chiefs of Staff that the Chiefs were absolutely against British military involvement in defence of Korea, and were urging that a warning be given to the United States Government about Britain's 'considerable misgivings' in regard to American policy, especially over Formosa.

For by now it was Formosa as much as Korea that was causing the flutters in London. According to the Chiefs as reported by Dixon, American action with the Chinese over Formosa would have 'repercussions' which would enlarge the area of conflict and might indeed lead to a general war . . .':[60]

From a military point of view [Dixon further quoted the Chiefs as telling him] we consider it essential to tell the United States that the United Kingdom are [sic] in no position to wage a general war in the Far East or to defend these islands. Nor do we consider that Europe could offer any effective defence.

From a political point of view an outbreak or development of war on the issue of Formosa would find the anti-Communist Powers divided.[61]

While the Chiefs recognized the dangers to Anglo-American relations of so bluntly warning the United States, they thought it had to be done. However, the Foreign Secretary had already instructed the British Ambassador in Washington to express his misgivings to Acheson, especially about Formosa:

I think that Mr Acheson and the United States Government should appreciate, and I put it to them very frankly, the way I see the situation as follows. Whereas the United States have the whole-hearted backing of world opinion in the courageous initiative they took to deal with the aggression in Korea, I do not believe they could rely on the same support for their declared policy in connexion with Formosa . . .[62]

Acheson's reply to this démarche serves to reveal how far he and the State Department were now moved by moral passion rather than guided by strategic appreciation of state interest:[63]

1 We have faced squarely a calculated act of aggression and in so doing we are profoundly convinced that we are acting for the protection of the entire free world. The future peace of the world in our view hangs directly upon the success we expect to achieve in defeating the first overt act of aggression since the end of the war.

2 . . . We believe the tragic history of the 30's demonstrates beyond any doubt that the sole hope of preserving the peace of the world is to halt before they spread initial acts of aggression of this character.[64]

Next day the American Ambassador to the Court of St James's, Lewis Douglas, conveyed to Bevin a rebuke from Acheson the terms of which should have enlightened the British as to the truth both about their own importance and about the nature of the cherished 'Special Relationship':

> I have been asked particularly to emphasise Mr Acheson's view that the implications of your message and its possible consequences on the relationship between your country and mine might become very serious indeed.[65]

Within the Foreign Office the tone of Acheson's message and of Douglas's 'obscurely worded menace'[66] was judged to be 'characteristic of the Americans when under the stress of emotion. It reflects the mood when the Americans feel that they are shouldering the burdens of the world and are being criticised by others whose burden they are carrying.'[67] On 14 July Bevin, that bruiser of a working man, resorted to soothing Acheson like a suitor in a personal telegram via the Washington embassy. Addressing the need to remove 'any misunderstanding', Bevin wrote that he knew he could explain without troubling their relationship 'exactly why we have been seriously worried here about the implications of the President's declaration about Formosa.' However – gentle reproach this time – he was sorry that

> it was not possible for you, no doubt owing to the speed of events, to consult us in advance on a step which is of such close concern to us, particularly in view of the undertakings which we exchanged when you and I met in Washington in last September and again in London in May to consult on matters affecting China. We are, as you know, in a very vulnerable position in Hong Kong, and we have vast Chinese communities in Malaya where we have a long drawn campaign on our hands . . .[68]

But the issue of Formosa was to continue to divide the two countries. As Sir Pierson Dixon shrewdly wrote, there was 'a good deal of muddled and wishful thinking' in Washington with regard to China.[69] During the Second World War the United States had displayed a weird solicitude for, and weirder faith in, Chiang Kai-shek's corrupt and incompetent Kuomintang regime. Even now, in 1950, Washington's influential 'China lobby' refused to accept the reality that Chiang Kai-shek had been totally defeated, and that all mainland China was now ruled by the Communist 'People's

Government'. Unfortunately, the US Administration shared this wilful myopia, coupling it with ideological hostility to Communist China.

Such prejudice was to wreck whatever chance there might have been to bring about a quick end to the fighting in Korea by diplomatic means. The British Ambassador in Moscow, Sir David Kelly, reported on 13 July after a meeting with Gromyko, the Soviet Foreign Minister, that there might be a possibility either that 'they [the Soviet Government] are looking for a peaceful solution' or that they 'have not in fact made up their minds.'[70] Five days later Kelly signalled the Foreign Office that the Soviet Government 'could not be talked into calling off North Koreans without *quid pro quo*.'[71] The evident *quid pro quo* was the admission of Communist China to the UN Security Council in place of the rump Nationalist regime in Formosa. This had already been proposed by India. It would be, after all, merely a recognition of a political fact. However, on 18 July the British Cabinet agreed that the Soviet proposal of a deal could not be accepted, on the somewhat naive grounds that there was 'no necessary connection between the stopping of aggression in Korea and the admission of the People's Government of China to the Security Council . . .'[72] But the real reason was, as Kelly acknowledged, that 'we cannot offer any *quid pro quo*'[73] – meaning because of America's ideological intransigence.

For the most dangerous factor in the present international crisis lay in the profound American conviction that the United States was not simply the latest in a succession of imperial powers but instead a moral mission. The roots of this conviction can be traced back via the United States constitution, inspired as it was by the optimistically liberal principles of the eighteenth-century Enlightenment, to the very founding of the original seventeenth-century colonies as Puritan experiments in living righteously.

By now, a fortnight into July 1950, it was beginning to dawn on Whitehall and Downing Street just what the aid to South Korea so blithely voted in the Security Council on 25 June at America's urging might entail in the event. The Cabinet Defence Committee sombrely concluded that 'in view of the American intention to push the North Koreans back to the 38th Parallel, it was evident that the Americans would become involved in a protracted and considerable operation . . .'[74] The Committee took glum note that the United States was already starting on the mobilization of the National Guard and of industry as well:

> It was desirable [minuted the Committee] that the possibility of similar action should be examined in the United Kingdom, and the Chiefs of Staff should consider the full implications of the situation in which the Americans now found themselves of the probability of a long and costly campaign in Korea . . . and to report, in consultation with the Joint War Production Committee, what measures would be required to get our own forces into appropriate shape . . .[75]

As Air Chief Marshal Sir John Slessor pointed out in a letter to a colleague (and passed on to the Prime Minister, Clement Attlee), the Americans might even have to re-invade Korea:

> Indeed [wrote Slessor] it is somewhat bizarre that, to liberate a country about which no-one cares very much (except on a point of principle), and restore a regime which was a pretty rotten one, the United Nations should have to undertake a major effort which cannot fail to weaken their ability to meet other 'Koreas' elsewhere – to say nothing of a major Soviet attack.[76]

This could hardly be bettered as a succinct analysis of the scrape into which the United States was propelling itself and its dollar-dependent satellites such as Britain. Yet bizarre though the scrape might be, every passing week – even every passing day – saw these satellites haplessly dragged deeper into it. As the Prime Minister's Private Secretary, W. S. Hunt, minuted on 15 July, the British problem with regard to contributing a land force to the campaign was

> essentially political rather than military. Do the political arguments in favour of sending a token land force outweigh, first, the difficulties of sending anything at all, and second, the fact that the token force would be so small that it would have little or no military importance?[77]

The question was now the more urgent because Lord Tedder and Sir Oliver Franks were shortly due to hold talks with the State and Defense Departments in Washington, thanks to President Truman's condescending response to a request from Attlee. Franks himself warned that the 'wrong way to handle the matter would be by sending a purely negative response to the appeal of the Secretary-General [of the UN for military aid to South Korea] without prior discussion with the Americans.'[78] Unfortunately Franks himself shared London's twin delusions that there did exist a 'special relationship' between Britain and the United States beyond mere sentiment (perhaps partly because he was a personal friend of Dean Acheson, the Secretary of State), and that Britain remained a first-class world power in fact as well as facade. He wrote to Attlee on 17 July to say that he regarded the President's agreement to the Prime Minister's request for talks 'as the assertion by us and the acceptance by the United States of our partnership in world affairs.'[79]

> This would have been impossible three or even two years ago: then we were one of a queue of European countries. Now, with new strength and vitality in our association within the Commonwealth, a reviving, more flexible and much stronger domestic economy, and a great improvement in our overseas payments, we are effectively out of the queue, one of two world powers outside Russia . . .[80]

But then Franks came to the question of the down payment needed to secure this exalted position:

> I feel that the Americans will to some extent – and I know this to be true of the Defense Department – test the quality of the partnership by our attitude to the notion of a token ground force. I go further and think that what we do on this, and when, will make a difference to the intimacy and success of the forthcoming talks . . .

He warned that 'Washington in emotional overdrive is a capital at war', and that 'their mood is one of the things that have to be taken into account in estimating the effect on Anglo-American relations of what we decided to do or not do . . .'[81]

Yet Franks had also advised London that the Americans 'will expect us to begin with a thorough examination of the European position and possibilities . . .'[82] Examination of the Far East and Middle East would follow 'in this context.'

At the Washington talks the British were to find themselves more and more oppressively squeezed by American pressure to offer a ground force for Korea. On 21 July the Head of the American Department of the Foreign Office, R. H. Scott, reported a hint from the US Embassy in London that there would shortly be a request for such forces: 'It is obviously desirable that we should not return a blank refusal to the Americans.'[83] He signalled the Washington Embassy: 'From the military point of view we would of course find it extremely hard to provide even a token force. But we realise that the question is at least in part, if not mainly, political . . .'[84] Scott proceeded to explain what he meant by 'political': '. . . we should be influenced in our attitude to this problem if it was likely that an offer of British ground forces would strengthen our hand with the Americans . . .'

It was Bradley, the American Chairman of the Joint Chiefs of Staff, who formally put the request to Tedder, on the score that British participation would emphasize the United Nations nature of the Korean operation. As Franks reported to London, the request 'also flows from their general policy springing equally from idealistic and practical motives to maintain and strengthen the United Nations Organisation . . .'[85] Franks emphasized that the Americans saw it as essential to the UN character of the campaign that it should not be fought by United States forces only; and that they considered Great Britain as the key to the action of others. Hence, in Franks's judgement, the 'great importance' attached by the US Administration to a British offer of ground troops. Bleakly Franks explained how small was the room for manoeuvre enjoyed by Britain, that country proclaimed by himself only a few days earlier as one of the two world powers outside Russia and a partner of the United States in world affairs:

> For these reasons I should expect the reaction of the United States Administration to a negative decision by us to be deep and prolonged. I am not thinking primarily of the effects which it would have on relatively short term matters, however important, such as additional appropriations for European defence and the third appropriation of E.R.P [Marshall Aid]. The important consideration is the effect our decision will have on the basic relationship of the two countries. I believe that because of the rational and irrational elements in the American mind about this for them unparalleled undertaking

to act as a policeman in the world, a negative decision could seriously impair the longterm relationship.[86]

The British might have reflected at this juncture that, damn it, the Americans had taken it upon themselves, uninvited, to turn the North Korean invasion of South Korea into a UN Security Council matter and likewise to commit their own troops. The British could have reflected too that later the Americans had chosen to assume full political and military control of the campaign which they now wished to dress up as United-Nations 'peace-keeping'. But as it was, the British simply altered course to follow the West's self-appointed flagship.

On 24 July, the day the talks in Washington ended, the Prime Minister told the Cabinet Defence Committee that 'there were now strong political reasons for sending a ground force.'[87] The Chief of the Imperial General Staff, Field-Marshal Lord Slim, reported that the Chiefs of Staff had reconsidered the question:

> Although in their view it was still militarily unsound, they recognized the strong political arguments in favour. In their view it would be wrong to send less than a Brigade Group. Nothing less could achieve the political objective . . . It should be a mixed force – perhaps an Armoured Regiment equipped with Centurion tanks, an Anti-Tank Regiment equipped with 17-pounders, a field regiment and three Infantry Battalions . . .[88]

To this the Defence Committee agreed: a fateful first step.

But there also remained American quixotry over Formosa to worry about. As Scott, Head of the American Department of the Foreign Office, wrote on this same day, 24 July, 'if we were to side openly with the Americans it would lead to a rupture with China, Hong Kong would become untenable.' But then again if the Chinese were to attack Formosa, 'and if the Americans want our assistance, we would have no option but to support them . . .'[89]

By now the combination of existing imperial commitments (Hong Kong being a prime example in the present crisis) and the new decision to send a brigade group to Korea had brought into question a fundamental aspect of total strategy – that of defence expenditure and its burden on the economy.

On 22 July the Minister of Defence recommended that in order to 'strengthen our immediate defences, and thereby, I hope, reduce the risk of war,' completion of existing orders for equipment ought to be speeded up and new orders placed. This would bring the defence estimates for 1951–52 up to £950 million, a rise of £170 million on the present level. Moreover, supplementary estimates of £30 million were needed for the current financial year.[90] The Minister of Defence warned, however, that if the present crisis did not pass away in time, and it therefore proved not possible to revert to a situation where 'war need not be foreseen for some years ahead,' it was clear that 'a major rearmament programme will be involved, with expenditure on a very large scale . . .'[91]

A major rearmament programme! Expenditure on a very large scale! For a nation not yet fully recovered from the Second World War and still living on tick this was a dire prospect indeed.

Yet America's zeal for international righteousness continued to deepen the crisis. A fresh US resolution tabled in the Security Council by the US (but not in the end passed) condemned the North Koreans 'for their defiance of the United Nations and called on all states, not only to use their influence to prevail on the North Koreans to cease this defiance, but also to avoid any action which might have the effect of extending the area of conflict.'[92] In tabling this resolution, the United States had yet again simply barged ahead on its own, as Kenneth Younger, Minister of State, reported to the Cabinet on 1 August:

> although the Americans had shown us the resolution in draft, they had not allowed us sufficient time in which to make effective criticisms of it, and although we had counselled delay, they had in fact tabled the resolution late on the previous evening . . .[93]

In this same meeting the Cabinet again agreed, in the Prime Minister's words, that 'we should not be party to any bargain in the Security Council by which a settlement of the Korean situation would be made conditional upon a change in China's representation in the Council . . .'[94]

Three days later the Chiefs of Staff gloomily reported on the military implications of possible hostilities between America and China:

In undertaking to send a field force to Korea we have scraped the barrel of our existing resources . . .

We conclude that, on military grounds, it is to the advantage, both of the United Kingdom and the United States, that we should stand aside in a conflict over Formosa. This would offer the best chance of localising the conflict . . . If, however, the conflict is prolonged we may be forced to join in.[95]

Meanwhile the North Koreans were continuing to inflict a humiliating rout on the Americans. On 20 July the 24th Regiment of the US 25th Division (the second to be deployed in Korea) broke and fled.[96] Still the retreat went on. By the beginning of August the Americans and South Koreans were back to a bridgehead some thirty miles deep round the south-eastern port of Pusan. Even though America was busily mobilizing manpower and industry at home, General MacArthur thus stood in desperately urgent need of 'men with rifles' there in the field. When Tedder in Washington signalled this need to London, the Chiefs of Staff decided (on 17 August) to recommend to ministers that two infantry battalions should be sent to Korea from Hong Kong in utmost haste.[97]

On 10 August the Secretary of State for War, John Strachey, informed the Minister of Defence that the British brigade group would start to leave the United Kingdom on 1 November, with advanced echelons arriving in Japan or Korea by 10 December and the whole force and its kit in Korea by 1 January 1951. But Shinwell immediately directed that embarkation must begin a month earlier, on 1 October.[98] Already the brigade group's expansion into a Commonwealth Division with Australian and New Zealand contingents was being discussed.[99]

Yet although Korea remained the focus of such intense effort, it had by now dwindled strategically into just one sector of what the United States Administration in its 'emotional overdrive' saw as a global battle-front where Soviet-directed Communist armies might be launched forward at any time anywhere.

As Dean Acheson told the Senate Committee on Appropriations, the North Atlantic Treaty powers could no longer afford to base their defence policies on surmises about Soviet intentions. Instead: 'The capabilities of the Communist movement for further acts of aggression must be the measuring rod by which we judge the adequacy of our defensive strength.'[100] It was Western Europe which Washington feared above all might be the scene of such 'further acts of aggression', even though in cool retrospect it is hard to discern why a conflict between the two Koreas should make it more likely that Soviet tanks would rumble en masse across the inner German border.

Nevertheless, in its belief that the 'Communists' had, in Truman's words, passed 'beyond the bounds of subversion to conquer independent nations and will now use armed invasion and war,' the United States now announced a colossal defence programme aimed at meeting a supposed maximum time of danger in 1953–54. The programme was embodied in National Security Document NSC-68, as much a classic of American moral rant as an exercise in strategic analysis. NSC-68 had been inspired by the successful Soviet test of an atomic device in August 1949, which had led Washington planners to fear that once the Soviet Union could match the nuclear striking power of the United States she might then exploit her own huge superiority in conventional forces. Hence NSC-68 urged that the United States vastly expand her own conventional forces as well as maintain her nuclear superiority. Although NSC-68 had been originally approved by President Truman early in 1950, it had then stalled because of the cost. Only now, thanks to the 'emotional overdrive' provoked on and off Capitol Hill by North Korean aggression, was it passed by Congress.

On 15 September 1950 the North Atlantic Council met in New York to discuss, first and foremost, the defence of Europe and the future role therein of a rearmed West Germany. On that same day MacArthur successfully carried out an amphibious landing at Inchon on the west coast of Korea, far behind the North Korean front – a bold and brilliant stroke that was quickly to bring about the collapse of the North Korean army and the re-conquest of all South Korea. The news of the landing and of the advances that then followed day after day could only enhance America's moral ascendancy over her junior partners in the North Atlantic Council. More, MacArthur's plucking of glorious victory out of shameful rout could only boost

America's 'emotional overdrive' as she strove to mobilize the West against Communist aggression.

To the North Atlantic Council meeting in New York President Truman now announced that American forces in Europe were to be strongly reinforced. He followed this with a flick of the Presidential whip at America's European dependants:

> A basic element in the implementation of this decision is the degree to which our friends match our action in this regard. Firm programs for the development of their forces will be expected to keep full step with the dispatch of additional United States forces to Europe.[101]

In the same meeting the North Atlantic Council willingly agreed, as America wished, to establish 'an integrated force under centralised command', so commencing the transformation of the North Atlantic Treaty from mere parchment into NATO. In December the Council appointed General of the Army Dwight D. Eisenhower as the first NATO Supreme Commander in Europe (SACEUR), with the task 'to train national units assigned to his command and organise them into an effective, integrated defense force.'[102] In January 1951 the transformation was completed with the setting-up of Supreme Headquarters Allied Powers Europe (SHAPE).

In hindsight it seems clear that this creation of an integrated multinational military structure in Europe and the approval by Congress of the huge NSC-68 defence programme mark the true beginning of 'the Cold War', as distinct from the diplomatic skirmishing of 1946-9 – if by 'Cold War' is meant that obsessive mutual fear between the United States and the Soviet Union and the consequent relentlessly sharpening rivalry (political, military, technological, and, above all, nuclear) which was to last until 1989.[103] These were mighty consequences to flow from the invasion, no doubt ill-considered, of a minor country to which the United States at the outset 'did not attach overwhelming [strategic] importance' (see above, p. 13).

For Britain herself the declaration of (cold) war on the Soviet Union by the United States meant that her pretensions to be 'the second power in the world outside Russia' were now to be cruelly put to the proof.

Her dilemma was no longer whether or not to contribute a 'token' land force for Korea. Events had already made their sour comment on that, for between October 1950 and January 1951 the British 27th Brigade had first taken part in MacArthur's rash headlong chase over the 38th Parallel (the dividing line between the two Koreas) and on through North Korea to the Chinese border, and then distinguished itself (together with 41 Independent Commando, Royal Marines) in the grim retreat back again in the face of the massed onslaught of the Chinese army. On New Year's Day 1951, a second British brigade, the 29th, was deployed in the line. That January Australian, New Zealand and Canadian units were linked with the British brigades to form the British Commonwealth Division. Some token force!

No, the dilemma for Britain now was how to reconcile 1930s-style rearmament on the grand scale with the health of a still convalescent and already overloaded industrial economy that was facing ever fiercer competition in overseas markets.

2. 'The Principal Partner of America in World Affairs'

As early as the end of July 1950 the US Government had asked its North Atlantic Treaty allies 'for information concerning the nature and extent of the increased effort both as regards increases in forces and increases in military production' which they were 'willing and able to undertake . . .'[1] It peremptorily called for 'an immediate reply in a form that could be published'.[2] Within ten days the British Government had obliged, promising a three-year programme costing £3.6 billion, but adding the cavil that they did not feel able 'to undertake consistently with the objectives indicated by the United States Government so full a diversion of productive resources to defence purpose unless the United States can offer financial assistance.'[3] Put in less Jeevesian language, this meant that America's 'partner in world affairs' already had her hand out again, palm uppermost.

For Britain was still beset by a cash-flow problem – an uneasy position for the banker to the Sterling Area that she wished to remain. On 12 July the Economic Section of the Treasury, commenting on prospects for the balance of payments in 1950–51, had pointed out: 'Our reserves are entirely inadequate to meet the drains which are liable to fall upon it [sic], if not in 1950–1, then subsequently . . .' The Economic Section reckoned that Britain needed double her present level of reserves, and they gloomed that dollar prospects for the future were 'uncertain'.[4]

Through the summer and into the autumn of 1950, diligent men toiled in lofty but war-shabby rooms within the soot-black Victorian and Edwardian palaces of Whitehall to work out the details of Britain's brave £3.6 billion offer. They pondered how to find the money and the industrial resources. On 12 October 1950 the Minister of Defence (Shinwell) was able to recommend to the Cabinet Defence Committee that it should accept the report of the Chiefs of Staff on a three-year expansion and re-equipment of the armed forces at a total net cost of £3.7 billion (sic).[5] Nonetheless, the Minister was 'by no means satisfied' that the Chiefs' proposals would in fact meet what he called 'our essential defence requirements'.[6] In particular they fell 'far short of what would be needed if we were to contribute our quota towards the N.A.T.O. Medium Term Defence Plan.'

For the figure of £3.7 billion merely represented (according to a joint memorandum by the Foreign Secretary and the new Chancellor of the Exchequer, Hugh Gaitskell, on 23 October) a guesstimate of 'the most that our productive and other resources are capable of providing without mobilisation measures . . .'[7] But the NATO Medium Term Defence Plan was based on what the military authorities 'consider to be needed' – a very different matter.[8] Though final totals had still to be settled, wrote Bevin and Gaitskell, it was 'clear at the outset that the United Kingdom defence budget over the next three years, on the basis of the Medium Term Defence Plan, would far exceed £3,600 million', and might even go as high as £6,000 million.[9]

How could Britain foot such a bill without cruel harm to her still precarious post-war economic recovery? The Foreign Secretary and the Chancellor could already foresee the kind of damage that would be inflicted by 'the addition of very substantial amounts of defence expenditure.'[10] Domestically it would mean 'a direct burden on the Budget' and, 'in the context of an inevitable rise in the cost of living, the political and social difficulties of increased taxation or renewed inflation . . .' Far more serious, however, was the probable injury to Britain as a trading nation and a banker:

> Rearmament will compete with exports for our production, and at the same time the rapidly rising price of imported raw materials is causing a further deterioration in the terms of trade. It will therefore become increasingly difficult to avoid a deficit on the United Kingdom overall balance of payments, which will show itself in a rise in our overseas sterling liabilities. It will be still more difficult to

attain that surplus which our external commitments require if we are
not to run into debt.[11]

What then to do? Well, Britain could turn once again to the
Americans to be bailed out, as in 1941, 1945 and 1948. Indeed it
appeared that the Americans were ready 'to offer us assistance so
that recovery should not be dislocated and halted by the heavy
impact of rearmament.'[12] But here came the catch, shrewdly
detected by the oddly yoked intellects of the Wykehamist Gaitskell
and the veteran trade union bargainer Bevin:

> If by accepting direct aid for military purposes we were to forfeit our
> economic independence we should lose the position we were just
> regaining as the principal partner in world affairs of the United States.
> We shall be back again in the European queue, and our loss of power
> and influence will reflect itself in many ways. It will be more difficult
> to hold the Commonwealth together. Our position in Europe will
> be weakened.[13]

Economic independence! Principal partner in world affairs of the
United States! Power and influence! Holding together the Commonwealth! Our position in Europe!

Could this be the country still on the drip of Marshall Aid and
with doubtful balance-of-payments prospects? Could this be the
Commonwealth which only functioned as a collective entity during
a war, but which at all times remained a net strategic and economic
drain on the Mother Country? And what *was* this position in
Europe that might be weakened, Britain having just excluded herself
from the new Coal and Steel Authority, the first step towards a
European union?

In 1944 Lord Keynes had written that 'All our reflex actions are
those of a rich man.'[14] In 1950 the language used by Bevin and
Gaitskell (and by officials) demonstrates that Whitehall's reflexes no
less remained those of a grandee. The latter reflexes, having bedevilled British foreign policy and global strategy since 1945, were
now to bedevil rearmament policy.

In the first place, the new programme was designed to bolster
the existing world role as much as to defend Britain-in-Europe.
According to the Chiefs of Staff, almost a third of the active army's

strength in 1951 would be deployed in the Middle East and Far East.[15] When the Royal Air Force's expansion had been completed in 1954, a fifth of its strength would be deployed in the Middle East and Far East – a higher proportion than in Germany.[16]

Secondly, it had occurred to neither ministers nor public servants (black-coated or uniformed) to restrict rearmament to the modest level that could be readily afforded by a hard-up and indebted country, or be produced by British industry without grievous harm to exports or investment. That would certainly have been a level far, far lower than the £3.7 billion so promptly offered to the Americans back in the summer.

But in any case it had never occurred to Whitehall simply to calculate what minimum offer of rearmament might suffice to secure American protection (especially nuclear) of Western Europe. For here, as in their attitude to the Commonwealth and the Sterling Area, ministers and public servants were inspired by a high-minded sense of moral responsibility towards the world at large. This was another legacy of the past, in the guise of values bequeathed by the Victorian religious revival and transmitted down the generations by the public school and the Nonconformist chapel.[17]

It could therefore be said that in 1950 the British governing elite suffered not only from the reflexes of a rich man and a grandee but also from those of a school prefect. Yet the latter reflexes were just as ill-adapted to Britain's present fallen state, just as much obsolete kit overdue for scrapping.

In any case, members of the Labour Cabinet were strongly influenced by their own peculiar mental legacy. They remembered in repentance the stubborn opposition of the Labour movement in the 1930s to timely British rearmament against Nazi Germany, on the doctrinaire grounds that this would mean 'a new arms race' instead of 'collective security' through the League of Nations.

But were ministers now in 1950 simply proposing to re-fight the last peace? Did Soviet Russia really pose a threat of aggressive war comparable to that posed by Nazi Germany? When Hitler came to power in 1933 he had done no more than reach the start-line for a future drive to destroy the peace settlement of 1919 and restore Germany's lost lands and military might. By contrast, and thanks to the installation of satellite Communist regimes throughout eastern

Europe, Stalin in 1950 had already secured his main objective, that of a defensive territorial glacis up to the Iron Curtain. And while Germany in 1933 possessed the most powerful industrial machine in Europe, with immense warlike potential, this could hardly be said of the Soviet Union in 1950, only five years after her stupendous human and material loss in the Second World War.

At the end of November 1950 the Joint Intelligence Bureau of the Ministry of Defence supplied the Cabinet with a set of tables ('intelligent guesses')[18] comparing the national incomes and defence expenditures of the Soviet Union and the members of NATO. At first glance, the Cabinet might have felt that these tables justified their alarm about a Soviet threat. For it appeared that the USSR was spending 13 per cent of GNP on defence as against America's 9.9 per cent and Britain's 8.3 per cent. But these percentages were misleading. When it came to *total* annual defence expenditures the JIB estimated the Soviet Union's at less than £2.5 billion, as against America's at £7.9 billion, and £1.7 billion for all the European members of NATO together.[19] As for the economic potential for military expansion, the JIB put the net national income of the Soviet Union at £19.1 billion, as against the United States' £79 billion.[20]

Nonetheless, the Cabinet, preferring to count divisions (the Soviet Union was believed to have 179) rather than coolly appraise overall total-strategic capability, did not dissent from America's present conviction that Stalin was another Hitler, with a bigger moustache, and that the West must rearm hugely and in haste to deter him from attacking.

Yet the ambitious scale of rearmament chosen by Britain inevitably meant that she must have recourse to American bounty. How, then, was this fresh dependency to be reconciled with the 'world-power' independence which Whitehall presumed that Britain now once again enjoyed? Already, back in November 1949, the Cabinet Defence Committee had felt deep unease about the onerous conditions proposed by the Americans under their Military Aid Program:

> on paper at any rate it would appear that the liability of this country to provide reciprocal aid would be almost unlimited; in return for

any equipment, material or services our arms export trade would be placed under the most embarrassing restrictions similar to those we had experienced under Lend-Lease . . .[21]

'Embarrassing'? The word preferred by civil servants in briefing the Committee was 'ruthless'.[22]

Nevertheless, in October 1950 Gaitskell and Bevin came up with an ingenious answer to the new puzzle of how to touch the Americans for a suitcase full of bucks to pay for rearmament while preserving Britain's status as a sovereign great power. It lay in a scheme drawn up by Paul Nitze (Director of Policy and Planning in the State Department) whereby the rearmament measures needed to implement NATO's Medium Term Plan would be collectively allocated to the twelve NATO members and the burden of the cost fairly distributed among them. Such a distribution, wrote Bevin and Gaitskell, could involve 'financial transfers' or 'equipment produced in one country [being] used in another,'[23] but, in their words, 'in neither of these cases should the transfers be regarded as "assistance" or "aid" . . .'[24] No, no, of course not.

Thus, instead of cadging directly from the United States, Britain would make a case to NATO. Instead of America inserting dollar bills straight into the British breast pocket, the handout would arrive indirectly via collective NATO rationing-out under the Nitze plan. That is, except for two lots of £100 million worth of dollar components (such as factory equipment) from the US which had already been negotiated in order to help with high-priority production programmes.[25]

But even Bevin and Gaitskell came close to acknowledging that in regard to rearmament Britain's 'independence' was once more just self-delusion:

On the one hand it is clear that the Nitze proposals offer virtually the only hope that the economic burden we shall have to bear will be tolerable in itself, and equitable in relation to that borne by others. On the other hand, the starting point of the Nitze memorandum is the adoption of the Medium Term Defence Plan . . . We know that our share of [that] involves a military effort for the United Kingdom far in excess of our £3,600 million programme . . .[26]

In other words, he who chooses a style of life he cannot afford and who in consequence must sponge off a rich but ruthless patron enjoys less true 'independence' than a poor man who lives humbly within his means.

This truth was to be brutally demonstrated at the beginning of December 1950 when Attlee flew to meet Acheson and Truman in Washington. The State Department and the White House were now John Wayne, striding up the world's main street with hand hovering over a holstered nuclear bomb towards the evil Communist outlaw. On 30 November President Truman even alluded openly at a press conference to the possibility of dropping the bomb in Korea. This occasioned a lively frisson in Europe. As Sir Roger Makins of the Foreign Office told the American Chargé d'Affaires in London next day, 'The President's statement about the use of the atomic bomb had precipitated suddenly a feeling of uneasiness about the conduct of the war in Korea which had been building up for some time.'[27] Washington's overwrought mood at this time no doubt owed much to MacArthur's current rout at the hands of a totally unforeseen Chinese offensive which began in the last week of November.

Even though Attlee's team included the Chief of the Imperial General Staff (Field Marshal Lord Slim), the Chairman of the British Joint Services Mission in Washington (Marshal of the Royal Air Force Lord Tedder), and the British Ambassador, Sir Oliver Franks, they proved quite unable to budge the Americans. Whereas Attlee argued the folly of excluding Communist China from the United Nations, Dean Acheson – with his bristly 'mustache' and homburg hat a Hollywood caricature of an English gent – believed that China 'was little more than a Russian satellite.' He and Truman regarded the making of any concessions to China in an attempt to detach her from the Soviet Union as 1930s-style appeasement.[28] And so, even if (as Franks believed) Attlee may have greased the cogs of 'the special relationship' and calmed the Americans down a little, he flew back to London having failed on every substantive issue.

Worse, the Prime Minister returned from the summit meeting, like Chamberlain from his at Bad Godesberg twelve years earlier, with unwelcome new demands from his host to communicate to the Cabinet. The difference lay in that whereas in 1938 the demands had been made in respect of a third party, Czechoslovakia, now they were being made on Britain herself. As Attlee explained to his Cabinet in his clipped, concise way, in his toneless middle-class professional man's voice, 'he had undertaken to consider the President's request that this country should increase its defence effort.'[29] In terms reminiscent of Chamberlain telling his Cabinet after his first flight to Germany how well he had got on with Herr Hitler,[30] Attlee assured his colleagues:

> In his talks in Washington, [he] had persuaded the Americans to accept Anglo-American partnership as the mainspring of Atlantic defence. Much of the advantage which we had gained would be lost if we were now to be treated as merely one of the European countries which were being urged by America to make a larger contribution to the common defence effort. We should align ourselves with the Americans in urging others to do more. One could not ignore the risk, however remote, that the United States might lose interest in the defence of Europe . . .[31]

Attlee therefore asked the Cabinet to authorize the Foreign Secretary to tell the Americans that the British Government had decided to 'increase and accelerate their defence programmes still further.'[32] The Cabinet tamely agreed. The Chiefs of Staff were asked to frame detailed proposals. Washington and the North Atlantic Council in Brussels were duly informed.

On 15 January 1951 Aneurin Bevan (then still Minister of Health) told the third Cabinet meeting of the New Year that he was 'sceptical of appreciations submitted to the Government by their military advisers regarding the strength and equipment of the Russian forces . . .', as also about the likelihood of some Russian (external) coup.[33] In his judgement it was the Russian tactic to induce the democracies to overload their economies with defence costs. Bevan no doubt had it in mind here that the Soviet Union's preferred strategy probably lay in internal subversion of Western Europe by means of the powerful French and Italian Communist Parties and trade unions, or even perhaps the Communist shop stewards who spasmodically disrupted British industrial life (see below, Chapters 9–13). As he explained to his colleagues, he 'therefore thought it would be folly for the democracies to adopt vast defence programmes which would put such a strain on their economies . . . as to give the Soviet Government the opportunity which they sought.'

A week later the Cabinet Defence Committee began to measure this strain. Before it were five weighty departmental reports[34] on the proposed new defence programme of £4.8 billion, some 33 per cent larger than that agreed in the previous October. In an echo of warnings at the start of the pre-war rearmament programme in 1936[35] the Committee was informed that 'the major physical difficulty' in carrying out the production programmes lay in 'the provision of adequate supplies of machine-tools and raw materials . . .'[36] So far as essential but scarce raw materials were concerned, it had been apparent since the beginning of December 1950 that in the scramble Britain was being shouldered aside by the United States. As the Chancellor of the Exchequer had then reported to the Cabinet Economic Policy Committee, 'we have at present little means of bargaining with them even over materials which they need from the Commonwealth . . .'[37] Now in January 1951 the Defence Committee was told that raw materials for the rearmament programme would have to be found by depriving export industries and civil consumption.[38] They were also told – the first note of a major theme in a relentlessly minor key – that the machine-tool gap could not be closed by switching from civil production. Perhaps Europe could help out?[39]

Sombre was the Chancellor's advice to the Defence Committee on the broad economic impact of the new programme:

> The increased expenditure . . . had to be undertaken at a time when the terms of trade were moving heavily against the United Kingdom. It would be necessary to forego the target of a surplus in our balance of payments, and accept instead basic equilibrium. But, for the rest, we should strive to carry as much as possible of the necessary sacrifices on current consumption, rather than to burden the future by any serious reduction in investment or the incurring of overseas debt.[40]

Those 'necessary sacrifices' would, he judged, do 'least damage' if inflicted on the production of consumer goods such as television sets, radios, refrigerators and certain kinds of vehicles. With the technological and marketing insight to be expected of a Wykehamist intellectual (first-class honours, Politics, Philosophy and Economics, at New College, Oxford), Gaitskell had picked on the very products that would constitute the fastest-growing world market of the near future: the market where Germany and Japan would successfully wage their new wars of conquest.

The Defence Committee plucked its lip: 'It was clear that the measures required . . . were both economically and politically so difficult that the Cabinet would have to consider them most attentively . . .'[41] Some anonymous member or members of the Committee even expressed the view 'that the dangers against which we were proposing these preparations were not so great and so urgent as to warrant such far-reaching measures.' But Kenneth Younger, the Minister of State, brought them back to the chill realities of Britain's position as 'the principal partner of America in world affairs':

> there was considerable pressure from the Americans for the United Kingdom to announce its increased defence programme as soon as possible, so that General Eisenhower, in particular, could report to Congress the substantial efforts being made by the United Kingdom in the common cause . . .

Indeed, Attlee himself was to admit in an interview in 1959: 'Pressure on rearmament was very heavy from the United States. I think they were inclined to press too hard.'[42]

Now it was up to the full Cabinet, meeting twice on 25 January 1951, to make the final decision.

With admirable candour the Chancellor reminded his colleagues that the economic strain on the country would be made even worse by an adverse shift in the terms of trade, a shortage of imported raw materials, and by the absence of any 'general financial aid' (further ERP payments being now suspended) from the United States.[43]

> The main weight of the programme would fall on a few industries – primarily engineering, building and textiles; and of these the engineering industry would bear the heaviest load. This meant that exports and investment would both be seriously affected, since the engineer-

ing and building industries were important contributors to those programmes.

Gaitskell asked (and it was a very good question even if he failed to answer it): 'How much of this burden could we afford to carry by accepting a worsening of our balance of payments situation?'

Nonetheless, he had a strategy to offer: 'a double diversion of industry – first, from civil to defence work; and second, from manufacture for the home market to exports.' Yet such a strategy, even if successful in terms of rearmament itself, must inevitably cause enormous incidental disruption to industry. And this would happen just when Britain was losing her post-war head-start in export markets to her resurgent trade rivals. Some unidentified but acute mind in the Cabinet did indeed question whether exports could be maintained at the level hoped for by the Chancellor.[44]

It is therefore the more remarkable that Gaitskell could so openly acknowledge the economic perils of so vast a rearmament programme and yet still urge his colleagues to approve it. Perhaps he did so for no better reason than to back the Americans politically at all costs.[45]

When the Cabinet met again that afternoon for yet more anguished debate, it was the doubters like Bevan (now Minister of Labour) who eventually lost to the 'principal partner of America in world affairs' men like Gaitskell, Morrison, Dalton, and of course Attlee. £4.7 billion over three years it was going to be.[46] On 29 January the Prime Minister announced the programme to Parliament.

Thus was Britain finally swept away by the wind and tide of American anti-Communist passion towards that lee shore, as yet distant, of total-strategic bankruptcy where she had come to shipwreck once before during the Second World War.

Of course it told a hard-luck story and for the usual reason, to touch a wallet if not a heart. But it did not really exaggerate the suppliant's ever more worrying plight. Entitled 'The Burden of Defence on the United Kingdom', it was the British submission for 'the Nitze exercise'; and it was dispatched to NATO's Economic and Financial Working Group in March 1951.[47]

According to the submission, the three-year £4.7 billion programme would entail a doubling of the annual defence expenditure
before the Korean War. At its peak in 1952–53 the programme
would amount to 12 per cent of GNP.[48] It would demand the
conversion of 25 per cent of the metal-using industries to munitions
production. 'These are the industries which in recent years have
provided over 90 per cent of gross fixed investment in plant,
machinery, vessels and vehicles, and nearly one half of total commodity exports . . .'[49] Rearmament at its apogee would swallow 11
per cent of the active population either in defence work or in
uniform.[50]

The predicted worsening of the terms of trade meant that Britain
would have to export 7.5 per cent more in order to pay for a given
quantity of imports.[51] But at the same time the increase in defence
production would mean 'a sharp reduction in supplies of many
engineering products for civil use both home and export'.[52] Even
so, it would not be easy to make up the shortfall in exports with
consumer goods because those industries would be handicapped by
shortage of raw materials and by losing labour and capacity to
defence production.[53] Moreover, at the end of 1951 Britain was due
to start repaying the 1945 American and Canadian loans. All in all,
reckoned the submission for the Nitze exercise, a substantial balance-of-payments deficit in the future was more likely than a
surplus, and a mere equilibrium the best that could be hoped for.[54]

But all this, according to the submission, only amounted to the
short-term predicament. Once the rearmament programme was
completed, Britain would then face 'the grave trade and industrial
problems' of redeploying its industries 'to meet the longer-term
market opportunities for United Kingdom goods'.[55] Unstated, however, was the corollary: if the Germans and Japanese and others had
not by then seized those opportunities.

In any event the submission made clear that the weight of the
rearmament programme was not going to be borne by a strong and
resilient economy but instead by one which 'has been working at
full stretch for eleven years', and for the first six of them 'sustaining
a total war effort'.[56]

Ironically enough, the submission's survey of the five *post-war*
years of 'full stretch' constitutes an unwitting admission by the

Labour Government of its own folly in pursuing, while the country was broke, the twin dreams of the world role abroad and 'New Jerusalem' at home.[57] For the submission describes how playing the world role militarily, with 'substantial forces' in the Middle East and Malaya as well as in Germany and Austria, had compelled the United Kingdom to devote a greater proportion of national resources to defence since 1945 than any other member of NATO.[58] Furthermore, she had 'contributed 22,000 men to the United Nations campaign in Korea . . .'[59] Then again, the submission spelt out how playing the world role as banker to the Sterling Area and benefactor of backward parts of the Commonwealth had kept Britain at 'full stretch' too. For she had emerged from the Second World War with her 'capital position' weakened by about £4.5 billion, thanks to loss of overseas investments and new debts. Since then she had incurred further debts in dollars of £1.3 billion.[60]

If the United Kingdom's 'many and varied external obligations are to be financed', wrote the submission, a substantial surplus in its overseas accounts of at least £100 million a year was 'essential'. But – here came the burden of Empire again – 'new obligations, such as those to be incurred in connection with the Colombo Plan for economic development in South-East Asia and growing investment needs particularly in Commonwealth countries make a considerably larger surplus desirable . . .'[61]

It was all heart-melting, wallet-opening stuff; or at least intended to be so. Nonetheless Britain's Nitze submission omitted to mention Britain's old obligations to the Commonwealth, such as the 'sterling balances'. These were the huge debts owed to India and Pakistan (the wartime India of the Raj) for logistic support to British forces fighting an imperial war from their soil against the Japanese. Britain was now nobly paying the debts off by means of British exports supplied buckshee.[62]

But also left unexplored in this crucial document was the more general and insidious damage inflicted on the British economy since 1945 by what it noted in passing as 'Britain's many and varied external obligations'.

Ever since the war the Labour Government had been obsessed by the need to build up large enough reserves of gold and dollars to run the Sterling Area and also finance Britain's own strategic and economic commitments overseas. They had therefore watched the balance of payments as if gazing at a fever chart, fearful that poor figures would lead to a run on the pound – as indeed happened in the summer of 1949, when sterling had to be devalued against the dollar by a third. Because export prices were pumped up by domestic inflation, the Government had been equally concerned to hold back the pressure of demand on the British economy.

And what simpler way to achieve this could there be than restricting capital investment in industry and infrastructure? With inflation thus controlled and the balance of payments buoyant, the Sterling Area could be kept in business and Britain could retain her top-table seat as its banker. There would be no need to make such drastic cuts in the defence budget as must entail the withdrawal of the squadrons and garrisons in the Mediterranean and Middle East which Bevin believed to be the buttress of Britain's position as 'a great power'. In fact, there would be no need all round for Britain to cease playing the grandee in the world. And no need either to chop back ruthlessly the construction or running costs of 'New Jerusalem', such as the ambitious programme of building new council houses[63] and the new National Health Service, where the projected 1951–52 budget stood at well over twice times the original 1945 estimate.[64]

And so in pursuit of all these vain hopes and despite the impassioned protests of departmental ministers about out-of-date and dilapidated industries, roads, railways, ports and telecommunications, the Labour Government had doled out annual rations of capital investment like gruel in a workhouse.[65]

The same perverse order of priorities had governed the British spending of Marshall Aid, in waste of a unique opportunity. First had been placed the maintenance of the gold and dollar reserves for the sake of remaining banker to the Sterling Area. Second came use of the Aid as a general subsidy to support the world role and domestic consumption. A mere runner-up was capital investment in modernizing Britain's industrial machine and national communications network. Britain in fact devoted a third less of her Marshall Aid to such investment than did West Germany.[66]

The consequences by 1950 of the Labour Government's past

total-strategic choices were spelt out bluntly enough in the Government's own submission for the Nitze exercise:

> by absolute standards the amounts invested in British industry and in social capital were still substantially below requirements. It seems unlikely, for instance, that in terms of industrial capital per worker employed the United Kingdom was reducing the gap between it and certain other countries which had widened during the war years . . .[67]

But the new defence programme, remarked the submission, was actually going to make this neglect 'even more serious', by hogging investment in plant, machinery and vehicles:

> Industrial investment in industries producing for essential civil purposes for home and export will, therefore, fall a long way short of the levels desirable for the long-term economic welfare of the country.[68]

Yet the submission predicted that despite such crippling sacrifices the United Kingdom's own production programme would *still* not be sufficient 'to provide complete scales of equipment and reserves for all the forces which it is planned to raise. It is hoped, however, that the United States will be able to make available very substantial quantities of equipment . . .'[69]

Largely barren proved the hope. All too accurate proved the prediction.

As early as the second meeting of the new official Committee on Productive Capacity on 19 February 1951[70] the supply of machine tools emerged as a key problem, just as it had during the Great War, during pre-1939 rearmament and during the Second World War.[71] The Committee concluded that machine tools for home investment would have to be cut from 25,000 annually to 14,000. This sacrifice 'would fall most heavily on the motor industry and its ancillaries, and on transport and electrical plant . . .', with as yet incalculable effects on exports.[72] Moreover, the chief bottleneck in expanding British production of machine tools was likely to lie in shortage of skilled labour – another old theme.

On 6 March this Committee agreed, in a further echo of the

past, that Britain would need a minimum of 3,500 American machine tools 'of types unprocurable at home'.[73]

On 2 May the Ministry of Supply's Engineering Advisory Council was told about 'some serious bottlenecks in components, such as bearings and electronic valves'; and that, as a result of the disruption caused by switching industry over to defence, production in the automobile industry 'was falling, labour was being dissipated, and it was becoming more difficult to maintain exports'.[74]

Next day the Committee on Productive Capacity pondered how to meet a rise in the possible total demand of the rearmament programme for machine tools to 35,000. Orders had already been placed in Europe for 8,000, and in America for 12,000. So it was that for the third time in her twentieth-century history Britain could only overcome her shortage of machine tools by recourse to imports, again to the benefit of Britain's competitors. The remaining 15,000 tools would be British-made, orders having so far been placed for 8,000, on some of which 'there might be a problem of delivery.' As for the rest, they would have to be obtained 'at the expense of civil users'[75] – the biggest victim being the vehicle industry, followed by manufacturers of textile machinery, oil engines, transport equipment, consumer goods and possibly marine engineering.[76]

By this time too a shortage of ball, roller and taper bearings was once again – just as in 1914–16 and 1936–40 – menacing both the expansion of industry and the production of military equipment. On into 1952, even 1953, the officials of the Ministry of Supply would be devoting vast time and trouble in trying to solve this problem in liaison with the manufacturers, the most important of these being anyway the British outstations of American or Swedish firms.[77] In a repetition of the technical problems before the Second World War in developing a tachometric high-angle fire-control system for the Royal Navy,[78] no manufacturer could be found in the United Kingdom who could fabricate special high-precision bearings for the fire-control boxes of new frigates. The orders had to be placed in America.[79]

On 19 May 1951 the Minister of Defence submitted to his ministerial colleagues his first periodic report on 'The Progress of Rearmament': more doleful tidings. A shortage of skilled labour, 'which is likely to persist,' had already led to 'clashes between defence and export demands for labour in a few areas'.[80] There existed in particular 'a serious shortage of skilled draftsmen and other professional and drawing office staff'. The Minister took pains to enlighten his fellow ministers about the machine-tool bottleneck and the consequent need to interfere 'considerably with non-defence orders'. He reported that for certain special types of tool Britain was 'entirely dependent on the United States'.[81]

On 7 June the Committee on Productive Capacity pondered a report from the Ministry of Labour that 'labour for the defence programme was not being found in sufficient numbers, because many firms attempted to superimpose defence contracts on their normal civilian production . . .' The Ministry advocated that such firms should be 'persuaded' to man their defence work by curtailing civilian production.[82]

On 8 June the Chancellor was informing his ministerial colleagues that 'there is a real danger of an unregulated scramble for raw materials which will produce quite disproportionately serious and widespread shortages and bottle-necks'. The difficulties, he said, were particularly acute in the engineering industry 'which is so much concerned with defence, exports and investment . . .'[83] He therefore advocated a system of allocating raw materials in order to give priority to defence production. This drew on the same day an objection from the Minister of Fuel and Power, Philip Noel-Baker, who argued that 'in the extremely difficult circumstances in which we find ourselves', the Chancellor's scheme was 'misconceived'. It would 'inevitably lead to the most serious difficulties' by starving the energy industries of steel. They needed this steel, wrote Noel-Baker, for building new production plant in order to expand their output of coal, gas and electricity. Already requests from some firms on defence production for extra gas and electric current had had to be refused.[84]

On 3 July the Committee on Productive Capacity turned its attention to the supply of labour to the Standard Motor Company in Coventry for the production of Avon jet engines (essential to the Royal Air Force's three-year programme), and to other defence contractors in that heartland of British light engineering. If the necessary 10,000 men were to be found, it could only be at the expense of diverting a quarter of the 1950 labour force engaged in civil motor car production, which 'would have a very serious effect on the export trade'.[85] This raised a question of national importance:

> In 1950 522,000 cars and 263,000 commercial vehicles had been produced in this country. Of this total 400,000 cars and 145,000 commercial vehicles had been exported. In the first five months of this year 200,000 cars and 110,000 commercial vehicles had been produced, out of which 155,000 cars and 71,000 commercial vehicles had been exported . . .

Hence 'it would be a very serious matter if exports of vehicles were reduced . . .'

> [but] the very nature of the requirements for the defence programme meant that those firms which provided the highest exports would be the first to suffer a drop in civil production and that the firms which did not export in large quantities would continue to produce the same level of orders.[86]

On 13 July the Committee pondered how far the experience and methods of wartime state control of production might be relevant to the rearmament programme.[87]

On 8 August the Minister of Defence minuted the Prime Minister that industry was reluctant to adjust to meet defence orders at top speed 'where this has meant interference with established business for exports or the home market . . .'[88] Experience so far, he went on, reinforced the view that 'if the plan is to be carried out in full, substantial interference with home consumption and some interference with exports will be inevitable . . .'

On 27 August labour requirements for the entire defence programme came – not for the first time – before the Committee on Productive Capacity. Air defence contracts (already behindhand for want of labour) would demand a net increase of 169,000 men and women. The needs of the army's programme could not yet be estimated because only 50 per cent of the contracts for radio equipment and 60 per cent of those for munitions and other supplies (including vehicles) had so far been taken into account.[89]

On 26 September the Committee's concern of the day was the shortage of nylon, especially needed for field telephone cable and driving bands for projectiles. Though nylon was a valuable export, 'supplies for that purpose would be prejudiced by the need to meet requirements for defence'.[90] The Board of Trade representative therefore pleaded that

> every effort should be made to ensure that an impossible burden was not thrust on the industry in the future. The vulnerability of the industry should be borne in mind, since there was only one source of production of polymer and one source of production of nylon yarn in the United Kingdom.[91]

As a means to avert such an 'impossible burden' the Board of Trade could only propose drastic cuts in exports and home consumption. This evoked a groan from the Treasury spokesman:

> In view of the deteriorating balance of payments position the Treasury were greatly concerned at the proposal to cut down on exports which were at the present time contributing over £20 million per year. A reduction of 400,000 lbs in nylon exports would mean an annual loss of about £1,250,000.[92]

The 'deteriorating balance of payments position' – yes, indeed. For this, threatening yet another national cash-flow crisis, had now become the gravest of all the problems that had ramified from Britain's original entanglement in the Korean conflict.

Month by month through 1951 the white breakers on the lee shore of economic disaster could be more and more plainly seen. In April the Labour Cabinet itself split asunder over the scale and cost of the rearmament programme. The Chancellor, Hugh Gaitskell, in an attempt to control swelling national expenditure in his forthcoming budget, proposed to save £13 million on the social services by making charges for false teeth and spectacles. Back in 1949 an earlier threat to the principle of a completely free health service had awakened the fundamentalist ire of Aneurin Bevan, the Minister of Health and creator of the service. Now, in the new situation created by headlong rearmament, he became even more angry, not least because he, Bevan, a man of passion and son of a miner, personally detested Gaitskell, that priggish, rectitudinous Oxford intellectual and sprig of the imperial governing elite. On 9 April (the eve of budget day) Bevan told a Cabinet meeting in the Prime Minister's room at the House of Commons (chaired by Herbert Morrison in Attlee's absence in hospital with a duodenal ulcer) that if these charges were imposed, he would have to resign. But not only that:

> he would feel obliged to make clear that his differences with his colleagues had not been restricted to this question of charges under the National Health Service. He was also gravely concerned about the economic consequences of the increased defence programme . . .[93]

His concern extended, moreover, beyond Britain's own programme to 'the pace and volume' of Western democracy's rearmament in general:

> He believed that, by trying to do too much too quickly in response to United States pressure, the western democracies were in grave danger of undermining their economic strength. The United Kingdom Government would in his view make a double mistake if they allowed the increased defence programme, not only to distort the national economy, but to do this at the expense of the social services.[94]

Although Bevan's vision of the welfare state might be steamed over with idealistic emotion,[95] his judgement was cool and clear enough in regard to the American belief that the Soviet Union posed a urgent threat of full-scale attack on the West. For instance, he could not understand how a state commanding an annual steel production of 30,000,000 tons could think of taking on an alliance commanding one of 140,000,000 tons.[96]

In contrast, Gaitskell in relation to the 'Cold War' acted within the Cabinet as the influential voice of subservience to America, as a British quisling. In January 1951 he had even been instrumental in securing British support for so calamitous an American act as a resolution in the United Nations General Assembly branding China as an aggressor. The passing of this resolution offended not only the Chinese (so hardly helping towards any possible deal that might end the now stalemated Korean War), but also many other Asian countries.[97] Since Gaitskell thus wholeheartedly embraced America's anti-Communist crusade and the Western rearmament driven by it, he was resolute that expenditure on defence must be preserved at the cost of the Health Service. And so in his budget it was.

The resignation of the enraged and defeated Bevan followed on 22 April. Both he and Harold Wilson, who resigned as President of the Board of Trade with him, used their resignation speeches in the Commons to seek to explain to the British public that the rearmament programme of £4.7 billion was more than the economy could bear without crippling damage, not least to exports.

As early as June 1951 it was becoming grimly apparent that they were right. On the 22nd of that month Gaitskell himself minuted his Cabinet colleagues:

> The economic situation is serious. We face the possibility of quite a heavy deficit in our overall balance of payments [up to £400 million in 1952] and perhaps a difficult dollar position a little later on. Prices are rising faster at home than we expected and the inflationary 'spiral' is in operation . . .[98]

He was convinced that the key to the problem of inflation lay 'in holding down import prices'. Though Gaitskell was too reticent to say so even to his ministerial colleagues, these prices had been puffed up by the American-led scramble for raw materials to feed Western rearmament. But the Chancellor did go so far as to express the hope that another British mission to Washington might persuade the Americans 'to agree on an effective policy for stabilising commodity prices in world markets',[99] or, *en clair*, to stop being so greedy and selfish.

On 27 July the Minister of Defence, circulating a detailed shopping list of the defence programme's needs and costs, remarked:

> The extent to which requirements can be met during the three years is obviously limited by production possibilities and the necessity to leave adequate capacity available for the manufacture of exports and essential goods for the home market.[100]

Obviously!

But this did not stop the Minister from asking that the production programme be enlarged still further.[101]

On the same day the civil servants and economists on the

Economic Steering Committee gave sign that their stomachs too were becoming queasy in the rising economic swell:

> The more detailed defence programme which has now been worked out must be considered against the background of a considerably weaker economy than was expected when the original exercise on the increased defence effort was done at the beginning of the year. This weakening takes the form primarily of a deterioration in the balance of payments but is also due in part to a worsening of the prospects for steel and coal production; and it reduces the capacity of the country to bear the economic burden of carrying out the programme on time.[102]

On 31 July 1951 the Chancellor passed his own sour judgement on the Minister of Defence's new shopping list:

> He had no doubt that this production programme would mean a greater burden on the national economy, especially as the balance of payments situation was now less favourable than when we had first undertaken the £4,700 million programme . . . this additional burden could not be accepted . . .[103]

Britain was already doing proportionately more than the rest of the NATO, admitted Gaitskell, 'not excluding the Americans'. £4,700 million was 'our absolute limit'.

On 4 September came confirmation of this judgement from the British representative on the NATO Financial and Economic Board (the body charged with implementing the Nitze 'burden-sharing exercise'), Eric Roll. In reporting on the board's work so far,[104] Roll too had no doubt that Britain was making a greater proportionate effort than any other NATO member, even the United States. Some other countries, such as Canada, Belgium and Denmark, were getting away with programmes that were 'inequitably low.'[105] Moreover, the American representative had perforce concurred in the board's judgement that the United States' own level of rearmament would not damage her already high standard of living, which would in any case resume its upward trend in about eighteen months' time.[106] Nevertheless, Roll reported, this had not deterred the Americans from pressing the Europeans to adopt even larger defence programmes.[107]

On 8 September 1951 a brief for the Chancellor on 'Economic Questions in the N.A.T.O.' for a forthcoming meeting of the NATO Council took an even gloomier view of Anglo-American differences. Whereas Britain wanted the 'burden-sharing exercise' to recognize that her £4.7 billion programme was 'an equitable discharge of our N.A.T.O. obligations and the maximum tolerable over the next three years', the United States wanted NATO members to commit themselves to carrying out the full 'Medium Term Defence Plan' (which in the British case would amount to £6 billion).[108] The Americans comfortably believed that 'the economic impact of the present defence programme is not as great as some European countries think'.[109] This was the reverse of the British view, as the brief for the Chancellor made clear:

> The United Kingdom is undertaking a defence programme which we now expect will impose the most severe strain upon nearly all aspects of our economic life and to involve [sic] serious sacrifices, both in the standard of living and in our industrial re-equipment, and even more important, to endanger our external solvency . . .[110]

In fact, Britain was 'already experiencing strains which for many other countries are still things of the future'.[111] Yet despite such exertions Britain still remained dependent on America 'for a considerable amount of end-item supplies to meet the full requirements of our forces'.[112]

It was in this same month of September 1951, when the adverse economic wind was strengthening towards gale force, that the Americans chose to present a bill (to be paid in dollars) to Britain for stores, equipment, transport, and hospital and other services provided to the two British brigades taking part in the American-inspired and American-controlled UN campaign in Korea. That campaign had now come to rest in protracted stalemate after months of indecisive attack and counterattack. Although armistice negotiations had begun in July between the American (so-called 'UN') command and the North Koreans, it would in the event take another two years to reach agreement. Thus was fully borne out the Cabinet Defence Committee's fear back in the summer of 1950 that the campaign in Korea would prove 'long and costly' (see p. 23 above).

The Americans coupled their surprise invoice for logistic support of the British forces in Korea in 1950–51 with a draft agreement for Britain to sign 'whereby His Majesty's Government agrees to accept and carry out the directives and policies of the Commanding General'.[113] Asked the Treasury: 'Should we accept any liability whatever?'[114]

> The fact that we sent two brigades to Korea must be taken as meaning that we undertook to maintain them there, failing any prior reservations on that point. No such reservations were made. The presentation of a bill by the Americans comes as an unpleasant shock and we certainly must question closely the scale of the charges [author's note: an initial charge of $2 million, and $2.3 million per month for maintenance]; but since we reached no prior agreement with them under which they would undertake to waive charges, it is entirely within their discretion to do so or not as they choose.[115]

In any case, according to the Treasury, if Britain refused to cough up for her forces in Korea, then America might suggest that her troops, air forces and bases in the United Kingdom ought to be paid for by Britain.[116]

Nor in the Treasury's judgement was this present bill necessarily the end of the matter. What about further dollar-costly military entanglements in the future?

> The possibility of operations such as those in Korea, perhaps on a larger scale, with the subsequent burden on our balance of payments, is certainly alarming, since it implies the creation of great dollar liabilities if we send troops to any theatre of operations in which the Americans are supplying [author's note: i.e., contributing] other U.N. forces . . .[117]

In this same month of September 1951 it was being predicted that next year the Sterling Area would incur a deficit of $1.1 billion. The Government therefore decided that the British family must make do in 1952 with smaller rations of meat, eggs, tea, sugar and cheese as its contribution towards plugging this colossal hole. Concurrently ministers began to ponder various quid pro quos and other stratagems for extracting enough dollars from the Americans to reduce the deficit by at least half.[118] Thus in October the idea was canvassed that the Americans should make off-shore dollar purchases of British engineering goods. But the Ministry of Supply had to point out that this dodge suffered from the disadvantage that the engineering industry was already stretched to the limit, with defence demands in 1952 likely to bite yet more deeply into production for the home and export markets.[119] The effect of further cuts to these markets in order to supply the Americans would, in the Ministry's judgement, be calamitous. In regard to the home market,

> even this year's £700m of capital equipment has been little enough when measured against a demand from industry for more efficient equipment and the exceptional need to supply machinery and plant for the switch-over to defence production. To the extent that the supply of capital goods to U.K. industries is cut down the efficiency of industry is jeopardised . . .[120]

As for reducing exports,

> already the overseas markets for all types of engineering goods are being invaded by German and Japanese manufacturers – not always because they can offer lower prices but because they are able to offer better deliveries. If we were to neglect these markets in order to use the productive capacity for earning dollars through offshore purchases, we might find we had lost the markets for ever.[121]

By November 1951 the economic gale had reached storm force, with an overloaded, underpowered Britain haplessly drifting off a lee shore in the third and worst balance-of-payments crisis since the war.[122]

On the last day of the month a new Chancellor of the Exchequer in a new Conservative Government fired the distress rockets.

3. 'Trying To Do Too Many Things At Once'

The rockets took the form of a report which despite its misleadingly innocuous title of 'Our Economic Objectives and Prospects'[1] served starkly to illuminate for ministers the entire scene of imminent national shipwreck. What, for a start, had been the Labour Government's grand objectives at the start of the rearmament programme last January? As tersely summed up now by the new Chancellor (R. A. Butler), they had been 'to achieve adequate security and to maintain a sound economy, on which our military power and political influence ultimately depend . . .'[2]

Externally 'a sound economy' had meant achieving at least an equilibrium in the British balance of payments and the Sterling Area's gold and dollar account. Even so, the Labour Government had taken, in Butler's view, 'a calculated risk' in settling for a mere equilibrium rather than a surplus.[3] At home 'a sound economy' had meant controlling inflation and getting enough coal, steel and raw materials to feed industrial expansion. It had also meant winning even more coal so that it could once again become a major British export. But most of all 'a sound economy' had required holding a balance between the conflicting demands on the engineering industry made by exports, defence, investment and other home uses.

Now, however, less than a year on, it appeared that this admirably comprehensive strategy had developed a tiny snag. It was that, in Butler's own words, 'we have fallen far short of achieving these objectives both on the external and on the internal sides'.[4]

Instead of a balance in our external accounts the United Kingdom will have a deficit this year of about £500 million. Against the objective of a balance in the sterling area's gold and dollar accounts and the maintenance of our reserves, our reserves will have [sustained] a loss over the year of $1,000 m.[5]

In 1952 Britain was likely to fall an extra $1,000 million into the red, in contrast to the pre-rearmament target of about $560 million per annum in the black. And a surplus of this size was 'not a frill', Butler wrote, 'but . . . a basic necessity if the United Kingdom is to retain its stability and if sterling is to be maintained as an international currency'.

At home, he gloomed on, coal was having to be imported instead of becoming a major British export and bargaining chip. Shortage of steel was throttling industrial expansion. Worse:

> The aggregate load on the engineering industry has now proved to be excessive. In consequence the defence programme is not being fully achieved, the output of the engineering industries is ceasing to expand and our exports of engineering goods are threatening to fall.

Why, then, had the Labour Government opted for so unrealistically grand a post-Korea rearmament programme? Butler's own answer was that they had expected the 'Nitze burden-sharing exercise' to bail Britain out.

> We hoped that it would be shown that the burden we were undertaking in carrying out the defence programme was so much beyond our fair share that the Americans would supply us with the necessary dollars for the economic support of our economy and, in addition to this, with the end items which are required to fill the gap in our programme.[6]

Thus Britain had solicited the United States for handouts of $600 million for the first half of 1952 and $1,000 million for 1952–53, as well as 'some assurance' about continuing economic aid to support the long-term costs of defence. She had also asked for American steel to bring British imports in 1952 to 1.5 million tons more than in 1950.[7]

It appeared, however, that despite 'the special relationship' the Americans had not been in the giving vein: 'In none of these respects have we received the assurances for which we have asked

... It has been impossible to extract from the Americans any assurances of a long term character.'[8]

Or as a Treasury brief was to put it:

> Our whole experience since their [the Americans'] first approaches on rearmament in July 1950 has been most unfortunate. Indeed, the results of United States actions – stoppage of Marshall Aid, tin and rubber policy, virtual abandonment of burden-sharing ... failure to find means to finance U.K. defence production ... and the repeated changes of front on the $300 million [Defence Aid in kind] – would be more readily understandable if their purpose was to weaken the U.K. economy, rather than to strengthen it.[9]

When Butler turned from Britain's present plight to her future prospects, he took on the doomsday tones of an auditor reporting to the board of a company fraudulently trading at a loss:

> Against all these uncertainties we are now committing ourselves to patterns of production for a long way ahead which will put it beyond our power to cope with the economic problems that confront us ... This situation carries with it the gravest dangers.
>
> It is of cardinal importance that the United Kingdom should be able to show that it is in control of its affairs. The United Kingdom is the hub of the sterling area. Unless we can show ourselves in reasonable balance in our external accounts ... we cannot hope to maintain cohesion in the sterling area or maintain sterling as a sound international currency ...[10]

Clearly the Chancellor had profited from Mr Micawber's famous financial analysis: 'Annual income twenty pounds, annual expenditure nineteen pounds nineteen [shillings] and six [pence], result happiness. Annual income twenty pounds, annual expenditure twenty pounds ought [shillings] and six [pence], result misery.' However, at the best of times it was no easier for Britain than for Micawber to achieve the desired happiness, as Butler went on to explain:

> We are particularly vulnerable to changes in [import] prices. As bankers to the sterling area we are also vulnerable to fluctuations in

the earning capacity of the other sterling area countries, which puts the central gold and dollar reserves in great hazard.[11]

Without some remedy for Britain's economic overstretch, Butler continued,

> we shall inevitably continue in a situation of crisis, dependent on American aid for an indefinite period ahead. There are many serious dangers in such dependence. Interference in our internal affairs is unavoidable . . . The commitment to our present defence programme gives a rigid shape to our economy preventing us from meeting changes in external circumstances. We sacrifice our export markets. In this respect we are reproducing, though on a smaller scale, the sacrifices which we imposed on ourselves when, in return for war-time Lend/Lease, we virtually abandoned our export trade. Finally, we run the continual risk of the withdrawal of American assistance, which would leave us in a position both exposed and unbalanced.[12]

But Butler had so far only sketched Britain's short-term future prospects, drying to the mouth and moistening to the palms though these were. He clearly found just as disturbing – perhaps even more so – the long-term outlook. For this 'would present many grave dangers', even if Britain could weather the next few years with American help:

> We should emerge from the rearmament period with inadequate reserves, with no assurance of further U.S. aid, with our export markets reduced, with a continuous and possibly increased claim on our resources for defence, with German and Japanese competition at full blast and finally, with industrial efficiency in a relatively worse position compared with that of the United states than it is now.[13]

Butler's paper could hardly be bettered as a critique of the total strategy whereby a hard-up island state with only a third of America's population and a mere eighth of her GNP[14] had been trying to play in the same world league. But when he came to explore possible remedies, he showed himself to be as much in thrall to Britain's past as the Labour Cabinet in its time.

For just as that Cabinet in 1948 (in planning its use of Marshall Aid) had given the priority to maintaining the Sterling Area and keeping Britain's top hat on as its banker, so too did Butler now. And he did so despite what he himself called the 'hazards', such as 'the unpredictable changes in the demands of the Rest of the Sterling Area on us'.[15] Hence he insisted that the gold and dollar reserves must be rebuilt as soon as possible. Hence 'we must establish the principle that exports are a first charge on our resources . . . In particular, we must make available more engineering products for the export markets.'[16] Hence there was a need to bring 'order into the competition which now exists between exports on the one hand and home demand on the other for defence, investment and consumption'.[17] And hence, in Butler's own words, 'We must also reduce home investment in engineering products by £100 million per annum at 1950 prices below the current level.' The load on the construction industry would also have to be held down to the level of 1950.[18]

So here, played now on a Conservative fiddle, was a fresh variation on the Labour Government's leitmotif in industrial policy from 1947 onwards.[19]

But it was in the very last paragraph of his report that Butler, in his own words, 'raised the fundamental question'. And that was: 'whether it is practicable for the United Kingdom to pursue simultaneously the twin objectives of maintaining economic solvency and re-arming on the scale hitherto contemplated.' His answer, delivered in veiled language expressive of a subtle (some said too subtle) intellect, was that 'some diminution and re-balancing of the defence burden is inevitable'.[20]

Next day Butler supplemented his deeply depressing discourse on 'Our Economic Objectives and Prospects' with a breakdown of state expenditure (excluding defence) according to the existing estimates for 1951–52. This showed the running cost of the Labour Government's proudest achievement, the new welfare state, as £715 million (£400 million for the National Health Service and £315 million for National Insurance and National Assistance). When housing subsidies and local grants (£130 million) and food subsidies (£400 million) were added, 'New Jerusalem' would be swallowing a total of £1,245 million in 1951–52, or nearly 60 per cent of the national budget other than for defence.[21]

Butler's two reports were now to serve as briefs for a newly created Cabinet 'damage control party' (as it would be dubbed in a stricken warship). This 'Sub-Committee on the Economic Situation'[22] was charged with recommending which items of state expenditure should be jettisoned in order to save the overloaded economy from foundering.

They faced much the same kind of problem as the Labour Government after the enforced devaluation of 1949. That Government at Attlee's behest had then adopted the principle of simply slicing 10 per cent off every field of spending, even including capital investment in industry and infrastructure. It was a ruse that had enabled them to shirk radical but painful choices that might have put an end to Britain's overstretch – like running down global defence commitments, or phasing out the function of banker to the Sterling Area; and, at home, making drastic cuts in 'New Jerusalem' or even deflating the economy at the sacrifice of full employment.[23] But such choices had lain far beyond the bounds of the politically thinkable, let alone politically possible, for Labour ministers shackled both by their idealistic creed and by the commitments which they had made to an expectant British people in the 1945 General Election.

Calamitously, however, the new Conservative Government were now to prove just as shackled by their own political faith and by the pledges which they in turn had made in order to win the October 1951 Election.

For in regard to world affairs the Conservative manifesto, in its own words, 'put first the safety, progress, and cohesion of the British Empire and Commonwealth of Nations'; second, the unity of the English-speaking peoples; and third, a United Europe.[24] Britain, it promised, would be brought back to her rightful place in the world: i.e., what it called the pre-eminent position she had held at the end of the war.

But what else could be expected of Winston Churchill, the seventy-seven-year-old party leader? After all, was he not a ministerial veteran of the British Empire's brief consummation in the Great War as a cohesive political and military power? Had he not served as Prime Minister in the Second World War when Britain outwardly remained equal partner with the United States? Was he not a romantic believer in the destiny of 'the English-speaking peoples'? And was he not the actual author of the 1951 Conservative manifesto's Edwardian imperialist sentiments and its Edwardian-baroque turns of phrase alike?

For that matter, abdication of Britain's traditional world role could hardly be expected of Anthony Eden, now Foreign Secretary again. He had been a prominent pre-war 'moralizing international-ist' and champion of the League of Nations,[25] and a post-war founding father of the League's successor, the United Nations Organization. After all, the UN Security Council now provided the splendid stage on which Great Britain as a permanent member and Eden himself as Foreign Secretary could play the global grandee and prefect.

Furthermore, 64 per cent of Conservative candidates' addresses in the 1951 General Election had also blown the bugle for 'the Commonwealth and Empire'.[26] It was, after all, less than seven years since Australian and Canadian airmen had flown with the Royal Air Force over Germany; since Canadian divisions had fought alongside British from Normandy to the Rhine; since New Zealand and Indian divisions had completed the long slog up Italy with the Eighth Army. So now – just as always with the Empire – sentiment and kinship pulled in one way while the stark realities of geography and of British strategic and financial overstretch pulled in another.

Nor was there any suggestion in the Conservative manifesto of drastically remodelling the vast institution of 'New Jerusalem', in the well-staffed care of which a dependent British people now felt so comfortably sheltered from the world and its stresses. Rather, the manifesto promised that even better health services would be provided for the same amount of money, and that pensions would be reviewed sympathetically. The Conservatives also undertook not to make radical changes in the level of the food subsidies[27] which by artificially keeping down the price of staple foodstuffs enabled the industrial working class to spend more of their wages on wrecking their health with cigarettes and alcohol, so in turn adding to the bill for supplying 'free' health care.

As for 'full employment', that admired achievement of New Jerusalem but also accelerator of wage inflation and brake on technological change,[28] the Conservatives had already in the 1950 General Election committed themselves to its preservation. Even so, in October 1951 no fewer than 69 per cent of Conservative election addresses made a point of reaffirming this promise.[29]

It appeared, moreover, that in one respect New Jerusalem was going to become even bigger and better under the Conservatives, since their manifesto promised that housing would be given a priority second only to defence, with a target of 300,000 new houses a year.[30] Here was an ill omen for investment in re-equipping industry and infrastructure, a topic which attracted no mention either in the Conservative manifesto or the candidates' addresses.[31] Clearly parlours must yet again come before plant.

Given all these political constraints, it is little surprise that the Cabinet's Sub-Committee on the Economic Situation could only do in 1951–52 as the Labour Government had done in 1949, and seek to chip bits off various commitments rather than make ruthless total-strategic choices between them.

For a start, there could be no of question of reneging on the basic principle of unlimited free health care on demand, even though the 1942 prediction of the wartime Chancellor of the Exchequer, Sir Kingsley Wood, had already come true that the Beveridgean welfare state would demand a subsidy from the taxpayer 'which will grow in the course of time to immense proportions'.[32] On present policies, Butler informed his colleagues, the National Health Service was going to cost £32 million more to run in 1952–53 than the current year's £399 million budget,[33] itself two and a half times Aneurin Bevan's original 1945 estimate (for the whole UK) of £162 million a year.[34] All that could be hoped for, according to Butler, was to hold the total down to the £399 million (the Labour Government itself having set a limit of £400 million).[35]

How then to cut out £32 million? With hacksaws and spanners at the ready the Cabinet damage-control party tackled the nuts and bolts of health care.[36] A 1/- charge on prescriptions would save £12 million. A 'hotel charge' for patients in hospital would be worth £14.25 million at 2/6d a day; £17.5 million at 3/- a day.[37] A flat charge of £1 for dentistry would save £7.25 million. Charges for certain appliances, for 'amenity' beds and for the use of day nurseries would bring in £1.25 million. Total: £34.75 or £37.75 million, depending on the level of 'hotel charge'.

However, Butler had to point out that if 'mental defectives', nearly 50 per cent of the hospital population, were exempted from the hotel charge, the saving would be about halved.[38]

Much time was now spent by the Sub-Committee on the Economic Situation in debate of these alternative tinkerings at the problem, although at least the shilling charge for prescriptions went through on the nod.[39] At a meeting on 7 December the idea of a 'hotel charge' for hospital patients was dropped, despite the comment of an unidentified hard man (surely Lord Cherwell, the Paymaster-General: see below) that, in view of the objective of substantially cutting Government expenditure, 'it was disappointing that in this field . . . the best that could be secured appeared to be virtually a continuation of present expenditure'.[40] Asked this hard man: 'Should not an attempt be made to obtain more drastic economies?'

But where? The Minister of Health, Harry Crookshank, pertinently reminded his colleagues that

> while there was no moral obligation to maintain expenditure at the £400 million 'ceiling' imposed by the former Government, it would be difficult politically to justify any substantial decrease below that level. It was clear, however, that in the present economic situation *expenditure should not be allowed greatly to exceed it* [added emphasis].[41]

The Paymaster-General, Lord Cherwell (Frederick Lindemann, educated at the Darmstadt Hochschule and the Physikalisch-Chemisches Institut, Berlin: a Germanic technocrat among British small 'l' liberals), offered his own alternative to what he called 'the proposed piece-meal economies' – simply charge the public with any excess over £400 million by bumping up their National Insurance contributions. However, the Chancellor objected that 'this method would have the disadvantage of offering no deterrent against extravagant use of the service . . .'

When on 12 December 1951 the Sub-Committee met to decide finally on the minor items to be hacksawed off the Health Service, Cherwell repeated that 'he was not satisfied that a cut could not be made in the very heavy costs of the hospital service: a flat cut of 15% in these costs would make all the other savings proposed unnecessary and would raise much less difficult political problems . . .'[42] A flat cut of 15 per cent! Oh dear no! His horrified colleagues pointed out that 'further savings on the scale suggested might result in the closing of hospital beds . . .'[43]

The Sub-Committee eventually agreed to recommend to the Cabinet such daringly radical measures as charging a shilling for prescriptions (£12 million saved); suspending both the free dental service except for 'priority' cases (£20 million saved, rather than the previously proposed £7.25 million) and the 'Supplementary Ophthalmic Service' (£5 million saved); and imposing the 'minor' charges on the customer (£1.25 million saved). Total saved: £38.25 million annually, or less than 10 per cent of the 1951–52 budget. However, if instead of suspending free dental treatment altogether it was decided to make a flat charge of £1, the total savings would shrink to £25.5 million.[44]

On 20 December the Cabinet duly agreed to the proposed 1/- prescription charge. But they winced at the political pain of suspending the free dental and ophthalmic service, and opted instead for the charge of £1 for all treatment other than false teeth and related work (saving only £7.5 million instead of £20 million).[45] They settled for charges for certain appliances, for amenity beds in hospitals and for use of day nurseries, these saving the colossal total of £1.25 million.

Thus the Chancellor's initial hope of saving £32 million and the 'damage control party's' recommendations of saving at best £37.75 million and at worst £34.75 million had been whittled down in the end to £20.75 million – a ludicrously small result from so much ministerial time and effort.

But this did not conclude the matter. On 10 January 1952 ministers whose election manifesto had promised to restore Britain to her rightful place in the world pondered such means to securing that place's financial foundations as a charge of three quid for surgical boots, a quid for a truss and a fiver for a pair of wigs.[46] Though they duly endorsed these and other footling levies, they knocked half a million off the proposed cuts in the dental service by exempting children and expectant or nursing mothers from the £1 charge.[47]

This brought the final saving to only £20.25 million, or less than

5 per cent of the existing Health Service estimate of £431 million for 1952–53. Put another way, the service's cost in the current year 1951–52 was not going to be cut, not even going to be held to £399 million, but was actually going to rise by £11.75 million.

This would hardly restore buoyancy to a stricken economy currently carrying a civil budget of £2.1 billion and a rearmament programme totalling £4.7 billion over three years. The Cabinet's 'damage control party' had therefore also been diligently searching for bits that might be chopped off other types of gear and thrown overboard.

Education was one obvious choice for chopping, since it was of supreme national importance, provided the key to the future developed intelligence of the British people, and had already suffered for six years from the Labour Government's niggardliness (see below, Chapter 22). On 4 December 1951 the Chancellor of the Exchequer canvassed such economies as increasing the charge for school meals by tuppence; lowering the school-leaving age back from fifteen to fourteen or raising the school-entry age from five to six; or reducing long-term programmes of capital investment from £468 million to £378 million, which would save £2 million in 1952 and £4 million in 1953.[48] These and various other trimmings would save about £24 million in a full year.

However, the Minister of Education (Florence Horsbrugh) objected to raising the charge for school meals, both on the score that children might not get enough to eat (suggesting a deep suspicion of working-class housewifery) and also because of the 'political difficulties'.[49] She likewise pointed out to her colleagues that changing the ages either for entering or leaving school would raise 'social problems and would be extremely unpopular'.[50] In the end the Minister, the Secretary of State for Scotland and the Chancellor compromised over the charge for school meals. It would be raised by one penny instead of two. Further pettifoggeries brought the 1952–53 education estimates for England and Wales down to £204.3 million compared with the current year's £200.2 million. In a wonderfully bold and constructive move, an extra £2 million would be saved by doubling the proposed cut in capital investment in schools and further education colleges in 1952–53.

But at a later meeting even one penny on the school dinner was ruled out because of the 'political difficulties'.[51] The Chancellor observed disconsolately that

> it seemed that substantial savings in expenditure on education could be obtained only either by dismissing a large number of teachers or by charging fees to pupils. It would be a very serious matter to do either of these things, but it might be necessary to consider them . . .[52]

Whether politically a very serious matter or not, it was estimated that a charge of a mere 1/- per week per pupil, about half the price of a packet of ten cigarettes, would have yielded £13 million a year.[53]

Since for the purpose of the present exercise the Sub-Committee assumed that food subsidies would remain next year as in 1951–52 (£410 million),[54] it therefore turned out that after all the laborious study and protracted debate the biggest fields of civil expenditure by far were still going to cost broadly the same in 1952–53 as in 1951–52.

What else, then, could go overboard? The Ministry of Aviation offered a cut of just over £5 million on a projected 1952–53 budget of £18 million – £3.7 million of that cut accounted for by estimated reductions in subsidies to the nationalized airlines for flying un-economic British-made airliners.[55] The Board of Trade could only find a saving of £289,180 on a budget of £6.6 million.[56] Other departments such as the Ministry of Works offered similarly meagre slices off small budgets.[57] It was like trying to trim a dangerously listing ship by throwing the wardroom crockery overboard.

Could any money be saved by shedding some of the 168,000 tax-eating civil servants required to administer all the regulations and to process all the paper involved in the welfare state and the 'planned economy'? The Chancellor reminded his colleagues that a reduction of 25,000 in the desk-ridden would save about £11 million.[58] However, the Sub-Committee on the Economic Situation guessed that shedding 15–20,000 was the best that could be hoped for, since the proposed exemptions to the new health charges would actually require extra clerks to shuffle the forms.[59]

When all the items proposed for throwing overboard were totted up, Government civil expenditure *as a whole* (but excluding civil defence) in 1952–53 would therefore be still no smaller than in 1951–52.[60] This was as far as the Sub-Committee on the Economic Situation could wriggle within the narrow cage of what ministers took to be the politically possible. The Sub-Committee could only seek solace in reflecting that since expenditure had been rising in recent years by about £100 million annually and costs were likely to rise by 10 per cent next year, 'it is a greater achievement to keep expenditure stationary than appears on the face of the figures . . .'[61]

Just the same, this 'achievement' alone could hardly free Britain from the total-strategic dilemma into which she had been floundering ever deeper since the outbreak of the Korean War. The essential nature of that dilemma had been defined by this same Sub-Committee back in December 1951 with an accuracy which contrasted brutally with the rhetoric and reassurance peddled by the Conservative manifesto[62] to voters in the General Election only two months earlier:

> The basic fact is that we are trying to do too many things at once; to re-arm, to maintain our standard of living and social services, to carry out our international commitments, to assist in overseas development and to maintain the sterling system . . .[63]

Since it was proving impossible to cut Government civil expenditure radically at home, what about the overseas costs of British total strategy?

But even in the face of the Chancellor's warning that their decisions 'must be adequate to meet a menacing situation . . .',[64] ministers could not bring themselves even to contemplate shedding the greatest overload of all on the economy: the world role, financial as well as military.

For them just as for their Labour predecessors the preservation of the Sterling Area and of the pound sterling as an international currency still came first and foremost in economic priority, no matter what the ensuing sacrifices at home. Wrote the Sub-Committee on the Economic Situation in its draft report:

> We should definitely announce our view that it is absolutely necessary for the soundness of the United Kingdom economy and of the

sterling area system for the United Kingdom to have a surplus on current account as a regular feature of its economic life.[65]

Since it was now reckoned that the balance of payments deficit in the second half of 1951 might be some 30 per cent bigger than earlier estimates and the gold and dollar deficit in the fourth quarter of the year alone 40 per cent bigger, the prospects for 1952, reported the Sub-Committee, were 'considerably worse than previously thought'.[66] With this rate of bleeding, the reserves would be down by mid-1952 to the level they were when the Labour Government devalued in 1949. In short, there could be 'no argument about the magnitude of the problem which faces us'.[67]

It followed that 'our major objective must be to stop or reverse this trend of our balance of payments and in the gold and dollar reserves as soon as possible'.[68]

But how?

The Sub-Committee's answer was hardly novel: 'The Government must establish and observe the principle that exports are a first charge on our resources.'[69] The aim should be to build up the volume of exports by at least £100 million a year, even though it would be 'difficult if not impossible to attain this figure during 1952–53'.[70]

Perhaps learning from the Labour Government's vain efforts to boost 'the export drive' by means of preachy advertising campaigns in the newspapers and on hoardings, the Sub-Committee observed that exhortation alone 'is not enough'. Yet as they acutely pointed out,

> a nation which was seeking to carry out a large defence programme, to maintain consumption levels at home, and to sustain investment upon a scale beyond its monetary and material resources, has little chance of increasing exports at the same time – quite the contrary.[71]

The Sub-Committee went so far as to acknowledge, even if back-handedly, that British industrial capacity was simply too small to support British world-power pretensions:

> the main reason why we cannot export enough to close the external gap is the excessive load of home demand on the engineering and metal-using industries. We cannot sell more consumer goods overseas

for lack of customers. We cannot sell more coal or raw materials because we are not producing enough. Only the engineering industries can provide the really substantial increase in exports we need. The production of these industries is held down by shortage of steel. Consequently more for export means less for the home market. But the home market is demanding more not less; primarily for defence, but also for investment and consumption. Unless the home demand is reduced, exports will fall instead of rise.[72]

As the Sub-Committee's report made clear, this circular loop of an economic predicament was worsened by inflation – partly resulting from sheer excess of home demand over available supplies, but mainly from 'the wage-price spiral'. There was now 'a serious danger that this will get out of hand'.[73] In the twelve months from October 1950 the index of weekly wage-rates had jumped from 111 to 122.

It was obvious enough that the flame under this particular pressure-cooker was supplied by 'full employment'. In the Chancellor's own words,

in conditions of full employment, such as we have today, it is clear that the bargaining power of Trade Unions is very strong. Employers in general can sell all they can produce profitably and are afraid that they will never get their labour back if they once lose it. Workers know that there is plenty of work available. Thus there is no real obstacle to the steady increase in wages, which in turn leads to corresponding increases of prices.[74]

Wrote Butler: 'I must tell my colleagues that I do not see any easy answer to this problem.'[75] In fact, an easy – or at least, operationally effective – answer did exist: simply turn down the gas under the flame, or, in other words, deflate the economy. This would have ended 'full employment' and so destroyed the unions' bargaining strength. It would also have made it harder for firms to make a profit, so weeding out the inefficient through bankruptcy and in this way toning up the performance of British industry as a whole.

But such deflation lay far beyond the bounds of the politically possible for a new Conservative Government committed to 'the postwar consensus'. Butler had to acknowledge that the wage-price spiral 'cannot be arrested purely by budgetary means unless these are pushed so far as to create much more unemployment than is economically or socially desirable'.[76] Small 'l' liberal as he was and an appeaser by deep instinct,[77] he looked instead to the reasonableness of what he called 'thoughtful people' for an answer to the wage-price spiral:

> My own view is that this is a problem which can only be dealt with if it is fully understood by the whole nation. Great benefits have been gained, both by employers and workers, from the virtual disappearance of unemployment. It is inconceivable to me that the country would wish to throw away these benefits through a violent inflation, if the issue were squarely placed before them.[78]

He therefore advocated that a White Paper be published 'setting out the problem of inflation in simple language . . .'

> It would explain what the people themselves have to do if we are to keep full employment and a reasonable stability of prices at the same time. My hope would be that such a document would lead to wide discussion and the creation of a public opinion in which the problem could be managed.[79]

It would be unfair to condemn Butler for his faith in human reasonableness and his neglect of the nasty realities of greed, power and leverage, for his naivety was to be shared by governments of both political parties during the next three decades, always to their ultimate disillusion.

Since, in his words, 'taxation has reached, if not exceeded, the limits which can be imposed in peace-time',[80] he saw only one other possible means of reducing the inflationary excess of consumers' demand over supply. That was to put the brakes on that basic welfare-state process whereby money was confiscated via taxation from the better-off (and potential savers) and then stuffed into the pockets of the poor (and probable spendthrift seekers of instant gratification).[81] But he recognized that the reduction of what he delicately called 'transfer payments' would raise 'serious political and social difficulties', or, in other words, was out of the question.[82]

So the Conservative Government was left with only one major expedient with which to lighten the general load on the economy, accommodate the rearmament programme (even as rephased over four years instead of three), and at the same time drive up exports for the sake of a large enough balance of payments to enable Britain to go on playing banker to the Sterling Area. It was the expedient which Butler had put forward in his initial report on the current crisis on 30 November 1951, and the same as the Labour Government had employed year after year – simply curb investment in re-equipping old-fashioned British factories and building new ones, in developing new technologies, and in modernizing Britain's anti-quated and ill-maintained roads, railways, docks, and telecommuni-cations net. Instead, export the engineering products thus saved, even if that meant helping other nations to modernize their own industries to Britain's later disadvantage.[83]

On 17 December 1951 the Investment Programmes Committee (civil servants) turned in their detailed homework on a directive from ministers that civil building work must be cut back enough to permit £90 million of defence building, and that investment in plant, machinery and vehicles at present approved for 1952 must be cut by £140 million.[84] The heaviest sacrifices were to fall on manufacturing industry and transport/communications, with gross fixed investment in 1952 set at 18.5 per cent lower than in 1950.[85] In contrast, defence capital investment even as reduced under new plans for 1952 would be more than three times as high as in 1950.[86]

What these cuts would mean for Britain's obsolescent industrial system and crumbling infrastructure soon became apparent. For example, the Investment Programmes Committee, loyal to ministe-rial instructions, was compelled to disregard an 'extremely strong' case by the Railways Executive that it was 'now imperative to restore the full efficiency of the track [and] to repair a large number of structures which, if left alone, will become more and more dilapidated . . .'[87] The Committee also had to accept that it would only be possible to start 'very few new road works' in 1952, and that these would in any case not be improvements to strategic routes (at present mostly asphalted meandering Anglo-Saxon cow paths) but serve the social experiment of 'new towns'.[88] They likewise had to accept that the ports programme 'would not enable any new works to be started in 1952'.[89] Moreover, even though shortage of steel was throttling Britain's entire economy, the steel industry's permitted investment in 1952 meant postponing large-scale new developments.[90] As for manufacturing industry, the Committee reported that they had 'no doubt that [their] proposals were far below what it would be profitable and desirable to invest . . .'[91]

So now it was not only the wardroom crockery that was at risk but also the modernizing of the ship's engine room.

On 28 December 1951 the Cabinet broadly endorsed these proposed cuts, although as the Chancellor acknowledged, 'the serious implications . . . were becoming increasingly apparent'.[92]

When the ministerial Economic Policy Committee met for the first time in 1952 on 2 January, departmental ministers bleated as loudly as the Labour predecessors at their short rations of investment. The Minister of Supply (Duncan Sandys) complained that the steel industry's 'already inadequate' development programme would suffer through delays or abandonment of schemes now in hand. The Minister of Agriculture (Sir Thomas Dugdale) was unhappy about suspending schemes of rural electrification. The Assistant Postmaster-General (David Gammans) argued that 'it would be impossible to provide a telephone service adequate to match the expansion of production at which the Government was aiming'. The Parliamentary Secretary to the Board of Trade (Henry Strauss) groaned about 'the serious consequences' to industries sponsored by the board.[93] The President of the Board of Trade (Peter Thorneycroft) had put it even more strongly in a paper the previous day:

> I am most anxious that my colleagues should fully appreciate the crippling effect of the proposals on these industries – which comprise over half of private manufacturing industry . . . possibly one-third of projects approved and in progress will have to be stopped and these are projects of the first importance, either as dollar earners or savers, or to meet basic needs.[94]

In February the Cabinet relented just a little when finally fixing the investment programme for 1952. But only a little. For instance, the British Electricity Authority was to have its ration increased by no less than 0.66 per cent for the sake of rural electrification. Ports were to get an extra 7.94 per cent; the Post Office an extra 0.78 per cent; and iron and steel even an extra 14.54 per cent.[95]

Yet capital investment in manufacturing industry was still to be cut from the 1950 figure of £420 million to only £348.7 million in 1952; in transport and telecommunications from £365.4 million in 1950 to £294.2 million in 1952.[96]

Thus did the new Conservative Government come to sacrifice the long-term strength of Britain for the sake of scraping through an immediate economic crisis and at the same time preserving the Sterling Area.

Yet the crisis entirely owed its origin to the Labour Government's decision under American pressure to pile rearmament on top of the existing British total-strategic overload. And that decision had followed in turn from the Labour Government's initial reluctant committing of a 'token' land force to Korea, equally under American pressure.

It is therefore the outbreak of the Korean War in June 1950, not the change of government in October 1951, which for Britain marks the true turning-point of the post-war decade. Henceforward this 'small island' (as Churchill himself described her in 1952), underpowered and obsolescent as she was, would have to carry the double top hamper of Cold War rearmament *and* the historic world-role. This must slow her progress in fine economic weather and threaten to capsize her in foul – until and unless those on the bridge, belatedly awakening to reality, decided to jettison most of that top hamper.

PART TWO

Our Status as a World Power

. . . a choice of the utmost difficulty lies before the British people: they must either give up for a time some of the advantages which a high standard of living confers upon them, or by relaxing in the outside world see their Country sink to the level of a second-class power . . .

(Anthony Eden, the Foreign Secretary, 18 June 1952)

Expenditure on the social services was inevitably rising, and he had hoped that it would be possible to keep defence expenditure level so that part of the increase in the national product could be used . . . for profitable investment . . .

(R. A. Butler, the Chancellor of the Exchequer,
19 October 1955)

4. 'A Choice of the Utmost Difficulty'

Reality? When on 2 June 1953 Elizabeth II, 'by the Grace of God, Queen of this Realm and of her other Realms and Territories, Head of the Commonwealth, Defender of the Faith', was crowned in Westminster Abbey, the day's ceremonial followed the form choreographed for the coronation of Edward VII as King-Emperor in 1902, a much grander and more polished production than the ill-rehearsed crownings of Queen Victoria and her Hanoverian predecessors. The coronation procession through the be-flagged streets of London, colourful with contingents from the armed forces of the Commonwealth as well as the Household Cavalry and the Foot Guards in their late Victorian costumes, re-enacted Queen Victoria's Diamond Jubilee procession in 1897, itself specially contrived as a public celebration of Britain's imperial greatness. Television – new technology in the service of old pageantry – brought the splendour of the day, though not the whiff of mothballs (metaphorical as well as actual), to twelve and a half million people. Coronation mugs given out to the nation's schoolchildren displayed the new monarch in crowned glory, along with her consort in the full-dress gold-laced tail-coat of an Admiral of the Fleet. One of Her Majesty's New Zealand subjects (with some assistance from a Nepalese) became the first man to reach the crest of Mount Everest, there to raise the Union Flag. Brave talk abounded about 'a new Elizabethan age'.

The symbolic message of the day was clear: Britain was still what she had been, and would remain so in the future. It was an affirmation of the continuity of Britain's history and the stability of British institutions from which the nation could justly draw powerful moral reassurance.

But where lay the border line between moral reassurance and flattery of the nation's prideful illusions?

For the coronation served to cast a veil of romance and emotion over the disagreeable truth that in terms of power the Britain of 1953 was not at all what Britain had been in 1897 or even in 1937, when the new Queen's father had been crowned. In such circumstances the British public cannot be blamed for preferring prideful illusion to disagreeable truth. But the new Queen's ministers can.

On 18 June (Waterloo Day) 1952, her Foreign Secretary, Anthony Eden, had turned in a homily on 'British Overseas Obligations'[1] which went so far as to admit that Britain's foreign policy was driven more by history than by present and future needs. 'The United Kingdom', he wrote, 'has world responsibilities inherited from several hundred years as a great Power'.[2] He put this first of three 'fundamental factors' which determined British policy, the second being that Britain was not 'a self-supporting economic unit,' and the third that Britain and the rest of the non-Communist world faced 'an external threat.'[3]

Eden acknowledged that the nation's inherited role and her present power might not match:

> The essence of a sound foreign policy is to ensure that a country's strength is equal to its obligations. If this is not the case, then either the obligations must be reduced to the level at which resources are available to support them, or a greater share of the country's resources must be devoted to their support.[4]

From this it followed, so Eden wrote at his grand Victorian desk in the Foreign Secretary's grand Victorian chamber, that 'a choice of the utmost difficulty lies before the British people . . . :'

> they must either give up for a time some of the advantages which a high standard of living confers upon them, or by relaxing in the outside world see their Country sink to the level of a second-class power with injury to their essential interests and way of life of which they can have little conception.[5]

A second-class power! But Eden here only echoed A. V. Alexander, the Labour Minister of Defence who in 1949 had asserted that to adopt a defence policy (and hence an international role) based on what the country could readily afford 'would bring very close Britain's extinction as a first-class Power'.[6] It says much about the reluctance (or inability?) of politicians to draw unwelcome conclusions from unpleasant facts that Alexander had been talking in the midst of the run on the pound which led to devaluation, while Eden was writing in the immediate aftermath of the winter economic storm of 1951–2.

Even a younger member of the new Cabinet, Harold Macmillan, the Minister of Housing and Local Government, could believe (in his words in July 1952 to colleagues preparing for the forthcoming Commonwealth Conference) that there 'should be three equal political partners in the free world – the Commonwealth (including Canada), the United States and Europe'.[7] And in November 1952 the Prime Minister himself, Winston Churchill, told the boys at Harrow, his old school: 'We *in this small island* [added emphasis] have to make a supreme effort to keep our place and status, the place and status to which our undying genius entitles us.'[8]

So under the Conservatives in the first half of the 1950s as under Labour in the second half of the 1940s the same battle would be fought between the 'world-power' lobby in Whitehall and the unfortunate Chancellors of the Exchequer who had to find the money to pay for the 'supreme effort to keep our place and status.'

To the Chiefs of Staff the holy Cold War declared on Communism by the United States in 1950 continued to provide renewed justification for Britain's old imperial military entanglements. On 17 June 1952 the Chiefs scratched the politicians' nerves with a report on 'Defence Policy and Global Strategy'.[9] Far from being coolly commonsensical in the Wellington mode, it could have been composed in the Pentagon, so unmilitary was its rhetoric. Under the heading 'The World-Wide Threat', it trumpeted: 'The Free World is menaced everywhere by the implacable and unlimited aims of Soviet Russia . . .' Worse, 'Russia and China are working hand–in–glove to extend Communist influence throughout the world . . .' To thwart them, wrote the Chiefs, was the object of Allied policy. The means were 'to restore the economic strength of the Free World and by rendering aid to the backward countries to lessen their vulnerability to Communism . . . to build up alliances against aggression and to build up military strength by rearmament, so enabling aggression to be halted and Communism to be contained.'[10]

However, it appeared from the report that these alliances related mostly to the same backward (and therefore militarily dependent) countries that also received 'development' baksheesh from the West: a double liability.[11]

What of the Foreign Secretary himself, Anthony Eden, diplomacy's answer to Ronald Colman, dapper, weakly handsome, a charming smile that verged on a simper; petulant, highly strung, vain? Thanks to his first-class Oxford-honed brain he was able in his state paper of 18 June 1952 to combine romantic vapourings about 'our Imperial Heritage' and about the need to maintain Britain's 'status quo as a world Power'[12] with a clear appreciation that 'rigorous maintenance of the presently-accepted policies of Her Majesty's Government at home and abroad is placing a burden on the country's economy which it is beyond the resources of the country to meet . . .'[13]

He therefore addressed himself to the problem of whether that burden could be reduced or partly off-loaded onto other states, 'without impairing too seriously the world position of the United Kingdom . . .'[14] It hardly astonishes that Eden, after running through what he took to be possible options, came to the conclusion that there were 'few ways to effect any reduction in our overseas obligations which would provide immediate relief to our economic difficulties.'[15]

But the reason why he could only see 'few ways' was because his mind remained a prisoner of the givens by which he had lived as a mature politician, a winner of the Military Cross as a young officer in the Great War, and an Eton schoolboy in the Edwardian heyday of Empire. He could no more imagine Britain giving up her inheritance as a world power because she was now hard up than for a similar reason having to exchange his own Savile Row suits for a reach-me-down from the Fifty-Shilling Tailors. Moreover, he similarly took it as given that the world role must be vital to the wealth and security of the realm.[16]

Hence withdrawal from any major overseas commitment was in

his belief out of the question because this 'would affect the international status of the United Kingdom':

> By reducing the value of the United Kingdom as a partner and ally, it would undermine the cohesion of the Commonwealth and the special relationship of the United Kingdom with the United States and its European partners and allies. Their attitude towards us will depend largely on our status as a world Power . . .[17]

Like Bevin in his time, Eden was entranced by the mystique of 'prestige', but, like Bevin again, confused 'prestige' with 'bluff':

> Finally, there is the general effect of loss of prestige. It is *impossible to assess in concrete terms* [added emphasis] the consequences to ourselves and the Commonwealth of our drastically and unilaterally reducing our responsibilities; the effects of a failure of will and relaxation of grip in our overseas commitments are incalculable. But once the prestige of a country has started to slide, there is no knowing where it will stop.[18]

But why did Eden find it impossible to assess in concrete terms the consequences of shedding overseas responsibilities, or (to reverse the question) the profit, if any, of retaining them? This is the more puzzling since he could and did put a figure on the direct military *cost* of so retaining them: £140.6 million in 1952 in foreign currencies spent on our armed forces overseas, and another £100.9 million in foreign currencies for purchases either for British defence production or for the armed forces in the United Kingdom – total: £241.5 million.[19] This amounts to nearly two-thirds of the balance of payments deficit in 1951 which had caused the great winter economic gale.[20] Moreover, Eden acknowledged that in any case the figure of £241.5 million did not cover the full cost of overseas deployments (including sterling expenditure) in the way of rations, stores, and supply and trooping transport by sea and air.[21]

Eden's case for the inevitability of overstretch naturally failed to cheer Butler, the Chancellor of the Exchequer, who commented dolefully to the Cabinet Defence Committee that it was clear 'that there was little hope of savings from any curtailment of British overseas [strategic] obligations, with the possible exception of Trieste . . . the situation in the Middle East offered no prospect of relief . . .'[22] However, the Minister of State, Selwyn Lloyd, sought to console him by saying that the Foreign Secretary hoped to engage United States assistance in the Middle East and South-East Asia, so that the United Kingdom could share the burden in the same way as in Europe via NATO.[23] Thus did hope, that whore of fortune, still beckon the innocent.

To the distress of the 'world-power' lobby, Butler in 1952 – like Dalton in 1946–8 and Cripps in 1949 – proved eccentric enough to want first of all to determine what the country could afford to pay for defence without damaging her economic future, and *then* to frame grand strategy accordingly. In response the Minister of Defence (another Alexander, this time Field Marshal the Earl Alexander of Tunis) and the Chiefs of Staff offered certain economies, though not without misgivings:

> The reductions which we recommend in the build-up and equipment of the forces can be undertaken only by incurring real and serious risks. These risks are only justifiable on the face of the threat of economic disaster.[24]

Their reductions took the form of a slower build-up of forces for a shooting war, and of designing such forces for 'the first few intense weeks' of war rather than for protracted conflict. For the Chiefs now believed that the deterrents of 'atomic air power' and adequate forces on the ground in Europe would lessen the likelihood of war. But they could not, they wrote, recommend any reductions in the provision of forces 'to protect our world-wide interests in the Cold War', on the score that the Foreign Secretary had pronounced that 'our world-wide commitments are at present inescapable'.[25] Here again was the perennial confusion between an 'interest' and a 'commitment'.

And what were these 'commitments' anyway?

For the Royal Navy in peace and Cold War the first and foremost among them (according to a top-secret report on 24 September 1952 by an ad-hoc Committee on the Defence Programme) was to provide 'support where necessary to the Foreign and Colonial Policy of Her Majesty's Government and supporting British interests, influence and prestige throughout the world . . .' In second place came the commitment to combat Communist

84

aggression wherever it occurred, such as in Korea and Malaya; in third place, to set 'an example to other European NATO powers and thereby encourage them to build up effective forces . . .'; and lastly, 'behind these overt functions' to maintain 'a balanced fleet structure capable of expansion to meet the immediate requirements of war . . .'[26] In the latter contingency, the navy must not only keep open 'our vital sea lanes' in home waters and the Atlantic, but also defend sea communications in the Mediterranean. 'These are our worldwide commitments which must be met on the outbreak of war, *particularly in the Far East* [added emphasis].'[27]

All this could have been written in 1932, ten years *before* the 1942 collapse of the facade of British imperial power, instead of ten years *after*.

In the case of the army, which, said the report, 'bears the brunt of the Cold War', out of its grand total of 11.33 (equivalent) divisions the equivalent of five divisions was at present deployed in Europe facing the Soviet threat, while the equivalent of another five was stationed in the Middle East and Far East.[28] Moreover, the report equally made clear that, just as in the Second World War, the army's strength in a future major conflict would have to be split between the European theatre (defence of the United Kingdom plus 'fighting the land battle alongside N.A.T.O allies') and global commitments such as reinforcing and defending the Middle East, and defending Hong Kong and Malaya.[29]

As for the Royal Air Force, its peacetime role (other than to act as a deterrent) was to serve 'as a means of upholding our influence in world affairs'.[30] Hence its strength too was dispersed across the Middle East and Far East as well as at home and in Europe.

So here yet again, but now much worsened by the aftermath of the Korean War, was the old quandary: how in peace and possible conflict to meet from limited national resources the competing demands of Europe's (and Britain's) defence on the one hand and the world-and-Commonwealth role on the other. Neither the National Governments of the 1930s nor the Labour Government of the late 1940s had found an answer. Could the present Conservative Government do better?

In October 1952 began a duel in the Cabinet Defence Committee between the Chancellor and the Minister of Defence over the latter's proposed defence budget for 1953–54. The duellists made an odd pair: the ambiguous Butler, sly of smile and shrewd of brain, with his curious visage somewhat reminiscent of a trodden-on trilby hat; Alexander, an imposingly elegant Guardsman but intellectually only as good as those currently doing his thinking for him. Whereas Alexander asked for £1,645 million (down from a previous offer of £1,719 million)[31] Butler told him that 'the country could not afford it; the most he could provide was £1,570 million'.[32] Alexander protested that 'it will be impossible to disguise either the magnitude of the cuts which will be made or the fact that for economic or other reasons we are adopting a course which must imperil our position in world affairs and our preparedness for war'.[33]

He backed his objection with a fresh report by the Chiefs of Staff, this time detailing exactly what forces where in the world would have to be shrunk along with stocks of warlike stores and production programmes for up-to-date ships, aircraft and weaponry. The reduction in the active fleet would be 'broadly equivalent to the whole strength of our Fleet now employed in the Far East, including Korea; or alternatively, the equivalent of the whole cruiser strength on all foreign stations'.[34] The shrinkage in the active army by 1.5 divisions 'is more than the total garrison planned [at present] for the Middle East and is equivalent to the combined garrison of Korea and Hong Kong.'[35] The Middle East Air Force 'would be reduced to a token force of 80 aircraft (less than at any time since 1915) and the Far East Air Force to the same. The Mobile Reserve of fighters, designed for reinforcement of the Middle East, would not be formed.'[36]

In a reference to the active army that equally applied to the other two armed services, the Chiefs warned that 'any reduction . . . must be balanced by a corresponding reduction in our Cold War commitments . . . It is not possible to spread the reduction and to continue on a reduced scale all our present tasks without risking disaster everywhere.'[37]

So what about imagining the unimaginable, such as liquidating commitments not directly related to the vital security of Europe and the United Kingdom? But the Chiefs too were still dreaming imperial dreams:

All over the world we are under the greatest pressure to hand over our responsibilities and our possessions. Any evidence of readiness to quit will start a landslide which we shall be quite unable to control. Are we, for instance, to cancel our Treaty and pull out of Iraq just as we embark on a Middle East Defence Organisation? Or are we prepared to deprive ourselves of the ability to intervene quickly to protect British lives in circumstances such as those prevailing in Kenya [author's note: where the Mau Mau terrorists were active]? What is the good of even discussing a Federation of British Central Africa, if we are to begin by proving to Her Majesty's subjects in Africa that we are quite powerless to protect them in trouble?[38]

But then, with the military directness so often unwelcome to politicians, the Chiefs stated the bleak total-strategic choice: '. . . either Her Majesty's Government must change their policy, or they must provide the military resources required to carry it out'.[39]

What was more, Her Majesty's Government would also have to decide how much could be spent on defence research and development. For the Minister of Supply (Duncan Sandys) pleaded at the beginning of November 1952 that to cut the R&D budget in 1953–54 from around £118 million to £100 million, as part of the Chancellor's desired overall reduction in defence expenditure, 'would have the most grave consequences'.[40] It would mean slowing down 'precisely those' projects which were 'the most important, namely, high priority work on aeronautics, jet engines, guided weapons and electronic equipment'.

Any relaxation of effort in these fields would not only prejudice our military position in years ahead, but might well have serious effects upon the progress of British civil aviation whose present technical lead has to a large extent been made possible by research and development undertaken or paid for by the Ministry of Supply.[41]

Combat was therefore joined across the tables first of the Defence Committee and then the Cabinet Room to decide whether the Minister of Defence should have his £1,645 million in 1953–54 or whether the Chancellor could lop £75 million off the defence costs of keeping Britain's place and status in the wide world. On 5

November the Chancellor attempted to wean the Defence Committee on to solid realities:

> Too much of our economic resources were being absorbed in unproductive commitments like defence and housing at a time when exports were falling and increased productivity was essential . . .[42]

In vain: the argument being inconclusive, the Prime Minister said that the final figure must be decided by the Cabinet at a meeting two days later.

Here Field Marshal Lord Alexander pleaded that his figure of £1,645 million for 1953–54 represented two successive cuts from an original estimate of £1,838 million. 'He was satisfied that it would be impossible to fulfil all our overseas commitments and our obligations to our Allies in the North Atlantic Treaty Organisation (N.A.T.O.) if the budgetary figure in 1953 were reduced below £1,645 million.'[43] But Butler still contended that this was 'more than the country could afford . . .' Nonetheless, he said that he was now prepared

> to accept a figure in the neighbourhood of £1,600 million for 1953, provided a radical review of the future pattern of our defence effort was undertaken at once, with due regard not only to strategic needs and foreign commitments but also to economic and financial factors . . .[44]

Butler pointed out that the Government's proposed savings in civil expenditure, including the welfare state, would no more than offset the increase demanded by the Minister of Defence. 'He [Butler] would thus be left with no means of enabling industry to increase its productivity and competitive power . . .'[45]

It was the President of the Board of Trade (Peter Thorneycroft) who reminded the Cabinet that the demands of defence in 1953 on the metal-using industries (the key alike to exports and the re-equipment of British factories) would amount to £480 million.[46] This was equivalent to nearly half the total value of their exports in 1952.[47]

But haver as ministers might, they could not in the end produce any answer better than another classic Whitehall fudge: a defence budget of £1,610 million for the financial year 1953–54, being £35 million less than desired by the Minister of Defence, and £40 million more than the Chancellor had originally stipulated.[48] The fudge signified that yet again the armed services would have some slices carved off them while all the entanglements which maintained Britain's traditional 'status quo as a world Power' (in Eden's phrase) would be preserved, if not extended.

The furthest away of such entanglements was ANZAM, an Australian dodge of the late 1940s (to which the Labour Government in Britain acceded in 1950) for collectively planning the regional defence of Australia, New Zealand and British colonies in South-East Asia. In time of war ANZAM would become a joint military organization with representatives of the British and New Zealand Chiefs of Staff sitting in Canberra with the Australian Chiefs of Staff.[49] But mercifully, as it might have been thought, the United States (which actually had the forces available in the Pacific to protect Australia and New Zealand) had later signed the Pacific Security Treaty (ANZUS) with these dominions. Moreover, British representation was excluded from ANZUS by wish of the Americans.

Funnily enough, the British Chiefs of Staff did not see this effective supersession of ANZAM by ANZUS as a happy release from a possible repetition of the British strategic nightmare of the 1930s and 1940s, that of having to fight simultaneous wars in Europe and the Far East. On the contrary, they advised Conservative ministers in December 1952 that since the United Kingdom had 'a great stake in the Far East', it was therefore necessary to ensure that Britain 'has an effective voice in whatever body prepares plans and controls strategy for the Pacific'. They also thought it important that ANZAM remained in being and was 'recognized as a Commonwealth Command or Commands, within whatever framework for overall command is ultimately agreed . . .'[50]

Here then, although reduced now to a piece of paper and an aspiration, were the old Australian–New Zealand and Far Eastern 'world zones' dreamt up by the Chiefs of Staff in 1946 as part of their fantasy of a global British and Commonwealth defence structure.[51]

In that structure the Middle East had constituted the central 'world zone', or grand-strategic cowpat. In the early 1950s it still remained so,[52] even though the cowpat had shrunk considerably since 1946 – not because of far-sighted choice in London, but because of irresistible circumstance. Although Libya still remained under British garrison, Palestine (once deemed by the Chiefs of Staff to be the essential eastern buttress of the 'world-zone') had gone in 1948. The Nile Delta, main British base during the North African campaign in the Second World War, had been evacuated in 1947, and the British Middle East main base now lay in the desert alongside the Suez Canal. Its dismal sprawl of cantonments, depots, workshops, hospitals, airfields and power stations had cost (over three and a half years) nearly £300 million, while its 700,000 tons of stores and 14,000 vehicles accounted for another £200 million:[53] in total more than twice as much as invested in 1952 in Britain's own transport system and telecommunications.[54]

But what apart from historical habit and world-power hallucination kept Chiefs of Staff and Cabinet ministers still wedded to this whole Middle East entanglement stretching from Tripoli to the Persian Gulf?

There was of course the Cold War, and Britain's satellite role in America's post-Korea policy of 'containing' Communism as if it was an outbreak of scarlet fever. Although in their Global Survey of June 1952 the Chiefs of Staff accepted that 'at present there is no direct threat of Soviet military aggression in the Middle East', they proceeded to offer a pick-and-choose assortment of reasons why the region was 'of great importance to the Free World in the Cold War', and why 'any excessive reduction – let alone a complete withdrawal – of British forces would result in the rapid spread of Russian influence throughout the area . . .' It was the land bridge between Europe, Asia and Africa, and hence 'the keystone of the defence against Communist infiltration into Africa'. Its oil resources – particularly the Persian Gulf oil – were of 'immense value'. With Turkey 'firmly' in NATO, it was important to prevent 'a chaotic power vacuum' arising on her southern flank. Moreover, the Middle East was the centre of the Moslem world, which – from Pakistan to Morocco – must be retained in the Western orbit.[55]

The Chiefs then adroitly shifted their ground from religious culture to bombers, arguing that Middle East airfields were 'essential to the Allied Strategic Air Offensive'. And lastly, and for good measure, the Chiefs reverted to the Victorian 'Great Game' between the British and Russian Empires in the Levant and Near East, averring that it was 'necessary to frustrate the traditional Imperialist Russian aim of expanding her influence southward to the Dardanelles, the Persian Gulf and beyond'.[56]

There was just one tiny drawback to all this, as the Chiefs were honest enough to acknowledge: 'Nevertheless, we are faced with the fact that the United Kingdom cannot afford to maintain its present forces in the Middle East . . .'[57]

But why should Britain, for her part, be so keen on keeping the Soviet Union out of the Middle East, other than the 'vacuum theory' of international relations?[58] If entanglement in the Middle East meant strategic and financial overstretch to Britain (as it did), then logically it must mean the same for the Soviet Union (as indeed was to prove the case in the 1960s and '70s during the Soviet Union's costly and futile 'pink-on-the-map' phase of expanding its 'influence' in Africa).

A much more convincing reason for retaining the Middle East strategic cowpat lay in the need to secure the oilfields of Iraq and Iran. In the Second World War these fields had merely fuelled the Commonwealth forces in the Mediterranean and Middle East theatre itself, while the British war effort at home (together with the strategic air offensive, the Battle of the Atlantic and the campaign in North-West Europe) had depended on supplies from the Western hemisphere. But since 1945 the reluctance of British miners to dig coal and Britain's desperate need to earn dollars had together served to turn on an oil-gush. Output from the Iranian fields on the Persian Gulf owned by the Anglo-Iranian Oil Company had doubled from 16.6 million tons in 1945 to 31.72 million in 1950 – ten times larger than Iraq's production – and accounted for over a third of total British supplies and two-thirds of British-controlled production in the Eastern Hemisphere.[59] The refinery at Abadan had become the largest in the world. Hence, as the Labour Minister of Fuel and Power had warned in July 1950, any interruption of Persian oil exports would have 'immediate and far-reaching consequences on the British position, strategically, politically and economically.'[60] Surely, then, Iranian oil was a British asset worth protecting? Surely that alone must justify the British military commitment to the Middle East?

It might seem so, only that already by 1952 the Middle East Land Forces, the Middle East Air Force, the Mediterranean Fleet and the Royal Navy's squadrons east of Suez had not in the event been able to protect the asset – simply because they had proved politically unusable.

5. 'An Area of Vital Importance'

On 2 May 1951 a new Iranian Government under Dr Mossadeq, an anti-Western patriot, nationalized the Anglo-Iranian Oil Company after months of abortive negotiations between the previous government and the Labour Government in Britain over a new and fairer sharing out of the profits. By June, with the oilfields and refinery (and their British personnel) in peril of physical seizure by the Iranians, the new Foreign Secretary, Herbert Morrison (who had replaced the dying Bevin on 9 March), an unlikely admirer of Lord Palmerston, was pondering armed intervention.

However, the Joint Planning Staff had reported back in March that even to take and hold Abadan itself, without operating in the oilfields, would require a cruiser, one or more frigates, and a whole division plus air component. The land force would amount to the equivalent of Britain's entire Middle East garrison, 'committed', so wrote the Joint Planners, 'to a task the scope of which might well grow and withdrawal from which, once committed, would be difficult . . .'[1] The Joint Planners remarked that 'the forces so employed would be entirely out of position in relation to the requirements of our Middle East strategy as a whole'. Moreover, they would have to be replaced in their present stations by troops from the strategic reserve in the United Kingdom.[2]

As if all these factors were not discouraging enough, the Joint Planners also saw a high likelihood of Soviet intervention under the 1921 Treaty between Persia and the Soviet Union. The consequent risk of contact between British and Soviet forces would carry with it the further risk of global war.[3]

The Chiefs of Staff concurred with this glum assessment,

especially since the United States had already refused to cooperate in any use of force. Instead the Chiefs settled for Operation Midget, a contingency plan for the evacuation of British personnel from Abadan by air and sea.[4]

But by July 1951, with British personnel in Abadan in peril of being forcibly seized by the Iranians, Midget had grown into Buccaneer, a contingency plan to secure the Abadan refinery after all.[5] Nonetheless, the Labour Cabinet, plucking their collective lip, decided on 2 July that such an operation would 'involve very grave political risks', and that therefore it would be 'inexpedient' to undertake any 'overt preparations'.[6]

Ten days later they were listening to Morrison repeat his Palmerstonian case for resolute action. In his belief, popular feeling at home was all in favour, while 'evidence of our readiness and ability to protect our interests would raise our prestige, notably in the Middle East'. Thirdly, a show of force would, he reckoned, be 'the quickest and most effective way of bringing the Persians to their senses'.[7] His cautious colleagues were still not convinced: they still felt that it was 'undesirable to take military action except to protect British lives . . .'[8]

On 17 July 1951 it was the turn of the Chiefs of Staff to discourse on the melancholy effects of a failure to defend British interests against Mossadeq and his hostile mobs:

> It might be objected that the tying-up of forces in Persia was playing the Russian game; it was an equally and perhaps more valid answer that the weakening of our position in the whole Middle East and the very serious loss of prestige in the Arab countries, with all its long-term consequences, would even more be playing into the hands of the Russians.[9]

But there was still no decision. Instead, the crisis dragged on into the autumn in anxious debate in Whitehall and mounting tension at Abadan. On 27 September Morrison attempted for the last time to persuade the Cabinet that Britain must live up to her pretensions to be a great power, particularly in the Middle East:

> If the remaining British staff in Abadan were expelled and the Government's handling of the Persian dispute appeared feeble and

ineffective, the repercussions throughout the Middle East and elsewhere would be very serious. Egypt might be emboldened to take
drastic action to end the military treaty and possibly bring the Suez
Canal under Egyptian control.[10]

But Attlee punctured such brave talk by reporting to the Cabinet
that he had been told by the United States President that America
would not support 'any action involving the use of force to maintain
the British staff in Abadan . . .'[11]

In fact, from the beginning of the crisis the United States, in the
shape of Acheson and the State Department, had applied ruthless
pressure on London not to take military action for fear of provoking
a Soviet invasion of northern Iran, and instead to abandon the
oilfields and the Abadan refinery to the Iranians. This pressure was
presumably by way of showing gratitude for British support to the
United States over Korea the year before; or perhaps by way of
aiding American oil companies to grab profitable business in what
had been solely a British sphere of interest. Nevertheless, Acheson's
torsion of the British arm was not to be resisted, given that at the
time Britain was living in hopes of further large dollar tips under
the Nitze exercise to help defray the cost of rearmament.

With America's support (or, *en clair*, her permission to the British
to act) thus finally withheld, Attlee had to tell his Cabinet at the
meeting of 27 September 1951 that it would be 'inexpedient' to use
force.[12]

And so the Cabinet could only decide to refer the matter to the
Security Council[13] – about as useful an exercise as posting a letter
down a drain.

On 4 October the last British managers and technical personnel
left Abadan. There followed more than a year of fruitless negotiations by the new Conservative Government with Dr Mossadeq
(more cunning than his bizarre costume of floppy pyjamas might
suggest) and of equally futile pondering of the case by the UN
Security Council and the International Court at The Hague.[14] In
1952 the loss of Iranian production cost Britain some $215 million
worth of dollar earnings, equal to two-thirds of Britain's dollar
balance-of-payments deficit that year.[15]

In regard therefore to Britain's one truly important material interest in the Middle East,[16] her expensive strategic cowpat and all its soldiers, sailors and airmen had proved no more use than a Butlin's holiday camp and its staff 'red-coats'.

Perhaps even more to the point, the Abadan crisis gave proof that Britain was not at all the independent great power (meaning able to take her own decisions in pursuit of her own interests) that her governing elite had liked to think she still remained.

Would this elite now take heed of this proof? To do so would mean having to junk the fundamental assumptions that had determined post-war British total-strategy. For them personally that would mean a denial of their whole preparation at public school and Oxbridge for a life of high responsibility (or, to put it in less flattering fashion, a life of going around being important) as the leadership of a world power.

There could only be one way to escape so profoundly shattering an experience – simply ignore the proof and carry on as before. And that is what the governing elite in 1952, Conservative ministers and Whitehall mandarins alike, chose to do.

Their wilful deafness to the lesson in the realities of power shouted at them by the Abadan crisis is the more deplorable because by now the Middle East strategic cowpat and all its baggy-shorted military denizens had also proved useless even as a means of securing the future of the British Middle East main base itself in the Canal Zone.

In October 1951 (the deathbed month of the Labour Government) the Egyptian government had unilaterally abrogated the 1936 Anglo-Egyptian Treaty by which Britain was permitted to station forces on Egyptian soil. With British installations under threat of guerrilla attacks, Herbert Morrison as Foreign Secretary had again wanted to make a show of force in order to convince the Egyptians that, in Morrison's words, 'we stay in Egypt'.[17] The garrison of the Canal Zone would be reinforced by a parachute brigade flown in from Cyprus and by an infantry brigade shipped in from Britain. A further infantry brigade in Britain would be placed on stand-by along with the Guards Brigade in Libya. But once more Attlee overruled the would-be sword-brandishers, emphasizing 'the need to avoid provocation . . .'[18]

Next month the problem passed to the new Conservative Government. In the first half of 1952 the British garrison was reinforced to 80,000 men because of riots in the Canal Zone towns and attacks on British base installations. A rant of latterday Gordons and Kitcheners on the Conservative backbenches known as 'the Suez Group' urged (as they were to go on urging for the next two years) that Britain should hold on to the Canal Zone by force if necessary.[19] After all, did there not come a time when a great power had to put the wogs in their place? But Anthony Eden was convinced that Britain could best uphold her historic role in the Middle East (and at the same time keep the pushy Americans out) by soliciting Arab goodwill, and that meant negotiating with the Egyptians.[20]

Even the Prime Minister, who had witnessed the Fuzzy-wuzzies being mown down at the Battle of Omdurman in 1898, came to recognize that it was politically impossible to use the 80,000 soldiers in the Canal Zone as a means of clinging on to the base. When in March 1952 the Chief of the Imperial General Staff, Field Marshal Lord Slim, repeated to the Defence Committee that Egypt was essential to the defence of the Middle East in war, Churchill pointed out that the 1936 Treaty with Egypt would in any case expire in 1956, and that therefore the Chiefs of Staff 'should work out a detailed plan, with an estimate of the cost, for stationing British troops in Gaza [Gaza!] and Cyprus'. The Committee agreed.[21]

In other words, even though the Canal Zone might follow the Nile Delta and Palestine into the dustbin, even though the Iranian debacle had proved the British military presence in the Middle East to be useless as an instrument of policy, Britain must still have a main base in the region somewhere, anywhere. Indeed, she remained loath to let go altogether of the Canal Zone and its £500 million worth of fixed assets, equipment and stores. In December 1952, the Chiefs of Staff, briefing ministers for forthcoming negotiations with the Egyptians, asserted:

> No effective Middle East defence can be undertaken without a suitable base to support it . . . Only in Egypt can such facilities be found on the scale required, and nowhere else in the Middle East

could existing facilities be expanded to form a substitute except at prohibitive cost.[22]

Britain therefore needed 'a working base in Egypt in war'. However, this 'cannot function except with Egyptian good will'. In the opinion of the Chiefs, the best of four possible negotiated solutions would be for the Canal Zone area to be handed back to Egypt, while the base itself remained under sole British control (on the analogy of American bases in Britain), though with British servicemen reduced to some 7,000 maintenance personnel.[23] This solution would enable British forces to return immediately in case of war. The worst or 'last ditch'[24] solution, should the Egyptians prove obdurate, would involve removing all possible stores, vehicles and kit, 'leaving the remainder to the Egyptians and possibly writing off the loss against the Egyptian sterling balances . . .'[25] In these circumstances it would take more than six months for the base to become fully operational again.[26]

Avowed the Chiefs: 'the paramount object of our negotiations' must be 'the use of a working base in Egypt in war . . . In addition, our Naval forces will require the use of Alexandria, Port Said and Suez.'[27]

Like the Chiefs' global survey of June 1952 (see above, p. 90), this appreciation too might have been written in 1932 or 1902, or even 1882, when General Sir Garnet Wolseley took an expeditionary force from England to defeat Arabi Pasha at the Battle of Tel el Kebir, so inaugurating the British imperial entanglement in Egypt.

In the event, Britain in her negotiations with successive Egyptian leaders did no better than an unwary tourist bargaining with a Cairo street vendor. Under the treaty eventually signed in autumn 1954 all British forces were to be withdrawn from the Canal Zone base within twenty months, and be replaced by British and Egyptian civilian technicians who would act as caretakers and maintenance men.[28] This was no better than the Chiefs of Staff's 'last ditch' solution (see above).

Did the new treaty mean the final drying-up of the Middle East strategic cowpat and related commitments in peace and war, so greatly easing the global overstretch of the British armed forces and relieving the Chancellor's anxiety about the defence budget? It did not. For Britain had secured Egypt's agreement that British forces might return to the Canal Zone base in the event of an armed attack on Egypt or on any other member of the Arab League, or on Turkey.[29] Moreover, in November 1954 the Minister of Defence (now Harold Macmillan) and the Chiefs of Staff recommended that a new combined Middle East Headquarters be set up in Cyprus, complete with sea, land and air commanders-in-chief 'of rank, experience and prestige' (to cite Macmillan's lofty job description) enjoying the 'status to deal with Ministers and Chiefs of Staff of foreign states . . .'[30]

It is clear from the Chiefs of Staff's own memorandum on the topic (sent by Macmillan to the Prime Minister and circulated to the Cabinet Defence Committee) that the hapless fate of the Anglo-Iranian Oil Company and of the British main base in the Canal Zone had taught them nothing:

> The Chiefs of Staff assume that Her Majesty's Government continues to regard the Middle East as an area of vital importance to our interests and that their policy is directed to improving the stability of the area in peace and defending it in war. At present the United Kingdom alone can provide the leadership and authority necessary to ensure those ends.[31]

On these assumptions Britain's basic strategic aims in the Middle East must be, they wrote,

> (a) to maintain and strengthen the influence and position which we have at great cost built up over the years and thus support our widespread political and commercial interests;
> (b) to provide the nucleus for a successful defence of the area in war, to protect the right flank of N.A.T.O., and to be in a position to fulfil our Treaty obligations to Iraq, Jordan, Libya and the Persian Sheikdoms [sic].[32]

Yet such continuing strategic bombast consorts oddly with the sober realism of the Chiefs' directive to the three Commanders-in-Chief, Middle East, back in March 1954. This stated Britain's strategic aims in the Middle East 'in war' as, firstly, to meet the requirements of the Allied strategic air offensive; secondly, to secure Turkey's southern flank; thirdly 'to protect as much of the Middle East *as possible*'; and fourthly, 'to secure *at least a proportion* [added emphases] of the Middle East oil'.[33] Tepid language indeed! But then followed the veritable cold douche:

> We realise that the full attainment of these aims will be beyond our resources, and the defence of oil in the Persian Gulf – although an integral part of our strategy – cannot therefore be undertaken during the foreseeable future.[34]

As for the Prime Minister, he had convinced himself that the withdrawal of British troops from Egypt 'could be fully justified on military grounds', on the score that our requirements in the Canal Zone 'had been radically altered by the admission of Turkey to the North Atlantic Treaty Organisation and the extension of a defensive Middle East front as far east as Pakistan'.[35] This newest of all Churchill's Levantine and Middle Eastern fantasies since 1915 had been inspired by a security pact of February 1954 between Turkey and Pakistan. But the pact was mere parchment, possessing (in the Chiefs of Staff's opinion) 'no military value at present'.[36] Nonetheless, the Chiefs still advised that Britain must take part in any planning that might take place under the pact 'because we provide the one directive and cohesive force in the area for which there is no substitute'.[37]

In 1955 this mirage of a new defensive front from the Bosphorus to the borders of India was to become yet more alluring – and potentially dangerous. For Britain alone of Western powers chose to sign up to the Baghdad Pact, by which Iraq had joined Turkey and Pakistan in an expanded security pact, the Middle East Security Organization. But why did Britain so choose, apart from the mere habit of 'status' in the region?

The specific motive lay in a hope of preserving the British right to maintain air bases in Iraq after 1957, when the present Anglo-Iraqi Treaty expired.[38] These bases dated from the 1920s when Britain had been an imperial power administering Iraq under a League of Nations mandate, and the Royal Air Force's biplane bombers had served as the chosen instrument for disciplining recalcitrant natives. Now it appeared that in future the bases would be needed to help fulfil British obligations under a pact signed by Britain in order to preserve the right to use the bases.

In another part of the Middle East theatre, too, Britain was becoming more entangled in 1955 rather than less. From April that year a Greek-Cypriot terrorist group, EOKA (Ethniki Organosis Kuprion Agoniston, 'National Organization of Cypriot Fighters'), set out to persuade the British by sabotage and murder to quit their colony of Cyprus, the site chosen for the grandly reincarnated Middle East headquarters. EOKA terrorism marked an attempt to emulate the 1946–8 campaign of the IZL (Irgun Zvai Leumi, 'National Military Organization') against British rule in Palestine. Just as in Palestine with Arab and Jew (or, for that matter, earlier in India with Moslem and Hindu), the British in Cyprus faced the added dilemma of trying to hold a balance between mutually hostile communities: in the present case, Greek Cypriots and Turkish Cypriots. By October 1955 the British garrison of the island had risen to 12,000 soldiers, and by early 1956 to 17,000.[39]

But this was not the only new addition by 1955 to the British burden in the wider Middle East 'world zone'. Far off in Kenya, where Ernest Bevin had once wanted to locate the British Middle East main base, Mau Mau terrorists had been slaughtering fellow Kikuyu tribesmen and the odd British settler ever since 1952. In 1955 no fewer than 5,000 British soldiers (plus 5,000 askaris)[40] were busy combing villages and the bush for the Mau Mau, all for the sake of beans for British coffee-pots and preserving the privileged way of life of a few thousand white landowners whose reputation was smirched by a notorious minority of drunks, snobs and adulterers.

In July 1956 a new generation of Chiefs of Staff (Admiral of the Fleet Earl Mountbatten, General Sir Gerald Templer and Air Chief Marshal Sir Dermot Boyle) submitted to the Defence Committee of Anthony Eden's Cabinet a bleak enough analysis of how total-strategically futile had proved Britain's entanglement in the Middle East since the Second World War:

Up to 1945 the United Kingdom enjoyed great influence in the Middle East. This rested on our physical control of many of the key countries in the area, our economic strength and the absence of any serious competition by other great Powers. Since the war, however, a number of changes of great and lasting significance [have been on balance] greatly to our disadvantage and have produced a vicious circle in which a reduction in our ability to influence events leads to a loss of prestige. This, in turn, creates both the incentive and the opportunity for countries hostile to us to take action harmful to our interests.[41]

Warned the Chiefs: 'This will continue unless we determine our long-term essential requirements in the area and shape our policy accordingly.'

What then in their opinion were now those long-term requirements? They were hardly novel: 'Our essential aims in the Middle East are to safeguard our vital oil supplies, prevent war and support the Baghdad Pact . . .' The Chiefs acknowledged that Britain 'could no longer rely solely on the threat of military force to attain political stability . . .', and that instead she would have to look much more to non-military means. Even so, the Chiefs still recommended that Britain should retain troops in Libya and Aden, and 'station a permanent force in Kenya' to protect British interests in the Arabian peninsula and East Africa. As for Cyprus, site of the new Middle East Headquarters, the Chiefs had to admit that 'political changes could damage its value to us . . .'[42]

Taken all in all, these uninventive recommendations for the future hardly followed logically from the Chiefs' own analysis of 'the great and lasting changes' that had undermined the British presence in the Middle East and vitiated its purpose over the last eleven years.

As it happened, the very day after this report the Secretary of State for Air (Nigel Birch) put in a memorandum on 'The Indian Ocean Air Route' that reads like a production by the Edwardian Committee of Imperial Defence after miraculously finding themselves in the age of long-distance air travel.[43] Britain, he wrote, needed a military air route to the Far East for trooping, carrying freight (including material for nuclear tests in Australia and the Pacific), rotating combat aircraft to the Far East Air Force, and emergency movements of troops and aircraft. But he warned that Egypt or Syria, even India or Ceylon, might put a stop to British aircraft overflying their territories. Hence there was a need for a route to the Far East via Libya (El Adem), Central and East Africa (Entebbe in Uganda), then the Indian Ocean islands of Gan and

Coëtivy. Construction of airfields on these islands was 'urgently required to enable us to fulfil our Commonwealth commitments in emergency, and to preserve the link with the proving and testing grounds [for nuclear weapons and ballistic missiles] in Australia and the Pacific . . .'[44]

At the same time the Conservative Government had not been neglecting the oceanic communications that traditionally linked the Mother Country to the far-flung Empire. In September 1954 the Minister of Defence, the Commonwealth Secretary and the First Lord of the Admiralty jointly put to the South African Minister of Defence

> a comprehensive plan of naval defence and communications. In war there would be a strategic South Atlantic Zone with a United Kingdom Commander-in-Chief at the Cape, linking up with the separate commands on the one side in Gibraltar and on the other in Trincomalee and Mombasa . . .[45]

Who would guess from such ambition that only six months later the Defence Committee would be debating whether to downgrade the Royal Navy's only three fleet carriers to light carriers in order to save £2.5 million annually on the cost of operating strike aircraft and another £2.5 million on the cost of new types of such aircraft?[46] In the event the Minister of Defence successfully blocked this proposal, thanks to so original an argument as the importance, yes, of 'prestige' and 'influence':

> The removal of our heavy carriers from the [NATO] Striking Fleet and the limitation of their use to a trade protection role would seriously reduce our influence in overall naval strategy, and deprive us of a say in the employment of the [NATO] Striking Fleet . . .[47]

Would the financial saving, asked the Minister, 'justify a course of action which must be damaging to the efficiency and the prestige of the Fleet?'[48]

Far beyond the Middle East 'Zone' and the South Atlantic 'Zone', Britain in 1956 was also still flying the flag militarily and/or politically in the Australia–New Zealand and Far Eastern strategic 'Zones', although in plain truth these were peripheral to the security of an island up to 12,000 miles distant off the north-west coast of Europe. But, after all, did not they complete the grand strategic architecture of British world power? Did not imperial history plus the habits of noblesse in the grandee and of public duty in the prefect oblige Britain to fly the flag there?

But what about hard economic interests of the United Kingdom in these distant zones that might justify the continued military or political commitments? In fact, only in a single case in the whole Far East and Pacific area were British armed forces deployed in preserving an asset truly valuable to the prosperity of the kingdom. That was Malaya's dollar-earning tin and rubber, where in 1955 some twenty-three battalions (mostly Gurkhas) were gradually winning a war of jungle ambushes with Chinese Communist guerrillas.[49]

But Korea, the proximate cause of Britain's present total-strategic overload, continued to be an entanglement devoid of profit. Here Communist and Western forces were staring each other out along an armistice line that seemed as if it could last until Judgement Day. In January 1954 the Minister of Defence, Earl Alexander, had mooted the suggestion of pulling out two British battalions, along with Dominion units, on the score that until 'we began to reduce our commitments we had no chance of building up a strategic reserve, or of keeping within the total expenditure on defence which the Chancellor of the Exchequer found it necessary to propose'.[50] But the Defence Committee was of opinion that in view of 'the many other difficulties which we need to discuss with the Americans at the present time, it would not be opportune to raise the question of reducing the Commonwealth Division'.[51]

Nearly two years later, in November 1955, the Prime Minister, Anthony Eden, is found complaining to his colleagues that 'it was deplorable that such large numbers of our troops [author's note: 4,500], who were badly needed elsewhere, should continue to be locked up in Korea for no good military purpose and at great cost . . .'[52]

Indeed, as if Korea were not enough, the United States had actually sought in the early months of 1954 to inveigle Britain into a second Asian morass.

★

The Secretary of State in President Eisenhower's administration, John Foster Dulles, a lawyer sour of face and stern of puritan principle, constituted a living reminder that America had been founded in bigotry as well as righteousness. Dulles burned even more fiercely with anti-Communist fervour than Acheson, and especially towards Mao Tse-tung's China.[53] In January 1954 he had threatened 'instant retaliation' if China were to intervene in the eight-year-old war in Indo-China between France (the colonial power) and Vietminh Communist insurgents. By the beginning of April 1954, with Washington in a fresh spasm of 'emotional over-drive', Dulles was urging Britain to back the United States in a decision to launch American airstrikes against the Vietminh besiegers of the French fortress of Dien Bien Phu, now in danger of falling.[54] He wished to couple this with a joint warning to China not to intervene, on pain of military reprisals.

Here was June 1950 – Korea and Formosa – all over again, with Hong Kong once more a British hostage to China. Yet this time the crisis was potentially the more dangerous. For the Chairman of the American Combined Chiefs of Staff, Admiral Radford, did not discount the early use of nuclear weapons, even though the Soviet Union now possessed them too.[55] It was the British fear that nuclear war, once started, could so easily engulf Europe, a much easier target than the United States for the Soviet Union to hit with its as yet small nuclear strike force.

On 13 April 1954 Dulles gave an alarming public demonstration of how rigid within its corset of ideology was his foreign policy. At a press conference in London he stated that his idea of a 'satisfactory settlement' of the Indo-China question was that the Communists should completely withdraw from the country, and abandon 'their apparent desire to extend the political system of Communism to South-East Asia'.[56]

Mercifully, however, Eden in the spring of 1954 was better placed to resist American pressure over Indo-China than Bevin in the summer of 1950 over Korea. Britain had now ceased to sponge on America except for a dribble of defence aid,[57] while the British economy was currently sailing through a brief and delusive interlude of fine weather, with the gold and dollar reserves actually rising.[58]

And whereas in summer 1950 there had been some doubt in regard to United States commitment to the defence of Western Europe, there now existed the NATO command structure under an American Supreme Commander, General Dwight Eisenhower (but see p. 110, below). Thus Britain was for the moment no longer looking quite so eagerly for American patronage.

Moreover, Eden enjoyed a second advantage over Bevin. The Indo-China crisis was burning on a slow fuse, giving him time to negotiate, or prevaricate, with the United States about what best to do. By contrast Bevin had been subjected to a bum's rush[59] by the sudden detonation of the Korean crisis by the North Korean invasion of the South, immediately followed by the fait accompli of America's committing her own forces to battle.

Thus in the event Eden was able to save Britain from another Asiatic mess. He refused to back Dulles in a decision to launch American airstrikes against the besiegers of Dien Bien Phu or to join him in uttering threats to China. Instead, employing his high skill as a diplomatic fixer (to the peeved Dulles's discomfort or even chagrin), Eden arranged a deal over the future of Indo-China at the Geneva Conference in May–July 1954, attended by all the interested parties, including the Chinese. Vietnam, largest constituent state of Indo-China, was to be divided between a Communist North and what soon became an American client regime in the South. In this way the colonial burden in Indo-China which France now shed with relief was taken up by the United States of her own free choice – the first step, as it was to prove, towards the most stunning national defeat and humiliation in American history.

Nevertheless, Britain did not entirely escape a further entanglement in Asia at American instigation. In September 1954 she signed up to Dulles's wheeze of a South-East Asia Treaty Organisation, on the analogy of NATO, completing (if only on paper) a global cordon of 'containment' of Communism.[60] Mercifully, however, the British insisted with success that there be excluded from the treaty the states of former French Indo-China: Laos, Cambodia – and Vietnam.

It is true that under this SEATO Treaty, as under the Baghdad Pact and ANZAM, Britain was not required to make any down payment by way of an immediate military contribution, but only to promise to rally to the defence of the treaty area in the event of a threat of attack from outside. However, as the 1925 Locarno Pact and Chamberlain's 1939 guarantee to Poland go to show, blithely issued promissory notes of this kind are prone to be presented for encashment at some inconvenient moment in the future. By 1955 Britain stood exposed to the risk of such presentations occurring anywhere from Jordan to New Zealand, and this in addition to her actual world-role deployments in Gibraltar, Malta, Cyprus, Libya, parts of Africa, Iraq, the Persian Gulf sheikdoms, Aden, Malaya, Hong Kong, Korea, and the seas between.

Simply to maintain on the ground or at sea such worldwide deployments cost the nation dear: pay and allowances (a huge item); the repair, upkeep and fuelling of ships, aircraft and vehicles; rations and ammunition; upkeep of far-off bases, cantonments and airfields; training; running costs of the troopships and storeships that plied constantly between home ports and the Middle East and Far East. Moreover, until the rearmament programme should deliver new equipment, money was having to be spent on retaining in service obsolescent and time-worn ships, tanks and aircraft (many dating from the Second World War), just to keep up the numbers required by the world role.[61]

It all amounted to an immense sprawl of politico-strategic top hamper for 'this small island' still to be carrying ten years after the end of the Second World War, the more so since most of it was as outmoded in concept and as redundant in function as the full rigs of sail carried in the steam-driven late-Victorian battlefleet.

Yet at the same time Britain was also having to bear the weight of her own vital armour: the security of the realm itself and (integral with that) of Western Europe. For this, as always, remained her single truly vital strategic interest.

6. 'To Know When to Retreat'

Before 1914 imperial isolationism had rendered it unthinkable for Britain to keep an army on the Continent in peacetime or even formally to commit herself to dispatching one in case of German aggression. Yet such an army, buttressing a political alliance with France, might have prevented the Great War.[1]

In 1929, in a fresh return to isolationism, Britain had prematurely withdrawn her post-war army of occupation from Germany. A French withdrawal (under British pressure) in 1931 had left the Rhineland (demilitarized under the Treaty of Versailles) defenceless against violation by Germany.

When in 1936 such violation took place without counter-moves from a nerveless France and Britain, it destroyed the Versailles Treaty's fundamental security guarantee. Yet through 1937 and 1938 Britain refused to contemplate committing an army to the Continent even in the event of renewed war between Germany and France, let alone in peacetime.

Not until the spring of 1939 did Britain accept the evident historical truth that France and the Low Countries were vital to British security, and more so than ever in the age of the bomber.[2] But by then it was altogether too late to create a large, well-equipped British army and install it on the Western Front in time to meet the German onslaught.

So in 1940 the British Expeditionary Force of only ten infantry divisions (compared with Field Marshal Sir Douglas Haig's army of sixty-one divisions in 1918) proved too weak to save a heavily outweighted France[3] from defeat and capitulation. Britain had lost her outer bulwark, to her ensuing mortal peril from air attack and invasion. Only thanks to the military power of the United States had this bulwark been re-conquered in 1944.

After 1945 the role of the new British army of occupation in Germany had gradually changed from that of guard against a revival of the German menace to that of Cold War deterrence against the Red Army. Nevertheless, and in the face of all experience, the Chiefs of Staff in the late 1940s had remained reluctant to commit extra forces to Europe in case of war. In fact, they amazingly repeated the 1930s error of giving priority to reinforcing the Middle East.[4] Only in March 1950 did the Chiefs at last come to recommend that in an emergency a corps of two divisions should be dispatched to augment the British Army of the Rhine.[5]

But here too the outbreak of the Korean War marked a turning-point for Britain. For it panicked Western leaders into believing that massed Soviet troops would at some chosen moment kick down NATO's flimsy fence protecting Western Europe. However, the only means of turning that fence into a living wall of armoured divisions lay in rearming West Germany. Unsurprisingly France took vast alarm at this prospect. In October 1950 the French Prime Minister, René Pleven, therefore proposed that the new West German army be integrated into a supra-national European Defence Community (effectively a single European army) to include Great Britain.

The Labour Government were even less enthused about this proposal than about the Coal and Steel Authority, which they had already refused to join.[6] The Conservatives, rhetorically pro-European in Opposition, proved in Government just as suspicious as their Labour predecessors. How could the United Kingdom, with her global responsibilities as a first-class power at the head of the Commonwealth, allow her armed forces to be swallowed up in some Continental mish-mash? How could she be expected to yield control over defence, the very soul of sovereignty?

Unfortunately in 1951–2 the United States (in the person of Dean Acheson as the Secretary of State) so esteemed Britain as a world power and so valued the 'special relationship' as to press the Conservative Government to join the European Defence Community.[7] For it consistently remained Washington's policy to encourage the ever closer integration of the nation states of Europe (yes, including the United Kingdom) in order to create a strong second pillar to the Atlantic alliance. This hardly accorded with London's conviction that Britain, far from being part of the common European ruck, served via the 'special relationship' as the essential bridge between the United States and Continental Europe.

In January 1952 Anthony Eden responded to persistent American prods by proclaiming in a speech at Columbia University, New York, that

> if you drive a nation to adopt procedures which run counter to its instincts, you weaken and may destroy the motive force of its action . . . You will realise that I am speaking of the frequent suggestion that the United Kingdom should join a federation on the continent of Europe. This is something which we know, in our bones, we cannot do . . . For Britain's story and her interests lie far beyond the continent of Europe. Our thoughts move across the seas to the many communities in which our people play their part, in every corner of the world. These are our family ties. That is our life: without it we should be no more than some millions of people living in an island off the coast of Europe, in which nobody wants to take any particular interest.[8]

Sadly this stirring romantic stuff, so evocative of the verse of Sir Henry Newbolt, failed to change Washington's disenchanted view of Britain's present and future status as a power. At the same time such utterances by a British Foreign Secretary were interpreted in Europe as a desire to return to Britain's old strategic isolation. Britain therefore found herself doubly squeezed, by impatient pressure from America and by anxious demands from Europe for a cast-iron British military commitment.

In May 1952 Eden partly gave way and joined the United States in a treaty guaranteeing the EDC against either internal or external threats. But even this could not allay the profound French unease about climbing into the same sleeping-bag with a Germany again in uniform. In December 1953, with German rearmament still the elusive prize, Dulles (now Secretary of State in succession to Acheson) warned the French Government that America would be forced to undertake an 'agonising re-appraisal' of its role in Europe if the EDC plan were not ratified soon. As for Eden, he was at this time quite resolved not to accede to French demands for a British guarantee to keep, in his own words, 'X number of troops on the continent for Y number of years'.[9]

Yet this was exactly what he volunteered ten months later following the refusal of the French National Assembly on 30 August 1954 to ratify the EDC Treaty.

He did so in order to clinch a deal over his own ingenious proposals for solving the problem of German rearmament now that the French had killed the EDC. These proposals, put to a conference in London in September 1954, embraced the expansion of the Brussels Treaty of 1948 between Britain, France and the Benelux countries into a Western European Union to include Germany and Italy. All members (with the exception of Britain – of course) would accept verification by the Union of the size and deployment of their forces. At the same time the Federal Republic of Germany would join NATO as a full member and assign her troops to the NATO command.

Yet the French fear of German jack-boots once more tramping westward still needed to be assuaged if France were to be brought to agree. And so on the eve of the London Conference Eden promised that Great Britain would maintain an army of four divisions and a tactical air force on the Continent as long as a majority of the WEU members wished it.[10] The promise worked; the deal was done; in October the French government signed the Paris Treaty establishing WEU; and the French National Assembly ratified it in December 1954.

For the first time in the twentieth century Britain had accepted a formal obligation[11] to keep a field army on the Continent in time of peace. She had now done for immediate political reasons in relation to an ally what she had long refused to do for long-term strategic reasons in relation to potential enemies: an irony indeed.

The Paris Treaty marked Eden's greatest triumph as a diplomatic fixer, the more so because there would be after all no 'agonising re-appraisal' of the United States commitment to the defence of Europe, since Dulles (now pally towards Eden rather than peevish as he had been over Vietnam) supported the deal as an acceptable alternative to the defunct EDC.

Yet the triumph owed nothing to any supposed 'status', 'influence' and 'prestige' allegedly conferred on Britain by her extra-European politico-strategic entanglements. It was due entirely to Eden's own personal skills, here deployed as Foreign Secretary of a European power principally in negotiation with another such power, France, and about a purely European problem.

Unfortunately the Chancellor of the Exchequer could not solve his own problem in defence matters by similar adroit tactics, linguistic finessing and deployment of charm.

In October 1955 (with Eden now as Prime Minister) there began the last Whitehall battle of the post-war decade over the design and cost of British defence policy – and in a more profound sense, about the future place in the world to which an economically limping island-state of fifty million people might aspire. For economically limping – and in urgent need of a thoroughgoing industrial refit – Britain still remained (see below, p. 398). In 1955 British exports of manufactures rose by only 7 per cent by value over 1954; those of the United States by 9 per cent; of Germany, by about 18 per cent; and of Japan by about 27 per cent.[12] In the summer of 1955, according to the Economic Survey for 1956, 'the economy was . . . disturbed by serious strikes. The trade balance remained heavily adverse. There was a loss of confidence in sterling, and the gold and dollar reserves began to fall again.'[13]

In the five years since the outbreak of the Korean War the current balance of payments had yawed between surplus and deficit: £386 million in the red in 1951;[14] £138 million in the black in 1952;[15] £115 million in the black in 1953;[16] £178 million in the black in 1954;[17] £79 million back in the red in 1955.[18] More disquieting still, the trade balance in goods had fallen £186 million into the red in 1954 and £359 million into the red in 1955.[19] In this last year the gold and dollar reserves leaked away by over one-fifth.[20]

Far from cheerful, therefore, was the economic background when on 14 October 1955 the Minister of Defence, now Selwyn Lloyd (a worthy, decent but dull lawyer, one of nature's butlers; Fettes and Magdalene College, Cambridge), submitted to the Cabinet Defence Committee his proposals for the United Kingdom's defence programme from 1955–56 to 1962–63.[21]

★

Ten years and two months earlier, as the Second World War ended with Japan's surrender, Lord Keynes (the then chief Treasury economic adviser) had given Attlee's new Labour Government a double warning: firstly, that the way 'we undertake liabilities all over the world and slop out money to the importunate represents an over-playing of our hand'; and secondly, that any substantial reductions in the cost of Britain's overseas defence commitments 'will require drastic revisions of policy'.[22]

How ineffective had proved Keynes's warnings during the ensuing decade is summed up with unconscious irony by a boast in September 1955 by the Cabinet Defence Committee: 'Taking account of the burden of our overseas commitments it could be argued that we were doing more than any other nation had ever done in peacetime.'[23]

In fact, according to the Minister of Defence, 'the burden of defence on the national economy' had only dropped from 10.5 per cent of GNP in 1952–53 (at the peak of post-Korea rearmament) to 9.5 per cent in 1954–55.[24] This compares with the 7.7 per cent projected by the Labour Government before the outbreak of the Korean War.[25]

Lloyd reckoned that if over the next four years the defence budget were held at 9 per cent of a GNP rising at 3.5 per cent annually, this would still be well short of meeting the cost of the armed forces' desired programmes.[26] For this reason, said Lloyd, he had put in hand the previous July a radical defence review. The objects of this review were 'to achieve a properly balanced programme' and 'to reduce expenditure to a realistic level . . .'[27] It was to be based on the assumptions that 'the danger of global war in the next few years had receded, that the cold war will continue . . .'[28]

It might seem, therefore, that this was the moment to follow Keynes's 1945 advice at long last and carry out 'drastic revisions of policy'. In 1955 such revisions would have surely meant at last beginning to throw overboard the obsolete top hamper of world-wide commitments and instead limiting outlay on defence to the security of Britain-in-Europe. This might have brought the defence budget down year by year to, say, the 4 per cent of GNP now being spent annually on defence by Britain's ever more formidable trade rival, West Germany.[29]

But no, habit still imposed its fetters, nostalgia still cast its spell, as is all too clear from Selwyn Lloyd's initial brief to the armed service departments. Britain 'must maintain an active fleet capable of supporting *this country's influence and interests as a world-wide Power and the leader of the Commonwealth* [added emphasis].'[30] The army 'should be primarily organised so that it can bring force to bear quickly in cold or limited war', and hence 'balanced forces must be *retained overseas* [added emphasis] . . .'[31] The Royal Air Force 'should provide our contribution to the nuclear deterrent in the shape of strategic [sic] weapons and a medium bomber force capable of delivering them. The force should be restricted to the minimum necessary *to maintain our position in world affairs* [added emphasis].'[32]

Lloyd also laid down that 'we must be prepared for the outbreak of limited war in the Middle East'. But in any case the Chiefs of Staff themselves meekly followed their predecessors in giving priority to the Middle East and the Far East over Europe. It was their view that the present size and equipment of British forces committed to NATO were 'dictated as much by political as by military reasons', and hence that this was where cuts could be found 'with the least military risk'.[33]

Lloyd had stipulated to the service departments that they must base their review on an average budget of £1,580 million (based on 1955 prices) annually over the next seven years.[34] But could his neo-Edwardian grand strategy be reconciled with such an annual budget? The service departments were certain that it could not. On the contrary, as Lloyd reported back to the Defence Committee, they were of one mind that such a budget meant that the sizes and roles of the armed forces would have to be severely curtailed. For a start, the active fleet would dwindle from the present eighteen ships of cruiser-size and larger to only six by 1965, and all units would have to be concentrated in home waters and the Mediterranean, 'except for a few small ships specially detached to the Persian Gulf and the Far East'. In particular, 'we should be unable to contribute more than a token force to the naval defence of the ANZAM area . . .' By 1958–59 the navy's bases in Ceylon and Singapore would be closed, and those in Malta and Hong Kong reduced in capacity. Gibraltar would become only a docking and storing base with no repair facilities, while at least one home dockyard would have to be closed.[35]

As for the army, 16 Parachute Brigade Group would be reduced to two battalions, perhaps only one. The strategic reserve would then consist of just one division, a brigade 'for Imperial policing', the Commonwealth Brigade Group in the Far East and a number of battalions in the United Kingdom. Reductions in war reserves of equipment and stores 'might entail the British Army of the Rhine having to lose as much as 75 per cent of its reserves in the event of a limited war requirement in another theatre, and might involve a serious risk'.[36]

In the case of the Royal Air Force, the bulk of the economies would fall on production of new aircraft. This would compel the future medium (nuclear V-bomber) force to be cut from 240 aircraft to 176; the frontline strength of the Canberra force from 124 to 84; Fighter Command from 576 to 252; all-weather aircraft in 2nd Tactical Air Force in Germany from 64 to 48; and day fighter/ground-attack aircraft from 266 to 72. The deployment of guided weapons would be reduced to the minimum required for training and trials. RAF Coastal Command would be cut from fifteen squadrons to five.[37]

When Selwyn Lloyd turned to defence R&D, he groaned that any reduction to the budget at present proposed for 1956–57 'would make it impossible to avoid the cancellation of major research projects, aircraft engines and helicopters, in the aircraft field; cancellation of at least one major guided weapons project, and all-round reductions in electronics and munitions'.[38]

Taken all in all, this 1955 report remarkably echoes the conclusions reached by a tri-service committee back in 1949 when asked to consider what kind of defence policy would be possible on a budget about a fifth less than that being projected at the time.[39] They too had portrayed inevitable shrinkages in the armed forces, leading no less inevitably to drastic curtailment of Britain's overseas deployments. The Labour Minister of Defence, A. V. Alexander, had passionately and successfully pleaded with his colleagues to reject such a policy of shrinkage, on the score that it would mean Britain's relegation to the status of second-class power.[40] Now, despite the discouraging experiences of the last six years, Selwyn Lloyd made a similar plea and in remarkably similar language:

> I do not believe that my colleagues will find these consequences acceptable, for the following reasons:-
>
> (i) We should lose our position as a world-wide naval power, weaken our air power in relation to the United States of America and U.S.S.R., reduce the effectiveness of our cold war strategy, and jeopardise the continued existence of ANZAM, on which our present Far East strategy depends.
>
> (ii) We should be unable even to make a pretence of honouring our commitments under the Paris Treaty.
>
> (iii) We should so reduce our contribution to the North Atlantic Treaty Organisation and so shake the confidence of our North Atlantic Treaty Organisation partners that we should put at serious risk the continued existence of the North Atlantic Treaty Organisation as an effective military alliance.
>
> (iv) There would be grave repercussions on the morale of our own people.[41]

Having thus found the consequences of an average annual budget of £1,580 million 'unacceptable', Lloyd put in a bid for £1,610 million for 1956–57, £1,665 million for 1957–58 and £1,695 million for 1958–59.[42] This would permit the navy's and air force's budgets to be upped by 15 and 14 per cent for 1958–59.[43] The navy's extra cash would enable it to start building new ships as the foundation of 'a comparatively small but modern and well-equipped Navy for the 1960's,' with a cruiser strength of twelve instead of six as under the budget now deemed unacceptable.

But on what criteria did Lloyd's naval advisers determine the future number and type of ships? The need to defend the vital Atlantic sea-lanes against Soviet submarines or surface raiders? No: because, in Lloyd's words, 'it would be just enough for a world-wide Navy. We could continue to be represented in the ANZAM areas and to retain most of our overseas naval bases.'[44] Nonetheless, Lloyd had to admit that such a role did involve a 'calculated risk', though one which he was prepared to accept:

By deploying this small fleet world-wide, however, we should be unable to concentrate in European waters enough ships to enable us to meet in full our present North Atlantic Treaty Organisation contributions . . .[45]

As for the Royal Air Force, the increased budget would permit inter alia a future strength of 200 medium bombers (i.e., nuclear-armed V-bombers) instead of 176. Lloyd suggested that the main issue for decision here was whether the British contribution to the Allied deterrent was 'of the right order of magnitude', bearing in mind firstly 'the need for our voice to be heard in planning the use of the Allied force as a whole', and secondly, 'the size of the job to be done in the initial phase of global war'.[46]

Thus Lloyd's memorandum, far from belatedly embodying Keynes's long-shelved 'drastic revisions of policy', was content to reprise the motto theme of British foreign and defence policy since 1945: 'Clinging On'. It merely looked for ways to orchestrate it for a smaller orchestra.

When the Defence Committee came to ramble round the memorandum five days later, the Prime Minister alone questioned the Chiefs of Staff's judgement that of all British world deployments it was Britain's contribution to NATO that could be cut 'with the least military risk'. Said Eden, pointing out the historically obvious to those blind to it, 'The maintenance of forces in Europe was essential to the defence of this island.'[47]

It fell to Butler to play a Chancellor of the Exchequer's customary part, of the finance director of a company whose board was wedded to plans beyond the company's present or future resources and little related to its profitability. He pointed out that if the Minister of Defence's proposals were approved, 'we should be mortgaging a large part of the prospective increase in the national product':

Expenditure on the social services was inevitably rising, and he had hoped that it would be possible to keep defence expenditure level so that part of the increase in the national product could be used for the many opportunities for profitable investment which were becoming available.[48]

He shrewdly noted that the Minister of Defence's figures

> did not fully reflect the strain on the economy that the programme
> would involve. Some £125 millions were to be spent in the next
> three years on the military aspects of atomic energy, but only a
> proportion of that total would be reflected in the defence
> budget . . .[49]

In point of fact, it was not merely a question of *general* strain on the
economy. As Butler pointed out elsewhere, it *directly* cost the
balance of payments £150 million a year to maintain British forces
overseas.[50] And in any case defence was by no means the only aspect
of the world role to impose economic stress. The colonial empire
(memorably described by Hugh Dalton in 1950 as being composed
of 'pullulating, poverty-stricken, disease-ridden nigger communities')[51] sucked on a complaisantly self-sacrificing Mother Country's
tit to the extent of £45 million a year in grants, loans and other
assistance.[52] Interest and capital repayments on the 1945 American
and Canadian loans took another £77 million (in dollars). Releases
from the so-called 'sterling balances' (debts owed to India and
Pakistan in regard to wartime costs incurred by Britain for the
privilege of defending the Indian subcontinent against the Japanese)
drained away another £27 million annually. Special credits to Iran
and Pakistan by the Export Guarantee Department alone cost £17
million, while a loan of £18 million for the construction of the
Kariba Dam had been granted to the ephemeral Federation of
Rhodesia and Nyasaland, one of the more futile British attempts at
political construction in Africa. These and other overseas liabilities
were, as Butler justly observed to the Cabinet in November 1955,
'serious in relation to the current and prospective state of our actual
net earnings overseas . . .'[53]

In any case, when making a judgement about future defence
budgets the combined costs of playing the world and Commonwealth power had to be added to the domestic burdens on the
Exchequer. In turn the impact must be weighed of this total load
on Britain's future as an industrial country up against ever tougher
competition.[54] Patiently the Chancellor tried that autumn to explain
such complexities to the Minister of Defence and other colleagues.[55]

Firstly, spending on the social services would increase in the next three years from £1,361 million to £1,524 million, or by an average of about 4 per cent per annum, even if there were 'no extension of services'.[56] Secondly, Government expenditure other than on defence or welfare would come to £1,806 million in 1955–56. While Butler assumed for present purposes that such expenditure would still be the same in 1958–59, this was, he said, 'a very optimistic assumption'.

The total increase in state expenditure (including defence at Selwyn Lloyd's figures) therefore came out at £121 million per annum.[57] This compared with an increase of only £100 million per annum in GNP in 1952–4 in real terms at 1954 prices.

The Chancellor proceeded to give his colleagues an even more dismal lesson in arithmetic. The prospective swelling in defence expenditure and in social service costs 'show annual rates of increase 80 per cent. and 60 per cent. respectively higher than the rate, in real terms (2.5 per cent.), at which the national product has recently been increasing'.[58] In absolute figures, he went on, the annual increase between now and 1958–59 in the total cost of defence and the social services would be about 20 per cent higher than the increase in *all* government expenditure over the previous three years.[59] If such increases were accepted, he wrote,

> it will mean that no margin will be available for any increase in the share of the consumer (through further reductions in taxation . . .) or in fixed capital investment . . . Moreover, at a time when our problem is to relieve the pressure of home demand and to allow more domestic resources to be devoted to exports, it would be wrong for the Government itself to adopt policies or programes [sic] which so far from relieving the situation seem likely to involve a Government demand for a *greater* share of the national product.[60]

Butler was therefore convinced that the government 'must reduce the rate of expansion of both Defence and Social Services expenditure . . .'

Just the same, the question for decision at the moment was, he said, 'whether we can safely contemplate Defence expenditure of £1,695 millions in 1958–59; and the answer must be that we cannot.'[61] The average annual rate of increase must therefore be brought down from the Minister of Defence's £67 million to not more than £40 million, thus cutting the 1958–59 total to £1,615 million (sic) – even if this 'may require a further re-examination of the assumptions and policies on which his proposals are based'.[62]

From this tangle of argument offered by the Chancellor and the Minister of Defence the nits were now to be picked at length by the mandarins of the Ministry of Defence, the Treasury, the three service departments and then again by the Chancellor and the Minister of Defence.[63] But the entire debate was, like all its predecessors back to 1946, about marginal revisions of policy, not radical ones. Butler's suggested increases over the three years to 1958–59 were only 40 per cent smaller than those proposed by Lloyd – and in any case were still *increases*, not reductions in real terms.[64] This was a far cry from, say, setting out to halve the defence budget down to the West German proportion of GNP, with commitments run down accordingly.

In fact, Whitehall's collective approach to defence policy and its cost continued to resemble nothing so much as Adolf Hitler in his years of defeat shuffling battalions when he ought to have been taking the decision in good time to withdraw whole army groups to a shorter front. But then Britain's world policy as a whole since 1945 had followed Hitler's example in clinging to ground at all costs. And it had done so out of the same kind of motivation as Hitler's: unwillingness to accept the fact of strategic overextension; dread of loss of standing among allies and enemies.

When the Duke of Wellington was asked what was the best test of a great general, he answered: 'To know when to retreat and dare to do it.'[65] It was a test which between 1945 and 1955 a Labour Government and two Conservative Governments had lamentably failed at proof.

The 1956 White Paper on Defence (published in February) reveals a British governing elite still deeply immured in their reality-proof mental bunker, still choosing to read the global liabilities on the wall-map as strategic assets. The armed forces' primary task was 'to make a contribution to the Allied deterrent sufficient in quality and size *to maintain our standing as a world power* [added emphasis]'.[66] They must 'play their part in the cold war. By their mere presence they can contribute to the stability of the free world, and the security of overseas territories whose peaceful development may be threatened by subversion . . .' They must be 'capable of dealing with outbreaks of limited war', and of 'playing their part effectively in global war should it break out'.[67]

The Royal Navy, proclaimed the White Paper, 'is able to play an important part *in upholding our interests and influence in peacetime in distant parts of the world* [added emphasis]'. In the case of limited war the navy 'planned to make immediately available in any part of the world a force of aircraft-carriers equipped with modern aircraft and supplemented by cruisers and escorts'.[68]

As for the army, the White Paper reported in so many words that the future defence of traditional strategic 'cowpats' like the Middle East would rely much less on large standing garrisons on the spot and much more on troops flown out from the United Kingdom. Thus the enforced withdrawal from the Canal Zone in 1954 becomes, in the White Paper's quaint Whitehall dialect, 'redeployment', opening the way for progress in building up the strategic reserve at home. 'Its strength at any time will, of course, depend on variations *in our overseas commitments* [added emphasis]. We have recently, for example, reinforced the Middle East . . . a large part of it [the strategic reserve] is trained and organised for transport by air.'[69] Thus new technological means would, it was hoped, fulfil old pretensions at a bargain price.

And a bargain price was badly needed. Publicly admitted the White Paper (no doubt at the insistence of the Chancellor and his Treasury accountants): 'The economy of the United Kingdom has been overstrained during the past year by the demands placed on it, and in consequence the balance of payments has worsened and the gold and dollar reserves have been depleted . . .'[70]

And so:

> The total of the defence budget proposed for 1956–57, before deducting receipts from American Aid is £1,548.7 millions as compared with £1,537.2 millions in 1955–56. After deducting American Aid, the figures are £1,498.7 millions for 1956–57 compared with £1,494.2 millions for 1955–56.[71]

Since the Minister of Defence had put in a first bid for £1,610 million in respect of 1956–57,[72] the final award marked a significant victory for the Chancellor. Yet it must inevitably worsen Britain's chronic strategic overstretch, for her future global commitments remained as grandiose as ever.

Back in 1890 the American admiral A. T. Mahan had commented in his classic work *The Influence of Seapower Upon History*[73] on the disparity between such inherited worldwide commitments and the current strength of the mother country – but with reference to eighteenth-century Spain. Whereas in that epoch, he writes, 'the might of England was sufficient to keep alive the heart and members [of Empire] . . . the equally extensive colonial Empire of Spain . . . offered so many points for insult and injury.'[74] By a doleful paradox, his description of eighteenth-century Spain's predicament had come to apply exactly to the Britain of 1956. This was freshly demonstrated in July when the revolutionary leader of Egypt, Abdul Gamal Nasser, took advantage of one of the 'many points for insult and injury' offered by Britain's worldwide commitments, and nationalized the Suez Canal (see below, Chapter 23).

Yet, as Mahan also perceived, the extensiveness of historic entanglements is only one factor in the total-strategic equation. The other lies in 'the might' of the mother country. The might of Georgian England celebrated by Mahan had consisted in seapower and the wealth from seaborne trade to pay for it. By the 1950s all that had long since vanished beneath the waves of history. Now the extent of Britain's present and future 'might' was determined by her performance as an industrial country up against ever more energetic foreign challenge. How well, then, would she perform?

The answer to that must depend first and foremost on what share of the national product Conservative governments chose to allot to investment in replacing those many parts of her industrial machine which were worn-out or obsolete.

PART THREE

The World's Largest Debtor

If one drives about the country and sees how much goods traffic is immobilised, or slowed down, every day because of our narrow and winding trunk roads, and our congested towns, it seems fairly clear that a major roads programme is a basic economic necessity for us – and not, as is sometimes suggested, a luxury.

(Lord Swinton, Lord President of the Council,
12 July 1954)

Investment in productive industry in the United Kingdom was suffering at the expense of non-productive investment such as defence, housing and education . . . The investment rate of productive industry was being reduced year by year . . .

(Peter Thorneycroft, President of the Board of Trade,
13 June 1952)

7. The Starving of Productive Investment

With the encouraging words 'It is a gamble – [it will] make or mar your political career. But every humble home will bless you if you succeed',[1] Winston Churchill in October 1951 appointed as his Minister of Housing and Local Government a snaggle-toothed, straggly moustached, droopy-eyed cuckold[2] and phoney Edwardian English gent (actually grandson of a Scottish peasant) equipped with small 'l' liberal prejudices, slippery political cunning, and remorseless ambition. Harold Macmillan took up the job with a resolve that, whether or not every humble home came to bless him, it would indeed make his career.

His opportunity sprang from an extraordinary happening at the Conservative Party Conference (usually as spontaneous as a Nuremberg Rally) in 1950 – a revolt from the floor which forced the leadership to commit the Party to building 300,000 houses a year if and when it next formed a government. The revolt has to be seen in the context of long memories about the fate of Lloyd George's promise after the Great War of 'homes fit for heroes to live in', and the Labour Government's election promise in 1945 to build 5,000,000 dwellings in ten years, whereas in the event it never did better in a single year than the 200,000 completed in 1950.

The Conservatives' pledge may well have helped towards the 1 per cent swing from Labour which gave them their narrow victory in the 1951 general election.[3] But now in office they were stuck with it. On the other hand, if Macmillan could fulfil it, what a marvellous vote-winner next time round!

There was just one snag, soon apparent. The launch of Macmillan's housing drive coincided with the great 1951–2 economic storm, and the Government's emergency measures to keep Britain out of the breakers. It also coincided, in both the short term and the longer term, with the rearmament programme. By March 1952 the Government's Chief Planning Officer, Edwin Plowden, was reporting that 'there is ... a direct conflict between housing, defence, and industrial investment'.[4]

This was a conflict which Macmillan set out to win, fighting right from the start to preserve in its ambitious entirety the housing programme adopted by the Cabinet: 230,000 houses in 1952, 260,000 in 1953, and 300,000 in 1954.[5] To him in his present post it seemed absolutely right that re-equipping Britain's widely old-fashioned and worn-out engine room ought to come second to installing commodious new cabins for her crew and passengers. As early as 13 December 1951 he vigorously attacked the Chancellor's cautious views on the total investment that the country could afford or steel supplies permit. Warning that ministers should not be misled into 'defeatism' by the Chancellor's desire to achieve a balance between resources and production, Macmillan scornfully wrote: 'The perfect balance is at zero. When one is dead the tempo of work is beautifully matched with the resources available.'[6]

More to the point personally, perhaps, was his further assertion that 'If it is decided not to build more houses in 1952 than in 1951 then there is no justification for the Ministry of Housing, and the Government as well as the Minister will be discredited.'[7]

As for 'the great bottleneck of steel', opined Macmillan, the 'obvious thing to do is to put more emphasis on that part of the building industry which makes no great demand for steel, viz., house-building, conversions of houses into flats, and essential maintenance.'[8]

To no avail did the Chancellor of the Duchy of Lancaster (Lord Swinton) point out in January 1952 that new housing estates required iron or steel for gas and water mains and that the houses themselves required steel for household kit like cookers and space-heaters, even for locks and hinges. To no avail did he point out that a much larger demand for dollar timber would hit the already disastrous balance of payments.[9] In vain too did the President of the Board of Trade (Peter Thorneycroft) plead at a meeting of the ministerial Economic Policy Committee in April for a switch of investment into industry. Proclaimed Macmillan:

> provided that sufficient steel and timber were available it might well be possible in 1953 to build more than the 260,000 houses now envisaged. He was not in agreement with the theory that orders must be reduced in order to prevent overloading; unless the housing drive was energetically pressed and the industry kept fully employed the houses we needed would not get built. Any suggestion that a change of policy was contemplated would be politically unwise, and would take the spirit out of the present active implementation of the housing programme.[10]

These tussles only marked the beginning of a fierce year-by-year scrimmage for investment resources between, on the one hand, the ministers responsible for Britain's manufacturing industry, transport systems, telecommunications and (for that matter) education, and, on the other, Macmillan at the Department of Housing and Local Government. It was a replay in different club colours of similar matches in the late 1940s (likewise uncomfortably refereed by Chancellors of the Exchequer) between these ministers' Labour predecessors and Aneurin Bevan, Minister of Health, as passionate promoter of new council houses.[11] Just as Bevan, a miner's son, knew at first-hand the grim terraces of South Wales pit villages, so did Macmillan, as pre-war MP for Stockton, know the North's barrack-hut sprawls of back-to-back dwellings in soot-dark brick run up in the Industrial Revolution to house the forebears of their present inhabitants. In consequence Macmillan, like Bevan, was moved by genuine concern as well as by ambition. This honed the blade of his argument in cutting at colleagues who still believed that up-to-date export industries and a modern transport network should come before domestic contentment.

Even in November 1954, with the economy showing fresh signs of overload, Macmillan fiercely objected to suggestions that council housing might be cut back, as being 'difficult politically to justify if other building was going ahead'.[12] In fact, what he called 'other' building was only going ahead because the Government had lifted direct licensing control over private builders, who were now free to erect as many dwellings as they could sell. Governmental grip on the level of investment in housing was therefore now limited to the construction by local councils of subsidized working-class estates and townships. The most that Macmillan even now would concede was that he would try to bring the number of new council dwellings down 'towards' 140,000 a year:

> but if this were to be done, it was important to omit the reference in H.M. the Queen's Speech on the Opening of Parliament to an active campaign to clear the slums. Slums could not be cleared unless the local authorities could build houses for the people who would be rendered homeless.[13]

Undaunted by Macmillan's heart-wrenching allusion to the slums, the critics of the ever greedier housing programme gave battle again. The Minister of Education (David Eccles) observed that

> there was nothing the Government could do to prevent about 360,000 houses being built in 1955, and, if present trends continued, something like 380,000 would be completed in 1956. If, by taking action now we could reduce this figure by 60,000, we should save capital investment of about £100 million . . . there would be ample room to accommodate the increased requirements for health, education, and the beginnings of the expansion of the road programme, the main burden of which must come after 1956.[14]

The President of the Board of Trade pointed out that 'the secondary effects of a large programme of Government investment increased inflationary tendencies and [that] this affected our ability to export'. He too therefore thought that 'some room for manoeuvre by means of a reduction in the housing programme was desirable'.[15]

And this time the critics did indeed partly carry the day. In the event, only – only! – 324,000 new dwellings were to be built in 1955 instead of the 360,000 feared by Eccles, whereas in the single year 1954–55 investment in plant and machinery jumped by 14 per cent, and investment in the motor industry, the panzer striking force of exports, nearly doubled.[16]

Yet such last-minute governmental repentance could not make good the damage already done.

★

During Macmillan's time as Minister of Housing, in the three calendar years 1952–4 new dwellings' share of Britain's *total* gross fixed investment increased by nearly 3 per cent, while manufacturing's share shrank by nearly 4 per cent.[17] This is one measure of his success in the annual scrimmages with his colleagues. Another is the actual sum of money invested in new dwellings, which soared by 34 per cent between 1952 and 1954, as compared with a mere 9 per cent increase in the amount put into manufacturing, transport and communications.[18] The niggardliness of this increase cannot, of course, be blamed on the housing drive alone, for the Conservative Government followed its Labour predecessor in ruthlessly squeezing industrial investment in order to accommodate the defence costs of world-power pretension and now the demands of post-Korea rearmament.

Nevertheless, some industries were spared the squeeze. First among these was steel, the very sinew of an industrial society, but in Britain a sinew that had proved in peace and two world wars too weak for the demands laid on it, not least owing to partial senility.[19] A month before Germany's surrender in 1945 the steel industry was pronounced by the President of the Board of Trade and the Minister of Supply in the wartime coalition Government to be 'in urgent need of modernisation'.[20] In consequence the new Labour Government had backed an initial five-year plan for switching production from a litter of small, aged and high-cost works to a few giant modern plants. But the plan fell behindhand because of operational problems and muddles, so that the largest single project, the Margam integrated strip-mill in South Wales, did not come on stream until 1952.[21]

Shortage of steel had therefore throttled all types of manufacturing and construction ever since the war: a major constraint on national investment. The advent of the huge post-Korea rearmament programme could only exacerbate this problem. Hence Conservative governments from 1951 onwards ungrudgingly backed investment in plans by the industry to reach an output target for 1957–58 of 20–21 million ingot tons compared with 16.3 million in 1950.[22]

The aircraft industry also proved specially favoured under the Conservatives as under Labour. For the Conservative Government too was inspired by the naive hope that, with a third of the all-round resources of the American industry and an unquantifiable fraction of the commercial punch and cunning, it could win a major share of the market for transatlantic and other long-distance airliners. Surely Boeing and Douglas would be seen off by the turbo-prop Bristol Britannia and the jet-propelled De Havilland Comet? – once, of course, the habit of the Mark I Comet of falling into the sea from a great height had been cured (see below, Chapter 17). Unstinting investment in the aircraft industry was no less ensured by the need of a present and future first-class world power like Britain to design and produce all her own military aircraft of whatever type required, to say nothing of novel guided weapons.

As for the energy industries, no government could forget the ice-age winter of 1946–7 when factories had shut down and households had shivered in the dark because of the power cuts. Nor could any government forget the debacle of Abadan, when production of refined petroleum from the largest British-owned refinery in the world was stopped by a funny old chap in pyjamas. And nor, for that matter, could any government be oblivious to the habit of British miners of taking a day off from time to time or going on strike if miffed about something or other, with consequent depressing effect on the output of coal. Hence followed the enthusiastic post-Abadan construction of oil refineries in the United Kingdom and the hopeful development of atomic energy (which was in any case part and parcel of developing a British 'independent' nuclear bomber force). Electricity generation and transmission too got their desired rations of investment.

The losers in the Whitehall scrimmage for capital resources in this era of 'the managed economy' continued to be the ministers responsible for manufacturing, for the road and rail networks, for telecommunications, and even for education. They are found in the 1950s making just the same kind of unavailing protests at their meagre rations as had their Labour predecessors in the late 1940s. In fact, Conservative departmental ministers were the more justified in protesting because it was now six, seven, eight, nine, *ten* years after the war, and yet so much that was antiquated or verging on the derelict had still not been replaced.

Even in regard to such a basic necessity of a modern industrial economy as good road communications, the Secretary of State for the Co-ordination of Transport, Fuel and Power (Lord Leathers) told the House of Lords in July 1952 that

> in the matter of road maintenance we are just about at rock bottom, and that any economy below the present level is a delusion. Our policy for the future will be to do our best to maintain the present standards as a minimum . . .[23]

Ten months later the same minister, together with the Minister of Transport (Alan Lennox-Boyd), was protesting against the Chancellor of the Exchequer's decision not to allow even a modest increase in expenditure:

> There is a growing volume of criticism of Government policy in regard to roads. We are adding materially to costs of production . . . by completely failing to adapt the road system to its legitimate needs. For many years our road system has remained static or worse and although it is an essential part of the machinery of production it is becoming increasingly obsolete . . .[24]

Bluntly the two ministers pointed out that the housing drive was blocking the creation of a modern strategic road system:

> virtually no new road works can be undertaken other than those arising from the New Towns and blitzed cities programmes, even though the needs of industry and agriculture cry out for new or better roads, and there are the most obvious and illogical contrasts between, say, the roads on the new housing estates and the public highways leading to them, which are sometimes little better than narrow muddy lanes.[25]

It appeared that this was not the only absurdity:

> Risks have to be taken with weak bridges or uneconomic detours or traffic restrictions imposed. Sometimes when the Railways Executive have had to repair a bridge to prevent collapse, it has been necessary to accept its reconstruction to the old and inadequate width instead of widening it to take the increased traffic.[26]

In October 1953, after exactly two years of Conservative government, Lennox-Boyd (now with the title of Minister of Transport *and* Civil Aviation) explained the situation to his colleagues:

> The case for increasing the proportion of our expenditure devoted to the roads could be made on safety grounds, but he felt that the stronger aspect of the case was the contribution which better roads would make to industrial efficiency; there was little point in pressing for greater productivity in the factories without looking at the efficiency of the transport of goods to and from them.[27]

He might here have reminded his colleagues that in 1948 the Labour Government had daringly raised the speed limit for heavy goods vehicles from 20 m.p.h. to 30 m.p.h., on the score that the existing seventeen-year-old limit was detrimental to their design and construction. Thirty miles per hour![28] The outrageous proposal had evoked fierce but vain opposition from cyclists' and pedestrians' organizations, and from the Transport and General Workers' Union. In 1950 the same Government with equal daring had proposed to increase the maximum permitted length of a single-decker four-wheeled bus or coach from 27 feet 6 inches to 30 feet, in order to give British manufacturers a better chance in export markets, where vehicles much longer than 30 feet had long been operated. This reckless initiative had been opposed by almost all police authorities, the County Councils Association and the Minister of Transport's own technical advisers, on the score that buses of this un-British length would not be suitable for quaint British roads.[29]

The trouble was, as Lennox-Boyd now sought to impress on his Cabinet colleagues, that in 1953 the roads remained just as quaint, and on present plans would so continue. In the financial year 1953–54 a total of £3 million was being spent on new roads or improvements, with £4 million in prospect for 1954–55.[30] To put this tiny investment in perspective, it amounted to just a ninth of the sum being slopped out annually in grants for colonial development.[31]

But then came a surprising turnabout. In December 1953, the Minister of Transport actually won his colleagues' agreement to a nine-year roads programme at a total cost of £140 million.[32] So finally, eight years after the war, Britain was to do better than minimum make-do-and-mend. Or was she? For the Cabinet decided not to announce this complete programme because of, in the Chancellor's words, its 'sensational effect' (so un-British!). Instead a list of projects would be made public, starting with an increase in expenditure on new roads or improvements to £7 million in 1955–56, £12 million in 1956–57, and £14.5 million in 1957–58.³³ The 1955–56 figure came to no more than twice the investment in 1954 in building work for the police, fire services, and prisons.³⁴

Notably welcome among the listed projects was the Dartford Tunnel under the Thames, a crucial strategic link first decided upon before the war but postponed ever since. At last! But since the tunnel was not due for completion until 1963, long-distance traffic could still look forward to many more years of queuing patiently on crumbling wharves for the slow and aged ferry between Tilbury and Gravesend. In any case, the entire nine-year programme still did not include a Forth road bridge, a Severn road bridge or a single long-distance motorway. No sensational effects! Nothing so bold or vulgar! Yet again a government had struck the authentic British note of timidity and preference for the piecemeal.

Seven months later, in July 1954, Lord Swinton, the Lord President of the Council, was writing in a memorandum to the Cabinet Economic Policy Committee: 'One cannot but be struck with the small scale of our road programme, when one finds that even a project for widening a few miles of the Great North Road ... cannot go ahead with the finance we so far have in view'. He went on:

> Briefly, I consider that the country needs a large programme of new road construction, and 'major improvements' – bypasses and bridges; exits to, and roads through, towns: probably some new 'Motor Roads'. If one drives about the country and sees how much goods traffic is immobilised, or slowed down, every day because of our narrow and winding trunk roads, and our congested towns, it seems fairly clear that a major roads programme is a basic economic necessity for us – and not, as is sometimes suggested, a luxury.³⁵

The Chancellor of the Exchequer 'agreed that much could be done to improve our road system'. However, he went on to express a typical Chancellor's cavil, in this case arising from the Government's chosen order of priorities:

> It was, however, undesirable on general economic grounds to begin extensive new construction at a time *when the housing programme was rising to 400,000 houses a year and defence expenditure remained at a very high level* [added emphasis]. There was now some danger of our economy being overloaded; employment was at the highest figure ever, and there were signs of a return of inflation. He hoped that it might be possible to make some reduction in the housing programme and to moderate defence expenditure, in which case it would be useful to have a road programme ready.[36]

In the event, Britain's first stretch of motorway – the Preston bypass (a source of national wonder, although only eight miles long) – was not opened until 1958, more than twenty years after the construction of the first long-distance European autobahnen and the American parkways.

But apart from this and other snippets of double-tracking, the British road network – 'system' would be too strong a word – at the end of the first post-war decade still presented a picture of traffic struggling along narrow, twisty defiles in town and country alike, and bottlenecked at river crossings and estuaries by medieval bridges or the wait for intermittent ferries. To cite just one notorious example among many, the A5 trunk route that linked the capital to Birmingham (centre of British light engineering) and the industrial North-West passed through the tightly narrow village street of Markyate in Hertfordshire. Despite a speed restriction of 15 m.p.h., heavy trucks constantly knocked the corners off the overhanging upper storeys of its thatched cottages.

The railways fared no better. Not until the beginning of 1955 was the nationalized British Transport Commission enabled to put forward (at the request of the Minister of Transport) a modernization plan on the scale of those which Continental European countries had actually embarked on some seven years earlier and by now largely completed.[37]

The Commission's case for their fifteen-year plan at a cost of £1,200 million serves backhandedly to sum up the consequences of the lack of investment in the railways by governments of both parties since the war.[38] Every long-distance main line in the country was still steam-hauled, whereas in France, West Germany, Italy and the Netherlands electric or diesel traction prevailed. Most goods wagons were still loose-coupled and individually hand-braked four-wheelers instead of bogied stock fitted with continuous air-braking – meaning that British freight trains could only move at a crawl, so impeding all other traffic. Marshalling yards were small, local and antiquated. Key sections of main-line track were still controlled by semaphore signalling forty years old. No centralized traffic-control centres existed. No main line was fitted with automatic warning devices. Track maintenance below pre-war standards, coupled with Victorian tight curves and confused junction layouts, meant severe speed restrictions. Almost the whole stock of (often dirty) passenger coaches needed replacing.

The Government announced its backing in principle for the Commission's plan (though actually more a botch-up of bits and pieces than a 'plan' as Louis Armand of the SNCF or den Hollander of the Nederlandse Spoorwegen would have understood the term),[39] and even agreed that £800 million of the cost might be borrowed in instalments from the Treasury.[40] This colossal average annual sum of £53 million of taxpayers' money to be invested in a vital British asset amounted to little more than a third of the money directly spent overseas each year on the armed forces supporting the pretensions to a world role.[41]

Although the modernization plan now got under way, it did so very slowly, rather like a contemporary British Railways express on an incline behind a labouring, wheel-slipping steam-engine.[42] Various piecemeal schemes were put in hand, such as ordering multiple-unit diesel trains to replace branch-line puffers. But this being mid-twentieth-century Britain, the major proposals for the modernization of the long-distance passenger and freight routes became stuck in the sidings of two-years-long committee meetings and correspondence within Whitehall and between Whitehall and the British Transport Commission.

Much of the argy-bargy related to the fraught question of how far British Railways workshops should build the new diesel and electric main-line locomotives, and how far the private manufacturers. The question had its technical fascination too because, this again being mid-twentieth-century Britain, neither nationalized nor private sectors generally enjoyed the expertise or equipment to build such novelties, both being still stuck in the Stephenson age[43] (see below, p. 299).

So eighteen months after the British Transport Commission's original submission the Cabinet is found appointing a Committee under the Lord Chancellor to consider practical proposals for 'increasing the efficiency of the railways' which 'could with advantage be included in a White Paper'.[44] In September 1956 the BTC therefore put in a fresh set of proposals,[45] which, at the Lord Chancellor's urging, the Cabinet accepted 'as practical and necessary'.[46] Thus it was only in the closing months of 1956 that the ancient semaphore signal of Whitehall decision-making finally clanked from red to green.

Nevertheless, even under the British Transport Commission's now approved plan the London (Euston)–Manchester–Liverpool main line would not be electrified until 1967, twenty-two years after the end of the Second World War, and that from London (King's Cross) to Leeds and York not until 1970.[47] In shaming contrast, European main lines from Paris to Lyons, Hamburg to Basel, and Milan to Naples had all been electrified by the early 1950s, thanks to use of Marshall Aid 'counter-part' funds, which the Labour Government in Britain, on the advice of academic economists seconded to Whitehall, had chosen instead to devote to writing down the National Debt.[48]

It followed that in Britain in the late 1950s and early 1960s even 'luxury' long-distance travel on the railways meant thirty-year-old Pullmans wreathed in smoke and steam rattling and rocking along at start-to-stop speeds of around 60 m.p.h., while in France, for example, luxury now signified the stainless-steel coaches of the Mistral sweeping along continuously welded track behind an 8,000-horsepower electric locomotive at a start-to-stop speed of over 80 m.p.h.

On the Continent the new railways and their elegant modern stations served as the public face of post-war national recovery. In Britain there was no such equivalent, except for the Festival of Britain Exhibition on London's South Bank in 1951, a brief flash of brilliant colour and bright imagination amid the shabbiness and sepulchral shades of the British scene, but by 1955 an empty and neglected site.

★

> The basis of the Post Office proposals was that in 1954 a definite start should be made to overtake the large outstanding arrears of telephone development. Post Office civil investment had been restricted or cut back ever since the war . . . the low level of investment in 1952–3 resulted from an overall stringency and from the increase in the Post Office defence programme.[49]

Thus in November 1952 did a Post Office spokesman make a plea to the Whitehall mandarins of the Investment Programmes Committee for money in 1954 to start modernizing and expanding Britain's worn-out and overloaded civil telecommunications system. As he explained,

> It would be nine years after the end of the war that the Post Office were suggesting making a determined attempt to reduce the telephone waiting list . . . No less than one third of the 450,000 subscribers on the list had been waiting 3 years or more, and one third of the list consisted of applications for telephones for business premises . . .
>
> Because of investment restrictions and of the need in the past to devote a high proportion of capital to defence projects . . . connecting new subscribers had had to take second place. The position in regard to local line plant was serious and the whole cable system was in need of overhaul.[50]

Three months later the Postmaster General himself (Lord De La Warre) was protesting that the skimpy capital investment for 1953–54 recommended by the Cabinet's Economic Steering Committee would force him to make up leeway in the trunk (long-distance) telephone services at the expense of local lines.[51] A month later still, in March 1953, he was explaining to his colleagues that whereas his short-term problem was to prevent a rise in the waiting list for telephones,

> his long-term problem was to prevent the growing deterioration of the trunk service . . . Ever since the war the Post Office had had to

rely upon expedients to maintain the service; the time had now arrived when a planned programme of development was essential, or there would be a serious danger of breakdown . . .[52]

The Economic Steering Committee relented, but only in part. In 1953 an extra £1 million would be invested in the national telecommunications net. £1 million on a budget of £43 million! And that budget in any case came to only about a third of the grants and loans authorized by Britain for development in the sterling Commonwealth that year.[53] Just the same, the ESC refused to grant the increase of £2.2 million requested for 1954 by the Postmaster General.[54]

Whether bestowed or withheld, these were trifling sums. They signified that at the end of the first post-war decade British business-men would still be waiting and waiting for their turn to have urgent long-distance calls put through inadequate cabling by good ladies shoving jacks into the switchboards of ageing manual exchanges. As for the private customer, years of patience – yes, years, for some had been waiting as long as seven[55] – might well bring her or him the boon of a party line – and, if their luck was in, a line not shared with one of the neighbourhood's champion gossips.

On the buoyancy of manufacturing industry and its exports every-thing else must be carried: the world-power top hamper (financial as well as military), the heavy combined cargo of house-building and the welfare state, even the weight of the minimal investment in infrastructure. In 1948–51, under the Labour Government, Britain had invested per employed worker in new plant and equipment in manufacturing industry less than a third of the United States figure.[56] Still more discreditably, Britain had invested per worker in manufac-turing industry in 1948–50 (the period of Marshall Aid) less than half the Swedish total and less than five-sixths of the French total.[57]

This neglect by the Labour Government rendered it more urgent than ever in the early 1950s that Britain should on the boldest scale build new factories and modernize the old, and develop new products that global customers would want to buy. Indeed, the urgency was now even greater because fast steaming up astern of Britain in export markets were newly refitted foreign rivals such as

Germany. Soon Britain would lose what was left of her colossal competitive head-start after the war as the only European country not to be fought over, defeated and subjected to enemy occupation.

Calamitously, however, the severe restriction of investment in British manufacturing (either by direct Treasury control in the case of the nationalized industries or through Building Licences and the Capital Issues Committee in the case of private enterprise) imposed by the Labour Government continued under the Conservatives. The justification remained the same: the need to make room for the demands of defence and house-building; the need to steer capital equipment into export markets; and the need to relieve the general inflationary pressure on the economy caused by full employment and the wage-price spiral.

Rationing under the Conservatives began with the emergency measures of early 1952, by which manufacturing industry was to be allowed in that current year only about two-thirds of the investment it had received in 1950, that being in any case reckoned to be some 20 per cent below what was really needed. Reported the official Investment Programmes Committee, if such rationing continued into 1953 in order to accommodate both the housing drive and rearmament, 'it would be damaging to the industrial efficiency of the country and to our future competitive power in foreign markets'.[58] Although the President of the Board of Trade (Peter Thorneycroft) accepted these cuts for 1952 in relation to industries sponsored by his board, he did so only with the gravest disquiet:

> I am most anxious that my colleagues should fully realise the crippling effect of the proposals on these industries – which comprise over half of private manufacturing industry. It may be expected ... that possibly one-third of projects already approved and in progress will have to be stopped, and these are projects of the first importance, either as dollar earners or savers, or to meet basic needs.[59]

The projects at risk included many ICI plant developments for chemical products and dyestuffs, new plant for Courtaulds and other companies for producing artificial textiles, fibreglass, photographic film, and a high-speed testing ground for the motor industry – even new facilities for Lloyds in the City of London, whose invisible earnings topped $20 million a year.[60]

In May 1952 the President of the Board of Trade and the Minister of Supply (Duncan Sandys) sought in a joint memorandum to persuade their colleagues that more money, lots of it, must be put into Britain's wealth-creating machine:

> The successive Balance of Payment crises have emphasised the importance of the continuing modernisation and development of productive industry in this country. This is essential to meet our basic needs and reduce demands on imports; it is even more necessary to secure the great volume of exports on which our whole national economy and our standard of living depend.

The two ministers pointed out for the benefit of colleagues deficient in technological understanding that those exports

> cannot be secured unless United Kingdom industry can compete successfully in world markets and for this purpose it must keep abreast, if not in advance, of modern development elsewhere . . . To do so requires investment, much more investment than manufacturing industry has been permitted this year, and indeed more than manufacturing industry has had for several years.[61]

And why had manufacturing industry been on short rations for so long? Wrote Thorneycroft and Sandys:

> Unfortunately, our capital investment resources have never been sufficient to meet all the calls which have been made on them since the war, viz, repair of war-time losses, power services, new houses, improved health services, more schools, to which has now been added the rearmament programme.[62]

In the judgement of these two ministers, the rations of investment allowed to manufacturing industries for new building in 1952 amounted to only just over half of their real needs.[63] They cited the particularly depressing case of Terylene, an ICI invention and 'probably the best of our new textiles, with great potential export sales':

> After many delays the first part of the project has at last started, but there seems little prospect now of permitting the second stage, planned to take production up from 5,000 tons to 20,000 tons a year,

to go ahead next year as planned. Meanwhile the United States firm, Dupont, who bought the U.S.A. rights of this new fibre invented in this country are going ahead at full speed.[64]

When in June 1952 the Cabinet's Economic Policy Committee came to discuss across-the-board proposals for investment in 1953, Peter Thorneycroft banged it home that

> investment in productive industry in the United Kingdom was suffering at the expense of non-productive investment such as defence, housing and education ... The investment rate of productive industry was being reduced year by year. He found himself in an embarrassing position when asking industries to increase their efficiency while he was at the same time unable to license improvements.[65]

Lord Leathers, the Secretary of State for the Co-ordination of Transport, Fuel and Power, for his part, contended perfectly reasonably that manufacturing industry should not enjoy extra investment at the expense of equally important energy supplies and transport. But it was the Minister of Supply (Duncan Sandys) who pointed the finger at the common enemy, unkindly observing that a continuation of the housing programme 'on its present scale was undoubtedly difficult to reconcile with our balance of payments difficulties'.[66]

Eight months later the President of the Board of Trade was reporting that he did not know how much industry was likely to invest in 1953 or 1954, because that depended on too many factors outside his control, but that his guess was that they would invest too little. And why? Because the Government's restrictive monetary and fiscal policies 'have placed severe checks on private investment . . .'[67] Brilliant! So as well as directly holding back modernization by limiting licences for new building or restricting new capital issues, the Government had undermined industry's own zest for investment by its blunt-instrument attempts to combat the inflationary effects of general economic overstretch.

In any case, the President of the Board of Trade in this same paper of February 1953 pleaded for an end to the entire suppressive

141

post-war system whereby a government licence had to be obtained for any industrial building work to cost more than £2,000:

> I believe it has been suggested that, if we ease up in this field, we must ease up in all. I do not accept this argument. The distinction between productive industry and social investment such as local authority building or schools seems to me quite a clear one which the public would accept.[68]

Nevertheless, the Chancellor, no doubt in pursuit of the Tory ideal of free enterprise, refused next month to abolish the licensing system.[69] He did however recommend that investment in new building in manufacturing industry in 1953 and 1954 be raised by £10 million in each year.[70] This would bring the total in industries sponsored by the Board of Trade and the Ministry of Supply to two-thirds of what had been estimated the previous year to be really needed.[71] Brilliant again!

Even capital investment in a field so fundamental to Britain's industrial future as education and training was crippled under the Conservatives because of the priority given to house-building and rearmament on the chosen scale.[72] The damage to Britain's long-term future was the worse because it followed six years of neglect of educational investment by the Labour Government for very similar reasons – priority in 1946–50 to council house construction and militarily playing the world power, and then, in 1950–51, priority to the £4.8 billion Korean War rearmament programme.

In their panic measures to save the ship in the winter storms of 1951–2 the new Conservative Government cut projected capital investment in education for the six years 1952–58 from £468 million to £378 million (see above, p. 67). Within this constricted budget the building of bright new primary and secondary schools in Macmillan's bright new housing estates was put first, at the expense of desperately needed improvements to inner-city schools where after six years of a Labour Government the children of the underclass (to apply a 1990s term to a similar phenomenon of the 1950s or, for that matter, 1850s) still sat in classes of up to sixty (see below, Chapter 22). Likewise provision of new schools on Macmillan's estates came before investing in further and technical education. In consequence such education found itself condemned to further years of 'make-do-and-mend' – and this despite the fearsome deficiencies (as compared with American or European institutions) exposed back in 1945 by the Percy Committee on Higher Technical Education[73] (see below, Chapter 22).

Two years after the Conservatives came into office the House of Commons Select Committee on Estimates was reporting that because of lack of investment the situation in this vital sector remained 'still roughly the same as it was in 1947'.[74] What did 'roughly the same' signify? The Committee proceeded to explain: 'Many of the buildings fall short of the requirements necessary for good educational instruction'. For example, in the case of Birmingham Technical College, at the centre of the car industry:

> Experimental work in the internal combustion department has some-
> times to be stopped in bad weather, owing to the need for covering
> the machines with tarpaulins to protect them from the rain.[75]

In fact, only one new technical college had so far been completed since the war.[76] The Select Committee reckoned that at the prevailing rate of investment a programme for producing minimum facilities 'cannot be put in hand by 1959–1960 as had been hoped'.

In December 1955, more than a decade now into the post-war era, the Minister of Education, David Eccles, was calculating that the total capital cost of future needs in technical education (including new colleges) amounted to £72 million, whereas in fact only £9 million had been authorized for new starts in 1956–57.[77] He warned: '. . . if we continue at this annual rate we shall not solve our problems as quickly as we must. Many of our technical colleges have old and inadequate buildings . . .'[78]

It was only in February 1956 that a White Paper on Technical Education[79] announced a major programme of development, including the creation of twenty-five 'Colleges of Advanced Technology'. At longest last Britain was to start creating the type, and number, of first-class institutions which her industrial competitors had enjoyed for many decades. Or, again, was she? At the Treasury's insistence a cavil had to be inserted in the White Paper to the effect that in the years 1957–58 and 1958–59 the capital costs 'will, in

common with all other programmes, be subject to review if economic conditions require . . .'[80]

Yet, future 'reviews' or not, the White Paper – like the ten-
year roads programme and the fifteen-year railways modernization
plan – was no better than a death-bed repentance. It was now far
too late to create new institutions in time to turn out a highly
trained mass workforce for the coming crucial world-market battles
of the 1960s. In the event, such was the cracking pace set by the
British governmental machine that the first Colleges of Advanced
Technology opened for business in 1965, only eleven years after
Eccles's White Paper and a mere twenty years after the Percy
Report.

According to an OEEC Report in 1954, Britain in 1952 had devoted
12 per cent of GNP to gross capital formation, as against West
Germany's 25 per cent, and an OEEC average of 18 per cent. In
fact, Britain then tied with Éire in bottom place out of seventeen
members of the OEEC.[81] Whitehall economists chewing over these
figures in December 1954 took comfort from the 'many statistical
pitfalls' in such international comparisons. Nevertheless, there can
be no question that in 1950–55 Britain had been putting into gross
fixed investment (even *including* Macmillan's new houses, hardly
productive assets) a far lower proportion of GNP (perhaps as much
as a third lower) than Germany's average of nearly 24 per cent.[82]

Yet this tight rationing is not fully explained by a post-Korea
defence budget annually gulping twice the share of GNP as
Germany's after 1954 (when she began to re-create her armed
forces), or by a rearmament programme which in itself pre-empted
nearly half of Britain's own yearly increase in GNP.[83] Nor is it fully
explained by the need to hold down expenditure in order to
compensate for the inflationary pressures of full employment. There
was another factor. The Conservative Government like its Labour
predecessor hoped that restrictions on industrial investment at home
would serve to divert into export markets the very engineering
products British industry needed to modernize itself.

But why such a bizarrely self-defeating strategy?

Butler had affirmed on becoming Chancellor in the midst of the
balance-of-payments panic at the end of 1951 that the sacrifice was

essential in order that Britain achieve a current balance-of-payments surplus of £200 million a year.

But why so huge a surplus? It was hardly needed just to enable Britain, as an island industrial state, to trade in the black rather than the red. Was it, then, desired for the sake of directly enriching the British people? No such thing. The £200 million was simply what Butler in 1951 (following Gaitskell before him) had pronounced 'a basic necessity' if sterling were to be maintained as an international currency (see above, p. 58).

But why was this maintenance of sterling as an international currency (together with the Sterling Area) taken as vital? Was it primarily and directly for the sake of the wellbeing of the people of the United Kingdom? No again. In the words of a Whitehall paper of February 1956:

> Without a surplus of well over £200 millions on current account, it is evident that we cannot meet our commitments and maintain our currency and our position as the centre of the sterling system, and *retain our position as a world power* [added emphasis].[84]

8. Operation ROBOT and the Burden of Sterling

Our position as a world power! Of course! If overstretch signified 'power' in regard to Britain's political and military entanglements from the Mediterranean to the Pacific, why not in regard to the Sterling Area and the 'sterling system'? After all, the area for the most part consisted of the British Commonwealth in its purely economic guise (less Canada, a dollar country); and where would Britain's pretensions be without the Commonwealth to sustain them?

Thus British politicians, abetted by some of their civil servants, could be pitilessly sceptical about both the 1948–50 proposal for a European Coal and Steel Authority[1] and the project afoot in the early 1950s to develop the Authority into a European Common Market (see below, p. 484). Did not these European projects emanate from a conspiracy between the frightful Huns, beaten by Britain and the Commonwealth in the last war, and the despicable French, who had let us down so badly in 1940 by not fighting for us better? But the Commonwealth economic connection remained exempt from such intellectual demolition work. The Commonwealth was Family. Close blood relatives were the 'white' Dominions, especially Australia and New Zealand. Adopted children who had just left home were the new dominions of India and Pakistan. As yet still children under Britain's firm but kindly care in loco parentis were sundry tribes of Africa.

It would therefore have seemed unworthy to most of the British governing elite in the 1950s to deal with these varied members of the Commonwealth family in hard terms of relative economic advantage to Britain. Rather it seemed a question of Britain's own duties to them. As late as August 1956 (a month when under Eden's direction military planning was in full swing for an expedition to undo Nasser's nationalization of the Suez Canal) a Commonwealth Relations Office paper on the future of the Commonwealth in relation to commercial policy could say:

> It has to be accepted that the United Kingdom is the keystone of the Commonwealth arch. Without it, it is impossible to conceive the Commonwealth holding together for long. Nor is it easy to conceive any other Commonwealth country, however great its wealth and population, taking its place, even if the Sovereign were to move to it.[2]

Yet facts and figures gathered by Whitehall itself four years earlier plainly demonstrate that this arch was in economic terms constructed not of ashlar but of pieces of historical rubble ill-assorted in quality and strength:

> The members of the Commonwealth range from some of the most sparsely populated countries in the world to the some of the densest; from populations of British extraction to Asiatic peoples; from tropical countries to temperate countries; from countries which are among the richest in the world to countries which are among the poorest. Some, like the United Kingdom, Canada and Australia, are highly industrialised; others have only the beginnings of manufacturing industry . . .[3]

Thus noted Whitehall officials in July 1952, when preparations were in hand for the first Commonwealth economic conference for twenty years, just as promised in the imperially bombastic Conservative election manifesto. The Commonwealth's economic anomalies at that time are well enough illustrated by the case of Britain herself. Her national income per head was ten times larger than India's, eighteen times larger than the West Indies', and twenty-one times larger than West Africa's. But her dollar-earning exports per head were only a third of Malaya's, and her total trade was a third less valuable per head than Malaya's.[4]

Taken as a whole, this sterling Commonwealth which the Conservative Government evidently valued so highly was, wrote the same 1952 report, 'deficient in all basic food-stuffs'; it was 'short of oilfields, of forests, of agricultural land suitable for cereals and crops, of two plantation crops (cotton and tobacco) and of a number of important minerals'.[5] Some asset!

Ever since the Second World War all the sterling Commonwealth countries had successfully milked the United Kingdom of capital investment, 'a heavy burden' (according to this survey) carried 'at considerable expense to ourselves'.[6]

And over the six calendar years 1946–51 the sterling Dominions had run a balance-of-payments deficit to the tune of £700 million, nearly £600 million of which had been financed by the poor old United Kingdom.[7] It is true that in the same period the Colonies had chalked up a surplus of about £300 million – but only because of British military expenditure in them, British handouts of some £80 million on development and welfare, and various British grants.[8]

In what sense, then, could the Commonwealth be regarded even collectively as an economic 'arch'? In no sense: 'less than one-half of the trade of the sterling Commonwealth as a whole is with other members of the Commonwealth. Countries within the sterling Commonwealth, as a group, conduct more trade with countries outside than with the countries within the group.'[9] This was true of the United Kingdom herself, with 51 per cent of her exports in 1951 going to foreign states for which Britain was not obliged to assume burdensome military, financial or governmental responsibilities as with the Commonwealth.[10]

In any case, the still surviving 1930s system of Imperial Preferences was now more disliked than valued by the Dominions: Canada (economically so close to the United States) on the score that the system was outmoded; India, Pakistan and Ceylon on the score that it was a relic of colonialism.[11] Australia was currently refusing to discriminate in favour of British goods and against those from Western Europe. So was South Africa,[12] a country which in any case already granted only a few preferences to Britain, and those small.[13] Even the colonies, under direct British rule, did not all of them accord preferences to British imports; and Malaya, the richest thanks to her dollar-earning tin and rubber, accorded virtually none.[14]

Back in the early 1930s Commonwealth markets fenced by

Imperial Preferences had offered Britain a refuge from the world slump. But now in the 1950s these preferences, coupled with the obligation to pay off the sterling balances, were helping to trap Britain in too much trade with 'old' dominions whose populations were small, and 'new' dominions and colonies whose peoples, though numerous, were mostly impoverished subsistence farmers – hardly a boom market for, say, Mr Ken Wood's new electric food mixer. It therefore hardly astonishes that this Sterling Area market was expanding much more sluggishly than world trade in general, and Western European trade in particular.[15]

So a shrewd stockbroker in the early 1950s would have surely advised the United Kingdom that it was time to sell the Commonwealth, being a stock that was growing too slowly, giving too small a return, and tying up too much capital. Yet a group of Whitehall mandarins in September 1952 judged that the stock was still worth holding, on the grounds of the Commonwealth's supposed potential for development. However, they made clear that this potential could only be realized if in such a good cause Britain chose to strain her buckling economy further still. The 'already over-pressed' engineering industry would have to provide most of the capital goods required in 'any drive to intensify development'. Moreover, it would have to do so on top of 'meeting the capital requirements of British industry', making the United Kingdom's 'main contribution to increasing non-sterling exports', and remaining 'also the basis of our defence production'.[16]

> In order to carry our present overseas commitments it is estimated that we must plan to secure a United Kingdom overall balance of payments surplus of £300 million [sic] within a year. Of this about £150–£200 million a year would represent investment in the rest of the sterling area – releases from the Asian Dominions' sterling balances, other repayments of sterling balances, private investment . . . loans to colonial and other Sterling Area Governments, &c.[17]

But an accelerated Commonwealth investment programme 'might require perhaps an additional £50 million a year'.

> It would then be necessary to raise our sights and plan United Kingdom resources to provide a balance of payments surplus of £350

million a year. It must be borne in mind that at the present time we are barely in balance. It would be a formidable problem to build a regular surplus of £300 million a year; it is *pro tanto* harder to build a surplus of £350 million a year.[18]

The only way to achieve this would be by 'practising self-denial' (sic) – cutting spending on welfare or defence and keeping British consumers short of cash in their pockets or goods in the shops.[19] Even so, there might be 'some conflict between the demands for capital goods for United Kingdom productive investment and the demands from other parts of the Commonwealth'.[20]

The authors of this report (prepared at the request of the Chancellor of the Exchequer) were 'therefore under no illusion as to the seriousness of the risks involved in this question'. Nevertheless – after all, this was the Commonwealth, not Europe, one had to be positive – they concluded that in order to develop the Sterling Area's productive resources the United Kingdom ought to take these risks. She should be prepared to do without at home in order both to fork out the necessary capital investment and also to boost exports for the sake of the balance of payments.[21]

But how could merely pursuing further this so far barren policy resolve the basic paradox of Britain's plight, as acknowledged plainly enough in the same report? On the one hand: 'We are the main source of capital for the Commonwealth and much of our economic and political strength [sic] derives from this position.' On the other hand: 'Our balance of payments is at best precarious . . . We are the world's largest debtor, and our reserves are ludicrously inadequate to cope with even minor fluctuations.'[22]

For the problem went much deeper than whether or not to punt even more on an underperforming stock like the Commonwealth. It resided in history's bequest of rich Victorian England's role of world banker to out-at-the-elbows post-war Britain. In vaults once crammed with gold there had been ever since 1945 much distressingly vacant space. Even the bank manager's watch and chain had been pawned to pay for the Second World War. How, then, does a banker in such a sorry state continue trading without his Sterling Area depositors (Commonwealth or other) storming the doors for their money – money which he actually cannot pay out?

Thus far the problem had been artificially contained by an apparatus of controls and fudges comparable to that which similarly protected Britain's post-war domestic economy from the pains of radical change.[23] For instance, the natural urge of the native British possessor of capital to shift it out of highly regulated and highly taxed Britain and invest it more profitably in some thriving 'hard currency' country was thwarted by exchange control.[24] The foreign or Commonwealth states whose national reserves were banked in London were prohibited from converting their sterling into dollars, however much their citizens might prefer, for instance, cheap and powerful Chevrolets to dearer and feebler Austins.

But at the same time the international value of sterling was artificially pegged at $2.80 – fixed rates for all currencies being an integral part of the world financial system set up at the Bretton Woods Conference in New York in 1944, and now monitored by the International Monetary Fund. To allow sterling to be convertible into dollars at a rate of $2.80 in Britain's present straitened circumstances would certainly lead to depositors rushing to change their pounds for real money. This could quite literally expose Britain to bankruptcy, as so nearly happened in 1947 when, in compliance with the terms of the 1945 American loan of $3.75 billion, Britain did make the pound convertible, at the rate of $4.03 – only to strap the corset of inconvertibility on again in short order.

Nevertheless, even this corset could not answer Britain's other problem in 1952 over sterling. Whenever the Sterling Area (including the United Kingdom) ran into deficit with its dollar balance of payments (as happened every other year or so), Britain as central banker had to plug the gap with her scant gold and dollar reserves at this fixed rate of $2.80. She was like a general who, having ordered that an exposed frontline position be held to the last, can only make good the consequent heavy casualties by robbing his *masse de manœuvre*.

The rapid disappearance of the gold and dollar reserves in such crises not only brought on acute flutters in Whitehall and Threadneedle Street, but also caused an understandable restlessness among Britain's Sterling Area clients. Always looming darkly in the minds of the Treasury and the Bank was the fear that Britain might have to devalue the pound yet again, as in 1949. What would this do to sterling's status as an international currency and to Britain's status as a world power? Yet, for that matter, how long could sterling retain its international standing if it could not be freely converted into 'hard' currencies like the dollar?

From 1945 up to the current crisis British governments had believed that the only way to cope with this baffling quandary lay in maintaining the corset of exchange controls and inconvertibility – while at the same time striving for a balance-of-payments surplus big enough to fatten the reserves to a point where the pound could actually be made convertible. But the vain struggle to achieve such a permanent surplus had already entailed seven years of national self-denial. Even now, in 1952, when European shops were again filled with abundance, the British housewife still went shopping with ration book in hand, compelled in this way to do her bit to save on dollar imports of food.

But far more damaging than a grey life for the consumer had been the squeezing of home investment, both for the sake of switching industrial products into overseas markets and also, more generally, for the sake of combating the domestic inflation which, by puffing up British export prices, worsened the balance of payments and endangered the pound.[25]

Was there, then, no answer to this joint problem of the Sterling Area, the balance of payments and the gold and dollar reserves other than everlasting controls and yet more national self-sacrifice?[26] At the beginning of 1952 ingenious intellects in Whitehall (including Butler's own) and in Threadneedle Street devised a conjuring trick by which, so they believed, the problem could be solved at a stroke. And for ever.

The idea of 'Operation ROBOT' (as the conjuring trick came to be dubbed on the Treasury file)[27] was born of the desperate winter of 1951–2 when Britain was enduring her third and worst economic crisis since the Second World War. ROBOT would be fiercely argued over by the same politicians and mandarins who were simultaneously trying to agree on emergency measures for keeping Britain out of the breakers (see above, p. 000).

The chief inventor of ROBOT was a forty-two-year-old Treasury Under-Secretary, R. W. B. ('Otto') Clarke (Christ's Hospital and Clare College, Cambridge; wrangler), a roman candle of an intellect spewing out bright stars as soon as a theoretical problem lit his touchpaper. Very much a member of the small 'l' liberal establishment, the author of Fabian pamphlets before the war, Clarke wholly believed in the post-war 'planned' economy and its artificial maintenance of 'full employment'. This rendered his invention of ROBOT the more surprising, because its essential gimmick was to abandon a fixed rate for sterling and allow it to float instead on the international currency market. Clarke believed that if a floating rate were coupled with certain stern safeguards it would enable sterling to be made convertible without the dreaded haemorrhage of the reserves.

On 25 January 1952 Clarke put forward his wheeze to Whitehall colleagues in a thirty-three-paragraph paper, the key arguments of which were to finish up before the Cabinet themselves next month in the form of a report by the Chancellor of the Exchequer (see p. 160, below). 'I cannot help feeling', opined Clarke in his first sentence, 'that we make very heavy weather of convertibility' – partly, he reckoned, because of 'dogma' derived from the Bretton Woods agreement of 1944, and partly because 'our 1947 experience was so disastrous . . .'[28] Convertibility 'came in a number of guises': it could mean the swapping of sterling for dollars by foreign banks or individuals, by Sterling Area central banks or individuals, or even by United Kingdom citizens. But full convertibility, wrote Clarke, implied all of these.[29]

> The crucial issue is whether you mean convertibility at a fixed or floating rate. There is nothing sacrosanct about a fixed rate . . . It is obviously much easier to be convertible at a floating rate than a fixed rate. Theoretically, with a floating rate, the rate falls to the point at which supply and demand for sterling cancel each other. You need not lose any gold at all. The extent to which you become convertible depends on how far you are prepared to see the rate fall.[30]

On the other hand: 'With a fixed rate, the equilibrating factor is the loss of gold, and the extent of convertibility which you allow is determined by the size of the gold reserves.'[31]

Clarke ruled out the option of remaining formally and permanently inconvertible, on the score that 'it was a nice idea to have a great sterling-based world system, embracing everybody except North America. But we are obviously not strong enough to run it. It was fundamentally escapist . . .'[32]

Then what about combining a fixed rate with 'controlled' convertibility, meaning that some of Britain's banking clients could change some of their sterling for dollars, while the rest of their balances was blocked? Clarke accepted that such a course implied major changes in trade relations, such as countries ceasing to discriminate in favour of British exports. However: 'I am pretty sure that it is, in the long run, detrimental to our earning power to have other countries discriminate in our favour, so that we have soft markets.'[33]

Clarke also foresaw that while such changes were taking place under a fixed rate Britain

> would take an awful beating . . . We've got to go through this stage of fighting our exports against the Americans, Germans and Japanese. There is no escape in restrictionism. But we should lose an awful lot of gold in the process. And here is the difficulty . . . if we had a lot of gold we should just run through it without doing the fighting and the economic adjustment; whilst if we have no gold we immediately collapse. In fact, the only way to get the reserves which are necessary to enable us to become convertible in this sense is to get a big loan from U.S.A., and *if we had these reserves we should not use them as a fighting fund to cover inevitable losses while we were becoming competitive but squander them on sugar and canned salmon* [added emphasis].[34]

Was Clarke here thinking of the way that Britain had frittered away too much of the 1945 American loan and later Marshall Aid on current national expenditure instead of investing more in industrial reconstruction?[35] It would seem so, because he added later in his paper:

> If we get the gold from the Americans, we shan't make the adjustments because they are much too painful to be made except under the strongest pressure of events (cf. my old note 'Food versus Sterling versus Defence') . . .[36]

Then again, according to Clarke, there were the 'intolerable difficulties' as to what to do with the Sterling Area countries if Britain tried to make sterling convertible at a fixed rate. 'Either they must work 100% with us and make big adjustments voluntarily – with great pain. Or they will be a drag upon us and prevent us from succeeding . . .'[37]

All these problems with convertibility at a fixed rate led Clarke to urge that Britain should instead allow the pound to float on the international currency market, so finding its natural exchange value. Moreover, Clarke favoured floating not only for the sake of convertibility in itself but also because it would automatically subject to severe discipline a hitherto soft, slack and protected British domestic economy. In his own words:

> The advantage of a floating rate is that the fact that the rate moves sets up equilibrating pressures on the economy. The rate falls; import prices rise; there is stimulus to exports. The whole economy feels these movements, and adjusts itself to them. If we had had a floating rate in the last six months, sterling might have fallen from $3.50 [sic] to $2 or even lower. The price of food would have gone up by 25% – ditto the price of raw materials; we should have got reduction in consumption; or exporters would have improved their business. We should now have been in great pain, but adjustment would have been going on.[38]

For an ex-Fabian in the Whitehall of 1952, this was an astonishingly Thatcherite 1980s analysis. No less so was Clarke's diagnosis of the debilitating effects on the nation of the present regulated economic environment:

> But we can lose $1,400 million of gold without anybody noticing it at all – and no adjustment until the government decrees it; and then it is the government's fault, imposing artificial restrictions, and the *real* conditions of life go on as before. It is literally true that after 31st January, no-one will have any more incentive to reduce his consumption of food or raw materials, or to export, than he had six months ago. Nor is it by any means obvious how this can be provided, except by complex fiscal measures, or by new controls, which take months to work out.[39]

What, then, switch off the protective systems that made the denizens of the British economy feel so secure? Open all the doors and windows to the cruel, if bracing, blasts of economic reality? The stuff of revolution indeed!

Clarke did, however, acknowledge 'formidable difficulties' with a floating rate, which again would affect both sterling as a reserve currency and also Britain's own economic life at home. The most serious of these difficulties lay in the groggy state of the Sterling Area economies taken as a whole, for in Clarke's judgement they were 'in such disequilibrium, with such rooted structural problems, that it is very dubious whether a rate exists at which anything like equilibrium is possible.'[40]

> The rate might fall to very low levels indeed, creating internal instability on a self-defeating scale. Without reserves, it would not be possible to support the rate, and our food prices and internal and political structure would be at the mercy of the market. It is only fair to say that if this argument is true, we should lose all our reserves protecting a fixed rate anyway.[41]

Then again, the Sterling Area countries might choose to float their own currencies against a floating pound, which would 'really disrupt the £ area . . .'[42] If they did this, 'it would really force the situation in which we treated R.S.A. [Rest of Sterling Area] countries like foreigners'. But why would this be a bad thing? Clarke did not say.

Instead, he proceeded to put forward his detailed plan for achieving convertibility 'at a fairly early date'. First came a floating rate. This would be coupled with freezing (and funding) all sterling balances held by non-Sterling Area countries except for limited current working balances. All non-residents of the United Kingdom would be free to convert pounds into currencies of their choice. Exchange control would be kept on capital transactions both in Britain and the rest of the Sterling Area. Britain and the Sterling Area would impose 'tight' licensing control on imports from outsiders. There would be 'working deflationary action throughout the sterling area'. Any Sterling Area country running an independent rate or 'not taking action to put its house in order would get "foreigner" treatment'.[43]

Clarke signed off by admitting that there were 'terrific risks in all this, but if we have blocked balances effectively, and are adopting a *really* scarce money policy, and the R.S.A. is taking it all seriously, it might be a starter. . . .'[44]

In referring to 'terrific risks', Clarke had hardly chosen a selling line most likely to appeal to the bulk of the Whitehall establishment, sober chaps weighted down by their public-school sense of prefectorial responsibility, as cautious by temperament as they were orthodox in outlook. The first instalment of a sustained critique of Clarke's clever dodge was offered on 12 February 1952 by his fellow Treasury Under-Secretary, E. R. Copleston (Marlborough College and Balliol College, Oxford; and from 1932 to 1942 a toiler in the Inland Revenue, that home of entrepreneurship). However, what Copleston called his 'worst fears' about Clarke's proposals really amounted to a single fear that the fixed and familiar post-war economic scene abroad and at home might be swept away. The first result to be expected from Clarke's scheme would be:

> utter disruption of U.K. trade, with the most stringent restrictions both by and against us: probably ½ million to 1 million unemployed within 6 months; general shortages and high prices . . .[45]

The scheme would lead to

> disintegration of the Sterling Area, on the basis of near-repudiation of debts, and the complete repudiation of C.F.M. [Commonwealth Finance Ministers'] policies, and probably disintegration of the Commonwealth as well . . .[46]

It could even lead, warned Copleston, to the 'disintegration and collapse of Europe . . .'[47]

Only after uttering these doomsday prophecies did Copleston come to the fundamental – the real – objection to Clarke's strategy, as all the critics (including Cabinet ministers) were to perceive it:

> the move would be violently controversial and contrary to the trend of economic thought since Keynes. There would be severe industrial unrest, and it would be political suicide for the Government – the discipline of the gold standard, the rule of the Bankers etc.[48]

In short, wrote Copleston fearfully, with a floating rate Britain would either have to allow the currency to depreciate 'or take more violent internal action than otherwise required . . .'[49]

Already privy to ROBOT were the Governor and Deputy-Governor of the Bank of England. The Governor, Cameron Cobbold (Eton and King's College, Cambridge), was for his part caught between a desire to do something drastic to relieve the strain which the Sterling Area imposed on his bank, and an acceptance that the bank, and Britain, could not default on the obligations dumped on them by history. 'Sterling is our currency,' he wrote sternly to the Chancellor on 13 February 1952, 'and we are responsible for its management.'[50]

> We have a fiduciary responsibility towards overseas holders of sterling. This responsibility is particularly clear in relation to the colonial territories whose policy we direct and to a somewhat lesser extent in relation to independent members of the Sterling Area who keep their reserves in sterling and who by and large have played in with our general policy.[51]

Noting that the 'unity and common interest of the Sterling Area' had been reaffirmed at the recent conference of Commonwealth finance ministers, Cobbold pronounced that 'it is our duty in reaching decisions to take full account of the interests of the Sterling Area and to carry them with us as far as possible in the necessary decisions'.

Thus clamped between historic duty and the fact of Britain's chronic (and at present acute) pecuniary embarrassment, Cobbold came up with a diagnosis and a suggested cure that amounted to Clarke-and-water. Sterling was 'under a cloud' because 'our overseas sight liabilities . . . are far too big in relation to our reserves . . . there is always the risk that at moments of crisis a greater load than we can bear will be put upon us'.[52] Then again, 'an increasing volume' of international trade was being carried on through transferable sterling at a discount, which 'throws continuous and growing doubt on our ability to maintain our official rate'.[53] All this led to doubt 'whether we can in fact hold the present rate'.[54]

> If we reach the conclusion that the present basis will not hold we should, in addition to internal measures, consider a bold and determined effort to deal with these other matters as well. This would be a most disagreeable process for us and everybody else, but it is greatly

to be preferred to waiting for worse disasters to be imposed on us and on them by the facts of life.[55]

In Cobbold's view such a plan must include 'a definite freezing and/or funding of a large bulk of non-U.K. holdings of sterling, leaving not more than say 10% or 20% of existing totals in the form of sight liabilities'.[56] The unfrozen portions 'should be freely transferable throughout the world and thus enjoy *some degree of convertibility* [added emphasis]'.[57]

Yet Cobbold made clear that his 'some degree of convertibility' would entail reviewing the exchange rates of sterling against the dollar and gold. He noted that devaluation to a new fixed rate had already been ruled out. As for a floating rate, 'we have hitherto always stood out against [this] . . . which, until the fundamental troubles are being firmly dealt with, could only mean progressive depreciation'.[58]

Was there a third option? The Governor thought there might be:

> If however a New Deal could be envisaged, including determined internal measures in the United Kingdom and throughout the Sterling Area, and also radical changes in our exchange rate system on the above lines, a sterling/dollar rate floating *over a much wider range* [added emphasis] than at present around a fixed parity might prove the best solution and might be the necessary protection for the degree of transferability and/or convertibility envisaged.[59]

Cobbold recognized that in any case some means would be needed of strengthening the reserves behind the new transferable sterling. But it 'should be our ambition' not to use any credits or drawing rights (from the IMF? from America?) for this purpose.[60]

Like 'Otto' Clarke, Cobbold did not imagine that his suggested strategy would provide an easy escape hatch. On the contrary:

> The difficulties both political and technical of such action are prodigious and nobody can predict its outcome. If, however, we form the judgement that the alternative is a wasting disease we ought to face the difficulties, take the decisions and do our best to carry the Commonwealth with us.[61]

Four days later Cobbold's sketch of a strategy was filled out in detail (complete with a countdown to a launch date of 4–6 April) by his Deputy Governor, Sir George Bolton, under the title 'Plan for "Overseas Sterling"'.[62] Bolton was careful to assure his readers that

> we do not propose action which would inevitably lead to a break-up of the Sterling Area and we would hope that the urgency of the situation would persuade the Sterling Area authorities *to agree to co-operative measures* [phrase underlined in pencil by a reader in the Treasury].[63]

The fervency of this hope cannot be doubted. In the very next sentence Bolton gives the net total of the United Kingdom's sterling liabilities to the rest of the Sterling Area as no less than £2,615 million.

For the benefit of the Head of the Treasury's Overseas Finance Division, Sir Leslie Rowan (Tonbridge School and Queens' College, Cambridge), Otto Clarke summarized the Bank's 'Plan for "Overseas Sterling"' in terms which confirm that his own scheme and the Bank's were essentially the same:[64] a floating rate of exchange; blocking of about 90 per cent of sterling balances; all unblocked sterling to be convertible.[65]

With Rowan, another of the grander mandarins of the time, also in favour, ROBOT now clanked forward on to the political stage. At a meeting on 22 February 1952 the Chancellor of the Exchequer verbally briefed fellow ministers[66] and handed them a re-hash (drafted for him by Otto Clarke) of the Clarke–Bolton–Cobbold scheme under the title 'External Action'.[67] Given that Britain 'cannot rely upon avoiding a major catastrophe to our economy in the next few months', Butler urged that 'we should act now, in the most effective way which is open to us. I am supported in this view by the Governor of the Bank of England and by my official advisers.'[68]

The Chancellor then proceeded to lead his colleagues on a trudge through the various options, even including the most drastic of them all, that of winding up the Sterling Area altogether:

> The sterling area, as at present constituted, is a source of both strength and weakness. Half our total trade is with other sterling area

countries, and the institution has become of *great political importance* [added emphasis]. The proposal which I am making seeks to control the greatest weakness in the sterling area system – the sterling balances. To go further than this and disrupt the whole system – certainly at the present stage – would create a major dislocation which I do not believe we could stand.[69]

A major dislocation which we could not stand? But this is mere assertion, not an appreciation (in the military sense) which thoroughly explores the likely course of events and weighs the probable outcome. Perhaps to Butler and his advisers a winding-up of the Sterling Area lay too blatantly beyond the limits of the politically possible to seem worth examining more deeply.

The Chancellor acknowledged that he was proposing 'a complete reversal of the policies of the last twelve years', with the Bank of England no longer required to provide foreign exchange at a fixed rate. Instead of the gold reserves taking the strain whenever the Sterling Area ran into a balance of payments deficit, the floating rate would take it instead – though of course in such circumstances actually by sinking. This meant that a balance of payments deficit 'falls immediately and directly on the internal economy, in rising prices of food and raw materials'.[70]

Hence, as Butler proceeded to make clear, the exchange value of sterling would depend on how lean, taut and efficient was Britain's own economy:

> The more effective our own action to deal with our balance of payments deficit, the higher will be the rate, and the lower the cost of living. On the other hand, if we fail to deal with our internal problems effectively, and fail to organise the economy in a way which releases sufficient resources for exports, the rate will fall and the cost of living will rise accordingly.[71]

Nor, it appeared, could the British economic system hope, as in the past, to shelter in a cushy billet thanks to US handouts:

> When we had gold reserves (and American aid) to take the impact of our balance of payments deficit, it was possible to insulate the economy from the failure to pay its way. This is no longer possible,

and failure to pay our way will be felt by every family in the country in a rise in the cost of living.[72]

Since this must have sounded to his ministerial readers like a sure prescription for losing the next election, the Chancellor hastened to cheer them up by pointing out the tonic effect on the British economy of being posted from the said cushy billet to the exhilarating front line of global market realities:

> It is true to say, on the other hand, that this process itself sets up forces which tend to bring the economy into balance. The rise in the price of imports will reduce the consumption of imports, and the fall in the exchange rate will increase the competitive power of our exports, and encourage the concentration of industry on exports . . .[73]

But here he wagged a stern finger:

> If we continue to use industrial resources for other purposes – defence, housing, etc. – thus preventing the diversion of resources to export work, the rate will continue to fall.[74]

He followed this single-sentence indictment of the main thrust of British economic strategy since the war by making brutally plain that the 'post-war consensus' as a whole would be squashed beneath ROBOT's iron feet:

> the basic idea of internal stability of prices and employment, which has dominated economic policy for so long will not be maintainable. It will not be possible to maintain stable prices and wages; it will not be possible to avoid unemployment. There will be a continuous process of change and adjustment, and much of this will be painful.[75]

Did Butler *really* mean that even if unemployment rose well above the present level of 2 per cent because of ROBOT the Government would refrain from inflating home demand in order to restore 'full employment'? Did he really mean that Britain would emulate West Germany, which instead of 'Keynesianism'[76] had chosen as the *Schwerpunkt* of economic policy the suppression of inflation by combined monetary and fiscal means? Such does at least seem to be implied, though only implied, by what he and other proponents of

ROBOT (like Clarke) had to say about the need for financial and economic rigour at home.

The drawback lay in that Britain had no equivalent of the Bundesbank, an independent institution charged with the duty of defending the domestic value of the currency. Far from it: the Bank of England had become since nationalization in 1946 a mere creature of politicians responsive to popular prejudices and desires. The danger therefore was that if the discipline of ROBOT's 'floating' exchange rate led to firms laying off workers, the government of the day would simply puff up inflation in order to restore 'full employment'.

Under ROBOT without an accompanying Bundesbank-style monetary regime Britain in the 1950s would therefore have been vulnerable to the kind of disaster triggered in the early 1970s by Edward Heath's Government, which even in the face of soaring world prices for oil attempted to combine a floating exchange rate with a 'Keynesian' full-employment policy. This led to inflation peaking at 28 per cent – whereas Germany's at the same period peaked at just 8 per cent.[77]

Butler himself had to acknowledge to his colleagues that his proposals constituted 'a formidable departure of policy, with great risks and considerable uncertainty as to the outcome'. But, said he, 'I am convinced . . . that it is necessary.'[78]

So politically sensitive was his memorandum that ministers were asked to return copies to Butler at the end of the meeting.[79] Indeed, all documents in the ROBOT files were understandably classified 'Top Secret' at the time.

Since of those present at this ministerial meeting only Lord Cherwell voiced any doubts,[80] ROBOT now appeared to be getting into an unstoppable forward lurch. Horrified, the anti-ROBOT forces in Whitehall began to mobilize. Their horror was inspired not only by ROBOT in itself but also by the need to rush a decision in order that the scheme could be advertised in the forthcoming budget, due on 4 March 1952. Even the postponement of the budget for a single week hardly helped to calm their fears. Wrote Robert Hall, the Director of the Cabinet Office Economic Section, and another grand mandarin of the time (an Oxford man who read classics at Magdalen College and later became lecturer in economics at Trinity), 'the action proposed will have such drastic and far-reaching effects that it is a matter of grave regret that a decision has to be reached so quickly ... extensive studies are normally made of much less important questions'.[81]

Hall was himself another close prisoner of the prevailing ortho-doxy of the 'post-war consensus', especially in regard to 'full employment'. In his own words: 'The effect of all the measures proposed is to abandon the whole attempt to adjust ourselves to changes in world economic circumstances without resort to unem-ployment...'[82] Even so, he had to accept that with a floating exchange rate imports and exports 'at some point ... would certainly come into balance', because in the event the rate would sink, so making imports dearer (and hence smaller) and exports cheaper (and hence bigger). But:

> The cost to ourselves would be the loss of production caused by unemployment and the reduced standard of living due to the higher cost of imports in terms of our own products. It would be very rash, however, to put the level of unemployment at less than 1 million, compared to about 400,000 today.[83]

Nevertheless, Hall did concede that the wage increases which in recent years had inflated British export prices 'would no doubt be less violent owing to the increase in unemployment than they have been'.[84]

In regard to other industrial consequences of a floating pound too Hall seemed similarly caught between belief in the post-war consensus and an awareness of its drawbacks. 'The least efficient firms', he wrote, 'go first in a depression and many people think that industrial discipline is improved.'[85] Did he mean that the bankruptcy of the inefficient was good – or bad? It is hard to tell. For he went on to argue that in such a situation 'the argument that [with full employment] there is no danger of "working yourself out of a job" loses its force.'

It was clearly beyond Hall's imagination that the unemployment caused by ROBOT might in time serve as a means of curbing the present power of the unions to hold down productivity and obstruct technological change (see below, Part Four). On the contrary, being a true small 'l' liberal appeaser, he wrote that it 'would presumably be necessary to enlist the co-operation of the workers in the national emergency if industrial relations are not to suffer. A coal strike, for example, could quickly produce disastrous results.'[86]

In the end Hall came up with a washy compromise which he hoped would avoid such dreaded consequences of ROBOT as 'a general deflationary effect in many parts of the world, leading to unemployment and dislocation there', the break-up of the Sterling Area 'if this [i.e., the Sterling Area] is regarded as a good thing', and at home 'a good deal of unemployment'.[87] He would retain the fixed exchange rate. He would not block Sterling Area balances, but only sterling held by non-area countries. He would suspend the present right of Sterling Area countries to convert a tight ration of sterling into dollars.

As for Britain herself as banker, Hall would have her cut her imports (including food rations) down even further in order to achieve a dollar balance. He would have her take 'more drastic action to secure the export of a large volume of engineering goods'.[88] To tide the banker over while such measures were put into action 'vigorously', it would be, averred Hall, 'a justifiable risk' to cadge a loan from the IMF.[89]

In short, this noted Whitehall brain could only offer a variation on a tried, tested and failed recipe.

As it happened, Anthony Eden, the Foreign Secretary, was then absent in Lisbon at a meeting of the North Atlantic Council, where the United States was persuading its junior partners to adopt a programme to expand NATO ground forces to a total of fifty divisions that year, seventy-five in 1953 and ninety-six in 1954.[90] With him was the Government's Chief Planning Officer and Chairman of the Economic Planning Board, Sir Edwin Plowden (third-class degree in economics at Pembroke College, Cambridge), another small 'l' liberal grandee of the time and (no surprise) believer in the post-war 'managed' economy.[91] To Plowden came an anguished letter from the 'very much disturbed and unhappy'[92] Robert Hall conveying his fears about the domestic and overseas effects of adopting ROBOT, especially what Hall termed 'the gravest consequences', those of touching off 'considerable political difficulties abroad'.

Hall confessed to Plowden that he felt 'very much puzzled and perplexed. It is extremely hard for me to believe that the Foreign Office have yet grasped the implications for them of what is proposed.' Disturbed and unhappy in his turn, Plowden persuaded Eden that he must not allow a decision over ROBOT to be taken while he was still abroad, and drafted for him a letter back home to the Prime Minister. This repeated the anxieties of the anti-Robotics about unemployment and also about the implications of ROBOT for British foreign policy. It successfully recommended that more time should be spent on looking at less drastic alternatives.[93]

By now a formidable Whitehall alliance against ROBOT had solidified under the ministerial leadership of Lord Cherwell (the Paymaster General), 'The Prof', the man who since wartime had enjoyed the freedom of Churchill's ear. As well as Plowden, Hall and Copleston the alliance included Frank Lee (Permanent Secretary at the Board of Trade) and Donald MacDougall (Chief Adviser, Prime Minister's Statistical Branch, and working for Cherwell). Moreover, Hall had consulted one of his predecessors as Director of the Cabinet Economic Section, Lionel Robbins, now Professor of Economics at the London School of Economics. Robbins was described by Plowden in his memoirs as 'one of the most widely respected academics of the time.[94] This clearly gave his opinion the weight of a front-row forward in the present scrimmage. Robbins was against floating the pound on the economic grounds that currency fluctuations would mean that exporters would have to guess their future delivery prices. But he also opposed ROBOT on the moral grounds that blocking the sterling balances 'involved bad faith',[95] something which he confessed to Plowden years later had 'shocked' him so much that he 'lay awake long into the night worrying about the loss of international credit which might occur if it were done'.[96]

Robbins's ethical qualms were shared by Sir Arthur Salter, Minister of State for Economic Affairs (and former Gladstone Professor of Political Theory and Institutions at Oxford), who dispatched to the Chancellor the most morally passionate of all Whitehall attacks on ROBOT. Salter accused the Chancellor's memorandum of failing to examine 'fully or profoundly' each of the 'grave consequences' which it acknowledged could result from the proposed strategy; 'the general impression left is, I believe, far short of the reality . . .'[97]

> We are to block 90% of all foreigners' private balances. This is the banker shutting his doors. 'Devaluation' was in effect a cancellation of part of our obligations. But it was a scaling down not a 90% blocking . . . It was justified, and the resentment reduced, by the fact that we were acting under indisputable force majeure.[98]

As for the official sterling balances, at least 80 per cent were to be immobilized – not merely the old wartime accumulations, but also 'ordinary short-term borrowings by us used for ordinary consumption'.

> Among the economic effects, in the Commonwealth, may be famine in India and the disruption of the Australian economy, the immediate responsibility appearing to rest entirely upon ourselves . . . In Europe the 90% blocking . . . will have profoundly disruptive effects on the economy of a number of European countries.
>
> E.P.U. and all the efforts at inter-European liberalization will be killed stone dead.
>
> Elsewhere, Iraq will probably leave the sterling area. I cannot judge the effects on our oil interests there.[99]

While Salter found 'beyond exact assessment' the possible *political* effects of ROBOT overseas, he guessed that they might be 'of the utmost gravity', and especially 'if the action is sprung at once':

> What will be the effect on the tenuous Commonwealth relationship of India and Ceylon?
>
> What will be the effect in Australia, both on the internal political situation, and in the tendency to orientation towards the U.S.A. rather than Great Britain?
>
> In Europe, already so resentful of our attitude, the results may be quite devastating.
>
> Not least is the possible (and perhaps probable) effect on all the N.A.T.O. plans (and the effect also on our relations with the U.S.A.).[100]

When Salter turned from his public-spirited concern with the likely impact of ROBOT on other nations to the more relevant question (for a British minister) of its effects on British life at home, he asserted that these would be 'equally serious'. A floating (i.e., in effect sinking) exchange rate could add 15 per cent to the cost of living:

> This, in spite of the Budget reliefs, will throw great numbers across the 'semi-starvation' line, it will force many who have struggled on independently to resort to national assistance, it will make the increases in the assistance scales, calculated on other grounds, inadequate.
>
> Unemployment too may be of very serious dimensions . . . I fear too that the classes of workers displaced may be to a very large extent untransferable into such industries as are expanding.[101]

The Government must therefore consider, thought Salter, 'whether, in the above circumstances, we shall be able politically to carry through the policy to the point where it will bring its rewards'.[102]

> There will of course be the most bitter and fierce attack by the opposition. That by itself we could stand. But the attempt by the more responsible Labour leaders to restrain political strikes, already uncertain of success, will probably – if continued – fail. And, in these circumstances, shall we in fact be able to hold even our own people? Twenty abstentions of Conservatives would bring us down at any time. And a General Election would result in a defeat . . .[103]

By way of a coda Salter expressed his 'ultimate anxiety' that if in this 'year of peril' ROBOT were to disrupt disarmament, cause resentment in Europe, the Commonwealth and America, and create a political crisis at home, it might perhaps 'tip the scales' in Moscow.

This was flesh-creeping stuff – but what did Salter propose as an alternative to ROBOT? It was that 'before we have seen the effect of the Budget' we should not 'exclude the possibility of *getting over the hump* [added emphasis] and maintaining our position'.

> It is surely not beyond hope that, *if* [Salter's own emphasis] we could *get over this year* [added emphasis], we could, in co-operation with America, bring our economy back to the self supporting basis which is now contemplated without the violence that would be inevitable under the present plan.[104]

On 25 February it was the turn of Cherwell, Hall and Mac-Dougall to submit a reply (over Cherwell's signature) to the Chancellor's paper, a copy of which the Paymaster General had cannily retained for close study. This reply made clever debating use of such damaging admissions by the Chancellor as that 'we cannot pretend to predict just what the consequences [of ROBOT] will be', that 'the basic idea of stability of prices and employment will not be maintained', and that 'no-one can guarantee the success' of the scheme.[105]

Cherwell's general critique of ROBOT unsurprisingly owed much to Robert Hall's already circulated apprehensions. A floating pound might well result in 'a constant devaluation of sterling' which would only end when speculators decided that it was so cheap as to be a bargain. Such devaluation would drive prices of food and raw materials in Britain sky-high. Although 'this harsh and clumsy method would certainly in the long run diminish the demand for imports and thus in time reduce the deficit in the trade balance' it might cause 'suffering and unemployment'.

> In a free and flourishing economy such a mode of control – which has the specious lure of being automatic – might be tolerated. But in a hard-pressed community like ours this form of rationing imports by the purse can surely scarcely be promulgated as Conservative policy.[106]

Although Cherwell averred that he 'was as anxious as anyone to move away from controls and to let economic forces play their part, . . . this time of crisis is not the moment for such a gamble'.

He asked the Chancellor to look at the effects of ROBOT abroad:

> Only a month ago the finance ministers from the Dominions were cheerfully concerting plans to help us round the corner. Now almost as soon as they reached home they are to be faced with an ultimatum. Nor is only the Commonwealth concerned. Half the trade of the world is carried on in sterling. To revolutionise the basis of half the world's trade at a few days [sic] notice without consultation will cause consternation and chaos far beyond the limits of the Sterling Area. We shall be pilloried, and justly, throughout the world. And

for what? In the hope that some financial juggle, some financial magic will enable us to escape from our predicament without toil and sweat.[107]

But when Cherwell came to make positive proposals 'definitely preferable to a leap in the dark', he (and his back-room boys) could only suggest yet again fingering the Americans for a loan, and this time the International Monetary Fund as well; and meanwhile slashing Britain's dollar imports and trying to persuade the other Sterling Area countries to do likewise. At the same time, 'we should offer inducements and exert pressure on exporters' to attack hard currency markets willing to pay high prices. At home Britain should raise the bank rate and take 'such budgetary action as we can to prevent a fall in confidence' – in other words, the 'Stop' phase in what would by the 1960s become known as the 'Stop-Go' cycle.

In Cherwell's opinion these all-too-familiar short-term expedients would, if taken 'firmly and rapidly', give Britain 'a very good chance of getting round the corner'.[108] Getting round the corner! It was the second time in the memorandum that Cherwell (or his ghost writers) had used the phrase, so wonderfully encapsulating the British penchant for muddling through, yet here appearing over the signature of a Teuton. And there had been so many corners since 1945 – was it enough simply to get round another one?

On the same day Hall and Plowden themselves favoured the Chancellor (at his request) with their own alternative to ROBOT.[109] This spelt out in detail the recommendations concurrently sketched in the broadside by Cherwell which they had helped to draft, including the maintenance of the present fixed rate for sterling. But the two grandees were also full of creative ideas as to the sacrifices which Britain could make for the sake of her role as international banker. They proposed introducing a severe budget; raising the bank rate; reducing food rations to save imports; making 'a real cut in the investment programme' in order to 'stimulate immediately the export of engineering products'; making 'a real cut in the defence programme'; and promoting bigger exports of coal even at the cost of supplies to British industry.

Just in case Butler failed to get the point, Hall also had his own personal go at the Chancellor,[110] again wringing his hands about the 'political consequences' of ROBOT, 'in so far *as these put strains on the sterling area, the E.P.U. and the ability of Europe to carry out the N.A.T.O. defence programme* [underlined in ink by the Chancellor]'.[111] Butler drily wrote at the top of Hall's offering: 'This should be filed for further reference as we drift slowly downstream.'

In the meantime Sir George Bolton had been passing on to Butler the Bank of England's second thoughts. These coupled 'a strong budget' and other curbs on the home economy (à la Hall, Plowden and Co.) with sterling allowed to float within limits set at 40 cents either side of $2.80.[112]

On 28 and 29 February 1952 the battle over ROBOT reached the Cabinet Room in No. 10 Downing Street: three tense meetings under the chairmanship of the senescent seventy-eight-year-old Prime Minister who as a fifty-year-old Chancellor of the Exchequer had returned Britain to the gold standard in 1925.[113] The ministers ranged round the long table had already received and presumably read Butler's memorandum on 'External Action' (now revised) and Cherwell's counter-blast, as well as a second paper by Butler outlining a conventional alternative strategy if ROBOT were turned down.

In talking his colleagues through 'External Action', Butler pointed to a cunning ploy by which 'we should publicly accept the principle of a variable exchange rate', but privately (apart from telling Commonwealth banks and governments), 'we should resolve to use the sterling area reserves for keeping the rate initially . . . within a range of $2.40–$3.20'. Rather in the manner of a teacher at a blackboard in front of a class of slow learners, Butler explained how a floating rate would take the strain of a balance-of-payments deficit instead of the gold and dollar reserves; how the consequent fall in the pound's exchange rate would reduce imports by making them dearer, boost exports by making them cheaper, and so eventually bring the economy into balance. But he went on to admit with the manly frankness so typical of him that the plan 'would mean a large new departure in policy and would involve serious risks'. Blocking sterling balances

> would be a shock to the Commonwealth members of the sterling
> area, and might bring one or two of them to the point of deciding

to leave the sterling area altogether. It would disrupt the European Payments Union, and would therefore be viewed with mixed feelings by the United States Government.

In regard to the internal economy of the United Kingdom, a floating exchange rate would mean

> abandoning the principle of stability in internal prices and wages; there would in the initial stages be some rise in the cost of living and some measure of unemployment; and there would be a continuous process of change and re-adjustment, much of which would be painful.

Nevertheless:

> the plan offered an opportunity for the United Kingdom Government to take a constructive and powerful initiative in the world economy; and all the indications were that, if this opportunity was not taken in the near future, we should be forced at a later stage, when the gold and dollar reserves had fallen to a much lower level, to take action which had all the unfavourable features of the plan now proposed without any of its favourable possibilities.

The Paymaster General, Cherwell, in presenting the now well-rehearsed case against ROBOT, sought to persuade the Cabinet that 'there were no sufficient grounds for the violent reversal of policy proposed by the Chancellor'. The emergency measures adopted by the Government in November 1951 had never been expected to produce results before the end of the present February, while there had not yet been time to introduce the further measures agreed by the Commonwealth Finance Ministers in January. 'Rather than run the risks involved in the Chancellor's plan,' suggested Cherwell,

> the immediate crisis should be met by still further reductions in imports, by a further expansion of exports, by borrowings from the United States and the International Monetary Fund, by Budgetary action to prevent a further fall of confidence in the pound and above all, by strong pressure on other sterling area countries to reduce their imports from hard-currency countries.

In other words, the 'get round the corner, over the hump or through the year' strategy.

The Paymaster General contended that Butler's plan would not make it easier to achieve a trade balance but more difficult, because if the exchange rate fell by 20 per cent, 'we should have to export 25% more in order to pay for the same quantity of imports'.[114]

Nonetheless, Cherwell's fundamental criticism of ROBOT, and in Cabinet the most damaging, was not economic at all:

> So far as concerned our internal economy there were grave political objections to the Chancellor's plan. If it helped to improve the balance of our trade accounts, it would do so only by increasing the prices of imported food and materials to an extent which compelled people to restrict their consumption. This method of rationing by the purse would be difficult to defend, and in any event would not produce results in time to solve our problems.

The ensuing long-drawn-out Cabinet discussions for the most part simply chewed over the same arguments for and against ROBOT that had already been exhaustively propounded in the Whitehall memoranda and correspondence.[115] But one anonymous minister pointed out that sterling (at its present official rate) was overvalued, and hence no one would hold it if he could avoid doing so. 'In these circumstances the large sums at call in the sterling balances were a grave threat to the stability of the currency.' And according to another minister the main factor in this particular threat lay with our Commonwealth kith and kin in Australia. It was 'unreasonable', said he, that the British people should be asked to accept 'increased hardships and sacrifices' for the sake of the balance of payments when all their efforts could be frustrated by unrestricted drawings by countries like Australia from their sterling balances. There was 'a strong case' for limiting Australia's right to draw down the central reserves of the Sterling Area.

But this was neither an academic seminar on economic policy nor a meeting of the board of a Bundesbank, but a tableful of politicians heading a recently elected government with a majority of just seventeen. Therefore the fate of ROBOT really hung on the Cabinet's perception of the limits of the politically possible, or even desirable. Those limits were in turn set by the current prejudices of

the electorate, whether about Britain as a world and Commonwealth power or about Britain's post-war 'full employment'
economy.

Even so, one true-blue voice did go so far as to suggest that a
'moderate' rise in import prices (thanks to ROBOT's floating
pound) would have 'a salutary effect' in bringing home to the
British people 'the reality of the economic situation in which they
were living' – better, he thought, for them to do the adjusting in
accordance with the price mechanism than for Government to take
the responsibility under a planned economy. But overwhelmingly
the Cabinet shrank away from the political and social implications
of ROBOT.

It was the Lord Privy Seal, the Marquess of Salisbury (Eton and
Christ Church, Oxford; a former Secretary of State for the Colonies,
and diehard devotee of the Commonwealth), who most forcefully
articulated their fears:

> The adoption of the plan would give rise to very great political
> difficulty. Public opinion in this country was wholly unprepared for
> such measures. The sudden reversal of the economic policies which
> had been pursued for the last twelve years . . . would come as a
> severe shock to public opinion. Under democratic government with
> universal suffrage such violent reversals of policy were hardly practi-
> cable. Even if the case for this change were abundantly clear on the
> merits, there would be very great difficulty in persuading the public
> to accept it.[116]

This intervention proved enough to blow ROBOT's circuits. After
more roundabout debate the Prime Minister told his Cabinet that
he had come to the conclusion that

> *at the present time* [added emphasis] there was not within the Cabinet
> a sufficient body of support for this plan to enable the Chancellor to
> launch it with the confidence that he had behind him the conviction,
> as well as the loyalty, of his colleagues.

At a third and final meeting the Cabinet endorsed the Chancellor's alternative 'get-round-the-corner' proposals for squeezing the
home market and industrial investment in order to reduce imports

and boost exports, and in this way 'check the deterioration in the United Kingdom balance of payments'.

ROBOT was now scrap metal, even though in a formal sense the Cabinet had only ruled it out 'at the present time', even though Whitehall grandees were to go on exchanging views about it through the summer of 1952, even though the Chancellor himself was to moot it again in July, and even though its essential ideas were briefly canvassed in October during preparations for a Commonwealth economic conference.[117]

Yet it can hardly be doubted that Salisbury's political judgement was correct. It would have been as mentally out of the question for the institutionalized Britain of 1952 to opt for exposure under ROBOT to (in Butler's phrase) 'a continuous process of change and adjustment . . . much of it painful'[118] as it would have been for France and the French army of 1939 to abandon the imagined security of the Maginot Line in favour of armoured manoeuvre in the open field.

Even looking back no one can say for certain what would have been in the event the ramifying effects of adopting ROBOT (with or without strict monetary control over inflation), had it proved politically a runner. However, its backers and its opponents alike were of one mind that for good or ill it would have put an end to so-called 'Keynesian' full-employment policy at home – that is to say, some thirty years earlier than the actual Thatcherite revolution. They were equally agreed that at least ROBOT would have relieved Britain from the immediate strains of acting as banker to the Sterling Area while herself short of the readies and stuck with a fixed but overvalued rate for the pound.

But what of the wider possible impact so bitterly disputed in Whitehall at the time?

Paradoxically, two of the worst consequences of ROBOT as feared by its opponents could have proved its greatest benefits: the break-up of the Sterling Area, followed by that of the Commonwealth itself. For a collapse of these delusory facades of collective strength would have starkly revealed to foreigners and to the British themselves the truth that Britain was a mere sham of a 'world power'.

Such a shock to the British national psyche might perhaps have set in motion a second painful process of adjustment (to paraphrase Butler), in this case to an acceptance that in real weight Britain ranked as just another European industrial state like West Germany or France or Italy.

From that acceptance must surely have followed sweeping changes in British overseas policy – towards Europe and its developing institutions; towards the 'special relationship' with America; towards Britain's existing extra-European political and military entanglements, whence a timely retreat could perhaps have halved the load of the defence budget on the economy. And these changes in turn might have awakened the nation to a renewed sense of its own identity, formed by a heritage far older and richer than the passing pomp of empire.

All this would have amounted to telescoping into the first half of the 1950s by timely conscious decision the actual course of Britain's affairs – hapless, piecemeal – over the next four decades.

As it was, with ROBOT scrapped, Britain would bid no speedy farewell to her time-expired role as a global grandee and prefect. After all, would not the Government's emergency economic measures 'get Britain round the corner' without the political anguish of violating the nation's self-delusion? And would not the problem of the balance of payments (and hence of carrying the Sterling Area and paying for the world role) be neatly solved by a huge expansion of exports? For British factories, British managers and British workers would do the business – while also, of course, supplying the industrial and military hardware for the huge Cold War rearmament programme.

Or so the chateau generals of Whitehall hoped.

PART FOUR

Industry – the Workers

The leaders of the agitation had thereupon organised what they called 'panzer gangs' who were prepared to use intimidation to the point of violence to stop all sections . . .

> (Report of Regional Industrial Relations Officer on a strike at
> the Ford Motor Co. plant in Dagenham, 21 June 1952)

One firm tried to introduce a loading truck which required the services of two workers instead of the three teams of seven men each required by established methods. The men agreed that the trucks might be introduced but only if the three gangs continued to be employed on trucking.

> (Report on the London Docks, May 1950)

9. 'The Leaders of the Agitation': Motor Vehicles

At 3.30 in the afternoon of 20 June 1952 some 10,000 workers trudged twenty abreast out of the Ford Motor Company plant at Dagenham, the only one in Britain which could compare in scale and integrated operation with those in Detroit or, for that matter, the Volkswagen plant at Wolfsburg. The throng surged across the Southend arterial road, blocking all traffic, to Princess Green, a stretch of waste ground amid the industrial squalor and the pebble-dash sprawl of semi-detached houses that make up the sad landscape of south Essex. Here they were harangued by Con O'Keefe, the Communist convenor of the ninety-five-strong shop stewards' committee at the Ford plant, as good-looking and cheery a bloke as ever came out of County Cork with the gift of the blarney. When the ranting was done, the meeting decided, according to the shop stewards' interpretation of a show of hands, to continue with the token one-hour daily strike and the ban on overtime that had begun a week earlier.

It was, after all, the role of purblind converts like O'Keefe to fulfil the task assigned to the British Communist Party by its Soviet paymasters, that of causing as much industrial disruption in Britain as possible.[1] And what better opportunity than in Britain's biggest and best motor-car plant producing her most successful export models? For that matter, what better moment than when the British car industry was having to compete with the rearmament programme for steel, machine tools and skilled workers, and at the same time fight against ever keener foreign rivalry in overseas markets? And, though more by luck than contrivance, what better moment to damage the precarious balance of payments?

179

The dispute at Ford had been detonated by a unofficial strike over a wage claim for 9d. an hour at the neighbouring Briggs Motor Bodies plant, owned by Ford but under separate management. This plant was also supplying the rearmament programme with jerrycans, ammunition boxes and dies for jet engines. When the supply of car bodies from Briggs to the Ford plant temporarily dried up, the management sent 240 press-shop workers home. The shop stewards' committee thereupon demanded that these men should be paid in full for idle time. This being refused by management, the shop stewards' committee called for token one-hour daily strikes, just for a start.

Gloated the Soviet-subsidized Communist paper the *Daily Worker* over the consequent 'stop-start' working days: 'Looking for some way out of the chaos, the management closed down any department affected by stoppages in other parts of the factory.'[2]

It could not be said that in general the Ford rank and file felt much loyalty to, or reposed much trust in, the Ford middle or senior management. For these were another tribe: clean-fingernailed men in suits aloof from the clangour of the shop floors, on salaries instead of hourly rates, and exempt from being laid off and rehired as the demand for cars ebbed and flowed. Nonetheless, some groups of the rank and file had shown a regrettable lack of appetite for stopping work and losing money in order to be harangued by O'Keefe. Clearly more persuasion had been needed. 'The leaders of the agitation', reported the Regional Industrial Relations Officer back to the Ministry of Labour, 'had thereupon organised what they called "panzer gangs" who were prepared to use intimidation to the point of violence to stop all sections . . .'[3] And so O'Keefe was able to command a full house on Princess Green that June afternoon.

From his desk in the Ford plant supplied by management and known as 'the Kremlin',[4] and from which he did no work at all for the company, O'Keefe proceeded with his fellow plotters to work up a trivial dispute into a major industrial battle. For as he had told the mass gathered on Princess Green, 'We stand for maximum pressure against the management for our claim with minimum loss to our members.'[5] Our claim? This was no longer for full pay for a handful of workers sent home for a few hours because the flow of car bodies from Briggs had temporarily dried up. It was for a 9d.

increase in the hourly rate of pay (just as at Briggs) and a holiday bonus of £20 – allegedly to make up for alleged harm to the workers' standard of living because of the new NHS charges and the cuts in food subsidies introduced by the Chancellor's emergency 'get Britain round the corner' budget in March. Since the official unions at Ford were already negotiating with Ford for a wage rise, O'Keefe and his cronies had by hijacking the claim challenged them as well as the company.

On 26 June the *Daily Worker*, gleefully reporting a further mass meeting, wrote that over 15,000 workers (a huge exaggeration) 'downed tools yesterday afternoon, streamed out of their factory, and decided to stop work until tomorrow morning at least'.[6] They had done so at the fresh instigation of O'Keefe and his fellow agitators on the so-called 'Committee of Seven' (shop stewards, six of whom were Communists), this time in protest at the temporary laying-off of 400 men by management. Yet these men had only been rendered idle because of a hold-up in production brought about by the shop stewards' own overtime ban!

In the morning before this latest walkout, the official trade union negotiating committee in the Ford plants, routine-minded bureaucrats not so much closer to the rank and file than the management, had feebly attempted to regain control of the situation. At noon a letter from the secretary of this committee was handed to O'Keefe deprecating the overtime ban and wild-cat strikes, pointing out that the unions had been asked to convene a meeting of shop stewards in order to secure an early resumption of normal working, and instructing that in the meantime work should continue. But O'Keefe neatly outmanoeuvred the union officials by failing to display this letter on noticeboards and at clocking stations as intended.[7] It was a measure of the tactical grip and acumen of these union bureaucrats that they had neglected themselves to make sure that their letter was so posted.

In the event, only a third of the Ford workforce actually turned up at the critical meeting on 25 June, evidence of a widespread apathy that would have shamed a herd of bullocks. Nevertheless, at the behest of the shop stewards those present voted on a show of hands for an all-out strike to win the wage claim of 9d. an hour.

Now, while the Volkswagenwerke continued remorselessly to

pump out Beetles, the entire Ford works (including the Briggs body plant next door) came to a standstill, with all 23,000 men idle; and at a standstill it remained. Nine days later the Communist *World News and Views* was trumpeting: 'This is a lead to the country for the wage demands of millions and the anti-Tory fight'. For, as the same journal proclaimed, the immediate objective of the Communist Party lay in 'the development of a mass movement to bring down the Tories and force a general election'.[8]

The bullocks, however, began to be restive. The stoppage being unofficial, they were receiving no strike pay. This meant dipping into savings or doing odd jobs. One man even resorted to singing at a dog track. It had also dawned that Communists had their own reasons for fomenting trouble at Ford. A fresh 'mass' meeting on 4 July, this time of 7,000 men, proved the scene of angry muttering, scuffles in the crowd, punch-ups round the platform sorted out by the police, and heretical questions to the shop stewards as to the provenance of the money needed to organize the strike. Only one anti-strike speaker was allowed the use of the platform microphone. Otherwise protesters had to shout above the tumult. When O'Keefe put a resolution to the meeting that the strike should continue,[9] it evoked loud cries of 'No!'. There followed a demand for an amendment in favour of a return to work. The platform neatly ruled this out of order. A show of hands as assessed by the platform confirmed that the strike would go on.[10]

Meanwhile a private meeting of 700 chargehands in the Central Hall, Dagenham, had decided not to try to brave the picket lines for fear of violence. Already some chargehands had been man-handled and one of them even frogmarched to the Thames and thrown in because he had attempted to go into work.[11]

Just the same, on 7 July 1952, as cars, trucks and cyclists queued outside the gates for interrogation by the pickets, about a hundred men did have a shot at breaking through under strong police escort, and about thirty succeeded.[12]

But two days later the bullocks finally ceased to be docile and tractable. At yet another open-air meeting the Ford strikers rejected O'Keefe's call to continue the strike and instead agreed on a show of hands to accept the advice of Harry Nicholas, official of the

Transport and General Workers' Union, to go back to work. An end to the Briggs unofficial strike soon followed.

The Ford Motor Company of Great Britain had lost 247,000 man-days of production,[13] to say nothing of the strike's impact on punctuality of deliveries of new vehicles, nor of the harm inflicted by so much disruption and ill-feeling on the quality of manufacture.

Could it all be blamed on a Communist plan 'to bring down the Tories'? This would hardly explain a very similar unofficial strike at Ford back in March–May 1946, under a Labour Government then working to fulfil its election promise of 'New Jerusalem' and at the same time beseeching the nation to export to the uttermost in order to wipe out the fearsome post-war balance-of-payments deficit. That strike had blown up out of a demand from a handful of workers in a single department for a wage increase. A similar demand from another group had been coupled with a threat of a strike if the claim was not settled promptly, this being a clear breach of a 1944 agreement between the company and the unions about negotiating procedure. Next day the militants had paraded through their shop floors to coerce their mates into stopping production. In an integrated assembly-line plant like Ford's such partial dislocation led inevitably to a total stoppage. For good measure, the strikers had also forcibly prevented a ship from being loaded with tractors for export to Denmark. The company had received no approach of any kind from the trade unions proper, and the stoppage had no official union sanction.[14]

Three days after the trouble began, the Hornchurch branch secretary of the Electrical Trades Union (then controlled by Communists)[15] had written to George Isaacs, the Minister of Labour ('Dear Sir and Comrade'), to explain that the strike 'is one provoked by the Ford management purely to sabotage the Governments [sic] production plan'.[16] Of course! He demanded 'full T.U. recognition of the strikers', and urged the Government 'to speed their plans for the nationalization of the motor industries'.

It took some six weeks of skirmishing before Arthur Deakin, trade union chairman of the joint negotiating committee at Ford and the grandest of the trade union barons of the period, was able to announce on 1 May 1946 a deal to end the strike – a five-day working week and higher pay. To the workforce Deakin expressed the hope that in return they would increase their output per man-hour 'related, as a first step, to pre-war achievement'.[17]

Were Ford particularly prone to shop-floor discontent because they were an American-owned company which entertained the weird idea that management's prime task lay in getting maximum production at minimum cost (and hence lowest prices for their vehicles in world showrooms) out of their investment in plant and machinery?[18]

As it happened, on 3 July 1952, in the middle of O'Keefe and Company's stoppage at Ford, all 1,000 employees of the entirely British Park Royal Motor Vehicles of Willesden, north-west London, also came out on unofficial strike in breach of negotiating agreements. As well as making the buses for London Transport and fulfilling export orders, the company was engaged in 'super-priority' production of radar components for the rearmament programme. What was the tremendous grievance that had brought this company to a halt? Twenty-two men in the roofing section of the finishing shop had struck over a bonus payment for a particular job affecting just six workers.[19] When this stoppage dislocated production else-where in the plant the management had had to lay off seventy-eight other workers. This was the signal for all the 'lads' at Park Royal to walk out.

The usual kind of circus now followed: a march through the factory belt of north-west London behind a pipe band; a open-air meeting outside the Rotax factory; much self-righteous rant. In this case the strike was backed by the relevant unions, the Amalgamated Society of Woodcutting Machinists (founded in 1834, its 'period' letterhead in 1952 still sporting Gothic characters and a florid coat of arms) and the Communist-dominated National Union of Vehicle Builders. This meant that the strikers, henceforward benefiting from strike pay, would feel much less acute financial pressure to go back to work. More marches followed. O'Keefe came over from Dag-enham to address a mass meeting. The strike committee issued the familiar kind of manifesto to the working class at large about their 'justified demands'. It proclaimed that they would win 'sooner or later victory', and that they fought 'to defend our standard of living' and 'strengthen the unity of the working class for jobs with decent wages'.

Unlike the fortnight-long Ford strike, that at Park Royal Vehicles proved a protracted war, with vain negotiations dragging on through July and August 1952. An attempt at peace-making by the Chief Industrial Commissioner of the Ministry of Labour at a joint meeting of the embattled sides on 19 August came to nothing. By now serious damage was being inflicted on the export of buses, and, worse, on the fragile European reputation of the British bus industry. In 1950 Associated Commercial Vehicles (ACV), the group to which Park Royal belonged, had beaten Scania-Vabis to win a contract in Sweden to supply buses to Linjebuss for its domestic and European routes. It was hoped that this would open the way to wider British successes in the Swedish vehicle market. But owing to labour troubles at ACV in 1951, the first deliveries had arrived too late for Linjebuss's peak season, with the result that Linjebuss suffered both financially and in goodwill because of cancelled tours.[20] Nonetheless, Linjebuss were persuaded by a British export agency to place fresh orders in Britain for sixteen coaches for delivery by the end of May 1952 at the latest. But by August only seven had arrived, the shortfall being this time due to the strike at Park Royal.[21]

On 25 August the Minister of Labour set up a committee of investigation under the Conciliation Act of 1896. This explored the dispute and its constitutional niceties in great detail, cross-examining spokesmen from all the parties. It reported on 4 September that, in sum, Park Royal Vehicles Ltd were blameless, whereas the unions had breached various agreements and procedures. The report recommended that the unions forthwith instruct their members to resume work.[22] The General Secretary of the National Union of Vehicle Builders accepted this outcome of what he described as a 'fair hearing'. The central strike committee did not. On 16 September a mass meeting in Acton Town Hall voted to keep the strike going.

The ACV group as a whole had now become the strikers' target. With the Commercial Vehicle Show at Earl's Court due to open to prospective British and foreign buyers in a week's time, they therefore stopped painters and carpenters from working on the five ACV stands. After all, what action could better safeguard the workforce's long-term employment than sabotaging ACV's main sales effort of the year?

The strikers finally went back to work on 8 October 1952, followed next day by the seventy-eight men originally laid off. Park Royal Vehicles had been at a standstill for fourteen weeks, the last five of them after the Committee of Inquiry had reported.

Yet the NUVB did even better in 1953, when for eleven weeks it disrupted production at one of the largest of the native British car manufacturers, the Austin Motor Company of Longbridge, Birmingham, with knock-on effects on Austin's outside suppliers such as Dunlop, Pressed Steel, Lucas and Lockheed. The casus belli of this strike, lasting from mid-February to early May and rendering idle a total of 2,271 NUVB members and some 6,800 other Austin workers (a third of the total workforce), lay in the dismissal of one individual, a Mr J. McHugh.[23] But it must be borne in mind that McHugh was a very, very important individual, in whose cause it was well worth dislocating one of the nation's major earners of foreign currency and at the same time aiding European car makers in their attack on British overseas markets. For McHugh was the NUVB's chief shop steward in the Austin plant.[24]

The trouble started to smoulder in August 1952, just after the Ford strike had ended but while the strike at Park Royal Vehicles was still going on. The Austin management informed union officials and shop stewards that, because production of the A90 Atlantic sports car was coming to an end, some 700–800 men would shortly become redundant, on the principle of 'last in, first out'. On 5 September McHugh received one week's notice, among the last to do so. However, when the District Organizer of the NUVB was told by the company that there was no alternative employment for McHugh, he chose to believe that McHugh had been fired only because he was the union's chief shop steward. His dismissal therefore must constitute an attack by Austin on the union.

As recently as May 1952 McHugh had been involved in a three-day strike in the paint shop while working on the assembly track for the Austin Sheerline, a pseudo-Rolls-Royce. It was when production of this unwieldy beast had to be curtailed because of falling orders that McHugh had been transferred to work on the A90 Atlantic, a stylistic abomination dreamt up for the American market and now doomed by that market's failure to appreciate it. Thus the case of McHugh demonstrates how an inept design and production strategy (see below) could have repercussions on employment and labour relations.

McHugh's dismissal marked the beginning of five months of deadlocked negotiations in both local and national conferences between the union and the company, and between the Confederation of Engineering and Shipbuilding Unions and the Engineering and Allied Employers' National Federation. On 17 February 1953, a final ultimatum from the union to Austin to reinstate McHugh having expired, the strike began. On 23 March a mass meeting endorsed the decision of the national executive of the NUVB to ask the Minister of Labour for a Court of Inquiry. On the same day Austin issued a notice that the strikers would be dismissed if there was no general return to work by 27 March. On 28 March, 1,583 strikers were duly sacked. On 2 April the Minister of Labour announced the appointment of a Court of Inquiry. Two days later a mass meeting accepted a recommendation from the union national executive that they should re-register for employment at Austin: i.e., go back to work. Since Austin still refused to re-employ McHugh, this marked a final and utter defeat for the union.

On 7 May 1953 the Court of Inquiry reported that there had been no victimization of McHugh; that the NUVB's district organizer had wrongly sought preferential treatment for McHugh; and that the strike was unconstitutional, not being in accordance with the rules of the union.[25] The court chided both Austin and the union for adopting 'a regrettably inflexible attitude' and neglecting 'reasonable possibilities of compromise'.[26]

The barren battle over Mr J. McHugh's job had caused the loss of 239,000 man-days at Austin alone.[27]

Nor can these strikes in 1952–3 by the National Union of Vehicle Builders (with or without the Amalgamated Society of Woodcutting Machinists alongside) be put down to defence of the working class against a cruel Tory Government. For in April 1948, under the Labour Government, the two unions, having persistently refused to submit a wage claim to arbitration, had brought out all their 'lads' in the vehicle building industry, 23,000 of them.[28]

The month-long strike had been in fact illegal under the still-extant wartime Order 1305 (to be abolished in 1951) enforcing compulsory arbitration, for the dispute had been formally referred to the National Arbitration Tribunal on 31 March 1948. As usual with major strikes during this post-war decade of constant anxiety over exports and the balance of payments, the problem had quickly reached the desk of the Minister of Labour, then George Isaacs, and thereafter the table of the Cabinet Room. On 7 April 1948 Isaacs had advised the Prime Minister, Clement Attlee, that by continuing with the strike the union was attempting 'to force concessions direct from the employers, in spite of the fact that the claim is no longer before them'.[29] In fact, as the *Manchester Guardian* pointed out, the union's defiant illegal action threatened the whole future of the system of compulsory arbitration set up in 1940. Fortunately, however, the NUVB at least had the sense to withdraw this particular claim before the National Arbitration Tribunal met.

But in October 1949 (in the aftermath of the great balance of payments crisis and the Labour Government's devaluation of the pound) NUVB members were at it again, walking out on unofficial strike at Barker of Coventry, the coachwork branch of Daimler, the famed maker of pompous cars for customers such as lord mayors, foreign princelings and the royal household.[30] This time the lads were aggrieved because of the dismissal of ten men for refusing to perform certain jobs for which piecework prices had not yet been agreed. It turned out that one of those dismissed was a Communist shop steward. Although the strikers went back to work after eight days, the Regional Industrial Relations Officer was reporting to Ministry of Labour headquarters on 1 December 1949 that an official strike backed by the NUVB was likely to start at the beginning of January 1950, the issue now being the sacking of the shop steward. This development, groaned the RIRO, had 'the makings of a widespread dislocation in the Motor Car Industry'.[31]

Was the union acting in defiance of agreed 'procedure' by launching the strike? Did the present case anyway fall within the terms of agreed 'procedure'? In a ritual so characteristic of British industrial relations, the barrack-room lawyers on all sides now argued such constitutional niceties at length. In April 1950 the Minister of Labour referred the question to the National Arbitration Tribunal for settlement. Only on 17 July was the dispute at Barker at last resolved by the tribunal's award that they were 'unable to recommend' that the shop steward 'should be re-employed by the company'.[32]

Yet output of motor vehicles, this panzer spearhead of post-war exports, could be disrupted by other means than stoppages at the manufacturers' own plants. On 9 November 1951 (a Conservative Government now) some 1,100 craftsmen and labourers at ENV Engineering, in north-west London (one of Britain's twentieth-century industrial areas), trudged out to begin a strike that would eventually last more than thirteen weeks.[33] ENV was a key supplier of gear and back-axle assemblies to the motor industry, including tank manufacture under the rearmament programme. By the middle of December 1951 the drying-up of supplies from ENV had stopped truck production at Austin in Birmingham and at Commer in Luton; shut down the production of Comet trucks at Leyland Motors; held up output of helicopters at Westland Aircraft; suspended exports of the Jaguar XK120 sports car and of Guy Motors trucks; more than halved output of the new Centurion tank; curtailed output of aero-engines at the Bristol Aeroplane Company; and was threatening further standstills at International Harvester (tractors and hay bailers) and Dodge trucks. Especially damaging was the impact of the strike on Volvo of Sweden, whose entire output of cars, trucks and tractors depended on components exported by ENV.[34]

According to the Regional Industrial Relations Officer, the strike at ENV had to be considered against the background of two similar recent stoppages at firms producing key components for other industries. In the case of Alfa-Laval, which supplied just such a part for more than 90 per cent of oil-burning vessels built in Britain,[35] the firm had 'cracked'[36] after many weeks of struggle because shipyard workers on the Clyde refused to allow a new 20,000-ton ship to carry an Alfa representative on her trials. In the second case, the firm of Coldair, a subsidiary of GEC, had found its production strangled by a strike at Change-Wares Ltd, again the sole suppliers of an essential component. But shop stewards had warned that if Coldair laid off any workers there would be strikes throughout the GEC factory and, if need be, in all other light-engineering factories along the Great West Road, London, another of Britain's newer industrial districts. Pressure from Coldair and the Engineering and Allied Employers' Association forced Change-Wares to capitulate. Both cases had marked a victory for the Amalgamated Engineering Union and Communist shop stewards.[37]

Now this same alliance was conducting the battle against ENV Engineering.

The nature of the dispute between union and company and of the actual casus belli which transformed argument into war neatly encapsulate British industrial relations in the mid-twentieth-century in all their head-banging intransigence, mutual suspicion, raw sense of grievance, and blind lack of concern with competitiveness in the face of foreign rivalry. In June 1951 the union had complained to management that a certain foreman, a Mr H. Gray, was being high-handed over the question of who out of 'viewers' and 'inspectors' should do what and at which rates of pay. In September and October this problem of long standing had come up again. Then, on 8 November, a further meeting between the shop stewards and this short-fused foreman (stupidly standing on his rank rather than showing true leadership) ended in a furious row. As the meeting broke up, Gray (according to a report by the Regional Industrial Relations Officer of the Ministry of Labour) told the convener of the shop stewards that he, the foreman, was not going to be 'a bloody dumb cluck' just to please the stewards.[38] A pamphlet issued by the strike committee alleged that Gray had been more forthright still, assuring the stewards that 'I'M BLOODY WELL RUN-NING THE SHOP, I'LL SHOW YOU WHO IS THE BLOODY BOSS.'[39]

There followed a union demand that Gray be dismissed. Management refused to do so, on the score that hiring and firing supervisory staff was their prerogative. The convener of shop stewards, a Communist by the name of McLoughlin, forthwith called the workforce out on strike. He did so without recourse to agreed procedure for settling disputes, and despite the receipt of a grovelling letter – 'my sincere apologies for losing my temper' – from Gray; and despite, for that matter, an endorsement of the apology by the Works Manager on behalf of ENV.[40]

On 28 November 1951 the Executive Council of the AEU decided to back the stoppage. This meant that, being official, it would now be fuelled with strike pay. The AEU made it truculently plain that only the sacking of the domineering Gray could bring about a return to work.

Now the strike committee, with three Communists (including 'Brother' and 'Comrade' McLoughlin) and one Trotskyist out of eight members,[41] eagerly set out to do their bit in the class war. Manifestos were issued; a North London Campaign Committee was set up, allegedly representative of twenty factories; deputations were sent to the Engineering and Allied Employers' National Federation; there were noisy marches through the local factory belt. It all made exciting 'front-line' copy for the *Daily Worker*.

On the last day of the year took place outside the ENV factory one of those scenes of angry intimidation of would-be 'scabs' by massed pickets (400 of them on this occasion) and of scuffles between pickets and police[42] that were to become so drearily familiar in the 1960s and 1970s, and which were only to be brought to an end in the 1980s by the unions' final nationwide defeat by resolute and ruthless management backed by a resolute and ruthless Government, neither being on offer in the 1950s.

On 4 January 1952 it was reported to the Ministry of Labour that Volvo had said that in view of 'the obvious hazards' they would have to cancel all future business with ENV, a loss of an annual turnover of £1 million to ENV and the nation's export trade.[43]

An attempt by the Ministry of Labour to broker a meeting between the warring parties was stymied by the same issue that caused the strike in the first place – Mr Gray the ill-tempered foreman. The employers would not shift him while under duress, but only after a settlement and a return to work. However, the union would only agree to negotiate 'if the foreman in question is not operating in a supervisory capacity whilst the discussions are proceeding'.[44] The Volvo board in Sweden must have noted this impasse with despairing bewilderment.

It took the direct intervention of the new Minister of Labour,

Sir Walter Monckton, to persuade ENV Ltd and the AEU on 22 January 1952 to accept in advance the recommendations of a Committee of Investigation which he now proposed to set up. The committee reported on 31 January that in their opinion,

> the substance of the dispute under review in no way justified the action taken by the shop stewards' convener and later supported by the Unions. We see no reason why the normal disputes procedure of the Industry should not have been operated, and we strongly deprecate the use of strike action in this case.
>
> We find that the foreman was at fault in that his attitude was not always strictly in accordance with the best interests of the Industry . . .[45]

The Committee therefore recommended that full working at ENV should be resumed without delay; that the foreman should be transferred to other work; and that the convener (Brother McLoughlin, the Communist) who had been in such haste to launch the strike should be removed from his convenership.

On 8 February 1952 the strikers began to traipse back to work. What did it matter if for three months widespread harm had been done to the motor-vehicle industry and its suppliers of components? One rude foreman in one shop in one smallish factory had been got rid of. That was the important thing. Wasn't it?

The battle at 'the Austin' in 1952–3 over the fate of Brother and Comrade J. McHugh had set a motor-industry record for size of strike within a single manufacturer.[46] Together with the Ford strike of 1952 and other lesser punch-ups such as between the NUVB and Park Royal Motor Vehicles, it marked the industry's first post-war peak of trouble (there were to be many more peaks, each time higher, in the coming decades). There now followed for two years a relative lull, marred only by another clash over the dismissal of shop stewards, this time at the Standard Motor Company of Coventry in 1954.[47]

But two years later, in April 1956, the joint shop stewards' committee at Standard launched a grand spring offensive against the company, whose provocation had been to announce that it was introducing into its tractor factory twenty-two automatic transfer machines, mostly German, of the kind now being installed in quantity in Mercedes-Benz, Opel and other German motor-vehicle factories, and, for that matter, at Ford of Dagenham.[48] Transfer machines enabled a complex component such as an engine block to be successively machined in one electronically-controlled automatic process instead of being shifted step by step round a series of separate machine tools separately manned.

This was therefore more than a mere matter of putting in new machines, a development anyway resisted by the trade unions since the 1790s whenever it meant displacing labour and especially traditional craftsmen. This was 'automation' (as it was already being dubbed). It signified a coming fundamental change in the way that the entire process of production in a factory was organized and carried on: in short, a new industrial revolution (see below, p. 366). It therefore posed a threat to the traditional culture of British engineering, that haphazard mosaic of hallowed practices, negotiating 'procedures', and customary rights bequeathed by long history.[49]

However, in the present case of the Standard tractor plant, the shop stewards declared war as much because of the immediate impact on their members as the long-term implications. For the company proposed to lay off some 2,500 workers while it halted production altogether for three months in order to install the twenty-two transfer machines (plus 220 other new machine tools) and the newest type of American electro-static paint plant. The changeover entailed shifting some 15,000 tons of machinery and completely reorganizing 950,000 square feet of factory space, all in readiness to produce a new and much improved tractor. Such a process of shutdown, retool and restart had long been routine in America, then the measure of 'world's best practice' in manufacturing.

As it happened, Standard's tractor plant was currently doing far better than the company's car division.[50] It supplied much of the output of the Canadian-based Massey-Harris-Ferguson Company, which owed its success in world markets to Harry Ferguson's brilliant innovation of integrating the tractor with a variety of interchangeable farm implements. This was why Standard was investing as much as £4 million in re-equipping the plant – a heavy cost for an under-capitalized company whose cars were losing market share even at home.[51]

When back in February 1956 Standard had discussed with the shop stewards the expected lay-offs, the stewards had instead demanded short-time working spread by rota across the 11,000 employees in both tractor and car plants.[52] The company vainly pointed out that the resultant daily rotating of workers from one task to another, often unfamiliar to them, must disrupt the smooth flow of work and components so essential to mass production. Quite apart from its effects on quantity and quality of output, short-time working (or shared work) could only result in increased costs which the company was in no position to bear. But the shop stewards were unconvinced, threatening to strike if there were any loss of jobs.

At the end of March a works conference on the question adjourned without agreement. On 25 April Standard informed the shop stewards that on 18 May some 1,900 workers at the tractor plant would be laid off. On 26 April the strike began. On the 27th, according to the *Manchester Guardian*,

> No cars or tractors were made at the Standard Motor Company's Canley and Banner Lane factories . . . No wastepaper baskets in the offices were emptied; no meals cooked in the canteen. The company's entire labour force of almost twelve thousand production and maintenance workers are on strike and many of the workers spent the day registering their inactivity at their trade union offices.[53]

Although the unions were to argue later that 'automation' was not the issue, the same *Guardian* reporter noted that 'in the queues outside union offices to-day that hated word was heard frequently'.[54]

With car production at Standard halted, lay-offs followed immediately at Pressed Steel at Cowley (Oxford) and at Mulliner and Fisher & Ludlow in Birmingham (all companies which supplied Standard with car bodies), as well as at Lucas, the electrical components firm. Meanwhile hostile mass pickets barred out the builders and electricians who worked for the subcontractors responsible for retooling the tractor factory. In the words of one contractor's spokesman, it was 'not fair to ask them to face physical violence to get into work'.[55]

The freshly self-created strike committee, chaired by a Communist, made haste to dispatch emissaries to the main ports to appeal to dockers to 'black' Standard products due for export, and to other industrial centres to appeal for money and moral support. Reproachful letters began to whiz to and fro between the Standard management and the Confederation of Shipbuilding and Engineering Unions (CSEU). The Ministry of Labour kept an anxious eye on it all, meanwhile amassing press-cuttings as the national and regional newspapers covered developments at vast expenditure of column inches.[56] In short, that ever-favourite drama, the great British strike, was playing again to a packed house.

There was just one point: thus far the strike remained unofficial, for the shop stewards had rushed to pre-empt a forthcoming meeting between Standard and the local secretary of the CSEU. The strike equally breached an agreement between company and confederation that there should be no stoppage of work until the negotiating procedure had been exhausted. The company was particularly incensed because the workforce had walked out when there still remained three weeks of discussion time before the lay-offs were due to start.[57]

On 1 May 1956 a mass meeting obeyed the shop stewards' advice to stay out until Standard agreed to short-time working instead of redundancy. That night the Managing Director of Standard, Alick Dick, helped things along with an untimely and unwelcome public reminder of commercial reality:

> We are installing costly equipment to supply tractors not only, as at present, to Europe but to America as well on a competitive basis. We cannot carry the same number of employees for fun. We must prepare ourselves in these competitive markets. Whether we can take on those laid off when the tractor factory is working depends on the output of cars at the same time.[58]

Two days after this soothing statement there was held another mass meeting, on Hearsall Common (near the silent Standard car factory), one of those dreary open spaces which for decades were to witness agitators promoting the demise of the British car industry. Here the throng listened without enthusiasm to Harry Urwin, the District Secretary of the CSEU, announce that it would be another six days before the ten unions at Standard met to decide their attitude to the strike. In contrast, the Communist strike-leader, Brother Warman, won loud applause when he yelled through the microphone that the strike would go on until Standard agreed to short-time working instead of lay-offs; and even louder applause when he asserted that Standard workers welcomed 'any new scientific and technical developments to improve the productive efficiency of the British engineering industry'.[59] Who could have doubted it? Warman added: 'But we believe such improvements are of no value until the benefits are passed on to the workers as well as the shareholders and employers.' He did not, however, explain how this might be done.

On the same day the Minister of Labour, now Iain Macleod (Fettes College, and Gonville and Caius College, Cambridge), a coming man on the small-l liberal wing of Eden's Conservative Government, preached to an industrial conference in London: 'This country above all others must not be afraid of change. Change is our ally and we must welcome it.'[60] As with so many sermons, the uplifting sentiment did not altogether accord with the realities of human behaviour.

On 9 May 1956 the representatives of ten unions decided to ask Standard for an immediate meeting to thrash out the problem. In the meantime they instructed their members that they should go back to work on the same day that the company consented to such a meeting. On 14 May the 11,000 strikers, having paralysed Standard for nearly three weeks, duly tramped in through the gates of the Banner Lane tractor plant and the Canley car plant. However, this was not a peace settlement, merely an armistice. How long would it last?

At a meeting with shop stewards on 16 May the company made a major concession: a four-day week in the car factory in order to share out the work with 1,200 tractor men. Just the same, the company saw no hope at all of absorbing the rest of the tractor men to be laid off – some 2,600 – into car production, for this had dropped by 600 per week since February because of falling sales. Worse, further falls in the autumn appeared all too likely. Alick Dick therefore gave notice in a personal message as Managing Director to all hourly paid employees on 30 May that the 2,600 would be laid off in two stages, the first batch immediately and the second in three weeks' time.[61]

In an attempt to remind the workforce that there existed a wider world beyond Banner Lane and Canley, beyond even Coventry, or even England herself, he wrote that 'it becomes clear to us all that the number of people we can employ cannot be determined by strikes, or by our emotions; it depends entirely upon the demand for our products'.[62]

It would be hard to conceive a more shocking heresy than this in terms of what the *Manchester Guardian* had described in another context as 'the comfortable industrial thinking of the years of full employment – the idea that a man should be tenant-for-life in a particular job', let alone in terms of the related idea that, again in the words of the *Guardian*, there was 'some natural law which gives a man the right to be paid whether there is work for him or not'.[63]

Unsurprisingly, the only reaction of the 240 shop stewards at Standard to Dick's message was to demand that their trade unions should now call an official strike. 'No redundancy' remained as ever the cry. Many shop stewards in fact wanted an immediate walkout and to hell with waiting for an official union decision. Nonetheless, at a further shop stewards' meeting on 4 June 1956 one brave man went so far as to propose that the wishes of the workforce them-selves should be ascertained by means of a secret ballot. This scandalous suggestion was ruled 'out of order' by the chairman, Brother Warman the Communist.[64]

Now it was the turn of the Minister of Labour to try to mediate. On 7 June ten representatives of trade unions at Standard presented their case to him at the Ministry's headquarters in leafy St James's Square (so conveniently close to Macleod's clubs, White's and the Carlton). The President of the CSEU, Harry Brotherton, graciously conceded that 'there must be some mobility to meet this kind of situation', but this was, he went on,

> not merely ordinary redundancy, but large-scale changes in produc-tion methods. The Ford company had introduced new methods recently without redundancy being involved, and the Unions felt that the Standard Company appeared to be taking an unduly pessi-mistic view of the long-term prospects of the motor car industry.[65]

Although the Minister promised to pass on these points, he never-theless made clear that it was up to Standard to decide the size of workforce warranted by the demand for the company's products, and that the government would not apply pressure on the company to change its attitude. This savage pronouncement evoked a bleat in the *Daily Herald* (the newspaper owned by the Labour Party) that here was 'a knell to hopes that the Government would recognize its responsibility to men put out of work by automation or production losses . . .'[66]

On 11 June it was the Standard management's turn to meet the Minister, its team of four headed by the firm's chairman, Marshal of the Royal Air Force Lord Tedder. Alick Dick argued that the current problems were 'very largely due to the inflexible attitude adopted by the shop stewards towards any proposals for redundancy'.[67] The present short-time working was

> a very complex matter and involved teaching 1,400 men new jobs every day . . . This had already led to inferior production at higher cost, which was a serious matter in the competitive conditions now obtaining in the motor industry. The difficulties were particularly acute with a mass production line involving the use of very expensive machinery.

Dick added: 'As a result of the recent troubles the firm had suffered considerable financial losses, the full extent of which could not be disclosed publicly.'[68]

At Macleod's suggestion Dick later wrote him a letter for transmission to the unions, conciliatory in tone, but ruling out a tripartite meeting with them plus the Minister as serving 'no useful purpose at the present juncture'.[69] Wrote Dick:

> We have our responsibilities to our customers and to our distributors and beyond that, we have responsibilities to the British Motor Industry as a whole, for maintaining its good name at a time *when it is being relentlessly attacked for bad quality, service and spares* [added emphasis].

The happy result of these chats with the emollient Macleod was that company and unions agreed (after some seven weeks of dispute) to meet for formal face-to-face discussions. But there the happiness ended, for three hours of argument between them on 19 June ended in final deadlock, Standard refusing to introduce a complete share-out of work at its factories as the unions wanted.

On 25 June took place another long meeting, this time between union officials and the Standard shop stewards in Coventry, about whether or not to call an immediate official strike. During this choleric encounter a renewed request for a secret ballot was again squashed, no doubt for the good reason that the workforce were getting tired of the dispute and might well vote in a way awkward for the militant shop stewards. In 'quite dreadful' scenes[70] the union officials were fraternally greeted outside by abuse bawled by a rentamob.

On 27 June 1956 Standard's Production Director, H. S. Weale, wrote a letter to the District Secretary of the CSEU (for release to the press) that his board had decided that it was 'quite impossible' to negotiate while it was 'being put under duress by threats of strike action' and 'being pressed to submit completely to the extravagant demands of certain minorities'.[71]

> We are aware of the true position inside our factories, that despite pressure from certain Shop Stewards at Factory Meetings held within the works yesterday, out of a total of 24 gangs in all our factories, only four voted in favour of strike action.
>
> It is deplorable that we as a Company are threatened from outside with strike action, when the employees inside – who are expected to make the sacrifice – clearly expressed their view to the contrary.

With these votes the Battle of Banner Lane finally sputtered out.

Then came the ironic postscript. On 30 June Standard announced that it was going to introduce a three-day week for some 7,000 workers on its car assembly lines. Why? It was because of a collapse in sales, which the company blamed on cancellation of orders from Australia and on the Conservative Government's new hire-purchase restrictions and 'credit squeeze'.[72] For – yes, what a surprise! – the British economy was in the summer of 1956 yet again drifting alarmingly close to the breakers (see below, Chapter 23).

The turmoil at Standard provides an aptly mournful epilogue to a post-war decade in which the British car industry was disrupted by at least four times the number of strikes as in the equivalent period before the war, and lost nearly four times the number of man-days.[73] Worse still, not least as an omen for the future, was the acceleration in the number of man-days lost through strikes from 302,500 in 1945–9 to 683,500 in 1950–54.[74]

In contrast to this disorderly British scene of up to ten highly individualistic unions in each plant and of major disputes ignited by local grievances stood the 'rational'[75] pattern offered by the American car industry. Here one single union (the Union of Automobile Workers) from time to time fought grand set-piece battles with the motor car companies over the terms of long-term contracts, while otherwise production rolled as smoothly as a Cadillac on a parkway.[76] And virtually unknown in West Germany's car industry were instant unofficial strikes of the British kind. Even official strikes were rare indeed.[77] Instead, the officers, NCOs and other ranks of Volkswagen and Mercedes-Benz simply concentrated like good German troops on the *Schwerpunkt* of breaking through into world markets.[78]

The tragedy for Britain during this turning-point decade lay in that such strikes and simmering discontents were not unique to the motor-vehicle industry, important though this had become as the single most valuable source of exports. They were rife across the entire industrial scene.

10. 'Actual or Imagined Grievances': Aircraft and Much Else

While the German enemy was at the gate during the Second World War, the British striker had also been at the gate – of his factory, shipyard or colliery. For even a total war for the nation's very survival could not abate Britain's industrial malaise, as the Ministry of Labour and National Service's weekly 'strike charts' (the Ministry's own term) kept from 1940 onwards go to prove.[1] On the contrary: more working days were lost through strikes each year from 1942 to 1945 than in 1938, the last full year of peacetime.[2] But actual strikes only marked the acute phases of a chronic condition the other wartime symptoms of which included widespread absenteeism or, at the very least, turning up late for shifts and sliding off well before the end.[3]

It can therefore hardly astonish that even in the first two years of the post-war era, that period of national penury and direst need of exports, there were on average thirty industrial disputes (existing or new) in progress per month.[4] Barely a corner of the economy was left unscathed, for stoppages ranged from the aircraft industry to artificial silk; buses to boilermaking; civil engineering to cigar manufacture; cold storage to cotton; insurance to iron and steel; pottery to papermaking; and radios to rayon, road haulage and rubber tyres.[5] Almost as diverse were the grievances that provoked the strikes.[6] Management's 'unjust' dismissal of a shop steward or other worker for alleged misconduct was one favourite, lay-offs another. Unions also proved just as ready as in wartime to pick a fight in defence of their own customary property rights, whether a closed shop, a craft demarcation, or skilled work threatened by 'dilution' with the semi-skilled, or all three at once.[7] In January

1946 the Sheet Metal Workers' Society 'went slow' and then struck at Fisher & Ludlow's car-body plant in Birmingham simply because the company had dared to put 'croppers' trained by itself on to operating Magee wiring machines and rotary shears – *at semi-skilled pay*! For the society averred that these men must become its members and be paid at skilled rates. Although the strikers went back to work in February 1946, there followed four months of tortuous argument centred on alleged historical precedent before the National Arbitration Tribunal finally resolved the matter by making an award in the company's favour.[8]

Thanks to a similar clinging to precedent, this time by the Amalgamated Engineering Union, a new mechanical press stood idle at the Crewe works of the London, Midland and Scottish Railway from February 1946 until September 1947. For the union threatened to strike, and then in November 1946 did strike,[9] simply in order to prevent the company from manning this press with a grade 3 machinist instead of a technically unneeded skilled craftsman (a blacksmith) at a craftsman's rate.[10] Did this dispute fall within the terms of Paragraph 28, Note 3 of Schedule B and Paragraph 43 of Industrial Court Award No. 728 of July 1922? Or Clause 14 of the National Negotiating Machinery agreed in August 1927? Or an amendment made in November 1937 to the 'Scheme of Machinery for Railway Shopmen'?[11] Or an agreement between company and union in March 1943? First the Ministry of Labour and then the Industrial Court grappled with these arcane points, so relevant to productive efficiency in the late 1940s and yet so typical of the tortuously slow 'procedures' for resolving British industrial disputes. The court eventually pronounced on 10 September 1947 that the LMS was indeed justified in its proposal for manning the new press.

In the meantime, obsession with supposed precedent had dominated another squabble between the LMS and the unions, in this case over whether automatic welding machines at the company's Derby and Crewe works should be manned by semi-skilled workmen or by skilled welders. It again fell to the Industrial Court to clear a path through dense thickets of legalistic disputation, eventually awarding in favour of the company.[12]

Since the British worker was blessed with a highly combustible sense of his rightful due, questions of piecework prices and bonus payments, let alone basic pay and working hours, served as a ready match. In August 1946, for instance, the year of the 'Britain Can Make It' exhibition and the Labour Government's urgent drive for exports, the printing unions imposed an overtime ban in support of a claim for a forty-hour week (instead of the present forty-five hours) and two weeks' paid holiday, as originally agreed back in happier times before the war.[13] With the industry's work already much in arrears, the ban soon held up delivery of sales literature essential for the export drive.[14] It took until October 1946 for a Court of Inquiry to come up with a compromise acceptable to both sides.[15]

Yet not all early post-war strikes were provoked by what were – at least from the perspective of a shop floor shell-hole – big issues. In one instance in 1945, tools were downed in objection to a notice 'strengthening clocking arrangements';[16] in another, at Fairey Aviation in late 1946, because one man had worked overtime in breach of union rules.[17] And in October 1946 employees of an engineering firm in Bridgend, Glamorgan, had walked out because the company had suspended welders for refusing to use files.[18] Even the timing of the tea break or the dinner hour could be worth a go.[19] Similarly, a strike might involve fewer than a hundred workers over a day or so, or tens of thousands over weeks or months.

It was the nation's misfortune that the Ministry of Labour's decision in June 1947 to cease keeping a file of weekly 'strike charts' by no means signified an end to strikes themselves, let alone to overtime bans and 'go-slows' (actual or threatened). On the contrary, throughout this crucial decade when Britain's old trade rivals were reviving ever faster, British workforces in every kind of industry, from rail and road transport to textiles and pottery, construction to chemicals, continued to pursue their diverse ancestral disgruntlements.[20] A Ministry of Labour paper in 1956 located the causes in

> lack of leadership, ill-defined targets, frustrations, fear of shortage of work, ill-directed group loyalties, actual or imagined grievances, lack of incentives, either financial or non-financial, or, in a few instances, plain laziness.[21]

The culture of grievance could even infect an advanced technology like aircraft manufacture, a field where the post-war Labour

Government had vainly and expensively hoped that Britain could one day compete successfully with America.[22] In the first two years after the war alone the lads had already downed tools in dudgeon at one time or another at Handley Page, Hawker, Gloster, Fairey Aviation, Airspeed and Parnall Aircraft.[23]

In February 1951 (still under the Labour Government) it was the turn of Rolls-Royce Aero-Engines, the brightest star of British advanced technology, on which greatly depended the production of civil airliners and also of military aircraft under the post-Korea rearmament programme.[24] In the forenoon of the 14th shop stewards at the Hillington factory near Glasgow held a meeting in the canteen during the tea break to chew over an already existing gripe.[25] The company's Labour Officer pointed out that permission to hold this meeting had been neither sought nor granted, and refused a request to allow the meeting to continue for a further five minutes. When the convener of AEU shop stewards (a well-known Communist) announced that they would finish the meeting outside, the Labour Officer promptly sacked him, along with the T&GWU convener who had protested that his colleague could not be dismissed in this summary fashion. A day of rising tempers culminated with 3,000 out of the workforce of 4,400 walking out at 1615.

The Industrial Relations Officer (Scotland) glumly reported to Ministry of Labour headquarters in London that while trade union officials 'intend to go in and handle matters', it remained to be seen 'how far and how soon they will penetrate beyond the Strike Committee'.[26] He added that the two sacked conveners were associated with the so-called 'Shop-stewards Movement' which had succeeded in making the Hillington Industrial Estate generally 'a black spot' (sic) in regard to a recent wage agreement.

There followed next day a four-mile slogan-shouting mass march from George Square, Glasgow, to Govan Town Hall, where on a show of hands the strikers resolved to stay out until the two conveners were reinstated. In reporting this the *Daily Worker* was delighted to add in the same column that a factory-gate meeting outside the aero-engine firm of Napiers in Acton, London, had delivered a seven-day ultimatum to the company demanding a wage increase of 11s. 'all round [sic]' with the threat of a total ban on overtime.[27]

A week later a second meeting at Govan rejected the advice of the unions' national executive councils to resume work so that negotiations with Rolls-Royce could begin (the company having refused to negotiate under duress). On 20 February 1951 ninety-five shop stewards representing some 20,000 workers on Clydeside agreed to stage a mass demonstration on the morrow in support of the conveners. In the event, however, no more than 1,000 turned out. Strikers began to drift back to work as money grew short and indignation cooled. At yet another, and very rowdy, mass meeting on 27 February, this time held in St Andrew's Hall (the largest in Glasgow), it was decided by 1,346 votes to 761 in a ballot vote to end the strike.[28] Though the meeting opened at 1000, the vote was not taken until 1500, the delay being caused by a filibustering minority who also sought – in vain – to convince the meeting that the decision to take a ballot vote was unconstitutional.

Could Rolls-Royce now look forward to trouble-free production of aero-engines at Hillington? By no means. At the end of March 1951 there took place a token one-day strike of 647 workers because the company had 'locked out' some men who reported late for work.[29] Then in May the issue of the sacked and never reinstated conveners surfaced again like a bubble from the bottom of a septic tank. The National Executive Council of the AEU decided that the allegations of victimization were indeed well founded, and that a ballot vote should be taken for or against further strike action. But on 9 June there voted 692 against such action, 435 in favour, so ending this particular industrial skirmish[30] and freshly demonstrating why Communist shop stewards so much preferred a show of hands counted by them to a ballot.

Across the Irish Sea during the same months of 1951, the aircraft factories in Belfast and Newtownards belonging to Short Brothers and Harland (a nationalized company) had also been brought to a standstill by a similar dispute between management and militant shop stewards. One of these stewards belonged to the Sheet Metal Workers' Union, which in the middle of the Second World War had argued that because for centuries metal had been shaped by craftsmen banging away at a bench with hand tools, then shaping metal for Spitfires and Lancasters by the power-press and automatic tool must be manned, rated and paid as skilled work even though actually performed by the semi-skilled.[31]

The first sign of trouble came with a lunchtime mass meeting about bonus payments on 4 January 1951, harangued by the shop stewards of the T&GWU, the Amalgamated Engineering Union and the Sheet Metal Workers' Union (the latter being one Brother Barr, a Communist). This overran half an hour into the company's time, so eliciting a warning from the personnel manager.[32] Next day the company refused permission to the shop steward of the Electrical Trades Union (Brother McKernan, another Communist) and the stewards of the T&GWU to hold two further mass meetings. In defiance McKernan went ahead and addressed his own union members, again in the company's time. However, on 8 January a meeting voted down a proposal by shop stewards that bonus working at Short's should be abandoned.

But this setback did not signify the coming of peace at Short's. On 16 January the Sheet Metal Workers brought about an unofficial stoppage over the entirely different matter of a demarcation (or 'who does what') dispute; and Brother Barr, the union's Communist shop steward, persuaded some thirty workers to walk out. Two days later the company, having mulled things over, gave Barr the sack, whereupon he refused to leave the factory and instead convened further gatherings preached at by other shop stewards as well as himself. When despite a fresh warning these men called yet more meetings the company sacked ten of them. This did not prevent them from successfully leading most of the workforce out on a strike which was to last nine weeks, the issue now being the reinstatement of the 'victimized' shop stewards.

It was in March 1951 (the month when the Labour Government submitted to NATO its £4.7 billion rearmament programme) that a Court of Inquiry at last mediated a peace treaty between Short's and the unions, laying down in detail the rights and responsibilities of the parties, and specifying that the ten men 'shall be re-employed as workers and not in the capacity of shop stewards'.[33] On 19 March the *Daily Worker* reported the ending of the strike under the headline 'Going Back Victorious'.

Just as injurious to smooth industrial production as these quarrels with employers were the continuing squabbles of unions with each other over the exact boundary lines between crafts, like rancorous neighbours about a fence. Here too a favourite weapon lay in the appeal to time-hallowed practice. In March 1948 it was the turn of the Scottish Typographical Association and the National Society of Operative Printers and Assistants (NATSOPA) in Glasgow to clutch hold of this weapon in order to 'glass'[34] each other in a squabble over which union should rightfully have as its members the rotary-machine minders at George Outram, publishers of the *Glasgow Herald*. When this matter finished up before a Court of Inquiry under the Conciliation Act of 1896, the disputants based their cases on their own interpretations of trade 'custom' and of agreements made in 1915, 1929 and 1942. Meanwhile the STA had called its members out as a ploy in its fight with NATSOPA, whereupon Outram's found themselves the innocent victim caught in the middle.[35] It took until the end of September 1948 for the two unions to strike a deal after what the Regional Industrial Relations Officer of the Ministry of Labour called 'protracted, and at times heated, discussions'.[36]

In the spring and summer of 1951 came the turn of the fledgeling nuclear industry, the Labour Government's expensive bet on winning for Britain both a cheap source of limitless energy and a future as a militarily first-class world power. The Amalgamated Society of Woodworkers and the Amalgamated Engineering Union began to wrangle over who should fix the metal panels for interior partitions at the huge Capenhurst diffusion plant for enriching uranium.[37] The contractor having used fitters to do the work, the carpenters walked out on 24 April. Was the work 'building construction', so belonging to the carpenters of the ASW? Or was it metal work, and hence to be owned by fitters of the AEU? That was the question. Naturally, the parties (including the Ministry of Labour) looked to historical precedent for an answer. They found it in the minutely detailed technical analysis of a National Joint Emergency Disputes Commission hearing in 1932 which pronounced that erecting metal partitions was construction work.[38] But this did not settle the matter. Was Capenhurst a 'building industry site' or 'a civil engineering one'? Was the work 'metal partitioning' or really a series of 'insulated boxes'?[39] It complicated the issue even more that the cladding in question was itself a technological novelty. For nine weeks the work at Capenhurst stopped while the disputants argued the finer points: a notable example of a minor local dispute halting a grand enterprise. At last, on 3 July, it was mutually agreed to deploy 'balanced gangs' of craftsmen from different unions.[40] Eleven days later two joiners walked out because they would not work alongside fitters.[41]

Yet when it came to inter-union quarrels during this first post-war decade over who (and how many) should do what and with which tools, the Blue Riband was easily won by the shipyards.[42]

The shipbuilding 'mateys' began the decade as they meant to go on, with a dispute at the Bristol yard of Charles Hill and Sons that dragged on from October 1945 to March 1946 between the Boiler-makers' Society, the Iron and Steel Shipbuilders' Society and the Shipconstructors' and Shipwrights' Association as to who should operate an oxy-acetylene cutting lamp on repair work. In October about a hundred riveters belonging to the Boilermakers walked out because this lamp had been issued to shipwrights. The Shipwrights' Association, for their part, contended that the lamp was common to all grades, and that their members had the right to use it whenever necessary for their own work.[43] Although work was resumed while the two unions bickered, the local branch of the Boilermakers' Society informed their opposite number at the Shipwrights' Associ-ation at the end of January 1946 that they

> cannot agree to any departure from the practices and custom that have so long operated relative to the use of the Oxy-Acetylene Burning and Welding Plants in the Shiprepairing of the Bristol Channel Area.[44]

Threatened with a strike by boilermakers which would halt the yard, the company decided not to issue the provocative lamp to shipwrights for the time being. This meant that shipwrights would have to cut off bolt heads by hand with a hammer and cold chisel. But at the beginning of February 1946 the now disgruntled Bristol branch of the Shipwrights gave a fortnight's notice to the company after which no bolts would be cut by hand. This signified in effect a complete embargo on bolt-cutting. The unions having failed to arrive at agreement, an arbitrator finally pronounced in March that the shipwrights should after all be entitled to use the lamp for cutting bolts – when the bolts were actually attached to shipwrights' work.[45]

In 1947 the boilermakers were at it again, this time at a major British yard, Palmers Shipbuilding of Hebburn on the Tyne. The cause of the fracas again lay in who should operate a flame-cutting machine, whether a boilermaker (though technically no longer necessary) or an unskilled worker.[46] The edge of the boilermakers' self-interest was all the keener because the new machine would anyway replace a crew of several skilled men. On this dispute too history exercised its malign influence, for the shipbuilding employers had been lastingly intimidated by a victory won by the boilermakers back in 1943–4 over the very same issue at the naval yard of Vickers-Armstrong. In the August of 1944, the time of the climax of the Battle of Normandy, the boilermakers had taken their objection to semi-skilled men operating new flame-cutters at Vickers-Armstrong to the point of refusing to work on any material processed on the new cutters unless these were operated and controlled by their members. They had done so even despite the setting-up of a Court of Inquiry and a personal reminder from the First Lord of the Admiralty about the urgency of the war work now being paralysed.[47] The Boilermakers had only lifted their ban in December 1944 because the company took the semi-skilled men off the new flame-cutters and suspended the operation of the cutters for the time being.[48]

Like the broken-armed victim of a protection racketeer, the shipbuilding employers henceforward trembled before the obstructive power and ruthlessness of the Boilermakers. In the words of a report in June 1947 from the Regional Industrial Relations Officer (RIRO) in Newcastle to the Ministry of Labour in London about the threatened trouble at Palmers,

> It will be recalled that a prolonged strike of Boilermakers occurred during the War at Vickers-Armstrongs Naval Yard, Walker, when a similar machine was introduced and it was not until the employers undertook to withdraw the machine that the men returned to work. Since then, although it is understood that other yards on the Tyne, including Palmers, Hebburn, have had this type of machine delivered,

none of the machines have been put into operation because of the danger of a recurrence of the former trouble.[49]

As the suspicious Boilermakers got ready for another fight, a spokesmen of the Tyne Shipbuilders' Association told the Ministry of Labour's local conciliation officer that the machine was 'not ready for operation and no decision or pronouncement has been made by the employers as to who should operate the machine, and no such decision will be made *without due regard to the circumstances* [added emphasis] . . .'[50] Of course not!

Back in 1944 the First Lord of the Admiralty had warned Cabinet colleagues that the future of British shipbuilding would be threatened by 'any tendency towards what I may term the fossilisation of inefficiency'.[51] And who more potent fossilizers than the Boilermakers' Society?

In September 1948 the society chose to have another go at their old and equally metal-headed rival, the Ship Constructors' and Shipwrights' Association, this time at Pembroke Dock in Wales.[52]

Although Pembroke Dock had previously been an Admiralty ship-repairing base (and remained in naval ownership), it was at present leased to a company, R. S. Hayes Ltd, which operated it as a commercial yard repairing civilian vessels. This ambiguity of status now served to inspire the flat-capped shipyard lawyers in both the unions. Their opposing arguments are tersely summed up in a report by the Ministry of Labour's local Conciliation Officer for Wales:

It is the practice in Admiralty Dockyards for the shipwrights to do the iron work on hulls, which means they are the dominant body and members of the Boilermakers Society are relegated to a secondary place. In all other Bristol Channel yards on the other hand the Boilermakers Society has established a claim to most of this type of work . . . The Shipwrights branch officials claimed that the present division of work had been established by long custom and practice and they would not be prepared to surrender it. They say it is a proper division for a dockyard area and although the Admiralty has for the time being ceased operations there, Pembroke Dock is essentially a Government dockyard area.[53]

Actual or Imagined Grievances': Aircraft and Much Else

But the Boilermakers' local secretary contended (so the report went on) that

> the dockyard is now a commercial yard and should follow the working practices of other yards in the Bristol Channel. His complaint was that the Shipwrights had been arrogant and unaccommodating, and his members felt compelled to fight for a fairer division . . .

Hence the Boilermakers' present embargo on work on one of the two ships in the yard. With commendable restraint, the Boilermakers limited their demands to, in the first place, a mere monopoly over the entire work of removing plates and bars; and secondly, to 'a full squad of boilermakers' carrying out all burning of bars, plates, etc, all burning and removing of rivets, and all work on boilers (such as stays, tubes, furnaces, smoke box doors).[54]

As for R. S. Hayes, the unfortunate company, they felt (according to the Conciliation Officer),

> that it would be better to get out of the ship-repairing business before incurring serious financial loss and thought that if the present labour troubles were not speedily settled, they would be out of the dockyard by next summer.[55]

This prospect gave no joy in the town hall, for the dockyard was Pembroke's largest employer, and R. S. Hayes was all that stood between the yard and a return to the dereliction that had followed the Great War.

There ensued fifteen months (fifteen months!) of futile disputation. As a start, R. S. Hayes quickly caved in to the Boilermakers and agreed to adopt the custom and practice of commercial yards along the Bristol Channel, whereupon the Boilermakers kindly lifted their embargo. Whereupon the Shipwrights walked out. After the latter had been on strike for three months, the company warned that their work on ceilings of holds in a ship (the *Empire Tees*) currently under repair in the yard 'will now doubtless be done on the Continent'.[56] Moreover, the company had already had to turn away several contracts requiring the work of shipwrights.[57] In spring 1949 a meeting convened by the TUC between representatives of the two unions failed because neither would yield so much as a rivet's length. The quarrel was finally settled only in December 1949 by an award in favour of the Boilermakers by the Disputes Committee of the Trade Union Congress.[58]

Meanwhile, in August that year, the Boilermakers had picked another quarrel with Vickers-Armstrong at Barrow-in-Furness, brandishing an ultimatum in the company's face to the effect that if they did not remove drillers (belonging to the Shipwrights' Association) from machines welding bolts (or studs) for electrical installations, all boilermakers would stop work immediately. As the local Conciliation Officer later reported to the Ministry of Labour in London, 'a withdrawal of boiler making labour would have had very serious consequences and the firm could not face such a prospect.'[59] So Vickers-Armstrong crumpled and took the drillers off the machines in order to give time for a peace treaty to be mediated between the two unions.

A tripartite meeting on 2 September proving abortive, Vickers-Armstrong actually dared a fortnight later to put drillers back on to the bolt-welding machines again. Perhaps the company in their naivety thought that they owned both the shipyard and the welding machines, and even believed that they were responsible for running the production programme. Perhaps they had forgotten for a moment that this was not Bremen, but Barrow. For the result of their decision was that all the boilermakers now walked out in a huff.

There ensued the usual kind of brain-pulping legalistic dispute between the two unions, with the company as victim and the Regional Industrial Relations Officer, Manchester, as would-be peacemaker. What about, for instance, the two sides agreeing to local arbitration, while in the meantime the boilermakers went back to work and the offending machines were put in temporary cold storage? Not a hope. The shipwrights would not agree to the machines being placed in store, alleging that the boilermakers had had ample time to agree on arbitration and were simply using delaying tactics.[60] The boilermakers would agree to drillers temporarily remaining on the welding work if arbitration could take place while they themselves were still on strike. This the shipwrights rejected.[61]

By now the local 'Brothers' of both unions were evincing in

person that helpful spirit of open-minded compromise so characteristic of British industrial relations. According to a Ministry of Labour
memorandum, when the two District Committees discussed the
issues for three hours one evening, 'they fell out, the proceedings
became acrimonious, and the breach became much wider'.[62] On 4
October another Ministry memorandum neatly summed up the
impasse:

> The present position is, therefore, that the boiler makers object to a
> return to work to permit the setting up of an arbitration tribunal and
> the shipwrights object to going to arbitration while the boiler makers
> remain on strike.[63]

A fortnight later the RIRO was reporting that the boilermakers had
'indicated their intention to stay on strike indefinitely until the
employers took the drillers off the work on insulated spaces. A strike
lasting ten months was mentioned . . .'[64] What was more, the local
boilermakers' representative had stated that 'the position of Barrow
was being closely watched throughout the country and financial
assistance [to the strikers] was being received from other districts.
Pembroke Dock was mentioned.'[65]

Yet there was much more at issue than who should operate a
few bolt-welding machines in Barrow. For the two unions were
already squabbling over who should do what under shipbuilding
methods and technology undreamed of when the forebears of their
unions were first founded back in the late Hanoverian era.[66] And
their defensive reaction to the threat signified in turn more trouble
for British shipbuilding. As the RIRO, Manchester, reported to
London on 17 October 1949,

> the employers are apprehensive about the next major issue affecting
> shipwrights and platers. The work is described as sub-assembly.
> Sections of a ship are fabricated in the shed and taken on skids to the
> ship for assembly. An intermediate stage between the shed and the
> ship is sub-assembly. Several operations are apparently in dispute and
> each Union is said to be claiming part of the other Union's work.
> The issue appears to be a complicated one and discussion is not
> expected to produce a solution. It is anticipated that there may be a
> stoppage of work affecting shipwrights. It is stated that if this were to

occur, production would be seriously affected. In Moss's words [Moss was Vickers-Armstrong's Shipyard Director], 'Vickers will become a cockpit for the Industry . . .'[67]

In the meantime the question of stud-welding had still to be resolved. On 22 October 1949 the RIRO, Manchester, was able to report that unions and employer had agreed that a local arbitration panel should sit in Barrow Town Hall on the 26th. Only after much wrangling had the parties even concurred on the terms of reference: 'To determine the use of stud welding machines welding studs in insulated spaces.'[68]

As it happened, the Shipwrights' drillers had almost finished work on these spaces and were about to transfer their stud-welding operation to deck planking, their own unquestioned fief. Nonetheless, the dispute ended up with Barrow's equivalent of a Hollywood courtroom drama, with the Boilermakers' representative (a local alderman) at first conveniently claiming that he had not received an invitation to the hearing (not the first time he had alleged non-receipt of correspondence), and then stomping out in dudgeon simply because Vickers-Armstrong's representatives were present as observers.[69]

On 29 October the Arbitrator, Professor D. T. Jack, awarded that 'stud welding machines welding studs in insulated spaces shall be operated by drillers.'[70]

In March 1953 the two unions began to head-butt each other again, this time at the famous John Brown's Yard on Clydebank, which hoped to have the new royal yacht ready for launching in April by Queen Elizabeth II. This time it was a question of who should install a novel insulation system based on metal and fibreglass rather than wood in a new liner, the *Arcadia*.[71] Over four months the unions and the employers argued the toss, sometimes in three separate rooms while Ministry of Labour officials sought to mediate between them, and while work in the yard intermittently stopped and started. Aggrieved boilermakers at John Brown's congregated from time to time to resolve to 'stand firm': a mass of obdurate faces under flat caps (actually less flat than the shape of cowpats) against a background of the looming derricks.

The IRO (Scotland) himself was, according to an internal

Ministry of Labour minute, 'fearful of anything which would interfere with the launching of the Royal Yacht on 16/4. Such an important launching is he says a strong temptation to "some people." '[72] It further complicated the problem that at John Brown's a second strike, by platers' helpers, was also going on. Nevertheless,

> so far as the building of the Royal Yacht is concerned [reported the I.R.O. (Scotland) on 3 March], the firm have neutralised the effect of this strike by concentrating enough Platers working without Helpers on this Yacht. It appears, however, that a strike of Platers or Carpenters or Joiners or any combination of these would jeopardise the launching date which was very near.[73]

Four days later he was reporting that the Boilermakers' Society delegate was now objecting to a proposed conference because his shop stewards had discovered that the Shipwrights had fixed four plates on the disputed insulation work in the *Arcadia*. 'It transpired that the four plates had already been fixed when the dispute arose but were taken down. Evidently they had been put back surreptitiously.'[74]

Even though the new Queen was after all able to launch HMY *Britannia* on 16 April, this tragic farce was to continue for months until a compromise was finally cobbled together, and, in the sour words of the Industrial Relations Officer, Scotland, in 1955, 'the disputed work at Brown's Yard struggled to a conclusion.'[75]

However, not even such dire case-histories as this could shake the faith of union leaders that craft demarcations constituted a key competitive advantage of British shipbuilding. In March 1955 Ted Hill, General Secretary of the Boilermakers' Society and Chairman of the Ship-building Sub-Committee of the Confederation of Ship-building and Engineering Unions, said as much to the employers during a wages conference:

> You talk of demarcation. Well, my predecessors have all had a go at this, and so have yours, and it is still with us, and I suppose it will be with us when we die. There is this to be said about it. There is no doubt that the skill of the British shipyard worker is as good as anywhere in the world, and perhaps better than most, and we feel that some of the reason for this is the fact that there are these

demarcation difficulties. You have got better craftsmen, probably, than any other country in the world, and demarcations are sometimes responsible for it.[76]

Six months after this affecting statement came a fresh punch-up on the Clyde between these better craftsmen than any other country in the world. The hapless victim now was Stephen's Yard at Linthouse. Once again the quarrel was over who should do what in insulation work, and this time a third union, the National Union of Sheet Metal Workers and Braziers, joined the melee.

At a joint conference with the company and the IRO, Scotland (in the customary thankless role of would-be peacemaker), on 19 September 1955, both sides 'gave their usual historical review quoting precedents favourable to themselves',[77] while neither would agree to arbitration. They maintained this constructive position in meetings through October and November and December, when the dispute was referred to the unions' national executives for settlement.[78] This protracted exercise in institutionalized stupidity was finally resolved in April 1956 by the shipowner for whom the ship was being built. He now wanted the insulation work to be done with veneered plywood instead of sheet metal: clearly ship-wrights' work, as all conceded. Reported the IRO, Scotland,

> Veneered plywood has apparently been used successfully for this type of work in German shipyards, but for this particular vessel it is by way of an experiment for this shipowner.[79]

Meanwhile the Boilermakers and Shipwrights had squabbled again at Pembroke Dock, where R. S. Hayes had made the mistake of adding the construction of new vessels to their existing repair work, with the aim of expanding output – and employment – in the yard. But how should the minute craft demarcations in the new construction be drawn? The unions naturally could not agree. So if R. S. Hayes pleased one of them, they must alienate the other. Thus the company were forced to accept, in the words of a director, that

> there will at some stage during the new construction programme be a stoppage of work, and the firm cannot and are not prepared to allow it to take place. It is with regret, therefore, that they have

come to the conclusion not to proceed with the new construction programme in any way until these matters can be clarified.[80]

It took until the middle of October 1955 to mediate a detailed peace treaty which would allow the yard to continue to provide paid employment on building new vessels.

Just a month earlier had begun at Cammell Laird of Birkenhead the most notorious of all the 'who bores which holes in what' disputes to erupt during this fateful decade for British shipbuilding.[81]

11. 'This Long and Bitter Dispute': the Shipyards

As at John Brown's on Clydeside the casus belli was supplied by a patented system of insulation, this time in a banana ship (the SS *Leader*) being built for an American customer, the Pan-Ore Steamship Company Inc. How should the work of fixing aluminium sheets to wood grounds be divided up? On this occasion no fewer than three unions pitched into the scrimmage: the Amalgamated Society of Woodworkers (joiners), the National Union of Sheet Metal Workers and Braziers (sheet-metal workers), and the Ship Constructors' and Shipwrights' Association (drillers).[1]

The joiners struck the first blow by walking out on 12 September 1955. Five weeks later they walked back again thanks to a deal between them, the drillers of the Sheet Metal Workers and Cammell Laird mediated by the Regional Industrial Relations Officer. But the drillers objected to a separate deal by the company allotting the actual drilling of the sheets to the joiners, who had claimed that drilling aboard ship was their historic right. The shipyard manager for his part had only conceded this task to the joiners because he had it in mind that some 80 per cent of the work on the aluminium sheets would anyway be done away from the ship, cut, fitted, punched or drilled by sheet-metal workers in their shed. Only a minimum would thus be left to be carried out on shipboard. But naturally the drillers were not going to have the joiners do even this minimum. And so they now threatened a strike involving all members of the Shipwrights' Association in the yard. This 'persuaded' Cammell Laird to cancel the agreement with the joiners – who thereupon struck again on 11 November.

The usual kind of would-be peace conferences between the

belligerents chaired by Ministry of Labour officials now followed through November and December, the arguments turning on the equally usual factitious interpretations of past precedent. Did the 1912 agreement about the procedure for settling disputes by arbitration bind the Amalgamated Society of Woodworkers as well as the other shipyard unions? It appeared from their conduct that the society no longer thought so. Did not the 'demarcation book' for Liverpool and Birkenhead dating back to 1900 state that 'all insulation work is joiners' work'?[2] But did not this agreement only apply to shipwrights and joiners, excluding drillers?

After a meeting at the yard on 21 November 1955 the RIRO reported:

> It seemed from the explanations given that drillers had not in the past been called on to drill aluminium sheets on board ship because the holes were already in the sheets, having been punched or drilled by the sheet metal workers. If drilling on board had arisen drillers would have been employed.[3]

It sadly complicated these intricate discussions turning on a 'book' written in the penultimate year of the reign of Queen Victoria that the technology now in question was entirely novel – at least, in Britain:

> It was ascertained that the type of insulation work on the fruit vessel has never been undertaken before in this country. The method has, however, been used in German shipyards. It was also stated that this was the first occasion on which a complete hold in a ship has to be insulated by metal attached to metal. In doing this there will be need for a certain amount of drilling on board ship.[4]

In continuing stalemate the dispute at Cammell Laird saw out the end of the final year of the first post-war decade.

In January 1956 further attempts by the Chief Industrial Commissioner of the Ministry of Labour to arrange a joint meeting between the parties failed.[5] By now the trouble at Cammell Laird's had become a public scandal. On the 13th of the month the *Daily Mail* asked in a big black headline at the top of a long article: 'Who's to Have the Job of Boring the Holes?' Noting that '$20,000,000 contracts wait while shipyard workers argue', the article opined that the dispute would be 'Comic but for its effect on the nation's economy'. It reported that the 500 woodworkers had been out on strike almost continuously since September over an argument with some 100 drillers:

> Laughable indeed, if you have not studied your industrial history of the past few decades. But shipbuilders all – management and men alike – can never banish from their minds the ghosts of the lean times.

And what more effective way of averting a return of such lean times (it might be asked in distant hindsight) than stalling an important job for an overseas client, and so jeopardizing further contracts?

On 7 February 1956 the TUC attempted to mediate, but without joy.[6] Next day the Aluminium Development Association wrote to the Parliamentary Secretary to the Ministry of Labour on the topic of 'this wretched dispute at Cammell Lairds about the troublesome demarcation rules of the Unions', which could threaten the future use of aluminium in shipbuilding.[7] The Aluminium Development Association pointed out that the machining of aluminium could be essentially done with woodworking tools. Therefore, they wrote, a possible solution would be for the woodworkers to drill the holes when aluminium was to be used in conjunction with wood, but for the drillers to drill the holes when it was to be used in conjunction with steel, as in deckhouses. Ingenious, of course, but hardly a solution acceptable to the teak and steel intellects of the unions.

By this time, the customer for whom Cammell Laird was supposed to be building the banana ship SS *Leader* had begun to display that notorious North American impatience. On 19 January 1956 Mr F. A. Billhardt, Vice President of the Pan-Ore Steamship Company Inc., wrote to Robert Johnson, General Manager of Cammell Laird, to say that since mid-December

> we have been waiting expectantly for news that the joiner strike in your yard would be settled.
>
> This news has not been forthcoming, and we are every day becoming more concerned with the tremendous increase in charter and interest costs which we are incurring due to the delay in delivery.[8]

He estimated that this delay, from 1 December to – say – 1 March, would cost Pan-Ore some $360,000. Groaned Mr Billhardt: 'It is difficult for us to sit back and see this loss continue.' Would it be possible, he asked, 'to load all the component parts on board the ship and tow the vessel to Holland or Germany for completion, or could such an arrangement be made in England?'[9]

On 7 February 1956 the agent for the owners of another vessel, the SS *Calamares*, whose completion was likewise blocked by the hole-boring strike, also wrote bitterly to Cammell Laird with the suggestion that the work should be finished elsewhere:

> We would recommend that on completion of the machinery instal-
> lation and trials you endeavour to arrange for completion of the
> vessel by some shipyard on the Continent.
>
> The Bremer Vulkan Shipyard of Vegesack, Germany, is familiar
> with the installation of the aluminium sheathing and air ducts to be
> fitted in the CALAMARES. Three vessels with holds of similar
> construction have recently been delivered by this Shipyard to the
> satisfaction of the Owners.[10]

Cammell Laird made a point of copying these ominous letters to the Ministry of Labour headquarters in London, with a request that they be passed on to the TUC.[11]

On 7 March a deputation from the TUC went to see the Minister of Labour in person, who now appointed a Committee of Investigation under the all-purpose Professor D. T. Jack. However, the prime difficulty, according to a Ministry of Labour report, still remained 'the insistence of the A.S.W. [i.e., the joiners] that the agreement between them and the firm should be reinstated, but if that were done the other two unions would then have struck work in protest'.[12]

On 27 March the Committee submitted a report unanimously concluding that the partial and then complete strikes of the joiners were 'wholly unjustified' and 'in clear breach' of procedures under the 1912 General Demarcation Agreement.[13] On 3 April the joiners went back to work after their seven-month strike – with the question of 'who drills the holes' still unanswered and left to be negotiated under the 1912 demarcation procedure. Moreover, the strike had ended as it began, without a vote being taken among the rank and file.

When interviewed by a British newspaper, the President of Pan-Ore Inc. (owners of the *Leader*), Mr William White, failed to admire the shipyard Hampdens who with dauntless breasts had been defending alleged rights won in the industrial battles of long ago. In fact, he was quite hurtful about Cammell Laird and the unions, just because they had lost his company half a million dollars: 'The way I feel now, I wouldn't spend another nickel building ships in England. I don't ever want to hear of Birkenhead again.'[14] In his opinion, 'nobody gave a damn whether we got the ship or not, except us. All we got was excuses from the company, always more excuses, and fine words from the politicians.' To his interviewer he even cruelly quoted – 'Listen to this. It'll kill you' – the Old Etonian President of the Board of Trade (Peter Thorneycroft) describing the strike as 'deplorable and reprehensible'. Said White, 'Dig that: *deplorable and reprehensible* . . . ALL I WANTED WAS A SHIP AND ALL I GOT WAS A LOT OF FANCY GRAMMAR.'

As hot as a flame-cutter, White went on:

> This isn't the first time we've had a raw deal from Britain. In January, 1951, we placed an order for two shallow draught ore carriers of about 8,000 tons with the Burntisland Company [on the Firth of Forth]. In May, 1952, we placed an order exactly the same with some Swedish yards.
>
> What happened? One Swedish ship was delivered 21 months after signature of contract and the second, 26 months after signature.
>
> The British ships took 36 months and 52 months.

Why the delay? White proceeded remorselessly to explain why:

> The Burntisland Yard welders were on strike from March 2 to March 30, 1953. The shipwrights and shipwrights' apprentices struck May 11 to June 4. The caulkers were out from November 20 to January 14, 1954. During part of that same period the burners weren't working either. In March, 1954, the shipwrights had a slow-down to March, 1955, and the electricians had a five-week strike.[15]

Nor was White mollified by the attempt of the Commercial Minister at the British Embassy in Washington to explain how hard

Cammell Laird were now trying to make up for lost time over the SS *Leader*. As the Commercial Minister reported back to the Board of Trade in London, White was 'not prepared to forgive Cammell Laird'.[16] He quoted White as saying that

> his company would probably place their next order with Japan because they had had reports of very good workmanship there and it was possible to obtain both a firm price and a firm delivery date.[17]

It was the Chief Industrial Commissioner at the Ministry of Labour, Sir Wilfred Neden, who found the right word for this immediate consequence of the great hole-borers' strike: 'Depressing!'[18]

However, it turned out that there were more consequences still to come, these even more depressing. From 12 June 1956 onwards the drillers and joiners at Cammell Laird were at it again, over insulation work on the fruit-carrying ship *Calamares*, and this for the second time. The new stoppage provoked William White publicly to confirm that his own company had asked for bids from twenty yards in seven countries for building their next ships, but had specifically excluded Britain because of union troubles. 'I can only say that I think this shows we were right to ask for bids elsewhere. Wouldn't anyone feel the same?'[19]

Apparently someone did feel the same. On 8 August 1956 the Chairman of Niarchos (London) Ltd, speaking at Vickers-Armstrong's yard at Barrow-in-Furness at the launch of the last of ten oil-tankers ordered by Niarchos from Vickers-Armstrong, told the company:

> During the past few months we have endeavoured to negotiate with you for dry-cargo ships, bulk carriers and also tankers. But . . . you were unable to approach the prices and deliveries obtainable elsewhere.
>
> As a result we have in the past 15 months or so booked orders in other countries for nearly one million dead weight tons.[20]

And on the topic of the Cammell Laird strikes he had this to say:

> So far as I can see, the only result of this long and bitter dispute is that so many holes have been drilled by so many people in the hull

of the ship of prosperity that the unfortunate craft is in danger of foundering.[21]

This was – at least in the short term – an exaggeration. But how much of an exaggeration?

In 1953 Britain was building 36.6 per cent of the global shipping tonnage under construction – nearly three and a half times as much as Germany, her nearest rival.[22] In terms of exports of ships, Britain was building 31.2 per cent of the world total, as against Germany's 20.4 per cent, the Netherlands' 16.0 per cent and Sweden's 7.9 per cent.[23] The industry's existing order book, at 5.8 million gross tons, was more than four times its annual output.[24]

On the face of it, all this marked an astonishing revival after the death-bed years of the pre-war slump. Yet in truth the revival had owed itself less to the industry's own efficiency and creative design[25] than, firstly, to the naval demands of rearmament and war, and, secondly, to the need of the Allies in wartime and thereafter of all maritime nations in peacetime, to replace the huge tonnage of shipping sunk by the U-boat and surface raiders. It had owed itself no less to Britain's head-start after the war while Germany's yards were at a standstill and other European yards were recovering from bomb damage.

An altogether bleaker picture of British shipbuilding's current efficiency and forward vision emerges from the evidence given to a Court of Inquiry in January 1954.

In December 1953 the Confederation of Shipbuilding and Engineering Unions (the CSEU) announced – no doubt to loud cheers in Bremen and Yokohama – that as leverage behind their current claim for a 15 per cent increase in the minimum wage rates in the ship-building and engineering industries, they would impose a national ban on overtime and piecework in shipyards from 18 January 1954, and, even more damaging, throughout engineering as a whole.[26]

The Minister of Labour in Churchill's Conservative Government, Sir Walter Monckton, unsurprisingly concluded that the threatened ban would have 'serious consequences to the economy of the country generally, to our export trade, and to the mainten-ance of full employment . . .'[27] He therefore set up two Courts of

Inquiry with identical memberships and with Lord Justice Morris as their president: one for shipbuilding and the other for general engineering.[28] Recourse to such bodies had long served as the British industrial equivalent of referring a threat to world peace to the League of Nations in order to dodge a painful decision as to whether or not to go to war. The device worked again in the present case, for the CSEU now graciously called off their threatened overtime ban.

In their evidence to the Court investigating the shipbuilding claim the CSEU displayed a smug expectation that the industry's current world leadership would continue; after all, just look at the size of the industry's order book. Such optimism justified their argument that the shipbuilding employers could well afford to fork out a 15 per cent rise. It was the CSEU's contention that, far from company reserves being needed for modernization instead of being available as a jackpot for the workers, 'in a number of yards no further modernisation was necessary, because they were as efficient as any in the world'.[29] Were they really? In point of fact, British shipbuilding firms were investing on their fixed assets only some £4 million a year – barely enough to cover normal wear and tear, let alone match the current huge programmes of modernization and development in German and Japanese yards.[30]

Nevertheless, in further ignorance or complacency the CSEU spokesman, Ted Hill, even assured the Court of Inquiry that he

> had studied American shipbuilding techniques, but felt that this country had little to learn from them. The employers had made much of the alleged advantage of Continental competitors due to double shift working [NB: as against the British single shift], but the higher proportion of workers on piece work in Great Britain – the highest in the world – must be offset against this, and probably made the difference in costs between the two very small.[31]

Hill went on to assert that many of the new techniques which had raised productivity, 'such as improved methods of prefabrication and welding', could not have been introduced 'without the willing co-operation of the workers'.[32] This amazing statement hardly squared with his own remark to a productivity conference in March 1953 that he 'would not lift a finger to increase productivity' unless (in so many words) his members got their rake-off, or with the remark of a member of his National Executive at the same conference that 'Productivity Committees would be wasting their time in shipyards and that they had better look into the men's complaints of over-mechanisation . . .'[33] Over-mechanization! Indeed, far from offering 'willing co-operation' the boilermakers were, in the judgement of the RIRO (Newcastle) back in April 1953, 'officially resolved to be thoroughly awkward in the field of productivity'.[34]

This resolve did not hinder Ted Hill in now rejecting the shipyard employers' argument to the Court of Inquiry that, with many orders already being lost to foreign competition, a wage increase would price the industry out of export markets. He contended that where buyers of ships placed their orders 'was determined very largely by the length of delivery dates. The size of the British industry's order book entailed later deliveries and led to more orders being placed abroad.'[35] So that was all right, then. But in fact the size of the British order book should not have been so much a cause for self-satisfaction as for self-criticism. For what it really signified was a production process choked by inefficiency. In 1956–57, the year after the great hole-borers' strikes on the Clyde and at Cammell Laird, it would be taking twice as long to build a comparable vessel in a British yard as in a Japanese yard.[36]

In contrast to Ted Hill's self-interested complacency the spokesman for the Federation of Shipbuilding Employers, Sir John Boyd (the Vice President), no less self-interestedly harped on the keenness of the foreign rivalry now faced by his industry:

> our most serious competitors were Continental countries, particularly Germany, Holland and Sweden. These countries had the advantage of double shift working paid at ordinary rates, and could offer both lower prices and quicker delivery in many cases. Not only were they attracting orders for new ships which might have gone to British firms, but a considerable number of repair jobs . . . had gone abroad, particularly in the last three months of 1953.[37]

Orders for new ships received in 1953, said he, amounted to little more than 500,000 tons or less than half a year's work, and from that total about 200,000 tons had to be subtracted in respect of cancelled orders. Moreover, twenty-eight firms had booked no new orders at all.[38] Sir John Boyd omitted to say what part in this sad story might have been played by the calibre of shipbuilding management and by the paucity of investment in new plant.

The Court of Inquiry themselves sombrely remarked in their report: 'While any opinions as to the future must be uncertain we think that recent cancellations and the falling off in new orders constitute a warning which it would be imprudent to ignore.'[39]

What then would an increase of 15 per cent in the minimum wage rate do for the industry's future world-market prospects? Indeed, what would it imply for the wider national interest? By way of answer the Court did no more than wring their hands about 'upward thrusts in the inflationary spiral', about the dangers of 'imperilling our export trade', and about the broader menace of 'an accelerating movement of wages, costs and prices', not least in relation to 'something very like an annual cycle of wage claims'.[40]

But just the same, they still finally proposed a wage increase of one-third of the original claim. Since such an increase would add at least 3 per cent to the price of contracts placed in British yards,[41] it would hardly help either to avert cancellations of existing contracts or to win new orders. Nor, for that matter, could it prove a very effective brake on 'accelerating movements of wages, costs and prices'. The report of this Court of Inquiry was published as a White Paper in February 1954. As it happened, 1954 turned out to be the year when Germany sailed past Britain in annual tonnage of exports of new ships.[42] The following year, in a grimly appropriate end to a decade in which the shipyards had suffered from the worst strike record of any single manufacturing industry,[43] Britain would be outsailed in exports by Japan as well.[44]

Thus to the shipyard unions belonged the honour of being the first to help destroy a great British industry's post-war leadership in world markets. Yet their brother unions were apparently keen to do the same for the whole wide field of engineering.

★

When industrial unrest occurs in so important and diverse an industry as that of engineering, the economy of the whole country must be disturbed and the whole community involved. The public are therefore properly and naturally concerned.[45]

So pronounced the report of the second Court of Inquiry set up in December 1953, in this instance appointed by the Minister of Labour to investigate the demand for a 15 per cent increase in the minimum wage rates throughout the engineering industries. For 'engineering' now constituted by far Britain's most important industrial sector and earner of foreign currency, employing about 15 per cent of the total working population, and accounting for 41 per cent of British exports by value as against 26 per cent in 1938.[46] The present wage claim embraced 4,260 firms large and small spread across twenty-five different industries, from machine tools to aircraft; locomotives to scientific instruments; electrical machinery to textiles; valves and electric lamps to boilerhouse plant; and from agricultural machinery to what the Standard Industrial Classification quaintly still described as 'wireless apparatus'. The target of the CSEU's wage claim was therefore the very technologies on which depended whether or not Britain could hold on to her post-war place as the second industrial nation after America, and, for that matter, meet the manifold costs of her pretension to be a world power.

For its part, the CSEU wonderfully represented the higgledy-piggledy structure of British trade unionism, as warren-like as an old British industrial works patched, altered and extended piecemeal since the first bricks were laid in the Victorian age. For the Confederation represented no fewer than thirty-nine different unions and about 1,250,000 workers, of which some 500,000 belonged to the Amalgamated Engineering Union (over half that union's total membership), 100,000 to the Transport and General Workers' Union and 95,000 to the National Union of General and Municipal Workers.[47] A 'confederation' these thirty-nine unions might be for the purpose of a wage claim, but in day-to-day factory life they only signified fragmentation, that rich compost in which germinated like weeds the shop-floor squabbles so peculiar to British industry. In contrast, a single union (I. G. Metall) represented all German engineering workers.

As the CSEU's claim serves to illustrate, the pay structures in British engineering were just as much the higgledy-piggledy consequence of long industrial history as the unions themselves. The present demand was for a 15 per cent increase in the 'consolidated time rate'. Its application to time-workers' rates was thus simple enough: 15 per cent. But what about pieceworkers? Their pay embraced at least four main elements – the national minimum basic rate, the pieceworker's percentage or bonus, the piecework sup-plement, and overtime payments.[48] What was more, pieceworkers' pay was also linked, in the words of the eventual report of the Court of Inquiry, to 'the national or local consolidated minimum time rate, inasmuch as overtime premiums are calculated on that rate'.[49] Quite apart from complicating the present national claim, such intricacies provided yet more rich compost wherein petty local disputes could erupt overnight, in this case over bonuses or overtime payments or comparabilities.

Between 1938 and 1953 there had taken place twelve bargaining battles between the engineering employers and unions. Only on five occasions had a final deal been willingly struck: otherwise the disputes had had to be referred either to the National Arbitration Tribunal or (in 1948) to a Court of Inquiry.[50] As the report of the present Court glumly noted,

> In all cases these [wage negotiations] have resulted from demands for increases put forward by the unions; no wage advances have been volunteered by the employers. Wage negotiations seem in general to have been hard and protracted, giving rise sometimes to periods of tension and uneasiness, and as often as not have resulted in a deadlock which has been resolved by compulsory arbitration.

Wherein lay the strength of the CSEU's present claim, other than in the threat to jam the cog-wheels of the industries that contributed 41 per cent of British exports by value?[51] It fell to Jack Tanner, National President of the Amalgamated Engineering Union, to explain. He was the man who in 1944, the climactic year of the Second World War, had pronounced that inefficiencies of produc-tion and waste of man and machine were 'largely a matter of indifference to the worker . . . his prime concern being to fight for better wages and working conditions'.[52]

Now he argued to the Court of Inquiry that between 1946 and 1952 productivity in engineering had risen by some 50 per cent. He arrived at this figure by dividing output in those two years by the number in the workforce,[53] a simple sum which ignored the fact that 1946 had been a period of difficult transition from war production to peace when national output as a whole remained well below the pre-war level.

While Tanner accepted the employers' contention that better methods and new machines had boosted output, he breathtakingly pleaded that 'the successful introduction of new techniques depended on the wholehearted co-operation of the workers', and that the unions had 'won over the majority of the workers to co-operate in many of the measures designed to increase productivity'.[54] But, keen to have it both ways, Tanner then asserted that 'even if the increase in productivity had been entirely attributable to improved techniques and machinery, the workers would still be entitled to share in the proceeds arising from it . . .' By this he meant a rake-off over and above their automatic increases under the payment-by-results system that largely prevailed in the industry.

And, after all, could not the industry well afford to hand it out? Had not the industry's gross profits ('gross' making a more impressive figure than 'net') doubled between 1947 and 1951?[55] Had not the reserves of the 100 main companies in engineering risen by 1952 to more than double their nominal capital? Could not the wage claim be met in part by dipping into these swollen reserves? Hardly worth mentioning, of course, that *net* profit in 1952 after taxation amounted to less than a third of gross profit,[56] or that some two-thirds of the net profit was ploughed back into the industry rather than dished out to shareholders, or that the issued capital of companies was often stated in pre-war values while the post-war rise of their reserves was recorded in depreciated pounds. Also hardly worth mentioning was that, as the Court of Inquiry came to agree, 'reserves' represented working capital rather than liquid assets available to be handed out for such purposes as wage increases.[57]

Yet the CSEU's sophistry over profits and productivity took second place to their main argument, which, it turned out, had less to do with the engineering industry's current performance and prospects than with a belief in a kind of 'Divine Right' of workers. For they contended that their members deserved bigger pay packets simply because 'the rise in the cost of living during recent years . . . had led to a fall in the real wages of the majority of workers in the industry'.[58] To prove this contention the CSEU dextrously flashed comparative cost-of-living statistics and figures of average earnings going back to 1947. But whether the chosen comparisons happened to be true or specious[59] hardly mattered, for they were quite irrelevant to the essential question of what an export industry up against ruthless challenge could afford to disburse.

In fairness to the CSEU, however, it must be remembered that workpeople in all industries now shared this extraordinary delusion that they were owed a 'fair' wage no matter what the financial circumstances of their employer and no matter what their own restrictive practices. The general puzzle posed to Government by this delusion was well summed up by a Treasury minute in January 1955 on the particular case of a threatened rail strike:

> The issue presents itself to the ordinary man and woman as whether or not the Government and the Transport Commission can find some way of paying railwaymen a rate of wage nearer to what are now socially accepted standards. In fact the issue is much more whether or not the railwaymen will cease obstructing those measures which would enable their higher wage to be economic as well as 'fair'. But this has not been brought home.[60]

To the CSEU's partial credit, however, their evidence to the 1953 Court of Inquiry did not altogether ignore the question of the present and future competitiveness of British engineering in world markets. Nonetheless, it remained their comfortable belief that 'failing a world slump, there was no need to worry about export prospects for British engineering goods, and that the [wage] increase claimed would certainly not price them out of world markets . . .'[61] In the CSEU's judgement, British production costs were '*little if any higher*' (added emphasis) than those of competitors.[62]

> Difficulties in the export trade, insofar as they existed, were to be attributed not so much to costs as to our inability to grant extended credit terms, to ineffective export promotion, and other such factors.
>
> The employers had referred to lost orders. It was necessary to point out that in respect of one order from India for £11 millions-worth of locomotives which had been lost to continental competitors, the reasons were not only price but delivery dates.[63]

Touché! And it was touché yet again when the unions cited the journal *Engineering* as averring in January 1953 that there was a danger that 'industry in the United Kingdom, in contrast to the United States, will continue to retain outmoded machinery and to maintain itself in a competitive world only at the expense of the standard of living of the workpeople'.[64]

The Engineering and Associated Employers' National Federation failed to share the CSEU's smugness either about the industry's ability to carry a 3.25 per cent increase in its overall wages bill or about its future prospects in general.[65] On the contrary, the employers were all too aware that foreign rivals had now got this flagship of Britain's post-war exports well within range, not least because in 1951–3 she had been slowed by the drag-chain of post-Korea rearmament. The employers told the Court of Inquiry:

> export orders received had declined in value from £648 millions in 1950/51 to £564 millions in 1951/52 (a drop of 13 per cent) and to £450 millions in 1952/53, a further fall of 20 per cent . . . in 1953 orders to a value of over £50 millions had been lost to U.S., German, Japanese, Swiss and Belgian competitors, in respect of locomotives, textile machinery, electrical equipment, boilers, cranes, petroleum oil-well equipment, railway equipment, carriages and wagons, presses and miscellaneous engineering equipment . . . The Federation was most apprehensive of the ability of the industry even to maintain its exports if wages and prices were increased.[66]

So yet again the employers appeared to be paying a remarkable tribute to the success of their own entrepreneurship.

The Court of Inquiry, picking its way between the opposing cases, guesstimated that the cost of conceding the union's claim 'would be of the order of £50 to £60 millions annually'.[67] This would raise the industry's overall costs by some 8.2 per cent, and add about 3.5 per cent to the total sales value of its products.[68] On what was perhaps the most important of all the questions at issue the Court returned an especially helpful and clear-cut judgement: 'What it [the granting of the claim] would mean to the majority of engineering exports, we cannot say.'[69]

They did however add that it must be 'clear that any appreciable rise in costs if it could not be met out of profits would have a material effect on that trade'.[70]

But what about the national interest as a whole, that matter naturally of deep concern to the lads in a myriad local engineering shops? Opined the Court:

> any considerable or general increase in costs which might prejudice our export trade must be fraught with peril to our economy. These are considerations which will be of general acceptance. They are among the factors to be kept in mind when considering the present dispute.[71]

Furthermore:

> The perils of inflation and of adding impetus to its spiral effect are, of course, fully and widely recognised especially at a time when it was [sic] reasonable to hope that a halt had been called in the upward trend of prices.[72]

Despite all these cavils (and, it appears, irrespective of the ability of British industry to pay up out of profits), the Court nevertheless thought that 'great heed must be paid' to the effect of 'a material rise in the cost of living' in the case of 'the lower wage earning groups.'[73]

How then did the Court finally balance its generous sense of equity against the stern realities of the world market?

> ... we are agreed that there is justification for some increase in consolidated time rates but not to the extent claimed. We hope that the parties will resume negotiations with a view to agreeing some increase ... As a pointer which we hope will assist them, our view is that it should be something in the region of one third of the amount claimed.[74]

Why one-third rather than, say, one-half, or one-sixth, or nothing at all? A member of the Court later explained why to a friend:

> I think whatever the parties decide among themselves, we were right in our 'pointer' not only on the merits of the case, which, after all, was our main consideration, but also psychologically. I say this because if we had suggested one-half, cynics and others would have

said we had merely split the difference, the first rule of compromise, etc. This would not only have been bad in itself, but would have given further weight to the procedure of asking for more than is justified with a reasonable certainty of getting one-half.[75]

A fudge, then! But be the fudge ever so crafty, it nonetheless still implied a rise of 5 per cent in the consolidated time rate for CSEU members: well above the current rate of inflation of 3 per cent,[76] with 'me-too' claims from other workers expected to follow inevitably.[77] It signified an inevitable rise in the prices of British engineering products:[78] good news for Britain's ever more formidable competitors.

Nor was this all. By its recommended fudge of an inflationary rise in a key sector like engineering the Court of Inquiry could only make worse a national problem which it had itself recognized:

there is apparently being established something very like an annual cycle of wage claims — a process which must surely accelerate the movement [of wages, costs and prices] . . .[79]

What with their flatulent wage costs and their fractious workforces it might be thought that Britain's vanguard exporting industries were handicapped enough. But no, they also suffered from discontent elsewhere in the sullen British scene. For ever since the war such discontent had curbed output of the nation's basic fuel; it had again and again slammed the gates to overseas markets shut.

12. 'Custom Versus Development': Coalfields and the Docks

Ever since the mid-Victorian age the coal owners had been regarded as the most villainous of all the bloated, be-watchchained, cigar-smoking capitalists in top hats who lived off the sweated labour of the working man – not least because the victims of their exploitation had been those muscular heroes of labour, the miners. But when the flag of the 'socialized' National Coal Board was hoisted at each colliery on Vesting Day, 1 January 1947, to the exultant cheers of watching miners and their families, a new era was supposed to have dawned. For now the mines belonged to 'the nation'. Surely, therefore, the miner would now respond to the nation's desperate post-war need for coal in domestic grates, power stations and gasworks, and as an export that could rescue the balance of payments?

But 'socialization' (the Labour Government's preferred term for nationalization) had in fact changed nothing, nor would it except in the slowest of motion.[1] The industry was still that haphazard detritus of nearly two centuries described by the Reid Report of 1945 – some modern, mechanized, low-cost fields and collieries, but too many of the rest positively antique in kit, scale and methods, their coal highly expensive to produce, and yet three-fifths of national output.[2] Inherited from wartime was a national structure cumbersomely bureaucratic, over-centralized, remote from the frontline realities. Still running the pits under the new flag were the same old pit managers, men so often second-rate in personal calibre and professional education, stiffly authoritarian in style.[3] The pit itself remained as hard, dirty, health-destroying and perilous a way of life as ever. The community of the pit village, for its part, remained just as self-sufficient and inward-looking, its outlook still determined by the prideful memory of past struggle and the sour remembrance of past exploitation – worse, past defeat – at the hands of 'management'.

In that very first summer of socialization (it was also the summer of the great sterling convertibility crisis) the miners at Grimethorpe and other Yorkshire collieries, the heart of Arthur Scargill's barony in the 1980s, downed picks over a two-foot increase in the daily stint for face-workers. By the beginning of September 1947 no fewer than forty-six pits in Yorkshire were affected, with thirty-three brought completely to a standstill while the sullen throngs of pickets kept guard beneath motionless winding gear.[4] The miners, reported Shinwell, the Minister of Fuel and Power, 'were in an ugly mood'.[5] Appeals by him and by the leaders of the National Union of Miners fell on deaf Yorkshire ears. Only in the middle of September did the disgruntled strikers go back.[6]

These outbreaks proved merely the entracte for a decade of sporadic strikes or go-slows afflicting a variety of coalfields, and ranging in number between 1,528 in 1948 (costing 1 million tons of production) and 3,771 in 1956 (costing 2.1 million tons).[7] However, major strikes (those each involving between some 1,700 men, as in both 1953 and 1954, and 22,000, as in 1949) accounted for only a tiny fraction of the annual grand totals: six at the minimum (in 1951), and sixteen at the maximum (in 1947).[8] The tally of stoppages thus overwhelmingly represented sudden detonations of local grievances, when 100–200 men might walk out for a couple of days or so.[9] Since the coal industry's origins lay back in the very dawn of the Industrial Revolution, it particularly suffered from those bizarre complexities of wage structure so common in Britain, some grades of worker being on piece-rate and others on day-rate. In the collieries as in the shipyards and the engineering shops these complexities provided the lush climate wherein grievances could swiftly germinate.[10]

But more insidiously harmful to coal output than overt trouble was absenteeism, a deeply worrying feature of the industry even in wartime.[11] In the first five years of nationalization the rate of absenteeism across the entire labour force ranged between 11.5 and 12.4 per cent.[12] According to a report in October 1950 by the

Minister of Fuel and Power in the Labour Government (Philip Noel-Baker), absenteeism remained 'specially high in certain pits and certain areas'. In consequence, noted he, overall output per manshift (even though improving year by year) had still only reached 1.21 tons.[13] This compares with the 1938 figure for the Ruhr of 1.55 tons.[14] As Noel-Baker pointed out to Cabinet colleagues,

> Absenteeism often disorganises production planning by its irregularity, and thus reduces average output per manshift. If absenteeism could be 'regularised', e.g., if the miners could be persuaded to give notice of when they proposed to absent themselves, its effects could be better controlled. Without prejudice to their efforts to reduce the total absenteeism, the [National Coal] Board are considering where it could be regularised in this kind of way. The problem is one of great complexity and closely related to the whole problem of leisure and holidays . . .[15]

That both management and Government could believe that the only answer to wholesale skiving lay in giving it official recognition only serves to reveal their helplessness in a era of 'full employment' and of the need for coal at all costs. But what else could they do? They could, and did, try to render the miner's lot less harsh by providing more houses in pit villages and equipping more pits with showers and laundries.

Nevertheless, in 1950 alone 10,000 face-workers were expected to leave the industry for cleaner, safer jobs.[16] Crafty buggers, who could blame them? As the Minister of Fuel and Power reminded his colleagues in October 1950, falling manpower in the coal industry had been a 'secular trend' for over thirty years.

> It has, however, been greatly accentuated by full employment, which has given opportunities of work at good wages to many men who would otherwise have entered the mines . . . And with the competing claims of the armament industries we must expect the situation to deteriorate further.[17]

Then what about fattening the miners' pay packets as an encouragement to stay in the industry and wield their picks more zealously? In January 1952 (the winter of the economic crisis brought on by rearmament), Lord Leathers, the new Conservative Secretary of State for the Co-ordination of Transport, Fuel and Power, was hoping that a recent wages agreement with the miners, 'concluded in an extremely good atmosphere', made it 'favourable for a special approach' that he was proposing to make to miners' leaders for a rise in output.[18]

Why was he making this special approach? Because of a 'very serious' gap of 8.6 million tons between the coal industry's expected output and the nation's expected requirements of coal that year.[19] Britain would have to import American coal in 1952 if the 'politically dangerous'[20] contingency of a severe winter and a breakdown in householders' supplies was to be avoided.

By April it seemed that Leathers' approach had worked. Thanks to the recruitment of 25,000 new miners the prospect gleamed of raising output by 14 million tons in 1953–54.[21] But no: output in the latter part of 1952 fell instead, not because of the inexperience of the new recruits but because of a 'relaxing of effort' by the old hands.[22] Two years later annual absenteeism among workers at the coalface, where a shift meant sustained hard labour amid the lethal dust and the oppressive heat, had reached 14.36 per cent.[23] And every 1 per cent rise in absenteeism signified a yearly loss of about 1 million tons of output.[24]

On top of this, outright disputes were costing an average of around 1 million tons of coal annually. In fact, in 1954, when total output was nearly 1 million tons less than in 1952, a two-week strike in Yorkshire alone cost the industry 1 million tons.[25] In 1955 deep-mined output was actually lower than in 1951,[26] not least owing to the loss of well over 3 million tons of production through strikes. Nearly a third of this total was contributed by one strike starting in the Doncaster area and affecting eighty-four pits. What great grievance had provoked this rebellion? The answer: coal fillers' piece-rates; a revision of fillers' price lists, pit by pit, being under discussion.[27]

When lost output both through skiving and through strikes is added together, it is clear that the industry was falling some 12–13 million tons a year short of its potential output even in its present largely out-of-date condition. Those lost 12–13 million tons a year would have eliminated that chronic shortfall in the supplies of coal needed by power stations, gasworks, railways, factories, and homes which so perturbed Labour and Conservative cabinets alike.[28] They would have boosted exports to a coal-hungry post-war world, so doing much to shore up the precarious pound sterling. And if Bevin, Churchill and Eden had been able to carry an extra hod or two of coal in their luggage, their attempts to uphold Britain's 'prestige', 'influence' and 'status' as 'the third power in the world' must surely have carried greater weight.

As it was, the average annual tonnage exported in the period 1947–55 was little more than a third of the 1938 total, and, perhaps even more telling, less than half the 1889 total.[29] Worse, as the post-war decade neared its end, Britain was still having to bring in coal from abroad in order to make good supplies of certain grades to her own home users. In December 1954 the Minister of Fuel and Power was proposing imports totalling 4.2 million tons for the first four months of 1955 alone.[30] As his Labour predecessor had justly written back in July 1951, 'to import coal into England is a lamentable confession of failure. It is a disastrously wasteful use of foreign exchange . . .'[31]

Yet even if the miners had dug more coal, getting it to the overseas customer would have meant facing the same hazard as every British export – the British docker, even more personally strike-prone than the miner himself; indeed more personally strike-prone than any other group of workers.[32]

It was only three weeks after Nazi Germany's unconditional surrender on 8 May 1945 that the London dockers mutinied for the first time in the post-war era, when men at the Royal Docks began a 'go-slow' over changes from wartime work patterns to peacetime. Through June, July and August the go-slow spread to other docks along the Thames. With the hands now suffering from what a Dock Labour Board report described as 'an extremely unsettled and inflammable state of mind',[33] less flammable soldiers had to be sent in to unload urgently needed cargoes of timber. In October 1945 more trouble detonated in the Port of London. This same month 40,000 dockers on Merseyside walked out for nearly four weeks, their urgent tasks of unloading being performed by 21,000 soldiers.[34]

These early troubles in the docks served to provoke the new

Labour Government into re-enacting Lloyd George's abhorred Emergency Powers Act of 1920, and then, in March 1946, into setting up a civil-service apparatus to prepare contingency plans for dealing with industrial 'emergencies'. This was the Whitehall euphemism for possible major disruptions of national life by the working class who had loyally and hopefully voted Labour into power in 1945. Thanks to a truck drivers' strike in January 1947, disrupting road transport in the midst of that Arctic winter, the Cabinet decided to set up their own Emergencies Committee, chaired by the Home Secretary. The new committee's given tasks were 'To supervise the preparation of plans for providing and maintaining in any emergency supplies and services essential to the life of the community; and in any emergency to co-ordinate action for this purpose.'[35]

It had been the Labour Government's belief on coming into office in 1945 that the habitual bloody-mindedness of the dockers stemmed from the peculiar dockland system of casual labour. This dated back to the era when the Thames, the Avon and the Mersey had bristled with the masts and spars of densely moored sailing ships. It had thereafter been adopted in the vast new docks created by the genius of Victorian engineers to accommodate the steamships of the greatest trading nation in the world. Under the system a throng of dockers would turn up at the gates each day hoping for work, some then to be hired, some to be humiliatingly turned away without hope of reward. During the Second World War the system had been temporarily replaced by the Dock Labour Scheme, introduced by Ernest Bevin as Minister of Labour. This guaranteed every docker a weekly wage in return for 'attendance' whether or not there was work for him on a particular day. In 1946 casual labour was ended for good by the Labour Government's Dock Labour Regulation Act, a development of Bevin's wartime scheme. So never again would dockers' families have to live precariously on the edge of desperate poverty.

Yet it did not lie within the power of the Labour Government similarly to modernize the dockers' tribal mentality, maimed as it had been by past exploitation and insecurity, and hardened by memories of struggle going back to the great London dock strike of 1889 for a wage of 6d. an hour.

In March 1947 there began the dockers' first large-scale try in the post-war era at barring Britain's main gates. This attempt proved inadvertently well timed to trip up an overstretched economy already tottering from the effects of the dreadful winter of 1946–7, and now faced with the obligation under the terms of the 1945 American loan to render sterling freely convertible into any currency, including dollars, from 15 July.[36]

True to British industrial form, this major crisis was ignited by a parochial gripe. On 24 March dockers in the port of Glasgow struck because, on the authority of the Minister of Transport, 500 men had been made redundant (270 of them being selected because known to be shirkers) out of a workforce of 3,400, on the score of the reduction in the port's traffic since its wartime peak as a terminal for Atlantic convoys.[37] This strike, like all strikes in every industry at the time, was illegal under the still-extant Order 1305 of 1940 enforcing settlement of disputes by arbitration. By 5 April the RIRO (Scotland) was reporting that sixty ships were now stuck in the Clyde awaiting discharge of cargoes, so causing their owners 'serious financial loss' and inflicting 'serious inconvenience on industry'.[38] On 6 April the Scottish Transport and General Workers' Union held a mass meeting in Govan Town Hall, that favoured venue for letting off righteous indignation. The General Secretary, Michael Byrne, told his audience:

> this is a national issue, with the sacking of our 500 men as a test case. A leading Shipowner has stated that there will be 14,000 redundant dockers at British Ports within the next year. If we are beaten here, the men at other docks can pack it in when it comes to their turn.[39]

Six union apostles thereupon went off to preach the word at various English ports. In Liverpool this elicited a resolution supporting the Glasgow men 'in their fight' and calling for the Ministry of Labour to set up an inquiry into their case.[40] But no strike. Never mind: the apostles had better luck in London, where on 28 April some 10,000 members of the National Amalgamated Stevedores' and Dockers' Union and of the Watermen, Lightermen, Tugmen and Bargemen's Union came out in sympathy. Two days later the Minister of Transport, Alfred Barnes, reported to the new Cabinet Emergencies Committee:

> Of the 124 ships in the Thames, 27 are fully manned, 22 are under-manned and 75 are idle. There are 26 food ships, of which 9 are under-manned and 17 are idle. The strikers include various specialised categories of men, such as corn porters, coal porters and deal porters, resulting in a complete cessation of the discharge of grain ships, colliers and timber ships.[41]

Worse still, at a time when rations were more meagre than during the war, there would be immobilized in the port of London within a week (so another Whitehall committee was informed) sixty ships carrying 200,000 tons of foodstuffs, including 7,500 tons of perishable foods in danger of spoiling.[42]

From the early days of the Glasgow strike soldiers had been unloading rationed foodstuffs. Now, reported the Minister of Transport, they were to do the same in London. But even if port-operating troops were brought over from Hamburg to bring the military labour force up to about 400, this 'would be quite inadequate to cope with the number of ships awaiting discharge in London and might, of course, if introduced, result in an extension of the strike to members of the Transport and General Workers' Union'.[43]

Lamented the Minister:

> The continued immobilisation of shipping is involving serious waste of shipping resources, which can only be made good, if at all, by chartering foreign ships for dollars, and will dislocate our import programmes for timber, paper and other essential materials, besides food.[44]

In Glasgow, the General Secretary of the Scottish T&GWU had meanwhile been explaining in public why his union would refuse a request by the Regional Port Director to hold a ballot vote:

> It is quite out of [his] province to suggest such a vote. We could have taken a ballot on the redundancy issue at the very beginning, but we chose instead to ventilate the whole position by taking strike action.[45]

On 28 April the Ministry of Labour and National Service issued a conciliatory press statement promising that if the Glasgow men returned to work any discharged dockers who were pre-war dockers, estimated to be 204, would be reinstated; the remaining 296 can be given work without guarantee pending enquiry by the National Joint Council into the present labour position at the Port.[46]

The statement further expressed the minister's hope that 'the grave consequences' of disrupting trade 'at a most critical juncture in the Nation's economic position' would be 'fully appreciated by all concerned . . .'

Would this attempt at appeasement succeed? There now followed one of those episodes of confusion, anger and attempted manipulation so characteristic of the conduct of British strikes. At a three-hour mass meeting of the Dockers' Branch of the Scottish T&GWU in Glasgow on 1 May 1947 the union Executive Committee recommended a return to work on the basis of the Ministry's press statement. But the Committee of the Dockers' Branch objected strongly, demanding that all 500 discharged workers should be fully reinstated. The union President then called for a vote by show of hands, which – so those on the platform alleged – backed the Executive Committee's recommendation by a majority of 14. However, the Dockers' Branch Committee now objected that the vote was invalid because many of the storemen present at the meeting (but not members of the T&GWU) had put their hands up. After some ill-tempered argument a fresh vote by show of hands was taken, yielding a majority of 175 against the recommendation to return to work. This being to the evident fury of the Executive Committee,[47] they later decided to hold a ballot vote at the union's three sub-offices in Glasgow between 9 a.m. and 12 noon on Saturday and Sunday, 3 and 4 May. Why just the mornings and over two days? Because, according to a Ministry of Labour internal note, the union Executive 'feel that the ballot will not be completed by noon on Sat. [sic] and they cannot risk continuing after the pubs open!'[48]

In the ballot the recommendation to return to work was carried by no fewer than 1,596 votes.[49] By this time the London dockers had already gone back.

These timely outcomes saved the Cabinet Emergencies Committee from having to implement (at least for the time being) the decision taken at their meeting on 1 May to prosecute those responsible for strikes illegal under Order 1305.[50] All that remained was to appoint, on 27 May, a Committee of Investigation to 'inquire into the size of labour force required for the Port of Glasgow'.[51] It sat from 11 to 13 June.

The arguments put to the Committee by employers and union serve neatly to encapsulate Britain's general problem of adaptation as an industrial society. The spokesman for the employers pointed out that during the war 'the use of mechanical gear was developed to a very marked extent in the handling of general cargo, and more modern appliances were made available for the handling of bulk cargoes; and he contended that the numbers of men employed in the gang could, and should have been, reduced'.[52] In contrast, the Union's General Secretary (Michael Byrne) rested his case for the existing workforce of 3,400 partly on ingenious calculations of men, hours and tonnages,[53] but largely on historical precedent. He first cited the opinion in 1937 by the Secretary of the Standing Advisory Committee on the Port Industry that some 4,000 men were required to work the port. He then quoted an explanatory memorandum by the Minister of Transport in March 1941 in regard to the wartime Dock Labour Scheme, which stated that arrangements under the scheme had been made 'in relation to the *circumstances and traditions prevailing in the port* [added emphasis]'.[54] And by way of a clincher he referred to the wartime Act of Parliament guaranteeing the restoration in peacetime of pre-war trade customs and practices.

The Committee of Investigation for their part finally pronounced that the size of the labour force required in the port of Glasgow was 2,900 – signifying redundancies of, yes, 500 from the present workforce of 3,400.[55]

But the Committee's decision far from solved the problem. For the next nine months the dismissals were held in abeyance while the interested parties vainly sought to agree on a definition of 'Port Labour Work'.[56] When at long last the Glasgow Dock Labour Board announced that redundant dockers would be dismissed by the end of April 1948, and if necessary without the union's agreement, a union official warned that 'there was grave danger that a complete stoppage at the Docks would follow'.[57] So yet again the dismissals were postponed, this time on through May and June, pending the rigmarole of 'discussion at national level' and a tribunal's hearing of appeals against dismissal. For a whole year, therefore, the port of Glasgow had had to go on carrying some 17 per cent more dockers than it needed for efficient operation.

By an agreeable irony, those on the redundancy list who had only become dockers since the outbreak of the Second World War objected to the union's own policy of 'last in, first out', on the score that they, the later recruits, 'have clean records with no convictions [for pilfering] and are being sacked so that other Dockers and their sons – "hereditary dockers" – can stay in their jobs'.[58]

All this was, however, no more than the smouldering stumps of last year's scrub fire. By now the docks were ablaze with the far more dangerous discontents of 1948, a year when Britain incurred a net dollar-and-gold deficit of £254 million in the first six months alone,[59] and when Whitehall was therefore again desperately looking for rescue to American charity, this time under the European Recovery Act (or Marshall Plan).[60]

The first outbreak proved deceptively easy to douse. At midday on 5 April some 5,000 members of the National Amalgamated Stevedores and Dockers struck at the Surrey Commercial Docks, Millwall and India Docks, the Royal Group and Tilbury.[61] The fire was ignited by friction at Maconochie's Wharf between two gangers belonging to this union and thirty-four dockers belonging to the T&GWU. The employer had unwisely sought to cool the friction by transferring the unpopular gangers to jobs in the warehouse, though this meant that they would lose piecework earnings and their supervisory status. Confronted with such an outrage, what else could the Secretary of the Dockers' Section of NASD do but call his members out, so stopping work on forty-three ships in the Port of London, three of them loaded with perishable foods? After urgent to-ings and fro-ings between the parties, the NASD that evening consented to call off the strike at midday on the morrow, on the understanding that the two gangers would get their old jobs back. Just the same, many NASD members failed to turn up for work that afternoon after all, they being – so it was surmised within the Ministry of Labour – 'still in bed (or in pubs?)'.[62]

It was a month later, in June, that there broke out the grand dockers' conflagration of 1948. Like many such destructive events in British industrial relations, it began as a tiny local flicker of flame, when eleven men were reported to the National Dock Labour Board for refusing to load 100 tons of zinc oxide from canal boats in the Regent's Canal Dock, London, into a ship unless they got 5s. per ton instead of the 3s. 4d. which their own union (the T&GWU) told them was the standard rate.[63] After the men had refused on further occasions to perform the work at this standard rate, the Local Board of the Dock Labour Scheme (on which employers and unions were jointly represented) decided to suspend them for seven days and withhold their entitlement to attendance money for three months. On 11 June the men appealed against these penalties, which were then deferred while the appeal was being heard. Another small fire and soon hosed down? Not at all.

On 14 June, 750 dockers in or near the Regent's Canal Dock struck in sympathy. Next day the strike spread to the London and West India Docks, the number of strikers rising to 3,000. On 16 June, when the Appeals Tribunal had been reconstituted to hear the case, 7,000 men were on strike. On 17 June the tribunal in its politic mercy reduced the disentitlement to attendance money to a mere three weeks, a decision accepted by both employer and union. However, that afternoon union officials failed to get the shop stewards' support for a return to work. Instead the shop stewards passed a resolution in the standard style:

> That we the accredited delegates of the shop stewards recommend
> the men on strike that this punishment meted out by the Tribunal is
> a direct attack on all militant workers in the docks. Further, we
> cannot recommend acceptance of the Tribunal's findings . . .[64]

On 18 June the T&GWU convened a would-be mass meeting in Victoria Park, another of those sad stretches of urban grass that played such a part in episodes of British industrial unrest. The meeting proved a fiasco. No more than 1,000 strikers turned up, and even then mostly in order to boo and shout down the union officials. By now 13,000–14,000 London dockers were on unofficial strike. On the same day riverside cold-store workers joined in, while the ships' clerks (belonging to the T&GWU) came out in a body. This brought all ship work to a standstill because no checking of work in progress could be done.

On 19 June the militant shop stewards held their own mass outdoor meeting, attended by 2,000–3,000 strikers, which backed the shop stewards' resolution of the 17th and also unanimously resolved 'To stop out until the unjust punishment of the 11 men is withdrawn.'[65] By now a 'no name organisation' had been formed by the militants who were fomenting the strike. The organizer, one Van Loo, was believed to be a Trotskyist, and the Chairman (also chairman of the shop stewards), Brother and Comrade Pat Coleman, a Communist.[66] With no doubt deep sincerity Coleman told a *Daily Worker* reporter:

> We know the circumstances of the restrictions of food which are bound to be prevalent after a war, and no body of men in Britain are more prepared to give their all in blood and energy to improve conditions than the dockers . . .[67]

In his enlightened view the present trouble originated in 'the profit motive'.[68]

On 22 June members of the Watermen, Lightermen, Tugmen, and Bargemen's Union began to join in, along with more and more stevedores of the NASD. This brought the total on strike to over 19,000.[69]

On 23 June the Chairman of the Port Employers of London conveyed to the Minister of Labour their 'deep concern' at the continuation of the strike, 'which not only involves the port and the country in immediate and tremendous losses but will have grave repercussions on the import and export and coastal trades for many months to come'.[70] The employers, he went on, were suggesting to the unions that they should 'arrange a secret ballot of the men immediately'.

By now ministerial nerves, already taut, were beginning to twang in response to the scale and spread of the conflagration. On 21 June 1948 the Cabinet Emergencies Committee asked themselves what could be done to limit the blaze and prevent it from leaping to other ports. They could of course call out the soldiers, but if the Smithfield market men were then to strike in sympathy, it would be impossible to deal with the situation adequately unless a force probably in excess of 15,000 troops were made available, together with men who could perform the skilled work of stevedores and crane drivers.[71]

The drawback here lay in that the armed services could only offer 5,000 men, and it would take seven days to mobilize them. In the meantime, perishable food, including 20,000 cases of eggs (the current ration was two per head per week), would be going off. So what about asking the T&GWU to call for volunteers? This could only be a sign of desperation, given that the course of the strike had demonstrated that the officials of the union, and especially its baronial boss, Arthur Deakin, were despised by the dockers. What about suspending the Dock Labour Scheme and its guaranteed attendance money, either by Order in Council under the Emergency Powers Act or by a short Parliamentary Bill?[72] No takers. Then should the strike leaders be prosecuted for running an illegal strike? The thought led to much uneasy sucking of teeth, as ministers asked themselves whether the present dispute did indeed legally constitute a trade dispute, and whether the penalties imposed on the Regent's Canal Dock 'Eleven' were indeed strictly legal. The Committee invited the Attorney General to examine these delicate issues in consultation with the Parliamentary Secretary to the Ministry of Labour.[73]

On 22 June the Attorney General, Sir Hartley Shawcross, favoured the Ministry of Labour with a tortuous opinion on the legal status of the strike and on whether or not the leaders could be prosecuted. 'Clearly, however,' wrote he, 'the matter is one which will require careful consideration at a high level before any decision is taken.'[74] Clearly! Two days later Shawcross wrote further to say that 'I should myself be disinclined to prosecute, not only because of the possible legal doubt but *because of the serious repercussions which might follow* [added emphasis].'[75]

Meanwhile the Cabinet Emergencies Committee had gloomily accepted on 23 June that 'it was unlikely that any last minute appeal by the union or the Government would be effective', and that there was 'no alternative to the use of troops to deal with perishable commodities notwithstanding the risk that the strike might be thereby extended'.[76]

On the same day the Prime Minister confided to a packed and attentive House of Commons that he could not believe that

> the general body of strikers have hitherto realised the true conse-
> quences of their actions . . . The handling of the country's overseas
> trade normally stretches to the limit the capacity of our available
> shipping. A hold up of any length delays the turn-round of ships and
> cannot be made up subsequently. The stoppage cuts millions of
> dollars and other needed foreign currency off our earnings – and cuts
> them off finally. Already the prospect of attaining this month's export
> target is affected, the gap in our balance of payments is widened and
> the pace of national recovery slowed down.[77]

For Attlee thus to ask the strikers to see such consequences as more important than the fate of eleven penalized dockers might seem a further sign of desperation. But, prosecution of strike leaders having been ruled out, what else could the Government at the moment do? Their plight resembled that of a fire brigade with only a trickling hose.

On 25 June (a Friday) Arthur Deakin attempted in vain to persuade a noisy gathering of some 2,000 men in Southwark Park, Surrey Docks, to return to work. Next day a rival meeting held by the strike committee in Victoria Park attracted at least 4,500 dockers, their massed cloth-cowpat headgear making an impressive spectacle of proletarian solidarity.[78] After the militants on the platform had done ranting, a vote of confidence in the strike committee was duly passed on a show of hands. On Sunday 27 June at a joint meeting (again in Victoria Park) convened by the T&GWU, NASD and the Lightermen's Union, the Chairman declared that those present had voted for a return to work.[79] In vain; on Monday over 19,000 men remained on strike.

Worse, this was the day when nearly 9,000 dockers at Liverpool and Birkenhead struck in sympathy with the London men, immo-bilizing a further 65 ships on top of the 167 already stuck in the port of London. Where might the fire spread next? Britain appeared now to stand in imminent danger of a general blockade, with all the grievous economic consequences that must shortly follow for a hard-up and indebted country dependent on exports to earn its living and on imports to sustain its very national life.

In the face of such a prospect the Government nerved itself to resort to the revived Emergency Powers Act of 1920, and so at last transform a trickling hosepipe into fire-quenching force. On this same Monday (28 June) that the Merseyside dockers struck, the Cabinet Emergencies Committee met to discuss exactly how far-reaching should be the code of regulations to be made under the Act.[80] Their 'general feeling', in which even that passionate left-wing member of the Committee, Aneurin Bevan, fully shared, 'was in favour of taking reasonably wide powers even though the present stage of the dispute might not require them all to be used'.[81] Certainly they reckoned that the regulation dealing with sabotage was needed. So too was the whole of the regulation 'dealing with trespassing and loitering in premises or in the vicinity of premises used for essential services . . .'[82] As the Home Secretary and Chairman of the Committee, Chuter Ede, reported to Attlee, 'The first thing, notwithstanding the needs of the export trade, is to unload incoming cargoes.'[83]

At 3 p.m. the Prime Minister delivered to the House of Commons 'a most grim statement'[84] to the effect that the King on his advice had declared a State of Emergency. These tidings Attlee repeated in a broadcast to the nation on the BBC that evening. Next day was promulgated the daunting list of repressive powers now assumed by Government. It says much about Britain as an industrial society that all this uproar could originate in a matter so trivial as that of 100 tons of zinc oxide and the claim of eleven dockers for an extra 1/8d. per ton over the going rate.

Nonetheless, this belated show of governmental power and resolve instantly quenched the fire – not least in the bellies of the strike committee. At a meeting of 7,000 dockers in Victoria Park on 29 June 1948 all but 100 voted in favour of the strike committee's surrender resolution:

In view of the complete line-up of reactionary forces against us and considering the complacent attitude of the respective factions – the employers, the trade union higher officials and the Government – the strike committee are recommending all our men back to work as from 8 a.m. tomorrow, Wednesday.[85]

So ended the great dockland conflagration of 1948, leaving behind as its product nothing but the ash of failure and futility.

Yet this was only one episode in a dockland drama series that was to run throughout the first post-war decade. As with all such series the setting remained the same, a closed but instantly recognizable little world, here of wharves and cranes, corner pubs and drab little streets. The core members of the cast too remained constant: dockers embittered by the past, militant leaders addicted to the adrenalin of the class war, union bosses too grand to be in touch, government ministers baffled as to what to do. And, also true to form, the scripts simply reworked the same basic plot, although with extra twists that rendered some episodes more dramatic than others.

Thus in 1949 a renewed attempt by the dockers to paralyse the ports of London and Liverpool coincided with the rapidly worsening balance of payments crisis that in August was to compel the Labour Cabinet to devalue the pound sterling. At the peak of the strike between 23 June and 23 July – again illegal under Order 1305, again fomented by an unofficial committee, this time comprising six Communist members out of seven – nearly 16,000 dockers were out. On 11 July, with Britain's gold and dollar reserves fast draining away despite the inflow of Marshall Aid, the King on Attlee's advice again proclaimed a State of Emergency. This year the Government deployed as many as 15,000 servicemen as strike-breakers in order to free the docks from paralysis: they unloaded nearly 110,000 tons of imports and loaded over 29,000 tons of exports.[86] It lent a further twist to the 1949 episode that the strike had not been detonated by any native grievance of the British docker, but instead by an event 3,000 miles distant in Canada, where the Communist-led Canadian Seamen's Union had blacked a ship, the *Beaver Brae*. This had inspired Communist and other militant busybodies in British dockland to issue a successful summons to 'the rank and file' to support the Canadian Seamen's Union. Felicitously enough, the strike agitators set about organizing their blockade of the Port of London just a month after Stalin had lifted his ten-month blockade of West Berlin.[87]

While the strike achieved nothing in itself, it nevertheless did succeed – along with three other major strikes and twenty-five minor ones – in making 1949 a record post-war year so far in terms of worker-days lost in British docks: 467,300 as against 220,000 in 1948.[88]

In the thrilling 1951 episode[89] the background to the plot was provided by the £4.7 billion rearmament programme adopted in January by the Labour Government under American pressure (see above, p. 39). Since the Government's hopes of both sustaining this colossal programme and keeping the pound strong rested on a surge in exports, the economy was to be more vulnerable than ever to trouble in the docks.

The first big strike of the year began in Birkenhead on 2 February and soon spread to Liverpool and Manchester. This time the detonator did not consist in some minor matter like the Regent's Canal Dock 'Eleven' or a remote one like the blacking of the *Beaver Brae*, but in rank and file discontent at a national wage deal.[90] The stoppage being (like all strikes) illegal under Order 1305, the Labour Cabinet resolved this time to prosecute seven strike leaders in the criminal courts. Ministers had already taken such bold action during the previous autumn in the case of the leaders of a ten-day stoppage in London gasworks, resulting in sentences of one month's imprisonment, later reduced to a £50 fine.[91] In the present case the Cabinet's new display of toughness did not turn out to be a good idea after all. For on the day after the strike leaders were arrested – big headlines, dramatic reports – 5,000 London dockers stopped work in angry protest. In Liverpool the self-appointed unofficial Ports Works Committee trumpeted to a mass meeting that those present were 'the finest defence of our seven brothers . . .' Indeed, their stand would 'guarantee that the struggles and sacrifices of the past and the present are not in vain'. The Committee called for 'a mighty protest' that would deal 'a smashing blow for trade Unionism and the [Dockers'] Charter . . .'[92] By now nearly 7,000 dockers were out and sixty-nine ships were idle.[93] The seven brothers being duly fined by the court, strikes in protest sputtered on in various ports into April.[94]

Yet the affair of 'the Dockers' Charter' and the seven arrested 'brothers' constituted no more than a promising start to a year of six major and twenty minor strikes in the docks, involving a total cast of 55,000 and a loss of 452,000 worker-days.[95]

Just the same, 1951 was to be quite outshone in dramatic tension by the final dockland episodes of the post-war decade, setting new records in disruption unsurpassed until the 1970s. For 1954 saw sixty-nine strikes and 787,000 worker-days lost, a feat closely rivalled by 1955's sixty-eight strikes and 763,000 worker-days lost, these displays directly affecting foreign confidence in sterling.[96] It happened that in both these years the British balance of payments was yet again lurching deep into the red.[97] The dockers in the pubs naturally talked of little else, and by way of doing their bit to help the country they imposed in October 1954 a virtually total blockade on foreign trade for a month.

The trouble had started in Hull in August, when 4,000 dockers walked out on unofficial strike because of discontent over certain work practices. It spread thereafter from port to port until eventually it reached London.[98] The London strike, however, simply served as the fighting climax to a ban on overtime in the port of London begun as far back as 25 January 1954 by the National Amalgamated Stevedores and Dockers, soon supported by the Watermen, Lightermen, Tugmen and Bargemen's Union, and later embraced by the T&GWU.[99] What was this particular dispute all about? It was about a nice point of principle. While the unions accepted that overtime working in the port of London was functionally essential and inevitable, they insisted that it be formally recognized by the employers as voluntary and not compulsory. Clearly this was a principle of such importance as to be well worth throttling back the flow of exports (especially motor vehicles)[100] while the usual kind of alleged historical precedents were vainly traded month after month with the employers. The ban and the strike both failed of their purpose.

Between 1946 and 1950, the most desperate period of the post-war export campaign and of national dependence on American loans and handouts, there were sixteen major strikes in British docks, cumulatively involving nearly 137,000 workers and losing a total of over 1,000,000 worker-days.[101] Between 1950 and 1955, the period of post-Korea rearmament and the renewed export drive for the sake of the balance of payments and the Sterling Area, the dockers were out eighteen times playing the big matches and 168 times in instant and short-lived kick-abouts.[102] The big matches drew onto the pitch a cumulative total of nearly 155,000 players, costing nearly 2,000,000 worker-days.[103]

But mere statistics cannot properly record the ramifying harm inflicted on British industry and commerce by these repeated blockades. For they meant export delivery dates missed and foreign customers infuriated; factories held up for want of raw materials and equipment from abroad; wholesalers and retailers running out of imported foodstuffs; transport to and from afflicted ports backing up in standstill and confusion; telegrams and telephone calls crowding an out-of-date and already overloaded telecommunications net as victims of the blockades tried to sort out their troubles; and an immense waste of time and effort by ministers and civil servants in attempting to deal with the strikes and their immediate impact. More insidious still was the moral harm done to Britain at home and abroad by such spectacular mutinies, further helping to convey the impression of a nation without disciplined purpose, and instead blindly intent on self-mutilation.

Yet in dockland, as in other industries, strikes or even go-slows were simply outward pustules sporadically erupting from a chronic and enfeebling sickness within.[104] As a report for the British Institute of Management on the London docks remarked in 1950, 'strikes probably do not account for even the major shortcomings in the docks . . .'[105] This report and a concurrent one on the Liverpool docks[106] agreed that the seat of the sickness lay in 'the dockworkers' feeling of isolation from the outside world . . .'[107] The feeling 'has strengthened the [established] customs and relationships and this in turn has increased the isolation'. Long collective memory too played its part: even in 1950 some old people in dockland were known as '1912-ers', that is, blacklegs in the 1912 dock strike.[108]

From such a deeply felt sense of tribal solidarity arose what the Liverpool report described as 'the traditional antagonism between the employers and workers' – an antagonism which 'now colours their [the dockers'] relationship with any who hold a responsible position of authority . . .' These persons included – no surprise here – local trade union delegates, who, according to the Liverpool report, were regarded by the dockers as just another type of 'official'.[109]

It was thanks to the antagonism between employers and workers that there prevailed, according to the London report, an atmosphere of suspicion and distrust which rendered 'almost any action liable to misconstruction . . .'[110] It hardly helped to clear this foetid atmosphere that:

> forcing the other side into making concessions or into eating its own words becomes something of a game played for its own sake, rather than for the material results . . . For instance, successive groups of workers engaged in particularly dirty cargo with one firm, demanded facilities for shower baths. They were installed, and then remained unused.[111]

Yet such mistrust constituted only one powerful factor in the dockers' resistance to change in their working lives. The other lay in 'the social pressures in dockland', which 'alike at work and in the communities, are traditionally wholly and strongly against any deviation from the accepted norm, customs and social relationships'.[112]

It followed that any attempt to mechanize dock operations now performed by muscle, any attempt to change traditional practices for the sake of higher efficiency, ran into stubborn and often successful resistance.[113] In Liverpool:

> Attempts have been made to introduce such improvements as forklift trucks and cranes for speeding up operations inside the hold, but the men are very opposed to any such innovations and will only reluctantly accept them if they are assured that there will be no reductions in the size of the gang.[114]

In London:

> The refusal of the workers to agree to alter long established rules seems now so much to be taken for granted that many technical improvements are not even seriously considered by the employers.

Both workers and employers are preoccupied with written rules . . .[115]

In fact, even the gradual improvements introduced over the previous half-century had 'led to ever more detailed regulations, concerning manning, for instance . . .'[116]

> One firm tried to introduce a loading truck which required the services of two workers instead of the three teams of seven men each required by the established methods. The men agreed that the trucks might be introduced but only if the three gangs continued to be employed on trucking.[117]

Another firm wanted to introduce a new method of handling bulk cargo which it had seen in America, and which would eliminate heavy physical work. 'But the men refused to work it other than on the same [existing] eight-hour daywork basis, with no shift work and no overtime.'[118]

It was the informed guess of one insider in 1951 that some 30,000 out of a total workforce of 75,000 in British docks were surplus to operating requirements – given maximum mechanization.[119]

In terms verging on despair did the report on the London docks define the root problem: 'the immediate aims of employers and workers directly clash: the employers require flexibility; and the workers, lacking adequate security, need to circumscribe flexibility.'[120]

Yet all industries, no matter whether they be strike-prone or relatively peaceable, were afflicted by this same problem of – to borrow words from the London docks report – 'Custom versus Development'.[121] In fact, worse than a problem, it amounted to a general crisis of adaptation. The crisis had been triggered by the ever-faster pace of technological change in the mid-twentieth century. Nonetheless, there was nothing novel in British workers fearing and resisting change wherever it threatened current jobs or crafts. They had done so since the earliest origins of this, the oldest industrialized society in the world.

13. The Psychology of the Underdog

The interests of masters and men are as much opposed to each other as light is to darkness. The object of the one is to get as much labour for as little money as possible, and the other just the contrary: hence the unanimous feeling on each side to oppose the other.[1]

So pronounced a contributor to the *Trades Journal* in 1825 when already in the raw new factory districts of Britain a mass proletariat was fast being formed by the mechanical tyranny of steam and the human tyranny of self-made entrepreneurs. Yet though this proletariat might spend their long dreary days as mere adjuncts to manufacturing processes and to their employers' accumulation of riches, they still felt, in the words of the same writer, 'pride, envy, hatred, and all the passions which those do who style themselves their betters'. They were not, he went on, 'manageable beings who are to be regulated by their masters with as much ease as a horse or an ass'. And so: 'Before you can order Englishmen to be worked like cattle, you must first deprive them of all the natural passions and feelings which were implanted by God.'[2]

That this could not be done failed to deter the majority of 'masters' from nonetheless trying their best to work their 'hands' like cattle. Yet such daily coercion – humiliation – lastingly twisted the proletariat's 'natural passions and feelings' into the psychology of the underdog: prickly, suspicious, mulish, defensive. Why should they welcome new machines and new methods which would boost their employer's profits and buy him a grander mansion in a bigger park, but benefit themselves not at all, and at worst consign them and their families to jobless destitution?[3]

The struggle against new technology, even to the point of violence against men and machines, began in the eighteenth-century textile industries, first to feel the onset of mechanization.[4] As early as 1715 hand-loom weavers successfully opposed the introduction of a factory system in the Essex woollen industry. In the 1730s the women button-workers of Macclesfield burned engine looms threatening their traditional needlecraft. In 1776 a spinning jenny set up in Shepton Mallet in Somerset was smashed by an enraged mob. In 1796 hooting crowds menaced the erection of the first steam-mill in Bradford.

Along with these first skirmishes emerged local 'clubs', 'societies' or 'combinations' of workpeople, the humble precursors of the trade union movement which in the twentieth century was to apply such powerful brakes to the progress of British industry.[5] For it made obvious sense for those individually helpless to combine together in order to exert pressure on the masters. That pressure could often take the form of crude intimidation. When, for instance, the calico printers of Lancashire in the late eighteenth century found their jobs under threat from new printing machinery, they dispatched a thoughtful, though anonymous, warning that 'we are determined to destroy all Sorts of Masheens for Printing in the Kingdom for there is more hands then [sic] there is work . . .'[6]

By the start of the nineteenth century the spread of the 'masheen' in British industry and the worker's fear of it were together growing apace. In 1811 the hatred and the desperation bred by that fear exploded in the widespread outbreaks of machine-breaking known as 'Luddism' (so named after a mythical folk-hero, 'Ned Ludd').[7] In 1812, to cite one example, 'Ned Ludd' wrote to a Huddersfield woollen master to give him 'fair warning' to pull down 'those detestable Shearing Frames':

> you will take notice that if they are not taken down by the end of next week, I shall detach one of my lieutenants with at least 200 men to destroy them, and further more take notice that if you give us the trouble of coming thus far, we will increase your misfortunes by burning your buildings down to ashes, and if you have the impudence to fire at any of my men, they have orders to murder you and burn all your Housing . . .[8]

Since under the Combination Acts of 1799 and 1800 'societies' of workmen constituted criminal 'combinations' operating in restraint of trade, it demanded the most solidly loyal of troops to take the field against the tyranny of the master and his machines. So late Georgian knuckles thumped out for the first time another enduring theme of British shop-floor history: that of the browbeating of docile workers by militants. In 1802, for instance, the Thames Police Court Magistrate was reporting to the Under-Secretary of State in regard to a strike at the King's Shipyard, Deptford, that despite the assurances given by disaffected caulkers 'not to disturb or molest others, complaints have been made before us of violent assaults made on those who are disposed to work . . .'[9] And during a London dock strike in 1810, wrote *The Times*, 'such as were backward in approving the conduct adopted by the leaders were roughly treated. Constables were called in . . .'[10]

By 1840 the making of the first mass industrial proletariat in the world had been completed: a society apart from the rest of British life, cherishing collective values, resentments and fears that would be passed on down the generations.[11] To Britain's future misfortune, however, one such abiding legacy consisted in a dread of technological change as deep as that of the hand-loom weavers in their time, and just as well founded. For the majority of this new working class earned their bread by mere muscle or simple repetitive dexterity. Hence they were no more than temporary human substitutes for future machines. As a contributor to the trade union journal *Pioneer* lamented in 1833, 'Thousands of working men are weekly being displaced by the new inventions of machinery . . . Their condition is becoming more and more degraded . . .'[12] According to another radical journalist that same year,

> It [machinery] is a monster that devours the bread of thousands. It is an insatiable Moloch. It is callous to all feeling . . . The labour of the working man is his only inheritance; if you take from him that, you deprive him of all. Yet this the growth of machinery has done, or what is nearly the same thing, it has rendered his labour valueless, for he is denied adequate employment for its exercise . . . Machinery has made labour too cheap, because it has made it too plentiful; there is not sufficient demand for it.[13]

Left-wing writers of the time like these might dream of a proletarian revolution born of despair, or might imagine working men escaping the tyranny of the masters by erecting and running their own machines. But the only practicable remedy for the workers' helplessness lay in gradually applying cramps to the masters' hitherto untrammelled freedom to run their businesses as they pleased. And who better placed to apply the cramps than 'the gentry' of this far from homogeneous working-class world — that is, the skilled craftsmen who made, maintained and repaired the masters' machines? Moreover, might they not at the same time win fresh recognition of the historical status of craft 'mysteries', with wage rates to match? Might they not secure agreements with employers on levels of manning in excess of the minimum actually required by advancing technology? Indeed, might they not even seek a monopoly of certain jobs, to be enforced through the 'closed shop'? And once won, these lodgements in the enemy's territory could thereafter be ferociously defended against infiltration by the lowly unskilled.

Thus by the 1840s many trades (such as typographers, cutlers and flint-glass bottlemakers) were already seeking to fix the maximum number of apprentices in a works, and to enforce a closed shop through traditional rules of apprenticeship. Those who broke such rules could find their equipment sabotaged or even, as happened in 'the Sheffield Outrages' in the 1860s, suffer personal violence to the point of having their houses blown up.[14] And when in 1850 the Amalgamated Society of Engineers (ASE) was founded, Rule XXIII, paragraph 2, of its rulebook laid down as a major purpose of the society that steps

> be taken to abolish piecework, to destroy the practice of working more than one lathe or machine, to prevent a greater number of apprentices or admissions into one trade than are likely to find employment therein — apprentices to be in the proportion of one to four journeymen . . .[15]

An initial defeat in 1851 — at the hands of employers who locked out craftsmen refusing to accept more unskilled hands in the workshops — proved only the first encounter in the ASE's ultimately successful hundred years' war of attrition.

In the 1860s regional print unions too fought running battles for control over the introduction of new machinery, and over who, and how many, should perform what tasks in a printing works. Like other craft unions the printers chose as the *Schwerpunkt* of their offensives the achievement of the 'closed shop', this having the double advantage of being a property-right enforceable against brother unions as well as against an employer.[16] In this trade too mid-Victorian setbacks marked only the beginning of a protracted and eventually successful campaign. For the print unions were to become the most effective, and the most stubborn, of all obstructors of technological change in Britain: the 'Old Guard' which was to die but not to surrender in the final climactic Battle of Wapping against Field Marshal Murdoch in 1986.

In the late Victorian era the craft unions shrewdly widened their base of power through recruitment of semi-skilled workers, those hybrids bred out of technological innovation.[17] For as John Burns, one of the legendary working-class leaders of his generation, wrote in 1890, 'Labour-saving machinery is reducing the previously skilled to the level of unskilled labour, and they must, in their own interests, be less exclusive than hitherto.'[18] By this time every craft big and little had its union, with the result that British industrial operations had become finely parcelled out like medieval peasant allotments. And just as with the manorial system of agriculture, traditional rights meant preservation of ever more outdated and inefficient systems. Indeed, it remained the craft unions' central purpose to defend familiar patterns of work against technical or managerial innovation. To cite but one instance, they blunted the attempt in the early 1900s by the engineering firm Thorneycroft to emulate American practice by imposing feed and speed charts, introducing time clocks, and changing the organization and control of production.[19]

In the 1880s and 1890s the industrial struggle was joined by newly created general unions with mass membership, such as the gas workers, the dock workers, and the Miners' Federation of Great Britain, formed in 1889 out of the existing regional coalfield unions. Their objective too lay in wresting from employers greater control over their members' working lives, but in their case with particular regard to levels of wages and employment, neither of which, they contended, must decline even when trade was bad.[20]

Thanks largely to this addition of the muscled mass to the craft elite, membership of trade unions rose from about 100,000 in the early 1850s to 1,500,000 in 1890 and to over 2,000,000 by 1896.[21] Britain had become the most unionized industrial country in the world.

Now, however, came a further threat to the power of employers (no longer 'masters'): the arrival of *national* trade unions or federations of unions. So the employers too began to organize themselves on an industry-wide scale. Their purpose was well expressed by Colonel Dyer, the American leader of the Federation of Engineering Employers (founded 1896), in respect of his own industry. It was

> to obtain the freedom to manage their own affairs which has proved so beneficial to the American manufacturers as to enable them to compete . . . in what was formerly an English monopoly . . .[22]

Just how far that freedom had been cumulatively shackled by the past step-by-step gains of the trade unions was revealed by books and newspaper campaigns urging Britain to 'wake up' to German and American competition. In 1894 appeared the bestselling *British Industries and Foreign Competition*. In 1896 followed a 'Made in Germany' press panic, on publication of a book under that title. In 1901 the *Daily Mail* followed a *Daily Express* series entitled 'Wake up England!' with its own on 'American Invaders'. In 1900–1901 *The Times*, governing-class opinion incarnate, ran major articles on 'The Crisis in British Industry' and 'American Competition and Progress'. Technical journals critically examined the efficiency of particular industries. All exposed British owners and managers as now widely old-fashioned in outlook, lethargic in action, and smug. But also fully explored was the opposition of the unions to new machines and new methods; the shackling effect of union restrictive practices on efficiency and productivity.[23] All in all, these press campaigns could not have made it more bluntly plain that the industrial girders which supported the edifice of British world power were already beginning to rust. But who would take note at a time when that edifice's outward splendour was inspiring the kind of vainglorious pride epitomized by Queen Victoria's Diamond Jubilee celebrations?

★

In 1893 Government chose for the first time to intervene as mediator in a confrontation between capital and labour, successfully settling a sixteen-week strike by the Miners' Federation.[24] As a direct result there followed the Conciliation Act of 1896, designed to promote industrial harmony through formal negotiating procedures under state patronage. Yet this Aristotelian aim of harmony hardly accorded with the Clausewitzian fact that a fundamental conflict existed between the top hats and the cloth caps. As the Labour Correspondent of the Board of Trade pronounced in 1888 when introducing the board's annual *Strikes and Lockouts Report,*

> It is certain that all such industrial struggles represent the conflict of employers and workmen upon matters which one or the other consider to be vital to their interests, and while engaged in this, the participants concerned are really in a state of moral if not actual warfare . . .[25]

In the years running up to the Great War this warfare grew worse, not better, partly because its edge was now sharpened by ideology. For the pragmatic British struggle for greater union say in the workplace had become politicized into a movement to replace 'capitalism' with 'socialism'. 'Socialism' could mean an enchanting fancy of an ideal society of Christian-style brother- and sister-hood, of contented workers busy at their crafts or happy in their cottage homes in 'garden cities'. To realize this fancy peacefully and constitutionally became the inspiration and benign purpose of the nascent Labour Party.[26] But, far less harmlessly, 'socialism' could also mean a dictatorship of the proletariat to be brought about by a working-class revolution, as prescribed by a desk-bound Prussian ideas-man, Karl Marx, whose theorizing think-pieces the world was to take seriously.[27]

A workers' revolution! The capitalist, and with him capitalism, defeated in a class war fought within his own mills, mines, works and foundries! Each workforce taking over and running its particular industry, as preached by the syndicalists! These prospects allured the testosteronic young militants among Britain's industrial rank and file. Between 1910 and 1914 the old Georgian theme-tune of violence and intimidation was yet played again, this time orchestrated for massed bands.

It was all the easier for the militants because the one-time fierce legal sanctions against intimidation in the course of industrial disputes had long been relaxed, thanks to the softening attitudes of government and public opinion. Under the 1871 Criminal Law Amendment Act (echoing legislation of 1825), 'obstruction', 'intimidation' and 'threat' by workmen had constituted criminal offences. So too had 'persistently following' and 'watching and besetting' if done by 'one or more persons'.[28] In a notorious case in 1873 sixteen farm labourers' wives had been sentenced under the Act for hooting at, and therefore 'intimidating', blacklegs. In the face of indignant working-class uproar all such offences were abolished in 1875 by the Conspiracy and Protection of Property Act.[29] The way had been opened for much non-intimidatory 'hooting' at blacklegs in the next hundred years, to say nothing of a great deal of 'besetting', 'obstruction' and 'threat', these also being no longer crimes in trade union law.

The new class-war militancy made its angry debut in 1910–11 with a ten-month strike of 30,000 South Wales miners for a guaranteed wage even though productivity was falling. The strike was enlivened by aggressive picketing, riots, drafting in of police reinforcements from London, even troop movements. One striker died and some 500 were injured. In 1911 a strike which started with the seamen and the dockers and then spread to all kinds of transport workers exploded into looting, rioting, and local bloodshed. In Liverpool military escorts were required to ensure the passage of essential food supplies through the docks. On 'Bloody Sunday' a policeman was killed and many strikers injured in a clash between the organized working class and the troops. Two days later two Liverpudlian rioters were shot dead by soldiers.[30]

Such continuing violent unrest and the syndicalist rhetoric that often went with it did much to convince the comfortable inhabitants of the Howards Ends of Britain that a workers' revolution might not after all be far off.

But instead came the Great War. In 1914–15 the demands of the war submitted the British industrial system to a ruthless audit which revealed that its methods and capital equipment alike were widely out of date; and, worse still, that in the case of several key advanced technologies Britain had come to depend on German or American

imports.[31] There then followed in desperate urgency a state-directed
drive to mobilize and modernize existing industries, and create vast
new ones. Across the entire varied field of precision engineering
this drive meant installing American automatic or semi-automatic
machine tools on American-style assembly lines in new factories
built to a mammoth American scale. As *The Times* reported in
November 1915:

> One of the new factories has grown up on a spot which last
> November was green fields. Now there are 25 acres covered with
> buildings packed full of machinery. Most of the machines are of
> American make, and some are marvels of ingenuity. Herein the war
> will prove a permanent benefactor to Birmingham. For it would be
> flattery to pretend that the prevailing Birmingham type of workshop
> is anything to boast about. It is on the whole conspicuously
> antiquated.[32]

Tremendous was the shock of this instant new industrial revolution
to a workforce with minds still stuck in the era of the original
industrial revolution. For the craft unions the shock was even worse.
They had been able to tame the piecemeal technological change of
the past by negotiating favourable labour-loadings or even craft
monopolies with employers. But now they were abruptly faced, on
the largest scale, with automatic machines that had no need of a
group of male craftsmen to operate, just an unskilled woman. What
a threat to pride of craftsmanship was this 'dilution', as it was called!
What a threat to status, even manhood itself!

Yet with the national survival at stake, the Government was
resolutely determined to get maximum production with minimum
labour out of its huge investment in new plant. The old conflict
between technological change and the workers' fear of it came to a
sudden acute crisis.

The crisis was apparently resolved by a 'Shells and Fuzes'
concordat between unions and Government in March 1915,
whereby the unions accepted 'dilution' in state-sponsored factories
in return for a promise that every hallowed restrictive practice
would be restored at the end of the war. And so, in the words of
the official *History of the Ministry of Munitions*, '. . . standardised
repetition work or mass production took the place of the varied and

variable output characteristic of much of British manufacture before the war.'[33] The way was clear for the astonishing industrial transformation of 1915–18.[34] Moreover, this was a transformation from which the mass of the workers also benefited: airy, well-lit factories instead of cramped old works; canteens, medical care, good wages.[35]

Yet craftsmen – particularly in areas where existing technologies were the more old fashioned – remained deeply resentful of wartime 'dilution', temporary though it was.[36] Their pique served to fuel the shop stewards' movement, whose lasting character and purpose even into the 1980s were well defined by the Clyde Workers Committee in October 1915:

> We will support the [union] officials just so long as they rightly represent the workers, but we will act independently immediately they misrepresent them. Being composed of Delegates for every shop, and untrammelled by obsolete rule or law, we claim to represent the true feeling of the workers. We can act immediately according to the merits of the case and the desire of the rank and file.[37]

'Acting immediately' was really code for calling the lads out on unofficial strike. Such strikes at their peak in April and May 1917 involved 200,000 engineering workers across forty-eight towns, losing 1,500,000 working days in the middle of a total war.[38] The grievances? Traditional craft privilege was being further threatened by the spread of dilution into private engineering works. Even more alarming, the craftsmen themselves were threatened with military service thanks to stricter government rules about protected (or reserved) occupations. As a satirical verse had it:

> Don't send me in the army, George,
> I'm in the A.S.E.
> Take all the bloody labourers,
> But for God's sake don't take me.
> You want me for a soldier?
> Well, that can never be –
> A man of my ability,
> And in the A.S.E.![39]

Once the Great War had been won, and just at the moment when the oceanic British Empire was standing precariously on the pinnacle of its political coherence and military power, the wartime industrial revolution stopped short. Employers and workforce alike hastened to revert to ways that would have been familiar to their grandfathers. On the shop floor all the traditional restrictive practices were soon back in place, and coveys of craftsmen once again fiddled where a woman had worked. Each trade union rededicated itself to defending its members' proprietorial rights against encroachment either by 'the bosses' or by other unions. In 1929 (exactly midway between the world wars, as it turned out), the most thoroughgoing of all official investigations into the state of British industry, the Report of the Balfour Committee on Industry and Trade, pronounced:

> We are aware of no other country that suffers nearly so much as Great Britain from artificial and hard and fast lines of demarcations between different skilled crafts, or between workers of different degrees of skill, and this disability is more acutely felt than ever in a period of rapid economic change, when old lines of distinction are necessarily becoming less and less consistent with the realities of productive economy.[40]

Twenty years later, in another post-war era, all this would be even more true. During the Second World War the nation's desperate industrial need supplied the workforce's crowning opportunity. The craft unions successfully defended their property rights to outdated processes. General unions like the miners contributed to a strike record worse than in the previous five years of peacetime. Skiving abounded, from old technologies like shipbuilding to new ones like aircraft manufacture.[41] And the state proved helpless in the face of it all even though armed with Order No. 1305 prohibiting strikes.

By the end of the war, therefore, the working class had finally won their own war, protracted over generations, to free themselves from a humiliating helplessness in the face of the master and the machine. They had won power in the work-place, and especially power over the use of technology, existing and new.[42]

Yet success in world markets belongs to businesses which are free to exploit the latest technologies swiftly, and which can – just as swiftly

– adapt their organizations and production methods to match. Success belongs to industrial 'armies' highly trained and high in morale, where all ranks work together in disciplined endeavour. None of these criteria can be applied to the industrial Britain of the 1950s, which less resembled one army advancing with common purpose than two armies, raggle-taggle at that, confronting each other on an old and stalemated battlefield.

Despite the occasional 'big pushes' known as strikes, this battle-field remained in most sectors and for most of the time quiet except for minor raids and sniping. Such tranquillity did not, however, mean (as some might think)[43] that all was well, and that here were industries humming with dynamic efficiency. On the contrary, it signified – just as with 'quiet' sectors of the 1914–18 Western Front – a tacit pact between the two opposing sides to live and let live for the sake of an undisturbed existence in the comfort of familiar routines. That meant in particular a willingness on the part of employers to tolerate restrictive practices and to keep the technolog-ically redundant hanging around on the payroll.[44] This was sadly a special feature even of modern process industries like chemicals and oil-refining.[45]

In short, the truce left the workers in secure occupation of the ground won from employers during the past century of industrial battles. This ground was now defended in depth by all the manning and demarcation agreements, by the negotiating and arbitration procedures, and by the 'closed shop', that virtually shell-proof bunker.[46] It is thus hardly surprising that British management on the whole shrank from launching frontal attacks in hope of achieving technological breakthroughs. In any case, the strength of the union trench system did not constitute the only reason why management generally lacked appetite for battle. As an unsigned pencil note in a Ministry of Labour file put it in December 1957,

> It must also be taken into account that, up to 1957, on the threat of a major strike there has almost always been the strongest pressure political and public, upon conciliation and arbitration to find a settlement and avoid disruption . . .[47]

When a company did nevertheless venture on an offensive, either for the sake of technical innovation or of survival in the face of foreign competition, the attempt could lead to heavy loss in terms of output and profit.[48] All in all, it is easy to understand why, in the words of the Conservative Minister of Labour, Walter Monckton (in a paper of December 1953 entitled 'Efficiency and Output'), too many British managements were willing to accept 'a ceiling on efficiency and output at the level of their own comfort and convenience . . .'[49]

It was therefore Monckton's gloomy prognosis that unless action was taken soon, 'the nation will continue contentedly with "business as usual".'

Yet 'business as usual' in the British mode must mean that Britain would see finally eroded away her post-war head-start over defeated rivals like Germany and Japan. Between 1948 and the first half of 1953 manufacturing output per head in Britain only rose by some 14 per cent, as against rises of 20 per cent in America and Sweden, 27 per cent in France and the Netherlands, and a staggering 101 per cent rise in Germany (reflecting, naturally, her acceleration from stand-still).[50] Even as early as 1950 Germany had virtually caught Britain up in manufacturing productivity.[51] In fact, such productivity actually fell in Britain by some 3–4 per cent in 1951–2, just at the time when it was rising fastest in Germany. It only regained the 1951 level in 1953.[52]

Opined a Whitehall report in March 1954:

> No doubt the changes in productivity in these different countries can be attributed in part to particular causes. But the general moral to be drawn from them is that if the tendencies they reveal were to continue, the relegation of the United Kingdom to the second division in the industrial league would not be far off. At present there is not much visible reason for optimism, and a certain amount of rather disquieting evidence.[53]

Relegation to the second division in the industrial league! But how could a second-rank industrial economy afford a defence budget large enough for armed forces which were (in Eden's words in February 1956) 'sufficient in quality and size to maintain our standing as a world power'?[54] Or, at least, how could such an economy do so without sustaining future damage comparable to that already inflicted by post-Korea rearmament?

In any case, it was not so much industrial productivity in itself that mattered as the earning of the nation's living in export markets. And here the figures were even more dismaying. Between 1950 and 1952 the volume of British exports fell by 5 per cent (rearmament again), while German exports rose by over 50 per cent and American exports by about 20 per cent. In just those two years Britain's share of world trade in manufactures dropped from 26 per cent to 22 per cent.[55] By the end of 1954 it was down to just over 20 per cent.[56] In 1955 American exports of manufactured goods rose by about 9 per cent by value, Germany's by 18 per cent, Japan's by 27 per cent – and Britain's by 7 per cent.[57] In this final year of the post-war decade the United Kingdom's current-account deficit in visible trade with countries outside the Sterling Area reached a frightening £318 million, and the gold and dollar reserves drained away to the tune of £229 million.[58]

Yet Britain's disastrously lacklustre record in productivity at home and competitiveness overseas cannot be blamed solely on the workers, the shop stewards or the unions. As the industrial record since the Second World War went to show, their hard-won power in the work-place was purely negative: the power to obstruct and disrupt but not to create and innovate. They were still not the masters, still only 'the hands'. They enjoyed no positive say in decisions over investment, whether in research or new plant. They did not design and develop new products. They did not lay out the production lines or organize the inward flow of raw materials and components. They did not choose the markets, evolve the marketing strategies or set up the service networks. They were not responsible for their own training, or lack of it. Least of all were they responsible for exercising leadership over themselves in the interests of commercial success. All these were the functions of management, from the grandees in the boardroom down to the 'line' officers in the work-place.

PART FIVE

Industry – the Leaders

The outlook of many of our Managing Directors is to the effect that 'you can't teach management'. Why is this so? It stems from two origins, firstly from our 19th century heritage of industrial enterprise (where the individual with initiative forged ahead *without* training), and secondly, from the emphasis placed by our Public Schools and older Universities on building up character rather than imparting specialised knowledge.

(The Chief Education Officer of the United Steel Company,
February 1953)

... to the extent that the countries of the Commonwealth and the rest of the free world look to us for their supplies of aircraft (and of the electronic and other equipment that goes with them) they will tend to be linked with us militarily and politically, and our influence in world affairs will thereby be increased ...

(Duncan Sandys, the Minister of Supply, and Lord De L'Isle
and Dudley, Secretary of State for Air, 23 May 1952)

... if the weight of invention or discovery is one, the weight to bring it to actual development should be ten, and the weight to produce and market it should be one hundred.

(Masaru Ibuka, President of the Sony Corporation, 1983)

14. 'Good Management is a Fundamental Requirement'

In the 1850s Great Britain still constituted 'world's best practice' in commerce and manufacturing: the model from which other nations, slower to start the race to industrialize, must try to learn; the leader which they must endeavour to catch up, perhaps even – impossible though it seemed at the time – to overtake. A century later it was America which provided the measure of 'world's best practice'; America to which Britain, having let her own leadership slip away, must now turn for lessons in successful management. To that end, teams representing a spectrum of British industries had been visiting their American opposite numbers in 1949 under the sponsorship of the Anglo-American Council on Productivity.[1]

As it happened, the subsequent publication of many of their reports straddled the outbreak of the Korean War and the ensuing entanglement of Britain in that conflict, at first militarily and then industrially as well. Thus a key report praising the American internal combustion engine industry in comparison with the British appeared in June 1950, the very month the war began.[2] In November, when the British 27th Brigade was caught up first in MacArthur's reckless advance into North Korea and then in the smashing Chinese counter-stroke, there appeared the report of a specialist team on 'Management Accounting', the core technique of modern business.[3] As it also neatly happened, this was also the month that saw the Labour Cabinet deep in anguished discussions about how to find the industrial and financial resources to support a rearmament programme costing at least £3.7 billion (see above, p. 37).

The report *Management Accounting* put its finger on the fundamental issue:

273

An army equipped with the best weapons and having troops with the highest morale will not win battles unless properly led. Similarly, industry, no matter how well supplied with tools and equipment and possessing a skilful and conscientious labour force, will not be efficient unless managed by men who are good leaders and are properly trained. Good management is a fundamental requirement of efficient business.[4]

Yet it was the common theme of the reports made by the Anglo-American productivity teams that British industries did indeed suffer widely from a lack of 'good leaders' who were 'properly trained'. Hence followed the inferiority of these industries to American in so many aspects of organization and production. The theme was either stated implicitly through praise of the American model, or explicitly — sometimes very explicitly — in the form of blunt criticism of British practice.

'In the opinion of the Team, after very careful consideration [stated the report on 'Management Accounting'] the greatest single factor in American industrial supremacy is the effectiveness of its management at all levels . . .'[5] British trade union representatives, contributing to the report *Trade Unions and Productivity*, agreed with this broad judgement: 'Efficient management set the pace of productivity in American industry — not because of an altruistic belief in social progress but from necessity . . .'[6]

The productivity team on 'Internal Combustion Engines' was particularly impressed by

the alertness and enthusiasm of the executives, most of whom had worked their way up from the factory floor in the face of keen competition and had in consequence a sound knowledge of their jobs and a determination to hold them down. Here, as elsewhere in American industry, the criterion of efficiency is ruthlessly applied. Sentiment and personal considerations have no bearing on the selection of men . . .[7]

The same report noted the belief 'held by workers at all levels' that the secret of maximum efficiency lay in 'the competitive spirit'. It further noted that this spirit was inspired by the personal ambition of the American worker, pushed by his wife, constantly to strive to raise his standard of living.[8] The productivity team on 'Packaging' found the same: 'The American way of life was described to us as being dominated by "a continual dissatisfaction with the existing best and a constant striving for change and improvement . . ." '[9]

It followed from this high-geared approach to life and especially industrial life that 'in most American factories discipline was strict, especially in regard to time-keeping and "knocking off" . . .'[10] The task of maintaining such discipline fell in the first place to the foremen and shop-floor supervisors, just as in Britain. In Britain, however, the foreman's role was ambiguous and uneasy, halfway between manager (though a weekly paid wage earner, and not fully in management's confidence) and overalled worker. He was expected to supervise a group of some forty to fifty subordinates, twice the size of a military platoon and six times that of an infantry section. At the same time, his authority suffered from continual challenge from the shop stewards.[11] Moreover, according to a 1949 report on British foremen, there existed 'quite severe limitations in the abilities and personal equipment of people at the supervisory level'.[12] In America by contrast 'the foreman was recognized as a key figure in the management system and, in every plant but one, was on a [monthly-paid] staff basis . . .' He took a prominent part in production meetings.[13] He supervised a team of no more than ten to twelve workers.

In any case, good labour relations on the shop floor were fostered by the existence in most American plants of a single labour agreement instead of the intricate variety, rich in potential for dispute, common in Britain. Quite as important, 'care is taken [in America] to ensure that both the authority and the responsibilities of each member of staff are clearly defined . . .'[14] Such responsibilities were 'decentralised to the limit . . .'[15] All these findings were confirmed by a later productivity team which in 1955 spent three months studying American steel plants.[16]

Contrasting discreditably with this progressive and professional American approach to the human aspects of management was the British pattern, particularly in older industries. Here prevailed rigid hierarchies of rank (no first names, please, we're British) absurdly coupled with a failure clearly to define functional responsibilities. Add a stubborn reluctance to delegate and the result was a sour cocktail of inefficiency and grumbling discontent. In the nationalized (and essentially Victorian) railway system, for instance, a study in 1954–5 found that 'very little responsibility is entrusted to lower grades of management, station-masters, goods-yard managers etc. This becomes serious when it inevitably ends in administrative muddles . . .'[17] It hardly helped to sort out these muddles that there existed on the railways 'ineffective communication from the top downward and from lower levels upwards . . .'[18] A study of British colliery management in 1954–6 found similar confusions in regard to the roles of different types and grades of manager, similarly haphazardly developed structures.[19] And in this and other traditional industries it was not the able and thrusting who got promotion. That perk went strictly according to seniority, or, in the vernacular, 'Buggins' turn'.[20]

Worst of all, managements in Britain still widely failed to perceive the need for leadership, in the sense of systematically fostering enthusiasm and team spirit as practised in a good British regiment or American industrial company. They still cleaved to their great-grandfathers' notion that they were 'the masters'; that they could simply order 'the men' about (however ineffectually in practice); that they could butt it out with the unions head-to-head whenever shopfloor disgruntlement flared into strikes or go-slows. In the case of the old and long-troubled British shipbuilding industry, a study in 1959 noted that the employers 'have shown no attachment to enlightened management practices; it is rare to find any specialist staff concerned with personnel management, and communication of intention . . . is frequently faulty or altogether lacking . . .'[21] Just about the same could be also broadly said of that modern industry, motor vehicles, so helping to explain its proneness to shop-floor disruption.[22] The British steel industry too – nationalized under the Labour Government, denationalized under the Conservatives – had 'still far to go in this field', according to a report in 1955.[23]

If professional techniques of personnel management – leadership, in a word – were so little understood in major British industries, what could be expected of the inchoate litter of small manufacturers that contributed so much of the country's output?[24] Even in an army under military discipline the kind of uncomprehending labour relations widely practised by British management in the post-war decade would lead to mutinies. Who should therefore be surprised at the results of compounding into one unstable explosive the thick-headed arrogance of the blue-suited and the reciprocal resentments of the blue-dungareed?

The enlightened American approach to management extended to the production process as a whole, thanks to 'widespread use of standards against which the realised performances of men, machines and raw material can be measured at every stage of manufacture . . .'[25] Cost accounting and cost control (together with time-and-motion study) served as the basic tools of American management in this 'continuous measurement of performance against targets'.[26] It was the judgement of the productivity team on 'Internal Combustion Engines' that while a number of British plants operated costing systems similar to those in the US, 'their budget statements in many cases appear too late and are not acted upon so seriously by all departments as is the case in the U.S. . . .'[27]

It followed from the rigorous monitoring of costs and performance in American industry that (according to the report on 'Management Accounting') 'offices are obviously considered to be as important as production shops and the same detailed consideration is given to the planning of operations . . .'[28] This was why American offices were equipped with advanced technology on a scale that astonished British visitors. 'Comprehensive mechanised punched-card systems are widely used for securing efficiency and economy in many fundamental office procedures . . .' reported the productivity team on 'Electric Motor Control Gear'.[29] The 'Management Accounting' team concurred with this finding: 'To British eyes the provision of auxiliary office equipment, such as calculating machines, addressing machines and typewriters, seemed lavish . . .'[30] Moreover, this kit was at the disposal of almost everyone in the office. Then again, the British visitors found the American office scene as a whole positively futuristic: 'The trend is towards large single offices which make for much greater flexibility. Physically the offices are attractive. Many have sound-absorbent tiles, and lighting, ventilation and decoration are of a high order.'[31] It was a world away from the fusty and dimly lit main offices and the warrens of poky rooms common in Britain.[32] And the quality of the American office environment was matched by the quality of the staff, with a higher proportion of the first-rate and highly trained than in Britain.[33]

The visiting British teams were just as impressed with the environment on the American factory floor. 'In all factories visited,' wrote the 'Electric Motor Control Gear' team, 'working conditions were of a high standard. There was better lighting, heating and draught-proofing in all the plants than is usual in Britain . . .'[34] Wonder of wonders, there were automatic machines to dispense hot and cold drinks. Where the type of industry permitted, forklift trucks and power-operated tools swiftly and efficiently did the work laboriously performed in Britain by muscle.

All these findings about the American working environment merely echoed the wonder of visiting teams from British aircraft firms in 1942–3 on first encountering vast air-conditioned assembly shops, clean, spacious and well kept, brilliantly lit by fluorescent tubes; on being shown lavishly staffed design floors equipped with such advanced techniques as photocopying drawings straight on to metal.[35] Ten years later British aircraft factories had still not caught up (see below, pp. 341–2).

In the judgement of the productivity team on 'Management Accounting', American modernity sprang from American willingness to scrap old plant and junk old products:

> In one case a considerable investment in plant, with years of useful life still left, was entirely scrapped and new plant laid down to manufacture an entirely different product, because the management was convinced that the previous product had no future . . .[36]

Yet even where old plant and old equipment still remained in use, the rate of output was high, 'due to good executives, first-rate supervising staff, and the productivity consciousness of the operator . . .'[37]

The visiting teams discovered that the percentage of highly skilled labour on the American shop floor was actually lower than on the British shop floor. Instead, 'there was a much greater proportion of labour rapidly trained to execute a limited range of functions'.[38] In America top-grade craftsmen were reserved for tool rooms and maintenance work, rather than allowed, as in Britain at the behest of the unions, redundantly to clutter up production lines.

The report on 'Internal Combustion Engines' tersely summed it all up: 'The Team was convinced at the end of its tour that at least the majority of British plants had much to learn about the full utilisation of manpower and the efficient use of machine tools . . .'

Perhaps the most damaging single proof of this American superiority in all-round productivity lies in a comparison in September 1954 between steel output at the Inland Steel Company, Chicago, and the more modern Port Talbot plant of the Steel Company of Wales. For Inland produced about 260 ingot tons per man-year as against about 160 ingot tons per man-year at Port Talbot.[39] It was a foretaste of the even more horrifying comparisons in the 1970s, 1980s and 1990s between productivity at identical car plants in Britain and on the Continent.[40]

Yet this American 'full utilisation of man power' only reflected equally clear-cut planning of the actual manufacturing process. Here the starting point lay in simplified product ranges and standardized designs.[41] According to the report of the visiting British team on 'Electric Motor Control Gear',

> The outstanding lesson to be learned from our tour is that circumstances [sic] have enabled the American Control Gear Industry to effect simplification and standardisation to a much greater degree than has been possible in this country . . .[42]

The British productivity team specifically charged with investigating 'Simplification in Industry' noted that one American manufacturer of radios had reduced his pre-war range of 160 models to just twelve. The team found similar reductions in the types of kit or types of parts in many other industries too, such as earth-movers, nuts, bolts and rivets, steel reinforcing bars, and diesel-electric locomotives.[43]

A second report by this team, in August 1950, *Simplification in British Industry*, revealed a dismaying contrast:

> It is apparent . . . that the true cost of producing in any individual firm a wide range of products – a common practice in British industry – is not generally known. In particular there is little accurate

information about the undoubted connection between profusion of
type of product and high overhead cost . . . It is recognised that the
special or short-run line creates a higher burden of overhead expenses
than the comparable long-run item, but we found that in general this
is not reflected in the final cost and selling price.[44]

The team pointed to the damage done by the vagueness of this
quaintly old-fashioned, almost amateur, British approach to the
business of production for profit:

> we are convinced that much needless variety is being maintained and
> encouraged by inaccurate costing. The results are prices which do
> not reflect accurately the manufacturing and management effort
> involved and the inefficient use of capital resources.[45]

The classic example of such neglect of accurate costing is that
romantic British legend, the Mini, launched by the British Motor
Corporation in 1959. Ford stripped down a specimen Mini and
costed every part in American style (which BMC had unbelievably
failed to do), and calculated that at the selling price BMC were
making a loss of £30 on every vehicle sold.

The best that the 'Simplification in British Industry' team could
say in its 1950 survey of seventeen industries in Britain was that in
several cases – for instance, iron and steel, motor vehicles, locomotives, plastic mouldings, ball bearings, paint – the industry in
question 'claimed' that it was actively studying, or promoting, or
was in the process of introducing, further simplification and standardization. In the case of motor vehicles, that vanguard of exports,
'the pre-war range of 48 types of dynamos is *in the process* [added
emphasis] of being reduced to 3, starters from 38 to 5, distributors
from 68 to 3, headlamps from 133 to 2, and batteries from 18 to
3.'[46] What did this say about the quality of the car industry's
management up to this time? In fact, only a manufacturer of gas
cookers (thirty-two models already cut to one) and the aircraft
industry won the team's full approbation. Nonetheless, while the
aircraft industry might well have simplified and standardized components, it certainly had not managed to simplify either itself or its
range of finished products. According to a memorandum by the
Minister of Supply just four days after the outbreak of the Korean

War, no fewer than thirty-five highly different aircraft types were currently being manufactured and a further thirty-five were under development. Moreover, the aircraft firms themselves numbered nineteen.[47]

The findings of the 'Simplification in Industry' team were borne out and amplified by other studies sponsored by the Board of Trade and the Ministry of Supply.[48] In May 1949 a report on the recently nationalized industries remarked of coal that 'pit tubs in a very wide variety of sizes remain in use to-day and there exists an even greater variety of pit tub components such as wheels and axles, couplings and links'.[49] The report noted similar traditional anomalies in the design of railway motive power, rolling stock and signalling equipment; in gas components; in coke ovens. In short, opined this report, in each nationalized industry 'a wide diversity of equipment is often purchased for the same essential purpose'.[50]

In October 1949 appeared the heavyweight *Report of the Committee for Standardization of Engineering Products* (the Lemon Report, after the Chairman, Sir Ernest Lemon),[51] covering seventeen sectors of the engineering industry. It patted some on the back, such as metal-box (or can) manufacture and the aircraft industry, but wagged a finger at others 'where relatively little has been done, and where there is scope for major improvement in productivity. . . .'[52] However, it seemed that once again the process of change was bogged down in Britain by the clinging clay of history, for the Committee gave as the first two of eleven main reasons for 'the wide and often excessive variety' of products and parts:

i) The long established pattern of production based on methods in use before automatic machinery and bulk production techniques were developed.

ii) The persistence of selling methods and ranges [similarly] derived. Companies have often preferred to compete with each other by offering to meet the exact requirements of customers (each of whom may hold different views on detail) rather than by offering standard articles at lower prices . . .[53]

Echoing the productivity team on 'Simplification', the Lemon Committee could only note hopefully that 'in a number of cases active steps to improve the position are already in hand'.[54] Lemon himself had explained to the Engineering Advisory Council back in March 1949 why these 'active steps' were in fact failing to exceed the pace of lead-booted divers on the seabed:

> the main problems facing the B.S.I. [British Standards Institution] in producing standards were the time taken by the present system of working and the power of veto which could be exercised by any section of an industry affected by a proposed standard.[55]

Hence followed the warning in his Committee's final report that in the case of standards affecting a wide cross-section of industry, 'progress is inevitably slow'. Inevitably! No Yank hustling over here! Evolution not revolution the British way!

So it was that in January 1951 it was being remarked in the Ministry of Supply that the office-machinery industry had only got as far as setting up a committee and three sub-committees to ponder standardization of components.[56] The same minute recorded that 'no great strides had been made towards standardisation' in internal combustion engines, while the manufacturers of printing machinery, having 'given a lot of thought to the matter', had concluded that, first of all, the printers must standardize the sizes of paper in place of the existing 'many standard sizes and innumerable bastard [non-standard] sizes . . .' In the case of contractors' plant, such as bulldozers, crawler tractors, and scrapers, some twelve committees under the auspices of the British Standards Institution were now pregnant with draft recommendations.[57]

In May 1951 bureaucrats in the Ministry of Supply lamented that standardization of mechanical handling equipment 'presents a difficult problem'. Never mind, a sub-committee of the trade association was keeping the question under review. Also 'continuously under review' by its trade association was standardization in the motorcycle and bicycle industries.[58] The electric-motor industry, for its part, had by now got as far as deciding to adopt the American standard dimensions. And so it went, and across virtually the entire spread of British industries. Only telephone equipment presented an outstanding exception to this broad scene of inherited shambles and present sloth, and that was thanks to the existence of a monopoly purchaser, the Post Office.

The truth was that the attitude of too many British managements towards simplification of components and standardization of products is exactly summed up in the old Chinese saying that it is better to travel hopefully than to arrive.

Yet when it came to the management of the business as a whole, British companies likewise found it more agreeable to travel hopefully than to arrive (probably tired and shaken) at the destination – that is, 'world's best practice' as portrayed by the Anglo-American productivity teams. Half a decade after the publication of these reports Britain's industrial shortcomings still remained the stock-in-trade of such well-meaning proselytizers as the British Productivity Council and (within Whitehall) an array of ministerial and official bodies like the Productivity and Conditional Aid Committee. Ministers of the Crown continued to preach upliftingly at lunch meetings for businessmen on what must be done to enable Britain to draw level with America in efficiency and keep ahead of the Europeans.[59] As good sermons should, these discourses reminded the congregation of their sinfulness and need to repent. Thus for his speech at the Cutlers' Feast in Sheffield in March 1954, the Minister of State was briefed beforehand:

> Industry in Sheffield is largely carried out on in small units which by many standards would be regarded as backward and indeed as 'backyard'. This is particularly true of the cutlery industry which is frequently spoken of as being thoroughly unmechanised and backward in taking to new techniques such as the use of mechanical aids, work study and so forth.[60]

The Minister, so continued the civil servant's brief, 'may wish to point out that it is obviously desirable in our present situation of increasingly fierce competition that firms should keep an eye on the development of new methods . . .'

Was there some simple reason for persistent managerial torpor despite all the clanging of alarm bells? On its return home the British team which in 1954–5 spent three months investigating the American steel industry offered an explanation: 'In this country we have attempted to find excuses for [avoiding] any radical changes that have been proposed, and appear to have lulled ourselves into a false sense of security about our efficiency.'[61]

But why had management so chosen to find excuses for inaction? Why had they so lulled themselves? Why, indeed, did their conduct of business operations at the end of this turning-point post-war decade still fail to match 'world's best practice'? The answers lie in the very nature of British managers themselves: who they were, where they came from, and what they knew. And these were things determined by a peculiarly British blend of social class and type of school, each serving to reinforce the other.[62]

By American or European standards the general ruck of British managers from boardroom to the 'line' in the 1950s were still little better than ill-trained amateurs self-taught on the job.[63] This was especially true of the owners or managers of the tiny enterprises employing between ten and fifty workers each, which accounted for a quarter of the total labour force in manufacturing.[64] Despite all the increasingly shrill warnings since the great Royal Commission reports of the late Victorian era,[65] formal training in management at every level in the United Kingdom remained a random and sketchy patchwork of courses long and short.[66] In 1956 (the year of Eden's Suez Canal adventure) a research study into a sample of 3,327 managers found that as many as 82 per cent had no professional (as distinct from educational) qualifications whatsoever.[67] True, 19 per cent of the sample did at least have degrees. But half of the degree-holders were scientists and technologists from red-brick universities: men with pens and a slide-rule stuck in the breast pockets of their white coats, more often confined to specialist departments than found in general management.[68] And only 40 per cent of chief executives in Britain had degrees, as against 89 per cent in France and 78 per cent in Germany.[69] In one American steel company even a third of the foremen were holders of first degrees![70] The British offering in 1952 of only thirty-five university first-degree courses on management and commerce plus seven one-year post-graduate courses[71] compares with the American record during the academic year 1949–50 of 617 institutions offering courses in business and commerce, and awarding 76,530 degrees.[72] As late as 1968–69 there would be only some 2,400 students studying for first degrees in management in Britain as against some 500,000 in the United States.[73] For the mass of managers or would-be managers down to the level of supervisors and foremen, British technical colleges were offering in 1952–53 just seventy-one 'Intermediate Certificate' courses and twenty-nine diploma courses in management studies, and in the previous three years had awarded a total of no more than 915 certificates and 118 diplomas.[74] Otherwise, hopefuls had to cram management skills and 'foremanship' in a scattering of residential courses lasting from two to five days.[75]

The truth was that in appointing or promoting managers British firms placed far less value than their American rivals – or German or French rivals – on highly trained proficiency. The Chief Education Officer of United Steel openly admitted this in a lecture in February 1953, and explained why:

> Whereas in the United States they are conscious of the need to integrate a philanthropy [sic] of industrial relations with their technology, over here there is an ingrained suspicion of technique. The outlook of many of our Managing Directors is to the effect that 'you can't teach management'. Why is this so? It stems from two origins, firstly from our 19th century heritage of industrial enterprise (where the individual with initiative forged ahead *without* training), and secondly, from the emphasis placed by our Public Schools and older Universities on building up character rather than imparting specialised knowledge.[76]

What 'character' really meant was 'the right sort of chap', socially and personally. This very British criterion was established from the top. In 1951–2 (as it happened, the climactic years of the industrial overload caused by post-Korea rearmament), research into 445 large joint-stock companies found that out of a total of 1,243 directors responding to a questionnaire, 58 per cent had been educated at a public school. Eton, Harrow and Winchester alone accounted for 8 per cent.[77] Moreover, 20 per cent of directors in these companies were Oxbridge graduates – not bad going since in total Oxbridge men only numbered 1 per cent of the graduate managers in Britain.[78] Within this privileged Oxbridge contingent the scientists and technologists were outnumbered two to one by arts graduates[79] – further proof of a British preference for the all-purpose amateur.

So at the summit of the industrial system stood an elite predominantly blessed with the accent of the officers' mess: men bowler-hatted or homburged, wearing suits of military cut either bespoke or at least bought from such approved outfitters as Aquascutum or Simpsons of Piccadilly; gentlemen indeed, confident of manner, instantly recognizable by stance and gesture. They lived in large detached houses on a couple of acres of garden in the suburbanized countryside that surrounded the great cities or within 'exclusive' private estates adjacent to the golf course. They drank gin and tonic; had lunch in a directors' dining room resembling as near as possible a club in St James's; dined in the evening; drove a Humber, Rover, Alvis, Lagonda or perhaps a Rolls-Royce; and were married to ladies who played bridge.[80]

However, the existence of this uniquely British brand of industrial elite (which in major companies would include the top layer of management as well as the directors) marked a surprising paradox. For the public schools and Oxbridge had long existed to produce another kind of elite altogether, by high-mindedly educating recruits for such respectable careers as the professions or public service, whether at home or in the Empire. The early Victorian vanguard of reforming headmasters, all clergymen, had indeed perceived their mission as one of emasculating the sons of rudely vigorous entrepreneurs into Christian gentlemen.[81] Even as recently as the 1930s (when the directors of the 1950s were at school and university) British upper-middle-class young were still receiving a narrow and highly academic schooling in the humanities (meaning above all Greek and Latin) or 'pure' science, supplemented by team games and daily chapel.

How then did products of this entirely un-technocratic education come to dominate the British industrial elite?

Could it be – at least in part – because nearly 30 per cent of the fathers of directors in the survey mentioned above were, or had been, directors themselves, and 19 per cent even directors of the same firms?[82] Could it also be that industry served as a dim second choice for those public school and Oxbridge arts men who failed the exactingly academic entrance examination to the civil or diplomatic services? Thus, even though they might have forfeited the chance of a prestigious career with a chance of a 'K' to crown it, they could at least look for a billet in some large company with a bureaucratic culture more akin to the British public service than to a pushily commercial American corporation.[83]

It therefore hardly astonishes that the 1951–2 research found that, out of the total of 1,243 directors, only 14 per cent had begun their careers in engineering and 4 per cent in a skilled trade. These miserably low percentages compare with the 22 per cent of directors who started off as 'executive trainees', 14 per cent in clerical work, 13 per cent in accounting, 11 per cent in 'other professional' and law, 4 per cent in administration, and 4 per cent in salesmanship.[84]

Once hired, the public school and Oxbridge contingent would then be propelled to the top more by being the right sort of chap (a rugger Blue perhaps? Low golf handicap?) than by technical or professional qualifications alone. And so, in the words of a survey of more than 670 managers in Lancashire and north-eastern Cheshire in 1958, the best combination of personal advantages 'consisted of belonging to a controlling family, having attended a major public school and possibly one of the older universities, and [possessing] the confidence and the contacts useful to a man wanting a successful career . . .'[85] Ninety years earlier a House of Commons Select Committee on scientific instruction had found much the same, reporting that 'the training [sic] of the capitalists, and of the managers of their class, has been that of the higher secondary schools' – 'secondary' in this context meaning the leading public schools and their 'liberal' education.[86]

Despite some notable exceptions like Rolls-Royce's aero-engines division the boardrooms and the top layers of management of major British companies in the 1950s were therefore thin on technologists,[87] thick with arts men with commercial or accountancy experience and sporting the right neckties, be they school, college, club or regimental.[88] After all, it would hardly do to imitate foreigners like the Germans or Swedes or Swiss and to have the business run by those who actually knew all about the product, its design and manufacture. Such plumbers were best left to get on with it on their own. The 'plumbers' for their part reciprocated with sour contempt for their ignorant 'superiors'.[89] It all made for close and happy teamwork.

Yet there was a further ingredient in that dearth of managerial drive noted again and again by the Anglo-American productivity teams. In the 1951–2 survey of 1,243 directors (average age 55.5) no fewer than 41 per cent had stuck with a single firm all their working lives, while another 31 per cent had changed jobs only once, and then early in their careers.[90] Once appointed to the board they stayed there for an average of nearly thirty years.

Why were these men content with such unadventurous careers? Was it because of a yearning for security born of the pre-war years of slump and unemployment? Only think of the pension! But, whatever the reasons, such long service meant that the denizens of a British boardroom became prisoners of their company's customs and culture, mentally shackled by corporate chains of history: stale and set in their ways.

But much the same was true of the broad mass of British management below the boardroom. A 1956 survey covering middle as well as senior managers found that of the sample of 10,000 some 44 per cent had been happy to plod on in one company for all their working lives. Only 33 per cent had joined their firm after the age of thirty. Only 12 per cent had even changed their field of function within the firm during their careers.[91]

As with the directors, the ranking within this spread of managers remarkably corresponded with social origins and schooling. Those who most successfully hogged the prospects for promotion, the 28 per cent of managers (in one survey) who had been to a grammar school and the 19 per cent who had been at a public school,[92] lived in detached houses with about half an acre of back ('rear'!) garden in a well-treed housing estate convenient for shops and town. These were the senior specialist staff – technical, accounting, legal, person-nel officers – and the 'executives' of middle management. Far less likely to be promoted high were the unfortunates who had only been to a state elementary school, leaving it at the age of fourteen without any skill or qualifying piece of paper: victims of a cut-price red-brick education for the children of the red-necked. These unfortunates amounted to a fifth of the 3,327 managers researched in the 1956 survey. Another third of the sample had attended what was described as an 'ordinary secondary school', entering the job market at age sixteen with or without the vocationally useless Schools Certificate.[93] In other words, over 50 per cent of this large sample of British managers belonged to the lower-middle or lower classes, dwelling in the semi-detached houses that monotonously lined the 'Closes', 'Walks', 'Drives', 'Gardens', and 'Avenues' of British suburbia. Indeed, status could be even more precisely identified by the size of the semi and its garden, and the relative prestige of the neighbourhood.

Nevertheless, there was a good reason why this middle ruck of managers attached such importance to such badges of status. It lay in the snobbery of the socially unsure. With the exception of the public-school men, these managers were all denizens of that unchartable sea that lay between the two well-defined shores of the upper class and the working class. All spoke in regional or plebeian accents, with the original roughness sandpapered down to a greater or lesser degree; they ate dinner at midday (though this was changing); bought their ready-made suits from Meakers, Dunn's or Horne Brothers; wore at the weekends blazers with breast pockets adorned with the crests of such un-crack regiments as the Royal Army Service Corps; drove staidly respectable motor cars like Morris Oxfords or Austin Dorsets; and were blessed with 'lady wives' who were proud of their well-furnished 'lounges'.[94]

These were not driven men, exerting themselves to the limit and beyond like their American opposite numbers in order to acquire this year's model of car (and a bigger one at that), an even larger refrigerator, a more ingenious washing machine, a double-oven cooker, and all the rest of the glamorous goods colourfully advertised in American magazines. On the contrary, they were for the most part content to jog along decade after decade in the same cosy working and domestic routines. If they cherished aspirations, it was for the established and leisured existence (as they imagined it) of professionals such as solicitors and academics.[95] Status and security – there lay the prize!

Such were the managers and such were the directors whose responsibility it was to steer British industry out of the past and into the Future.

15. 'Inward-looking Traditionalism': Old Technologies

By the 1950s industrial management in the United States had long since accepted Henry Ford's dictum that history was bunk, and also its corollary that the past should be sold for scrap in order to make way for the future. In Britain, however, things were not so simple. For a start, there coexisted in the one country what amounted to two industrial systems, the old and the new, rather as within the German army in 1940 the elite of fully motorized panzer divisions coexisted with the mass of marching infantry and horse-drawn guns and transport left over from a previous era.

The old system could be defined by the nature of its technologies, all survivals from the first industrial revolution, all now embodied in dense agglomerations of brick, stone and iron. Or it could be defined by geography: the squalid urban wastelands, smoke-corroded, of the North and the Celtic fringes. Or it could even be defined by the prevailing character of management: in professional and personal calibre well below 'world's best practice' or even Britain's best practice; elderly in disposition if not necessarily in actual age; men loyal alike to a traditional product or an existing old works. For that brash American style, that American craze for the newfangled, held little appeal in dark-panelled British boardrooms adorned by portraits of be-whiskered founders. If change must come, then let it be so gradual that no one would feel the pain.

And nowhere was that sentiment more deeply felt than in the recently nationalized coalfields. Their managers had long become accustomed not only to the physical encumbrance of much ancient plant but also to the absurd commercial encumbrance (imposed by Government) of wages and prices averaged across all collieries no matter what the true local operating costs might be.[1] Tucked up safely in a state monopoly as they now were, managers suffered no fear of competitors selling better and cheaper coal. Nor did they face the need to find new markets or devise novel ways to exploit the product, for their fuel-famished customers lay at their mercy.[2] Profit? That indecent word had been replaced since nationalization with, yes, 'surplus'.[3] Call it profit or surplus, either way it mattered little, because between nationalization in 1947 and the end of the post-war decade the NCB turned in an average annual loss of £2 million.[4] Where then were the spurs to dynamic innovation?

The inertia of managers in the coal industry was compounded by their often poor personal calibre. According to the 1955 *Report of the Advisory Committee on Organization* (the Fleck Report, after the Chairman, Sir Alexander Fleck, head of ICI),

> At every level . . . and in most departments, there is a serious shortage of able people equipped with the right qualifications and experience . . . Quick promotion has come to more people than is good for them or the industry . . . While in some appointments – we have instanced Colliery Managers – the turnover is too rapid, in many others it is too slow. Too many men settle down early to a career in the department in which they started . . . Once people have been put into a post there is little planned training for them and virtually no scheme designed to teach them the art of management . . .[5]

As if they were not already personally overstretched enough by the mere business of running a colliery from day to day,[6] these untrained managers also had to cope with the endless grudges and grievances of one of the most truculent workforces in the country. Their deficiencies in the leadership of men no doubt contributed significantly to the coal industry's abysmal post-war strike record (see Chapter 12, above). A zest for innovation? A belief that the existing best is not good enough? It would be unfair to expect it.

It could hardly even be expected at the level of the divisional directors of the NCB. Those rare individuals among them who might personally wish to act like entrepreneurs in an open competitive market could not do so, for they were imprisoned in the role of civil-service-style administrators in a nationwide bureaucracy. They were free neither to initiate major programmes of investment on their own say-so, nor to shut down uneconomic pits. After all, even plans emanating from on high to run down high-cost production in Cumberland and West Durham had to be slowed because the ultimate bosses, the governing politicians of the day, shrank from the political repercussions.[7] For under nationalization the stultifying layers of bureaucratic decision were stacked beyond the National Coal Board in London itself up to the Ministry of Fuel and Power, the Treasury, the Cabinet Production Committee, and the Cabinet.

This amalgam of constipated decision-making and wide managerial incompetence explains why by 1955 the nationalized coal industry had still not got very far with fulfilling the revolutionary 1945 report of the Technical Committee on Coalmining, chaired by Sir Charles Reid (the Reid Report). Reid and his team had called for a 'vast programme of reconstruction of existing mines and the sinking of new ones', together with sweeping closures of inefficient, high-cost pits.[8] Not until the end of 1950 did the National Coal Board get around to publishing its own 'proposals' for a 'National Plan for Coal'. Why the delay? According to one insider, 'our lack of technical staff of all categories in the early years [of nationalization] badly delayed the task of preparing the essential reconstruction plans . . .'[9] Only in spring 1951, after the usual British palaver of committees and consultations, in Whitehall and out of it, did the Board formally submit *Plan for Coal* to the Minister of Fuel and Power. Only in July 1951 was it approved by the Cabinet Production Committee.[10]

Nevertheless, this approval did not mean that the Plan had now been safely loaded onto a rapid conveyor belt towards implementation. Instead the conveyor belt trundled all too slowly at first, the brakes being applied by the Labour Government and then by the Conservatives as part of their common policy of restricting industrial investment in order to accommodate the rearmament programme (see Chapter 00, above). Expenditure on *Plan for Coal* in 1951 came to only 57 per cent of the total projected; in 1952 (supposed to be a peak year) to 64 per cent – in real terms much the same as in 1949. Not until 1953–5, with annual expenditure trebled, did the conveyor belt speed up.[11] Nonetheless, of 281 major schemes in *Plan for Coal*, only 20 had been completed by the end of 1955.

This sluggardly performance can only be blamed in part on the whims of politicians. Technical troubles coupled with technical incapability made their own dismal contribution too:

> the inherent problems of the quality of the coal reserves and the development of the mining equipment were greater than anticipated. An example of the latter was the tunnelling machinery essential for the creation of the level horizon roadways [instead of the conventional British way of following the seam] . . .[12]

It hardly helped to solve such ticklish problems that according to a Coal Board study in 1954–5 the industry was still suffering from

> a serious lack of engineers, which would become more acute with the introduction of planned maintenance and further mechanisation; most engineers were fighting a losing battle to deal with breakdowns and were carrying out too little routine maintenance.[13]

With the managerial mind as narrowly directed as a miner's lamp onto problems of current output, it is understandable that progress in technical innovation was slow in coming. Only in 1948, a year after nationalization, was a Coal Research Establishment created to examine chemical questions. Only in 1952 did a Mining Research Establishment (located in the well-known coalfield of Isleworth, west London) follow, charged with investigating problems of operations underground. Not until 1954 did the NCB inaugurate the Central Engineering Establishment near Burton-on-Trent specifically for research into mechanical engineering, that key to raising productivity and lowering costs.

It was all rather belated, for the most important new machine to be introduced underground in the British coal industry in the post-war decade had already been invented in wartime Germany by the Gewerkschaft Eisenhutte Westfalia: the Panzerforderer, later known in Britain as the AFC (Armoured Flexible Conveyor). This huge Tiger tank of a machine represented a vast improvement on existing belt conveyors because it could carry the immense weight of coal sheered quickly off a long face.[14] In 1952 the Panzerforderer was followed by a creditable exercise in British ad-hockery. On the initiative of the Coal Board's Area General Manager in Lancashire, James Anderton, a small team seconded from coal production – one mechanization engineer, two fitters, a blacksmith and a draughtsman – improvised the prototype of the Anderton Shearer Loader for speeding up the cutting of coal and loading it on to the conveyor (at that time still done by hand).[15] Two years later the German firm of Eickhoff exhibited their own purpose-built version of the ASL at the Essen Trade Fair. In 1955 began series production, with Eickhoff sharing the NCB contracts with a native British firm, Anderson (Strathclyde), and the American-owned British Jeffrey Diamond company.[16]

To invent and develop the ASL was an admirable achievement in itself. But to bring one new machine to the point of manufacture did not make a technically transformed coal industry. Nor did one bright design team make a world-class management. Ten years after the Reid Report, the industry was still awaiting drastic curative surgery. In the meantime, it remained the misshapen offspring of long history, some limbs strong, others crippled: shambling, confused, torpid-brained.[17]

In no better state than the coal industry during the first half of the 1950s was its valued customer, the likewise nationalized British Railways. Here too 'socialization' had laid a new central bureaucracy on top of existing managements already stiff and slow enough. Here too the industry had long lost its freedom to price its products according to their varying costs of operation and profitability.[18] And here too the geographical pattern of the industry was Victorian, the haphazard result of competing ventures eager to turn a quick guinea for the punters. Thus even long-distance trunk routes were sometimes duplicated, while the local lines, laid down long before the coming of tarmac country roads and motor transport, formed an intricate cat's-cradle along which still puffed antique tank-engines pulling one or two equally antique carriages, Lincrusta-ceilinged, and now often empty or nearly so. Amazing were the statistics in 1952 of this working museum of nineteenth-century transport history: 19,500 miles of track; 8,300 stations and goods yards; 19,000 steam locomotives; 42,000 carriages; 1,110,000 goods wagons (mostly hand-braked four-wheelers); 609,000 employees.[19]

Before the Second World War the private railway companies had lacked the imagination and ruthless willpower needed to close down operations that lost money and concentrate on those that made it. Instead they had been, absurdly, more concerned with maintaining or increasing the sheer volume of traffic carried. The consequently precarious finances and wobbling profits induced the companies to give priority to shareholders' yearly dividends over long-term investment. In any case, investment on the scale needed to create a twentieth-century railway would have entailed lavish borrowings, and who would want to lend money to these obsolescent undertakings?[20] The famous steam-hauled 'streamliners' of the late 1930s – the Silver Jubilee, the Coronation and the Coronation Scot – merely served to disguise the creeping decrepitude of the network as a whole, and even these 'shop-windows' could not equal the start-to-stop average speeds of German diesel-powered flyers.[21]

Since the Second World War, and thanks to direct Treasury control through nationalization, the railways had suffered from crippling Government limits on expenditure that had prevented them even making good the arrears of maintenance and repair, let alone embarking on large-scale re-equipment. These shackles were first imposed by the 1945–51 Labour Government[22] and then continued up to 1955 by the Conservatives as one way of making room for the costs of the world role and rearmament (see above, Chapter 7). Nevertheless, this enforced preservation of an already out-of-date railway system was by no means the whole of the trouble. For the mind of the railwayman, from the bowler-hatted in the boardroom to the greasy-overalled on the footplate, was equally out of date. His vision of the future lay in the restoration of an imagined glorious past: pounding pistons, fiery furnaces, proud banners of smoke streaming in the wind. There was no wish to emulate the Continental example and electrify the main long-distance routes. There was no thought of replacing steam by diesel-electric traction, now almost universal on American railroads, even though this could have been done step by step and without the need for the huge capital costs of electrification.[23] So it was that in 1951, at the Festival of Britain exhibition in London, British Railways proudly showed off their major post-war technical innovation: the Britannia, the first of a new standard class of express steam locomotive. It was now two years since the French national railways had built their *last* steam engine.

It is easy to understand why the management of British Railways, from directors to engineers and line controllers, felt emotionally coupled to the steam engine and its past glories. All of them had all been brought up in the age of steam. Many of them were also hereditary railwaymen. A report in 1955 on a BTC study course held on 'Human Relations in the Railway Industry' recorded:

> The outstanding impression is the very considerable degree of pride in the industry felt by all grades of management and workers on the one hand, and on the other the tendency to regard themselves as a race apart, coupled with much resistance to any kind of change.[24]

It served to enhance this institutional in-breeding that (according to the same report) promotion went 'strictly by seniority. It would appear that the quality of the senior people has for years suffered in consequence.'[25] Even such bread-and-butter innovations as pilot schemes of interviewing for promotion by group-selection methods and of the training of interviewers in interviewing techniques 'were thought to be little short of a revolution'.[26]

The Railways Executive, the governing body of the nationalized industry, was itself loaded with men professionally bred to steam and loyal to it. This made them all the readier to heed the insistence of their engineers that (in the words of an authority on the history of the railway) 'really worthwhile economies could be achieved by one more reappraisal of steam locomotive design . . .'[27] The continued faith of the engineers themselves in steam was, in the same writer's opinion, 'symptomatic of the inward-looking traditionalism of the industry'.[28]

If there was to be a revolution that would topple belching, snorting, cinder-spitting, labour-intensive steam in favour of soullessly humming electric locomotives or rumbling, boringly efficient diesels driven like cars, it would have to be forced on the industry from the top.

But at the top, on the footplate of the British Transport Commission, the body responsible for the whole nationalized transport bureaucracy covering road haulage, London Transport and the inland waterways as well as the railways, stood in 1951 a sixty-eight-year-old former civil servant, Sir Cyril Hurcomb. This classic British administrator (Oxford High School and St John's College, Oxford; his interests fishing, birds and nature conservation) had served as Permanent Secretary at the Ministry of Transport before the war and then as Director-General of the Ministry of War Transport. Being innocent of anything so vulgar as a background in business or engineering (but a sound chap, good at chairing committees), he had been the obvious choice in 1947 (when aged sixty-four) for the job of first Chairman of the Commission. He was followed in 1953 by the fifty-seven-year-old General Sir Brian Robertson, whose business experience amounted to a spell as Managing Director for Dunlop in South Africa in the 1930s. Otherwise his personal and professional qualifications for revolutionizing so hidebound and so huge an organization as British Railways lay in experience as Chief Administrative Officer to the wartime Allied Commander-in-Chief in Italy, and later as a peacetime commander-in-chief himself in the Middle East. But another sound chap, of course.

In 1946, meanwhile, the French, in their curious fashion, had appointed as Director-General of the Societé National des Chemins de Fer the forty-one-year-old Louis Armand, a graduate of the École des Mines, a member of 'Les X' (or top *Polytechniciens*), an *Immortel* of the Académie Française, and a former engineer with the Paris–Lyons–Mediterranée railway.[29] Armand was, or would be, author of numerous papers on topics such as the direct use of industrial current for electric propulsion, on education, and on the future of Europe – no doubt also the staples of Hurcomb's and Robertson's conversations at their clubs. Armand's personal qualities included high managerial ability and a remorseless will in driving change. He was, in short, a leader. By 1955 his railway showed it. From Paris electrified main lines stretched to Lille, Toulouse and Lyons, and the catenaries were being strung further fast. Multiple-unit diesel expresses served Normandy, Brittany, and the Auvergne. New colour signalling had been widely installed; new marshalling yards built; old passenger stock replaced by new, including the air-conditioned stainless-steel coaches of the Paris–Nice Mistral; old goods trucks had been scrapped in favour of new bogied and air-braked wagons. Tracks had been realigned to allow fast running.

And behind Armand as he drove this great programme lay the full horsepower of the French state, willing to allot him the lavish investment resources he needed, including Marshall Aid funds in a category which the Labour Government in Britain instead constructively used to write down the National Debt.[30]

Not until May 1954 did the British Transport Commission get round to setting up a 'Planning Committee' (what else? No Louis Armands here; we're British) to work out a 'plan'. According to a historian of nationalized industry, this long delay in even beginning to contemplate modernization was 'quite inexcusable . . . on the part of a body supposed to be devoting its whole energy to matters of major policy'.[31] Under this Planning Committee (on which were represented all main sectional interests of the nationalized network) no fewer than sixteen specialist committees now set to work.[32] The resulting botch-up[33] was submitted to the Minister of Transport at the beginning of January 1955.[34] And botch-up it was. According to one critic within the Treasury, 'it was quite clear that the Commission had not yet worked out a firm plan at all, but had merely put together an assortment of ideas and projects put forward piecemeal by the various regional railway authorities . . .'[35]

Reported the Minister of Transport to his Cabinet colleagues, the fifteen-year plan at a cost of £1.2 billion 'would enable substantial progress to be made in the abandonment of steam propulsion in favour of electric or diesel power . . .'[36] 'Substantial progress?' No more than that? No more than that. The British Transport Commission envisaged that even as late as 1970 half of railway motive-power units would still be steam locomotives.[37] In further proof of their low professional calibre the Railways Executive proposed to buy in up to 200 mainline diesel locomotives of varying designs[38] simply for the purpose, in the acid words of a Treasury civil servant, of 'fooling around for 4 or 5 years experimenting' instead of getting on with the re-equipment of the system.[39] After all, the Americans had long been producing highly reliable diesel locomotives. Why not simply choose from these proven models, and adapt them to the British loading-gauge? Not invented here, of course.

In a long handwritten minute of April 1955 to Burke Trend,

Under-Secretary at the Treasury, a civil servant devastatingly identified the root cause of all the bumbling and torpor not only at the top of the BTC, but also at the top of British industrial policy-making in general: it lay in the 'mentality' of 'the ageing body of men like the Transport Commission' who were in charge. 'They are cautious about spending money; they fear the recurrence of slumps; they do not believe in progress; and the spirit of resignation and defeatism at the top rapidly spreads down the line.'[40]

Nonetheless, it was not the fault of ageing steam-headed rail managers but of a procrastinating Conservative Government that only in autumn 1956 was an updated rail modernization plan (daring stuff, this: London to Manchester electrified by 1967; London to Leeds and York by 1970) finally endorsed in a White Paper (see above, p. 134).[41] Already nearly two years late in chuffing out of the station (ten years late in comparison with French developments), British Railways' modernization plan was in any case far too slowly timetabled in terms of future progress.[42]

> No doubt the real bottleneck to development [wrote a Treasury civil servant] lies in shortage of trained technical staff on the railways – engineers, surveyors, architects, draughtsmen, telecommunications experts and so forth.[43]

But whose fault was this shortage other than that of railway management in general? Theirs was the responsibility for foreseeing corporate needs and hiring specialist staff accordingly, and they had failed to do so – another mark of their poor calibre and blinkered vision.

Unfortunately British Railways were more than a transport service; they also constituted an important branch of the heavy engineering industry in Britain. But the managements of the Victorian workshops that built the locomotives and rolling stock were just as mentally stuck fast in the age of the Stephensons as the men who ran the trains. And equally stuck fast were the plant and the craftsmen. The rail modernization plan called for 2,500 mainline diesel locomotives. But British Railways workshops were only equipped for the manufacture of steam engines. They were incapable of the large-scale production of mainline diesel locomotives.[44] This was why all but thirty of an initial order of 171 such locomotives had to be placed with private firms. British Railways workshops only accepted the order for the batch of thirty on the basis that they would fabricate the mechanical parts, and buy in the power equipment from outside. It logically followed that these antique railway workshops, equipped only to bolt together great chunks of steel, brass and iron castings, should be shut down. In any case, as Den Hollander, head of the Nederlandse Spoorwegen, put it in 1955, 'a railwayman's job is to run trains. It is not his job to be a caterer, hotelier, painter, or builder of locomotives.'[45] Shut down the railway workshops, monuments as they and their craftsmen were to the heroic age when the steam engine constituted high technology? Not a hope. Only think of the uproar that would be raised by the railway and engineering unions! Only think of the political repercussions! As a Treasury mandarin minuted to Burke Trend in June 1955:

> The fact is that the railway workshops will have to be kept going not only because they exist and the people working there must be reassured, but it is inevitable that the railways must have their own repair shops and it must therefore be economical for them to do a good part of the assembly work here.[46]

Trend agreed, but pointed out the quandary that must result:

> Quite clearly the BTC's own workshops can't be shut down: and equally clearly the BTC must be guided, in placing orders for the new locomotives, by considerations of cost and efficiency.[47]

The BTC had their answer: they would buy in the advanced technology such as diesel engines and electric motors, and install them on the cruder bits that could be made in the railway workshops, such as the chassis frames and running gear.[48] But this raised another problem, calling into question the vision and competence of management in British engineering in general. The private firms capable of manufacturing diesel-electric traction equipment were too few and too small to supply what was needed.[49] Metropolitan-Vickers's annual production of mainline diesel locomotives only came to around 50; English Electric's production to about 120.[50] In fact, according to one Whitehall report in 1955, English Electric was the *only* British firm capable of building complete mainline diesel locomotives.[51] In any event, BTC proposed to carry out extensive trials of two foreign diesel engines – Sulzer (Swiss) and MAN (German), now made in Britain under licence.[52] But what about the rest of the private locomotive manufacturers in Britain – North British, Vulcan, Beyer Peacock, Robert Stephenson & Hawthorne Ltd? They had remained just as stuck in the past as the railway workshops, making steam engines only.[53] Yet even in this traditional field they were losing overseas markets to foreign competition, especially German.[54] Nonetheless, the North British Company had bravely begun to look to the future – for it was they who had acquired the British rights of the MAN diesel engine, as well as the rights of a German design of hydraulic transmission.[55] But what if the German manufacturer could supply diesel-hydraulic locomotives cheaper than the home-made – a peril that had already manifested itself in the case of a possible order by the Great Northern Railway of Northern Ireland?[56]

The much grander problem vexing Whitehall departments lay in how to share out the contracts under the modernization plan between the railway workshops and the private manufacturers. For 'fairness' and the desirability of maintaining employment in ailing industrial areas such as Lancashire and Durham alike demanded that all should have their due ration. Tackling the problem naturally called for yet another consultative committee, which this time consisted of representatives of the BTC and various manufacturing associations.[57]

In France, Louis Armand with the backing of the state made his own decisions about the kit best suited to his new railway, and then bought it from a capable indigenous industry. In America, private-enterprise railroad companies made ruthless commercial decisions as to who should supply their motive power and rolling stock. By the same pure criteria of railway modernization and of efficient future operation the only sensible decision in Britain in 1955 would have been to buy the mainline diesels from English-Electric and from American manufacturers like General Motors,[58] and the mainline electric locomotives from Europe (with subcontracting of components to suitable British firms like GEC). Instead, the future equipment of the national rail network of a 'world power' was to be entrusted to a rabble of suppliers, big and small, who in most cases would have to learn a new technology from scratch on the job.[59] In this way the green light dimly showed through the fog of British managerial muddled thinking for a botched-up plan to go ahead, and turn eventually into the expensively botched-up railway of the 1960s, with all its brand-new obsolescence.[60]

What was true of the management of the coal mines and the railways was also true of their peers elsewhere in those begrimed conurbations where the choral societies performed better than the industries. For in the shipyards of the Tyne and the Clyde, in the cotton mills of Lancashire and the woollen mills of Yorkshire, in the Potteries, also dwelt minds walled in by tradition: stubbornly suspicious of the newfangled, whether in the design of the product or the technology of production.

Thus even 'progressive' shipyard managements were a decade behind the Americans and the Germans in large-scale adoption of the system of prefabricating hull sections off site and welding them together on site as a stage in flow-line production. The Americans had first developed the system in wartime on the largest scale for mass-producing 'Liberty' ships, and the Germans had done likewise for mass-producing U-boats.[61] Similarly British shipyard management in the 1950s lagged behind their rivals in Germany or Sweden in such technical innovations as one-tenth-scale lofting and those novel materials and methods for fitting out the interiors of ships which caused the endless ructions with the shipwrights and the boilermakers (see above, Chapter 11). Then again, shipbuilders in Britain spent virtually nothing themselves on research and development, relying instead on the work of state-supported research associations in the industry – which anyway spent a mere fraction of the shipbuilding research budgets of other countries.[62] Likewise now lapsed into fat complacency was the marine engineering industry. The old-fashioned designs of Parsons, once the bold pioneer of the steam turbine, had been shown up in the Second World War when the performance of British warships equipped by them proved humiliatingly inferior to those of American ships equipped by suppliers of industrial power-plants.[63] Although in 1944 a rightly anxious Admiralty had sponsored a new research association to remedy this inferiority, the resulting designs up to the 1960s still performed worse than foreign makes.[64] More seriously still, Britain was also being left behind in the market for marine diesel engines, this being where the future lay. Between 1950 and 1959 the proportion of large marine diesels built in Britain to foreign design rose from 25 per cent to 46 per cent.[65]

As for the cotton industry, the manufacturing wonder of Europe a century and a half earlier, its managements now rivalled those in the shipyards for elderly unwillingness to change. According to the report of a visiting United States productivity team in 1952,

> large elements of both management and labour are dominated by an inertia which prevents them from seeing the future clearly. Their main effort at the moment seems to be directed towards the protection of the least efficient producers and the preservation of antiquated arrangements.[66]

The managements of the cotton industry clung – with a few commendable exceptions – to an outdated individualism, refusing to amalgamate their little firms into large-scale groups integrating the processes of spinning, weaving and dyeing. Even in so 'progressive' a company as Tootal Broadhurst Lee Ltd the boardroom preferred the unexacting status quo to the radical structural changes proposed by their Chairman, Alan Symons, who in consequence resigned in 1957.[67] Meanwhile, the industry also remained loyal for the most part to types of machinery long outmoded in America. Perhaps there was some excuse for this: when the management of J. & P. Coats Ltd did introduce costly new spinning frames at their mill in Paisley, the resulting battle with the National Union of Dyers, Bleachers and Textile Workers over work-stints lasted from 1954 to 1958, ending up before an Industrial Disputes Tribunal.[68] Coats's experience no doubt provided a source of Schadenfreude to mill managers elsewhere who remained content with grandfather's technology. In 1954 this prevailing self-satisfaction provoked a German-born banker to write in the *Manchester Guardian* that 'a few little Sherman acts in Lancashire would make all the difference to the industry's willingness to re-equip'[69] – Sherman being, of course, the Union general who in 1864 marched through Georgia disturbing the serenity of Southern life with fire and sword. But in any case the makers of the textile machines were no better than the manufacturers of the fabrics, though again with rare exceptions which only showed up the torpor of the rest. Designs were conservative, quality of manufacture often slack, export marketing neglected in favour of passively relying on the traditional soft markets of the Commonwealth.[70] It was in 1957 that the British share in world exports of textile machinery, hitherto steady at around 30 per cent, was overtaken by West Germany: the prelude to decades of precipitous decline.[71]

And in the potteries of north Staffordshire, still recognizably the same stiflingly narrow provincial world portrayed in Arnold Bennett's novels of the 'Five Towns', managements remained smugly proud of famous brand names, smugly satisfied with traditional patterns and markets. Back in the eighteenth century Josiah Wedgwood had been an outstanding commercial innovator and taker of risk: advanced production methods, novel designs, new markets. Now, in the 1950s, the company that bore his name proved as content as the rest to jog along with the familiar (aside from a few genteelly timid attempts at the 'contemporary' style), and leave it to foreign competitors like Rosenthal of Germany to win fresh markets with wares by world-class designers such as Raymond Loewy and Walter Gropius.

But surely at least the managements in iron and steel, the very sinew of industrial strength in times of war, Cold War and rearmament, presented a creditable exception to this prevailing inertia? After all, they had drawn up their national modernization programme ten years earlier than the railways. Now, in the early 1950s, the new plants were coming on stream, in South Wales, in the Midlands, in the north-east and north-west: blast furnaces, rolling mills, tube mills, tinplate mills.[72] Yet this modernization plan had been – like that of the railways – less a coherent overall strategy than a totting-up of various piecemeal projects.[73] It was flawed by a failure to envisage ruthless culling of time-expired plant run by time-expired men. In any case, the industry's leaders had only cobbled together their 'plan' because of pressure from a wartime coalition Government justifiably worried that a future shortage of steel could shackle Britain's post-war recovery – as it was to do in the event. And would the boardrooms of the private steel companies have embarked on such enormous projects as the new rolling mills at Margam in South Wales without the backing of the state? After all, it was only because of state sponsorship and state finance during the 1936–9 rearmament drive that Britain was able to enter the post-war era with at least a few world-class modern steel plants amid the picturesque sites of industrial archaeology that still supplied much of the national output.[74] For the previous overall record of the industry from the 1930s back to the 1890s had been one of supine management haplessly resigned to see America and Germany take the lead.[75]

Even by 1955, and despite what had been accomplished since the war, iron and steel still epitomized the two co-existing British industrial systems, ancient and modern. Quaint old handmills and cramped old foundries[76] bizarrely contrasted with new plant on an American scale. Brilliant research into steels to meet the demanding requirements of jet engines contrasted in the same city of Sheffield with the handicraft of back-street cutlers. In nearby Rotherham in 1952 the United Steel Company opened the Swinden Laboratories, then the largest research centre of its kind in the world.[77] Yet all the major post-war innovations in the technology of steel *production* in Britain came from abroad: the Kaldo, Rotor and LD processes (the latter named after the Austrian steelworks at Linz and Donawitz, where it was developed).[78]

Moreover, the demands of the steel modernization programme for new plant and equipment served – just like the equivalent plans of the coal industry and the railways – to expose the managerial lethargy present elsewhere in the British industrial system, particularly in engineering. Thus the constant delays in the construction of the new steel plants over the years were, according to the Board of Trade in 1957, 'largely due to difficulties in the supply of castings, forgings and electrical equipment . . .'[79] Moreover, the British steel-plant construction industry suffered from what the Board of Trade called 'two major weaknesses':

The first defect was that most of the design for large plants had to be imported from America; the industry could make no design effort comparable with that of either the Germans or the Americans. The second defect was that such ability as there was to design and manufacture the largest plants was concentrated in one firm [Davy and United Engineering]. In comparison the German plant industry was perhaps three times as large as that of the United Kingdom and contained several major firms capable of undertaking work of any nature.[80]

The Americans! The Germans! *Yet again!* Such repeated contemporary mentions of their technological prowess can only constitute a backhanded indictment of the boardrooms in all Britain's first-industrial-revolution industries. But what of her other industrial system – the twentieth-century technologies largely concentrated in the Midlands and the South? For it was on *their* management's energy, imagination and zest for change that above all depended Britain's future performance in the markets of the world, and, in turn, her ranking among the powers.

16. The 'Practical Man', Science and *Technik*

In 1983 the President of the Sony Corporation, Masaru Ibuka, was to enunciate in one sentence the strategic principle that had by then enabled Sony to win dominance over the world market in consumer electronics: '. . . if the weight of invention or discovery is one, the weight to bring it to actual development should be ten, and the weight to produce and market it should be one hundred.'[1] But in the first decade of the post-war era the British weighting was virtually the opposite. Here invention and discovery won first prize, not only because they were thought to be high-minded, not to say noble, activities in themselves, but also because under the label 'science' they were even seen as the key to future national success.[2] For the British elite and the British populace alike loved to flash the famous names which by the start of the post-war era had put the island race in the scientific forefront of the world: Sir Alexander Fleming, Howard Florey, Ernst Chain and penicillin; Sir Robert Watson-Watt and radar; Sir John Cockcroft and nuclear fission; Sir Frank Whittle and the jet aircraft engine; Alan Turing and his 'Colossus', wrongly believed to be a true computer and a British 'first'. Had not Trinity College, Cambridge, produced more Nobel prizewinners in the twentieth century than France?

So it was that in the scale of British values mere vulgar success in the marketplace came a poor second to supposedly brilliant scientific innovation or supposedly superior technical ingenuity. An outstanding example of such perversity lies in the gas-cooled reactor installed in the world's first (yes, another wonderful British 'first'!) large-scale nuclear power station at Calder Hall, Northumberland, in 1956, and thereafter in all British nuclear plants up to the 1990s. The United

Kingdom Atomic Energy Authority believed this 'Magnox' design (and its successor, the AGR, or Advanced Gas-cooled Reactor) to be technically superior to the American reactor design based on cooling by pressurized water. Solely for this boffin's reason the UKAEA persisted with development of the Magnox and then the AGR even though they well knew that other countries, including the French, were going to build the American design under licence because it was cheaper to construct and run. Not a single 'Magnox' or AGR was ever built abroad.[3]

Then again, while Fleming might have discovered penicillin in 1928, and Florey and Chain might have demonstrated its potential as a potent cure for bacterial infections in 1940, Britain finished up paying royalties to the American pharmaceutical companies that had developed the techniques for mass-producing the drug. And though ICI might have invented Gammexane, a superior insecticide to Geigy of Switzerland's DDT, it was nevertheless DDT which became the world's favourite wartime and post-war slayer of bugs.[4]

The British elite's veneration of 'science' led the Labour Government to set up in 1947 an Advisory Council on Scientific Policy. What was meant by 'scientific' policy? As the Advisory Council explained in their seventh annual report in 1954,[5] it meant 'the strategy of scientific affairs'.

> This, in a very real sense, is part of national policy, for a country's wealth and power are to-day largely determined by the extent of its scientific knowledge and by its capacity to use that knowledge. The deliberations which led to the establishment of our Council were dominated by this thought.[6]

So in the Council's opinion it was 'scientific knowledge' which provided the key to national wealth and power – not what the Germans call *Technik*, that process of designing and making things for the market which Masaru Ibuka reckoned to outweigh invention and discovery by a hundred to one in importance.

The truth was that the Advisory Council on Scientific Policy simply lacked awareness of *Technik* as a supremely important field of human endeavour in its own right. This was hardly surprising, since on the Council over the period 1947–64 the great academic chams of original research outnumbered the industrialists by nearly two to one. This surely explains why the Advisory Council relegated the role of *Technik* to a second-class category of 'applied science' and the 'exploitation' (their words) of scientific discovery. Even though they recognized that a gulf existed between 'science' and its 'exploitation', they firmly laid the blame for this on industry, rather than on 'science', especially academic science, in its frequent remoteness from the marketplace.[7]

Yet there was nothing novel about the Advisory Council's failure to distinguish science proper from *Technik*. Such mental confusion had long been common enough among academics and bureaucrats. It had bedevilled the 1946 report of the Committee on Scientific Man-power (the Barlow Committee, after the Chairman, Sir Robert Barlow, and also stuffed with academics),[8] which advocated a vast state-funded expansion of 'scientific' research and 'scientific' education, all for the sake of future national prosperity. For the Barlow Committee had categorized as 'scientists' all those holding degrees in mathematics, physics, chemistry and biology – no matter whether they might be engaged in academic 'original' research or in the development of potentially profitable new industrial products and processes.

Similarly, the Advisory Council on Scientific Policy's Scientific Man-power Committee was urging in 1952 (when the new Conservative Government was grappling with the peak load of post-Korea rearmament) that 'every effort' was needed to boost the numbers of 'scientists' (sic) such as chemical engineers, electrical engineers and mechanical engineers![9] Then, in 1954, the Advisory Council themselves formally widened the definition of 'scientist' to embrace 'all scientists, *engineers and technologists* [added emphasis] who are trained to university level or its equivalent'[10] – in American, German or Japanese terms a palpable nonsense of a definition.

From this confusion, common to academe, Whitehall and Westminster, stemmed the belief that in 'science' lay the starting point of growth, wealth and power. In turn, it followed that (as the Barlow Committee had recommended) there must be a huge increase both in the output of science graduates and in the amount of scientific research. To the glee of universities and their laboratories, the hapless taxpayer was duly compelled by both the Labour and Conservative Governments to shell out for this noble programme.

In 1954 it was estimated that state spending on civil research in the year 1954–55 would rise to nearly £20 million, five times more than in 1939–40.[11] Moreover, the Barlow target of 5,000 science graduates per annum by 1955 had been reached by 1950. Two years later the total number of graduates in what the Advisory Council on Scientific Policy delicately called 'pure science' had risen to 5,710 – 86 per cent higher than in 1938.[12] A wonderful achievement? In fact, it was not so wonderful, for the number of graduates in the year 1952–53 in the second-class category of 'applied science' – and that embraced architecture as well as engineering and other technologies – amounted to no more than 3,636, or less than 50 per cent up on 1938.[13]

So it far from flabbergasts that whereas in 1954–55 Britain produced 5,666 science graduates to West Germany's 2,762, she only turned out 2,666 technology graduates to West Germany's 3,243, and France's 4,142.[14]

Meanwhile, the 1945 Report of the Percy Committee (after Lord Eustace Percy, its Chairman) on Higher Technological Education, calling for a vast expansion of technical education, to include German-style 'Colleges of Advanced Technology' equal in status to conventional universities (see below, Chapter 22), had come to nothing: the victim, unlike 'science', of tight restrictions on educational investment imposed by Labour and Conservative cabinets in order to make room for the costs of the world role and rearmament.

The British bias in favour of 'science' over *Technik* is therefore beyond question. Indeed, it may even help to explain how it was that Britain in this period spent a higher proportion of GDP on civil R&D than her rivals, especially Germany, and yet her rate of economic growth was poorer.[15] For contemporary statistical records do not distinguish expenditure on 'R' from expenditure on 'D', but lump them together. It may therefore be that the British total conceals a greater spending on high-minded 'R' and less on market-oriented 'D' in comparison with other countries.

But how did the elite of Whitehall and academe come to believe in the first place that a Britain menaced by foreign competition would be saved in her hour of need by the magic of Merlin in a white coat? After all, it was not the scientist but the self-taught 'practical man' – whether entrepreneur or craftsman – who had brought about Britain's triumph in the first industrial revolution. He had done so by exploiting a happy set of historical and geographical coincidences – plenty of investment capital, absence of internal trade barriers, abundant water power, coal and iron conveniently adjacent to each other, and plenty of labour because enclosure of the common fields was evicting the peasantry from the land.

In any case, science in the eighteenth century was in its earliest infancy: the hobby of curious amateurs. Much more valuable to industrial progress was trial-and-error experimentation by such entrepreneurs as Josiah Wedgwood, and directed at producing a technically better and more saleable product.[16] Nor did there yet exist a snobbish distinction between an industrialist and a 'scientist', for Wedgwood himself was a Fellow of the Royal Society by 1763.

By the 1840s, however, science in the modern sense had taken shape as a coherent and growing body of knowledge and theoretical principles. To enlarge that knowledge and deepen understanding of those principles through organized research had now become a major purpose of European universities, especially German. Yet, just as important, Britain's emerging competitors were also forging science into a practical tool of industrial progress: in short, *Technik*. From the start of their industrialization the *Schwerpunkt* of the Europeans – and the Americans – lay in *Technik* and training in *Technik*. The French École Polytechnique for engineers dates from 1794; the Berlin Technical Institute from 1821; the technical high schools at Karlsruhe from 1825, at Dresden from 1828, at Stuttgart from 1829. The importance accorded to *Technik* by the Europeans extended to the thorough training of their industrial NCO corps and even other ranks. By 1851, for example, there were in Prussia alone twenty-six trade schools (*Fortbildungsschulen*) giving compulsory post-school training. For adults there were *Fachschulen* to train foremen, craftsmen and junior managers.

At the apex of national systems in training in *Technik* stood in France the *Grandes Écoles*, and in Germany formidable university teaching departments in chemistry, metallurgy, physics and engineering which dispatched into industry a broadening stream of graduates. These were the men who were developing the sophisticated technologies that would supersede the simple machines and processes devised earlier by the British 'practical man'. As a consequence, this worthy pioneer was by the 1840s beginning to seem to British critics and foreign visitors alike a primitive soon to be left behind. In 1842, for instance, a young French industrialist reported home that British 'managers do not at all understand the important theory involved in the [manufacturing] processes . . . In certain works in Newcastle, for example, they do not even know how much coal each furnace burns.'[17]

And yet, paradoxically enough, Britain in this same period was becoming strong in fundamental science, thanks to such distinguished minds as Sir Humphry Davy (inventor of the miner's safety lamp) and Michael Faraday (who in 1822 discovered how to generate electricity by rotating a coil in a magnetic field). Moreover, British science was backed by effective sponsors, in the Royal Society (1660) and the Royal Institution (1799). Even the universities of Cambridge and Oxford (those most important and influential of English clubs) created – respectively – a Natural Sciences Tripos in 1848 and an Honours School in Natural Sciences in 1852. Surely nothing could more convincingly prove that pure science was the coming thing – almost as intellectually respectable as the classics, and just as untainted by relevance to 'trade'.

And yet already the British mind was confusing science with *Technik*. In 1853 was founded in London the national museum of *technology*. Yet its formal title was 'the National Museum of *Science* [added emphasis] and Industry'. This was soon shortened to the name by which this institution (now crammed with ingenious mechanical and electrical artefacts) is known today: 'the *Science* Museum'. Another notable example of such confusion of mind lies in the lasting belief that Faraday's discovery of the principle of the dynamo marked the birth of the age of electric power and electric propulsion. Surely, therefore, Faraday's experiments vindicate the prime importance of fundamental research, i.e., of science? But in fact, Faraday's apparatus was no more than a laboratory toy. It was a Belgian engineer who in 1873 developed the first practicable electric dynamo; an American engineer who in 1881 inaugurated the first power station; another American who in 1885 developed the induction motor which today powers all factory machines; and a German, Werner von Siemens, who in 1879 demonstrated the potential of the electric motor for tram and railway traction. It was

the Americans and above all the Germans who by the opening years
of the twentieth century had created powerful and profitable electrical industries making everything from heavy machinery to household gadgetry. It was the Europeans who by then had electrified
major railway routes, such as through the Alpine tunnels. All this
marked a triumph for *Technik*, and – except for Italian-born but
British-based Guglielmo Marconi's development of radio-telegra-
phy,[18] and Sebastian de Ferranti's innovation of the large-scale
power station serving a wide urban area – foreign *Technik* at that.[19]

That Britain's competitors had stolen a march by breeding a new
kind of technologically trained 'practical man' was publicly revealed
at the Paris International Exhibition in 1867, when Britain took
only ten out of ninety prizes, fewer even than Belgium.[20] Alarm at
this poor showing spurred intensive investigations first by a House
of Commons Select Committee in 1867–8 and then by a Royal
Commission in 1868. Their reports, extending as they did beyond
training in *Technik* itself to basic schooling, could only add to
national disquiet. In the prophetic words of the Schools Enquiry
Royal Commission:

> . . . we are bound to add that our evidence appears to show that our
> industrial classes have not even the basis of sound general education
> on which alone technical education can rest . . . in fact, our
> deficiency is not merely a deficiency in technical education, but . . .
> in general intelligence, and unless we remedy this want we shall
> gradually but surely find that our undeniable superiority in wealth
> and perhaps in energy will not save us from decline.[21]

In 1875 and 1884 there followed two more Royal Commission
reports, the first on Scientific Instruction and the Advancement of
Science, and the second on Technical Instruction.[22] Both were
designed to be heavy enough and explosive enough to smash
through the masonry of British smugness. The report on Technical
Instruction not only indicted British managers from boardroom to
foreman for their professional ignorance compared with their European opposite numbers, but also sought to bring home to its
readership that Britain had now ceased to be the measure of 'world's
best practice' in technology and business methods.[23] It compared
the nationwide provision in European countries of well-equipped

technical colleges and evening schools with the formless scatter of low-grade local institutes in Britain; and it urged that Britain must emulate the Continental example. The Royal Commission on Scientific Instruction and the Advancement of Science, for its part, saw Britain's salvation from foreign technological rivalry as lying in a vast expansion of, yes, scientific instruction and expenditure on the advancement of science.[24] And no wonder! For the Commission was little more than a lobby of scientific grandees, including the Chairman himself, William Cavendish, Duke of Devonshire (founder of the Cavendish Laboratory in Cambridge), a passionate believer in science and especially university science.

What then was the sequel in the coming decades to this salvo of heavy-calibre reports fired off in 1868–84? The answer is simple: a considerable expansion of universities and university science, and a failure to match the Continentals in education in *Technik* at any level.[25]

Oxford and Cambridge, with their immense prestige, set the scene. Although the Clarendon Laboratory at Oxford was founded in 1870, followed by chemistry laboratories in 1877–9, a chair in engineering had to wait until 1908. The Cavendish Laboratory in Cambridge dated from 1870, prelude to a continual creation of other science laboratories. Although Cambridge to its credit founded a chair in engineering as early as 1875 (only about half a century later than comparable European developments), it was not until 1892 that 'mechanical sciences' (sic) became a Tripos subject, taken by fewer than 3 per cent of examinees. A private conference in Cambridge in 1903 heard the Vice-Chancellor and the Professor of Chemistry agree that Cambridge did not provide an education suitable for future businessmen.

Meanwhile the humanities, proudly cockscombed with Greek and Latin, were still crowing their dominance over both the ancient universities. Ludicrously enough, until 1919–20 even would-be scientists and engineers had to qualify in Greek in order to be accepted as students. The public schools and their imitators, the grammar schools, naturally conformed with Oxbridge's priorities, given that the successful grooming of boys for Oxbridge entrance constituted their major selling-point. In the 1870s only 18 out of 128 endowed schools were equipped with laboratories. Of all public-school headmasters over the entire century between 1860 and 1960 less than 2 per cent were scientists, let alone technologists. Only a single public school, Oundle, adopted *Technik* as the *Schwerpunkt* of its education.[26]

Although certain Cambridge scientists in the late Victorian era did perform some useful work for industry,[27] the institutional thrust of Cambridge science lay in the advancement of fundamental research. By the end of the nineteenth century the university had become a world centre for such research, especially in physics: an astonishing achievement in only a few decades. But a Massachusetts Institute of Technology or a Charlottenburg Physikalische-Technische Reichsanstalt was the University of Cambridge not. The creation of a true British equivalent to these foreign institutions, the Imperial College of Science, Technology and Medicine in London, had to wait until 1907.

Nor were the provincial universities and university colleges founded after 1870 (often thanks to the benefactions of local industrialists) *technischen Hochschulen* on the Continental pattern, even though their scientific and engineering departments fulfilled a similar function of collaborating with industry. For owing to the malign prestige of the humanities in British elite culture, these new universities were compelled to spread their limited resources over useless knowledges as well as science and technology. At Birmingham University in 1910 there were 185 students in engineering and other technologies, but 396 in the arts; at Manchester, 70 in engineering, 385 in the arts; at Liverpool, 122 in engineering and technology, 270 in the arts.[28] It worsened this imbalance that there were in any case more students studying science than the technologies.

Thus even by the eve of the Great War Britain still trailed far behind her major challenger, Germany, in higher technological education, with Germany's total of 17,000 students in the technical high schools alone almost equalling the non-Oxbridge British total of 19,000 university students in all subjects.[29]

The British disdain for trained technological skill is perhaps even more blatantly revealed by the failure between the 1880s and the Great War to create a European-style country-wide network of high-quality polytechnics, trade schools and evening institutes, as recommended by the 1884 Royal Commission on Technical

Instruction. Certainly there took place an impressive expansion from 1890 onwards, both in numbers of technical colleges and of candidates for the qualifications offered by such examining bodies as the City and Guilds of London Institute. But this was impressive only in comparison with the contemptibly small British provision beforehand – not in comparison with the scale and spread of European technical education. The figures say it all: fewer than twenty first-class technical schools were built in Britain between 1902 and 1918.[30]

It was Britain's misfortune that systematic training in *Technik* was as much disdained by the 'practical man' in British industry as by the grand intellectual elite: a double bind, and a lasting one. To the 'practical man', be he employer or trade union craftsman, 'training' was the rule of thumb you learned on the job from your elders and betters: the way we do it, the way we've always done it. As the Board of Education reported in 1910:

> The slow growth of these technical institutions is, however, in the main to be ascribed to the small demand in this country for the service of young men well-trained in the theoretical side of industrial operations and in the service underlying them.[31]

Four years later the demands of total war against Imperial Germany revealed to Government, if not to the public, how disastrously Britain had allowed *Technik* to languish between high science on the one hand and the hidebound 'practical man' on the other.[32] In the case of steel, the basic sinew of industrial strength in peace and war, Britain was now forced to import huge quantities from America and Canada because her own industry was too small and technically backward. With imports of special steels (such as for high-speed cutting tools) from Germany cut off, Britain would have to look to Sweden for rescue. And this despite all the distinction of metallurgical research in Britain.

Nor had the similar excellence of university engineering 'sciences' saved Britain from depending in peacetime on Germany for sophisticated semi-automatic machine tools. It was because the machine-tool designs of the British 'practical man' had yet to emerge from the Victorian age that Britain in wartime had to buy in large quantities of modern tools from the United States, Sweden

316

and Switzerland in order to equip her new 'national' munitions factories. As it happened, Britain could not at first make the fuzes for shells either, because she had failed to develop light-engineering industries capable of fabricating miniature mechanisms to fine tolerances, such as clockwork toys. Nor could Britain supply herself with products basic to the new era of the internal combustion engine and the motor vehicle such as magnetos and ball bearings. These too had been largely imported from Germany in peacetime, and now in wartime would have to be bought in from Sweden and Switzerland until Britain could create her own new industries. And in 1914 Britain could not even manufacture aero-engines, relying instead on imports from France.

Yet another gulf between academic science (in this case chemistry) and Britain's industrial capability was revealed by the wartime need to fill shells with explosive if they were not to remain, in Lloyd George's phrase, harmless steel vases. For distinguished research notwithstanding, Britain had failed to develop an organic chemical industry which could be switched to making explosives on the grand scale. In peacetime she had depended on Germany even for the dyes for the Royal Navy's blue rig and the army's khaki uniform. More than this, she had depended on Germany for drugs like aspirin, novocaine and Salvarsan (all of them developments of German Technik). The only place in Britain where novocaine and Salvarsan could be made before the war was the Ellesmere Port works of a subsidiary of Farbwerke Hoechst.[33]

This by no means inclusive catalogue of shortcomings in advanced Technik go to demonstrate how little impact on the nature of British industrial production had been made by university science in the years leading up to the Great War. But from the middle of 1915 onwards the British and their leaders were goaded by national peril in a total war into carrying through a remarkable industrial revolution – remarkable not only because of the scale of the deficiencies that must be made good, but also because the revolution was driven through at utmost speed.[34] By 1918 Britain had created an organic chemical industry that was the basis of the future ICI; a vast aircraft and aero-engine industry; and new factories to make aircraft instrumentation, ball bearings, magnetos, optical and scientific instruments, and much else besides. Electric power output had been doubled and the average capacity of a power station increased by thirteen times. All this constituted an astounding achievement, marred only by the diehard stand of the craft unions against novel production methods and 'dilution' (see above, p. 262). The achievement owed itself to an unprecedented partnership between the state, private industry and the education system.

Yet every one of the wartime accomplishments in *Technik* necessarily denotes an equivalent peacetime dereliction.

Nowhere was this more true than in the case of the universities, their staffs and laboratories, for now these were fully mobilized in the service of industry for the first time in their history. Academic 'science' for its own sake gave way to the development of desperately needed new products and processes: in short, to *Technik*. Academic 'education' gave way to the training of industrial personnel, another field of relative British neglect before the war. In the apt words of the report of the Board of Education for 1914–16, 'The War has brought the professor and the manufacturer together with results which neither of them are likely to forget.'[35]

It was thanks to University College, London, that Britain developed a new process for fixing nitrogen, a basic ingredient of TNT. This enabled the government to build a main production plant at Billingham, to be taken over by ICI in the 1920s. It was Chaim Weizmann at Manchester who discovered how to mass-produce acetone by fermenting starch – essential to the production of cordite and for 'doping' aircraft fabric. The effectiveness of the British gas mask owed itself to experiments at Oxford and Bristol universities. Research at Manchester and Cambridge led eventually to a process for producing mustard gas which by the end of the war gave Britain an output thirty times larger than Germany's, and at one-thirtieth of the cost. It was owing to close collaboration between university research and industry that Britain also caught up in the production of drugs, the key to treating the sick and wounded. To cite one example, St Andrews University devised a means of producing novocaine at half the cost and a fifth of the time of the German Hoechst method.

In aeronautics too, the universities played a truly vital role, with work on light alloys, on aerodynamic design and instrumentation. It was mathematical studies on aircraft structure that led to British combat aircraft like the SE5 being much more stable than their German equivalents, with resulting advantage in the dogfights over the Western front.

Then again, the development of British-made magnetos owed much to Bangor University; of radio to Royal Holloway College, which developed the thermionic valve adopted by the Royal Navy; of Morse radio for communication with submerged submarines to Birmingham University. The hydrophone, that major step forward in detecting submerged U-boats, was developed thanks to research by Queen Mary College, London.

Only this triumph of mobilized *Technik* on the home front made possible the winning of final victory in the field in 1918. But would it provide a model for peacetime? It would not – any more than would the rest of the wartime experience, such as the suspension of trade union restrictive practices or the coming together of the British Empire as a cohesive political and military power under London's leadership.[36]

Instead, with academic science returning to its own curiosities, the professor and the manufacturer went their separate ways again. Between the world wars the pursuit of success in world markets was to be backed by only a fraction of the talent deployed on *Technik* in 1914–18 in pursuit of victory.[37] Within industry itself the bulk of peacetime R&D was contributed by only some twenty out of 200 major firms, with Imperial Chemical Industries (created in 1926 from Brunner, Mond and that legacy of wartime, the British Dyestuffs Corporation) in the lead. Elsewhere, and with some creditable native exceptions such as Marconi and Pye in electronics and Glaxo in pharmaceuticals, it was the trans-national concerns like Shell and Unilever or the present and former out-stations of foreign *Technik* like Burroughs Wellcome, Westinghouse, Siemens, AEI and EMI which shone in developing marketable new types of product.[38]

But otherwise, within the wider sprawl of works and mills and small-to-middling manufacturing companies that made up the bulk of Britain's industrial base, the 'practical man' just plodded on through the 1920s and 1930s in the same old ways, still ignorant of *Technik* as the Europeans and Americans understood it, and a world away from university science and its lofty concern with such questions as nuclear physics.[39] Indeed, the British motor car industry, the largest in Europe between the world wars, was assembled by a new wave of 'practical men', such as William Morris (a bicycle maker educated at a village school), William Rootes (a former apprentice) and Herbert Austin (a former foundry apprentice): complete throwbacks to the entrepreneurial style of the first industrial revolution. Graduate technologists and managers? R&D and design departments? Cost accountants? Never! You bought in the parts cheap, and on assembly lines copied from Ford and General Motors clapped them together into vehicles mechanically primitive (by American standards),[40] and priced by the simple device of undercutting your main British rival by a few pounds.

As for the British elite, culturally and socially so distant from the brash workshops of Cowley and Longbridge, they once again prized the liberal arts over science, and science over *Technik*. The depressing evidence lies in the comparative percentages of university students in different subject areas during the inter-war period. In the five years 1920/21–1924/25 the technologies were studied by 13.5 per cent of students, as against 17.0 per cent in 'pure science', and no less than 39.8 per cent in the arts. By the period 1935/36–1938/39 technology students had dropped to 9.7 per cent, whereas arts students had actually risen to 46.5 per cent of the total. Even when students in 'pure science' (at 16.3 per cent) and technology are lumped together, their joint percentage in 1935/36–1938/39 comes to not much more than half that of the arts.[41] Thus did the legacy of Victorian intellectual snobbery continue to blight the university scene.

For the socially second class, however, a second-class part-time route to higher technological qualifications had been opened in 1920, in the form of Ordinary and Higher National Diplomas. By 1938 this half-cocked British reply to European technical high schools and engineering schools had produced a cumulative total of only 3,317 OND passes and 1,668 HNDs.[42] The forty-six German engineer schools alone were annually turning out 2,000 qualified practical engineers in the late 1930s.[43]

In any case, the general standard of the buildings and equipment of British technical colleges on the eve of the Second World War remained, in the judgement of a 1943 Whitehall report, 'deplorably low'[44] – all because of a lack of investment stemming from the governing elite's renewed disdain for *Technik*.

Defence research was another matter. Even in 1930, at the peak of pacifistic disarmament and romantic faith in the League of Nations, the state spent on this at least a third more than the whole of industry spent on civil R&D.[45] Here lay another penalty of being the Mother Country of a vulnerable Empire. Yet in defence too the old fissure had reopened between what 'science' could invent and what the 'practical man' could manufacture. Why, for instance, did the Admiralty, despite all the R&D resources available to it, choose before the Second World War an anti-aircraft fire-control system which guessed at an attacking aircraft's movements rather than precisely measured them like the 'tachymetric' system adopted by the United States Navy? Answer: because 'the practical men' of British engineering could not fabricate to the fine tolerances required by the American system.[46] More damning still, the Admiralty had to scour the country to find any firm even capable of making the cruder British design – which was then delivered late. In any case, the ships' anti-aircraft guns themselves – Oerlikons and Bofors – had to be bought in from Europe, for Vickers' attempt at such a gun failed under test.[47] Similarly, the existence of the Admiralty's research departments failed to save new British warships from being equipped with steam propulsion machinery so crude in design and manufacture (compared with American) as grossly to waste fuel, with crippling effect on operating range.[48]

As for the Air Ministry, this spent in 1930 nearly half as much again on research as the Admiralty. It enjoyed a first-class scientific service in the Royal Aeronautical Establishment at Farnborough (a legacy of the fright generated by the Great War). Yet when the rearmament of the Royal Air Force began in 1935–6 the airframe and aero-engine industries proved technically incapable of manufacturing the latest designs of all-metal monoplane fighters and bombers. In consequence there were immense delays in planned deliveries while the industry equipped itself with sophisticated new machine tools (from America and Germany) and learned new production techniques.[49] Meanwhile, the gulf between research and *Technik* in aviation was further displayed by problems in manufacturing powered gun-turrets, and even more by the need to buy in aircraft instrumentation of all kinds from abroad until new British factories could be built and equipped (shades of the opening years of the Great War).[50]

Weaknesses in *Technik* similarly marred one of British science's most celebrated achievements before and during the Second World War: radar. It was Robert Watson-Watt's original research into radio and the cathode-ray oscillograph which led to the first British trial of radar in 1935, and thereafter to the building of the 'Chain Home' series of early-warning stations which in 1940 enabled Fighter Command to win the Battle of Britain. Yet the radar sets themselves were only completed thanks to thermionic valves imported from Holland and America, for the 'practical men' of the British radio industry proved unable to make enough quickly enough.[51]

The 'Chain Home' stations were followed by a wonderful series of wartime innovations in the field of radar by teams of scientists mobilized from the Cavendish and Clarendon Laboratories, from Birmingham University and from the Telecommunications Research Establishment at Malvern: 10cm radar sets for detecting surfaced U-boats; devices like Oboe and H2S, which enabled Bomber Command to strike home in darkness or foul weather; proximity fuzes which burst an anti-aircraft shell when close to its target; gunnery radars for the army and the Royal Navy.

When these secrets were revealed after the war they were hailed as triumphs for British science. Yet in truth wartime radar development provides yet another doleful case-study in the alienation of science from *Technik* in Britain. Tucked away in their laboratories the scientists invented their ingenious new devices without benefit of any comprehension of production engineering or the advice of production engineers. Their brilliant prototypes were therefore not easy to adapt for series manufacture. But in any case the manufacture of kit as technically sophisticated as radar found the British radio and engineering industries wanting. Equipment like 10cm radar and H2S were delivered months late, even a year late – partly because of bottlenecks over key precision components and partly because of sheer incompetent production management. From this fresh failure of *Technik* Britain had to be rescued by American industry, which sent over huge quantities of thermionic valves[52] (including the magnetron) and other components, as well as advanced plant for 'high speed machine controlled production'.[53] Finally, in 1943, shortage of technologists on top of troubles in manufacture compelled Britain to consent to America taking over the main responsibility for future radar research and development.[54]

In contrast to post-war vainglory about British genius in radar and related electronics, the Government was being warned in 1944–5 that in the future peacetime market for mundane telecommunications equipment Britain could be eclipsed. According to one expert report, two American companies, GE and ITT, had before the war controlled 60 per cent of all telecommunications and electrical firms in Britain, France and Italy combined.[55] The only European rival of comparable weight had been the German firm of Siemens & Halske, employing some 120,000 people and possessing many research laboratories staffed by a total of some 2,000 engineers and specialists.[56] The British Government was advised by this expert that it was important that Britain, not America, took over Siemens & Halske, for 'control of that company would advance this country technically very much nearer to the high position held by America, by providing the Research facilities and Techniques which England lacks'.[57]

It has to be said that the record of the Second World War indicates that British *Technik* as a whole had actually lost ground relatively since the Great War. By 1917–18 British industry could not only make in abundance every kind of aircraft, warship, weaponry, munitions and medical equipment needed by the armed forces of the British Empire, but also could lavishly supply its allies, including the United States forces in Europe. But in 1944–5 Britain depended on America for bulk supplies of trucks, tanks and self-propelled guns; for escort aircraft carriers; for Very Long Range anti-U-boat aircraft; for electronic components; and for key items of advanced industrial technology. Even development of that other wartime wonder of British invention, the jet engine, depended on American turbine blades and impellers.[58]

Nonetheless, in the euphoria that followed victory over Germany in May 1945, no one doubted that, in the words of the *Daily Mirror*, 'as the secrets of the war are revealed, British achievements take on a new glamour . . .' Was not radar, in the words of the *Daily Mail*, 'a British discovery developed by British scientists and engineers into the biggest single war-winning factor produced for many years'? More to the point, did not the course of the air war as a whole constitute, as a *Times* headline had it, a 'Triumph for Science'? And the Prime Minister himself in his victory broadcast on the BBC reminded his listeners that 'our scientists are not surpassed by any nation in the world . . .'[59]

So that was it – 'science' had won the war. Clearly, then, the key to national success in the post-war era lay in yet more science and more scientists. But in particular 'science' and scientists were seen by the governing elite as the keys to a grand effort to catch up the United States in certain advanced technologies (radar, aeronautics and the atom bomb being the outstanding examples).

In order to drive this grand effort the Ministry of Supply was kept going after 1945 instead of being abolished at the peace like its Great War predecessor, the Ministry of Munitions. The effort – and with it the Ministry of Supply's own directing role – became grander yet after 1950 thanks to the ambitious post-Korea rearmament programme. By the mid-1950s nearly half of all R&D carried out in industry was being funded by the state for military purposes.[60] So for the first time in peacetime history the British state had taken on a general responsibility for masterminding the development of new technologies, new industrial capabilities and new products.[61]

It marked a momentous departure. But it suffered from just one drawback. Its *Schwerpunkt* lay in realizing the dream of Britain as a future world power in the same league as the United States. It did *not* lie in winning future global markets. Indeed, this new state-sponsored military-industrial complex was positively to damage Britain's prospects in those markets, by devouring the best of the nation's limited resources in *Technik* and managerial talent.

And the greediest single devourer of those resources – and of taxpayers' money – was that gross and lumbering bird, the aerospace industry.

17. 'Not Wholly Unsuccessful': the Aircraft Industry

It was the wartime coalition Government that took the original fateful decision that Britain in the post-war era should not only manufacture all types of aircraft and missiles required by her armed forces, but also compete with the United States in making and marketing civil airliners. They did so even though they well knew that the British aircraft industry enjoyed only about a third of the all-round resources of the American industry. They further decided that British constructors should not limit themselves to short-haul passenger aircraft, even though this 'niche' market offered better chances of foreign sales, but instead challenge the Americans head-on in the most competitive field of all, that for large long-distance transports. They came to this decision even though the Americans by 1944 already had a potential transatlantic airliner, the Lockheed Constellation, in series production as a military transport.[1]

Why did the wartime coalition and thereafter the Labour Government between 1945 and 1951 so choose to pour scarce resources (especially scarce scientific and technical personnel) into such a high-risk investment? There is no evidence that they based the decision on a comparative cost-benefit analysis between putting so many golden eggs in one precarious basket and other possible fields for national investment. Instead, the Whitehall records make clear that the wartime coalition and the post-war Labour government alike simply took it for granted that being a world leader in aviation rightfully belonged to Britain's inherited status as a first-class power.

Thus it was on the grounds of British 'prestige' that Labour ministers again and again justified their continued backing of such ever more evident turkeys as the commercially flightless[2] Bristol Brabazon intended for the Atlantic route. Even when in December 1950 (the month of disastrous retreat in Korea) the Labour Government finally accepted that the Brabazon would never carry a paying passenger, they still decided to complete a second prototype for 'research' purposes, on the grounds that 'cancellation would be damaging to our prestige . . .'[3]

'Prestige'! This same favourite governmental word of the time was also repeatedly used by Labour ministers to justify compelling the nationalized airlines in the late 1940s to fly converted wartime bombers at a loss (carried by the taxpayer) when foreign rivals were flying real airliners, American-made, at a profit.[4]

As commercial hopes of the Brabazon and another monstrosity, the SR-45 ('Princess') flying boat, died at the end of 1950 (combined cost to the taxpayer by 1955: £19.45 million),[5] new hopes were already lifting the wings of ministerial optimism. At the 1950 Farnborough Air Show Britain had shown off – to the wonder and acclaim of spectators – the prototype of the world's first jet-propelled airliner, the de Havilland Comet. Particularly impressed was the President of the Boeing Aircraft Corporation, whose own jet airliner project was still years behind the Comet. And the Comet would be shortly followed by the turbo-propeller Bristol 175 (later stirringly named 'Britannia'), another British first.

These freshly airborne hopes of the Labour Government were fully shared by Winston Churchill's Conservatives after their election victory of October 1951. After all, although the Germans and Japanese were now becoming ever greater commercial threats in less glamorous technologies, they had since the war been forbidden to manufacture aircraft – lucky for them, as it turned out. The French, for their part, were still rebuilding their aircraft industry. That left the Americans as Britain's only rival in the air. But what a rival! Just the same, the new Conservative Government still believed, like its Labour predecessor, that the British aircraft industry could play and win in the same league as the American giant. They reckoned that the size of the potential jackpot justified the gamble, huge though that evidently was. And they too, like Labour, were obsessed with aeronautical 'status' and 'prestige'. For in mid-twentieth-century Britain old-fashioned patriotism had been reinvented as romantic faith in British advanced technology: 'Reach for the Sky', and all that.

> During the next few years the United Kingdom has an opportunity, which may not recur, of developing aircraft manufacture as one of our major export industries. On whether we grasp this opportunity, and so establish an industry of the utmost strategic and economic importance, our future *as a great nation* [added emphasis] may to no small extent depend.[6]

In these ringing terms did the Minister of Supply (Duncan Sandys, Churchill's son-in-law) and the Secretary of State for Air (Lord De L'Isle and Dudley) on 23 May 1952 open their case for continued state backing for the industry and its development of new aircraft. After all, they went on, aircraft were 'a most attractive export' since the ratio between the cost of materials and the value of the finished product was only excelled by precision products like watches.[7] Moreover, expansion of aircraft exports would boost Britain's global importance:

> to the extent that the countries of the Commonwealth and the rest of the free world look to us for their supplies of aircraft (and of the electronic and other equipment that goes with them) they will tend to be linked to us militarily and politically, and *our influence in world affairs will thereby be increased* [added emphasis] . . .[8]

Nonetheless, the two ministers did not neglect to plug the enticing commercial prospects: 'If we can win over foreign and Commonwealth air lines from their present American allegiance we should be able to arrange production on a scale that would put us in a fully competitive position.'[9]

> In short, we have in the aircraft industry an asset of enormous importance to the future of our economy. If we can once obtain a large share of the world trade, it will not be easily taken from us; firstly because having once adopted British aircraft, with the spares, equipment, tools etc. that go with them, an air line will not readily change to foreign types, and secondly because in this particular industry we are less exposed to the competition to which we are vulnerable elsewhere.[10]

But surely there were some snags in all this? The first and biggest, glibly overflown by the two ministers in their vaunting of British technical innovation, was that (to adapt their own argument and language in regard to Britain's own future prospects) America had in fact already obtained a large share of the world trade. This (further to paraphrase the two ministers) would not be easily taken from her because foreign airlines, having adopted American aircraft, with the spares, equipment, tools, etc. which went with them, would not 'readily change to another supplier': viz., Great Britain.

How then did Sandys (Eton and Magdalen College, Oxford) and De L'Isle (Eton and Magdalene College, Cambridge), two gentlemen innocent of technological or business training, conceive that the British aircraft industry could nevertheless overcome this daunting handicap – the more daunting because of the size, technical resources, and marketing power of the American industry? In the first place, they did not even accept that a daunting handicap existed, assuring their Cabinet colleagues: 'Potentially, the competitive position of the United Kingdom is very strong.'

> There is no doubt of our ability to produce aircraft and aero-engines of the highest quality. Of existing types, the Comet and Viscount air liners and the Canberra light bomber, and of types shortly to be produced, the Bristol 175 [Britannia] air liner, the F.3. fighter and the Valiant medium bomber, are widely admitted to be the best in their classes in the world. We are acknowledged to lead the world in the design of aero-engines.[11]

Despite their smug and very British belief that innovative design and technical excellence as such supplied (along with lower costs) the keys to commercial success, the ministers did concede that the export market 'will not be secured without some risks and sacrifices':

> It is no use having the best and cheapest aircraft in the world unless you can offer timely and reasonably assured delivery . . . there is no doubt that we could sell substantially greater numbers of Viscounts overseas if they could be produced in the reasonably near future and with the introduction of the Comet into scheduled service there is every indication that the same situation will occur in the case of this type also . . . Our problem is to ensure that, *from our limited capacity*

[added emphasis], we can offer deliveries at the rate necessary to obtain the orders.[12]

Although the ministers failed to mention it, this 'limited capacity' was fragmented between twenty aircraft companies (even the six biggest being dwarfed by Boeing or Douglas) and spread over the production of over thirty-five very different types of aircraft (military and civil), with a further thirty-six types under development along with an array of fancifully named guided weapons or ballistic missiles.[13] Moreover, the technology of aircraft systems and instrumentation was ever faster becoming ever more complex, which must test the industry's network of component suppliers to the utmost, and especially in electronics and precision engineering. No matter: Sandys argued to his colleagues on the Cabinet Economic Policy Committee that, thanks to Britain's technical lead in jet airliners (with the larger Comet Mark III due in service by 1956 and the airliner version of the Vickers Valiant swept-wing bomber by 1957), 'there is no reason why we should not capture a large part of the world market from the Americans'.[14]

However, he reminded his colleagues that Britain's technical lead was 'due in large measure to the fact that the Government has financed the development of new types, and it is vitally important that in the critical three or four years ahead, this assistance should continue.' Sandys therefore recommended to the Economic Policy Committee – successfully in the event[15] – that the Government should both fork out financial support to promising development projects (in particular for the Comet Mark III and the airliner version of the Valiant), and also 'take some share in the [commercial] risk' by placing orders to cover a proportion of the production runs.[16]

Thus did a new government clear for take-off a renewed flight into the blue yonder by the aircraft industry. But would the management crew turn out to be any better at piloting the industry in the first half of the 1950s than they had in the second half of the 1940s?

At least the boardrooms and executive levels of the aircraft companies were dominated by engineers[17] rather than by the accountants and salesmen customary elsewhere in Britain. This pattern might seem encouragingly to resemble that of American or German manufacturing leadership. Yet the resemblance was only superficial. In both America and Germany the engineer who had become a senior manager would also have studied business administration and cost-accounting, either as part of his graduate engineer's course or in a business school (of which Britain in the early 1950s still possessed not a single example). He would thus be able to set his engineering expertise within a wider framework of commercial understanding and strategic vision.[18] But this was rarely the case at the top of the British aircraft industry, where 'engineer' meant no more than just that. The elite of graduate engineers, especially those from the University of Cambridge and Imperial College, would have studied the subject in its narrowest and purest form as theory, and certainly without any leaven of business economics. Those senior managers who were former workshop-trained apprentices with a part-time degree or Higher National Diploma were very much nuts-and-bolts engineers in the old 'practical man' British tradition. All in all, therefore, this was a culture that conceived of future aircraft in terms of technology for its own sake rather than of costs, customers and the market. Surely the world would rush to buy a marvellous piece of innovative design?

In military aviation the 1950s began well enough with the delivery to the Royal Air Force in 1951 of the English Electric Canberra jet-propelled light bomber. By the end of 1954 the company had delivered 472 aircraft. In proof of its rugged dependability the Canberra was to be still in service as a photo-reconnaissance aircraft over forty years later. But, sadly, one Canberra did not an aeronautical summer make. The years 1951–5 marked a dragging anticlimax in the development and delivery of other new types of military aircraft, as was gloomily documented in a report by the Minister of Supply, now Selwyn Lloyd, in January 1955 in response to an urgent request from the Prime Minister, Winston Churchill, and submitted to him personally.[19]

Of the new swept-wing or delta-wing 'V' bombers (Valiant, Vulcan and Victor), classified in 1950 as of 'supreme importance'[20] because their role would be to carry the 'independent' British nuclear deterrent, only the Vickers Valiant was likely to be delivered in 1955. It would receive 'limited clearance' for operations in January, its delivery to the Royal Air Force being four months behind forecast.[21] Why the delay and why the 'limited clearance'? They were due to aileron vibration when flying at high speed at high altitude. Although the Valiant was designed to fly at 90 per cent of the speed of sound, it would now be limited to 80 per cent. In the case of the Avro Vulcan, the first of two prototypes had completed about a third of its flight test programme, but the second prototype had been 'extensively damaged in a forced landing' in summer 1954, and was still on the ground.[22] Clearance of the Vulcan for service was not now expected before March 1956. As for the Handley Page Victor, the first of its two prototypes had been totally destroyed in a fatal accident. This setback followed on from a three-month delay in the test programme because 'a large amount of faulty material' had to be replaced in both prototypes. Limited clearance of the Victor was not expected before about September 1956.[23]

The record for new fighters had turned out just as disappointing. Although the turbo-jet Vickers Venom had been delivered in quantity by the end of 1954 in its two versions of single-seat day fighter-bomber and a two-seater night fighter with radar, Selwyn Lloyd had to report that 'many troubles have been experienced'. Nevertheless he reassuringly added that 'action to remedy those troubles has been taken . . .'[24] As for the single-seat swept-wing Hawker Hunter, the first two marks were now in service and 'reasonably satisfactory'. Nonetheless, they suffered from 'a man-oeuvring limitation and an inconsistent performance with the Avon engine in the Mark I'.[25] A more powerful version of the Avon would give later marks of the Hunter a better performance, but only at the cost of lending 'greater significance' to the manoeuvring limitation. In any case, a much more serious problem with the Hunter lay with its armament:

At present the aircraft have not been cleared for gun firing in the Service. There are two main difficulties. First, the ejected links are causing damage by striking the airframe and a collector system is being designed to overcome this. Secondly, at high altitude, gun firing interferes with engine performance. The problem is being tackled energetically, but it will be several months before the aircraft will be fully operational in service.[26]

Also seriously delayed (in this case because of the loss of two aircraft during flight testing) was the development programme for the Gloster Javelin delta-winged, two-seater, twin-jet, all-weather fighter capable of launching the Blue Jay guided weapon. Limited clearance was expected in April 1955, reported Selwyn Lloyd in January, with a forecast of 120 aircraft delivered by the end of March 1956.[27] But in December 1955 another Javelin crashed on test, the victim of a vicious spin peculiar to its experimental delta-wing, which set back the whole programme.[28]

Yet all these troubles amounted to mere passing turbulence compared with the ultimately doomed flight of the Supermarine Swift swept-wing fighter, first ordered in 1950. This was designed to have a greater range than the Hunter and to be more versatile, with variants capable of tactical and photo reconnaissance and also of delivering Blue Sky, Britain's first air-to-air guided weapon. In January 1955, Selwyn Lloyd had to tell Churchill that the Swift 'is suffering from major aerodynamic troubles'.[29] It would, he said, be necessary to decide 'within a couple of months' whether it would be 'wise to continue with the full production programme [of 100] or to reduce it.' That one Swift variant was being developed to carry Blue Sky (the first aircraft to do so) alone rendered it 'a serious matter to abandon the Swift altogether'.[30] But abandoned it finally was in 1957, except for twenty-five photo-reconnaissance versions.[31]

Since Britain in the 1950s still aspired to the role of global seapower, the aircraft industry had also to develop and manufacture new types for the Royal Navy's carriers and shore stations. By the end of 1954 nearly 300 Seahawk fighters/fighter-bombers had been delivered: 'an excellent deck-landing aircraft,' reported the Minister of Supply to the Prime Minister, 'but there are still serious limitations on performance above 35,000 feet for which technical remedies are being urgently studied.'[32] Deliveries of the Sea Venom Mark 20 all-weather fighter were expected shortly, although the 'most important Service limitation to date has been the lack of a carrier release ... Severe flying restrictions have been imposed pending essential modifications to prevent fire.'[33] The Mark 21 was not yet cleared for service, the navy having criticized the absence of ejector seats for pilot and observer. Wrote Selwyn Lloyd: 'A trial installation with a light-weight seat is in hand.'[34] In the case of the Fairey Gannet anti-submarine aircraft, service with an experimental squadron since February 1954 had revealed 'a serious engine control trouble, which, though now cleared, has delayed the delivery programme'.[35]

As for the new ballistic missiles and guided weapons, from Red Shoes to Blue Cheese,[36] the Minister thought that there was 'a fair chance that the planned dates will be met although in some cases the margin of time remaining against unforeseen development troubles is uncomfortably small'.[37] However, the Secretary of State for Defence, Harold Macmillan, had to warn the Prime Minister that Blue Sky, Red Shoes and Red Duster 'are unlikely to be brought into use operationally . . .' and would only serve for training purposes.[38]

All in all, the Minister of Supply had told a glum story, himself admitting in his Jeevesian way that the position was 'unsatisfactory in some important aspects'.[39]

Why then had the managements of Britain's pride, the aircraft industry, made such a muck of military aviation? Or had it been the management of politicians and bureaucrats in Whitehall who had made the muck?

The Minister of Supply sought to furnish the Prime Minister with answers:

Several years had been lost after the War, first by the decision not to experiment with manned supersonic aircraft but to rely on models, and by our failure to provide the extremely expensive advanced test facilities such as high-speed tunnels, and finally by the delay in proceeding with swept-wing fighters until after the Korean war had started.[40]

He might have added in all truth that the Labour Government had economized on such high technology in order to find the money for the traditional worldwide bases, garrisons and squadrons required to bolster their neo-Edwardian foreign policy.[41]

When the Korean crisis arose [Lloyd went on] production orders for most of our aircraft had to be placed before it had been finally decided what weapons and equipment should be put in them. Certain manufacturers quickly became overloaded, *having regard to their technical and managerial capacity* [added emphasis].[42]

It then became the disruptive practice to modify designs with the latest improvements even when production programmes were well advanced.[43] In any case, not enough prototypes were ordered for thorough testing, while the crippling aerodynamic defects encountered were largely due to the British lack of wind tunnels. Moreover, admitted Lloyd, the speed of technical change led the Ministry of Supply itself into making a functional muddle of its relations with the service departments and the industry.[44] And finally:

The financial arrangements [costs plus a fixed profit] under which aircraft are developed and produced are such that that manufacturers suffer little penalty for failure. There is not enough financial difference between failure and success.[45]

Six months later the Secretary of State for Air (still Lord De L'Isle) was even more caustic:

Our present relative inferiority [to the Americans and Soviets] in the fighter field thus indicates that we are behind in the whole field of the practical application of aerodynamics . . .[46]

In April 1953 the Vickers Viscount short-haul airliner, its propellers powered by four Rolls-Royce Dart gas-turbine engines, made its inaugural commercial flight from London to the British colony of Cyprus via Rome and Athens. To the passengers the Viscount's pressurized cabin offered a novel comfort and quietness. To BEA (British European Airways) and then the foreign airlines worldwide which bought it, the Viscount offered reliable and profitable operation. With 438 eventually sold in various versions,[47] the Viscount proved to be the outstanding commercial success of the British aircraft industry in the second half of the twentieth century.

Yet one Viscount in the field of civil aviation, like one Canberra in the military field, did not a summer make. In May 1952 the BBC, the British press, and cinema newsreels had given vast and braggartly coverage to a wonderful British feat of aeronautical pioneering – the first commercial flight of the world's first jet-propelled airliner, the de Havilland Comet Mark I. How fast! And so smooth that you could balance a coin on edge on a cabin table. The Comet I's sleek lines, with jet engines concealed within the swept wings, seemed to epitomize British design at its elegant best.

Meanwhile, Boeing's jet airliner (later known as the 707) still lay in the development stage. This much larger aircraft was specifically intended to fly the most lucrative airline route of all, across the Atlantic, which America at present dominated with piston-engined aircraft like the Lockheed Constellation and the Boeing Strato-cruiser.

The Comet I, however, had not been designed for the North Atlantic. Its range was too short and it could only carry thirty-six passengers. Instead its designated role was to fly the old imperial routes to South Africa, India, and Singapore, and do so in stages of around 1,500 miles. Here once again were the British advancing into the future with gaze firmly directed astern into their past.

But in any case, the jubilation over Britain's technological 'first' soon gave way to hangover. In April 1953 a Comet crashed on take-off from Karachi, killing all eleven on board. In consequence the wings were modified to give extra lift. Then, on 2 May 1953, exactly a year after the triumphal inaugural flight, a second Comet fell to the ground while taking off in a thunderstorm from Dum Dum airport, Calcutta, killing all forty-three on board. A court of inquiry hazarded the guess that the aircraft's structure had been 'over-stressed' by the storm. But then, on 10 January 1954, a third Comet I plunged into the Mediterranean off Elba after taking off from Rome airport. The six crew members and all twenty-nine passengers lost their lives. This time every Comet was grounded while the Royal Aeronautical Establishment at Farnborough investigated wreckage recovered from the seabed by the Royal Navy. Two months later the Comets were cleared for commercial flight again. And within a fortnight, on 8 April 1954, yet another had crashed into the sea when climbing high out of Rome Airport. The Comet I was grounded again. It took 9,000 hours of testing of an intact aircraft to simulate the cumulative effect of all the take-offs and landings experienced by the lost Comets before the investigators found the crucial flaw in the Comet's design and fabrication. Thanks to metal fatigue, a hairline crack at the corner of a square escape hatch window (all the Comet's windows were square, a truly catastrophic error of design) suddenly ripped into an eight-foot-long fissure. This meant that the pressurized fuselages of the lost Comets had literally exploded in the air.

Was this simply an example of (in the curiously dismissive words of the Minister of Supply, Selwyn Lloyd, in December 1954) 'the hazards that must accompany any venture of this nature?'[48] It was not. The Court of Inquiry blamed the fatal defect on lack of sufficient experimental testing in the development stage, and especially on the fact that only two prototypes (just as with the 'V' bombers) had been built for this purpose: effectively derelictions of management.

The Comet I disaster necessitated radically re-designing the much larger Comet III, with a consequent prolonged delay in bringing it into service. In the words of the Minister of Transport and Civil Aviation, John Boyd-Carpenter, in February 1955, it had been 'expected that the Comet III would be available years earlier than will now be the case . . .'[49] Worse still, by 1957–8 (likely timing for the Comet III's entry into service) non-stop transatlantic flights would have become the norm instead of the current stopover at Gander, Newfoundland.

In the event the Comet (now the Mark IV version), with a passenger capacity of eighty-one, did not enter transatlantic service (with a stopover) until October 1958. Only twenty-three days later Boeing introduced on the same route its non-stop 179-passenger 707, soon an outstanding commercial success in itself, and in due course the progenitor of a prosperous family of 727s and 747 'jumbos'.

The Comet and the 707 symbolize two manufacturing philosophies. De Havilland's beautiful bird had been solely designed as an airliner. It marked an adventurous leap into what were for the company hitherto unexplored technologies. The Boeing 707 by contrast was adapted from a contemporary design of a United States Air Force mid-air refuelling tanker, itself largely based on the well-tried but aerodynamically advanced B-47 long-range jet bomber. Equally characteristic of this workaday American approach was the mode of installing the Boeing's jet engines: not gracefully faired into the wings like the Comet's, but hung beneath on brackets whence they could be swiftly unbolted for maintenance or replacement. In short, technically and in market terms the Comet to the 707 was a Jaguar sports car to a Chevrolet sedan.[50]

So by the end of the first post-war decade Britain had decisively lost her chance of dominating the future market for transatlantic jets. Yet, astonishing as it may seem, Whitehall and the British aircraft industry had since the late 1940s pinned their transatlantic hopes on another type of airliner altogether – the turbo-propeller Bristol Britannia. In terms of the Atlantic route the Comet III had been merely regarded as 'as a re-insurance against delay or failure of the Britannia';[51] a role which by 1955 the Comet III could no longer fulfil either on delivery date or on endurance.

This appeared to leave all British bets riding on the Britannia alone, which in the opinion of the Minister of Transport and Civil Aviation, John Boyd-Carpenter, would entail 'too great a risk over B.O.A.C.'s North Atlantic service'.

My view that that risk is too great constitutes no reflection on this aircraft. But it remains the fact that neither Bristols nor any other British manufacturer have as yet built a transatlantic airliner and only the earlier mark of Britannia has yet flown at all. The Britannia 100 is a fine and impressive aircraft but the long range model with different engines and wing structure and the longer fusilage [sic] is not yet in existence, and the possibility of delay in delivery cannot be excluded.[52]

For BOAC this possibility could only be highly disquieting. They therefore asked for government permission to buy nineteen American Douglas DC7Cs as re-insurance on the North Atlantic, this being not only the airline's most profitable route, but also where they faced the fiercest foreign competition.

In a memorandum of 14 December 1954 on 'British Aircraft and World Markets' the Minister of Supply, Selwyn Lloyd, helpfully defined for his colleagues the trickiness of the problem now confronting them:

The Comet disasters and B.O.A.C.'s disclosure of their interest in an American competitor with the Britannia have together put in jeopardy the Government's policy of building up the manufacture and export of British civil aircraft. Issues that may gravely affect the future of the British aircraft industry and the balance of payments need to be considered.[53]

So the Conservatives now found themselves in the mid-1950s impaled on the same dilemma as the Labour Government in the late 1940s[54] – having to choose between the commercial viability of the nationalized long-haul airline and the enforcement on it of a 'Buy British' policy as life-support for the aircraft industry. Had not Conservative ministers chosen in 1952 to continue trying to develop the industry into a major exporter? Had they not then believed that on the success of this endeavour 'to no small extent depended our future as a great nation'?[55] And what would public opinion now think if the national airline bought American yet again? As Boyd-Carpenter reminded ministers, 'there had been very strong feeling in the House of Commons about this question'.[56]

It rendered the Government's dilemma still more acute that a private operator, Air Charter Ltd, had requested a licence to import three second-hand American DC4 Skymasters.[57] Such licences were of course still obligatory because the Conservatives were the government of free enterprise and the free market, in contrast to Labour's love of state regulation. The Minister of Transport and Civil Aviation was for his part

> convinced that it would be practically and politically indefensible to allow a private enterprise company to buy American aircraft for an unspecified purpose and, on the other hand, to refuse to allow a nationalised corporation to buy the aircraft it feels it needs for the purpose of competing effectively on the intensely competitive North Atlantic Route.[58]

The reluctant agreement of ministers to allow Air Charter to import their Skymasters[59] only opened up an anguished governmental debate as to whether or not BOAC should now have their Douglas DC7Cs.

Selwyn Lloyd fought for his clients, the aircraft manufacturers, just as stoutly as his Labour predecessor, George Strauss, in 1948–50. In his memorandum of 14 December 1954 he pleaded that the industry should continue to be copiously refuelled with money pumped from the taxpayers' bowser. He opposed allowing airlines the freedom to buy foreign aircraft at will. Instead, he urged that the state should continue to regulate the purchase of aircraft in order 'to ensure that British operators, including the Corporations, use British aircraft so far as this is possible and reasonable':[60] i.e., unless, in his words, 'they were demonstrably and markedly inferior to those available elsewhere'.[61]

In fact, the minister had a special, if surprising, reason for wanting to ensure that BOAC and BEA bought British: these nationalized corporations were needed as testers for the aircraft industry's new products.

> Every aircraft has teething troubles and foreign buyers usually hold off until the domestic operator has eradicated them. The American industry, with its large domestic market, both civil and especially military, can take this problem in its stride. For example, the American military order for the Boeing jet refueller will give the Boeing Company an invaluable start in catering for the commercial market for the Jetliner, which is the civil aircraft being developed in parallel.

But:

> We cannot afford a military transport force on a scale anything like that which the Americans have and the British industry must look therefore largely to the two Corporations to carry out this essential process of proving and running-in new British aircraft.[62]

These remarks appear to tear the wings off the fundamental assumption of United Kingdom governments since the war that Britain could take on America in the air, and win. Just as destructive proved Selwyn Lloyd's own historical summary of this ambitious venture.

'It had always been realised', he wrote, 'that to reach our objective [of breaking into the world market for large transport aircraft] we should have to take risks and commit to the venture large sums of public and private money.' These 'large sums' now totalled £60 million of public money, while Bristol had bet £18 million of their own money on the Britannia, de Havilland £20 million on the Comet, and Vickers £18 million on the Viscount.[63] Although 'a proportion' of the public funding would come back to Government, depending on the degree of success in selling current types of airliner, the minister had to admit that 'the return so far has been small'. But, he hastened hopefully to add, 'as an example of the success that can be achieved we shall recover from the sales of the Viscount already ordered at least the full sum of our contribution'.[64]

The Minister of Supply's facts and figures hardly constituted the kind of balance-sheet or chairman's statement that would cheer a shareholders' meeting. It is no wonder, then, that the tepid best he himself could say of British civil aviation policy since 1945 was: 'The effort has not been wholly unsuccessful.'[65]

> We have achieved outstanding success in the Viscount and we have a thoroughly useful article in the [Airspeed] Ambassador; in the Comet we have encountered the hazards that must accompany any venture of this nature; in the Britannia we have a project still in the stage of great promise.

And so:

> The major problems now are how to re-establish the Comet and how to secure the future of the Britannia. The ultimate success or failure of the whole enterprise will depend on the steadiness and faith we now show. It is not misleading to say that the commercial future of the British aircraft industry, for at least the next ten years, depends upon a successful solution to the Comet and Britannia problems.

Faith! Steadiness! These were strange words to use in relation to what should have been a commercial decision based on cost–benefit analysis and realistic assessment of market prospects. Clearly the record of the past decade had taught Lloyd nothing.

In contrast, the Minister of Transport and Civil Aviation, John Boyd-Carpenter, was, like his own Labour predecessor in the late 1940s, concerned above all that the nationalized airlines should compete profitably in a tough world market. He argued that if these corporations were to be obliged to buy British aircraft unless these were 'demonstrably and markedly inferior' to foreign, it would raise the question 'as to whether on this point the commercial judgement of the Corporations is to be overridden on the basis of other opinions, and, if so, whose'.[66]

Two days before Christmas 1954 Selwyn Lloyd and Boyd-Carpenter argued their cases in person to the Cabinet Economic Policy Committee, chaired by R. A. Butler as Chancellor of the Exchequer. True to form, the Committee flinched from a decision, referring the matter back instead for further study and a fresh recommendation.[67] By the third week of February 1955 the two ministers had agreed jointly to recommend that BOAC should be allowed to buy ten DC7Cs (instead of the nineteen wanted by the airline). It was the view of the ministers that this conventionally piston-engined American aircraft enjoyed 'reasonably firm prospects of meeting its estimated performance', whereas until the long-range Britannia with its new turbo-propeller engines had flown, it was 'not so certain' that it 'will be able to meet manufacturers' guaranteed figures of performance'.[68] BOAC (reported the ministers) were now going to order a mixed fleet of ten DC7Cs, fifteen Britannia Mark 100s, eight Britannia Mark 300s, ten Britannia long-range Mark 300s, and twenty Comets – just the recipe for economical simplicity in crew training, operations and maintenance.[69]

On 21 February 1955 the Chancellor of the Exchequer, R. A. Butler, had the final word, telling the Cabinet Economic Policy Committee that

> in view of the balance of payments position [N.B.: again grim, with loss of confidence in, and a run on, sterling][70] he was reluctant to permit the purchase of these American aircraft, but he accepted that B.O.A.C.'s competitive position on the North Atlantic route must be maintained.[71]

So was perpetrated the final aeronautical fudge of the decade. Bristol would be encouraged (at the taxpayers' expense) to go on developing and manufacturing an aircraft with acknowledged 'problems', even though the company's only assured customers for it were BOAC and RAF Transport Command.[72] And BOAC were to be allowed to purchase only half the quantity of American aircraft that they really wanted.

This final fudge marks the moment when all that remained of

the post-war British attempt to outfly the Americans in the world market for airliners was a column of smoke rising from the wreck, and ever-optimistic ministers trudging back to their drawing-boards. For, with the exception of the Viscount and the smaller Ambassador short-haul airliners, not one of the aircraft which had inspired Labour and Conservative Governments with such romantic hope, from the Brabazon to the Britannia, was in the service even of a British airline in 1955, let alone managing to 'win over Commonwealth and foreign airlines from their present American allegiance'.

In the mid-1950s state spending on civil and military R&D in the aircraft industry amounted to almost as much as the total spent on R&D by all nationalized and private industries. But this was a matter not just of money, but of trained talent too. Even in 1959, when the post-Korean War rearmament boom had long subsided, the aircraft industry was gulping 16 per cent of the qualified scientists and engineers engaged in research and development in British manufacturing industry, and no less than 11 per cent of all qualified scientists and engineers employed in *any* function in manufacturing industry.[73] To what extent, therefore, was the national commitment to aerospace R&D sucking in qualified personnel who might have been more usefully employed in the actual process of production in other, less glamorous, industries?

Yet the awful paradox was that the allotment of money, talent and material resources to aerospace in 1945–55, though vastly disproportionate in terms of British industry as a whole, had proved quite inadequate to cover the multitude of ambitious projects embarked upon. In May 1956 the Minister of Defence, writing with particular regard to the military aircraft programme, said as much:

There is no doubt that, taken as a whole, the industry is trying to carry out more R & D work on aircraft and their equipment than it has the resources to complete in time to meet our military and economic requirements, and that the delays which the overload causes are increasing. The position is similar in the electronics field, where the firms, together with the aircraft firms, have an immense programme of work in guided weapons as well as radar systems for aircraft and other uses. The companies are competing with each other and with Government establishments for scientific and technical manpower, the supply of which is limited. This process is simply putting up the costs of R & D projects without any increase in the available effort or benefit to the programme.[74]

It follows, therefore, that the tally of cancelled projects, technical setbacks and crucial delays (costing irrecoverable market opportunities) cannot be blamed solely on company managements who lacked the calibre and business training to bring complex products from the design studio to market or to squadron service. There was a more profound and yet very simple cause, one all too familiar – national overambition leading to overstretch of national capabilities. And the blame for this once again lay with British management at the highest level of all – ministers of the Crown, be they at the time Labour or Conservative.

Yet they learned no lesson from the aerospace debacle of 1945–55 and its corollary, the futile splashing-out of public money.[75] In particular, they could not grasp even now, would not grasp, never were to grasp, that there is much more to marketing airliners against American competition than the technical excellence (sometimes doubtful) and the innovative nature (sometimes dangerous and always costly) of the product.[76] Nothing demonstrates the continuing prideful unrealism of the politicians more vividly than the creation in 1956 of a Supersonic Transport Aircraft Committee, composed of representatives of the Ministries of Supply and of Transport and Civil Aviation, the Royal Aircraft Establishment at Farnborough, and the manufacturers of airframes and aero-engines. This self-serving conspiracy would in due course advocate that design studies be started (at taxpayers' expense) on an amazing new project which (just as had been hoped of the Comet in its time) would leave the Americans trailing – a supersonic long-distance airliner, with potential world sales of no fewer than 500! The romance of it! Britain in her rightful future place as a great nation, at the forefront of science and technology![77]

Meanwhile, 1956 saw British management decisively out-generalled in a twentieth-century manufacture which lacked any romantic cachet of technological pioneering, which carried no superfluous

343

patriotic luggage about Britain's future as a great nation, but which happened to be her largest single earner of foreign currency.[78] For this was the year when the United Kingdom was overtaken by the Federal Republic of Germany in the output and export of that workaday artefact, the motor car.

18. Dependence on America:
Business Systems and More Besides

'Rely upon it, the strength of Great Britain is within the United Kingdom', pronounced Gladstone in 1879. It would be even truer to say that in the 1950s the strength of America lay within the United States, for, unlike late Victorian Britain, the latter-day United States constituted a virtually self-sufficient continental economy: a vast single market. And the actual strength itself consisted in an industrial machine powerful enough to satisfy all the wants of such a market. It consisted in the managers and technologists who drove the machine with such ruthless energy and questing commercial imagination.

Since the outbreak of the Korean War in June 1950 and the adoption of NSC–68 (see p. 29, above), this machine had fulfilled both a huge rearmament programme and the American consumer's swelling appetite for every kind of material comfort and convenience. Nonetheless, still more impressive had been America's record back in the Second World War, when her production expanded so vastly and so rapidly that she not only met all the lavish needs of her own armed forces and many of Britain's needs as well, but also raised the living standards of her own people at home.

In 1948 the European Recovery Programme (Marshall Aid) had connected a jump-lead from this massive industrial engine to the stalled economies of war-ruined Western Europe. When in 1951 the jump-lead was removed, the European economies began to motor under their own power, gathering speed as every year passed. In West Germany the rubble and ruin left behind by a lost war were steadily replaced by glittering new city centres in the revived modernist style of the Bauhaus. The shops filled up with goods and

345

shoppers. The restaurants and *Konditorei* were thronged with the greedy, eager to forget the post-war years of near starvation. So it was also in France, in Italy, in the Benelux countries.[1] The consumer boom was under way that would materially enrich the lives of the peoples of the Western world (and that must include Japan) beyond previous imagination. Shopping would shape society as religion had shaped it in the Middle Ages.

In the process, the demands of the shopper would serve as the locomotive that hauled in succession every echelon of productive industry. For manufacturers of actual consumer goods would (if enterprising) want to equip their assembly lines with the latest machines. They would want the newest business systems to handle orders, stock control and accounts. They would want forklift trucks for their warehouses; fleets of heavy goods vehicles and vans to ship the product from factory to retail shop. So for the makers of all these twentieth-century technologies a bountiful future world market would also beckon.

Yet they in their turn would need the products of traditional trades like iron and steel, coal, heavy engineering, just as the field forces of an army on the offensive depend on base workshops and ordnance depots far behind the front. And as the advance of an army depends on logistics, so too would exporters need road, rail and telecommunications networks – ports as well – that were modern, efficient, and able readily to cope with swelling traffic.

On the statistical face of it, Britain was better placed than any other country except America to profit from the burgeoning consumer boom and all the industrial demands that would ramify from it. Was she not in 1950 comfortably the leading industrial power in the world after the United States, with a GDP per head a third higher than France's, two-thirds higher than West Germany's, twice Italy's, and nearly four times higher than Japan's?[2] Did she not account for a quarter of world exports of manufactures, well over double the share of her nearest non-American rival, France, and a third larger than that of West Germany?[3]

Yet these impressive figures, like the annual report of a long established 'blue chip' company, could prove a misleading guide to long-term future prospects, especially in regard to creating new markets by means of novel products. A better guide lay in operational realities such as the state of the plant, the present and planned range of products, and, above all, the energy and creative imagination of management.[4]

Analysis of these factors would have suggested to a shrewd investor that this was the time to sell, rather than buy, Great Britain (Twentieth–Century Products) Ltd.

In the first place, British manufacturers of such products, whether for the family out shopping or to re-equip office and factory, suffered handicaps not of their own making. They were hampered by the ill-managed and union-lamed performance of their own suppliers in the old heavy industries of the North and Celtic fringes (see Chapter 15, above). They were hindered by obsolete logistic services – ports, and road, rail and telecommunications networks – starved of investment by politicians[5] keen to save money for more important things such as new houses or 'developing' backward colonies or paying for the world role, financial and military. And they found themselves freshly handicapped after the outbreak of the Korean War by a rearmament programme on a scale proportionately more obese than adopted by any other European member of NATO (see Chapter 2, above). In 1953, 10 per cent of the labour force in all kinds of manufacturing industry in Britain were employed on defence contracts; 18.6 per cent across all engineering industries from the heavy end like marine machinery to watches and clocks.[6]

Especially harmful because ubiquitous in its impact was the overload laid by rearmament on the manufacturers of ball- and roller-bearings. For these were components vital to every kind of twentieth-century machine, from colliery conveyors and rolling-mills to internal-combustion engines, gas turbines, and machine tools, from electric motors in locomotives to electric motors in vacuum cleaners and food mixers, from the axle-boxes of railway rolling stock and motor vehicles (including farm tractors) to the axles of the humble bicycle and perambulator. An article in the *Economist* in 1952 proclaimed that 'Defence Runs on Bearings'. It would be equally true to say that the twentieth century ran on bearings – ball, roller and taper.

At this period no less than 95 per cent of United Kingdom capacity consisted in the outstations of foreign firms like Skefko

(Swedish), Timken (American) and Hoffman (American): an indictment of native British lack of entrepreneurship in this key technology since the beginning of the century. But in any case United
Kingdom capacity was only large enough to meet home demand,
'although', in the words of a Ministry of Supply memorandum in
1948, 'export potential is very large'.[7] So British-based firms certainly could not cope with the double load of producing for civilian
industry at home *and* the rearmament programme, let alone also
exploit the marvellous opportunity for exports presented by the
current world shortage of bearings.[8]

For the rearmament programme alone required an annual production rising to a peak of 2.8 million bearings,[9] and of types
ranging from 6in diameter and over for heavy vehicles (including
tanks), airscrews and ships' rotating radar scanners down to miniature versions for precision instruments. Year by year from 1951
onwards the Ministry of Supply struggled to reconcile these huge
orders with the needs of civilian industry and civilian goods, and to
overcome the resulting bottlenecks and late deliveries.[10]

It did not help the flow of deliveries that the 'extra-precision'
bearings produced by British-based companies proved inferior in
quality to American or Swiss,[11] so signifying a higher percentage of
rejects; signifying too that British production management in a
crucial high-technology manufacture was defective. Nor did it help
the flow of heavy tank bearings that the Ministry of Supply had to
fight a protracted battle with the Ministries of Labour and of Town
and Country Planning over the location of a new plant for British
Timken, and with the Treasury over whether or not the scheme
merited state capital assistance. Back in 1949 Timken had been
denied a development certificate to build at Coleshill, near Birmingham, by that post-war curse on industrial flexibility, Whitehall's
Location of Industry Informal Committee. Timken had responded
by resolutely refusing to build in a 'development area', meaning
some decayed industrial district suffering from unemployment.[12] By
July 1951, with the rearmament programme in full swing, a new
plant for tank bearings appeared to be a necessity, and so the
Coleshill proposal was revived. For the next seventeen months the
arguments within Whitehall about the proposal trundled round and

round. Finally, in mid–December 1952, Timken was told that the bureaucrats had decided not to proceed after all. The company no doubt took comfort from a civil servant's assurance that 'the inconvenience caused . . . is unavoidable and regrettable'.[13]

By the end of 1953 Britain had been robbed by rearmament of her one fleeting opportunity of building a great export trade in ball bearings before the Germans and Japanese could get started again, for by then West German output was already some 50 per cent higher than the 1936–8 average for the same territory, and still climbing fast.[14] In fact, Britain was even having to import German bearings,[15] as well as Swedish, Swiss and American, just as she had before 1939, just as she had before 1914. The same dreary pattern had now occurred with machine tools: large imports of special types from abroad; the letting slip of the post-war opportunity to replace Germany as the principal European exporter. By 1956 West Germany's exports of machine tools stood at £55 million as against Britain's £21.4 million.[16]

In the case of 'wireless apparatus'[17] of all kinds the demands of rearmament proved even more commercially damaging. In that same year of 1953 those demands were sucking 32.6 per cent of the radio industry's labour force,[18] just at a time when a vast new world market for domestic radios and televisions was about to tune in. In 1955 the total value of British exports of these items (plus 'gramophones')[19] still only amounted to a paltry £10 million.[20] The particular culprit here lay in the nostalgic belief of politicians that Britain – being of course a first-class world power – could and should supply all the advanced military equipment (especially in the field of radar and guided weapons) which she needed to wage the Cold War as an equal partner with America. So the best of British firms in electronics and precision-engineering had to stretch – overstretch – their resources in management, R&D, and manufacturing in order to fulfil government contracts for the guidance systems of such marvels as Red Shoes, Blue Cheese, and Blue Sky, and at the same time cover as best they could the consumer market at home and abroad.[21]

As if all this were not overstretch enough, some of these firms – EMI, Ferranti, and English Electric (who bought Marconi in 1946)

– were also trying to cover yet another field of R&D, one of immense promise yet inevitable American rivalry: the electronic computer.[22]

Popular British myth has it that the wartime Colossus used to break the German Enigma ciphers was the world's first computer in the modern sense. It was not; it was a giant electronic calculator designed for the special purpose of breaking the German Enigma ciphers. The first true general-purpose computer was invented by a German, Konrad Zuse, in 1941. However, both this and the comparable American Harvard Mark 1 computer of 1943 were electro-mechanical in operation. The decisive breakthrough came in 1945 with the invention of the theoretical 'architecture' of the electronic stored-program computer by John von Neumann and his colleagues at the University of Pennsylvania. This served as the foundation on which the post-war computer industry was built. To Britain, however, belongs the credit for first building and putting into operation an electronic stored-program computer, a small experimental machine (nicknamed 'Baby') put together at Manchester University in 1948 by two young scientists, Tom Kilburn and Freddie Williams.[23] That university collaborated with Ferranti Ltd to develop a full-scale version, the Ferranti Mark 1. When completed in 1951 it became the world's first commercially available computer. Meanwhile, a team at Cambridge University led by Maurice Wilkes (formerly in wartime radar R&D) had developed the EDSAC (Electronic Delay Storage Automatic Calculator). When it began to run on 6 May 1949, it was the world's first fully operational stored-program computer.[24] In 1950 the third major British centre for computer research, the National Physical Laboratory at Teddington, ran its experimental model, Pilot ACE, for the first time. This was based on a design by Alan Turing, the brilliant mathematician and a wartime member of the Government Code and Cypher School at Bletchley Park.

Wonderful! Here was Britain seizing the lead from America in a new technology which (though no one could foresee it at the time) would transform the functioning of human society, as steam power had transformed it during the first industrial revolution.[25] For the computer would first become universal in industry, commerce, and all types of administration, and then in the households of the Western world, so making it (along with the television set and the motor car) a quintessential consumer good of the late twentieth century. And what a fillip the British 'firsts' of 1948–50 were for the university-based, state-funded scientific research so admired by the university scientists on the Cabinet's Advisory Council on Scientific Policy!

Yet it was exactly this high-minded academic approach, valuing the computer primarily as a tool of mathematical calculation in universities, which supplied one crucial reason why Britain by the late 1950s would have blown her chances of dominating the future world market. An eminent British computer theorist occupying the Chair of Mathematical Physics at Cambridge (and thus obviously an expert on the market potential of new technologies) had counselled a senior manager of Ferranti in 1948 that

> all the calculations that would ever be needed in this country could be done on the three digital computers which were then being built – one in Cambridge, one in Teddington and one in Manchester. No one else . . . would ever need machines of their own, or would be able to afford to buy them. He added that the machines were exceedingly difficult to use, and could not be trusted to anyone who was not a professional mathematician, and he advised Ferranti to get out of the business and abandon the idea of selling any more.[26]

Certainly the R&D teams in British universities and the National Physical Laboratory each had their link with a selected industrial or commercial firm: Manchester with Ferranti, Cambridge with J. Lyons Ltd the caterers, the NPL with English Electric (whose Chairman, Sir George Nelson (later Lord Nelson of Stafford), sat on the NPL executive committee). Moreover, the National Research Development Corporation (NRDC), set up in 1949 by the Labour Government[27] to foster the commercial exploitation of British inventions, was keen to do just this for computers. The NRDC's first Managing Director, Lord Halsbury, had indeed come back from a visit to America in 1949 convinced that IBM (International Business Machines) would sooner or later market a commercial computer, and that Britain must therefore make haste.[28]

But even at this early stage Britain's chances were beginning to be queered by an old British malaise infecting even new technologies. The familiar symptoms consisted in the smugness, parochial vision and jealous individualism of company managements, and the institutional creakiness that beset any peacetime attempt in Britain to bring about change. Halsbury himself wished to create a 'critical mass' behind the development of commercial computers by bringing together the business-systems firms and those electrical-engineering companies capable of making the computers. It took six months before he could get their senior managers all round a table, in December 1949. However, this Advisory Panel on Electronic Computers only met once. All the manufacturers claimed that

> they were individually in positions to tackle the problems of an electronic computer development project as well as, for example, the International Business Machines Corporation in the United States . . . It was apparent also that the manufacturers were not willing that the Corporation [i.e., the NRDC] should take the initiative in launching a development project . . .[29]

So instead of a *Schwerpunkt* there followed disparate, and (by American standards) small-scale attempts at advance, with a total of nine different types of computer being under development between 1951 and 1956 by no fewer than five different British companies.[30]

The firm of J. Lyons Ltd, who had backed Cambridge University's research project EDSAC by seconding one of their engineers and donating £3,000, developed their own version of EDSAC for use in processing the company's pay-roll, stock-control, and distribution of bakery products. LEO (Lyons Electronic Office) made its inaugural run on 5 September 1951: the world's first routine commercial operation.[31] Another British 'first'! And in itself LEO proved completely successful, not only in vastly speeding up Lyons' own administrative and logistic operations, but also eventually working part-time for the Ford Motor Company, Kodak, Tate & Lyle, the Meteorological Office and the Census Office. It even carried out ballistic calculations for the Ordnance Board in regard to the Black Knight and Blue Streak guided missiles,[32] both of which nevertheless turned out to be sodden fireworks rather than terrors of the Soviet Union.

Yet LEO was not the prototype of a production series, but a

single bespoke job hand–crafted by Lyons for their own company's use. Only in late 1954 did Lyons' management decide to market an updated version of LEO through a new subsidiary, Leo Computers Ltd. Such marketing proved hard work, as LEO's historian relates:

> Potential customers had little understanding of computer technology or the potential of the machines. The long-term uncertainties of replacing conventional and familiar systems with automatic processing were, for many, extremely difficult. The generation of [British] managers of the late 1950s were far more cautious and had less capital at their disposal than the more adventurous types of pre-war manager.[33]

Would the savings in time and efficiency pay off the capital cost? How many clerical staff could be dispensed with? What would the unions say – and do? Among the managements of potential customers for LEO there was much plucking of the lips. Not until May 1958 was the first LEO (a LEO II) delivered to an outside customer, the steel firm of Stewart and Lloyds of Corby, Northamptonshire.[34] Only nine LEO IIs were ever sold. And not until 1962 were Leo Computers Ltd to sell their first LEO III, an advanced model, to an outside customer – in South Africa. No more than fifty-nine LEO IIIs were ever manufactured, and no more than nine of them exported. Moreover, with American computer firms now strongly competing in all world markets, Britain included, Leo Computers Ltd were losing money. The end of this particular technological cul-de-sac was to be finally reached in 1970 when Lyons, the parent company, themselves opted for IBM equipment.[35]

The original LEO project remains a tribute to admirable boldness of vision on the part of Lyons' management. But Lyons' main business lay in cafes and food products, not business systems or advanced engineering. For them computers could never be more than a fringe activity. If Britain were successfully to exploit in world markets her early technical lead over America, it would be up to other, more relevant, industries, such as electronics.

Yet here again British cultural snobberies proved the wrong kind of mental programming. Just as the educated elite prized 'pure' science above *Technik*, so the managements of electronics companies in the

1950s prized advances in computer *Technik* for their own sake rather than for their money-making potential. None of these managements (let alone their research departments) would have empathized with the vulgarly commercial dictum of the President of the Sony Corporation in 1983 that 'if the weight of invention or discovery is one, the weight to bring it to actual development should be ten, and the weight to produce and market it should be one hundred.' Thus even by 1955 neither English Electric nor Ferranti had for sale any data-processing computer suitable for business operations, but only kit designed for scientific research.[36]

The supreme example of this British fascination with the technology of computers as an end in itself is provided by the ATLAS, jointly developed by Ferranti and Manchester University during the late 1950s, partly funded by the NRDC, and eventually launched in 1961. A brilliant exercise in technical pioneering, the ATLAS was very high speed in operation and incorporated various design features probably two years ahead of current American rivals. However, it had not been designed as a business data processor but as the British rival to the American STRETCH and LARC computers as a mincer of complex calculations in nuclear and other defence research.[37] Between 1961 and 1963 only two ATLAS I computers (at £2 million a copy) were sold, one of them to the United Kingdom Atomic Energy Authority and the other to London University, although Manchester University was later to acquire a third. ATLAS II, a cooperative venture with Cambridge University, was to fare even worse, with only a single copy ever sold – to the United Kingdom Atomic Weapons Research Establishment at Aldermaston.[38] According to a scientist who joined the ATLAS project in 1961, Ferranti

> was not a very commercially-minded operation. We undertook the development of Atlas jointly with Manchester University mainly as a prestige venture, with government backing, because the UK had aspirations at that time of being a leading country in the development of computers . . .[39]

The hope that ATLAS could compete successfully with the IBM STRETCH computer in selling to American defence establishments crashed

354

due to lack of investment in marketing and our very limited production capacity – at one time we had a US prospect for three machines and these would have taken Ferranti's total production capacity for two years! We were a small British company, and with hindsight there was no way that we could compete successfully with an enormous corporation like IBM or sell into key US markets.[40]

In short, the ATLAS project does not belong to the history of the computer as an eventually ubiquitous tool and a huge global market, but to the history of the British governing elite's costly post-war delusion that Britain could play the technological great power in the same league as the United States.

By the late 1950s the long collaboration between electronics companies and university or government research units had resulted for the most part only in a splatter of experimental or prototype computers which (like ATLAS in its turn) were to lead commercially nowhere in coming decades[41] – certainly nowhere in comparison with United States competition. By 1955 fewer than twelve computers had yet been installed in Britain (other than one-offs for scientific research).[42]

For that competition was primarily coming not from the American electronics industry, but from manufacturers of business systems (calculators and punched-card data processing), where America had long dominated the world market. To them the computer was not so much a technical wonder, let alone a scientific tool, as potentially the everyday business system of the future, with consequently immense opportunities for sales and profits. It makes the contrast with the British scene all the sharper that it was two leaders of a university research team who in America first perceived these commercial opportunities, and, in 1946, formed their own company to exploit them.[43] The result was the UNIVAC of 1951, the first widely marketed computer.

In meeting this new challenge Britain was, however, handicapped by yet another legacy from her past: the long-standing weakness of her business-systems industry compared with its American rival, not only in sheer weight of technological resources, but also in managerial vigour and vision.

★

355

In the 1880s the one great area of work throughout the industrialized world still untouched by the machine had lain in the office and the counting-house. Here handicraft still prevailed, with drab legions of Bob Cratchets toiling over ledgers and letters pen in hand. Yet only a quarter of a century later these legions had in America been largely swept away by ingenious mechanical invention enthusiastically embraced by business management.

The typewriter came first, introduced by Remington, the small-arms firm and hence expert in precision engineering. By 1880 the company had only sold 1,000 machines; by 1890 sales were running at 20,000 a year. By 1900 Remington had sold more than 250,000.[44] The first operationally effective calculating machine, the Compto-meter, again American, was launched in 1887, and was eventually to sell in millions. Next, in 1888, came the adder–lister machine patented by William Seward Burroughs, another American. Sales climbed from a mere 284 in 1895, its first year on the market, to 13,314 in 1907, by which time it was available in fifty-eight different configurations to fit every line of business.

The year 1889 saw the birth of the electro-mechanical 'punched-card' machine for sorting and tabulating complex data, when the system invented by Herman Hollerith, a graduate of the Columbia School of Mines, New York, and former instructor at MIT, won the competition to process the 1890 American national census. In 1896 Hollerith entered the commercial market by leasing his machines to the New York Central Railroad to process its annual 4,000,000 way-bills, a task beyond even an army of clerks. Although by 1908 Hollerith's Tabulating Machine Company had still only acquired some thirty customers, its business grew thereafter at the amazing rate of 20 per cent per half-year. In 1911 it became part of the Computing-Tabulating-Recording Company, retitled in 1924 International Business Machines, or IBM: initials that were to resonate down the century. According to a contemporary American report

> The [Hollerith] system is used in factories of all sorts, in steel mills,
> by insurance companies, by electric light and traction and telephone
> companies, by wholesale merchandise establishments and department
> stores, by textile mills, automobile companies, numerous railroads,

municipalities and state governments. It is used for compiling labour costs, efficiency records, distribution of sales . . . production statistics, day and piece work. It is used for analysing risks in life, fire and casualty insurance, for plant expenditures and sales of service, by public service corporations, for distributing salesmen and cost figures as to salesmen, department, customer, location, commodity, method of sale, and in numerous other ways.[45]

This quotation could serve just as well to describe the general revolution in management techniques in the United States brought about in the early 1900s by all types of office machine. Yet credit is equally due to the senior managers across commerce, industry and public administration who were so quick to adopt the machines and embrace the revolution. Thereafter supply and demand were to revolve ever faster in a virtuous cycle of enterprise, typically American.

Great Britain, however, produced no Remingtons, Holleriths or Burroughs in the late Victorian era; no native business-machines sector at all. And commerce and industry for their part displayed little desire to replace Bob Cratchet with the faster and more reliably accurate machine. So revolved lack of supply and lack of demand in a vicious cycle of inertia, typically British. In the early 1900s at the Prudential Assurance Company, a giant (and supposedly innovative) concern,

clerical work continued to be carried on by methods not essentially different from those of thirty to forty years earlier. Records were still compiled by hand. Into ledgers almost too heavy for a junior clerk to lift, were carefully copied details of agents' accounts and every policy-movement. Industrial insurance policies were written by young ladies, while in the basement junior clerks numbered these policies on machines worked by foot.[46]

At the steel-makers Stewart and Lloyds in 1903

The only piece of modern equipment was the telephone, with a private line to the Glasgow office . . . But there was no other office machinery of any kind – no typewriters, adding machines, compto-meters, pay-roll listing machines, etc . . . Everything was hand-written . . .[47]

It is impossible to believe that such scenes were the consequence of any rational cost-benefit comparison between running Bob Cratchets and operating the new business machines. They could only stem from a prevailing culture of management in Edwardian Britain which flinched from change just as much as had Scrooge himself.

By 1914 the United States had achieved virtually complete world dominance in business systems, with only Germany among European countries able to offer some products of comparable technical merit.[48] Yet the dominance did not only spring from patented inventions or the economies of large-scale manufacture. There was another factor, one still to be decisive at the dawn of the computer age in the 1950s – the high importance accorded by the American companies to marketing and after-sales service.

As for Britain before the Great War, the only firms in the field were American outstations: the Powers Accounting Machine Company (grandly reincarnated in 1915 as the Accounting and Tabulating Company of Great Britain Ltd, or 'Acc-and-Tab' for short) and the Tabulator Limited (reconstituted in 1907 as the British Tabulating Machine Company), an offshoot of Hollerith's Tabulating Machine Company.

It was only during the Great War, some twenty years after comparable American developments, and under the spur of industrial mobilization for total war, that British commerce began to accept the new business systems. Of this there could be no more vivid a sign than the acquisition in 1918 by the Prudential Assurance Company of the rights to make and sell Powers machines throughout the British Empire. Next year the Prudential proved more daring still: it was instrumental in turning 'Acc-and-Tab' into a wholly British-owned company, putting in its own placemen as Chairman, General Manager and board of directors. In just as dramatic an initiative, both BTM and Acc-and-Tab now actually opened their own factories, modest enough by United States standards. At first these merely nutted-and-bolted American parts together, but later they fabricated complete machines.

So by the early 1920s the pattern was set. Although Britain now had her business-systems industry, it was the late-born offspring of American parents, and doomed to remain a dwarf by comparison. In 1925, for example, BTM employed only around 150 people, while IBM employed 3,900.[49] Until as late as 1949–50 the British companies were to operate uneasily under restrictive agreements with their American parents in regard to royalties, patent rights, sales territories, and supplies of machines and punched cards. BTM was almost entirely dependent on its American parent for R&D and the introduction of new models; the more innovative Acc-and-Tab (later Powers-Samas) less so.[50] Moreover, both companies grew much more slowly in the 1920s than their parents, largely because of their managements' amateurish approach to marketing: another British case of traditional values ill at ease with novel technology. According to the historian of BTM,

> Creating an aggressive motivated sales force in the British culture was no simple matter, and the general managers of the BTM and Acc and Tab were not well qualified for the task. Even sales commissions, for example, were viewed as ungentlemanly . . .[51]

Salesmen were recruited from accountants and such like, and then trained in punched-card technology by apprenticeship:

> their background was thus rather gentlemanly, and was technical rather than sales oriented. This was very different from Thomas Watson's ethos at TMC [Tabulating Machine Company, from 1924 IBM] in the United States: there the salesman was king . . .[52]

In the world market for typewriters too Britain remained an also-ran in the 1920s, with her exports amounting to around a tenth of Germany's and a fiftieth of America's.[53] The bravely named Imperial Typewriter Company was a runt compared with Remington, and even the British home market was dominated by American outstations importing or assembling American machines: a story familiar enough from other modern technologies. And exactly the same was true of calculating machines,[54] where the only native manufacturer was Guy's Calculating Machine Company, whose Britannic was operated by hand. Yet Germany in the mid-1920s came second only to America as an exporter of mechanized calculating machines.[55] And whereas Britain was at this period incurring a heavy trade deficit in all kinds of business systems, Germany was running a strong surplus. Even in the most basic of office technologies, such as loose-leaf filing systems, British manufacture was based on designs licensed from American firms such as Kalamazoo and Rand Kardex.[56]

Nor in the 1930s did the British business machines industry get around to transforming itself from an also-ran into a front-runner. BTM for example continued to depend almost entirely on IBM for new designs, importing either complete machines or parts for assembly.[57] As rearmament got under way in 1937–8 these imports rocketed. In fact, the efficient running of the British war effort, industrial and military, during the Second World War was only made possible by American-designed business systems. That included the processing of precious ULTRA intelligence data at Bletchley Park.[58]

Yet the end of the war in 1945 gave the United Kingdom business machines industry a unique opportunity to become a world-class player at last. There it stood with its capacity not merely undamaged but, thanks to state investment, greatly boosted, whereas its former European rivals in Germany and France lay paralysed by devastation and disruption. At home the industry faced no immediate American competition because hard-up Britain could not spare the dollars. With a pent-up demand at home and abroad to be satisfied, all the industry had to do was shove out to grateful customers its existing models – even though these might be pre-war designs now old-fashioned by American standards.[59] Production bounded, and so did profits.

It was all so easy – in fact, too easy, beguiling self-satisfied senior managers into neglect of long-term development. Not that they needed much beguiling: BTM, according to a future managing director, was then a company 'really run by English gentlemen, and I think the business came fourth after hunting, shooting and fishing'.[60] As for Powers-Samas (as Acc-and-Tab had become known after 1925), they were taken over in 1946 by Vickers, the engineering, aircraft and armaments conglomerate grown fat for years on cost-plus government contracts. Here the grandees of management were untainted by any tiresome American-style dynamism. When in 1952 a candidate (a banker!) for the part-time chairmanship of Powers-Samas was to question whether the job could be adequately done by a part-timer with many other commitments, the Chairman of Vickers, Sir Ronald Weeks (Charterhouse and Gonville and Caius College, Cambridge; wartime Deputy Chief of the Imperial General Staff), assured him: 'Well, Terence, I should think you will find no difficulty – just look in every Tuesday afternoon.'[61]

It was only in 1948, marking three years' loss of time, that the British business systems companies began to address such crucial questions bearing on their future as restructuring or market strategy or product R&D or even effective internal cost-control.[62] The then Managing Director of Powers-Samas, himself a rare exception to the prevailing managerial tweediness, wrote that

> future success depends in very large measure upon their correct appreciation and anticipation of the needs of the market *many years ahead* . . . Research is therefore *vital*, and on the same level as Sales and Production, and today it is behindhand.[63]

Yet Powers-Samas's new research division, unable to free itself from the mental shackles of the company's history as a manufacturer of mechanical systems, was largely to disregard electronics. Although expenditure on R&D more than doubled between 1950 and 1955, the company only progressed as far as falsely marketing as 'electronic' an electro-mechanical data processor[64] – just at the time when even truly electronic punched-card systems were about to give way to computers. Even the Powers-Samas Programme Controlled Computer launched in 1955 was really no more than a calculator.[65]

BTM, for its part, continued comfortably to look to its benevolent American uncle, IBM, for new designs – until 1949, that is, when a painful rupture between the two companies forced BTM at long last to take full responsibility for its own R&D. The BTM press release about the rupture only goes to show that a faintly desperate blowing of Britain's trumpet was not a post-war monopoly of politicians, for it welcomed 'this opportunity of proving that British effort and British skill can be matched successfully against any competitor in our business, whether national or international'.[66] It is sufficient comment on this bluster that within ten days IBM announced the creation of the IBM World Trade Corporation, its mission to conquer all markets everywhere, including Britain. So BTM's progenitor back in the 1900s and patron ever since had now become its most dangerous long-term commercial enemy.

Nevertheless, there followed in the first half of the 1950s a delusory happy time for BTM and Powers-Samas. Their output of conventional punched-card machines trebled and exports flourished, especially in the Commonwealth. The happiness was only marred by the calamitous failure in 1950–52 of Powers-Samas's attempt to invade the United States market, with only eight machines sold by the end of 1951: Dad's Army taking on the US Marine Corps and losing.[67] In mid-decade, however, IBM began its inexorable advance into the markets of the British companies. The performance of its new accounting machines eclipsed that of BTM's current design dating from before the war. It could deliver in six months as against two years for both British firms.

IBM's superiority did not only lie in technological innovation and sheer manufacturing capacity. Just as important were the power and skill of its marketing offensive, especially since this was carried out by shock troops of highly trained, highly rewarded and highly motivated salesmen.[68] In the face of this offensive BTM's overseas earnings dropped in 1955 alone from a quarter of total revenue to a fifth.[69] And the new accounting machine rushed out by BTM in 1956 as its riposte to IBM proved both unreliable in operation and inferior in specified performance.

Yet Powers-Samas was in even worse case. Its great hope, the Samastronic, turned out in 1956–8 to be a technical disaster leading to a sales debacle. That debacle in turn inflicted a mortal wound on the company itself, which in 1959 was compelled to merge with BTM to form International Computers and Tabulators Ltd (ICT): an apt valedictory tribute to the quality of Powers-Samas's top management.

That the British business systems industry was losing the current battle for sales of 1950s technology hardly boded well for its chances in the next battle, for this would prove a far, far more exacting test of its technological and marketing prowess.

In America in the late 1940s and early 1950s visionaries were already describing how in the business of the future every kind of operational data would whiz by wire straight into head office's 'electronic brain' for processing. Routine office staff, paper files and punched-card machines would all become redundant. But how far were these futuristic imaginings to be taken seriously by the manufacturers of business systems, and especially their R&D and marketing departments? The conundrum was the more baffling because 1950–55 marked the commercial heyday of the electronically operated punched-card machine. How far, then, should research be directed at exploiting this short- or medium-term market with improved or new designs? And how far directed towards the more speculative bet of data-processing by computer?

Attitudes in the research department of BTM towards 'electronic brains' at first varied between a shutting of the mind to their promise and outright hostility. Then in late 1950, and thanks to a bright new computer research team, the company decided to develop a small and relatively cheap 'semi-scientific' computer. The prototype HEC (Hollerith Electronic Computer)[70] was shown off at the 1953 Business Efficiency Exhibition at Olympia. Early in 1955 two HEC2M[71] pre-production prototypes were delivered. Although only six HEC2Ms were ever sold, experience with them emboldened BTM in 1954 to embark on a data-processing version, the HEC4. First introduced in 1956, it would sell over a hundred copies, so becoming the most commercially successful British computer of the late 1950s.[72] And in January 1957 BTM was to crystallize a future strategy of developing a three-fold range of computers: the successor to the HEC, the medium-price Atlanta, and the high-capacity Apollo, the latter two being collaborative ventures with Ferranti.[73]

Had they got it right at last? Only up to a point. One crucial weakness lay in the peripherals that a computer needed in order to do its job, such as printers and the magnetic tape for storing information. British electronics firms (including BTM itself) had either neglected the technical development of these items or made a muck of it because of what Lord Halsbury called 'their spirit of facile optimism'. As late as 1958, according to Halsbury, 'we have not a single tape-deck in the U.K. able to compete with U.S. equipment . . .'[74] And so, far from Britain exploiting the huge potential world market for peripherals, she was having to import printers and tape-decks from America.

But much more serious for the future ICT Ltd in the 1960s was a fundamental blunder of corporate strategy committed by BTM in the 1950s. The blunder was the product of a very British lack of ruthlessness in thought, decision and action, especially when it came to junking the familiar in favour of the novel. For the management of BTM treated the development of computers as a mere extra to the development of punched-card machines, which they still saw as the continuing core of the business long into the future. Writes the historian of the company: 'When it became obvious that computers were in the ascendant, ICT had neither the technical capability nor the organizational structure to react.'[75] The relative excellence of BTM (and later ICT) in R&D was to be no help at all when the traditional market for punched-card machines was brutally killed off in 1961–2 by mass sales of IBM's new 1401 computer. For ICT's problem lay in *Technik*: it was 'quite unable to switch its electro-mechanical production to electronic equipment and computer peripherals with anything like the necessary speed'.[76]

In fairness, it was only in the mid-1950s that the management of IBM in the United States came to recognize that the future of business systems lay with the computer. But in contrast to British floundering, the American company, once roused, proved swift in decision and ruthless in action. Thomas Watson Jr., who took over from his father as head of IBM, recalled later:

> We took one of our most competent operating executives with a reputation for fearlessness and competence and put him in charge of all phases of the development of an IBM large-scale electronic computer. He and we were successful . . .
>
> By 1956 it became clear that to respond rapidly to challenge, we needed a new organisation concept . . .[77]

This new concept was settled in the course of a carefully pre-planned three-day meeting of some hundred top executives. IBM would devolve the command and control down from the top in order to achieve maximum speed and suppleness in reacting to technical or market opportunities. BTM on the other hand was to remain head-office-heavy and tight-corseted by bureaucracy: the

Whitehall model instinctively emulated by the managements of so many large British concerns.

By the early 1960s British manufacturers of computers had completed their bungling of the post-war opportunity. The electronics companies who had developed the computer as just one among their several product lines would be marketing a jumble of models, some technically advanced, few designed primarily for commercial data processing, and all sold in small quantities.[78] The single British business systems company of any note, ICT, would for a time be reduced to importing and reselling American computers and peripherals to fill the gaps in its own inventory.[79] British manufacturers as a whole now lay some two years behind their American competitors in terms of the technology of computers, including peripherals and software (in itself a term current in America some two years earlier than in Britain). And no British company, not even BTM, had yet equalled IBM in appreciating the crucial importance of marketing and salesmanship.

Yet their own managerial mistakes and fragmentation of effort do not constitute the sole reasons why the British computer and business systems industries in the late 1940s and the 1950s had as a whole failed to approach 'world's best practice' as set by IBM. Management right across British industry and commerce must share the blame. For they were proving just as reluctant to adopt the computer in the mid-1950s as their predecessors to adopt punched-card technology in the 1900s. In some cases this was due to sheer ignorance: in answer to a Board of Trade questionnaire in 1956 on 'automation',[80] the British Tyre & Rubber Company wonderfully reported that it was considering the introduction of 'automatic computers, which will probably not be electronic'.[81] Only one oil company, British Petroleum, had then actually installed a computer (the DEUCE, made by English-Electric), while the British subsidiary of Esso Petroleum had only got as far as reckoning that 'future developments point to the *ultimate use* [added emphasis] of magnetic tape and computers'.[82] Although the British Insurance Association reported that 'a few companies' in their field had already ordered computers, with more to follow over the next five years,[83] the

British Bankers' Association had no such good news to convey: computers for clearing-house operations and centralized book-keeping were still in the stage of being 'envisaged'.[84] Several other industries had also got no further with computers than 'envisaging'. The nationalized Central Electricity Authority reported that the application of 'larger type electronic computers' to its supply and office operations remained 'still under consideration'.[85]

Yet it was the National Health Service, that cumbersome Stalinist-style bureaucracy created by Aneurin Bevan to dispense health care to the captive consumer, which had the furthest to go. Five out of fourteen Regional Hospital Boards in 1956 had not even got as far as central accounting and administration systems based on ordinary electro-mechanical punched-card machines – let alone electronic data processing, let alone computers. A civil servant noted in November 1956: 'Apart from one small electronic calculator, no electronic machinery has been introduced by Regional Boards . . .'[86] Two hospital boards did however report that they had each ordered a computer for experiment in electronic computation: one a BTM HEC, and the other stated to be a Powers-Samas, although in fact the company never made a true computer.[87]

The upshot of this prevailing British caution was that even by 1960 only 250 computers of all types had so far been installed in the United Kingdom, compared with over 1,000 in Europe and 3,800 in America (1959 figure).[88] In Britain, therefore, the other half of the equation of success, a ready market, was missing.

What the punched-card machine and the computer were to the modern office, so were instrumentation and automatic control systems ('automation') to the modern factory. In both these technologies (often coupled, or even conflated, in contemporary discussion) the pointers on the dials of performance proved disquietingly reluctant to move up.

Before the Second World War the instruments industry (in the strict sense of devices for measuring and monitoring) had 'lagged behind its foreign competitors, particularly Germany, in research and development'. So opined a Whitehall Report in July 1945 on the future of the industry.[89] Germany had dominated export markets partly because German instruments were so good and partly because

of 'highly organised methods of salesmanship'.[90] Now this toughest
of rivals lay temporarily closed down by national defeat. What, then,
did managements in the British instrument industry need to do in
order to seize their present chance? The Whitehall report could
only recommend improvement of 'overseas marketing facilities' and
of 'facilities for proper technical education', and the encouragement
of 'industry generally' to make 'fuller use' of the latest instruments.[91]
These and similar platitudes fell far short of a plan for rapid and
radical change.

But in any case the thought of rapid and radical change was to
prove just as distasteful to British boardrooms in this technology as
in others. According to a Cambridge expert in December 1953, 'the
instrument industry in this country is almost entirely composed of
small firms unable to cover a wide range of applications or to
maintain large enough research and development departments
to make real progress in this difficult field'.[92] The truth is that each
management far preferred to remain the boss of their own little
private army, however ineffective, than to accept coordination into
some kind of industrial panzer corps, however apt for defeating
foreigners in the market. Wrote one civil servant in the Ministry of
Supply to another in the Board of Trade in January 1954:

> The leading firms in this manufacturing industry have turned a deaf
> ear to all approaches by our Interdepartmental Committee on the
> Scientific Instrument Industry and by the British Scientific Instrument
> Research Association (and doubtless other bodies) to join in organ-
> ised research activities.[93]

Why the deaf ear?

> This is probably due in part to the fact that several of the manufac-
> turers of this equipment rely entirely on their American associates for
> information of this kind. Even when they have no American connec-
> tions U.K. manufacturers seem to prefer to work in isolation . . .[94]

Or as Lord Halsbury put it more broadly in the course of a
Whitehall committee meeting on instrumentation in April 1954,

> The instrument industry undoubtedly had certain weaknesses due to
> its mosaic structure. In addition certain criticisms which are made

generally of British industry by contrast with American industry tended to be particularly noticeable in the instrument industry.[95]

Could British manufacturers do better with control systems? In the aftermath of the Second World War, Whitehall had its doubts here too. After all, these manufacturers were in some cases one and the same as the makers of instruments per se who had competed so feebly against the Germans before the war. So in November 1947 eighteen representatives of the Department of Scientific and Industrial Research, the National Physical Laboratory, the Telecommunications Research Establishment, the Board of Trade and the Ministry of Supply met to discuss electronic systems, the latest control technology. The gathering came to the bold decision to set up a survey group 'to investigate the possibility of improving methods of control in industry, and report'.[96] They also reckoned that 'panel meetings representing a wide variety of interests might usefully be held at say six-weekly intervals to discuss work in the field.'[97]

On 9 February 1948 an even larger conclave of twenty-two scientific and bureaucratic brains met to apply themselves to the interim report of the survey group.[98] According to that report, while automatic *mechanical* controls were common in older industries, pneumatic and electro-pneumatic controllers were also in wide use, especially to regulate temperature. The obstacle to installing more of these conventional devices lay in 'shortage of production, and consequent long delivery . . .'[99] As for the newer electronic control systems, 'only isolated examples . . . have been seen in use in factories . . .'[100] Why so isolated? The report's answer flattered neither the users nor suppliers: 'There are relatively few firms engaged in the manufacture of electronic devices, and few such devices have been fully developed and marketed.'[101] Moreover, those devices now on sale 'frequently' suffered from 'poor engineering design'.[102] As for the users, their shortcomings consisted in 'lack of knowledge regarding electronic techniques', and 'lack of personnel with suitable knowledge and training to supervise the running and servicing of automatic devices, a difficulty aggravated by the inadequate "after-sales" service provided by the manufacturers.'[103]

How then to cure all these woeful, if familiar, derelictions? The conclave's high-wattage collective intellect produced a brilliant answer: an 'Advisory Committee on Industrial Instrumentation'. This was to accomplish its task by such shock measures as 'collection and dissemination of information' and 'education of the user industry in the possible benefits to be achieved from increased instrumentation'.[104] Bonaparte at Austerlitz! Wellington at Waterloo!

It was the outstations of American companies[105] that – just as with office machinery – provided the contrast to a prevailing native British inertia. Yet their output wholly depended on their American parents for R&D as well as imports of essential components or tools. In November 1951 one such American outstation, Bristol's Instruments Ltd, was brutally told by its parent company that 'you could not do the [R&D] work that we are doing for you even if you had 12% of our total personnel in the Engineering Department, or 12 men, do the work for you.'[106] At this same time Bristol's wrote to the Ministry of Supply to plead that without import licences for American components the company would be unable to meet demands for complete plant instrumentation from industries as disparate as rubber tyres, coke ovens, chemical works, and oil companies.[107]

The mention of the oil industry was shrewdly judged to make Whitehall wince. For a grand programme was just getting under way to build refineries and petrochemical plants on United Kingdom soil for the first time – partly because of the loss of the huge refinery at Abadan after Mossadeq nationalized the Iranian assets of the Anglo-Iranian Oil Company (see above, Chapter 5). This programme represented a laudable example of large-scale capital investment in a modern technology. It is thus more the pity that for control systems as well as instrumentation in the narrow sense the programme would throughout crucially depend on American expertise and American kit. In 1957 a Whitehall report on the oil-plant construction industry noted: 'Design "know-how" is, however, almost entirely in the hands of American consultants . . .' while a 'very considerable number of manufacturing and selling agreements have been negotiated by U.K. manufacturers with American licensors . . .'[108]

Nonetheless, Lord Halsbury (Chairman of the NRDC) argued in a letter to a colleague in the Board of Trade in January 1954 that 'you cannot expect the British Instrument Industry to produce out of their hat, as it were, instruments to control the behaviour of plant the like of which has never existed in this country before . . .' He considered that they were 'under a hopeless handicap when it came to instrumenting the new oil refineries'.[109]

Not their fault at all? In June 1954 the President of the Board of Trade (Peter Thorneycroft) was briefed:

> The equipment-supplying firms are in general too small to employ the large staffs and undertake the research and development necessary to enable them to design new equipment with confidence to meet new needs. The most experienced control engineers are probably with the large users, such as refineries and large scale chemical manufacturers, who have been obliged to solve their problems themselves.[110]

Yet with automatic control systems as with computers it would be wrong to lay all the blame on the manufacturers. How strongly did the managements of potential purchasers hunger for this technological revolution? For one thing, their appetites would not have been whetted by displays of diehard union resistance to various types of new technology, most notoriously in shipbuilding. In 1956 the Standard Motor Company had to fight an industrial battle of the Somme with the unions over automation at its Coventry car and tractor plants (see above, p. 192). The patchiness of the British response to the promise of automation is revealed by the answers to the Board of Trade's questionnaire in 1956–7.[111] Many respondents confused true 'automation' with the commonly installed mechanical or pneumatic control devices, and even with simple mechanization like belt conveyors. Over twenty respondents were content to report that they had either long been equipped with the latter kinds of kit, or were planning to install them.[112] The British Steel Wire Industries Association wonderfully believed that automation 'though a new word, more or less covers something the Steel Wire Industry has been practicing for a hundred years . . .'[113]

The process industries such as gas or chemical plants and oil refineries reported – unsurprisingly – that with them automatic control systems were already standard. However, answers to the questionnaire from manufacturing companies showed that automation of factory production through electronically-controlled transfer machines was still very much a novelty. For example, in so important a firm as the English Electric Company (Chairman: Lord Nelson of Colne, an imposing industrial viceroy of the period), 'transfer machines and automatic handling from say presses to heat treatment operations' were still only 'envisaged' by management.[114] And in that same month of November 1956, the managing director of Morphy-Richards Ltd, one of Britain's premier producers of household electrical goods, reported to the Board of Trade that although they were continuously increasing mechanization, they had 'no intention of introducing the techniques which you [the Board of Trade] clearly define under the heading of Automation.'[115]

Nevertheless, there were honourable exceptions to the lethargy of the native British control-systems manufacturers and many of their potential customers. In 1953 one such, Elliott Brothers Ltd, even took over Bristol's Instruments. Elliotts also distinguished themselves during the decade as technical leaders in the development of computers, especially for use in automatic control of industrial processes. This firm was, however, led by a dynamic and ambitious entrepreneur, Leon (later Sir Leon) Bagrit.[116] In 1957 he was to form Elliott-Automation, the first company in Europe to specialize in this technology.

Thus did an exotic chef demonstrate to the plain cooks what could be done with that widely available ingredient, opportunity.

That the twentieth-century industries which equipped office and factory had muffed their post-war chances rendered it the more essential that Britain should outstrip foreign rivals in the designing, making and marketing of wares which the Western family in shop or showroom would want to buy. For the fulfilment of that family's aspirations to the material good life had now become the end purpose of all peaceful Western industrial effort. And no British government of the 1950s could forget that on Britain's competitive success in this effort depended the balance of payments, the strength of sterling, and their own credibility in playing the world power game.

19. The Drive-train of Industrial Growth

While the battle-front in Korea was swinging to and fro in the first years of the 1950s, the patient housewives of the United Kingdom were still queuing up at the shop door with ration book in hand, or far along the street for such 'off-ration' delicacies as cod or bananas. Although the once-defeated countries of Continental Europe had by now abolished food rationing, British governments had gone no further than relaxing step by cautious step the severely institutional diet of the immediate post-war years. Yet this diet only marked the barbed tip of a regime of 'austerity' extending to personal and household goods in general. The regime had been at first enforced by means of a 'points' system of rationing (for clothes and household textiles) and latterly either through long waiting lists for scarce commodities or through the dampening down of demand by bumping up purchase tax.

These sacrifices were meant to help offset the cost imposed on the national economy (and especially the balance of payments) by the world role, financial and military; and, from 1951 onwards, also to help offset the burden of rearmament. To the intellects of Whitehall it appeared a cunning enough trick: throttle back imports of foodstuffs (especially from the dollar area) while at the same time diverting consumer goods as well as industrial products from the home market to exports, and Britain could happily combine solvency and self-importance. As Anthony Eden as Foreign Secretary put it in 1952, the British people

> must either give up for a time some of the advantages which a high standard of living confers upon them, or by relaxing in the outside world see their Country sink to the level of a second-class power . . .[1]

According to him, the people were therefore faced with 'a choice of the utmost difficulty.' But in reality they had no choice at all: the sacrifices were simply imposed on them by Government, whether Conservative or Labour. Guns before butter! Status before sirloins!

So it was not until 1954 that the ration book finally joined the rest of the lumber in the national attic, its abolition a sign that at last the long winter of austerity was yielding to the springtime of material abundance. Now sophisticates could actually cook Elizabeth David's Mediterranean recipes[2] instead of merely reading them with vain salivation. On their tables *bœuf en daube à la niçoise, pommes à la manière d'Apt* and a side salad supplanted the native Sunday roast garnished with 'greens' boiled to a mush that would still remain the choice of the gentry and the flat-capped.

Mediterranean cuisine proved, however, only one of the exciting European invaders of Britain in the early 1950s. If it was novel (whatever 'it' might be), if it was chic, it surely must be foreign; if it was frumpish, perhaps rather old-fashioned, it must be British.[3] Thus the teashop in its genteel chintziness found itself competing with the colourful coffee-bar decorated in 'contemporary' style: a case of the 'Copper Kettle' under attack from 'El Sombrero'. The huge tea-boilers in canteen and 'caff' made by Stotts of Oldham and resembling part of the engine room of an Edwardian battleship faced an upstart rival in the elegant espresso machine (invented by Gaggia in 1946) that equipped the coffee-bars. A new word, *cappuccino*, entered the English language.

The British motorcycle, essentially unaltered for five decades and intended for rugged proletarians willing to brave the weather swaddled in leather from helmeted top to booted toe, now also confronted a novel challenger: the motor scooter, which could be comfortably ridden in normal street clothes by both sexes and all ages. The scooter offered some protection from wind and rain, was nippy and convenient in town, and even provided a hook from which to hang a shopping basket or briefcase.[4] Was it manufactured in Birmingham or Coventry thanks to the vision of the managers of Norton, BSA, Triumph or Matchless? No, it was not; it (the Vespa, designed in 1946) was made near Genoa thanks to the vision of Enrico Piaggio, head of the eponymous engineering firm.

From Germany came the handy little two-stroke two-seater city mini-cars, the Messerschmitt and the Isetta, much cheaper to buy and to run than even the cheapest British family cars like the Ford Popular or Austin A30, and much more fun than those staid family conveyances. From Germany too came the Grundig tape-recorder, enabling British families to amaze themselves at the weird sound of their own voices.

True, foreign imports only amounted so far to a tiny fraction of the British consumer market. But, just the same, they were harbingers, and as such they merited alert appraisal by British managements. This they did not always receive, the smug self-satisfaction of provincial boardrooms being what it was.

Yet some British managements did bravely decide to junk what had served them well in the past and instead strike out afresh. In 1952 Sainsbury's opened the first self-service grocery supermarket in Britain. Their directors had made a personal reconnaissance of the supermarket operations in America successfully and profitably conducted since the 1930s, and they came home convinced that this must be the future shape of British retailing too. But while Sainsbury's went on to prosper mightily with their new American formula, rival grocers doomed themselves to extinction because their managements, mentally chained by corporate history, clung to the pre-war formula of many small branches and labour-intensive counter-service: high costs and high prices.[5]

There is a general lesson here. Boardrooms were not (and are not) inhabited by the classical economist's 'economic man' responding mechanically to market opportunities and competitive pressures, but by individual human beings who vary widely in creative imagination, flexibility of mind, and boldness of leadership. Moreover, the ordinary ruck of directors and senior managers were (and are) conditioned for good or ill by the prevailing business cultures of their company and country – be those conservative or innovative.

All these considerations are implicit in the reports on United States industries rendered by the Anglo-American productivity teams (see above, pp. 273–8). But they are made all too starkly explicit by America's global dominance over the marketing of novel consumer products between 1900 and the Second World War. The tally includes the electric washing machine; the zip fastener; the brassiere; Formica; lipstick; the electric hair-dryer; the food mixer;

the teabag; Band Aid and Elastoplast; paper tissues; the cotton swab on a stick; the pop-up toaster; ready-wrapped sliced bread; frozen food; Scotch Tape and Sellotape; tampons; the Brillo pad; the electric razor; the polythene container; and the parking meter. Humble though these products may be, they and all their fellows have cumulatively transformed everyday life, to the great profit first of their innovators, then their imitators, and finally of the Western economy as a whole. The comparable British contribution in 1900–1939, however, hardly goes beyond the Jubilee clip, the catseye road stud, and stainless steel.[6]

This dismal record is not the only sign of waning British creativity in the consumer marketplace. Before and after the Second World War the British housewife cleaned her home with vacuum cleaners supplied for the most part by British subsidiaries of Electrolux of Sweden and Hoover of America – just as she made her clothes and curtains with a sewing machine manufactured by the local outstation of the American Singer Company. She mostly did the washing-up and the laundry with soap powders and detergents marketed by an Anglo-Dutch company, Unilever, and a subsidiary (Thomas Hedley Ltd) of the American firm of Procter and Gamble. Her family washed themselves and cleaned their teeth courtesy of other American outstations, such as Colgate-Palmolive. It was the outstation of the Kellogg Company that supplied their favourite breakfast cereals.[7] Need to cure a headache? That meant Aspro-Nicholas, an Australian outstation in Britain. Morning shave for the breadwinner? That meant safety razor blades from Gillette, a Canadian outstation. And so it went.

It boded ill for Britain's long-term commercial prospects that during the first post-war decade British management proved just as lacklustre in devising new consumer goods that would create the markets of the future. To America belongs the credit for such novelties as the Polaroid camera (1946), aluminium cooking foil (1946), emulsion paint, hair-spray and the microwave oven (1949), and, in 1956, superglue (Loctite). The meagre British list consisted of the domestic rubber glove (1950) and the frozen fish-finger (1956), though the credit for this belongs to the local subsidiary of the American Birdseye Corporation. Whereas the roll-on deodorant was certainly a British invention (1955), it took the United States successfully to market it. In fact, when it came to humble innovations with high potential for sales and profits, even little Sweden and Switzerland did as well as Britain, with (respectively) the Tetrapak milk carton (1952) and the Velcro fastener (1956).[8]

It is remarkable that over the entire period from 1900 to 1956 the former 'workshop of the world' failed to produce a single industrial designer who matched in world stature and influence the likes of Raymond Loewy, Henry Dreyfuss, Walter Dorwin Teague and Charles Eames (American); or Erich Behrens, Walter Gropius, Marcel Breuer and Erich Mendelsohn (German); or Alvar Aalto and Eero Saarinen (Finnish). Despite Charles Rennie Mackintosh's own individual genius, he had little impact on the design of British products. Gordon Russell remained dowelled into the romantic arts-and-crafts culture of hand and tool, a world away from the industrial studios and clientele of a Loewy or a Harley Earl. Wells Coates, an outstanding designer in Britain before and after the Second World War, was himself highly untypical of the British scene, being Canadian by origin and both a graduate and a Ph.D. in engineering (Universities of Vancouver and London).[9]

And in regard to the 1950s in particular, the resounding international names in the design of all kinds of consumer goods from typewriters to armchairs were Italian when they were not American: a tribute equally to the designers themselves and to the manufacturers who had commissioned them.[10]

Why had Britain so persistently failed to become one of the global leaders in well-designed consumer products? The blame lay equally with the red-necked philistinism of British managements who (with rare enough exceptions)[11] scorned industrial designers, and the accursed high-mindedness of the British educational elite who, in their reverence for 'Fine Art', relegated industrial design itself to the lowly category of 'commercial art'.[12] Here was a new twist to the old story of the divide between the cultural values of common room and boardroom in Britain: a twist which explains why, for instance, Britain had never created its own version of the 1920s German Bauhaus. The nearest (though still very distant) British equivalent lay in the Royal College of Art in London. Yet only after Robin Darwin became its Principal in 1948 did this hitherto somnolent institution begin to shift its *Schwerpunkt* from pursuit of 'fine art' to training in design for industry. Even so, the College was not to be installed in its own purpose-designed building instead of a collection of huts until 1962,[13] a mere thirty-six years later than the construction of the Bauhaus.

By the time the Korean War broke out in mid-1950 the motor car was already fast becoming the West's supreme consumer product and both a measure and a drive-train of industrial growth. For the world motor-vehicle industry towed behind it a great complex of component manufactures, electrical and mechanical. It was a major consumer of electricity, gas and steel. Its products would make more and more use of the new plastics and synthetic fabrics created by the chemical and petrochemical industries. Hence a nation's share of the global output and exports of motor vehicles would in future serve both as a gauge of its technological horsepower and also as a speedometer registering how fast its economy was accelerating. If British management and British design could not above all get this one right, then the faith of the governing elite that Britain had a long-term future as an industrial power second only to America must prove mere self-delusion.

Yet in 1950 where lay the doubt? Every Briton knew that when it came to making motor cars 'British was best'. Was not the industry riding serenely ahead of its foreign rivals, just like industrial Britain as a whole? That year the United Kingdom made 523,000 cars as against France's 257,000 and West Germany's 219,000. It exported 399,000 against France's 89,000 and Germany's 69,000:[14] it even exported more than America. This glossy statistical surface concealed, however, corrosive rust working deep within the structure – again, just as with industrial Britain as a whole. For none of the deficiencies identified by the March 1945 Whitehall report on 'The Post-War Re-settlement of the Motor Industry'[15] had been put right five years later: the British car industry remained still fragmented between too many companies each making too many models with too many types of engines and components.[16] The industry's managements, conditioned by pre-war experience, still thought first and foremost of the British family motorist and the British road when conceiving new models. Not one mass-production car in 1950 could match an American 'auto' for combined robustness, comfort, power, and relative cheapness. Not one could match the Volkswagen for sheer reliability in all climates and over Continental distances; and not one native British car manufacturer could match Volkswagen in excellence of overseas after-sales service.[17]

The single advantage of the British car industry over its German, French and Italian rivals since the Second World War had lain in its head-start in getting back into production, and by 1950 that head-start was narrowing. Moreover, the happy time was now past when the overseas customer would gratefully buy any vehicle, however flimsy and old-fashioned in style, that the British car industry cared to shove abroad.[18]

The impressive grand total of exports in 1950 is even deceptive in itself: out of 399,000 cars exported, fewer than 65,000 went to the fast-growing European market, and fewer than 20,000 went to the United States, about the same as to New Zealand.[19] Overwhelmingly the United Kingdom car industry still looked to traditional but under-populated and slow-growing 'Empire' markets. Australia alone took 122,000 British cars in 1950, a fifth more than the whole of North America and more than a third of the entire export total. And in that North American market British sales to Canada, at 76,000 cars, were more than three times those to the United States.[20]

It was therefore high time that the industry at last accepted the challenge which it had shirked since the war – that of totally redesigning itself. It would, however, have to be quick about it, for the Europeans were every year driving up closer behind. But did management have either the desire or the strength of will to push the accelerator of change down to the floor?

The bare record gives the short answer. Each year from 1951 to 1955 the growth of Britain's world exports of cars proved sputteringly slower than that of her rivals. In 1952 total British exports were actually down to 184,500 from 399,000, with sales in Europe falling from just under 65,000 to just over 51,000; in Australia from some 122,000 to some 57,000; and in Canada from some 76,000 to some 21,000.[21] No doubt the industry was then suffering from the peak impact of rearmament on its manufacturing capacity.[22] But three years later exports to the booming European market remained stuck at virtually the same volume as in 1950: just under 66,000 cars.[23] Exports to all North America in 1955 amounted to little more than a third of the 1950 figure: 33,600 as against 96,260.[24] With Australian sales down to under 100,000 compared with 122,000 in 1950, only sales to New Zealand, up from just under 20,000 in 1950 to 37,650 in 1955, went a little way to redeem a distinctly underpowered performance.[25] Between 1953 and 1955 Britain's motor-vehicle exports as a whole rose by only a fifth in value, whereas Germany's more than doubled.[26]

What was going wrong? The answer is simple: just about everything that was wrong with the British industrial system as a whole. For a start, the car industry's Communist or Trotskyist shop stewards and unofficial strike committees were manfully doing what they could to disrupt production and hold up exports (see above, Chapter 9); and they were to do even better in the decades to come. Yet the main responsibility for what was going wrong lay with managements still held mentally prisoner by the industry's past.[27]

The single major act of reorganization between 1950 and 1955 lay in the merger in 1952 of Austin and the Nuffield Organisation (the two largest native British manufacturers) into the British Motor Company.[28] On paper this created a world-class enterprise, certainly in terms of scale. But it was on paper only, not in manufacturing reality. In the first place, Austin's output was based on a single large (by British standards) plant at Longbridge near Birmingham, while Nuffield's various badge-engineered marques were made in no fewer than fifteen factories scattered from Abingdon and Cowley (Oxford) to Birmingham and Coventry. Secondly, and obviously enough, there was no model and no engine common to both companies, and few components either. In consequence, it would be years before major economies could be brought about by rationalizing the factories and the model range, to say nothing of amalgamating the two dealer networks. In 1956 the British Motor Company (BMC) would be offering for sale no fewer than fifteen different models as against Volkswagen's one,[29] these ranging from ponderous pseudo-Rolls-Royces down to the Morris Minor. And thirdly, the new BMC's two constituent firms had long been the

379

bitterest of rivals, so that in terms of management the merger was less like putting two newly-weds into bed together than stuffing two aggrieved ferrets into one sack.

In any case, the merger of Austin and Nuffield still left the mass-production of cars in Britain split between no fewer than five major companies: BMC, Ford, Vauxhall, the Rootes Group, and Standard. This compares with one such company in Italy (Fiat), three in France (Peugeot, Renault and Simca), and four in Germany (Mercedes-Benz, Opel, Ford, and, far and away the largest, Volkswagen). It further splintered British mass-production that the Rootes Group by itself was offering (in 1954) eleven widely different models, the company being, like Nuffield, a conservator of the bonnet badges of venerated but defunct British makes.[30]

In motor manufacture, just as in other British industries, relatively modern large-scale operations contrasted with a covey of little firms stuck in a workshop mode more appropriate to the first industrial revolution than the second.[31] Although the names of these little firms – Lea-Francis, Alvis, Allard, Invicta, Healey and so on – are now largely forgotten, their cars attracted much respect at the time from motoring journalists and a public who admired individuality, success in international rallying, and the 'quality' believed to come from 'craftsmanship'.[32] Yet peak annual sales for Lea-Francis (in 1951) only reached 375; for Alvis (also in 1951) 538; for Allard (in 1952) 155; for Invicta (taken over by Lea-Francis, a case of minnow eaten by sprat) some fifteen. Fifteen![33]

In a different category from such highly personal ventures coupling technical enthusiasm with commercial amateurism were companies trying to survive on the borderline between workshop construction and the assembly line: companies too small and under-capitalized fully to exploit their own innovative ideas, yet each consuming their portions of scarce steel, machine tools and skilled labour. The Singer SM 1500 and its 1954 successor, the Hunter, won applause from the British motoring press for their performance and comfort even though their styling (if it could be called such) was so ungainly. Yet their annual production peaked at just 6,400 in 1951. In 1953 the company's new SMX Roadster was welcomed by the press as 'the car of the future' and Britain's potential opposition to Porsche. Production peaked at 580 in 1954. The cars were made in an archaic multi-storey factory in Birmingham, cramped in layout (so causing high handling costs), and equipped with belt-driven machines for fabricating engine-parts.[34] From 1946 to 1952 Armstrong-Siddeley, another distinguished name in British motoring, marketed the genteelly elegant (but at first under-powered and somewhat frail) Hurricane and Typhoon, of which a mere 1,267 were manufactured in 1952. Their successor, the Sapphire (produced from 1952 to 1959), was in its mechanical design, performance and passenger comfort far ahead of its time: later marks came complete with power-steering, overdrive and a top speed of 98 m.p.h. The Sapphire might thus have proved in world markets the British equivalent of the Mercedes saloons of the 1950s and 1960s – had it not been that annual production peaked in 1954 at only 2,800, and ceased altogether in 1960 after the company was swallowed up in the Hawker-Siddeley aircraft group.[35]

Similarly, the Jowett Javelin might have proved the British answer to the immensely successful Peugeot 203, had it been manufactured by a company as big as Peugeot and not by a little firm operating out of a poky two-storey factory in Bradford; and had Jowett enjoyed the resources to develop an engine and a gearbox equal to the advanced design of steering and suspension. As it was, the Javelin was betrayed by a modified pre-war long-stroke engine prone to failure of bearings and gaskets, and gears distinguished for either sticking fast in the box or jumping out. Annual production of this 'shining example of the better kind of family saloon' (to quote *The Autocar*'s gush) peaked in 1951 at just 5,658 cars.[36]

Yet the classic 1950s case of the British fascination with *Technik* and high performance per se must be those romantic legends in their lifetime, Sir William Lyons and his Jaguar XK120 sports car. A Sunday newspaper profile[37] in 1953 (Coronation Year, that festival of patriotic trumpet-blowing) lauded 'Bill' Lyons as 'the captain and sole selector' of the management team of Jaguar Cars; a team which he directed with 'a sustained and compelling intensity of purpose'. He was 'an example of individual enterprise on a scale uncommon in these days of impersonal corporate undertakings'. He was 'physically trim, immaculate in dress'. He had 'the aura of power but not its trappings'. Few of his employees, reported the article, 'recall a conversation lasting more than ten minutes. His interest is precise, kindly and aloof.' And when touring his factory floor his eyes 'search forward with the sweeping intensity of swift-moving head-lights'. An automotive Bonaparte! Yet Lyons was praised in this personal profile for much more than outward charisma: 'His under-standing of the whole complex of design and production is compre-hensive and exact . . .' while 'his most direct contribution has been in styling: his is the flair for line.'

The XK120 open-topped sports car, launched in 1948 and in production throughout the 1950s, superbly embodied that flair. A motoring correspondent who half a century later took an XK120 out on a nostalgic test-run remarked on her 'gorgeous shape, at once voluptuous and athletic', and pronounced that 'the Jaguar's beauty was still breath-taking . . .'[38] The Jaguar-designed straight-six engine made the XK120, at a top speed of 120 m.p.h., the world's fastest production car of the post-war decade. This magnificent beast was intended to clear the road for sales of Jaguar saloon cars as well, under the slogan 'Grace, Pace and Space'. In 1950 the company exported nearly 70 per cent of its production of over 7,000 cars.[39] In 1952 it shifted manufacture to a one-million-square-foot 'shadow' factory in Coventry dating from the pre-war rearmament pro-gramme. Here was success to warm British hearts in a chill econ-omic season. Here were new triumphs of the nation's technological genius to talk about in pub and club.

Yet reality did not accord with reputation. Firstly, even Jaguar were not immune to wilful trade union sabotage, for in spring 1951 the National Union of Vehicle Builders did their best to steer the company off the road with a seven-week strike that also progres-sively rendered idle the members of other unions in the plant. The NUVB had chosen their moment with their usual skill, as Lyons lamented to the Permanent Secretary of the Ministry of Labour and National Service:

> The tragedy of the whole thing is that we are losing most valuable dollar business. We are just on the eve of commencing delivery, on a substantial scale, of our new Mark VII to America and Canada, and it is estimated that we have already lost roughly two million dollars' worth of business. Our principal American Distributor, Mr. M. E.

Hoffman ... has advised us that as he is so very much dependent upon Jaguar, it is impossible for him to continue with the expensive sales operation which he has built up during the last few years.[40]

In Lyons's view, this threat to Jaguar's North American distributor and hence to future dollar exports was 'a most serious aspect' of the strike. Just a week after he wrote this letter, however, the malcontents returned to work, having, in accordance with the custom of the time, achieved nothing but passing damage to the operation that gave them employment.

But no union could be blamed for the failure of Bill Lyons and his company to match technical creativeness with quality of build, efficiency of production, and skill in export marketing.

On the characteristics of the XK120 as a motor car rather than metallic mistress a coolly objective light is cast by a report in the American journal *Consumer Reports* for November 1954.[41] The engine was praised for its flexibility, power and smoothness; criticized for being 'complicated and expensive to work on; it prefers premium fuel'. At normal road speeds 'even the hulking, big-engined Oldsmobile goes as far on a gallon of gas . . .' The report noted that while the Jaguar's basic chassis was 'ruggedly constructed', there was 'considerable weaving and shaking of sheet metal, with the resulting difficulty in preventing squeaks and rattles'. And although the XK120 'handles beautifully on the road', it suffered from a 'dead' (sic) ride which jarred on 'potholes, "washboard" surfaces and joints in concrete'. The journal's testers 'found the Jaguar's clutch stiff to operate, and the gearshift likewise very stiff, though solid and direct in action'. In major ways, summed up the report, Jaguar was 'all that a sports car should be − sleek, powerful, well engineered and a lot of car for the money . . . Bear in mind, though, that a Jag is neither cheap to operate, nor to maintain and repair.' In short, the Jaguar was 'for fun . . . not for a transportation vehicle'.

It renders this American evaluation of an English motoring legend the more enlightening that the same report also included a road test of the Mercedes 180 saloon. Sold at a similar dollar price to the Jaguar, the German car was the product of an utterly different design philosophy. Though its engine was still a low-powered pre-war side-valve, the car had a modern unit-construction body, with independent suspension front *and* rear (the XK120 had leaf (or cart) springs at the rear). 'High quality prevails throughout the coach work and chassis', pronounced *Consumer Reports*. 'The car is light for its size, but the structure is as solid and quiet as a bank vault; rough roads do not shake it.' The Mercedes offered 'an unequalled combination' of a soft ride over washboard or pot-holed surfaces and of steering, handling, and 'roadability' (sic), all at 'a high level of excellence'.[42]

Hindsight suggests that in this comparative American report of 1954 may be discerned clues to the long-term destinies of Jaguar and Mercedes-Benz. For Mercedes-Benz were always to put their faith in building cars 'as solid and quiet as a bank vault'. These qualities inspired the growth of Mercedes-Benz from the 1950s onwards into one of the world's greatest industrial companies,[43] manufacturing a technically coherent family of vehicles that ranged from luxury cars to diesel taxis that ran for ever.

William Lyons, however, had no such ambitions for Jaguar, although there was no inherent reason why his company should not have grown into a British Mercedes-Benz. For he saw his firm as simply a niche player, albeit a major one and a growing one, with its role limited to making sports cars and sports saloons. In 1954 Jaguar's output only amounted to 1.5 per cent of total British production;[44] and the company was never to turn out more than 20,000 cars a year.[45] Mercedes-Benz's annual output passed 42,000 as early as 1951.[46] Likewise, Lyons chose flair in design and exhilarating performance as his leading cards rather than boringly Teutonic exactitude of engineering. In consequence, Jaguar's build quality could be questioned even in the 1950s, as the *Consumer Reports* road test of the XK120 went to show. The new 2.4 litre Mark I saloon of 1955, the first Jaguar to have unitary construction instead of a separate chassis, rusted away fearsomely fast. The powerful 3.4 litre engine of its 1957 successor was ill-matched to feeble drum brakes, while thanks to a rear-wheel track narrower than the front the car became notorious for alarming moments of over-steering.[47] Only with the Mark II of 1959 was Jaguar to get things largely right. So instead of matching Mercedes-Benz's meticulously thorough product development, Lyons's company had fallen into the practice widespread in the post-war British motor industry, that of using the unfortunate purchaser as tester.

Nor was Jaguar always up to 'world's best practice' in bringing its products to market, especially in North America. In November 1954 a hundred dealers were invited to New York to see the new models – of which not one had yet been delivered west of the Mississippi, and only a few to Jaguar's main American agent in the East.[48]

But then, uncertain and unpunctual deliveries had for years been souring the overseas reputations of those who ought to have known the export business better than Jaguar – Britain's mass-production car makers.

If small manufacturers such as Jowett were blessed with creative imagination but handicapped by lack of capacity and capital, it was the very reverse with the four native British members of the 'Big Five' – Austin, Nuffield (Morris), Rootes and Standard. Theirs were the great assembly line plants, to which had now been added former state-funded 'shadow' aircraft and aero-engine factories. But theirs was also a stodginess of brain and body, a corporate conservatism, that laid them open to defeat by brighter foreign rivals.

The stodginess and the conservatism were proclaimed by the very names which manufacturers chose for the cars on sale in the early 1950s, evocative as these were of genteel English rural life or traditional elite institutions – the Devon and the Dorset, the Hampshire and the Somerset, the Cambridge and the Westminster (all Austin); the Oxford and the Isis (both Morris). Some new models carried on the names of their 1930s (or even 1920s) predecessors: the Morris *Minor* and the Hillman *Minx* and the Austin *Seven* and the Standard *Eight*. Clearly the manufacturers hoped thereby to tap the sentimental nostalgia of the middle-aged British family motorist. But what possible meaning could such names hold for a Swiss, a Dutchman or an American?

In their styling these cars fully lived up to the promise of their names. Not one of them rivalled Raymond Loewy's futuristic post-war body-shell for Studebaker, the sheer free-thinking eccentricity of the Citroën 2CV, the engineering 'rightness' of shape of the Volkswagen, or, for that matter, the fluent grace of Bill Lyons's

XK120. Instead, all aspired to be staidly 'respectable' family saloons, to be owned by a British suburban paterfamilias, polished with pride on a Sunday morning, and taken out for 'a drive' on Sunday afternoon.[49] In the cases of Austin and Morris, the two biggest native British producers, the styling (if it can be called such) of models in the showrooms in the early 1950s usually originated in the amateur back-of-an-envelope diktats of their ageing but imperious bosses, Leonard Lord and William Morris. Who can be astonished, then, at a report in the *Spectator* in 1955 that the Swiss called British cars 'old men's cars' because of their appearance?[50]

There were exceptions. The Standard Vanguard (first introduced in 1947, and still going strong in successive versions throughout the 1950s) aspired to live up to its name with a bulbous would-be American body squashed on top of a British wheelbase only 7 feet 10 inches long.[51] The Austin Atlantic convertible (1949–52), bedizened in chrome like a whore's chest with costume jewellery, was the hideous fruit of Brummagem's fantasizing as to what would appeal to the American buyer. In contrast to such amateurism, Ford of Great Britain launched in 1952 the Zephyr and Consul, straightforward scaled-down versions of current American Fords: clean designs still looking good half a century later. Vauxhall, the British outstation of General Motors, similarly offered in the Cresta and Velox series scaled-down versions of contemporary Chevrolet styling. The Rootes Group, for their part, were content simply to plagiarize American fashion for their Hillmans and Humbers, though sadly not American running-gear.

Beneath the dowdy exteriors of the native British mass-production cars lay technology just as dowdy: vague and wandery recirculating-ball, cam-and-roller or worm-and-peg steering instead of precise rack-and-pinion; cart springs at the back instead of independent or coil suspension; long-stroke instead of 'square' engines and, in some cases until the mid-1950s, side-valves,[52] although without Mercedes' excuse of having to re-start the company itself from scratch after the war. Morris's top-of-the-range Isis of 1955, for instance, broadly matched the Mercedes 180 and 220 in size and engine power, but, thanks to cam steering and leaf-springs at the rear, in nothing else. According to *The Autocar*, the 'combination of suspension and steering does not appeal to the driver who corners fast; must be driven with care when surface is wet.'[53] A critic wrote from Rangoon in 1956 about his experience of the Isis: 'Suspension produces excessive steering-wheel kick . . . also rattles, a disturbing knock underneath and then poor brakes in really heavy rain.'[54]

If this was a British mass-producer's top-of-the-range car ten years after the Second World War, what could be expected of the workaday transports? A comparison of the Morris Minor, the Peugeot 203, and the Austin A50 Cambridge provides the answer.

The Morris Minor was rapturously praised by British critics at its launch in 1948 for its advanced design, and it remains to this day a British legend. But what was advanced about it? Independent front suspension? American and some European cars had been equipped with this before the war, and in any case the Minor still had cart springs at the rear. Rack-and-pinion steering? This too had been common on pre-war European cars and was certainly standard on the Volkswagen and the Peugeot 203. But what else? It could hardly be the puny side-valve engine derived from a design of 1932. Only in 1953 did the Minor receive an Austin OHV engine as the first technical benefit of the merger of Austin and Morris into the British Motor Company; and only in 1956 was it finally equipped with an engine giving power adequate to the Minor's weight.[55] And it goes to prove the ad-hockery of its engineering that Alec Issigonis, its supposedly brilliant designer, decided at the last moment to widen the body by 4in (10cm), so making it necessary to bolt on a fillet to cover the resulting gap in the cut and widened front bumper of the production version.[56] Genius indeed!

According to a test by *The Autocar* in 1951, the Minor's top speed was 61 m.p.h. and it took 38.6 seconds to reach 50 m.p.h. Yet the Peugeot 203 in a road test by *Automobilia* in 1948 achieved over 72 m.p.h. (116 k.p.h.) over a flying kilometre, and took 22 seconds to reach 50 m.p.h. (80 k.p.h.).[57] In this test the Peugeot covered 166 kilometres of ordinary roads in two hours: an average speed of 52 m.p.h. The car was equipped with independent front suspension and coil-sprung rear axle; a 'square' (75cm x 73cm) OHV engine; and sound-proofed and insulated monocoque body, plus equipment for heating and de-frosting.[58]

Austin's A50 'Cambridge' too proved in all respects an inferior product to the 203 even though it was launched in 1954, eight years later than the French car. Its shortcomings included a long-stroke engine (73cm x 89cm), cam steering, and rear cart springs. According to an *Autocar* test in April 1955, the Cambridge's maximum speed was 71.7 m.p.h. – slower than the Peugeot 203 in 1948.[59]

It was not merely in technology that Peugeot outshone its British rivals; it was also in the general strategy of product development. Whereas the French company steadily developed the 203 as their *sole* product between 1948 and 1955 (when it was replaced by the equally successful 206), Austin, Nuffield (Morris) and then BMC between them designed and built no fewer than five different cars in the 203's capacity class.[60]

For the managements of the native British mass-manufacturers made not only a technical botch of developing new models but also a strategic hash of production planning and export marketing. The Morris Minor affords an outstanding example of these basic mistakes of management. It alone among British cars could have challenged the Volkswagen in export markets throughout the critical period 1948–55. But instead of making the Minor its *Schwerpunkt*, Nuffield spread its production resources over other Morris cars as well: the Oxford and its cheaper variant the Cowley (total output in the period: 96,083), and the Morris 6 (total output: 12,184).[61] Thus total output of the Minor over seven years only reached 387,000 – not much more than a third of the Volkswagen's total of one million cars in the same period achieved from a standing start in a bombed-out works.[62] In 1952 exports of the Volkswagen saloon and the mechanically identical Transporter, at 47,000, actually equalled that year's total output of Minors.[63] Add in the factors of Volkswagen's aggressive marketing and its justified reputation for after-sales service,[64] and it is easy to see why VW sales in the United States accelerated from 2,000 in 1953 to 55,000 in 1955, while in the same years the sales of the Morris Minor to America virtually conked out, down from 1,570 to a mere 700.[65]

It verges on the tragic that the British Motor Company was to repeat the same misjudgement with the Mini of 1959, potentially a success on the Volkswagen scale. At first badged as either a Morris Mini-Minor or an Austin Seven in sentimental deference to pre-war tradition, it too would have to share factory space with an assortment of other models, with the result that its cumulative output had only reached one million by 1965[66] – a figure equalled by the output of Volkswagens in that one year alone.[67]

In the late 1940s and early 1950s Austin's management – and this means the arrogant Leonard Lord – failed no less than Nuffield's to select a *Schwerpunkt* for production and marketing, and concentrate resources behind it. They too pursued a broad-front strategy, with the consequence that the A40 (the Devon and the Dorset), Austin's broad equivalent to the Volkswagen or the Peugeot 203, had to share assembly-line resources with the smaller A30 and the bigger A50 (Cambridge) and A70 (the Hereford and the Hampshire), to say nothing of the Atlantic. Thus the total output of the A40 and its variants between 1947 and 1954, at 456,835, amounted to less than half that of the Volkswagen over an equivalent period.[68]

Yet perhaps the saddest example during the first post-war decade of a British manufacturer throwing away a magnificent opportunity to create, and then dominate, a new global market lies in the Rover Car Company.

In 1948 Rover's engineers improvised the only rival in the world to the American Jeep. Launched as the Land Rover, this immensely tough yet cheap multipurpose vehicle therefore had the potential to sell overseas in immense quantity. But instead of investing in a major new plant devoted solely to the Land Rover and (in Volkswagen style) entrusting the company's entire future to this single winner, the Rover management chose to keep up production of their old-fogeyish saloons. The consequence was that the supply of the Land Rover was never to meet the demand. It took twelve years for total sales to creep up to a measly 250,000. Even after nearly forty years cumulative production had only reached 1,389,900,[69] a record which compares appallingly with the more than eight million sales in thirty-three years for the French equivalent, the Renault 4.[70]

Why did British managements persist in marketing miscellanies of vehicles rather than each specialize in a certain category, like the Continental European manufacturers? In 1957 Britain would be offering twenty-six different makes and models for sale in the United States, compared with six by Germany and five by France.[71] The answer must be that managements could not break free of a habit of mind formed in the pre-war era, when they had been competing against each other for the British home market, and had believed that to do so successfully they must satisfy a complete range of potential customers. In the very different circumstances of the post-war era, however, this ingrained habit led to the absurdity whereby British firms were competing not only against the foreigner in export markets but also against each other. In contrast, Volkswagen, Peugeot, Renault and Mercedes (Fiat, for that matter) were each the sole national flag carrier for a particular category of car. More-over, this incoherent British production effort also meant the penny-packeting of sales and service networks, not to mention a messy proliferation of components and spare parts. But then, did not penny-packeting and messy proliferation constitute the leitmotif of so much of United Kingdom manufacturing?

The British car industry was also losing the battle for Europe because of its mistaken strategies and technically stale models. As early as October 1951 it was reported from the Paris Motor Show that 'Continental-made cars, particularly German, [were] ousting British cars from the best markets in Europe, Belgium and Switzer-land . . .'[72] Two years later the German Federal Government's representative on the Volkswagen board was assuring an official of the Ministry of Supply that 'they had an absolute world-beater in the Volkswagen . . . He was particularly confident that the Volks-wagen would completely oust the British light car in Switzerland where they had already captured 52% of the market.'[73]

In passing this information on to the Board of Trade a civil servant in the Ministry of Supply remarked that the VW could be

> driven at its maximum speed, in excess of 60 miles per hour, all day long, without showing signs of stress . . . The Continental driver likes to be able to drive hard without worrying about repair bills. This is the quality that sells the Volkswagen.[74]

And after a trial run in the Standard Eight, a new but already obsolescent British offering, a colleague cheerily reported: 'it will not stand any comparison with the new Volkswagen under Conti-nental road conditions.'[75]

By the middle of 1953 a chill of anxiety was beginning to penetrate the duvet of British complacency. Sir William Rootes told a meeting of the National Advisory Council of the Motor-Vehicle Manufacturing Industry in July that all manufacturers 'were agreed that the outlook was disturbing. There was ample evidence of growing competition in overseas markets while at the same time there was the prospect of higher costs in this country.'[76] All too soon the industry was even feeling a twinge of alarm that the Germans might invade the British home market itself, since in 1953 Britain and Germany had agreed on limited bilateral trade in passenger cars. In December that year the Society of Motor Manufacturers and Traders (SMMT) anxiously telephoned the Ministry of Supply to ask whether the Volkswagen Microbus would count as a passenger car or a commercial vehicle.[77] The Microbus, a variant of the well-tried VW Transporter, was the original of what by the end of the century would be known as a 'people-carrier'. Since the British motor industry in its lack of imagination had failed to evolve any comparable mass-produced vehicle,[78] it is all too understandable that Sir William Rootes, speaking for the industry, should express the hope that the Microbus would be classed as 'commercial', so excluding it from the bilateral agreement. But opinion in the Ministry of Supply did not concur: '. . . protection of British industry is not to be arranged by a juggling of definitions and the quotas agreed with Germany for 1954 should stand . . .'[79]

'GERMANS BEAT US – IN BRITAIN' yelled a headline in the *Daily Herald* on 14 December 1953 above an article reporting that the Microbus could cruise at 50 m.p.h. with seven passengers, a driver and luggage; that it was popular on the Continent with hotels, factories, schools and hospitals; and that its British distributors 'have a long order list already'.

Four days earlier the SMMT representative for Europe had written to the Ministry of Supply to say that 'we cannot protest too strongly against any suggestion that a quota should be established by the U.K. for the importation of German commercial vehicles'. He proceeded to give the van and truck industry's good reasons for wishing to remain warmly tucked up in a protected home market:

> As you know, U.K. production of C.V.'s this year has dropped compared with last year, while there has been an even greater reduction in our exports.

It seems likely that both production and exports of C.V.'s will be lower still in 1954 than in 1953. Under these conditions, it is essential that the government should do everything possible to assist the industry, and not agree to any concession, such as the one suggested, which would not only seriously affect the home market, but also do incalculable harm generally to our exports.[80]

When a civil servant in the Ministry of Supply checked these assertions with Leyland, Rootes and the Chairman of the Heavy Vehicles Section of the SMMT, he found that they too 'all object strongly to a quota for German commercial vehicles, *for no better reason than that they feared competition* [added emphasis]'.[81] It did, however, somewhat weaken the British manufacturers' case that Germany had been quite happy to liberalize the import of British commercial vehicles some two years before.

From 1953 onwards the native British car firms became more and more twitchy about foreign imports into Britain even though the permitted quotas remained minute in proportion to the size of the home market.[82] After all, great breakthroughs can start from small bridgeheads. The manufacturers particularly fretted about the imbalance between German sales to Britain and British sales to Germany. Whereas in 1953 Britain imported 1,164 German cars, Germany only imported 305 British cars in return.[83] Yet the German market had been perfectly happy to take 2,037 French cars that year, and 1,929 Italian as well.[84]

Even the personnel of the British Control Commission and the British armed forces in Germany were often so unpatriotic as to prefer well-designed, well-engineered and well-serviced German cars to the home product. So recorded a cruelly critical report by the Commercial Counsellor at the British Embassy in Bonn in the summer of 1954 on 'The German Market for United Kingdom Passenger Cars'.[85] It appeared that the same went for British businessmen based in Germany. Groaned the Commercial Counsellor:

It is regrettable to have to record that the majority of them prefer to run German cars because of the difficulties they felt they would encounter if they tried to maintain British cars; this is a good example of the damage which is at present being done to our prospects by the lack of adequate servicing facilities . . . here is the real crux of the matter.[86]

For their part, German dealers handling British cars 'complained of difficulties in getting delivery of cars and spares and even getting adequate literature'.[87] No doubt it was, in the words of the SMMT's representative for Europe, 'absolutely fantastic that British Officers should be running around on official duties in Volkswagen and Mercedes Benz cars', but who in the circumstances and in their right mind would choose to buy an Austin A40 rather than a Mercedes 170 SV at the same price of DM7,950? Or a Morris Minor at DM5,950 rather than a standard Volkswagen at DM3,950?[88]

But of course, the faltering British performance in export markets for cars and commercial vehicles was in no way caused by shortcomings either in the product or in the competence of management. No, no! It was all due to such unfair commercial practices by johnny foreigner as undercutting British prices, to say nothing of bad light and a biased referee. Thus Rootes Motors had a complete answer to the devastating 1954 critique by the Commercial Counsellor in Bonn:

> It is depressing to note that the trend of import figures of cars from England [into Germany] is downwards. Two main reasons for this in our opinion, which are not propounded in the report, are: (a) The intensity of German Nationalism which has been drummed into them over the past seventy years, and particularly by Dr. Goebbels, that they must buy German, and this they are certainly doing; (b) Fear of lack of service and parts in the event of war . . .[89]

The Assistant Sales Manager of Nuffield Export Ltd wrote to the SMMT that the company 'most emphatically repudiate the suggestion that lack of spare parts or poor service has anything to do with it [poor sales to German nationals] . . .'[90] He too claimed that the Germans, being 'fanatically patriotic', would always buy German cars, mysteriously adding that it was 'hardly to be expected that we can compete with German vehicles on price'. As for British businessmen in Germany preferring German cars, continued this Nuffield spokesman, 'the inference here' was that 'their prejudice was based only on hearsay; and we think it probable that they use German cars mainly to create a favourable impression amongst their German business contacts'.[91]

In passing these letters on to the Ministry of Supply, Grant-Crofton (the SMMT representative for Europe) conceded that certainly 'servicing is the crux of much of the overall problem confronting the British motor industry'.[92] But he then followed with an exculpatory bleat that would have made Volkswagen laugh:

> I would only add that to provide the ideal service envisaged by those outside the industry would undoubtedly increase the initial costs of purchasing a motor car considerably and would price us right out of the market as it exists today. It is the old question of which comes first the egg or the chicken – the car or the servicing? Secondly, who is going to put up the money, the manufacturers or the local distributors? Literally millions of pounds could well be tied up in providing depots spread throughout the world.[93]

It is a curious paradox that British managements could be at one and the same time alarmed about foreign competition and yet still remain sure that there was nothing wrong with their own marketing and production strategies, let alone with themselves. Nonetheless, this very paradox provides the clue to the fundamental weakness of the British motor vehicle industry: arrogant self-regard and glaucomic insularity of outlook.

That managements were indeed effectively cushioned by these attributes from the potholes of criticism and the rough surface of world-market reality is demonstrated by their reaction to a draft PEP report on the industry back in 1948. This study, broadly repeating the thrust of the 1945 Whitehall report, 'The Post-War Re-settlement of the Motor Industry', had called for greater standardization of models and components for the sake of lowering costs and enhancing competitiveness in export markets.[94] When the PEP Engineering Group met to discuss the draft in May 1948, Sir Reginald Rootes said that

> he was alarmed by certain points which he thought would do the industry a great deal of harm if published. It would seem that one or

two preconceived ideas permeated the whole report and gave it a dangerous slant . . . Technical progress both in design and research had been far greater than would be gathered from the report. The industry had made great strides before the war and was now again developing rapidly. . . . He considered that throughout the report unfair comparison had been made between the British and American industries. Standardisation was supported by all manufacturers, but could not be carried out quickly . . . the report gave the impression that the M.G. and some specialist cars ought to be wiped out, which was ridiculous.[95]

He argued that 'if the industry was forced to standardise there would be no progress, and if there was no progress the motor industry was doomed'.

Sir Patrick Hennessy, Managing Director of the Ford Motor Company (of Great Britain), agreed with Sir Reginald, observing that the report 'seemed to put the industry in the dock. He thought that the tremendous achievements both before and during the war had been understated'. He considered the report 'an unfair and dangerous document'. In the export field 'the industry would have to build what the overseas markets called for, and this could only be found out by trial and error'. The President of the SMMT, Mr F. I. Connolly, concurred, stressing that 'overseas customers would very soon be influencing the type of cars to be produced, and that the industry did not require the expert advice of the government or any other body'.

Mr J. Masterton, of the components firm Joseph Lucas (which was later to earn the title in Canada of 'Prince of Darkness' because of the unreliability of their lighting systems), said 'he could speak from experience on the type of car demanded by overseas markets':

no market required only one model; most needed six or seven. A small car would meet the general requirements of most overseas markets where most of the users needed cars for travelling to and from their work on good road, and for pleasure purposes in parts of the country where motoring facilities were very good. Very few people motored for hundred of miles in rough country or spent weekends in the bush . . .

Six or seven models! Here was the same cart-sprung mentality which two years earlier had induced representatives of the British motor industry after visiting the Volkswagen plant at Wolfsburg to report that they saw no commercial future for its single model, and to recommend instead that the factory be demolished and the machine tools brought to Britain.

Mr H. W. Fulton of Albion Motors (representing the heavy vehicle manufacturers) for his part told the meeting that the adoption of standard types 'might handicap the industry in its efforts to cater for overseas markets . . . the heavy vehicle building industry's reputation rested on its ability to build a better custom-built vehicle than any of its competitors'. In short, no equivalents of Packard, Dodge or Mack mass-produced trucks, we're British.

Mr R. F. Hanks of the Nuffield Organisation

> asserted that the small car was the birthright of the British manufac-
> turer and to get America interested in the small car would be very
> dangerous indeed to the British industry. He stressed the lack of any
> reference in the report to the cost of the export drive to the industry.

Mr P. Eisler of Vauxhall Motors

> did not feel that competition made for a multiplicity of models; nor
> did he feel that the comparison with America throughout the report
> was quite reasonable, since the entire British output of cars was less
> than that of one American model.

Eisler did, however, strike the one mild note of dissent in the whole discussion, by adding that the need for concentration on fewer models was much greater in Britain than in America, since 'all American cars were of the same size, and that they could therefore incorporate components and equipment basically the same'.

It fell to the Second Secretary to the Ministry of Supply, Sir George Turner,[96] to give the blessing in this private service of thanksgiving for Britain's good fortune in enjoying the best of all possible automotive worlds:

> he did not consider this a good moment to publish a report of this
> kind. It would do the industry a dis-service by opening up all the old
> controversies which have now been closed. To him, the Summary

[of the report] was 'just another pamphlet'. He did not consider it
undesirable to have a large number of models and thought it would
be of little benefit from the point of view of manufacturing costs if
standardisation on a large scale was forced on the industry.

On the other hand, Sir George *did* consider that

The industry had rendered invaluable service during the war and the
small specialist firms had played a role to which there was no parallel
in the United States. The industry would be worse off if it carried
out many of the suggestions contained in the report.

A week later the Chairman of the PEP Engineering Group, Mr A.
K. (later Sir Alec) Cairncross, wrote to Gresham Cooke, Director
of the SMMT and Joint Secretary of the National Advisory Council,
Motor Manufacturing Industry, to assure him that the report would
be duly emasculated before publication (in any case delayed until
1950).[97]

So that was all right, then: the industry could bumble on undisturbed in the way of life to which it wished to remain accustomed.

Come May 1955, and the Ministry of Supply was trying to estimate
the consequences for the British motor industry if imports of foreign
vehicles and parts were freed from all restriction. The Ministry's
reading of the cards was gloomy, but, as the ensuing decades were
to prove, correct: 'if the U.S.A., Germany and Italy in particular
had absolutely free access to the British market, imports of passenger
cars might be greatly increased . . .'

Why? Because: 'The Motor Industry is not yet ready to withstand
the full impact of U.S. and Continental competition . . .'[98] After all,
only a decade had elapsed since the end of the war in Europe; only
seven years since the industry had scorned the PEP Report.

Nonetheless, the Ministry of Supply's pessimism was fully justified by the industry's current performance in world markets. In
1955 the British export total, at 373,000 cars, was actually lower
than the 1950 figure of 399,000, while Germany's total, at 320,000,
represented a virtual quintupling from her 1950 figure of 69,000.[99]
And 1956 saw Britain actually overtaken by Germany as an exporter
of motor cars: a bitter but apt denouement to ten peacetime years

of bungled opportunity. For Britain's lost lead was never to be regained.

Motor-vehicle manufacture was, however, only one ramshackle mechanism (albeit of cardinal importance) within the whole ramshackle, partly obsolete, industrial engine room propelling a national economy heavily overloaded by the world role and the welfare state. But while Britain had been wallowing along, her manufacturing rivals had been steaming up fast: and Germany above all, newly re-engined and lightly freighted. In May 1956, the month before Abdul Gamal Nasser nationalized the Suez Canal and threw poor Anthony Eden into such a fuss, a working party of officials submitted a report on 'German Competition with particular reference to the Engineering Industries'.[100] It made grim reading. Between 1953 and 1954 German exports rose by 40 per cent in volume and her share of world trade in manufactures rose from 13.3 per cent to 15.6 per cent, whereas Britain's share fell from 25.5 per cent to 19.8 per cent.[101] In those same years output per man in manufacturing 'improved almost twice as much in Germany as in the United Kingdom'.[102] What was more, Germany's performance 'cannot be explained, as could to some extent the expansion which also occurred before 1953, by the low level from which she started'.[103]

Warned the report: 'If this country fails to meet the German export challenge, it could fall into second place behind Germany as the leading exporting country in Europe, with all that this implies.'[104]

Back in 1951 Government had gambled that British industry could carry the rearmament-swollen defence programme (10.9 per cent of GDP at its peak in 1952–53, and still 7.9 per cent in 1954–55) and at the same time export enough to keep the balance of payments in the black, and sterling safe and sound. The gamble had not come off: in 1955 the United Kingdom's balance of payments had fallen into the red to the tune of some £100 million, while the gold and dollar reserves had plummeted by £229 million.[105] In January 1956 alone the balance went into the red by a further £74 million,[106] impelling the Chancellor of the Exchequer, Harold Macmillan, to prepare emergency plans to reimpose import controls and even full rationing, food and all.[107]

Yet Britain's 'slow-ahead' progress since the outbreak of the Korean War and its culmination in this present peril could not be attributed solely to deficiencies in her industrial engine room and its crew. The officers on the bridge – Labour and Conservative governments alike – bore their share of responsibility too, well meaning though their attempts had been to navigate the national economy in their charge.

PART SIX

Consensus and Impotence

. . . full employment was the cause of an irresponsible attitude to workers' discipline and to strikes . . . There was a greater inclination to strike because the workers felt that they were not at risk and could if necessary obtain other employment.

(Sir Walter Monckton, the Minister of Labour, June 1955)

. . . the chief part for the Ministry to play in connection with labour relations and labour disputes is to concentrate on supplying ample lubrication in the right places at the right times, and to refrain from action which might conceivably be criticised as Government intervention.

(Sir Walter Monckton's policy as Minister of Labour, according to a Treasury official, 1955)

20. 'This Pressing Problem' – Productivity

> I think the time has come when the Government should resume the productivity campaign, perhaps on more practical lines than during the Socialist regime.
>
> By appearing to drop it entirely, we have weakened our stand that wage increases can only be justified by increased productivity and efficiency.

Thus Walter Monckton, Minister of Labour and National Service in Winston Churchill's Cabinet, to his colleague, Peter Thorney-croft, the President of the Board of Trade, in August 1952, suggesting that their two ministries should 'work together on this pressing problem'.[1]

The problem was in fact the more pressing because it had been neglected while all hands in Whitehall had been at the pumps trying to save the economy from foundering in the great sterling crisis of the previous winter. Yet to raise industrial productivity and efficiency nearer to American standards must in any case be crucial to what Churchill in 1952 called the 'supreme effort' needed to keep 'the place and status to which our undying genius entitles us'.

But how to bring about the desired raising?

In October 1951 a Labour Government which did not really believe in socialism had been replaced by a Conservative Government which did not really believe in free-market competition. All that had happened was a shift of emphasis within the small 'l' liberal post-war consensus. Thus Labour in their time had chosen not to employ the one powerful lever ideologically available to them for enforcing industrial change – direct and detailed state intervention. They had left unreconstructed such shambles as the motor vehicle, cotton and shipbuilding industries. They had failed to set up state enterprises to develop such new technologies as computers and automation.[2] On the other hand, their programme of nationalization had merely laid a stultifying bureaucracy on top of industries mostly out of date and ill-managed, and, perhaps worse, put it in the Treasury's power to restrict investment in new plant and kit.[3] Only in the case of warlike technologies (including nuclear power) under the sponsorship of the Ministry of Supply had the Labour Government directly used the weight of the state to advance industrial progress. Otherwise they had put their faith in persuasion via such cloutless means as the National Research Development Corporation, the development councils due to be set up under the 1947 Industrial Organisation and Development Act, the British Institute of Management, and preachy public-relations campaigns.[4]

The Conservatives on coming into office also had a lever ideologically available to them for compelling drastic change in the ways in which British industry and commerce operated. It lay in the free-market competition celebrated by the Party's rhetoric. But what if rhetoric were to be turned into reality? This would surely demand, in the first place, carrying out Operation ROBOT, so putting an end to the British economy's post-war thraldom to sterling's international role. This in turn would cause (as the proponents of ROBOT acknowledged) severe deflation at home, so dooming inefficient, ill-managed companies on the margin of profitability and, by ending the era of artificially puffed-up full employment, blowing away the foundations of trade union power. No longer would the unions be able to enforce overmanning and archaic work practices, or to win wage increases unrelated to productivity. Instead strikes would become a form of working-class hara-kiri rather than a means of beating 'the bosses'.

But even for a Conservative Government it lay far beyond the bounds of the politically possible to bring about such a new and bracingly harsh economic environment, as the actual fate of ROBOT in 1952 goes to prove. Unlike Margaret Thatcher in the 1980s financially armed with the rake-off from North Sea oil, her predecessors of the 1950s possessed no 'war chest' to enable them to see through to the end a profound and painful transition in the national life, with all its inevitable attendant unrest among the workforce. On the contrary, the economy was so overstretched by the world role and rearmament, the balance of payments and the pound were so fragile, that even the actual level of damage inflicted on exports by strikes was enough to bring on palpitations in Whitehall.

In consequence, appeasement was to rule domestic policy in the 1950s just as it had ruled foreign policy in the 1930s, and for similar reasons: weakness of position coupled with a genuine small 'l' liberal horror of confrontation. Peace in our time! The post-war consensus rules!

What then could the Conservatives do, other than emulate the Labour Government's attempt to raise productivity by preaching? That would surely prove futile, as a civil servant in the Board of Trade was moved by Monckton's present proposal to point out:

> a productivity campaign which consisted simply of propagandist mass meetings addressed by Ministers spreading down to a whole series of purely exhortatory activities throughout the country through trade associations was getting increasingly useless, since both sides of industry had had so many injections of publicity about productivity as to have an allergic reaction to it . . .[5]

For all these reasons, wrote this civil servant, Monckton's initiative 'might have been rather embarrassing a few months ago'.[6]

Now, however, a new factor had come into play: the prospect of more dollar handouts from America under the 1952 Mutual Security Act.

The Act, a product of the Korean War, was designed to help the members of NATO complete their rearmament, but at the same time to support programmes for strengthening their economies and so render them better able to resist Communist subversion. Just as under Marshall Aid, participating nations would be obliged to make contributions in their own money equal to the dollar grants from America: so-called 'counterpart' funds. In the case of Marshall Aid in the late 1940s, Britain had chosen to waste her counterpart funds by simply using them to write down the National Debt, whereas

Continental states had spent theirs on useful practical projects like modernizing their railways.[7] This time, however, the Americans were not going to allow Britain to get away with it. As this same Board of Trade civil servant pointed out,

> the latest Mutual Security Act makes it a condition of our receiving part of our dollar aid from America that we spend the counterpart funds in sterling on various activities, of which the encouragement of productivity is likely to be the only one to find favour in our eyes.[8]

Therefore, in order to present a convincing picture to the Americans, 'something of a co-ordinated productivity programme', he wrote, 'had better be drafted'.[9]

Thus did Monckton's proposal begin to roll forward. Take-off was, however, to be long delayed owing to bureaucratic slush on the runway.

For a start, who in Whitehall was to coordinate the 'something' of a programme? Which department should run the productivity programme once decided? Week by week from August into October the files in fusty offices fattened with copious internal minutes and with wordy correspondence between the Board of Trade and the Ministry of Labour and the Treasury.[10] The grand mandarinate held joint seminars to try to settle matters. Parliamentary secretaries and even ministers fussed around, being 'extremely keen to "get things moving".'[11] There was resort to that old Whitehall standby, an interdepartmental 'working group', which held their first meeting on 30 September 1952,[12] eight weeks after Walter Monckton had first suggested the need for a renewed productivity campaign. October saw the Treasury, the Board of Trade and the Ministry of Labour each putting in an impressive statement of their existing roles in regard to productivity – more gobbets to be chewed over in meetings of the Working Group.[13] By the week before Christmas 1952 – what a rush! – the Group were ready to submit their report.[14]

They reckoned that it would be 'impracticable' to concentrate all government functions in regard to productivity under a single department. Instead, one department should be nominated 'to bear the co-ordinating and residual responsibility'.[15] Just in case the blade of decision-making had still not been blunted enough, the Working Group also recommended setting up 'a standing interdepartmental committee' to coordinate and 'review' departmental activities in regard to productivity, and 'report from time to time to Ministers'.[16]

There was just one small snag to this classic Whitehall solution: the Working Group could not agree which department should be charged with the central coordinating role.[17] So now it was up to the politicians to sort it out.[18] This took until the fourth week of February 1953, when at a meeting between the Chancellor (R. A. Butler), the Minister of Labour (Walter Monckton) and the President of the Board of Trade (Peter Thorneycroft), and thanks to the Chancellor's casting vote, the coordinating role was entrusted to the Board of Trade.[19]

A month later, and only half a year since Monckton's original initiative, Sir Thomas Padmore (Second Secretary at the Treasury) got round to starting 'action to call into existence an Inter-Departmental Committee on Productivity'.[20]

By now, however, the moves towards a productivity campaign had become 'hopelessly entwined'[21] with the handling of American 'Conditional Aid'. On this topic a Whitehall 'Mutual Aid Committee' had been negotiating with the London representatives of the Mutual Security Agency since August 1952 as to where best to spend the counterpart funds. The experience had proved less a meeting of minds than a clash of national cultures and temperaments. In the case of university-based research, for example, the Americans, George Patton-like, wanted a narrow thrust-line of investigation aimed at one specific objective: the impact of monopolies and restrictive practices on productivity and efficiency in designated industries.[22] But their intention faltered in the complex minefields of British institutions – bureaucratic, political and educational – and in the face of British cavilling and caution. Stonewalled a civil servant in the Board of Trade:

> the University Grants Committee would almost certainly feel that the endowment on a generous scale of research in a relatively small part of the economic field would unbalance the academic programme. It would not be easy to reconcile such a concentration of assistance on enquiries into monopolies with the British policy of granting public money to the Universities with no detailed control of the purposes for which it was spent.[23]

Worse still, 'the impression might be conveyed that the Government had departed from *its impartial attitude to monopolies* [added emphasis] and this would detract from the importance of the Monopolies Commission'. This Commission was a quasi-governmental wind-driven paper-mill set up by the Labour Government in 1948, and which in 1952 had still to deliver a report. Long into the future the Commission would harmlessly flap at monopolies and restrictive practices instead of grinding them up.

So instead of the MSA's un-British focus on research into monopolies, the civil servants representing Whitehall's Mutual Aid Committee deftly suggested a 'more catholic approach'. By this they meant research into 'the problems of the human relations between management and labour, of the social ecology of the worker in the plant, of the economic ideals which animate both sides of industry and so on'.[24] And, for good measure, what about some 'pure economic descriptive theoretical and statistical work' as well?[25] Yet all this high-minded academic fustian disappointed the American side, who acidly – and vainly, as it turned out – remarked that the outlined programme 'dealt only indirectly, and to a limited extent, with the encouragement of free private enterprise and the discouragement of cartel and monopolistic business practices . . .'[26]

Nonetheless, by January 1953 the two sides had reached a compromise outline agreement. While this repeated the earlier British fustian in much the same words, it also endorsed some research into 'the relative efficiency of competitive and monopolistic enterprise'.[27]

By March the Mutual Aid Committee was

> very busy establishing a network of committees in order to plan the whole programme in detail. The main body concerned will be an interdepartmental committee of senior officials under the chairmanship of the Board of Trade . . .[28]

In the event, this 'main body' would carry a crew of up to twenty assorted bureaucrats.[29] It would preside over as many as six other committees, on which were to be represented no fewer than twenty-one Whitehall departments or other bodies, such as the University Grants Committee and the Department of Scientific and Industrial Research.[30] In the meantime, these and yet further institutions had been asked to submit their ideas. The possibilities, wrote a civil servant, 'excited very considerable interest' in academic circles – no doubt because donnish nostrils had picked up the rich scent of fat grants wafting in the air.[31]

On 1 April 1953 a combined Productivity and Conditional Aid Committee was at last formally set up.[32] The plotting of the programme began to roll at – in Whitehall terms – full throttle:

> In all our deliberations [stated a progress report on 17 March 1953], we have in mind the necessity of producing to M.S.A. before the 30th June at least a general programme combined with firm commitments for, we hope, appreciable sums for individual projects in each of the different sections.[33]

In the event, the £3,011,543 programme as finally agreed with the Americans was published as a White Paper[34] in July 1953, a mere eleven months after Monckton had first proposed action to solve 'this pressing problem'. The whole performance bears witness to the special qualities of Whitehall's top managers and their first-class-degree intellects, as also to the remarkable nature of Whitehall's essentially late-Victorian/Edwardian command and control system.

Of the £3,011,000 budget a third was to be devoted directly to raising industrial productivity via a Revolving Loan Fund to assist firms in buying new plant and kit.[35] £457,000 was to go on technical and managerial 'advisory services' to industry and agriculture, to be run either by interested ministries or the DSIR, the BIM, the new British Productivity Council (see p. 411, below), and industrial research associations.[36] Sure to warm the hearts of the denizens of senior common rooms was the £589,000 to be invested in economic and social research projects more academic than operational in purpose.[37] Of this total, 'studies in monopoly and restrictive practices' got a sixth: £100,000. As for the eventual products of all this research, the White Paper stated that 'in certain suitable cases special arrangements will be made for their wider publication . . .' Otherwise, however, results were to be 'published in accordance with normal academic practice . . .':[38] i.e., specialist academic trade journals rather less likely to be read by industrial managers and workers than the *Sporting Life* or the *Daily Mirror*.

About a sixth of the total budget, £519,000, was to be allotted, usefully enough, to long-term improvement of vocational education related to industry and agriculture.[39] Three professorships or readerships in *Technik* were to be created, two of them at Imperial College in London. Of the latter, one would be in heavy electrical engineering, and the other in production engineering. Technical colleges were also to benefit by new teaching posts and scholarships.[40]

So the Conditional Aid Programme, this bureaucratic Brabazon, was at last airborne. But it would be a very long flight before it reached its planned destination of raising Britain's industrial productivity and efficiency. For adoption of the White Paper only meant that the elaborate rituals of committees and ever-thickening files of memoranda now proliferated from Whitehall to all the intended recipients of the largesse, such as the University Grants Committee and their clients and advisers.[41]

Come the end of October 1953, and Cranfield College of Aeronautics and Loughborough College of Technology had actually accepted endowments for new posts; London University had got as far as preparing the deed for their two chairs at Imperial College; Cambridge had merely been asked whether they would create a chair in production engineering; and Queen's University, Belfast, was in the course of consulting the city's education committee about advanced teaching in light electrical engineering.[42] A further eight months on, and the representative of the American Operations Mission in London (the body now responsible for monitoring the Mutual Aid programme) is found expressing 'considerable disappointment about the slow progress made over the educational sector of the programme'.

> so far as he knew only one lecturer had been appointed at Cranfield . . . His impression was that Queen's University authorities were moving very slowly indeed. Cambridge had only just settled some questions of the term of a grant which had been giving them a good deal of trouble and he did not see any prospect of their having their man in post for the next academic year.[43]

Even when all the posts had been finally agreed upon, they would have to be advertised, candidates interviewed, and winners chosen. There would then inevitably be further delays before the winners could take up their posts and begin to function. So it could be 1955–6 before the investment of counterpart funds in higher education even resulted in the beginning of academic work, and years after that before it actually began to yield a return, useful or not.

Clearly, then, the immediate attack on what Monckton in 1952 had called 'this pressing problem' of productivity must fall to another and more mobile division within the Conditional Aid Programme: the British Productivity Council.

This body had been set up in November 1952 as the successor to the Anglo-American Productivity Council, whose work was now completed. In accordance with British custom, the new Council was composed of the great and good: no fewer than twenty-six of them, drawn from 'both sides' of industry and commerce.[44] Unlike the 'productivity centres' set up as straightforward agencies of the state in some European countries, the BPC would therefore have to rely on the support of the very industries whose productivity it had been set up to improve. In consequence, as a civil servant was justly to write three years later, 'the nature of its membership must limit the Council to non-controversial matters'.[45]

It took a mere five months for the new Council and its permanent staff to frame an outline strategy, similar to the time taken in 1944 by Supreme Headquarters Allied Expeditionary Force to organize Operation Overlord. On 19 March 1953 the BPC announced its plans at a press conference, to the accompaniment of much flag-waving from the grandees on the platform about how in Britain 'we have the scientific and technical knowledge, the managerial ability and the basic commonsense which, properly applied, can solve our present problems'.[46]

Since the British Productivity Council, in common with other contemporary British institutions such as the Foreign Office, the BIM and the whole machinery of industrial conciliation, lacked actual leverage (or, in its own words, had 'no executive powers'), it would, like them, have to resort to 'influence'. Success, averred the Council, must depend on the part played by 'every working member of the community' throughout industry and commerce.[47] The Council therefore proposed to arouse 'every working member' to their personal responsibility by preaching the need for 'progressive change' in production methods, and the corresponding need on 'the human side' for 'full understanding'. As one way of arousal the Council looked to a propaganda campaign via the modern medium of film (both instructional and general interest) and such traditional means as the issue of improving tracts and the supply of lecturers. But its principal wheezes for transforming traditional attitudes and practices throughout industry lay in Local Productivity Committees and what it called 'the Circuit Scheme'. Both the wheezes owed their conception to the happy belief of the Council that there was 'great scope for enlisting local enthusiasm in the cause of higher productivity'.[48] The LPCs (to be set up in more than a hundred towns) would be manned by employers, trade union officials, persons in technical education, and members of professional associations. These human macédoines were to organize discussion meetings, lectures, and film sessions. Under the Circuit Scheme for Exchange of Team Visits, groups each consisting of two managers, two technicians and two from the shopfloor would learn on the spot how 'the other man does his job',[49] and how the other industry does its job too, for that matter.

In these hopeful strategies may be discerned a fresh manifestation of the naive small 'l' liberal faith that deep-seated problems, not to say conflicts of interest, may be resolved if only all the parties can be got talking round a table or subjected to some enlightening educative process. Surely mutual understanding must burgeon, and so lead to a shift in attitudes? Surely through exchange visits, discussion groups and instructional films even the most benighted on 'both sides' of industry must see the light, and become born-again apostles of technical change and high productivity?[50]

On this ideal scenario all too soon impinged the drab realities of organizational incompetence and sloth, and human apathy.[51] As early as June 1953, widespread criticism had arisen in government departments and regional agencies that 'the machinery of the B.P.C. works too slowly and that its staff is inadequate'.[52] Its favourite wheeze, the Local Productivity Committees, 'are having a very mixed reception', wrote a civil servant in the Ministry of Labour. 'In some cases it seems to be simply a general reluctance to set up yet more committees; in others there has been indifference if not opposition from the Trade Union Side.'[53]

Nine months later the head of the American Operations Mission in London, Francis Rogers, having done (in the words of a Board of Trade bureaucrat) 'a good deal of snooping on the B.P.C.'s activities',[54] was badgering the Board of Trade about the Council's lack of progress. According to the report of another Board of Trade civil servant on an interview with Rogers on 16 March 1954, it was 'quite obvious, and has been for some time, that F.O.A. has very poor opinion of the way the Council is doing its job.'[55]

> They consider it slow and inefficient. They hold that it might have been seen from the first to be a mistake to try and set up as many as 80 or 100 Local Productivity Committees and that it has so turned out in practice, that the television film programme is badly conceived and wasteful and the general administration is not very competent.[56]

It seemed that after visiting twenty-eight localities Rogers's snooper had reported that in general 'the Committees are not being supported by management, that up to 70% to 80% of them have had no guidance and visits from headquarters staff and that many of them are moribund'.[57]

Poignantly ironic it is, then, that the BPC should itself already be offering an exemplar of incapable British management and low productivity. Not only this, but it was also already going the way of so many institutions in British life, and becoming more concerned with preserving its corporate independence than with improving the quality of its service and product. Secrecy, that proven national means of fending off criticism, prevailed. Even the Board of Trade was 'being kept so much on the outside of B.P.C.'s activities'.[58]

In April 1954 the American frustration with the BPC led to another clash of national cultures and temperaments. Francis Rogers bluntly asked his British opposite number, S. A. ff. Dakin of the Board of Trade, how much the Board knew about 'what was going on inside the B.P.C.' (honest answer: not much); and 'did we consider the position satisfactory and if not were we prepared to do anything about it'.[59] Do anything about it? *Do* anything? What suggestion could have been more brashly American? Answered Dakin on behalf of his department:

we should be extremely reluctant to press any reforms on B.P.C. unless there were absolutely overwhelming evidence that the job was being done badly and that it would have been possible to do it better.

What could have been more limply British than this response? No wonder (as Dakin reported) 'Mr. Rogers seemed very disturbed about this . . .'

> He enquired what would happen if, say, towards the end of the year when the Local Productivity Councils had been going for about twelve months, we were to become aware that the majority of them were moribund; should we then cheerfully agree to paying a grant for the second year?[60]

Dakin replied that the Board of Trade could make use of 'certain rights of report and the withholding of grants under our Agreement with the Council', although he thought 'we should be very reluctant to do so'. The two men could only agree that Rogers, for his part, would have to continue pressing for the evidence needed to justify the way in which £120,000 of Conditional Aid was being spent.

Nonetheless, American impatience and Whitehall's own discontent with BPC's operations and secrecy did at least bear fruit in a new British-only liaison committee composed of departmental civil servants and representatives of the BPC. It met for the first time on 31 May 1954, hearing from the BPC delegation the kind of defensively evasive or merely glib explanations typical of a body under rightful criticism.[61] Nonetheless, instead of the sharp kicks up its great and good backside which Francis Rogers would have wished to give the BPC, the Liaison Committee was never to go beyond genteelly ineffectual prods.[62]

So the BPC trundled on. Although by August 1954 Local Productivity Committees numbered eighty-seven, only a few 'were making much of an impression'.[63] Estimates by Board of Trade Regional Controllers of the support enjoyed by LPCs from local employers and trade unionists varied from 'well supported' (North Midland Region) to 'considerable scepticism' (Eastern Region) and 'the apathy facing the creation of the committees was almost overwhelming' (Southern Region).[64] The BPC's own *Bulletin* for August 1954 reported that only 236,317 employees belonged to firms signed up for the Circuit Schemes of exchange visits[65] – 236,317 out of an insured working population of nearly 22 million!

In October Francis Rogers was telling his British opposite numbers that for all the old reasons and some new ones the FOA remained 'not at all happy about the development of B.P.C.'.[66] The original strategy of trying to set up 100 LPCs had been 'ill advised: there had been no attempt to see whether L.P.C.'s were needed in all the areas where they had been established . . .' Similar doubts about the effectiveness of the Council's strategies were to be voiced inside Whitehall right through 1955, and ventilated in the press in 1956.[67] Now, in October 1954, Rogers criticized the Council for failing adequately to support such LPCs as were active, and instead 'frittering away' funds on television films and other ventures.[68]

For while the BPC's two main inventions, the Local Productivity Committees and the Circuit Schemes, had been widely falling victim to grass-roots apathy (the very malaise they were intended to cure), the Council had also been expending much effort on conventional propaganda. Films, pamphlets, bulletins,[69] and exhibition stands had preached the gospel that (in the narcotic words of captions to the BPC stand at the 1954 Production Exhibition in London) 'THERE'S ALWAYS A BETTER WAY!', that 'The More We Produce the Better We Can Live', and that 'We Must Earn Our Keep with Exports'.[70] Eminent progressive talking-heads of the time such as the economist Graham Hutton were hired to write or preach inspirational sermons explaining to the grown-up children how 'We *can* prosper – if not as much, immediately, as the Americans or the Canadians or Swiss, then within a pretty short order . . .'[71]

One particularly ingenious BPC method of inducing a new zest for productivity on the factory floor had consisted of luncheons for up to ninety assorted chairmen or directors of companies and trade union barons, when over the coffee and cigars they could be droned at by the Council's Chairman and Deputy Chairman.[72] And for all the scepticism in 1952 about the practical value of political exhortation, ministers too had been doing their share of the missionary work.[73]

★

For the linked questions of productivity and competitiveness continued to haunt the Cabinet,[74] as year by year the balance of payments ebbed and flowed in and out of the red, and sterling and the gold and dollar reserves bobbed up and down accordingly. Ministers hardly needed a reminder from Walter Monckton in December 1953 that they 'must pay close attention to the levels of output and efficiency in export industry in view of the tough competitive times ahead'.[75] But should a government that espoused free enterprise go beyond 'paying close attention' – even to the extent of directly intervening in some way?

The question provoked sharp disagreement between Monckton as Minister of Labour and Peter Thorneycroft as President of the Board of Trade. Wrote Monckton: 'What we want above all is a substantial increase in efficiency and output in the right industries – not in a few years' time but now.'[76]

> The B.P.C. in its present form, is doing valuable and necessary work [sic] but cannot show immediate results. The organisations . . . of which it is composed, will move very slowly. They are unlikely to admit that anything serious is amiss amongst their own members. The government must, therefore, take upon itself the responsibility for sounding the alarm and giving a new impetus to output and efficiency.[77]

In this last recommendation Monckton was backed by a doomful report from the official Productivity and Conditional Aid Committee, which warned that if present comparative international trends continued, 'the relegation of the United Kingdom to the second division in the industrial league would not be far off'.[78] Nonetheless, Thorneycroft refused (in March 1954) 'to accept the suggestion of new public intervention by government in the work of productivity'.

> I am very doubtful whether this would ever be right; I am quite certain that we have not yet reached the point at which we can say that industry cannot and would not do the job for itself and that until this point is reached, if it ever is, it would be most unwise for the Government to appear to intervene.[79]

Retorted the Minister of Labour:

I do not think that the Government can avoid ultimate responsibility for success or failure in expanding national output. We should continue to devolve as much work in this regard as possible on to the B.P.C. but I do not think ourselves can remain silent. We can and ought to give leadership.[80]

But how?

The answer, according to Monckton, lay in 'telling the country the facts about efficiency and output, and trying to ensure that they become known not only to the leaders of industry but on the shop floor. This means taking a lead in regard to joint consultative machinery.'[81]

It now fell to the Cabinet Economic Policy Committee on 18 March 1954[82] to chew over the two ministers' contrary views, along with a weighty report by civil servants making their own recommendations on 'The Role of Government in Promoting Higher Industrial Productivity'.[83] The meeting ended in a characteristically opaque summing-up by the Chancellor, R. A. Butler. This was interpreted (conveniently?) inside the Board of Trade to mean that

> the President's view was adopted and that Government do not accept "the major responsibility of urging greater industrial efficiency" (Mr. Watkinson),[84] but will do all in their power *unostentatiously* [added emphasis] to help forward efforts made by national industrial or professional organisations, to further productivity.[85]

And this, together with ministerial speeches on appropriate occasions to industrial grandees, is exactly what happened.[86]

What then was the cumulative impact of the well-meant attempts since 1952 to tackle this 'pressing problem' of productivity? An answer depends in the first place on how productivity should be measured. In reports by Anglo-American productivity teams straight comparisons could be made between comparable British and American plants. That was easy. But productivity in general? To reckon it according to output per man-hour was distrusted within Whitehall, because this could vary for reasons quite unconnected with standards of production technique, managerial competence and workers' zeal. So the preferred practical measurement lay in output per man-year:[87] in other words, the quantity of production that emerged from a given workforce, no matter what might be the number of shifts worked or of hours in the working week.[88] That measure revealed that the overall productivity of British industry rose by 5 per cent in 1952–53 and by the same in 1953–54. Yet in 1953–54 productivity rose by 7.6 per cent in West Germany and 8 per cent in France.[89]

But, in any case, even by 1956 the functional results of the productivity campaign (if it may be so called) had been too slight and obscure to allay the disquiet felt by ministers about Britain's productivity and her competitiveness in export markets. The report on 'German Competition' circulated to the Cabinet Economic Policy Committee in July 1956 at the Chancellor of the Exchequer's request (see above, p. 398) is one long bleat about how much more creditable was Germany's industrial record than Britain's and why this should be so.[90] Germany's exports of manufactures were rising faster than Britain's, so boosting her world-market share while Britain's shrank. German output per man (or productivity) was increasing faster than wages, whereas the reverse was true in Britain. And so it went.

The report did however identify one crucial reason why Germany was doing better than Britain in terms of productivity, and it had nothing to do with hopeful propaganda campaigns by some German equivalent of the BPC. It lay in comparative rates of industrial investment. Over the years 1950–54 Germany had devoted 21 per cent of GNP in industry, Britain 14 per cent. In 1954 Germany had put 56 per cent of all investment in manufacturing into the key sector of the metal and engineering industries, Britain only 42 per cent.[91] But what else could be expected when the Conservative Government, like its Labour predecessor, had been such at pains to hold back investment in Britain's industrial system?

Yet this rationing was only one among the policies of commission – or omission – by which the Conservatives did harm to the nation's competitiveness far exceeding any good that might result from their puny attempts to improve it.

21. 'No Fear of Unemployment'

First and foremost among the instruments of harm must obviously
be the continuance by the Conservatives of the rearmament programme inherited from the Labour Government, even if spread
over four years instead of three at Butler's urging (see above,
Chapter 3). The efforts of a thousand Productivity Councils could
not have compensated for the damage directly done to British
export performance by the greedy technological demands of rearmament – nor for the damage likewise done by those demands to the
process of re-equipping Britain's own industries. But also to be
taken into account is the harm inflicted *indirectly* on British competitiveness by rearmament, in the form of the huge extra burden piled
onto a national economy already heavy laden with the year-in,
year-out costs of the world role. It was, after all, in order to
compensate for this double load (and also to make room for
Macmillan's housing programme) that in 1952–5 Churchill's
government chopped back investment in modernizing Britain's
outdated industries and infrastructure. Only in 1955–56 was there a
short-lived rise in such investment (see above, Chapter 7).

Yet the economy of West Germany, the trade rival most feared
by Conservative ministers and their Whitehall advisers, was suffering
from no comparable self-inflicted burdens. Nor, for that matter, was
it suffering like the British economy from a third and even more
pervasive handicap – so-called 'full employment', as artificially
maintained by state-puffed inflation. In 1950 unemployment in
Germany stood at 1.58 million, a figure that would have caused
political panic and public outrage in the United Kingdom. Even
in 1955 it had only fallen to 920,000, compared with 232,000 in

Britain, though the populations of both countries were of broadly similar size.[1]

For 'full employment' remained as ever an unshootable sacred cow of the British post-war consensus. But as well as yielding the warm milk of job security this cow also produced vast amounts of manure by way of undesirable economic side-effects. The constituents of this manure were acutely analysed by Hugh Gaitskell, the last Labour Chancellor, writing on 1 December 1950 – as it happened, the same day that the United Nations forces in North Korea began their pell-mell retreat before the massed onslaught of the Chinese People's Liberation Army. Before the Second World War, wrote Gaitskell, 'it was the existence of heavy unemployment, at home and abroad, which allowed employers to resist wage claims and discouraged workers from pushing them too far . . .'[2] What was more, 'wages were more under pressure in declining industries than in expanding industries . . .'[3] But under full employment there was 'very much less check on the upward movement of money wages', with the likely result that 'exports will cease to be competitive and there will be balance of payments difficulties. These can only be met, in the end, by devaluation', which, if often repeated, would destroy 'the international position of sterling . . .' Meanwhile at home, as Gaitskell acknowledged in so many words, full employment acted as an effective brake on industrial adaptation: 'The problem of the supply of labour to different industries is also more difficult because there is no reserve pool to draw on . . .'

And so:

> It is clear that a very difficult problem faces a country such as ours, which wishes to maintain full employment and yet to avoid the undoubted evils of rising prices at home and balance of payments difficulties abroad.[4]

After the General Election of October 1951 this problem and the linked one of union-imposed industrial arthritis were passed on by the Labour Government unsolved to the Conservatives. The diagnosis made by the incoming Chancellor, R. A. Butler, differed little from Gaitskell's. Thanks to full employment, wrote he, 'the bargaining power of Trade Unions is very strong': employers were afraid that they 'will never get their labour back if they once lose it'; and workers knew that 'there is plenty of work available'.[5] Result: 'there is no real obstacle to the steady increase in wages, which in turn leads to corresponding increases of prices.'[6]

Manure in plenty! So how best could the Conservative Government prevent it from clogging up the nation's economic progress? It fell to Chancellors of the Exchequer to go to work with shovel and bucket in regard to inflation (the so-called 'wage-price spiral'); to Ministers of Labour in regard both to strikes and to union restrictive practices, those crusted historical deposits kept in a state of preservation by full employment.

Sir Walter Monckton, Minister of Labour from 1951 to 1955, was the subtle lawyer who had acted as Jeeves to King Edward VIII's Bertie Wooster in 1936 when the royal master fell for a lady of dubious antecedents. With dark hair parted in the middle and slicked to the skull with brilliantine, and a narrow face, Monckton even resembled the Jeeves drawn on the 1930s dust jackets of P. G. Wodehouse's novels. And like Jeeves he was above all a fixer, not a man for a fight, which was exactly why Churchill gave him the task of keeping the Conservative Government on good terms with the trade unions. In this task Monckton succeeded, thanks to his conviction (as a Treasury civil servant expressed it in 1955) that

> the chief part for the Ministry to play in connection with labour relations and labour disputes is to concentrate upon supplying ample lubrication in the right places at the right times, and to refrain from action which might conceivably be criticised as Government intervention.[7]

Monckton's successor (in Anthony Eden's Cabinet in 1955), Iain Macleod, was no less a deft operator with the oil can, no less a member of the small 'l' liberal wing of the Conservative Party and an enthusiast for the post-war consensus – 'full employment', taxpayer-funded 'free' National Health Service, and all. Macleod even believed romantically in 'One-Nation' Toryism, in defiance of the historical fact that since the industrial revolution there had existed two nations in British society, the proletariat and the rest.

During their years in office both these men served congenially enough as the ultimate conciliators in that elaborate national apparatus of conciliation which, though it might eventually fudge a settlement of a particular industrial dispute, left unreformed the archaic, anarchic and sclerotic structures of British trade unionism (see above, Part Four).

Thus in regard to restrictive labour practices (rigid craft demarcations, overmanning, resistance to new technologies) Macleod advised his colleagues in February 1956 against appointing a public Committee of Inquiry, even though its purpose, innocuous enough, would be 'largely educational'. He did so on the grounds that to set up such a body would 'certainly be opposed by the trade unions and would not be received with enthusiasm by the employers' organisations'.[8] Since he deemed their 'goodwill and cooperation' (sic) essential if restrictive labour practices were to be diminished, he had 'serious doubts' about a move which began 'by risking the hostility of both sides of industry'.[9] It would be better, thought Macleod, to ventilate the problems in the National Joint Advisory Council (the domestic industrial equivalent of the League of Nations, and just as impotent), on which the TUC and the British Employers' Confederation were both represented. In any case, as he told his ministerial colleagues later that month, 'Legislation was out of the question; apart from any other consideration, it was impossible to apply legal sanctions in this field.'[10] Impossible?

So in place of a public inquiry a new committee of officials representing all Whitehall departments involved with industry was set up in April 1956 to puzzle out for the benefit of ministers what could be done, if anything, about the kind of nonsense that was currently threatening (to cite one scandalous example) the export prospects of the shipbuilding industry.[11] The creation of this body was inspired by the recent passing of an Act of Parliament (not so much toothless as equipped with an ill-fitting set of ineffective dentures) to limit price-fixing and market-rigging by companies.[12]

To the new Committee the Ministry of Labour submitted a comprehensively dismaying dossier on union restrictive practices and on strikes in recent years. All these regrettable happenings were, according to the Ministry,

intimately bound up with the whole nexus of working conditions, and under our system of regulating industrial relations through the bargaining of free and independent parties it is evident that the ultimate agreement of those parties to any change is essential.[13]

And so:

No third party judgment can be effectively enforced against the will of either of the parties without the introduction of a fundamental change in current generally accepted ideas of free association and free negotiation.[14]

'Free association?' The Ministry, it seems, was suffering a lapse of memory about the closed shop.

After pondering for some four months the Committee came to the limp conclusion that 'it would not accord with present-day thought to argue as if [the sale of labour] should be subject to the same kind of laws as the sale of goods'.[15] For the Committee now broadly shared the Ministry of Labour's sense of sympathetic understanding:

Restrictive practices by labour are generally manifestations of an underlying malaise rather than practices deliberately adopted as an end in themselves. To attempt to suppress restrictive practices by forcible means, even if they were successful, would not cure the underlying trouble, but would rather exacerbate it. All hope of better industrial relations would be lost, and the workers would be put in an unco-operative frame of mind, in which their productivity would deteriorate.[16]

The Committee therefore recommended that 'any general legislative action against restrictive labour practices is neither possible nor desirable'.[17]

In October 1956 Macleod in a speech to the Conservative Party annual conference at Llandudno publicly took the same flaccid line:

I believe firmly that the British system of free voluntary negotiation in industry, with the minimum of Government interference, is the best, and I believe firmly in the trade union system. Those views are fundamental to my political beliefs . . .[18]

So how and when might the historic trade union shackles on productivity be eventually loosened? The Committee on Restrictive

Labour Practices had reckoned that since these chains were 'a reflection of low morale in the industrial community', they would be 'reduced as and when industrial – indeed national – morale improves'. Therefore 'progress must be expected to be gradual'.[19]

There was only one drawback to this waiting game as favoured by the mandarins and the Minister. British industrial society was not an island unto itself, but part of the main of the world market. It was therefore not without relevance that the Committee on Restrictive Labour Practices had reported that they 'knew of no such practices' in Britain's most formidable challenger, West Germany.[20]

Meanwhile the related problem of disruptive strikes had also been perplexing the essay-writers and seminar-holders of Whitehall, not least because the problem was gradually getting worse as unions and shop floor increasingly sensed the coercive power lent to them by full employment and by Whitehall's well-known anxiety about the balance of payments. In Walter Monckton's words in June 1955,

> full employment was the cause of an irresponsible attitude to workers' discipline and to strikes . . . There was a greater inclination to strike because the workers felt that they were not at risk and could if necessary obtain other employment.

But what to do about it? That month the Prime Minister (now Eden) was stirred by a recent rail strike and current stoppages in the docks and ocean-liner terminals into setting up a special ministerial committee, chaired by Butler as Chancellor, to 'consider what action can be taken to check strikes and to improve industrial relations generally . . .'[21]

Monckton informed this body that the British Employers' Confederation 'were firmly against legislation to make unofficial strikes illegal'.[22] Ministers concurred: such legislation 'would be impossible to enforce . . .'[23] Impossible? The British Employers' Confederation also reckoned (so Monckton reported) that a legal requirement for a secret ballot before strike action 'might not be as effective as they had originally thought, since this would not prevent unofficial or illegal strikes'.[24] The best the BEC could suggest was to establish a legal 'period of reflection' before a strike was finally called, coupled with a fact-finding inquiry by a High Court judge. But how long a period? It had been twenty-one days under the old wartime Order 1305; it was currently eighty days in America under the Taft–Hartley Act, which also provided for a compulsory secret ballot before strike action. However, Monckton twanged his colleagues' delicate nerves by warning them that the American provisions 'were introduced in the teeth of trade union opposition in a way which would be politically impossible in this country'.[25] Impossible – that strain again! Monckton himself was 'sure that a legal requirement imposing statutory timing on the calling of strikes would only rarely assist in promoting industrial peace and would raise the usual awkward problems of enforcement'.[26] Moreover, the employers and the trade union leaders on the NJAC agreed with each other that such a requirement 'would do more harm than good'.[27] Instead, reported Monckton, the idea had been floated that 'both sides of industry' might draw up a code of industrial relations, 'which would impose some kind of moral obligation ... to observe agreements . . .'[28] 'Some kind of moral obligation'! It would have proved (as it did prove in the 1960s and 1970s) about as effective in industrial affairs as had the Covenant of the League of Nations in preventing international aggression during the 1930s.

What, then, if the liability of strikers to legal action were widened? Monckton saw 'serious objections' to this too.[29] There was 'no prospect of getting the trade union movement to agree to it'. It would be 'extremely difficult to undertake an extension of the existing restrictions on the right to strike in face of opposition from the trade union movement as a whole'. Monckton even believed it likely that 'a more vigorous enforcement of the present law [the Conspiracy and Protection of Property Act, 1875] would seriously exacerbate industrial relations'. As for the employers, Monckton reckoned that it was 'by no means certain' that they 'would like such action'. What was more, any stricter legislation 'would place both the Attorney General and myself in the dilemma of having to choose between large scale prosecutions or turning a blind eye to breaches of the law'. And lastly, of course, such legislation 'might prove embarrassing in conciliation work since there would be pressure on us to take legal proceedings rather than seek an agreed solution'.[30]

The case for appeasement had never been better made since

Neville Chamberlain, Lord Halifax, and Sir Nevile Henderson (British Ambassador in Berlin) practised their own version of conciliation work with Hitler's Germany in 1937–8. No doubt Monckton's advocacy of appeasement emanated from his personal character and his political philosophy. But was it justified by operational realities?

Certainly even the wartime Order 1305 had failed to prevent unofficial strikes, as Monckton justly pointed out: the year of the Normandy invasion, 1944, was the worst for stoppages in two decades.[31] Where strikers had been fined under the order, it had sometimes proved impracticable to collect the money – presumably because of a failure to deduct at source from pay packets. In 1950 unofficial strikers in the gas industry had been prosecuted under Order 1305 as well as the 1875 Act and sentenced to a month in prison (though this was later reduced to a £50 fine). Nevertheless, the case caused such an uproar of public indignation that the Labour Government revoked Order 1305 in the following year.

Clearly use of the criminal law to limit strike action, so creating martyrs in flat caps, was a disastrously wrong way to go about it. But no one in the Conservative Governments of the 1950s, or for that matter in the Labour Government of 1945–50, even *floated* the idea of a strategy like that successfully adopted by Margaret Thatcher in the 1980s – that of strict statutory limitations (cooling-off periods, secret strike ballots, outlawing of intimidatory and secondary picketing), which could be readily enforced by swingeing sequestrations of union assets or the assets of unofficial fomenters of strikes.

It might be argued that in failing even to float such ideas the politicians of the 1950s were simply motivated by a judgement, right or wrong, that at a time of full employment and a tottery pound the British state was too weak to wage and win an industrial war. Yet the written and spoken evidence of the time puts it beyond doubt that this was not at all their motivation, which was quite otherwise.[32] In the first place, Labour and Conservative ministers and their advisers all found conflict personally and ideologically abhorrent. In 1956 senior civil servants in the Ministry of Labour even persuaded Iain Macleod that it would be 'unwise' to introduce compulsory secret strike ballots (standard practice in Germany), because this would arouse 'very strong opposition and resentment' in the unions.[33] And, secondly, politicians and civil servants alike cherished a positive and fervent belief that policies inspired by a spirit of conciliation could do the trick. They looked hopefully to better mutual understanding between management and labour in the future, perhaps even a proletarian change of heart. But how were these desirable changes of attitude supposed to come about?

How else than by means of that small 'l' liberal cure-all of the time, enlightenment through some educative process? As Monckton explained to his colleagues in July 1955, it was 'desirable to educate public opinion about the problems of industrial relations in contemporary society, and particularly about the limitations of the strike as an industrial weapon'. In his view, 'much could be done' through discussions on radio and television 'to demonstrate that the problems were different with full employment . . .'[34]

Monckton (Harrow and Balliol) went on to amplify these thoughts in language that would have done credit to the original nineteenth-century progenitors of small 'l' liberalism[35] – educational idealists like Cardinal Newman, Dr Arnold and a host of later public-school headmasters; romantic dreamers like William Morris; the earnest chapel-goers who shaped the Victorian Liberal Party and, later, the Labour Party too: all those hopeful souls who ever believed that mankind might be redeemed from conflict and selfish greed for a life of brotherhood and harmony.

> We should aim [wrote Monckton] at education in the arts of working together in an industrial democracy . . .
>
> . . . education is required on the question of the responsibility of the individual, whether it be trade unionist or employer, for the economic health and social well-being of the state . . .
>
> Education on this basic problem is, of course, concerned with the moral fibre and social attitudes of the nation as a whole. It should be the concern of all men of goodwill who can influence public opinion, e.g., teachers, churchmen, newspaper editors, Members of Parliament.[36]

Just the stuff to go down well with the disgruntled troops on the shop floors of Coventry and Cowley and in the working-men's clubs and pubs of Sunderland and Glasgow!

Since Monckton's successor, Iain Macleod, proved broadly of

the same mind as he, it meant that the Ministry of Labour, in trying
to clear up the copious industrial-relations droppings from full
employment, had chosen to equip itself only with an india-rubber
shovel and a bucket with no bottom.

Yet at the same time a far worse problem was confronting Chancellors of the Exchequer and, behind them, the crack Treasury bureaucratic brains trust. For full employment also excreted a by-product
highly poisonous to the health of the nation's economy as a whole:
the so-called 'wage-price' spiral of inflation. This weakened the cost-
competitiveness of British exports, so in turn menacing the balance
of payments, the international standing of the pound, the survival of
the Sterling Area, and ultimately the grandiose but wobbly facade of
Britain as a world power. Moreover, even full employment's comforting warm milk of abundant pay-packets and easy profits only
served to render the British economy at home fat and flabby, so that
even dud companies (especially in older technologies) found it easy
to keep bumbling along.

All of this was perfectly well recognized year after year by
Conservative ministers and the civil service 'gentlemen's gentlemen'
at their elbows.[37] In July 1954, for instance, the Government's Chief
Economic Adviser, Robert Hall, is found percipiently observing
that 'the problem [of wages and full employment] is one of the most
fundamental of our economic problems to-day'.[38] Hall proceeded
to explain just why in terms that closely paraphrased Gaitskell's
analysis in 1950 and Butler's in 1952:

> When there was a good deal of unemployment, wages could be
> safely left to collective bargaining. But with full employment, there
> is no real resistance to a steady increase in wages. The workers are in
> a strong bargaining position, and the employers know that in the end
> the Government will have to see that business conditions are good
> enough to keep them busy; so that they have not much to fear,
> except perhaps in export markets, if they agree to higher wages.[39]

In short, 'there is a strong tendency for wages and prices to rise
continually and this is inevitable as long as full employment is a
main object of policy'.[40]

In March 1955 Butler scrawled an amendment in his own hand

on a typed draft letter from him to the Prime Minister: '*Running a full employment policy, and with increased profits and rewards for the enterprising*, we cannot pretend to secure reductions in the [cost-of-living] index . . .'[41] And a whole year later Robert Hall, briefing the Prime Minister for a meeting with the TUC on 5 March 1956, simply trotted out his July 1954 diagnosis again, but this time added that inflation arising from full employment was 'the reason why we import too much, export too little, and get into balance of payments difficulties'.[42]

In the same month the influential Head of the Information Division of the Treasury, S. C. Leslie, starkly warned that 'mastery of inflation is a life-and-death matter':

> let it be remembered that (i) we have in fact been steadily losing our *share* of world trade, and (ii) even when there have been no crises we have failed to achieve an export surplus.
>
> This surplus is essential *in the light of our commitments, upon the discharge of which depends the continuance of the entire British power-system in economics and politics* [added emphasis].[43]

And Anthony Eden himself, in the course of a prime-ministerial sermon at Perth in May 1956 on virtuous economic conduct, pronounced that the problem of the balance of payments 'has got to be solved':

> The truth is that our gold and dollar reserves are still too small for the *duty* [added emphasis] we have to perform as banker to the sterling area. Half the world's trade is carried on in sterling, a matter of which we can be *proud* [added emphasis].[44]

But how were we to fulfil our 'duty' and justify our 'pride'? Eden had thought of an answer: 'we must export more overseas and consume less at home'. He acknowledged, however, that 'of course' there were 'difficulties about this in what are virtually boom conditions'[45] – meaning, in other words, the state-puffed 'full employment' economy.

Yet in the face of all the evidence and all their own analyses the Conservative Government could not nerve themselves to slaughter this sacred cow. To allow the number of unemployed to rise above half a million, or 2 per cent of the insured population, was taken to be politically out of the question. As late as June 1956, when Britain's vulnerability to the German challenge in export markets had become a matter of deep concern, the Chancellor of the Exchequer, by now Harold Macmillan, was ruling out 'a severe deflation by monetary measures' on the score that 'the consequential damage would be very great . . .'[46]

So instead of such 'severe deflation by monetary measures'[47] the Government feebly prodded the brakes from time to time with 'credit squeezes', including such fiscal measures of 'disinflation' as juggling the rate of purchase tax in order to manage consumer demand. Unfortunately ministers had been taken in by those theoretical economists in Whitehall and the universities who conceived of 'the economy' as a grand machine to be judiciously accelerated or slowed down. In fact, some theoreticians of the time even built a model of 'the economy' out of glass receptacles and tubing, in which the effect of various economic pressures and possible governmental counter-pressures could be simulated by the displacement of coloured fluids. Yet outside this abstraction of 'the economy' lay a real world of factories and assembly lines, and of output planned according to estimates of future sales. For the Government abruptly to slam on a higher rate of purchase tax or tighten hire-purchase terms could only be damagingly disruptive to production and productivity – not least by compelling managements to lay off workers or put them on short time.[48] The impact was all the worse because Chancellors selected as the targets for their unwitting attack on productivity those very modern industries with the fastest-growing markets – motor vehicles, televisions, radios, and household white-goods such as refrigerators and washing-machines.[49] The first restrictions on the hire purchase of cars were imposed in February 1952 during the economic crisis caused by post-Korea rearmament.[50] They were lifted in July 1954; slammed back at a lower level in February 1955;[51] raised to the original levels in July when the balance of payments and sterling were again beginning to look dodgy;[52] and finally, in February 1956, made more swingeing than ever, with a initial deposit of half the purchase price.[53]

Neither this kind of unhelpful tinkering nor even Governmental brakes on capital investment in industry (see above, Chapter 7) were anywhere near capable of solving the 'life-and-death' problem of inflation, or, in other words, the problem of reconciling full employment with stable wages and prices. How then could the inherently irreconcilable be somehow reconciled?

Since coming into office in 1951 the Conservative Government, aided by the finest minds of Whitehall, had sought to crack the conundrum, their efforts being closely interwoven with their repetitive diagnoses that full employment caused inflation. Year after year this combined process of thought went round and round in circles, like a battleship whose rudder has been jammed by an unlucky hit from a torpedo.[54] Yet there essentially emerged only one single suggestion as to how Britain might enjoy full employment without a wage–price spiral. It was that the trade unions in the case of wage claims, and company managements in the case of prices, should show responsibility and exercise restraint.

Here was the same kind of hopeful, hopeless, small 'l' liberal fantasy that was being concurrently peddled in regard to solving the problems of lagging productivity, poor industrial relations and restrictive labour practices. For where was the leverage, and where was the bribe? It might be that it was in the nation's interest, or even in the long-term self-interest of workers and companies, that neither wages nor prices should rise. But this was quite irrelevant to the immediate realities of a company deciding to hike its prices to meet extra costs, or a union – perhaps a strike committee – deciding to put in a wage claim to compensate for a rise in the cost-of-living index.

At a meeting in June 1952 between a Government delegation led by Butler as Chancellor of the Exchequer and the barons of the TUC Economic Committee, Mr Lincoln Evans (General Secretary, the Iron and Steel Trades Confederation) had tried – as it turned out, in vain – to enlighten the unworldly Whitehallites:

> The fact must be faced that the ordinary wage-earner did not work out for himself the effects of higher wages on prices at home and in the export markets, however obvious this might be.[55]

It follows that much the same would be true of the 'ordinary' company's thinking in regard to the effects of higher prices. Nonetheless, in defiance of such human realities, the Whitehallites continued to delude themselves that a long-term voluntary policy of restraint by unions and management lay within the bounds of the practically possible.

What then could Government do to encourage the two sides in this joint exercise of civic duty? How about trying to educate them, and public opinion too, about the economic implications of full employment? And – apart from the usual kind of sermons by ministers[56] – what better means of education than a White Paper? This was bound to be a bestseller among workers and managers, or, at very least, be fully reported in their favourite newspapers, *The Times* and the *Manchester Guardian*. As Robert Hall put it with mandarin pomposity in July 1954 when this idea was first being mooted, 'it is the historic function of White Papers to inform the public of the views of the Government on important questions'.[57] After the customary many months of argy-bargy over the small print in committees of increasing seniority, this exhortatory document duly appeared in March 1956,[58] with all the impact of a dud shell falling into deep mud.

Nevertheless, the Government's main hope of restraint over wages and prices lay elsewhere – in directly brokering a voluntary policy with the TUC and the employers' organizations.[59] Three years of diplomatic exchanges with these important powers having produced nothing but platitudinous communiqués, the Prime Minister (now Eden) is found on 1 November 1955 receiving thirteen members of the TUC at No. 10 Downing Street, in yet another attempt at cajolery. The Chancellor of the Exchequer (still Butler) assured the trade unionists:

> There was no need to fear unemployment. The Government had no intention of resorting to a policy of creating unemployment in order to check wages. They had a reserve of works and many items of public expenditure which could always be used to counter unemployment. If anything, they erred on the side of pursuing full employment too vigorously.[60]

After emphasizing that 'the problem facing the country was inflation', the Chancellor observed that so far as the unions were concerned, 'he would like to see claims for wages allied to increases in productivity'. Unsurprisingly the TUC delegates proved less interested in this than in more 'planning' and a return to price controls. They did, however, usefully remind ministers – as had their predecessors in 1952 – that in any case the TUC General Council 'could not issue a general statement calling for restraint, since it would not be applicable to all unions':[61] i.e., not to those unaffiliated to the TUC. In fact, even affiliated unions lay under no obligation to obey the TUC. What was more, one other main target of governmental diplomacy, the British Employers' Confederation, also lacked the authority to dictate policy to its numerous members. The impotence of the participating powers might seem to put a dampener on this kind of summit diplomacy. Far from it: at the beginning of 1956 a new Chancellor of the Exchequer, an ersatz Edwardian boulevardier oozing with confidence in his own powers of charm and manipulation, bustled forth to achieve a long-term understanding with the unions and the employers over wages and prices that would finally break the spiral.

Harold Macmillan, promoted from Foreign Secretary on 21 December 1955, took up his new post just as there erupted a fresh economic crisis that had been brewing since midsummer. For the balance of payments was yet again flagrantly breaking the Micawber rule, so inducing a run on the pound and a consequent outflow of the gold and dollar reserves. These had now dropped below the level of late 1945 after the $3.5 billion American loan, and far, far below the post-Marshall-Aid level in mid-1951.[62] There were deeper causes for anxiety as well: Britain's loss of world market share in manufactures; her rising unit labour costs compared with her competitors; the German industrial challenge.

The immediate economic crisis was mastered by Macmillan with his own ingenious counterparts of the 'turning the corner' expedients adopted during the storm of 1951–2.[63] Among these counterparts was the torpedoing of the motor-vehicle industry by the imposition of an initial hire-purchase deposit of half the price of a car. Nothing like this ever happened to Volkswagen or Mercedes-Benz. But Britain's deep long-term problems, and that of full employment and inflation in particular, were another matter.

Before the Second World War Macmillan had belonged to the left wing of the Conservative Party: a back-bencher appalled by the unemployment in his constituency of Stockton, that technological

and social scrapheap left over from a defunct industrial revolution.
Now he was a man passionately committed to the ideals of the post-
war consensus. To him the maintenance of full employment constituted a prime governmental duty. He recorded in his memoirs how
in a speech in the Commons on 20 February 1956 he

> could not help contrasting the new problems of today with those
> which had confronted us between the wars. Then the cost of living
> had been at its lowest, but unemployment at its peak. Now we had
> full employment – some would say artificially full employment – but
> prices were rising all the time. I disclaimed altogether the idea that
> we were trying produce unemployment. Nor was I even ready to
> accept the 3 per cent unemployment which Lord Beveridge had laid
> down as a fair average and which even Gaitskell had been prepared
> in certain circumstances to accept.[64]

But Macmillan's devotion to 'some would say artificially full
employment' only made it the more urgent that he should achieve
his wished-for understanding with the unions and employers over
wages and prices.

He planned his offensive like a military campaign, using his civil
servants as an operations staff and the Permanent Secretary at the
Treasury, Sir Edward Bridges (a contemporary of Macmillan's at
Eton and in his words 'a humanist and scholar'),[65] as chief of staff.
Macmillan had, after all, served as an officer with the Grenadiers on
the Western Front in the Great War, and in the Second World War
had worked with Allied generals as Minister Resident in the
Mediterranean theatre. In the opening phase of the offensive, he
and the Prime Minister met the TUC on 5 March; the British
Employers' Confederation on 7 March; the heads of the nationalized
industries on 14 March; the Federation of British Industries on 19
March; and the TUC for the second time on 27 March.[66] At this
latter meeting, Macmillan rounded off a tour d'horizon of the
nation's economic predicament and the government's recent
attempts at remedy by calling for 'a truly national effort':

> But a lot needs to be done [so went his speaking notes]
> But if we can begin
> (a) to overcome inflation

(b) steady prices

(c) see [balance of payments] surplus grow

we shall feel it's worth while and that we are going along the right road.

Then things can be done to make us all feel better.[67]

That same day he wrote to the Prime Minister to reaffirm the *Schwerpunkt* of the campaign:

> Our long term objective is clear. We want stability of prices. To this end, with full employment, we need to restore realism in relation to price and, its necessary counterpart, realism in relation to personal incomes (salaries, wages and profits). The question to which we must now direct our thoughts is how fast it will be practicable to go. It is important to start in time to influence the annual union conferences which will be beginning very soon.[68]

It seemed to Macmillan that there were two alternative strategies:

> One is to attempt something like a voluntary standstill for some appreciable period. The other is to move gradually towards our end. I am afraid that I doubt whether a standstill in the near future is practicable.

In any case, he was shrewd enough to perceive – unlike some Conservative and Labour Chancellors of the 1960s and 1970s – that there existed 'disadvantages in a standstill irrespective of difficulty of timing':

> Unless economic conditions are such as to produce a climate in which prices and wages would naturally remain pretty steady, a policy which in effect holds them steady is of the nature of a freeze. But every freeze has to be followed by a thaw and past experience is that as soon as the freeze begins to break up the accumulation of water behind the ice block produces floods and in effect sets in motion inflationary processes all over again.[69]

So Macmillan argued that 'the most promising line' lay in a policy of 'gradual moves'. This would have the advantages that it 'might go on for a long time and be increasingly effective'; that it 'would seem more likely to obtain acceptance'; and, thirdly, 'and perhaps most important, it would have a flexibility which would enable necessary changes either in prices or in wages to be made part of the policy itself, and not as exceptions to it.'

Gradual moves? Was Macmillan's policy then merely a new design for a rubber shovel? In a prime-ministerial minute on 11 April Eden himself agreed with Macmillan that 'our policy must be flexible'. But how flexible?

> In other words, we ought to combine a policy of exhortation and encouragement to restraint, with one of remedial measures to take out excessive demand . . .
>
> Of course, I have never thought that we could or should achieve a standstill or freeze on wages or prices. On the other hand, short of taking deflationary measures to a length which is politically not tolerable, I do not see how we can hope to limit wage claims by removing pressure on the labour market.[70]

Eden believed that the bulk of wage demands sprang 'from the traditional and annual reaction of the unions to the continual upward creep of prices'. Therefore his preferred strategy was that 'we should do all we can to discourage wage demands – both by explaining that the true interest of the community lies in price stability, and also doing what we can to keep prices stable where they are in our control' (meaning the nationalized industries).[71]

'Discourage' by 'explaining'? – surely here was the Prime Minister's own version of the rubber shovel.

Within Whitehall, however, influential voices were by now urging that ministers take 'a positive lead' and put forward 'more concrete proposals than they have done so far'.[72] This urging bore fruit in a 'pretty blunt' though 'inoffensive' statement[73] due to be given to the TUC at a meeting in No. 10 on 10 May, to the effect that whether prices went on rising really depended on organized labour showing 'utmost moderation' in wage demands.[74] Yet a nervy Cabinet decided after all neither to hand the statement to the TUC nor to publish it.[75] It says much about the rarefied nature of ministerial minds that the meeting thought that an effective way of influencing 'moderate' trade union leaders would lie in 'a firm leading article in the "Times" newspaper'.[76]

At the conclave with the TUC on 10 May, Macmillan chose to

plug the total-strategic consequences of further rises in wages and prices:

> there was a real threat of devaluation. If this happened the sterling area would break up and we would become a small power, with our economic position very much worse. The prize of price stability was a great one.[77]

A TUC representative repeated the old warning that the TUC 'had very little control over Trade Unions',[78] which again called into question the utility of this kind of summit diplomacy. Otherwise all that came out of the day's chat was agreement 'that the problems needed to be studied industry by industry, and that care was needed to have this done in a calm atmosphere'.[79] Nelson at Trafalgar! Engage the enemy more closely!

On 11 May 1956 the Prime Minister himself gave the desired 'positive lead' in an inspirational speech in Perth: very much the headmaster addressing a school whose conduct was falling short of the founder's ideals. Eden ranged from the balance of payments, the 'reserves', and the Sterling Area to full employment, industrial disputes, the importance of welcoming automation, and the fact that wages were rising faster than prices. Perorated he:

> The quality, skill, thrift, courage and imagination which have marked our national history can carry us through triumphantly today. Timidity, sectionalism, selfishness, partisanship for its own sake, will bring us all to ruin. It is for the nation to choose.[80]

Less than rousing turned out to be the effect of this oratory, for, in the judgement of Whitehall publicity experts, 'There did not seem to be any awareness that the Government had got a policy any different from those of the past.'[81]

With his campaign for voluntary restraint stalling, and the wage-price spiral threatening to twirl upwards again, Macmillan decided that he personally must explain to the country the Government's strategy for combating inflation, and do so in forthright terms. In a speech to the Northern Conservative Club in Newcastle on 25 May he hammered home that it was entirely the responsibility of employers and trade unions whether prices went up or not. We were, he said, already on a plateau of stability; we could stay there if we chose:

> I do not say that there should be no flexibility or minor adjustments. As production rises and techniques improve, of course such changes are right and proper. But another general round of increases, such as we have had, cannot be repeated without disaster. It won't bring any benefit to anyone. It would only benefit men in a particular industry if they were the only ones to get it. But they won't be. If one starts, the others will follow. No one will gain anything, except more and more paper money, which will buy less and less.[82]

These were sentiments to be repeated interminably and vainly down the coming decades by Macmillan's successors as Chancellor, Conservative and Labour alike. Now, however, they were well received in the press. The *Manchester Guardian* said that the speech confirmed that the Government 'is issuing a specific appeal to the trade unions to forgo all wage claims in the immediate future'. The paper saw Macmillan's 'clarion call at Newcastle last night [as] in a sense . . . an attempt to recover from the false start that had been made'.[83] *The Times* praised the speech in the context of Britain's general economic frailty, especially in export markets now that German and Japanese competition was no longer eliminated by the effects of the Second World War. Macmillan, pronounced *The Times*, was right to point out that the trade unions could wreck the country's efforts.[84]

Nonetheless, there still ensued no breakthrough and no successful advance to the final objective, but instead a long hard repetitive slog all through the summer of 1956 and into the autumn: face-to-face negotiations with the TUC, the BEC, the CBI, and the National Union of Manufacturers; government statements; ministerial (especially Chancellorial) speeches; and, in bureaucratic bunkers behind the battle-front, immense efforts at planning and preparation.[85] Still Macmillan stuck to his hope (as he told the National Union of Manufacturers in June) that 'by stressing the serious disadvantages which flowed from continuing inflation', he could create 'a climate of opinion in the country against further wage awards unjustified by increases in productivity'.[86] But where even now was the leverage? Macmillan still barred a policy of deflation sufficiently ruthless to create such high unemployment as to fillet union power. For this option remained, in Eden's words, 'politically intolerable' to the Cabinet, and to Macmillan personally quite unthinkable. All that Macmillan could therefore offer to employers' organizations was 'so to use the monetary controls that employers could no longer easily afford increased wages'.[87] The employers must have found this a great comfort.

At the end of August the Chancellor fired off to a press conference yet another heavy-calibre statement about the need for restraint. His opening gambit was topical enough: an indignant denunciation of President Nasser of Egypt's recent nationalization of the Suez Canal.

> But the seizure of Suez is not the only present threat to the future of Britain and her people. There is another danger, more familiar, less dramatic, harder to realise, but just as deadly. It is the possibility that by our own short-sighted folly and sectional divisions we may drive ourselves out of the front rank of industrial powers.[88]

Macmillan reminded his audience that the Government had put this possibility plainly before the country, and had urged all sections in industry 'not to weaken our competitive power by driving up costs and prices through a policy of grab'. He flashed statistics showing that while German and American wage costs had remained steady over the last three years, British wage costs had risen by a tenth. But, oddly enough, Macmillan omitted to mention here the crucial fact that neither Germany nor America were operating a state-puffed full-employment policy.

What had Macmillan to say about the assumption underlying his whole strategy (and shared by his ministerial colleagues and by senior civil servants) – that to combine full employment with stability of wages and prices actually lay within the bounds of the possible? And what had he to say in justification of his further belief that this reconciling of the irreconcilable could be brought about by an appeal to the good sense of 'both sides' of industry?

> I am told that I have been foolishly optimistic in thinking that a straightforward account of our circumstances and the risks that confront us would evoke a reasonable response, in particular from

the Trade Unions. I am still optimistic – whether that is foolish remains to be seen.[89]

Within a week the annual conference of the Trades Union Congress at Brighton cruelly gave him the answer – by passing a resolution to break off all further discussion with the Government on the topic of wage restraint. The resolution was moved by the new left-wing General Secretary of the Transport and General Workers' Union, Frank Cousins, whose vision of a socialist Britain remarkably resembled the actuality of Europe beyond the Iron Curtain.

Thus in the autumn of 1956 the Conservative Government did not find itself, as it had hoped, entering a new era of industrial peace and of stable wages and prices. Instead, it faced the prospect of deepening conflict and an early round of greedy wage claims.[90] Even Macmillan himself had to acknowledge to the Prime Minister that

> our campaign ... received a set-back at the recent Trades Union Congress. As a result some unions may well be more militant about wage claims and we are already confronted with a prospect of considerable pressure in three main sectors, transport, mining and engineering.[91]

As it turned out, and thanks to wage claims already won, the average earnings in manufacturing industry would rise by 8 per cent in 1956 (fully as much as in 1955) compared with an increase of only 3.5 per cent in retail prices.[92] In 1957 they would rise by 6 per cent compared with an increase of, again, 3.5 per cent in retail prices.[93]

And, most important of all in terms of Britain's overseas competitiveness, her export prices would be 4.5 per cent higher in 1957 than in 1956.[94] Moreover, her total exports of manufactures would grow by only 6 per cent in 1957, as against a rise of 11 per cent in global trade in such goods, so signifying a further shrinkage in her world market share.[95]

Futile though had proved the Conservative Government's industrial policies of appeasement, and profoundly harmful their loyalty to 'full employment', it might be pleaded in their defence that they were shackled by the limits of the politically possible in the prevailing climate of national opinion.[96] But no such excuse can be offered for the utter failure of both Conservative and Labour Governments in the first post-war decade to remedy Britain's fundamental deficiency as an industrial country – a workforce from boardroom to shop floor less well trained, less well educated, than their rivals in America and Europe.

PART SEVEN

Towards the Fall

... our deficiency is not merely a deficiency in technical education, but in general intelligence, and unless we remedy this want we shall gradually but surely find that our undeniable superiority in wealth and perhaps in energy will not save us from decline ...

(The Schools Enquiry Royal Commission, 1868)

If we are to produce all the trained craftsmen and technicians and technologists that are needed, the pyramid of technical education must have a broader base of school-leavers than it has now.

(Technical College Development Plan; draft Cabinet paper,
November 1955)

... there is ... at the other end of the [socio-economic] scale, the larger families, low housing standards, poor school attendance, and children below average in intelligence and in physical development.

(Scottish Mental Survey Committee, 1953)

We have to pull into rational groups the existing scattered facilities for technical education ...

(David Eccles, the Minister of Education, 21 November 1955)

22. Education for Industrial Defeat

The Labour and Conservative ministers of the first post-war decade well knew what needed to be done. For they had served together in Churchill's coalition Government while the audit of total war was revealing how far short of the needs of an advanced industrial state fell the output of the British education and training system.[1] Ministers had been particularly concerned, for example, about the long delays and difficulties in actually manufacturing the brilliant devices in the radar field invented by Britain's tiny elite of world-class university scientists. Why the delays and difficulties? The answer lay in a lack of enough highly trained production managers, production engineers, and technicians.[2] As a result, Britain was compelled to turn to the United States for indispensable thermionic valves and precision components; and even to abdicate to the Americans the main responsibility for the future wartime development of radar. But what else could be expected when, for instance, the cumulative British output of graduate electrical engineers for the fourteen years 1925–39 amounted to less than double Germany's output for the single year 1937?[3] Other wartime industries in Britain, from coal to aircraft manufacture, similarly suffered from scarcities of trained high-grade talent at all levels of management and engineering; suffered too from workforces whose mental horizons stretched no wider than their own particular craft and their own corner of the local shopfloor.[4]

There was, or should have been, no mystery about any of this, given the national provision of education and training just before the war.[5] At the apex of the pyramid was a privileged handful of university students drawn overwhelmingly from the middle and

445

upper classes: one in 885 of the national population. In comparison, one in 275 of the population in the United States went to university, one in 480 in France and one in 604 in Germany.[6] At the broad butt end of the pyramid, and in shameful contrast, 99 per cent of working-class children left school devoid of any kind of qualification, scholastic or vocational: ignorant coolies for a world of rapid technological change.[7] It makes this statistic all the more gruesome that a Carnegie Trust study in 1937–9, *Disinherited Youth*, found that out of a sample of 1,800 young people between eighteen and twenty-five in three old industrial cities, more than a third in Glasgow and nearly a third in Liverpool were 'so deficient in physical and mental qualities' as to be totally unfit for training in a government centre.[8] To support and guide the nation's adolescents – including such no-hopers – there were in 1939 only 350 full-time youth leaders in the entire country, when, according to a wartime estimate, up to 6,000 were really needed.[9]

In the middle of the educational pyramid the secondary-school population aged fourteen to eighteen amounted in 1937 to less than a tenth of the entire national age group. Of the 80,000 youngsters in England and Wales who went on from elementary school to secondary school at age fourteen, only 47,000 remained after the age of sixteen, and 17,000 after the age of seventeen. In contrast, proportionately twice as many German youngsters stayed on to age eighteen, and two and a half times as many obtained the German equivalent of the Higher Schools Certificate as obtained the British qualification. Of those British youngsters who left school at sixteen only five-eighths obtained the Schools Certificate, a third-rate academic piece of paper valueless as equipment for a working life; valueless too as a leaving certificate, because, unlike its German equivalent, it did not provide a passport to further education or training. In any case, English state-funded secondary education as a whole existed primarily to turn out white 'babus'. A sixth of secondary-school leavers in 1937 went into local government, nearly a third became clerks in banks or insurance offices, and only one-sixtieth went into industry.[10]

Out of the grand total of 663,000 school-leavers in Britain in 1937 at all ages and from all kinds of state school (in other words, the future young employees of wartime), only the 13,000 at junior technical schools had received any kind of prior preparation for a working career. And whereas Germany had over 1.8 million young-sters in part-time vocational training in 1937, Britain had only 20,000.[11]

Britain had been no less backward before the war in providing full-time further education and training. For young people between thirteen and sixteen there were 214 junior technical and commercial schools with only 30,000 students, as compared with Germany's 1,233 *Berufsfachschulen* (full-time training colleges) with over 138,000 students. For those sixteen to twenty-one England and Wales provided 149 technical colleges with some 9,000 full-time students, as against Germany's 303 *Fachschulen* (technical colleges) with over 26,000 students. What was more, Britain possessed no equivalents of either the forty-six German engineer schools or the ten German *Technische Hochschulen* (technical high schools) with university rank.[12] It hardly compensated for this stunning German superiority that in Britain in 1938–9 a mere 1,111 students were studying part-time for the Higher National Certificate in technological subjects and 173 for the National Diploma.[13] In any case, the prevailing standard of building and equipment in British technical colleges was, according to the 1943 White Paper *Educational Reconstruction*, 'deplorably low'.[14] This verdict serves neatly to complement the wide-eyed wonder of a British team visiting Western European countries in 1935 at 'the amazing scale on which provision is made for technical instruction of all grades':

> The size, dignity, and spaciousness of the buildings are scarcely paralleled anywhere in this country and the provision of apparatus and equipment is much superior to the majority of our insti-tutions . . .[15]

Nor could the science and 'applied science' departments of Britain's universities make up the British shortfall in advanced training in *Technik*. Of a total of 50,000 university students in 1938–9, those studying 'the Arts' numbered 22,374, while 'Applied Science' (meaning *Technik*) accounted for only 6,331.[16] Whereas in a key field like machine-tool design the University of Dresden before the war produced annually six to seven experts at the highest level, no equivalent training existed at all in the United Kingdom. This was consequently to cause embarrassment when in 1944 the Viceroy of India requested Britain to train Indian graduates in machine-tool design. Likewise, there existed no technical institution in Britain which could adequately give higher training in refrigeration engineering, and before the war trainees had had to be sent to an advanced course at Karlsruhe.[17] Equally lacking in Britain was any advanced centre for the technology of gear-cutting.[18]

Then again, only since 1939 had production engineering been accorded academic recognition as a post-graduate course in certain universities (Birmingham, for instance) and as a National Diploma course in certain technical colleges. There was not a single chair of management studies in the country in 1939, although there were some university courses in 'business administration'. The nearest British equivalent to the Harvard Business School lay in the Department of Business Administration at the London School of Economics – with a capacity of only eighty students per year, and a staff of only six specialist teachers.[19] In the case of economics – this being the single arts subject of any apparent relevance to running a business – the total British output of graduates with first degrees in the academic year 1938–39 amounted to just 115. All in all, the British effort in the field of management training verged on the invisible in comparison with the 16,000 students of industrial administration in Germany and the 80,000 in the United States.[20]

It is clear, therefore, that Britain went to war in 1939 with an education and training system which fell a long way short of setting the standard of 'world's best practice'. Yet the leaders and the led of British industry during the first decade after the war were, willynilly, its products. For this reason the system's flaws and gaps serve as tarot cards accurately predicting that decade's record of bungled industrial operations and muffed market opportunities.

> . . . our deficiency is not merely a deficiency in technical education, but in general intelligence, and unless we remedy this want we shall gradually but surely find that our undeniable superiority in wealth and perhaps in energy will not save us from decline . . .[21]

So reported the Schools Enquiry Royal Commission back in 1868. By the outbreak of the Second World War their prophecy of relative decline was well on the way to fulfilment.[22] How was it, then, that the double national deficiency identified by them had never been remedied in the seventy years that had elapsed since their report?[23]

Part of the answer lies in the triumph during the Victorian era of a high-minded (and above all classical) academicism in education. This triumph led to a lasting bias in public schools, grammar schools and, later, state secondary schools against any course which smacked of practical preparation for life. Such idealistic pursuit of moral and cultural purity had begun in the 1820s with visionary Christian headmasters like Dr Arnold of Rugby, spread to Oxbridge colleges, and been successfully proselytized by unworldly prophets like Cardinal Newman, John Ruskin and John Stuart Mill. After the passing of the 1902 Education Act the responsibility for designing the curriculum of the new state system of secondary education disastrously fell into the hands of the humanist public-school-and-Oxbridge civil servants who then dominated the Board of Education.[24] Intellectual snobs as they were, these mandarins patronizingly believed that by imposing an academic curriculum they would be proffering to working-class children a ladder of advancement in society. They regarded technical and vocational education as of lower standing and lesser importance, and, what was more, intrinsically alien to the teaching of moral values. And despite some powerful criticism during the 1920s and 1930s, the entire British system of education – schools of all kinds and the universities – remained heavily biased in favour of the academic (and the arts above all) right up to the Second World War. Even the nit-ridden children of the slums in elementary-school classes of up to sixty pupils received a smudgy umpteenth carbon copy of a 'liberal education' rather than practical instruction which would have been both useful to them and much more interesting.

The second reason why by the outbreak of the Second World War Britain had still failed to remedy her double deficiency in technical education and 'general intelligence' lies in the profound national distaste for either clear-cut organizational 'wiring-diagrams' or for equally clear-cut strategies boldly carried out. In 1895 the Royal Commission on Secondary Education had indicted educational developments in Britain as never 'continuous or coherent', by which the Commission meant that they 'did not represent a series of logical steps or even connected sequences . . .'[25] Fifty years later the Commission's indictment remained just as apposite – in fact, even more so. For Britain went into the Second World War equipped not with a coherent system for educating and training her people but with an incoherent patchwork.

In the first place, Northern Ireland, Scotland and England (with Wales) had evolved their own distinct systems, with Scotland much closer to the Continental model. It was within England and Wales (four-fifths of the national population) that there existed the far greater incoherence. Thus responsibility for the schooling and further education of young people lay with the Board (later the Ministry) of Education, whereas responsibility for their vocational training lay with the Ministry of Labour. Apart from the inevitable administrative confusions and overlaps, this splitting of roles between two departments served to institutionalize the false dichotomy in the mind of the elite between 'education' and 'training'. Yet in reality these constitute the brace and the bit that together make the effective tool of personal and national capability.

But in any case the Board of Education, unlike a European Ministry of Education, enjoyed no direct executive powers even within its own supposed sphere of responsibility. The state elementary and secondary schools and the technical colleges were run by 146 independent local authorities, while the direct-grant secondary schools and the universities were all autonomous (though state-aided) bodies. As for the broad policy of university development, that lay in the jealously independent hands of the Committee of Vice-Chancellors and their eminent confrères on the University Grants Committee, the body which handed out taxpayers' money at its sole discretion to what it judged to be deserving academic causes.

Nor was there cohesion between what was actually taught by different institutions, or even taught *within* an institution, as was devastatingly pointed out in 1945 by the Chairman of the Special Committee on Higher Technological Education:

> In this country . . . we seem to be in some danger of falling between two stools, securing neither efficient courses nor coherent institutions. For instance, technical colleges do not usually teach Physics up to

'intermediate' standard for the Ordinary National Certificate in Engineering, but they teach it up to a higher standard to individual students reading for the London External B.Sc. Here there is continuity neither within the technical college itself, nor between the technical college and either secondary schools or universities.[26]

It followed from this halting and piecemeal development of educational structures between the 1870s and the Second World War that Britain always remained 'one beat behind the band' compared with Europe and America in terms of the quantity and quality of education and training provided to the mass of the nation.[27] Again and again it had taken some kind of a fright to jerk the governing elite into a spasm of proposals for reform – these being then normally half-cocked in the event.[28] In the late Victorian era the fright derived from British industry's dismal showing in international exhibitions, and from the subsequent blockbuster reports comparing the excellence of European technical education with the poverty and muddle of British. The Great War supplied the next great fright, prompting more blueprints (especially for further, vocational, and technical education) which nonetheless remained largely unfulfilled between 1918 and 1939. After all, this was now Britain in peacetime; and first-class facilities cost money. It took yet another fright, from Adolf Hitler, to spur the belated building of new technical colleges in 1938–9 in order to supply the skilled manpower needed for the rearmament programme.[29]

Finally, the even nastier fright of the Second World War provoked a grand slam of official reports from 1943 to 1946 covering secondary and further education, youth training, higher technological education, the supply of scientific manpower, and even management training. The basic issue facing all these 'blueprint' committees was tersely stated by one of them:[30]

Trained intelligence and ability are among the nation's greatest assets – as has been strikingly demonstrated in this war – and are destined to be of increasing importance. We are entering an age in which organising and scientific capacity may well make the difference between victory and defeat in war, between prosperity and decline in peace.[31]

451

The 1943 White Paper on Educational Reform had boldly proclaimed that the purpose must be to 'remould and unify the educational system' and not merely (as in the past) to 'patch and improve it'.[32] Yet remoulding and unifying is exactly what the various blueprints failed to achieve even on paper. For unlike the land, sea and air plans for the D-Day invasion of Normandy, they were not developed as components of a coherent master-plan. Far from it: the blueprints proved sharply at odds even over such fundamental questions as educational values and priorities.

Thus the 1944 Education Act itself, in opening up secondary schooling to all children in England and Wales to age fifteen, created a tripartite system of grammar, secondary-technical schools, and secondary-modern schools all supposed to enjoy parity of esteem. But the committee appointed in 1941 by R. A. Butler as President of the Board of Education to report on 'Curriculum and Examinations in Secondary Schools' chose to ignore secondary education in technical and modern schools completely, and pay exclusive attention to the academic curriculum of the grammar schools. Although Butler had asked the chairman of this committee to bear in mind 'future competition in practical and technical education',[33] the committee's report in 1943 (complete with a quotation from Plato's *Laws* in the original Greek on the title page) proved an amazing rehash of mid-Victorian high-academic prejudices.[34] It emphasized the role of the classics, especially for the study of Divinity, and dismissed with contempt the idea of a curriculum including such subjects as international relations, economic and political structures, local and central government, and the history and economic resources of other countries – let alone any vocational element.[35] Modern languages could not be viewed, so pontificated this Report, 'solely as one of practical utility in terms of employment or career . . .'[36]

But no one should be surprised at such unworldly cant when the committee's chairman was a former headmaster of Harrow, one Cyril Norwood, and its twelve members were either heads of very crack grammar schools or other equally high-minded academic chams, with no leavening at all from trade unions, commerce, industry or technical education.[37] Yet it may be that the Norwood Committee was the more eager to preserve the educational past because wartime had seen among pupils a remarkable swing of popularity away from the arts towards science. An unpublished official history of education written in 1944[38] noted that, in comparison with the technological excitements of aviation and mechanized land warfare, 'Latin and Greek, which even in peacetime had little enough obvious relation to the future careers of a great majority of pupils and required a severe mental discipline . . ., must have seemed to many intolerably academic and tedious.' Just the same, the Norwood Report took for granted that bookish learning, however academic and tedious, must of its nature be superior to developing practical capability, certainly so far as brainier children were concerned.

Nevertheless, the significance of Norwood's defiant manifesto does not lie in its mortar-board-and-gown prejudices as such. It lies in that it was drafted by senior representatives of that very elite who, by fixing the requirements for examinations and university entrance, determined what would be taught in schools. Thanks to this dominating role, the grandees of academicism would succeed throughout the post-war decade – and beyond – in preserving the Victorian-cum-Edwardian character of the grammar-school curriculum in England and Wales. But even more harmfully, they would also successfully ensure that in prestige (and, as it turned out, in funding) the grammar school would lord it over Butler's new tripartite system, relegating the secondary-modern and secondary-technical schools to the category of a second-rate education for mentally second-class children.

Yet the very kind of cultural indoctrination so prized by the Norwood Report was regarded by another wartime official 'blueprint' study group, the Special Committee on Higher Technological Education, as calamitously starving industrial life of the best of the nation's brains. Indeed, this committee was much concerned to find a means whereby 'the present tendency of the ablest boys to go through the Secondary School to the University and thence to the professions or to black-coated occupations could be corrected so that a proper proportion went to industry.'[39] It looked in hope to the future evolution of the secondary-technical schools and their envisaged sixth forms: 'the fundamental question is that of attracting to the Technical High School the type of boys who at present go to the Grammar school . . .'[40] Here was the Norwood Report flatly contradicted.

By way of adding still further to the cultural confusion, a third major report (by the Interdepartmental Committee on Further Education and Training, chaired by Lord Hankey) cannily – or muddle-headedly – placed a two-way bet. On the one hand, it took note that the Government

> have recognized the importance of securing to the country, after the war, the service and influence of persons highly trained in the humane studies, such as philosophy, the classics, history, law, economics, and the fine arts, and the Committee recognize that *their first duty* [added emphasis] must be to consider what is necessary to offset the reduction during the war in the number of persons with such training.[41]

But on the other hand the Hankey Report foresaw a post-war need for the highly trained technicians and administrators on which industrial development would depend; for scientists to serve expanded research; and, 'even more important perhaps', a greater requirement 'for persons with scientific and engineering qualifications suitably trained for managerial and administrative functions'.[42]

Could divisiveness of purpose go further? It could, for Whitehall displayed its usual brilliant flair for the piecemeal by setting up, one year after another, two separate 'blueprint' committees to recommend what Britain needed by way of a future technocratic elite, and how best to provide it.

First in the field was the Special Committee on Higher Technological Education[43] appointed by Butler in January 1944 to recommend appropriate reforms 'having regard to the requirements of industry'. Its report in 1945 constituted by far the most important document on the subject since the Royal Commission on Technical Instruction of 1884. But its investigation was partly sabotaged before it even began because, 'the requirements of industry' notwithstanding, the committee's terms of reference[44] were drawn up by humanist university-educated civil servants in consultation with two distinguished humanist dons (one a former Professor of Moral Philosophy, of all irrelevances)[45] rather than two industrialists. At the recommendation of these university grandees (experienced entrepreneurs, of course) 'commerce' was deliberately excluded from the terms of reference on the ground that it offered a 'very different and separate problem'. This was piffle, since R&D, production and marketing (i.e., commerce) should properly form a single integrated process.

But at least the Chairman of the Committee, Lord Eustace Percy, was himself an imaginative choice, being a man of puckish personality and strong views. As the present Rector of King's College, Newcastle, he saw the main role of his own college as meeting 'the postwar demand for an expanded production of scientists and technologists'.[46] Yet, surprisingly enough, Percy had himself been educated at Eton and Christ Church, Oxford, where he took a first-class degree in modern history (at Oxford, 'modern' meant after AD 410, the end of Roman rule in Britain).

On his committee there were five industrialists (including Sir George Nelson, Chairman and Managing Director of English Electric Ltd); three heads of technical colleges; two vice-chancellors and the Rector of Imperial College; the Cavendish Professor of Experimental Physics at Cambridge; and the Director of the National Physical Laboratory. It would be fair to say, therefore, that the weight of expertise of the university members of the Committee lay in high science rather than *Technik* in the German sense. This was to prove a serious drawback, for in this committee too a lobby of the high-minded was to fight hard for the purity of academic 'values'. In the present case, moreover, the lobby was also fighting to defend a corporate monopoly, since they took it for granted that within the field of higher education these values were exclusive to universities. Here were the twin issues, by no means relevant to 'the requirements of industry', round which eight months of investigation and discussion by the Percy Committee revolved.

The issues came up at the very first meeting on 28 April 1944,[47] when Percy told his colleagues that one of their principal tasks must be 'to find some allocation of function between Universities and Technical Colleges which would enable them jointly to meet [the] demand'. However, British technical colleges were at present (as the head of one of them[48] had to remind the Committee) for the most part rather dim local institutions with a stock-in-trade of evening classes and junior day classes. The number of such colleges in which the work was comparable in standard with that in the Universities was, averred this head, 'extremely small'.[49]

Thus there existed between these lowly institutions and the universities a chasm which in Europe was filled by the *Technische Hochschulen*. Hence the Percy Committee and its professional witnesses had no difficulty in agreeing[50] that, in the words of Sir Lawrence Bragg (the Cavendish Professor), 'a weakness lay in the lack of institutions in this country comparable to the Technische Hochschule abroad.'[51] They also agreed that this lack must be remedied.

But how? Should Britain's new *Technische Hochschulen* be created out of the present engineering departments of universities (as suggested by the Institution of Mechanical Engineers) or by developing selected technical colleges? Or, far more boldly, should the *Technische Hochschulen* be completely new green-field creations, as had been the original nineteenth-century European versions?

It took months of tortuous argument before the committee finally decided against hiving off university engineering departments, and instead settled for developing up to six (exclusive of the London area) of the better technical colleges into 'Higher Technological Institutions' or 'Royal Colleges of Technology'.[52] These were to teach 'technological courses of a standard comparable with that of university degree courses'.[53] Percy himself urged that these upgraded institutions be called 'Royal Colleges of Technology' (on the analogy of the foundations created as offshoots of the Great Exhibition of 1851),[54] in order to enhance their status in the face of academic snobbery.

This final strategy adopted by the Percy Committee signified, however, that the university lobbyists had won. Their technology departments were to be spared to go on educating 'the long-range thinker' (in Sir Lawrence Bragg's romantic description),[55] or, in other words (as one meeting of the Percy Committee agreed), the 'men of sound but not outstanding calibre' which 'the provincial universities tend to produce'.[56]

Meanwhile, the same covey of eminent academic lobbyists had been fighting just as tenaciously to preserve the exclusive right of universities to award degrees, as distinct from mere 'diplomas'. The representatives of the Committee of Vice-Chancellors in their evidence to the Percy Committee had stoutly backed their donnish colleagues on the committee in arguing that no 'single faculty' institution could rank as a university, 'though they were anxious to see the legitimate desires of Colleges of Technology satisfied and the value of their services properly recognised'.[57] What could be more gracious? In the view of the Vice-Chancellors, the 'ultimate goal' of the Colleges of Technology should be a 'high diploma . . . but not itself a degree or carrying the letters of a degree . . .'[58]

Yet such self-serving pedantry evoked fierce opposition, led by Percy himself. In his own words,

> if higher technological education is to be developed on the scale and with the intensity which we have been convinced is necessary to the well-being of the nation, it is natural to suppose that such higher studies, wherever pursued, should lead to a Bachelor's degree.[59]

It proved, however, impossible to resolve this fundamental disagreement, as the Committee had to acknowledge in their report. Percy himself felt so strongly about the intellectual and institutional snobbery prevailing in British higher education (as it did in secondary education) that he added his own personal note to the report:

> I do not share the view of those who feel it necessary to emphasise the essential differences between courses at Universities and Colleges of Technology, or to object to the grant of University powers to 'single-faculty' institutions. University institutions primarily devoted to technological studies should, indeed, provide for their students a wide range of such studies and should also provide teaching in the pure sciences and in such 'arts' subjects as history, English, modern languages and economics; but it does not follow they need be qualified to grant a B.A. or a B.Sc. degree. The degree of B.Tech seems to me perfectly appropriate to Colleges of Technology which are otherwise qualified for the grant of University powers.[60]

And in a coda to all his valiant efforts as Chairman, Percy looked still further ahead, and advocated that it should be government policy to develop suitable Colleges of Technology into 'major University institutions'. In his judgement, 'no policy would be more likely to enlist [the] active co-operation and . . . financial generosity' of industrialists than one 'deliberately aimed at the progressive development of a future system of fully self-governing University Institutes of Technology.'[61]

The second grand inquisition inspired by the war into Britain's future needs in higher technological education submitted its report in May 1946.[62] The 'Committee appointed by the Lord President of the Council entitled "Scientific Manpower"' had been set up in December 1945 by Herbert Morrison, Lord President in the new Labour Government, to consider 'the policies which should govern the use and development of our scientific manpower and resources during the next ten years'.[63] It was chaired by Sir Alan Barlow, Joint Second Secretary at the Treasury (Marlborough College and Corpus Christi College, Oxford); contained just one industrialist (Sir George Nelson, veteran of the Percy Committee) and one economist; and otherwise was packed with eminent scientists, including Professors P. M. S. Blackett and Solly Zuckerman.

As might therefore be expected, the Barlow Committee claimed for the universities a monopoly over the training of 'qualified scientists'. Nevertheless, it did handsomely recognize that Britain as an industrial power was not to be saved by university science alone:

> The close relationship between pure science and the various branches of engineering cannot be over-emphasised, nor the fact that ... whereas no one can doubt the value of our achievement in fundamental science during the war, we were not always so successful in those applications of science which lie in the field of engineering and technology.[64]

The Barlow Committee therefore 'cordially' supported the Percy Committee's recommendation of full-time technology courses to degree standard in selected technical colleges.[65] In fact, it went even further:

> We think that urgent consideration should be given to the development of two or three Institutes of Technology, preferably in University Cities, whose aim should be to provide graduate and post-graduate courses and to conduct research of a standard at least equal to that demanded of candidates for doctorate degrees in the Universities.[66]

But what about training in management (and especially personnel management), in which Britain was known to be so lacking compared with America? Both the Percy and Hankey Committees had accepted that the future competitive efficiency of British industry must depend on producing professionally skilled leaders to replace the self-taught 'practical man'. They therefore wanted management studies to be formally incorporated in all technology courses, no matter in what type of institution. The Barlow Committee even proposed that at least one centre for the post-graduate study of management should be created.[67] A Harvard Business School – in Britain!

Nevertheless, prescriptive measures of this kind were rejected by two other official committees[68] specially charged with reporting on the topic of management training. Instead, they saw it as one of the persuasive functions of their proposed 'British Institute of Management'

> in consultation with the Board of Education, the Scottish Education Department and the universities, to *consider* [added emphasis] what developments were needed from time to time in education in schools, technical and commercial colleges and universities.[69]

A German poet wrote in the early nineteenth century that German history was an unending prologue. Exactly the same might be said of the history of education and training in Britain from the mid-Victorian age to the Second World War. To move on beyond prologue merely required that in the post-war era Government should swiftly meld all the hopeful reports of 1943–6 (plus the provisions of the 1944 Education Act) into a coherent plot, then produce the play and launch it on a successful run. To the Barlow Committee belongs the credit for specifying the basic requisite of success in this endeavour – the development of 'a regional and national system . . . for knitting together the Schools, the Technical Colleges, the Higher Technological Institutes, the Universities and Industry'.[70] A regional and national system! Bonaparte sweeping away the historical haphazardness of the ancien régime!

But ten years later the ancien régime in British education and training survived virtually intact, like a patched-up old huddle of a factory to which the odd extra building had been tacked on in the meantime.[71] Unsurprisingly, the régime's human output still fell a long way short of meeting the needs of an advanced industrial society. That output presented as ever a contrast of extremes between a small up-market range of university graduates (with the de luxe models carrying the prestigious logo of the humanities or 'pure' science) and the mass production of crudely finished proletarians outclassed by their European or American rivals.

It was a tragedy for these young proletarians – and for the nation as a whole – that Butler's Education Act of 1944, setting up the tripartite system of secondary modern schools, secondary technical schools and grammar schools, had led in the event to the very opposite of what he meant to achieve. Instead of the three types of school enjoying parity of esteem, they had perpetuated in educational form the British class divide between 'blue-collar' (secondary modern and secondary technical schools) and 'white-collar' (grammar schools). Why had this come to pass?

The answer partly lies in the malign dominance of academic tradition as represented by the Norwood Report. Partly it lies in old and unsuitable school buildings that were not replaced because of the general scrimping of capital expenditure under both Labour and Conservative Governments in order to make room for the assorted costs of keeping up appearances as a world power. Since preferential rations of new schools were awarded to new housing estates and new towns, secondary education in older districts was largely compelled to operate from existing premises. This inevitably meant that 'secondary modern' schools in such districts started life in the buildings of the old 'senior elementary' schools, and the new secondary 'technical high' schools in the buildings of the old 'junior technical' schools. It was no wonder, therefore, that along with their predecessors' cast-off premises the new types of school also inherited their predecessors' low social and educational prestige.

Long-term and grievous proved the harm caused by this governmental betraying of the promise of the 1944 Act. At the close of the post-war decade a Conservative Minister of Education, David Eccles, is found setting out afresh to create the parity of esteem envisaged in Butler's original tripartite strategy, acidly minuting in January 1956 on a paper by his officials about technical education that 'the opportunity is not taken to state plainly my policy of equality [of secondary technical schools] with Grammar Schools'.[72]

Yet in any case Butler and his co-authors of the 1944 Act were too dazzled by their 'New Jerusalem' vision of free secondary education for all to foresee what would be the future practical reality in the classroom. Although by 1956 the percentage of children staying on in school after age fourteen was double that of 1937, 'secondary education' only signified for the vast majority of them a tedious extra year in the classroom that still led to no academic or vocational qualification.[73]

In a report in 1957 neatly entitled *15 to 18*, the Crowther Committee (after its Chairman, Geoffrey Crowther)[74] agreed that

> At the moment we had three different leaving ages all heavily loaded with class values – 15, 16 and 18. Present education organisation reflected a 'class' base in a way unknown in America and was itself the cause of a good deal of emotional stress (mainly for the parents but communicated to the children).[75]

This judgement is borne out by the statistics of school-leaving – statistics which at the same time reveal the blatant disparities in the quality of education (and hence of human output) between the 1944 Act's three supposedly equal but different types of school. Out of a total of 300,000 school-leavers in 1955 at the minimum age of fifteen, no fewer than 282,000 were from secondary moderns.[76] In fact, in that year only 1.2 per cent of secondary modern pupils stayed on after age fifteen, as against 54.6 per cent at grammar schools and 21.7 per cent at secondary technical schools.[77] Youngsters staying on beyond age sixteen into the sixth form amounted in secondary modern schools to less than one per cent of the original fourteen-year-old age group; in secondary technical schools to 5.8 per cent; and in grammar schools to 33 per cent.[78] Of the combined national age groups seventeen and eighteen the percentage of youngsters who still remained in school in England and Wales in 1956 was virtually the same as the German percentage in 1937: 10.9 per cent to 10.7 per cent.[79]

These are lamentable figures. But the human reality was even worse. The 1944 Act had failed in a main purpose of eradicating the educational handicaps derived from social class and passed on from parent to child. That failure is revealed by the fate of those children of unskilled or semi-skilled parents who *did* succeed in passing the eleven-plus examination and entering a grammar school, the academic queen of the tripartite system. According to a report on *Early Leaving* in 1954 by the Gurney-Dixon Committee (after its Chairman, Sir Samuel Gurney-Dixon) of the Central Advisory Council for Education (England),[80] more than half such children failed to obtain even three passes at 'O' Level, and a third left before the end of their fifth year at age sixteen. Moreover, only about one in twenty of these working-class children who went to grammar school passed in even two subjects at 'A' level.[81]

The Gurney-Dixon Committee hazarded a guess that in this poor performance 'educational sub-normality in parents may play a part':[82]

> Most of the [skilled, semi-skilled and unskilled] parents will themselves have left school at fourteen. It does not follow of course that they will lack a sense of the value of education; indeed this sense may be more keenly felt by a man who is conscious of what he has missed . . . But inevitably the continuance of full-time education to the age of sixteen, seventeen or eighteen cannot be taken for granted by such parents as it is by most parents of professional standing; and if it is not taken for granted by the parents it will not be by the children . . .

However, continued the Gurney-Dixon report, ideas were not only picked up in the home but in the neighbourhood:

> There is no doubt of the strength of pressure on even conscientious parents from neighbours who see no point in education beyond fifteen or sixteen, as the case may be; and if the pressure on the parents is strong it is much stronger on the children.[83]

This realistic diagnosis of the human damage down the generations by life in grim factory towns since the first industrial revolution was supported by evidence compiled by the Scottish Mental Survey Committee in 1953:

> there is, at one end of the socio-economic scale, the pattern of small families, older parents, more favourable housing conditions, with children above average in intelligence and physique, and at the other

end of the scale, the larger families, low housing standards, poor school attendance, and children below average in intelligence and in physical development.[84]

These mid-1950s reports are the more appalling because they essentially repeat the 1937–9 findings of the Carnegie Trust study *Disinherited Youth* (see above, p. 446). Worse, they even echo the verdict of the Schools Enquiry Royal Commission back in 1868 that Britain was suffering from a deficiency 'in general intelligence', and that unless this deficiency was remedied she would 'gradually but surely' find herself in decline. Nearly ninety years had now passed since that tocsin was sounded, and still it tolled with unfading resonance.

Of the 400,000 fifteen- to seventeen-year-olds entering insurable employment in 1954, over 80 per cent did so at the age of fifteen without having sat for 'O' Level examinations, and without any paper qualification whatsoever: not even a leaving certificate, for such did not exist.[85] In other words, just as in the 1930s so in the mid-1950s the school system was simply dumping on the labour market a young lumpenproletariat. And lumpenproletariat the vast majority would remain, owing to the want of training opportunities in the work-place and the still threadbare nature of the further and vocational education provided by the state.

For the saddest youngsters, those from the poorest homes and with the most culturally impoverished families, the pastoral care offered by the youth service remained all too sketchy. In 1955–56 the total of grants to voluntary youth organizations by the Ministry of Education was about a third smaller than in 1946–47.[86] As late as 1958 it was estimated that there were only 800 full-time youth leaders in the country, as against the wartime McNair Committee's recommendation of 6,000.[87] In 1960 a report on the youth service in England and Wales by a committee chaired by Lady Albemarle was to supply an appropriately sour epitaph for the years of post-war neglect:

> the question now should not be, ought there to be a Youth Service, but can this country any longer make do with one so plainly ill-equipped to meet the needs of the day.[88]

But far more serious for the future quality of the British industrial rank and file and NCO corps was the existence even in the mid-1950s of a vocational and further education system no less 'plainly ill-equipped to meet the needs of the day'.

It was a creditable achievement that the numbers of students in all kinds of further education and training were much larger by the end of the post-war decade than before the war. Nevertheless, an organization's performance is not to be measured against its own past record, but, as with a boat-race crew, against the performance of rivals. To cite one important category, although students aged fifteen to seventeen in full-time further or vocational education in English and Welsh technical colleges had risen from 27,000 in 1937 to 39,000 in 1955,[89] this latter figure still compares poorly enough with a 1937 German total of 138,055 post-school leavers in full-time national education in *Berufsfachschulen* for a population then only half as large again as that of England and Wales in 1955.[90]

Nor had Britain caught up with Europe in the provision of *part-time* further education and training. The 1944 Education Act laid down that new County Colleges were to be established by local authorities for this specific purpose. In 1955 not one of these colleges had yet been created.[91] In existing institutions in the year 1955–56 there were 383,600 part-time students aged fifteen to twenty in evening classes, plus 237,380 aged fifteen to seventeen in day-classes.[92] Although this latter figure was five and a half times as great as that for 1937–38,[93] it still amounted to a fifth of the 1.1 million fifteen-to-seventeen-year-olds currently attending *Berufsschulen* (vocational schools) in the Federal Republic of Germany, whose population was little larger than that of England and Wales.[94]

Indeed, the England-and-Wales total of 237,380 part-time day-students in 1955–56 failed even to match, proportionate to population, the German figure back in 1937–38 of over 1.8 million part-time day-students aged fifteen to eighteen in *Berufsschulen*. And of this pre-war German total no fewer than 1.7 million had been on *compulsory* day-release from employment (first set up under the Weimar Republic),[95] whereas in England and Wales in 1955 this was still limited to a single centre, Rugby – just as it had been in 1938. It was a sign of the perennially slug-like pace of educational developments in Britain that forty years after the 1918 Education Act had vainly provided for day-continuation schools[96] the Crowther Committee is found recommending compulsory part-time day-release to age eighteen on the German model.[97] Meanwhile, British employers, in token of their enlightened approach to the education of their workforces, were allowing as many as 210,000 youngsters (1955 figure) out of a national fifteen to seventeen age group of 1.2 million to attend classes in working hours.[98]

Just how badly England and Wales were still performing in the mid-1950s as educators and trainers of post-school fifteen-to-seventeen-year-olds is summed up by a single fact: about half the fifteen-to-eighteen age group were not in any form of grant-aided education or training whatsoever.[99] There was of course apprenticeship – for a minority.

And minority it was, for out of the grand total of 414,000 fifteen-to-seventeen-year-olds entering employment in 1955 no less than 71 per cent did so into dead-end jobs offering no craft or career training at all.[100] In any case, apprenticeship was being sharply criticized in the mid-1950s as a medieval survivor inappropriate to the systematic teaching of skills in modern technologies. The critics wanted it replaced by full-time training in British equivalents of the German *Berufsfachschulen* and the French *Centres d'apprentissage* – whenever these equivalents might be created.[101]

The authors of a draft plan for the Cabinet in November 1955 on future technical-college development therefore surely got it right when they pronounced that the present proportion of fifteen-to-seventeen-year-olds undergoing vocational training was 'not nearly sufficient':

> If we are to produce all the trained craftsmen and technicians and technologists that are needed, the pyramid of technical education must have a broader base of school-leavers than it has now. Our aim must be to attract 50 per cent of them into day-time attendance at the technical colleges.[102]

A broader base to the pyramid of technical education – exactly what the Schools Enquiry Commission had urged eighty-seven years previously! But what about the *middle* layer of the pyramid seventy-one years after the Royal Commission on Technical Instruction had pointed out how insubstantial that was? Ten years after the Percy and Barlow Committees had done the same with even greater urgency?

In February 1956 the White Paper on Technical Education[103] gave the answer:

> From the USA, Russia and Western Europe comes the challenge to look at our system of technical education to see whether it bears comparison with what is being done abroad. Such comparisons cannot be made accurately because standards and systems of education vary so much, but it is clear enough that all these countries are making an immense effort to train more scientific and technical manpower and that we are in danger of being left behind.[104]

Such progress as had been made in the field since the war in Britain was, so pronounced the White Paper, 'nothing like enough'. Who could disagree? Lord Eustace Percy's proposed Royal Colleges of Technology ranking as universities had come to naught. The single new comparable institution consisted in the College of Aeronautics at Cranfield, set up in 1945. In an initiative at once cut-price and timid, nine designated 'national colleges' each specializing in a particular technology came into being between 1945 and 1952 – but only within already overstretched and underfunded local technical colleges or polytechnics. The rate of progress with these selected 'colleges of technology' was damned by the Parliamentary Scientific Committee in July 1954 as 'slow, hesitant, hampered by controversy and not sufficiently in keeping with the urgency of the problem'.[105]

As it was, the continued lack of *Hochschulen* left the responsibility for training the nation's technologists split wide between the universities (speciality: 'the long-range thinker') and the catch-all local 'tecs' which also had to train the fifteen-to-seventeen-year-olds. But only one new technical college had been opened since the war, in Norwich. At full capacity the 'tecs' could only cope with 26,800 full-time technology students in 1954 aged eighteen-plus,[106] as against 57,300 in the German Federal Republic's *Fachsschulen* and 19,272 in *Technische Hochschulen*.[107] Even when the 10,000 full-time students of technology[108] at British universities are added to the balance, it still leaves Germany riding well ahead.

She was also leading Britain by a length or two when it came to the output of degree-level technologists and engineers. In 1955–56 her *Technische Hochschulen* turned out 3,760 graduates with diplomas or doctoral degrees. Universities in England and Wales managed a total of 2,300 degrees or diplomas in all kinds of technology, and the local technical colleges a further 959: a combined total of 3,259.[109] This was just over the Percy Committee's target for graduate engineers alone. And when it came to what the Germans called *electrotechnik*, that key area of advancing technology, Germany produced 830 graduates in 1955–56; British universities only 250.[110]

Nor could the output of local 'tecs' in Britain fill the gap. Only 531 students (1953–54 figure) took an external degree from London University, and a mere 332 the Higher National Diploma. The remaining 6,784 took the humbler Higher National Certificate, usually the result of part-time study.[111] To put the performance of the British 'tecs' in 1953–54 into perspective, their grand total of successful students, at 7,963, was less than the 1937 output from the German *Fachschulen* alone of 9,101 students with the *Erfolg*, to say nothing of the over 2,000 qualified engineers annually produced in the 1930s by the forty-six German engineer schools.[112]

The combined yearly output from British universities and technical colleges of some 10,000 holders of degrees, diplomas or national certificates in technological subjects appears even less adequate when compared with America's annual production in the early 1950s of around 50,000 graduate engineers alone.[113]

It might be pleaded that the output of 'scientists' by British universities in 1955–56, at 4,200 gainers of first- and post-graduate degrees[114] to Germany's 3,527 diplomas and doctorates, went a fair way to make up for Britain's lower output of degree-level technologists – especially since there must be considerable functional overlap between the two statistical categories. It might also be pleaded that it had been a creditable achievement to double by the early 1950s the pre-war production of university-trained scientists. Nonetheless, in 1955–56 the production of 4,200 such scientists lagged 800 below the annual target set by the Barlow Committee in 1946, and anyway only around a quarter of them opted for careers in private industry.[115]

Moreover, of those technologists (wherever trained) who did

choose to enter private or nationalized industry too few were prepared to make a career in actual production rather than in research or the design office. So groaned the Ministry of Education in 1953. The Ministry partly attributed this reluctance to the failure of 'sandwich courses' to fulfil their purpose, thanks to lack of co-ordination between college teaching and industrial experience:

> To the best of our knowledge there is not a single integrated course of college study and industrial training in operation; nothing comparable, for example, with the course for chemical engineering at Massachusetts Institute of Technology which includes, in addition to studies at M.I.T., a planned course of practical training in a works under the control of a teacher who is on the staff of M.I.T. and who instructs and supervises the student in the works.[116]

In the autumn of 1954 the Committee on Scientific Manpower reported that the most serious shortages of trained talent lay in chemists, physicists, chemical engineers, mechanical engineers and electrical engineers. There existed (according to this committee) a particular scarcity of physicists to work in radio, radar and electronics, and this was causing defence and civil R&D programmes to fall behind schedule. In the case of aeronautical, automobile, gas, marine, and mining engineers – production engineers too – 'there has been a continuous and unsatisfied demand since the end of the war'.[117]

So no matter how the categories and the total numbers of the scientifically and technologically qualified are juggled, the final pay-off remains the same: Britain's output of these valuable items of human kit at the end of the post-war decade in no way matched the present and future needs of the first-class industrial and military power which her elite believed her to be.

Just as vain had proved the hopes of the Weir and Baillieu Committees after the end of the war that management and business administration might become in Britain the highly skilled professions that they had long been in America and Germany. In May 1952 the National Advisory Council for Education in Industry and Commerce (or NACEIC), one of those impotent bodies of well-meaning worthies so beloved by the British 'establishment', took note that management studies formed an integral part of first-degree engineering courses in the United States; that there was a 'considerable number' of independent courses in management at first- and second-degree level; and that American universities and industrial companies maintained close links with each other.[118] By way of contrast, the British Institute of Management published in October that year a lugubrious survey of what Britain herself was providing in this field.[119] Out of 125 university courses that touched however remotely on aspects of industry and management, as many as 100 included general economics, 84 economic history, 61 political theory and philosophy, but only 35 'management' as such.[120]

Nevertheless, it would have been un-British, not to say unacademic, to take swift action to remedy this lamentable record. For one thing, to have done so would have meant ditching the intellectual high-mindedness proper to high tables, where the spirit of Newman and Ruskin lived nobly on. According to the Chairman of the BIM, Sir Hugh Beaver (also Managing Director of Arthur Guinness, Son & Co.),

> the University view is certainly that 'Management', in so far as it is yet understood and comprehended, has not that 'intellectual content' which alone justifies consideration of it as a subject for a complete course for a chair or a degree.[121]

At an informal meeting between Beaver and the Chairman of the UGC in 1953 it was comfortably agreed that

> the whole question of Management Education is one in which no quick solution is possible, and the subject will have to be tackled by experimentation, and not by laying down any firm principles nationally at this stage.[122]

The prophecy of 'no quick solution' duly fulfilled itself. By 1958 the University Grants Committee got as far as opining (in its report on the quinquennium 1952–57) that 'the development of management as an academic discipline represents a worthwhile challenge . . .'[123] Five years on again, in a chapter entitled 'The Universities and National Needs', the 1963 Report by the UGC on the quinquennium 1957–1962 listed 'Management Studies' last among the disciplines which it took to be relevant to such needs, adding defensively:

> The universities have been criticised to an increasing extent in the
> last few years for their alleged failure to develop management studies.
> This is a subject to which a great deal of thought has been given, and
> is continuing to be given, in the universities.[124]

According to this 1963 report the UGC had enquired in 1960 of all
universities what courses they would be running in 1960–61 'in
management studies (including business or industrial administration,
personnel management and marketing), and in commerce. Particulars were also requested of any courses of a general character.'[125]
Back came a depressing answer:

> there were a few undergraduate courses leading to degrees in business
> or administrative studies, in business economics, in textile manage-
> ment, and so on, but in the main these were not widely patronised.[126]

Even by the early 1960s the number of students on full-time one-
or two-year degree or diploma courses in production engineering
and management, and in personnel and industrial administration as
well, would only have reached 200 for the entire country.[127]

And once again the local technical colleges could not make up
the difference. Only after five years of dithering discussions and
consultations was finally implemented a 1947 proposal (by yet
another Whitehall committee)[128] for part-time courses in management studies. In 1953–54 the scheme turned out a mere 450 students
with Intermediate Certificates and 177 with Diplomas.[129] Otherwise
a variety of institutions was running a random scatter of short
courses – could be one week, could be three months; could be part
time, could be full time – for a mixture of customers ranging from
senior managers down to foremen, and on such topics as work-
study, labour relations, and production control.[130]

When measured against the 'staggering'[131] flow of graduates in
management or business administration into American industry, the
combined British effort resembles a village shop up against Sears
Roebuck. In the United States during the academic year 1949–50
as many as 617 institutions of higher education were offering courses
in business and commerce, and they granted 76,530 degrees.[132] Over
the broader range of commercial and economic studies the German
Federal Republic too was well outstripping Britain. In 1955–56 the

number of her students in this field in universities or in *Hochschulen* exceeded the total for *all* the humanities in British universities.[133] Moreover, she turned out in that year 1,679 graduates in the career-related subject of 'business economics' alone.[134]

As for the British Institute of Management, so hopefully set up in 1947 for the purpose of persuading tradition-bound British companies that they needed professionally trained managers, its fundamental flaw was pointed out in March 1956 by the Minister of Education, David Eccles. 'To a considerable extent', he wrote, the BIM was being subsidized by 'large and efficient firms, who make relatively little use of it', while on the other hand it was getting 'only limited support from the small firms which, however, need most help and stand to gain most from a body of this kind . . .'[135]

When nonetheless recommending to his Cabinet colleagues that the Exchequer should continue to bail out the BIM for a limited period, Eccles drily observed that 'the general case for raising efficiency in management is no doubt as strong to-day (or even stronger) as it was in 1946 . . .'[136]

This double-barrelled comment neatly bagged two birds at once: the prevailing quality of present British managers, and Britain's failure after ten peacetime years to match America or even West Germany in the training of future managers. It was just one more botched post-war opportunity among so many.

Why had all the educational blueprints of 1944–6 simply ended up as age-foxed paper curling at the edges? First and foremost, it was because Labour and Conservative governments alike – and whatever their rhetoric about the importance of education – accorded low priority to turning these blueprints into accomplished fact. How else to explain why all three Ministers of Education between the departure of Butler in March 1945 and the appointment of David Eccles in November 1954 were second-raters, has-beens or never-would-bes?

By the time of Ellen Wilkinson's appointment by Attlee in 1945 all that remained of the blazing left-wing crusader she had once been in the 1920s and 1930s was a human clinker burned out by middle age and ill-health. Intellectually she personified the values of the Norwood Report, being a humanist educated at the then equivalent of a grammar school and at Manchester University under a renowned medieval historian.[137] She was far less concerned with Britain's future competitive efficiency as an industrial society than with education as an aspect of 'New Jerusalem', Hence her prime objective, achieved on 1 April 1947, lay in raising the school-leaving age to fifteen and thereby admitting all children to a secondary education of a kind. She died the same year of a drugs overdose.

Her successor, 'little George Tomlinson', in Attlee's words, a man who would give you 'the ordinary man's point of view',[138] had left elementary school aged twelve. A former weaver and Lancashire County Councillor, Tomlinson had long served as a trade union stalwart and willing Labour Party dray-horse. And he was succeeded in October 1951 by the sixty-one-year-old Miss Florence Horsbrugh, just as much of a dull but safe Party dray-horse, except this time a Conservative, appointed as Minister of Education by Winston Churchill on forming his first peacetime Cabinet.

Not one of the three provided the ruthless and magnetic leadership, inside and outside the Cabinet, that was needed to drive through the drastic remodelling called for by the blueprints. For a start, they altogether failed to develop the Barlow Committee's desired 'regional and national system . . . for knitting together the Schools, the Technical Colleges, the Higher Technical Institutes, the Universities and Industry' (see above, p. 459). In April 1951, just about the halfway point of the post-war decade, the Permanent Secretary at the Office of the Lord President of the Council (Sir Max Nicholson) was writing to Sir John Maude, his opposite number at the Department of Education, that what was needed was 'a clear Government statement, accepted by the Universities, the Technical Colleges and the professional bodies, of national policy, and of the parts which the various interests are intended to play'. Alongside the words 'national policy', Maude scribbled: 'Which?'[139] It was a good question.

The failure to create a rational, well-articulated system and a clear strategy proved fundamental. There continued to flourish the disastrous British tradition of ill-related educational agencies each jealously guarding their own professional patch and pursuing their own agenda. To the end of the post-war decade, for instance, the University Grants Committee and other donnish lobbyists fought for a monopoly over teaching degree-level technology, fearing that Percy's 'Royal Colleges of Technology' might yet be created with the right to award degrees rather than diplomas. All the arguments over the future structure of higher technological education that had gone round and round during the meetings of the Percy Committee continued to go round and round between 1948 and 1955 within such bodies as the National Advisory Council for Education in Industry and Commerce and its committees.[140] Other bodies meanwhile debated and debated what ought to be done to improve further and vocational education for school-leavers, with much the same suggestions bootlessly coming up year after year.[141] How little had actually been accomplished in this field since the war is shown by the recommendations made in January 1958 by the King George's Jubilee Trust. For the Trust wanted the long-promised County Colleges set up 'at the earliest possible moment' to educate youngsters from when they left school to age eighteen. It urged that day-release by employers should be made compulsory, and that the Youth Service should be strengthened.[142]

Even within the monkish precincts of academic learning itself there took place another prolonged, circular and unresolved debate, this time over the merits of early, and narrow, specialization from the sixth form onwards, as in England and Wales, compared with the broader curriculum of the European baccalaureate combining the humanities and the sciences.[143] Was it right that at fifteen years of age youngsters should have to make a virtually irrevocable choice between science and the arts? Was it right that, having made this choice, the scientist should be educated in ignorance of the humanities, and the arts student in ignorance of science and technology? Since, however, the raison d'être of the grammar school (and the public school) lay in getting their brightest into university, and best of all Oxford or Cambridge, it followed that their curricula were determined by the requirements of university entrance examinations. So to widen a grammar-school education would have necessarily meant also widening that of the universities: as easy a task as bending granite.[144] As things were, the blinkered specialization in English schools and universities only made sense if the ultimate aim of the whole system was to produce professional academics: better still, Fellows of the Royal Society and the British

Academy, perhaps even Nobel prizewinners. This high purpose in effect relegated the common ruck of the graduate output to the status of mere by-products.

Nevertheless, the failure to implement after ten years the brave blueprints of 1944–6 cannot only be blamed on the inability of educationalists to make up their own minds (let alone concur on common strategies) or even on their incorrigible factionalism. To turn the blueprints into reality required unstinted capital investment.

This investment Helen Wilkinson, George Tomlinson and Florence Horsbrugh failed to persuade their Cabinet colleagues to sanction. After all, Labour and Conservative governments alike had to find ways to offset the costs of the world-power game and the vote-winning welfare state, and it seemed just as good a wheeze to do without a first-class national education and training system as to do without modernized industries and infrastructure. Against this order of priorities the three Ministers of Education proved quite unable to prevail, protest though they might, win the occasional concession though they might.

The battle was lost from the start. The projected capital investment in education for 1947–48 failed to provide for the new school building needed to raise the leaving age to sixteen as planned, or to make day-release attendance at County Colleges compulsory, or to reduce the 1,000 classes with over fifty children in them, or to build separate secondary schools (where these did not at present exist) for children over ten instead of keeping them in 'all-age' schools from five to fifteen.[145] As for technical education, the Ministry of Education submitted to the Investment Programmes Committee a long-term investment programme of £80 million, which, it pleaded, was the minimum required if the country was to retain its competitive position in world markets.[146] But in the aftermath of the world premiere in 1947 of that long-running hit, the great sterling crisis, the figure was chopped down to £50 million.[147]

In 1948 it was planned to allot to technical education next year only £3 million worth of building work out of a projected total educational building budget of £43.75 million. That total was itself no larger than the sums spent in each of the two years before the war.[148] The bureaucrats of the IPC had to acknowledge that the expansion in the number of part-time and full-time students in technical colleges since the war had been carried out 'in makeshift conditions and even so the facilities available are quite inadequate to meet the effective demands . . .' They therefore urged on the politicians 'that a programme for the provision of adequate facilities for technical education should be pushed ahead with vigour . . . if necessary, at the expense of some other part of the social investment sector.'[149] And, yes, further and technical education's share of capital investment for that year was raised from £3 million to £4.3 million. Even so, this was only some 10 per cent more than allotted to new facilities for school meals: an extraordinary balance of priorities.[150]

In January 1949 the IPC took note that the problem of school buildings in Scotland was

> acute in some of the industrial areas where even deplorable buildings could not be replaced as the emphasis had to be placed on providing more school places . . . There were at present a number of areas in which children were unable to start school until the age of six years . . .[151]

Nevertheless, the same committee five months later dismissed as 'completely out of proportion' George Tomlinson's bid for an investment of £113 million in education in 1952–53, and instead recommended to ministers not so much more than half that: £71 million.[152] This time Tomlinson raised bitter objections, describing the proposed cut as 'disastrous' and arguing that the Ministry's own figure was 'a bare minimum' which left out the replacement of old and bad buildings, the extension of the youth service or the establishment of the County Colleges.[153] But all he could win from his ministerial colleagues was the minor concession that the £40 million capital-investment budget for 1950 recommended by the IPC bureaucrats should be raised to £49 million – only to have that £49 million sliced later by £5.5 million.

This time the blame for the cut lay with the second great balance-of-payments panic of the post-war era, which blew up in summer 1949 and compelled the devaluation of sterling.[154] For in the aftermath of the panic, and in order to relieve the overload on the economy, palliate inflation, and restore foreign confidence in the British economy and the pound, the Labour Cabinet slashed national expenditure across the board. Prominent in that butchery was capital investment in Britain's future strength as a technological nation, from schools and colleges to factories and telecommunications.[155] Yet – thanks to the domination of the Cabinet by neo-imperialists – there was still no question of radically shrinking the world role and with it the excessive burden of defence costs.[156] In vain was the enduring fallacy of post-war British defence policy summed up in November 1949 by Herbert Morrison, the Lord President of the Council: 'We are, in fact, in danger of paying more than we can afford for defences that are nevertheless inadequate, or even illusory.'[157]

Come January 1950 and the Ministry of Education was pleading afresh that

> in the present economic situation of the country the need for further technical education to assist in raising productivity was very pressing. It was necessary to meet the demands of small firms who in many cases had not even adequate accommodation to provide practical experience for their employees, quite apart from theoretical tuition.[158]

The universities were doing no better than technical colleges. Of the £80 million capital investment judged necessary in 1945 only £7.5 million of building work had so far been completed. Despite this grim backlog and the urgent need to complete schemes for science and technology, the IPC only recommended £4 million of capital investment in universities for 1950–51 and £4.5–£5 million for 1951–52.[159] At that rate it would take some fifteen years before British universities were anywhere near equipped to 'world's best practice'.

Over this already blighted scene of niggardly investment in the future capability of the British people there spread from 1950 onwards the new and devastating blight of the Korean War. For education could not escape the cuts in all areas of national investment inflicted by the Labour Government in order to make room for the greedy demands of the rearmament programme (see above, Chapter 2).[160] In April 1951 George Tomlinson was protesting that the total investment of £60 million in 1953 in England and Wales proposed by the civil-service big-wigs of the IPC (as against the £65 million budget put in by his department) was below 'the minimum amount of building work necessary to carry out our minimum policies at the lowest possible cost'.[161] Such a total, he told the Cabinet Production Committee in May 1951,

> would make it necessary to lower the school leaving age from 15 to 14 or, alternatively, to undertake no investment at all in technical education, which would be quite incompatible with the carrying out of the defence programme and the present high demand from industry.[162]

He asked for, and in September was granted, £63 million:[163] big deal. In that same month the Labour Government published a White Paper[164] putting forward schemes for the piecemeal long-term development of higher technological education, but rejecting the idea of a new technological university à la MIT on the grounds of cost. While admitting that 'much new building is still needed', the White Paper tamely accepted that developments in the field would be 'limited by available resources' – really meaning the resources that government would choose to make available after other demands had been indulged.

The economic tempest of winter 1951–2, with Britain on her beam ends and yet again perilously close to the rocks of bankruptcy, ensured that capital investment in education would be more than ever 'limited by available resources'.[165] For in December 1951 R. A. Butler as Chancellor and Florence Horsbrugh as Minister of Education in Churchill's new government agreed to reduce the investment programme for the period 1952–58 in England and Wales from £468 million to £378 million. Scotland was to suffer in due proportion.[166] This was less of a 'cut' than a progressively deeper and more disabling long-term wound.

An early slash with the knife dispatched the proposal for a new technological university. Like their Labour predecessors, the Conservatives decided not to proceed with this at the present time because of lack of resources – and despite a powerful plea from Lord Cherwell that unless Britain caught up with other countries in the production of first-rate technologists, 'the future of our industry, especially in export markets, is black.'[167] Instead a bit more money was to be trickled into existing universities and technical colleges.[168]

In November 1952, almost a year after Butler's decision to chop the long-term investment programme, the need for extra school places in new towns and in the new housing estates being run up by Macmillan as Minister of Housing compelled the Government to enlarge the ration of capital investment for 1953 from £60.5 million to £62.2 million. But this did nothing for further and technical education, as the mandarins on the Investment Programmes Committee complained:

> The present programme was a very restricted one directed solely to projects which would help to increase technological efficiency and so lead to increased productivity and exports. Any cut in this sector would be difficult to justify or operate in view of the emphasis on increased productivity in industry.[169]

Ten months later the House of Commons Select Committee on Estimates returned a blistering indictment of both the post-war governments for failing to invest in education on the scale long known to be necessary.[170] They noted that back in 1947 the Ministry of Education, recognizing that 'for the most part there is a very great dearth of social and educational accommodation of every kind, from college to village hall', had asserted that it was time 'to plan boldly and comprehensively'.[171] In particular, it had by then become apparent, wrote the Select Committee, that much more money would have to be spent annually on further and technical education 'if developments in certain European and other countries were to be equalled or overtaken . . .'[172] Instead, and because of governmental tightfistedness, 'the position is still roughly the same as it was in 1947', with many of the present technical college buildings falling short 'of the requirements necessary for good educational instruction'. In the case of the Birmingham Technical College, at the centre of the Midlands automobile and engineering industries, noted the Select Committee:

> Experimental work in the internal combustion engine department has sometimes had to be stopped in bad weather, owing to the need for covering the machines with tarpaulins to protect them from the rain.[173]

The Select Committee plainly did not believe that ministers had yet repented of their past neglect: 'It is clear that the prospect of

478

replacing many of the unsatisfactory technical school buildings does not appear to be envisaged now for many years.'[174] Though five technical colleges were building, only one (in Norwich) had so far been completed since the war.[175]

The Select Committee clinched their indictment with some simple but telling arithmetic. In 1949 it had been estimated that 'a total post-war investment of the order of £50,000,000 [by 1959–60] would be necessary before the country could claim that it had minimum facilities for technical education'. But in terms of major building work, only about half that total, £26,083,000, had been approved and started between 1 January 1948 and 31 March 1954. Given that inflation had raised the original estimate of £50 million to £75 million, and given the past and present rate of investment, it was clear that the complete programme for producing minimum facilities 'cannot be put in hand by 1959–1960 as had been hoped'.[176]

But even this blast failed to propel the Conservative Cabinet forward in the right direction. Instead they decided in July 1954 to cut the planned building programme for higher technological education courses for 1955–56 by up to half:[177] one item in a chipping of bits off all public expenditure, from the NHS to defence. Why this fresh recourse to the old routine? The Cabinet was alarmed at a prospective budget deficit in 1955 so large as to necessitate an increase in taxation.[178] Only in November 1954 were the limits on new building starts in technical education as a whole for 1955–56 raised from some £4.5 million to £7.5 million.[179] Yet this was still a tiny rate of annual investment when measured against the scale of the problem posed by too few technical institutions, and these being cut-price and second-class by European standards even when built between the world wars or earlier still. To put this rate in perspective, however, *total* capital investment in the education system in England and Wales in 1956–57 – the youth service, all types of school, all further-education and technical colleges, all universities – would stand at £65 million,[180] which, after allowing for inflation, was about the same as in 1953. This meagre sum may be compared with the £40 million of public funds to be lavished in 1956–57 on 'free' school meals.[181]

The scale of the British educational backlog[182] and its impact on Britain's industrial competitiveness were fully grasped by the new

Minister of Education appointed in November 1954. In contrast to the worthy but dreary Horsbrugh, David Eccles – tall, sleek of head, handsome of visage – brought to the Ministry of Education a personal and intellectual elegance buffed to a high shine at Winchester and New College, Oxford. He also brought to the job a well-whetted ambition and a genuine zeal for drastic reform. Above all, he was seized of the importance of a functionally logical 'wiring-diagram' and a coherent long-term strategy:

> We have to pull into rational groups the existing scattered facilities for technical education, i.e., building up a few regional colleges doing advanced work surrounded by satellite colleges doing work of a lower level. To carry through such plans we need to see our way ahead. This is particularly so because of the complexity of the negotiations with Local Authorities and with industry.[183]

In 1955 he set forth an inquiry into future needs in technical education in England and Wales and the total capital costs of meeting them. The resulting report of September 1955 calculated these costs at £72 million, of which some £25 million was required for newly built colleges to replace old premises and for the development of existing technical institutes into full technological colleges.[184] Although the Government had agreed to lift expenditure on new building starts for 1956–57 to £9 million, Eccles made plain that this was still not nearly enough: 'if we continue at this annual rate we shall not solve our problems as quickly as we must. Many of our technical colleges have old and inadequate buildings . . .'[185] He therefore urged on the Cabinet that they should launch a programme of some £85 million (including £15 million for equipment), all of it to be started within five years.[186] His proposed programme included selecting and developing 'some twenty-five regional colleges where advanced technology would be taught up to university standards. Each such college would be the centre of a group of satellite colleges, planned to suit industry.'

In February 1956 Eccles's five-year-plan was published as a White Paper, *Technical Education*.[187] Admirably bold though the plan was, it nonetheless signified that a decade after the Percy and Barlow reports Britain had still got no further than the stage of blueprints.[188] The proposed 'Royal Colleges of Technology' would not become operational before 1964 – a lapse of almost twenty years since Percy had first proposed such institutions.[189]

Of all the squandered post-war opportunities to break the chains of history the most disastrous in the long-term must be the failure to turn the wartime blueprints for education and training into reality. For the 'system' as it remained in the mid-1950s and its human output – Britain's future leaders and led – together serve as a fresh set of tarot cards, this time foretelling Britain's defeats and retreats during the decades to come.

But no tarot cards gave warning that, before the year 1956 was out, a new war would submit Britain's national pretensions to judgement, and her power in the world to audit.

23. The Reckoning

On 26 July 1956 President Nasser of Egypt nationalized the Suez Canal Company, giving him control over the key bottleneck in Britain's historic route to her Indian Empire. But that Empire had been dumped in 1947. Nonetheless, British politicians and their advisers in uniform and plain clothes had ever since continued to be strategically obsessed with the route and with the geographical region that surrounded it. They had done so partly out of sheer habit, partly for reasons still current. Certainly the Canal offered a convenient short cut for the tankers plying to and from the oil terminals of the Persian Gulf. Certainly it provided the quickest sea passage to Britain's tin-and-rubber-rich colony of Malaya, the naval base at Singapore, and, beyond, Australia and New Zealand. Nonetheless, the experience of the Second World War had shown that the Suez Canal–Red Sea route was by no means indispensable, and that the long route round the Cape could serve adequately enough. In any case, however, Nasser had only nationalized the company; he had not blocked the Canal. And, unless provoked, why should he ever do so when it offered a source of much profit to a poor country?[1]

Nevertheless, the British and French governments were outraged at Nasser's cheek in nationalizing a private joint-stock company in which Britain held 42 per cent of the shares and which was predominantly French 'in character and style',[2] with its headquarters in Paris. On 27 July Britain and France lodged formal protests in Cairo: the first steps in an intricate round dance of international diplomacy prancing on through October. Among the steps to be clumsily performed was the setting up of a 'Suez Canal Users'

Association' in the hope of collectively impressing Nasser; a couple of conferences in London; and, of all proven fatuities, a démarche at the United Nations. The twists, twirls and turns are depressingly reminiscent of those executed by London after the Iranian Prime Minister Mossadeq nationalized the assets of the Anglo-Iranian Oil Company in 1951 (see above, Chapter 5). This time, however, Anthony Eden, in a high state of indignation, persuaded his Cabinet right at the start that if need be they would substitute guns for notes as instruments of diplomacy: very Clausewitzian.

In the imagination of Eden himself – a man vain, weakly handsome, petulant, strung-up, with a smile that verged on a simper, the very picture of an effete aristocrat[3] – the ghosts of Hitler and Mussolini (certainly Mussolini) were walking in the guise of Nasser. Was this not the beginning of a new sequence of aggression, just like Mussolini's attack on Abyssinia in 1935? At that time Eden, as Minister without Portfolio for League of Nations Affairs in Stanley Baldwin's government, had urged in vain that Britain must support the League in resisting this aggression, at the risk of war if need be. Now he was Prime Minister, free and able to act as he could not twenty years earlier. Throughout the unfolding Suez crisis, therefore, history was to gibber at his shoulder.

On 27 July Eden signalled President Eisenhower that Britain 'must be ready, in the last resort, to use force to bring Nasser to his senses'. He went on: 'I have this morning instructed our Chiefs of Staff to prepare a military plan accordingly.' He explained to the President that if Nasser were allowed to get away with it, 'our influence and yours throughout the Middle East will, we are convinced, be finally destroyed'.[4]

'Influence!' – it had been Ernest Bevin's favourite word as Foreign Secretary in the late 1940s, particularly in regard to the Mediterranean and Middle East: a favourite too of Anthony Eden as his Conservative successor at the Foreign Office in 1951–5. Here it was again, uttered now by Eden at the head of a government. No matter whether or not 'influence' had actually promoted the wealth and security of the British people at home, it supplied the real reason why Britain in 1956 was still clinging on to her Middle Eastern strategic 'cowpat', consisting of an armoured division and an air base in Libya; air bases and squadrons in Iraq; the vast military installations of the evacuated former Middle East main base in the Suez Canal Zone now under care and maintenance by the construction company Wimpey; the crown colony of Cyprus and its new Middle East main base; the Nelsonian naval bases of Gibraltar and Malta; and a Mediterranean Fleet.

And it had been for the sake of exercising 'influence' in world affairs beyond the NATO area that the share of GNP spent on defence per annum by Britain since 1945 had never dropped below 8 per cent, and in 1955–56 was still standing at just over 9 per cent – twice the average for the other European members of NATO. Similarly, the hankering after 'influence' had induced Britain to sign up for defence obligations in the South-West Pacific under the ANZAM pact with Australia and New Zealand, those prominent members of the 'old' Commonwealth.

In turn, it was for the sake of the Commonwealth connection, Imperial Preference, and the Sterling Area (those presumed buttresses of Britain's presumed status as a world power) that Eden's Government in November 1955 had rejected the idea of joining, and thereby shaping, the supra-national European 'common market' then being negotiated by the six members of the European Iron and Steel Community.[5] Let the French and the Germans get on with it; and anyway it was quite possible, so Whitehall comforted itself, that they would fail to make a go of it and the whole project would collapse.[6] For was it not Britain's status as an independent great power at the centre of the Commonwealth, was it not her military strength derived from the post-Korea rearmament programme, that confirmed her as America's principal partner in world affairs? That cemented the 'special relationship'?

Confident in their grandiose vision of Britain in the world, Eden and his Cabinet plotted to topple Nasser off his perch.[7] Step by step, however, the unfolding crisis was cruelly to reveal the vision to be a fantasy born of nostalgia.

In the first place, Britain at the outset of the crisis lacked the ready military means either at home or in the Middle East even to knock over a backward country like Egypt. When contingency planning began for Operation Musketeer ('Pop-gun' would have been more apt), an amphibious landing at Port Said and an advance down the Suez Canal, a sorry scene was revealed. The army's

Strategic Reserve in the United Kingdom was, according to a historian of the Suez adventure, 'dispersed, disaggregated, under-trained, on leave, with obsolescent equipment well below strength'.[8] The infantry units eventually dispatched to the Mediterranean had to leave behind their new anti-tank guns because of insufficient ammunition, and instead took Second World War design 17-pounders known to be ineffective against the armour of the tanks supplied by the Soviet Union to Egypt. For want of transporters, the tanks of the armoured brigade had to be taken to the embarkation ports courtesy of Pickfords, the removal firm.[9] Only two Landing Ships Tank were in commission, and the remaining thirty that made up Britain's total strength in these vessels had to be extricated from 'moth-balls' and rendered seaworthy. No more than fourteen could be made ready in time to load the Centurion tanks, so limiting to a mere ninety-three the number that could be taken to the Mediterranean.[10] In fact, there existed a desperate shortage of landing craft of all types. This determined the possible scale and location of an amphibious assault.

Yet all these deficiencies merely constituted the major items in a list covering every kind of military kit big and small.

The Royal Air Force was hardly better off. In July 1956 its first squadron of twenty-one V-bombers (Vickers Valiants) were still in the stage of forming, and due to production delays – what was new? – had not been equipped with their advanced electronic bomb-aiming equipment. Instead a substitute visual device had to be quickly shoved in. Although there were two hundred Canberra light bombers available, their own electronic blind-bombing kit could not be used in the Mediterranean theatre because the system had to be in range of two separate radio beacons. In any case, by no means all the Canberras could be deployed because of a shortage of enough airfields within striking distance of Egypt.[11] So the Royal Navy's carriers in the Mediterranean would have to provide much of the airpower that would bomb Egyptian targets and cover the seaborne expeditionary force against enemy attack.

Yet the navy too had its problems. At home the oxyacetylene cutters, welders and fitters were hard at work converting two escort carriers into emergency troopships complete with bunks, and later stripping out the bunks again in one ship to make room for helicopters. An operating theatre and other medical facilities were hastily installed in what might have to be used as a hospital ship.[12]

This ramshackle, rusty and unready military machine marks the bankruptcy of the defence policy so stubbornly pursued by Labour and Conservative cabinets alike, and specifically intended to support the world role as well as defend Western Europe. As an end-product of the £4.6 billion post-Korea rearmament programme and of defence expenditure averaging 8 per cent of GNP since 1946 and 9.8 per cent since 1951, it entirely vindicates Herbert Morrison's warning seven years earlier that we were 'in danger of paying more than we can afford for defences that are nevertheless inadequate . . .'

And when the actual planning of Operation Musketeer began, the costly Middle East strategic 'cowpat' was itself revealed as operationally near to useless. Cyprus had been chosen as the new Middle East main base even though it lacked a deep-water harbour, a disadvantage well recognized during the Second World War.[13] In consequence, the troopships, Landing Craft Tank, and escorting warships would have to be assembled in Malta's Grand Harbour, more than 900 miles from Port Said. At the start of the crisis only one air base on Cyprus (at Nicosia) was operational, though in the midst of reconstruction. An undeveloped relief airfield was liable to waterlogging in wet weather, and had to be hardcored and asphalted in great haste and at much logistical inconvenience. The main runway of the new air base at Akrotiri only became usable in August.[14]

The 10th Armoured Division stationed in Libya (actually little stronger than an armoured brigade) had been regarded by successive foreign secretaries, ministers of defence and Chiefs of Staff ever since the Second World War as an essential buttress to Britain's position in the Middle East – a position in turn regarded by all these worthies, and especially by Eden now, as the key to preserving her status as a world power.[15] The division was operationally capable (though with logistic difficulty) of invading Egypt from the West along Field-Marshal Rommel's old axis of advance. Nevertheless, it quickly became clear that to deploy it in battle would in all likelihood be politically out of the question. Even moving the division to eastern Cyrenaica for 'training exercises' had to be ruled out, since under treaty Libya's permission would be required, and to ask for it in the present crisis would provoke outrage from her government and people.[16]

This was surely the hour of need when the vast current and capital expenditure punted by politicians on the Middle East 'cow-pat' over the last ten years should have paid a handsome strategic dividend. Instead the payout was proving paltry indeed. The politicians in their dreams of grandeur had simply invested in a dud stock.

What about support for Britain in the present crisis from members of the Commonwealth, that cherished figment of British romancing, especially from the 'old' Commonwealth, and, more especially still, from Britain's co-signatories of the ANZAM Pact? After all, policy-making by British governments and their advisers had long been characterized by a high sense of moral responsibility for the defence as well as the financial and economic welfare of Commonwealth nations. Perhaps they might now recognize some reciprocal obligation? But the Commonwealth nations stood well back, like prudent men who see a friend rashly getting into a messy and potentially violent quarrel in a bar. Even Robert Menzies, the Australian Prime Minister whom London had long seen as a true Brit in sentiment and sympathy, advised against the use of force by Britain: by *Britain*, note – no question of Australian military involvement.[17] Only Sidney Holland, Prime Minister of New Zealand, responded as Eden had hoped, at least in words: 'I was able to tell Sir Anthony Eden . . . that Britain could count on New Zealand standing by her through thick and thin . . .'[18] This heartwarming message did not include, however, the promise of any troops. Could at least the cruiser HMNZS *Royalist*, at present training with the Mediterranean Fleet, take part in bombarding operations and air defence if the crisis should come to war? While Holland gave his consent to the ship remaining with the fleet, he insisted on a remarkable cavil, as the Admiralty signalled the C-in-C, Mediterranean: 'Mr. Holland is most anxious that this offer should not be known on any account and, if challenged, intends to deny it.'[19]

In short, the Commonwealth was proving about as valueless in terms of diplomatic and military support for Britain as it had during the Munich crisis in 1938. As always since the Great War the Commonwealth remained for Britain an entanglement, not a source of strength.

But what about the other 'special relationship' also sentimentally cherished by the British elite, and which since the catastrophe of 1940 had provided the guiding compass of British foreign policy? After all, Britain had turned out for America's war in Korea, even if under ruthless American pressure, and thereafter had embarked – even if under equally ruthless pressure – on a rearmament programme which her economy could ill support, and which rendered her vulnerable at a crucial time to reviving foreign competition in world markets. Could she now hope, if not for America's support, then at the very least for her forbearance, should the present crisis threaten to deepen into war?

She could not. John Foster Dulles, the Secretary of State, that ornament of the North American branch of Anglo-Saxon puritan priggishness, made it clear that he disapproved of the use of force even if Nasser blocked traffic through the Canal. In such a case the United States, said he at a press conference in September, would simply divert its own vessels round the Cape.[20] President Eisenhower was equally strong for the rule of international law and the avoidance of force. Asked by a reporter on 15 September whether America would back Britain and France if they finally went to war, he replied:

> I don't know exactly what you mean by 'backing them'. As you know this country will not go to war ever while I am occupying my present post, unless the Congress is called into session and Congress declares such a war. Now, if, after all peaceful means are exhausted, there is some kind of aggression on the part of Egypt against a peaceful use of the Canal, you might say that we would recognize that Britain and France had no other recourse than to continue to use it even if they had to be more forceful than merely sailing through it.[21]

Would Britain and France, he was asked, be justified in using force to restore a management acceptable to non-Egyptian employees? Eisenhower answered that though they had rights under the 1888 Treaty, this did not entitle them to use force: 'I think this. We established the UN to abolish aggression and I am not going to be a party to aggression if it is humanly possible.'[22] In short, since the American Government did not perceive United States interests to be involved, a Wilsonian regard for moral conduct and the international order could prevail. The 'special relationship' had turned out to be yet another of Britain's busted flushes of 1956.

As is the case with intimate relationships gone a bit sour, the party who had it in mind to be naughty henceforth kept his intentions concealed from the party who would be sure to disapprove. But, again as in such cases, the deceived soon came to realize that something dubious was going on, which only made them – meaning, in the present imbroglio, the American leadership – all the crosser. They were later to wreak their revenge.

For British ministers were flirting (to say the least) with the French Government. It is indeed a wondrous irony that in the Suez crisis Eden found his staunchest ally in France – the country which in 1955 Britain, for the sake of her special relationships with the Commonwealth and America, had contemptuously[23] refused to join in creating a European 'common market'.

On 15 September 1956 the British and French Governments, in an act of spectacular stupidity, did their best themselves to stop traffic through the Canal, by withdrawing all their specialist pilots. It was their arrogant belief that this would demonstrate to the world that the backward Egyptians could not run the enterprise they had nationalized. To Franco-British chagrin the Egyptians simply hired pilots from other nations to supplement their own, and the merchant ships and tankers steamed though as usual.

Britain's new French connection raised up, however, issues older and deeper than the current state of bankruptcy of the foreign and defence policy pursued by Britain since the Second World War. Unlike British cabinets (including Eden's own) or the dignitaries of the Foreign Office, the inhabitants of the Palais Matignon and the quai d'Orsay were not the small 'l' liberal heirs of a moral revolution wrought by Victorian Christianity and consolidated ever since by the public school, Oxbridge and the Nonconformist chapel.[24] Even the puny and transient prime ministers and foreign ministers of the Fourth Republic – in the present case, Guy Mollet and Christian Pineau – remained true to the operating principle of state policy as practised by Talleyrand or Richelieu or Louis XIV himself: pursuit of the interests of France by whatever means seems useful at the time.

The French therefore felt no qualms about secretly concocting with the Israelis a plan for a joint attack on Egypt. It made brilliant military sense: immediately after the Israeli army had launched an offensive westwards across the Sinai towards the Suez Canal, the French (and the British) would land at Port Said and take the Egyptian army in flank. The threat of an Egyptian invasion of Israel would be eliminated; Britain and France would regain physical control of the Suez Canal; and, a bonus, Britain could re-occupy her huge main base in the Canal Zone. The supreme prize would lie in the downfall of Nasser himself in the wake of so great a national disaster and humiliation. What could be more mutually profitable?

The deal between the French and the Israelis was struck in Paris on 1 October 1956. An eighteenth-century British cabinet would not have hesitated to join in. Indeed, in its secrecy and unscrupulousness the Franco-Israeli deal had much in common with the kind of tactics employed by Sir Alfred Milner, the British High Commissioner in South Africa in 1899, in preparing the way for a war against the Boer republics. In contrast, Eden's cabinet was riven by moral squeamishness; so too were the house prefects of the Foreign Office.

The irony lay in that the political and psychological shackles which the morally squeamish now found so uncomfortable had been forged by themselves. It was they and their predecessors who since 1918 had brought about the prevailing climate of opinion in which a state's naked pursuit of self-interest, if necessary by armed diplomacy, if necessary by war, was deemed a sin, even a crime. In furtherance of their romantic vision that a 'world community' ruled by law could, and would, replace the existing world arena of group struggle, they and their predecessors had first created the flimsy League of Nations and its futile Covenant, and then, after the Second World War, the United Nations Organization and its Charter. Since this document outlawed war except in clear cases of self-defence, it now supplied an peculiarly uncomfortable shackle for Britain, for here she was, a Permanent Member of the UN Security Council and yet secretly plotting to revert to realpolitik.

Eden as Prime Minister marvellously personified these ambiguities, being himself a pre-war moralizing internationalist and apostle of the League of Nations, and a statesman-founder of the United Nations Organization. Who can wonder that in the present crisis he was so edgy and indecisive? His were the dithers of a bishop nerving himself to enter a brothel.

The French deal with the Israelis was followed by a fortnight and longer of complicated and confused negotiations in London and Paris that more resembled the backstairs intrigues and secret treaties of the Stuart or Elizabethan eras than the soberly respectable diplomacy of the mid-twentieth century Foreign Office. The French Chief of Staff, General Maurice Challe, visited Chequers in civilian clothes as plain M. Challe, though not, so far as is known, wrapped in a cloak and wearing a mask. Officials were barred from delicate personal meetings between British and French ministers. The Foreign Secretary, poor dogged, decent, self-doubting Selwyn Lloyd, the honest son of a teetotal and strict Methodist family, was in the uneasy situation of a country solicitor who suddenly finds himself negotiating a big but shady deal with high-powered corporate lawyers. In short, where once a Castlereagh, a Palmerston, a Salisbury and an Edward Grey had self-confidently conducted the foreign policy of a truly great power, there now held sway a ludicrous blend of melodrama and farce. Nevertheless, the deed was done: on 16 October Eden committed Britain to the Franco-Israeli conspiracy. For obvious reasons the conspiracy remained in the highest degree secret. Nonetheless, on 24 October that Britain was soon to attack Egypt was helpfully leaked to the American Ambassador in London by that arch-appeaser and all-purpose cringer in the face of trouble, Walter Monckton.

The plotting being finished, the war could start as soon as the players were ready. At 0500 (local time) on 29 October the Israelis began their offensive with a parachute drop only forty-five miles from the town of Suez. It was the prelude to a blitzkrieg which smashed the Egyptian army in the Sinai to pieces and swept on towards the Canal. Next day France and Britain presented Israel and Egypt with an ultimatum to pull back their forces ten miles from the Suez Canal. The Egyptians, however, were also called upon to accept 'the temporary occupation by Anglo-French forces of key positions at Port Said, Ismailia and Suez'.[25] In the case of failure of the combatants to comply within twelve hours (a certainty in the case of Egypt), 'U.K. and French forces will intervene in whatever strength may be necessary'.[26]

According to the cover story trotted out first in the ultimatum and then repeated by Eden in the House of Commons and by the British representative on the Security Council (a haplessly embarrassed Sir Pierson Dixon), Britain and France were simply intervening to end hostilities between Israel and Egypt, and secure safe passage through the Canal. The story deceived no one.[27] In the Security Council the United States, in the sanctimonious person of Cabot Lodge, moved a resolution calling for an immediate Israeli–Egyptian ceasefire. Since this would have deprived Britain and France of their war, they vetoed it. It was the first time Britain had ever used her veto.

Already, on 27–28 October, the Anglo-French amphibious task forces, some 80,000 men strong, had begun to put to sea from Malta and Algiers. By the night of the 31st three British aircraft carriers and one French, with escorting cruisers and destroyers, were on station fifty miles off Port Said, uncomfortably shadowed by the immensely more powerful American Sixth Fleet. That same night Royal Air Force aircraft from Cyprus opened the bombing offensive against Egyptian targets. The old allies who in their former heyday as great powers in 1914–18 had defeated the might of Imperial Germany were again together going to war; and in Egypt, a backward country of poverty-stricken peasants, they were attacking a foe in keeping with their now shrunken sinews.

Yet Operation Musketeer in itself constituted only one of the components in what ought to have been a well-balanced total strategy: components neglected or mishandled by Eden in his jumpy, tetchy obsession with toppling Nasser. In the first place, if Musketeer did not suffer a flash in the pan but succeeded in hitting its target of reaching Suez at the southern end of the Canal, what then? How long would a 'temporary' allied occupation last? The 'temporary' occupation inaugurated in 1882 by Sir Garnet Wolseley's victory at Tel el Kebir had endured for seventy-four years. What size of garrison would be required even in the short term? Britain could be saddled with a costly and open-ended commitment. As not infrequently in twentieth-century British history, it was the military men, the Chiefs of Staff, who displayed a greater degree of practical common sense and foresight than many politicians or indeed civil servants.[28] On 25 October they had pointed out to ministers that the occupiers were bound to inherit a 'seriously damaged' Egyptian economy, with communications largely disrupted and disease rife.[29] If the question later arose of enforcing a change of government in Cairo and then supporting the new regime, a force of three to four divisions would be needed. This would indefinitely cut down the Rhine army facing the Soviet threat in Germany by one division and consume the Strategic Reserve in the United Kingdom. There would be nothing left to meet Britain's other global commitments in the event of trouble.[30]

Musketeer's land-force commander, General Sir Charles Keightley, raised similar doubts with Eden personally: was Britain going to be better off after a successful operation? It was a good question: the one question in all the debate, public and secret, about the proposed adventure that needed to be asked. By way of an answer, so Keightley later told Lord Mountbatten, 'Eden gave him (Keightley) a very severe dressing down and told him that these were questions with which military commanders should not concern themselves.'[31]

A crucial factor in a nation's total strategy, especially during the run-up to a war, now lay in the attitude of public opinion at home and abroad. This Eden and his colleagues failed to comprehend sufficiently, even though Musketeer and its preliminaries were taking place under the arc-lights of democracy and before the rolling television and newsreel cameras. Certainly Eden, an old-fashioned grandee, tried the old-fashioned 'establishment' method of exerting pressure behind the scenes on fellow grandees in the media: newspaper proprietors and editors, and the Director-General of the BBC. But there took place no sustained attempt to mobilize a popular consensus by means of the kind of propaganda mounted by the old wartime Ministry of Information.

Instead, as the weeks passed, public opinion shifted like shoal waters this way and that. On 10 August an opinion poll found that only a third of those interviewed were in favour of military action if diplomacy failed – even though nine out of ten did not think that Egypt could be trusted to keep the Canal open to all traffic.[32] On 31 August a Gallup poll in the *News Chronicle* found that 59 per cent of the people (77 per cent of Conservatives) approved of the Government's handling so far.[33] On 10 September Gallup found that 81 per cent of the public favoured going to the UN if Egypt would not agree to a plan put to her by a current conference in London. Only 34 per cent were in favour of a military ultimatum if the UN could not come up with a solution, and 49 per cent were against.[34] On the same day a separate *Daily Express* poll found that approval of Eden's personal handling of the crisis had slumped from 43 per cent in August to only 25 per cent, while disapproval had risen from 33 per cent to 57 per cent.[35] Eden was losing a battle on the home front before the first shot had been fired at Port Said.

Back in August even the Labour and Liberal parties and their newspapers had thought that right lay on Britain's side rather than Nasser's. They saw his unilateral seizure of the Canal as violating the spirit, if not the letter, of international law and the new world order. But when it became more and more plain what kind of deed France and Britain were getting ready to perpetrate, small 'l' liberals in Parliament and the media – not to say the intelligentsia – began to flush pink with moral indignation, always with them a source of pleasurable excitement.

The Anglo-French ultimatum on 30 October, so obviously the prelude to war, finally split national opinion. The progressive intelligentsia's outrage at Eden's policy was pungently expressed by a manifesto signed by 335 Oxford academics:

> We consider this action is morally wrong, that it endangers the solidarity of the Commonwealth, that it constitutes a grave strain on the Atlantic alliance and that it is a flagrant violation of the principles of the U.N. Charter.[36]

Among the newspapers only Beaverbrook's *Daily Express*, in happy disregard of the power realities of 1956, took a line of simple romantic patriotism: 'Military action has a clear motive which will commend itself to all the people: To safeguard the life of the British Empire.' In the belief of the *Daily Mail*, 'so grave a decision was reached only in the deep, sincere conviction that, if we had remained quiescent, Britain and the whole world would have suffered irreparable damage'. The left-wing *Daily Mirror* proclaimed to its mass readership: 'This is Eden's war. It can achieve nothing, it can settle nothing.' According to the Labour movement's own newspaper, the *Daily Herald*, 'The voice of the British people must din in the Government's ears the demand to call off this lunatic aggression.' *The Economist* shrewdly reckoned that the manner 'in which the crisis has been handled suggests a strange union of cynicism and hysteria in [Britain's] leaders'. *The Times*, in the pen of the editor, Sir William Haley, reproved Eden and Co. for misleading Britain's ally America.[37]

Yet it was an editorial in the *Observer*, the voice of the 'enlightened' establishment, which on 4 November 1956 most unequivocally based its condemnation of the Government on the issue of right and wrong rather than on the kind of practical concerns raised by Keightley and the Chiefs of Staff.[38] The editorial was written by Dingle Foot (son of Isaac Foot, the former Liberal MP, former President of the Liberal Party, and former Vice-President of the Methodist Church), and himself a one-time Liberal MP who had joined the Labour Party in July 1956. 'We had not realised', lamented this editorial, 'that our Government was capable of such folly and such crookedness . . .' Whatever the government now did, it 'can never live down the dishonest nature of its ultimatum, so framed that it was certain to be rejected by Egypt'. In the eyes of the whole world the British and French Governments 'have acted not as policemen but as gangsters'. The *Observer* combined these denunciations with a passionate sermon:

> Ever since 1945, there have been two cardinal features of British external policy. The first has been to uphold the rule of law with special reference to the United Nations. The second has been the steady progress away from imperialism, exemplified in the full emancipation of Burma, India, Pakistan, West Africa and the West Indies.

And:

> The Eden administration has shown that it does not understand the sort of world we live in. It is no longer possible to bomb countries because you fear that your trading interests will be harmed . . .

And:

Nowadays, a drowning man on a raft is the occasion for all shipping to be diverted to try to save him; this new feeling for the sanctity of human life is the best element of the modern world. It is the true distinction of the West . . .[39]

This exercise in hand-wringing could hardly be bettered as a statement of the small 'l' liberal outlook on world affairs now shared not only by the Liberal and Labour parties but also by many Conservatives. When on 3 November 1956, in a last-minute attempt to rally the nation, Anthony Eden spoke on BBC television – a flickery black-and-white image of Ronald Colman features adorned with officer's 'tache', an aristocratic drawl so fruity as to verge on parody – he shrewdly (but no doubt sincerely) sought to persuade his audience that his attack on Egypt was motivated by the purest of internationalist motives:

All my life, I've been a man of peace, working for peace, striving for peace, negotiating for peace. I've been a League of Nations man and a United Nations man and I'm still the same man with the same convictions, the same devotion to peace. I couldn't be other even if I wished. But I'm utterly convinced that the action we have taken is right.[40]

'Peace'! As he spoke, the allied forces were approaching the beaches and the bombs were continuing to explode on targets round Cairo and elsewhere. Even Gladstone, the founding father of liberal piety, had felt able to dispatch an expeditionary force to Egypt in 1882 in furtherance of British interests without having to resort to such hypocrisy. On 4 November Hugh Gaitskell, replying on television as Leader of the Opposition, tore Eden's flimsy cover-story apart: 'Make no mistake about it – this is war . . . it is not a police action, there is no law behind it – we have taken the law into our own hands.'[41]

In a troopship steaming towards Port Said – and no doubt in other ships too – men listened to Gaitskell's broadcast (so recalled the journalist Anthony Howard, then a National Service subaltern) with 'such expressions of fury and disgust and revulsion as I have rarely seen among grown men . . .'[42] They regarded Gaitskell quite simply as a traitor at a moment when they were about to go into battle against 'the wogs'.[43] They had not appreciated that their brand of simple 'Britain-first' patriotism was now out of fashion. Their angry voices went unheard. The small 'l' liberal elite, the 'enlightened' establishment, had once again presumed to speak for Britain. Their success in so doing may be taken to confirm the final triumph of righteousness over realpolitik, of sentiment over strategy, as the inspiration of British foreign policy.

The want of national unity[44] was serious enough. But what about the absolutely vital component of total strategy in time of war – economic and financial strength?

As ever, the health of the pound sterling and the reserves depended on the state of the balance of payments, which in turn so much depended on the performance of British exports. All through 1954 and 1955 and into 1956 ministers and civil servants had monitored this performance with mounting anxiety as Britain steadily lost ground in world markets to foreign competition.[45] As a working party on 'Export Trends' groaned in the autumn of 1955: 'Measured against the needs of the balance of payments, our recent export performance has clearly been inadequate.'[46] But why? The Whitehall situation reports in 1954–6 found a common answer in some very familiar villains: higher prices caused by the inflation resulting from full employment, a shortage of skilled labour in engineering industries, the pull of a soft home market, and in 1955 the disruption caused by rail, coal and dock strikes.[47] It really all came down to one simple truth: exports had been flagging because of the chronic, systemic, long-term malaise afflicting Britain as an industrial society, and which ten years after the Second World War still awaited radical treatment, let alone a cure.

On 20 February 1956 the Economic Steering Committee warned ministers:

> Without a surplus of well over £200 millions on current account, it is evident that we cannot meet our commitments and maintain our currency and our position as the centre of the sterling system, and retain our position as a world power.[48]

This was just what Butler as Chancellor had said during the crisis of 1951–2; just what his Labour predecessors had said during the crises of 1949 and 1947. And yet such a surplus lay as far beyond reach as ever. According to the Economic Steering Committee, 'the outcome for 1956 seems likely to be a repetition of the current deficit of £100 million suffered in 1955. Such an outcome would be serious. Our actual and potential commitments . . . are considerable.'[49]

As it happened, these commitments more than equalled the 1955 deficit, for they included over £100 million per annum in grants, loans and capital investment being poured down holes in jungle and desert in present and past British colonies in Africa and Asia[50] because of a British sense of 'special responsibility'.[51] To these gratuities have to be added the annual interest of £40 million on the 1945 American and Canadian loans and the annual capital repayments of £37 million.[52] The total burden of all this was, so the Chancellor had reported in November 1955, 'serious in relation to the current and prospective state of our actual net earnings overseas . . .'[53]

By early 1956 the Conservative Government had run into yet another full-dress economic crisis, with the January trade figures some £74 million in the red.[54] Macmillan as Chancellor told Eden on 8 February that though the reserves had shown a 'slight rise' in January, it was 'not as high as it ought to be'.[55] In a high state of agitation the Chancellor talked of possible autumn devaluations and even raised the question of reintroducing import controls. The panic passed, however, and, in a familiar Micawberish routine, things began to look up again. Nonetheless, the summer brought fresh worries. On 5 July 1956, three weeks before Nasser nationalized the Suez Canal, there was circulated within Whitehall that grim report on German competition (see above, p. 398) which noted Germany's rising share of world exports of manufactures and Britain's falling share, and which attributed this worrying trend to a faster rise in productivity in Germany than in Britain. Why this faster rise? Because Germany had devoted 'a substantially higher proportion of her national product to industrial investment than the United Kingdom'.[56] In 1955, gloomed this report, Germany's exports of ships by value had overtaken Britain's, while her exports of motor vehicles had doubled between 1953 and 1955 as against a British increase of only a fifth (in the current year, the year of Suez, Germany's exports of motor vehicles by value were also to overtake

Britain's). The report speculated that German success owed itself to a 'quite exceptionally vigorous' sales effort in overseas markets. This implies – quite correctly – that exceptional vigour in marketing and sales promotion was not exactly the common characteristic of British exporters.

On 17 July 1956, nine days before Nasser put poor Anthony Eden into such a flutter, the 'Prospects for the Balance of Payments' Committee's report for June[57] was circulated. It was far from sanguine: 'To regain in 1956 part of the £200 million loss of reserves which we suffered in the last six months of 1955 would be satisfactory in itself.' Even so, such a recovery would only be possible thanks to certain windfalls.[58] Summed up the report: 'Our underlying position is still precarious.'

Was, then, a precarious underlying position of the reserves (and hence of sterling) adequate as the keel of British total strategy in the coming war? In August and September 1956 the question was much debated by powerful minds in the Treasury, the Bank of England, and the Cabinet Office. They dismissed with a collective shudder the possibility of an autumn devaluation of the pound; even a floating rate would be better – an echo here of the ROBOT arguments of 1952.[59] Just the same, Macmillan confidently minuted on 12 August: 'It is clear we are pretty well armed for Suez . . .'[60] On 28 August the Cabinet discussed a Treasury report, too narrow in its focus, which optimistically reckoned that the cost of the military steps now in hand would not seriously disturb the economy, and that even the cost of a shooting war would not be heavy on the Budget in relation to the present scale of defence expenditure. Only if the Suez Canal were closed as a result of conflict and Britain had to buy dollar oil to replace cut-off supplies from the Gulf would the balance of payments and the reserves be hit.[61]

What advice did the Chancellor, Harold Macmillan, that devious, glib and shallow man, now give the Cabinet? Nasser could not be allowed to get away with it. The experience of Mossadeq demonstrated that with these countries one could not rely on policy being governed by commercial self-interest.[62] Macmillan was very much acting the old Great War Grenadier at this period of the crisis, eager to thump the Gyppos, and even putting forward plans (as Chancellor of the Exchequer!) for a bold pincer movement on Cairo from

Libya and Alexandria. This zest for war explains why he continued to ignore Treasury warnings that, in Sir Leslie Rowan's words, there was 'a very dangerous outlook for sterling in the coming months'.[63] It explains why he failed to heed advice that he should take timely precautionary measures, such as making use of Britain's drawing rights (rights to borrow) from the International Monetary Fund. At a Cabinet on 11 September Macmillan actually argued that from the viewpoint of the national economy it was highly desirable to bring the Suez issue to a head. A quick decisive victory would restore confidence in sterling![64]

On 26 October, the day *after* Eden won the Cabinet's reluctant acquiescence to the dispatch of an ultimatum to Israel and Egypt 'in the event of an Israeli attack on Egypt'[65] – effectively a commitment to war – the Cabinet met to discuss the present state of health of the pound sterling and the reserves. It was an extraordinary reversal of what surely ought to have been the logical sequence of discussion – especially since sterling and the reserves were already sickening as a result of the long crisis. Macmillan now warned – rather late in the day, it might be thought – that he expected the loss of gold and dollars in November to be as high as $300 million, which would cause a further shock to international confidence. Unless all the country's financial reserves were mobilized to maintain the fixed rate of sterling against the dollar, it would, said he, be necessary to float the pound. That would end sterling's role as an international currency and destroy the Sterling Area.[66] All this, and not a shot had yet been fired!

Thus in the last week of October 1956 did those two outstanding post-war British obsessions, the Middle East and the Sterling Area, finally conjoin in a very madness of a total strategy.

How was John Bull to free himself with one bound from this self-inflicted quandary? Macmillan had his answer. It was the standard answer ever since 1945 for a first-class world power temporarily short of the readies: touch Uncle Sam for a wad of greenbacks. 'Informal contacts with the Americans should be used', said Macmillan, 'to prepare the way for the substantial loans that would be needed if the existing parity were to be defended.'[67] Surely the 'special relationship' would pay out again?

On 31 October, the day the bombing began, a joint meeting of the Treasury and the Bank of England took note that the reserves had lost $50 million in two days. At this point came another crass misjudgement. Sir Denis Rickett, Second Permanent Secretary of the Treasury, advised Macmillan that the United States 'might oppose a drawing by us [from the International Monetary Fund], particularly if in the meantime the [UN] General Assembly had passed an adverse Resolution'.[68] Yet amazingly Sir Denis did not then recommend that Britain should grab the money while she could, but instead that a drawing should be delayed 'as long as possible to give tempers time to cool all round'. And Macmillan agreed. The French – the French! – had already cannily strengthened the franc in anticipation of war by making timely use of their own drawing rights from the IMF.

The war against Egypt and the crisis of sterling now developed in tandem. On 2 November the UN General Assembly adopted a resolution calling for an immediate ceasefire and a withdrawal of Israeli, British and French armed forces, pending the creation of a UN peacekeeping force. Eden and the French instead opted to hasten their attack. As Eden told the Cabinet 'Egypt Committee' on the 3rd, 'it was politically desirable to establish Anglo-French forces at key points along the Suez Canal at the earliest possible date'.[69] By this time Britain and France had received letters from Dag Hammarskjöld, Secretary-General of the UN, informing them that Israel and Egypt had accepted the ceasefire, and asking them if they too were prepared to accept it. Fortunately fresh news came in that Israel had actually refused to accept a ceasefire. This emboldened the Cabinet to decide unanimously to go ahead with Musketeer.

On 5 November the allied attack on Egypt opened with a drop of French and British parachute troops who in the British case jumped from obsolescent aircraft. Next day amphibious forces landed at Port Said and Port Fuad, winning a complete victory over the Egyptians, and opening a clear road down the Canal to Suez. Already, however, the run on the pound had turned to a nasty bout of Egyptian dysentery, with £31.7 million (or $85 million) of the reserves lost in that first week of November alone.[70] Panic now supplanted Macmillan's previous belligerence. Devaluation loomed!

The sterling area was going to collapse! Through the night of the 5th/6th the Chancellor frantically telephoned Washington to plead for a financial rescue. No luck! This time the 'special relationship' was not going to pay out on demand. Only if Britain arranged a ceasefire before midnight on 6 November would the United States support a loan from the IMF and help sterling in other ways. During a Cabinet meeting in the forenoon of the 6th Macmillan received confirmation that the US Treasury was indeed blocking British efforts to draw from the IMF in order to relieve sterling's dysentery.

Must Britain therefore conform with a UN resolution calling on all belligerents to accept a ceasefire on present positions? The French, with their usual Palmerstonian disregard for world opinion, and especially American opinion, urged that the allies should complete the job and reach the Red Sea at Suez. What to do? The disarray of the Eden Cabinet, its overwrought nerves and its bitter divisions, are poignantly reminiscent of another Cabinet which had believed itself at the head of a great power but then abruptly found itself confronted by the bitter truth: that is to say, Paul Reynaud's in 1940 in the last dreadful days of France's defeat and rout by Nazi Germany. Anthony Eden's own nerves were now not so much stretched taut as snapped and twanging free. Worse, he was also sick and intermittently feverish with an old bile-duct complaint, and under drugs, all this serving to exacerbate all his weaknesses of character and temperament. As for Harold Macmillan, his poses of insouciant Edwardian boulevardier and brave old warrior had vanished in the face of the unfolding disaster to sterling and the blank American refusal to help until and unless Britain fully complied with UN resolutions. Playing the part of Marshal Pétain in 1940, Macmillan now virtually demanded that Britain accept the ceasefire for the sake of sterling. This settled the matter. Only Selwyn Lloyd, Anthony Head (Secretary of State for War) and James Stuart (Deputy Chief Whip) were in favour of fighting on. Butler and Salisbury led the majority of ministers in favouring a ceasefire. Two small 'l' liberal Conservatives, Edward Boyle (Economic Secretary to the Treasury; Eton and Christ Church, Oxford) and Anthony Nutting (Minister of State for Foreign Affairs; Eton and Trinity College, Cambridge), had already publicly washed their consciences Persil-white by resigning.

The Cabinet's surrender to the UN ceasefire resolution – really to remorseless American pressure on the pound – was announced to the Parliament that afternoon, to scenes of equally uproarious jubilation and anger.

Nevertheless, the future of the Anglo-French force now squatting after the ceasefire with silent guns on the northern twenty-three miles of the Canal Zone had still to be decided. Negotiations in Washington and at UN headquarters in New York dragged on to the end of November as Britain and France sought UN sanction for their soldiers to remain in Egypt until a promised UN force of peacekeepers was fully deployed; perhaps even be allowed to contribute to that force. This at least would salvage dignity from defeat. But meanwhile the pound sterling's runs were getting worse. In the three months to the end of October, so Macmillan told the Cabinet on 12 November, $328 million worth of the reserves had already flowed out.[71] On 19 November the Treasury was predicting a further loss for that month of over $250 million, although the Deputy Governor of the Bank of England put the real figure as high as $401 million.[72] If on 3 December (the day when the November figures were due to be routinely announced) the total reserves had sunk below $2,000 million, this could precipitate a catastrophic flight from the pound.

Britain therefore desperately needed to draw the total British IMF quota of $1,400 million, as well as persuade the Americans to waive due repayments of the 1945 American loan. It did not help that Britain would have to look to American dollar oil to replace supplies of sterling oil from the Persian Gulf, now cut off because the Egyptians had blocked the Suez Canal with scuttled ships.

Still the United States (and its newly re-elected President, Dwight Eisenhower) remained implacable, and in particular George Humphrey, the Secretary of the Treasury. A home-spun moralist, he likened the British action over Suez to that of 'a burglar who had climbed in through the window, while Nasser was the house-holder in his nightshirt appealing to the world for protection'.[73]

On 23 November Eden amazingly and unforgivably went off to Jamaica to nurse his illness, leaving Butler in command of the stricken ship. Next day the UN General Assembly passed by 63 votes to 5 a resolution censuring Britain and France and demanding the withdrawal of their forces 'forthwith' from Egypt. The United States voted for the resolution. When the Belgians moved an amendment to delete the censure and make the withdrawal a gradual one, it was defeated by 37 to 3, the Americans abstaining.[74] Their abstention was still decisive, because if they had chosen to support the Belgian resolution they could certainly have mustered enough votes from client states to pass it. However, the United States was resolved to teach her erstwhile ally and partner in the 'special relationship' a lesson in humiliation and obedience that she would never forget. The Eisenhower administration threatened further attacks on sterling; it threatened to deny Britain dollar oil, so menacing the fragile British economy with paralysis. But if Britain proved a good little boy and abjectly repented, then kind and forgiving Uncle Sam would unbelt the greenbacks and open the tap on the oil.

On 27 November Macmillan told the Cabinet that because of the forthcoming obligation to reveal the extent of the drain on the gold and dollar reserves, 'it was desirable that we should have secured by then the support of the United States Government for the action we should need to take to support sterling'.[75] Next day he increased his torsion on the Cabinet's arm: American goodwill was essential to save sterling, but 'this goodwill could not be obtained without an immediate and unconditional undertaking to withdraw the Anglo–French force from Port Said'.[76]

More turmoil! – not only in the Cabinet but also among Conservative backbenchers when their views on this proposal (presented to them without its author's name) were privately canvassed. Nobody liked it, but what else could be done in view of Britain's pitiful plight as presented by Macmillan? On 3 December poor Selwyn Lloyd announced to the House of Commons the decision to withdraw. This caused the greatest happiness on the Labour and Liberal benches, and in the Government's own supporters a despairing rage.

Shortly before 1900 on Saturday 22 December 1956, the last of the British troops embarked in a landing craft at Port Said, followed shortly afterwards in another landing craft by the brigadier commanding 19th Infantry Brigade and two staff officers. The vessels made for the open sea; the Suez adventure was over.

Less than forty years separated this national rout in a petty conflict from Britain's triumph in the Great War. Then she had stood at the head of a world empire in arms. Then her sixty divisions on the Western Front had won the crescendo of victories in 1918 which compelled Imperial Germany to sue for an armistice. Then she had possessed the largest navy and air force in the world. Then her industrial machine was the most powerful in Europe, with old industries modernized since 1914 and new technologies created. And by Armistice Day Britain had already drawn bold blueprints for further strengthening the sinews of British power – plans to carry forward the new industrial revolution to fulfilment, to remodel the education and training of the nation, to exploit the natural resources of the colonies, and to weld the Empire into a closer political and strategic union.

The sorry and shameful feebleness of 1956 therefore attests to a tragic decline in Britain's fortunes since 1918: and tragic in the true dramatic sense of the word because it had been brought down upon the British by themselves.

For it was they (the leaders and the led) who had collectively failed between 1918 and 1939 to fulfil the wartime promises of a new industrial revolution and a new education system; they who in the Second World War had therefore proved incapable of equipping their armed forces with all the sophisticated weaponry and equipment that was needed; they who even in the midst of such a war for national survival had still pursued their internecine industrial strife; they who since the end of the Second World War had chosen to carry on with this self-mutilation; they who in these same post-war years had again failed to provide themselves with the education and training system vital to industrial success; they who had failed likewise to carry through a root-and-branch transformation of their industries modelled on 'world's best practice' as set by America; they who had expensively botched high-technology projects in aviation, computing and defence.

It was governments voted in by the British people back in the inter-war period who had failed to solve the problem presented by the British Empire, neither fulfilling the hopes of 1918 that the Empire could be welded into a cohesive political and military alliance, nor thereafter abdicating Britain's moral responsibility for its global defence: an obligation far beyond her actual or potential naval and military strength, and which in the 1930s distracted her in the face of Nazi Germany. It was the British people at large who nevertheless continued to cherish the romantic illusion that the 'cigarette-card' Empire on display at George VI's Coronation in 1937 constituted the buttress of British power, when in reality it was not a buttress but a predicament: one of the most outstanding examples of strategic overextension in history.

And it was the British people too who had allowed themselves to be taken in after the Great War by another romantic illusion – the small 'l' liberal belief of the intelligentsia and the governing elite that the creation of the League of Nations had rendered military alliances and the balance of power obsolete, and that nation states, having promised under the League 'Covenant' to be peaceful and law-abiding, would no longer commit aggression.

In this same era it was the British people who had just as tamely accepted the view of their small 'l' liberal betters that the Versailles Treaty had been unkind and unfair to Germany (who had, after all, merely caused the Great War), and that Germany's 'legitimate' grievances should be sympathetically addressed by policies of 'appeasement'. It was the British people who had likewise fallen for the myth propagated by the small 'l' liberal intelligentsia that the Great War did not mark a magnificent victory, and one achieved by a British army which by 1918 had become the most formidable and best-led fighting force on the Western Front, but instead a futile carnage, and one caused by a callous and incompetent high command. And it was by swallowing this myth and flinching at the thought of another mass land war on the Continent that the British people had provided a further powerful motive for 'appeasement', the fantasy of small 'l' liberal politicians in the 1930s that by means of timely concessions and a show of sweet reason a deal could be negotiated with Adolf Hitler. Had not the nation cheered Neville Chamberlain rather than stoned him for selling out Czechoslovakia at Munich in 1938 in pursuit of the 'appeasement' of Europe?

And it was the British people who had consented far too late to the rearming of Britain against Hitler: who had accepted far too late that Nazi Germany's territorial ambitions must be resisted by force if need be. Hence theirs must be the ultimate responsibility that in 1939 an unready Britain plunged into a war which the Chiefs of Staff reckoned she could only win if it were a long one, and which the Treasury reckoned she could only afford if a short one: an insoluble dilemma which ended with Britain becoming from 1941 onwards a warrior satellite of the United States, dependent for life itself on American handouts.

Yet it was once again the British people, leaders and led, who in 1945 succumbed — if understandably — to the illusion that Britain had been a victor in her own right in the war, rather than towed home by the United States while the Red Army was gutting the Wehrmacht. It was they who in their elation at Nazi Germany's defeat had failed to comprehend that British power in its historic Victorian and Edwardian form had finally vanished amid the stupendous events of the Second World War, like a ship-of-the-line sinking unperceived in the smoke and confusion of battle. It was their trusted leaders who instead had fallen victim to the fresh fantasy that, once Britain's supposedly short-term difficulties in the wake of war had been overcome, her traditional world role could, and should, be salvaged, refitted, and put into service again. It was therefore the British people at large who shared responsibility with their politicians for all the colossal overloads and overstrains that pursuit of this fantasy imposed on Britain between the end of the Second World War and the final self-deluding absurdity of the Suez adventure.

Yet it was they who no less shared responsibility for that second great cause of post-war economic overload, 'New Jerusalem'. For they had demanded, and the politicians had promised, that there be fulfilled without delay the wartime prospectus of state welfare from crib to coffin, 'free' health care, 'full employment', and an ideal home for every family. It was the British people, therefore, who ensured that during the turning-point decade after 1945, when other European countries and Japan were putting investment in industry and infrastructure first and foremost in readiness for commercial battles to come, in Britain new parlours had come before new plant and free false teeth before fast railways.

Where is to be found the key that explains this history of mistaken policy, delusive dreams, miscarried projects and frittered opportunity since 1950, since 1945, since 1918? Because it is character which, contending with circumstance, governs the destinies of nations, the key can only be found in the character of the British people themselves, as portrayed by the historical evidence.

And that evidence justifies, on the first count, a verdict that the British in the twentieth century during times of peace were collectively prone to muddle, both in thought and action. They preferred ad-hoc expedients to long-term strategies. They instinctively avoided the 'wiring-diagram' approach which integrates separate bodies or functions within the same field into a coherent whole. On the contrary, theirs was a genius for *dis*-integrating what could be a whole into independent splinter groups, each doing its own thing, often in rivalry with one another, and each stoutly defending its own little empire. All this was true of much of British business; true of British trade unions; true of the British education 'system'; true of Whitehall ministries; true also of 'quangos' like the University Grants Committee. There were no civilian peacetime organizations equivalent to the superbly integrated air defence system which defeated the Luftwaffe in the Battle of Britain, or of Western Approaches Command which defeated the U-boat.

Moreover, the British in their affinity for muddle were just as averse to that functional version of a 'wiring-diagram' which defines clear lines of responsibility and devolves leadership and initiative downwards. They instead preferred – and still prefer – foggy liaison arrangements; they preferred – and still prefer – to proliferate committees, often overlapping, and all with as many opinions as they had members. From this followed – and still follows – the time-wasting and decision-clogging procedures so typical of British private institutions and public bodies alike; the botching of so many technological projects.

According to Marshal Foch, '*Décider, c'est choisir*'. But in general the British in boardroom and Whitehall alike before and after the Second World War hated making choices. After all, if they chose a certain course of action, that would mean forgoing the possible alternatives. It would also necessarily mean incurring penalties, either by way of the drawbacks inherent in any course of action or by way of protest by those unhappy at what had been decided. Much easier, therefore, to try to have it all ways by means of a fudge. In the case of the mandarins of Whitehall and of many ministers in the post-1945 Labour and Conservative Governments, the inborn horror at making a decisive choice had been intellectually blessed by an Oxbridge humanist education, valuing as it did 'balance' and objectivity, and esteeming as it did the critical faculties over the constructive. This is why the papers written by these grandees so often read like waffly ('on the one hand, on the other') prize essays rather than plans of action proposed to a general by his staff.

The evidence also justifies a verdict that the British character in peacetime, repeat *peacetime*, lacked not only hardness of mind, but also (except perhaps among the trade union barons and the shop-floor mutineers) hardness of will. In a corruption of the virtue of tolerance into a vice, the British too readily put up with slackness; they shrank from weeding out and discarding the incompetent, whether these wore the executive homburg or the workman's overalls or the teacher's gown. They lacked, moreover, the dynamism powered in America by individual and corporate ambition and in post-war Germany by obsession with *Leistung* (achievement). For long since out of fashion in Britain was the restless energy displayed by British entrepreneurship in the full momentum of the industrial revolution. Instead, in the shrewd diagnosis of a distinguished economic commentator in 1963 (and fully justified by the historical evidence), 'The very niceness of the British, the national desire to do the decent thing . . . has become an enormous force for *immobilisme* . . .'[77]

'Niceness', the desire 'to do the decent thing' – these qualities constituted then, and still constitute today, the emotional essence of small 'l' liberalism. They are qualities desirable in a friend, a neighbour or a colleague, and admirable in the citizen of a democracy. But they serve ill as a guide to a nation's total strategy in a ruthless world of struggle. The dominance of these qualities over the British public mind and feelings therefore accounts more than any other factor for the contrast between British power in 1918 and British power in 1956. For the desire to be 'nice' and 'do the decent thing' lay at the heart of 'appeasement', whether of dictators in the 1930s or trade unions in the 1940s and 1950s; it explains why the British saw their colonial empire as a trust, a civilizing mission, rather than as a resource to be exploited if profitable, and dumped if not; it explains why the British saw the Commonwealth and the Sterling Area – indeed, world affairs in general – in terms of altruistic responsibility rather than of self-interested calculation. And it was this same desire to be 'nice' and 'do the decent thing', rather than a resolve to improve the competitive quality of Britain's human resources, which provided the inspiration behind 'New Jerusalem'.

All this signifies that, within the middle classes at least, the moral revolution begun by early-nineteenth-century religious fervour (itself a symptom of the romantic movement and its exalting of emotion over sense) had run its full course. It had softened into 'niceness' the muscularity of the national character during Britain's rise as an industrial power between 1750 and 1850. It had emasculated into a desire 'to do the decent thing' in world affairs the belief of the English political nation from Walpole to Palmerston that little mattered beyond the wealth and power of the realm of England.[78]

On 9 January 1957 Anthony Eden, nattily attired in a cutaway morning suit as if on his way to a society wedding, went off to the Palace to 'kiss hands' on resigning as Prime Minister. Eden's scheming successor, Harold Macmillan, and the new Chancellor of the Exchequer, Peter Thorneycroft, now embarked on yet another emergency audit of the national resources and liabilities like those of 1951–2, 1949, 1947 and 1945. This time, however, there was the novelty that the audit was not occasioned by a standard-issue sterling crisis, but instead by the utter collapse at Suez of Britain's post-war total strategy in its every aspect and assumption.

Would the British and their new government therefore at last scrap the scenario for national decline written in the dreams and illusions of VE-Day? Would they now write a new scenario consistent with the reality that Britain was a second-rank, problem-ridden, partly obsolescent industrial state located on an island off the north-west coast of Europe?

It seemed at first as though they might. For the new Chancellor bluntly told his colleagues where Britain had gone wrong since the Second World War and even more wrong since the Korean War:

> The truth which has been revealed is that our reserves and our resources are inadequate to our tasks and responsibilities as traders, bankers or preservers of the peace . . .[79]

He reminded his colleagues that at home too the national resources were just as overstretched:

> If Education is to cost more and we are to face some inevitable increase in the cost of pensions for the aged, we need to look again at the sum total of Social Service expenditure . . .

And Thorneycroft (a former President of the Board of Trade) fully recognized that, above all, Britain needed 'great and prosperous and expanding industries. Without them all else is vanity.'[80]

Would therefore the process of reinventing and repositioning Britain as an industrial country in the world at last begin which ought by now to have been completed?

It would not. For even the brutal shock treatment of Suez had failed to cure politicians and civil servants of their hallucination that global entanglements and obligations were the same thing as global power. And what prime minister, what foreign secretary, what cabinet, what diplomat, would not wish to believe that Britain still remained a global power? So even now – even now – there was no question of starting to chuck overboard the massive military and economic burdens loaded on the British economy by the world and Commonwealth role and the sterling area. On the contrary, Thorneycroft at the start of 1957 is found singing the old song: 'our principal aim should be to achieve the surpluses [on the balance of payments] requisite for the banker and principal investor in the sterling area'.[81] These 'requisite' surpluses were now guesstimated at up to £400 million per annum. Why so large? The answer only serves to underline the folly of Britain's unchanged post-Suez total strategy: such surpluses were largely needed in order to cover a combined overseas expenditure of some £400 million per annum on handouts to backward countries[82] and on the continuing deployments and bases of the armed forces beyond Western Europe[83] – to say nothing of the cost of creating and maintaining a British nuclear deterrent.

For radical though might appear the defence policy finally announced in the 1957 White Paper[84] – end of conscription; shrinkage of standing overseas deployments in favour of reliance on swift reinforcement by air transport; emphasis on nuclear deterrence – it really amounted to no more than new wheezes for supporting old pretensions. The leitmotif still lay in the quest for 'prestige' and 'influence', both these weasel words being freshly trotted out by the Prime Minister while the 'new' defence policy was being evolved in the Cabinet Defence Committee. For a start, there would be no reneging on what Macmillan called 'our worldwide policing obligations',[85] or, in other words, the treaties that entangled Britain in the Middle East and Far East, and the strategic 'cowpats' that went with them. For instance, Macmillan averred that if Britain were unable to maintain adequate naval forces in the Far East and the South Atlantic, there would be 'a serious risk' to Britain's position 'as the centre of the Commonwealth'.[86]

As if the continuance of all this old lumber would not be a heavy enough load on what Macmillan himself acknowledged to be 'an already overstrained economy',[87] he reckoned that the provision of an independent British nuclear bomber force, along with the technological back-up needed to produce both atomic and hydrogen weapons, 'must have first call on our [defence] resources'. Why? Firstly because, in his words, such a force would be 'an effective means of maintaining British *prestige* [added emphasis] throughout the world . . .'[88] And, secondly, because it would 'give us an independent deterrent *influence* [added emphasis]'.[89] In Moscow? Or in Washington? Macmillan did not say. But he did make clear that in any case Britain's nuclear strength would never be operationally employed in circumstances short of global war, whence it followed that 'we could, therefore, assume that we should not use strategic nuclear weapons except in alliance with the United States'.[90] Here was a stark admission that the 'independent' British nuclear deterrent neither was, nor even intended to be, independent in any meaningful political or military sense of the word. Yet at the same time Macmillan had to admit to his colleagues that 'the decision to remain a nuclear power would inevitably impose a greater relative burden on this country than on the other two nuclear powers'.[91]

Thus even in the face of the Suez debacle Macmillan's cabinet flunked the Duke of Wellington's supreme test of generalship, that of knowing when to retreat and daring to do it.

The continued 'world-power' defence effort was the more madness because politicians and civil servants were perfectly well aware of the deep wounds it must inflict on the British economy.[92] For one thing, defence would go on gulping some two-thirds of the nation's resources in R&D.[93] According to a brief for the British delegation to NATO in November 1958:

> The defence load –
> (i) makes the United Kingdom balance of payments more vulnerable;
> (ii) hinders the United Kingdom's economic growth;
> (iii) means the other vital claims on the economy must be sacrificed.[94]

Even by 1970 Britain's overall defence expenditure as a percentage of GDP would still be half as much again as the West German percentage.[95]

The failure of Macmillan and his colleagues to awaken from the 'world-power' hallucination led to wider consequences still. There obviously could be no question of Britain, grand with global responsibilities and entanglements, signing up to the 1957 Treaty of Rome inaugurating the new supra-national Common Market of seven states, that further step towards closer European political union. Yet she thereby threw away the chance to play a chief part in the shaping of the market's new institutions and policies – only to plead, and in vain, to be let in four years later, when the French and Germans had already constructed the market to suit their interests rather than Britain's. In the meantime, Macmillan and Co. would have cobbled together a rival European 'free trade area' of six minor states plus Britain.[96] The purpose of this flimsy expedient (first bandied about in Whitehall in 1956) was to preserve inviolate that sovereign British independence the functional reality of which had been so graphically demonstrated during the Suez adventure.

'EFTA' also saved the Government for the time being from the pain of having to choose between the Common Market and the Commonwealth.

The very keel of this essentially unchanged British total strategy after Suez lay, naturally enough, in 'the special relationship', even though America had proved so ruthlessly hostile towards Britain's show of national freedom of action over Suez.[97] Macmillan himself devotes a whole self-congratulatory chapter in his memoirs to his successful visit to Washington in 1957 to smarm the important and restore Britain to American favour. His Cabinet's collective sentiments were well caught by Thorneycroft when he wrote that the foundation of Britain's relations with the rest of the world beyond the Commonwealth and Europe must be 'friendship with the United States'. Even the main purpose of economic ties with a European free-trade area or with the Commonwealth was, wrote Thorneycroft, to 'strengthen ourselves in order that we may be a powerful and equal partner in the Atlantic Alliance'.[98] A powerful and equal partner in the Atlantic Alliance! The phrase repeats almost word for word the hopeful bluster of British diplomats at the time of the outbreak of the Korean War in 1950.

Obviously such an equal partnership between the powerful must mean that, in Thorneycroft's words, that there was 'much that we must share [with America] in defence and other matters'. But how could this intimate cooperation with the United States be squared with Britain's prized future sovereign independence? No one in Whitehall or Westminster chose to explain. This was just as well, because when the British long-distance nuclear rocket Blue Streak and airborne nuclear missile Blue Steel failed to fly on time and on budget, the Americans were in 1960 astutely to offer Britain their air-to-surface nuclear missile Skybolt. The allegedly 'independent' British nuclear deterrent then became first of all dependent on unilateral American changes of policy over the delivery-system (cancellation of Skybolt in 1962 in favour of the submarine-launched Polaris missile), and thereafter dependent on American Polaris technology, production and maintenance.[99]

'Friendship with the United States'? 'Powerful and equal partner'? In reality Britain was to remain for the rest of the century and into the next what she had been ever since the latter years of the Second World War[100] – a satellite posturing as an equal.

Nor was there was to be a radical change of total strategy at home after Suez either. Macmillan was himself very much on the small 'l' liberal wing of the Conservative party, a loyal creature of the so-called 'post-war consensus', an appeaser by deepest instinct, especially in matters of industrial conflict. His political speciality as Prime Minister (and one emulated by his Labour successor, Harold Wilson) would be to dose the populace with a comforting mixture of warm opium and treacle rather than dunk them in a cold but invigorating bath. Safe in his hands, therefore, would be the 'managed economy', cosily complete with exchange controls and Exchequer-inflated, union-empowering 'full employment'. Safe too would be the welfare state, though ever more greedy in its demands on the taxpayer, ever more corrupting in its encouragement of dependency. In 1957, after all, a general election was in the offing, and Macmillan was the last man at such a time to snatch the warm teat of state maternalism out of a sucking voter's mouth.

Thus had Britain comprehensively blown her very last chance to reposition herself as a power in the world and to reinvent herself as an industrial country before her eager competitors caught up with her. It marked the consummation of her long-term failure to repeat that triumphant transforming of the national life accomplished during the first industrial revolution. Instead Britain had finally settled into the rut of relative decline where she would remain stuck fast for at least the next quarter of a century.[101]

In 1879 Gladstone had pronounced that 'the strength of Great Britain lies within the United Kingdom'. In 1957 Thorneycroft as a new Chancellor of the Exchequer recognized afresh that the source of that strength could only lie in 'great and prosperous and expanding industries. Without them all else is vanity.' But into the twenty-first century Britain was to witness instead the shrivelling, and even extinction, of too many of her great industries, whether old or new in their technology.[102] And all else *was* vanity – the vanity of a governing elite who would not abate their 'world-power' posturing even as Britain's comparative national strength waned. And so the central theme of British total strategy would continue to be what it had been ever since the period between the world wars: overstretch coupled with underperformance.

The quarter of a century following the Suez debacle was therefore simply to witness a repetition over and over again of all the problems and patterns of the post-war decade – from strikes to sterling crises, from abortive 'prices-and-incomes' policies to bloated welfare costs, from botched technology to lost markets, from Commonwealth to Common Market, from flaccid management in the factories to limp leadership in Downing Street, from 'go' to 'stop' and from 'stop' to 'go'.

The novelist Joseph Conrad had memorably imagined Great Britain as 'a mighty ship . . . carrying the burden of millions of lives'. But for the remainder of the era of the post-war consensus and the rule of small 'l' liberal politicians, Britain would more resemble a ship with steering jammed by a self-inflicted hit from a malfunctioning torpedo and doomed to keep circling in her own wake, while the officers of the watch on the bridge scratched their heads and looked haplessly over the side, the crew below played cards or refused duty, and other nations steamed past and away.[103]

References

Notes

1. 'The Probability of a Long and Costly Campaign'

1. Routine described to the author by retired senior Foreign Office personnel.
2. CAB 21/1985. The Situation in Korea. From Washington to Foreign Office, 24th June 1950. Sir O. Franks. No. 1756, 24th June 1950. D: 1.15 a.m. 25th June 1950. R: 7.15 a.m. 25th June, 1950. IMMEDI- ATE. SECRET.
3. Cf. CAB 128/18, CM(50), June meetings, passim.
4. The concept of 'total strategy' was first stated by me in 1972 in the Preface to *The Collapse of British Power* (London, Eyre Methuen, 1972; paperback: Stroud, Alan Sutton, 1984): '. . . strategy conceived as encompassing all the factors relevant to preserving or extending the power of a human group in the face of rivalry from other groups.' Such interacting factors include foreign and defence policies, economic and industrial resources, technological capability, education and train- ing, national leadership and political institutions, and public opinion.
    It was similarly in *The Collapse of British Power* (p. 232) that I described the British Empire between the world wars as 'one of the most outstanding examples of strategic over-extension in history.'
5. I have read John Charmley, *Splendid Isolation? Britain, the Balance of Power, and the Origins of the First World War, 1874–1914* (London, Hodder and Stoughton, 1999), and regard as absurd his belief that instead of going to war Britain could, and should, have lived with Wilhelmine Germany's domination of western Europe. This is as glibly clever but actually preposterous as his claim in *Churchill: The End of Glory; a Political Biography* (London, Hodder and Stoughton,

1993) that Britain could and should have unilaterally withdrawn into neutrality in 1940–41.

6. Cf. CAB 16/109, DRC 14, Report of the Defence Requirements Sub-Committee of the Committee of Imperial Defence, 1934.

7. See B. Bond, *British Military Policy Between the Two World Wars* (Oxford, Clarendon Press, 1980), ch. 4, but especially pp. 121–5.

8. For an account of the failure between 1918 and 1931 of the British attempt to turn the Commonwealth into a cohesive political and strategic entity under her leadership, see Barnett, *Collapse of British Power*, part IV: An Imperial Commonwealth (pp. 123–233), and cited documentary sources.

   I know that my friend Paul Kennedy will not mind my pointing out that my 600-page analysis of British imperial overstretch in relation to the United Kingdom's industrial resources and technological capabilities appeared twenty-four years before his exploration of similar themes in his *The Rise and Fall of the Great Powers*.

9. See Barnett, *Collapse of British Power*, pp. 485–94, and *The Audit of War* (London, Macmillan, 1986, and Pan Books, 1997), pp. 63–75, 87–103, 107–12, and cited documentary sources.

10. E. J. Hobsbawm, *Industry and Empire* (Harmondsworth, Pelican Books, 1969), p. 211.

11. See Barnett, *Collapse of British Power*, pp. 237–98, and cited documentary sources.

12. Ibid., pp. 298–305, and cited documentary sources.

13. Ibid., pp. 350–408, and cited documentary sources.

14. CAB 13/31, COS 560, 21 February 1937.

15. Barnett, *Collapse of British Power*, pp. 476–85; Barnett, *Audit of War*, chs 7 and 8, passim.

16. Barnett, *Collapse of British Power*, pp. 551–2. See also G. C. Peden, *British Rearmament and the Treasury 1932–1939* (Edinburgh, Scottish Academic Press, 1979), pp. 60–149, and R. P. Shay, Jr., *British Rearmament in the Thirties: Politics and Profits* (Princeton, Princeton University Press, 1977), passim.

17. For a full account of the 1938 Czechoslovakian crisis based on the Cabinet records, see Barnett, *Collapse of British Power*, pp. 456–550. The work describes the motives behind, and the naivety of, Chamberlain's policy of 'appeasing' Germany, Chamberlain's misreadings of

Hitler's character, and his failure to perceive the implications for the strategic balance of Europe of abandoning the Czechs.

18. CAB 29/159, AFC1, 20 March 1939.
19. CAB 16/209, SAC4.
20. See Barnett, *Collapse of British Power*, pp. 581–93.
21. See Correlli Barnett, *The Lost Victory: British Dreams, British Realities 1945–1950* (London, Macmillan, 1996, and Pan Books, 1997), part 1: The Dream of World Power, for a detailed account based on Cabinet and Cabinet records, particularly those of the Defence Committee.
22. CAB 131/1, DO(46), 10 April 1946, cited in Barnett, *Lost Victory*, p. 58. See chs 4 and 5, passim, but especially pp. 58–69.
23. Ibid., pp. 100–102.
24. CAB 131/7, DO(49)69, 3 November 1949. Size and Shape of the Armed Forces 1950–53: memorandum by the Lord President of the Council.
25. See Barnett, *Lost Victory*, p. 365, and cited official sources.
26. CAB 131/7, DO(49)51 (draft), 27 June 1949, Size and Shape of the Armed Forces 1950–53 (Harwood Committee Report): memorandum by the Minister of Defence (A. V. Alexander) on the report.
27. See Barnett, *Lost Victory*, Parts Three to Five, but especially chs 10 and 20.
28. CAB 134/225, EPC(50)46, 9 May 1950, Forecasts of National Income and Expenditure. See also Cmd. 7915, para. 58.
29. CAB 134/225, EPC(50)46.
30. CAB 134/224, EPC(50)18th, item 1, 13 July 1950.
31. Alan Bullock, *Ernest Bevin: Foreign Secretary 1945–1951* (London, Heinemann, 1984), p. 791.
32. Ibid. In actual fact, as is now known from Soviet records, the attack on South Korea was not the result of Soviet initiative at all. It was only after prolonged wheedling by North Korea's leader, Kim Il Sung, that a cautious Stalin gave his consent. Mao Tse-tung, the Chinese Communist leader, was not in favour, being himself preoccupied with the question of Formosa (now Taiwan), but was finally pressured by Stalin into giving his support. See Sergei N. Goncharov, John W. Lewis, and Xue Litai, *Uncertain Partners: Stalin, Mao, and the Korean War* (Stanford, Calif.: Stanford University Press, 1993), ch. 5, and especially pp. 131–54; and John Lewis Gaddis, *We Now Know:*

Rethinking Cold War History (Oxford, the Clarendon Press, 1997), pp. 70–75.

33. CAB 21/1985, No. 1772, Washington to Foreign Office, 27 June 1950. For an analysis of differing opinions and evolving policy in Washington, see Michael Hickey, *Korean War: The West Confronts Communism 1950–1953* (London, John Murray, 2000), ch. 3.

34. Ibid.

35. CAB 128/17, CM(50)39th, 27 June 1950. For British agonizing about whether, and how far, to join America's crusade in Korea, see also Hickey, *Korean War*, ch. 3.

36. Ibid.

37. See Barnett, *Collapse of British Power*, pp. 298–305, 350–81.

38. CAB 128/18, CM(50)39th.

39. Cited in FO 371/83298, FC 1024/40, 3 July 1950, Memorandum re US policy towards Formosa.

40. CAB 21/1988, COS(50)96th, 27 June 1950, Confidential Annexe: Korea: Assistance of United Kingdom and Commonwealth Forces.

41. CAB 21/1988, DO(50)48, Situation in Korea – Memorandum by the Chiefs of Staff, and DO(50)11th, 28 June 1950.

42. FO 371/84082 FK 1022/66, 28 June 1950. See also FO 371/FK 1022/51, *Top Secret*, Signal from Commander-in-Chief Far East Fleet to Comseventhtaskfleet, 30 June 1950: 'I am at present instructed that British ships should not repetition not participate in operations relating to Formosa.'

43. FO 371/81655, AV 1075/1.

44. FO 371/83298, FC 1024/40.

45. Ibid.

46. Ibid.

47. CAB 21/1985, Note to Prime Minister citing DO(50)51, Report on effect of current events in Korea on British defence interests in the Far East and South East Asia.

48. Cf. FO 371/FK1022/56 and FK1022/152, Kelly to the Foreign Office, 6 and 18 July 1950.

49. Max Hastings, *The Korean War* (London, Michael Joseph, 1987), pp. 81–4; Hickey, *Korean War*, ch. 4.

50. CAB 21/1988, citing Confidential Annexe to COS(50)101st, 3 July 1950.

51. Ibid.

52. CAB 131/9, DO(50)50, 5 July 1950.
53. CAB 21/1985, 5 July 1950.
54. CAB 21/1988, DO(50)12th, 6 July 1950.
55. CAB 131/9, DO(50)50, 5 July 1950.

Appendix A listed the Royal Navy's Far Eastern deployment as:

> *Korean Waters*: 2 cruisers, 1 light fleet carrier, 2 destroyers, 2 frigates, 1 Australian frigate.
>
> *Japanese Waters*: 1 frigate, 1 Australian destroyer, 1 hospital ship, 1 stores ship.
>
> *Hong Kong*: 1 cruiser, 1 destroyer. 2 frigates, 1 stores ship.
>
> *On Passage*: 2 destroyers left for Okinawa on 4 July.
>
> *Refitting*: 1 frigate.

Appendix B listed the Army's global deployments:

> *United Kingdom*: 2 infantry brigades (1 in strategic reserve and the other part of the Middle East Land Forces' infantry division; all battalions below strength). 1 Parachute brigade (earmarked for internal security role if need be in West Africa). 6 infantry battalions (of which 3 on London duties).
>
> *BAOR*: 1 infantry division. 1 armoured division. 7 regiments Royal Armoured Corps. 1 medium regiment Royal Artillery. 2 infantry battalions.
>
> *MELF*: 1 infantry division less 1 brigade, plus 1 field regiment Royal Artillery. 2 regiments Royal Armoured Corps. 2 heavy anti-aircraft regiments. 1 field regiment Royal Artillery. 5 infantry battalions (committed to Aqaba and Eritrea).
>
> *FARELF*: Malaya: 1 Gurkha division. 1 Gurkha brigade. 1 British brigade and 1 Royal Marine Commando detached from Hong Kong. 2 British battalions. 2 armoured car regiments (1 belonging to MELF).
>
> *Hong Kong*: 1 infantry division less 1 infantry brigade. 1 armoured regiment. 1 medium regiment Royal Artillery. 2 anti-aircraft regiments.
>
> *Austria*: 1 infantry brigade. In BETFOR [Trieste]: 1 anti-tank regiment Royal Artillery and 2 infantry battalions.

Appendix C listed 'Present Dispositions of the Royal Air Force':

United Kingdom: 83 squadrons, of which 17 medium bombers and
40 day and night fighters [average of 8 aircraft per squadron].
Germany: 4 light bomber squadrons. 3 day fighter/ground attack
squadrons.
Middle East: 15 squadrons.
Far East: 14 squadrons.

56. Ibid.
57. CAB 128/18, CM(50)43rd.
58. CAB 21/202, Telegram No 3070 from the Prime Minister to the President, 6 July 1950.
59. Hastings, *Korean War*, p. 84.
60. FO 371/84082 FC1024/44, 12 July 1950.
61. Ibid.
62. FO 371/84082 FK1022/56G, Telegram No. 3092, para. 5.
63. The United States, like Great Britain, had been deeply moralized by nineteenth-century religion, President Woodrow Wilson being a notoriously disastrous example of the resulting application of moral idealism to foreign policy. See Barnett, *Collapse of British Power*, part I, All That Is Noble and Good, which analyses the long-term transformation of British attitudes to international relations brought about by the nineteenth-century religious revival, up to the creation of, and later faith in, the League of Nations. The book also touches on the crucial role of the sanctimonious Wilson in creating the League.
64. FO 371/84086, FK1022/111, 11 July 1950.
65. FO 371/84084, FK1022/77G, 12 July 1950.
66. Ibid.
67. FO 371/84087, FK1022/128. Pierson Dixon's memorandum of 12 July 1950.
68. FO 371/84086, Telegram no. 3186, 14 July 1950.
69. FO 371/84087, FK1022/128, memorandum of 12 July 1950.
70. FO 371/84088, FK1022/115/G, 13 July 1950.
71. FO 371/84088, FK1022/152, 18 July 1950.
72. CAB 128/18, CM(50)47th, 18 July 1950.
73. FO 371/8488, FK1022/152.
74. CAB 21/2102, DO(50)14th, 14 July 1950.
75. Ibid.
76. Ibid. Letter to Air Marshal Sir William Elliott (Deputy Secretary

(Military) to the Cabinet), 14 July 1950, passed by Elliott to the Prime Minister.

77. FO 371/84089, FK1022/165.
78. Ibid.
79. FO 371/84089, FK1022/165G, 17 July 1950.
80. Ibid.
81. Ibid.
82. FO 371/84087, FK1022/118, 14 July 1950.
83. FO 371/84090, FK1022/198G, Memorandum on 'Ground Forces for Korea', 21 July 1950.
84. FO 371/84090, FK1022/198.
85. FO 371/84091, FK1022/222, 23 July 1950.
86. Ibid.
87. CAB 21/1988, DO(50)15th, 24 July 1950.
88. Ibid.
89. FO 371/FC1024/51.
90. CAB 131/9, DO(50)56, 21 July 1950. National Defence: Memorandum by the Minister of Defence.
91. Ibid., para. 16.
92. As reported to the Cabinet by Kenneth Younger, Minister of State. See CAB 128/18, CM(50)52nd, item 1, 1 August 1950.
93. Ibid.
94. Ibid., item 2.
95. DEFE 5/22, COS(50)282, 4 August 1950: Military Implications of the Course of Action Open to the United Kingdom in the Event of Hostilities between the United States of America and Communist China.
96. Hastings, op. cit., p. 86.
97. CAB 21/1988, Signal COSSEA 760, Chiefs of Staff to BDCCFE, 17 August 1950.
98. Letters in CAB 21/1988.
99. Ibid., COS(50)123rd, 4 August 1950, and 124th, 10 August 1950.
100. Cited in R. E. Osgood, *NATO: The Entangling Alliance* (Chicago: University of Chicago Press, 1962), p. 70.
101. Cited in ibid., p. 71.
102. Ibid., p. 73.
103. See Gaddis, *We Now Know*, pp. 84, 101, and 107; also Christopher Andrew, *For the President's Eyes Only; Secret Intelligence and the American*

Presidency from Washington to Bush (London, HarperCollins, 1995), pp. 180–83; and Ernest R. May, ed., *American Cold War Strategy: Interpreting NSC-68* (Boston, Mass., St Martin's Press, 1993), passim.

2. 'The Principal Partner of America in World Affairs'

1. Cited in CAB 131/9, DO(50)91, 23 October 1950; The Finance of Defence: Joint Memorandum by the Secretary of State for Foreign Affairs and the Chancellor of the Exchequer, para. 4.

2. Ibid., para. 5.

3. Cited in ibid., para. 5.

4. CAB 21/2248, Note by the Economic Section on EPC(50)73 and 75, 12 July 1950. Their view hardly squared with that of the Foreign Secretary and the Chancellor of the Exchequer in October 1950, to the effect that Britain in the summer was economically doing rather well, what with a current surplus on the balance of payments and an increase in the reserves, so bringing her within sight of independence of 'external assistance'. See CAB 131/9, DO(50)91, 23 October 1950; The Finance of Defence.

5. CAB 131/9, DO(50)81, covering COS(50)409, 'Size and Shape of the Armed Forces, 1951–54'.

6. Ibid.

7. CAB 131/9, DO(50)91, 23 October 1950; The Finance of Defence, para. 7.

8. Ibid. The Plan had actually been approved in outline by the North Atlantic Council in April 1950, before the outbreak of the Korean War. The figure of £6 billion for the UK represented 'a purely hypothetical [British] exercise' for an abortive NATO costing exercise in October 1950. The basis of the Plan was readiness to resist aggression in 1954. See CAB 134/488, MAC(50)60, 13 December 1950 and Annex, The Medium term Plan.

9. CAB 131/9, DO(50)91, para. 7.

10. Ibid., para. 13.

11. Ibid., paras 13 and 14.

12. Ibid., para. 10.

13. Ibid., para. 11.

14. Cited in Correlli Barnett, *The Lost Victory: British Dreams, British*

Realities 1945–1950 (London, Macmillan, 1996, and Pan Books, 1997), p. 111.

15. CAB 131/9, DO(50)81, Annexe II. Middle East = 1.33 divisions; Far East = 2.33 divisions; total 3.66 divisions. BAOR plus Austria and Trieste = 4 divisions.

16. Ibid., Enclosure to Annexe III.

17. See Correlli Barnett, *The Collapse of British Power* (London, Eyre Methuen, 1972; paperback: Stroud, Alan Sutton, 1984), part II: All That Is Noble and Good.

18. CAB 134/488, MAC(50)49, 28 November 1950, Mutual Aid Committee: Comparative Defence Expenditure; covering note.

19. Ibid., The Atlantic Pact Countries and the U.S.S.R.: Population, National Income, Current Defence Expenditure, 'Index of Defence Effort' and Long-term Rearmament Programmes, Fiscal year 1950 or 1950/51, Columns 3, 5 and 7.

20. Ibid., column 3.

21. CAB 131/8, DO(49)21st, item 1, 21 November 1949.

22. CAB 131/7, DO(49)71, 17 November 1949, United States Military Aid Programmes – Bilateral Agreements – a note by officials.

23. Ibid., para. 19.

24. Ibid.

25. CAB 134/488, MAC(50)3, 20 October 1950, covering Final Text of the United States Aide-Memoire on Interim Aid for the United Kingdom Re-armament Programme, dated 6 October.

26. Ibid., para. 23.

27. FO 371/83019, F/1027/16.

28. See Kenneth O. Morgan, *Labour in Power, 1945–1951* (Oxford, the Clarendon Press, 1984), pp. 428–430.

29. Quoted in CAB 128/18, CM(50)87th, item 1, 18 December 1950.

30. See Barnett, *Collapse of British Power*, pp. 527–8.

31. CAB 128/18, CM(50)87th, item 1.

32. Ibid.

33. CAB 128/19, CM(51)3rd, item 3.

34. CAB 131/10, DO(51)1st, 23 January 1951. The five reports were: CP(51)16, Memorandum by the Chiefs of Staff on Defence Programmes 1951–54; CP(51)19, Memorandum by the Chancellor of the Exchequer on the Economic Implications of the Defence Proposals; DO(50)106, Memorandum by the Minister of Defence on increase of

tank production capacity; DO(51)1, memorandum by the Minister of Labour on the supply of National Servicemen to meet the needs of the Forces; and DO(51)3, Joint Memorandum by the Minister of Agriculture and Fisheries and the Scottish Secretary also on the supply of National Servicemen to meet the needs of the Forces.

35. See Barnett, *Collapse of British Power*, p. 477, and cited sources.
36. CAB 131/10, DO(51)1st.
37. CAB 134/227, EPC(50)125, 2 December 1950; Report on Raw Material Situation.
38. CAB 131/10, DO(51)1st.
39. Ibid.
40. Ibid.
41. Ibid.
42. Cited in Michael Foot, *Aneurin Bevan, A Biography*, vol. two: *1945–1960* (London, Davis-Poynter, 1973), p. 312.
43. CAB 128/19, CM(51)7th, item 4, 25 January 1951.
44. Ibid.
45. See Morgan, *Labour in Power*, p. 434.
46. CAB 128/19, CM(51)8th, item 2.
47. CAB 134/490, MAC(51)43(Final), 31 March 1951, covering the 40-page 'The Burden of Defence on the United Kingdom; Memorandum to NATO'.
48. Ibid., para. 3; see also para. 30, Table IV – Growth of National Resources.
49. Ibid., para. 35.
50. Ibid., para. 3.
51. Ibid., para. 37.
52. Ibid., para. 36.
53. Ibid., para. 38, and Table VII.
54. Ibid., paras 48–50.
55. Ibid., para. 39.
56. Ibid., para. 70.
57. See Barnett, *Lost Victory*, passim, but especially pp. 163–4.
58. Proportionate to GNP, this was correct.
59. CAB 134/490, MAC(51)43(Final), para. 2.
60. Ibid., para. 58.
61. Ibid., para. 48. Of all madnesses, Britain was proposing to increase

investment in the colonial empire during rearmament while decreasing it at home. See ibid., Appendix B, para. 7.

62. See Barnett, *Lost Victory*, pp. 109–12.
63. See ibid., ch. 8.
64. See ibid., ch. 7.
65. See ibid., chs 14, 15 and 16.
66. See ibid., ch. 19.
67. CAB 134/490, MAC(51)43(Final), para. 40.
68. Ibid., para. 42. According to Table VIII – Gross National Product and Expenditure 1949–53, domestic investment as a proportion of GNP was to fall by about 2 per cent between 1950 and 1952/53, and remain static in total at 1949 prices.
69. Ibid., para. 18.
70. CAB 134/114, CPC(50)2nd, item 1.
71. For machine tools in the Great War munitions drive, see Barnett, *Collapse of British Power*, p. 85; for machine tools in pre-1939 rearmament and during the Second World War, see Barnett, *Audit of War*, pp. 133–4, and 159–61. For machine tools in the post-war British economy 1945–50, see Barnett, *Lost Victory*, pp. 303–5.
72. CAB 134/114, CPC(51)2nd, item 1. On the continuing problem of the machine-tool shortage, 1951–52, see the Ministry of Supply files in SUPP 14/186.
73. CAB 134/114, MAC(51)3rd, item 1.
74. ED 46/753, EAC(51)25th meeting, 2 May 1951, paras 11 and 12.
75. CAB 134/114, CPC(51)7th, item 1.
76. CAB 134/114, CPC(50), 8th, item 2, 29 May 1951.
77. Cf. the voluminous internal and external correspondence in SUPP 14/80–92. See below, ch. 18.
78. See Barnett, *Engage the Enemy More Closely; the Royal Navy in the Second World War* (London, Hodder and Stoughton, 1991), pp. 47, 322 and 886–7.
79. SUPP 14/86, 22 May 1951, minute by G. H. Singleton, Engineering Industries Division, Ministry of Supply.
80. CAB 131/11, DO(51)58, 19 May 1951.
81. Ibid.
82. CAB 134/114, CPC(51)9th, item 1, with reference to CPC(51)24.
83. CAB 134/230, EPC(51)58, Economic Policy Committee; The

Defence Programme and Material Supplies; Memorandum by the Chancellor of the Exchequer.

84. CAB 134/230, EPC(50)57, 8 June 1951, The Fuel and Power Requirements of the Defence Programmes; Memorandum by the Minister of Fuel and Power.

85. CAB 134/114, CPC(51)11th.

86. Ibid. The problem of labour supply in Coventry was to baffle the Committee repeatedly into November 1951. See CAB 134/114, passim.

87. CAB 134/114, CPC(51)15th, item 3.

88. CAB 131/11, DO(51)97, Defence Programmes – Progress Report; Minute to Prime Minister from Minister of Defence.

89. CAB 134/114, CPC(51)18th, item 2.

90. CAB 134/114, CPC(51)21st, item 2.

91. Ibid. This section of the minutes was in fact crossed out and replaced with a blander version.

92. Ibid.

93. CAB 128/19, CM(51)26th, 9 April 1951.

94. Ibid.

95. See Barnett, *Lost Victory*, ch. 7, especially pp. 144–50.

96. Foot, *Aneurin Bevan*, vol. two, pp. 306–7. See above p. 36 and endnote 19 to this chapter for a comparison of Soviet and Western national incomes.

97. Cf. Foot, *Aneurin Bevan*, vol. two, pp. 313–15.

98. CAB 134/230, EPC(51)65, 22 June 1950, Economic Policy Committee: Memorandum by the Chancellor of the Exchequer, paras 7 and 32.

99. Ibid., para. 32.

100. CAB 131/11, DO(51)94, Service Production Programme 1951–4. Memorandum by the Minister of Defence.

101. Ibid.

102. CAB 131/11, DO(51)95, 27 July 1951. Memorandum by the Economic Steering Committee on the Report by the Joint War Production Committee on the Service Production Programme 1951–4.

103. CAB 131/10, DO(51)21st, 31 July 1951.

104. CAB 134/491, MAC(51)129, 4 September 1951, The Interim Report of the Financial and Economic Board of N.A.T.O. to the North

Atlantic Council; impressions by Mr Eric Roll, the United Kingdom representative.

105. Ibid., para. (v).
106. Ibid., para. (ii).
107. Ibid., para. (iv).
108. CAB 134/492, MAC(51)137, 8 September 1951, 'Economic Questions in N.A.T.O.: United Kingdom and United States objectives for the burden-sharing exercise contrasted': Final version of brief for the Chancellor of the Exchequer on the Report by the Financial and Economic Board of N.A.T.O. on the Defence Burden Exercise, paras 1 and 2.
109. Ibid., para. 2.
110. Ibid., para. 5.
111. Ibid., para. 19. On 13 September the Committee on Productive Capacity had considered reports on how best to cut back civilian output and consumption in order to lighten the load on industry and release more labour for defence production. See CAB 134/114, CPC(51)19th.
112. CAB 134/492, MAC(51)137, para. 20(i).
113. CAB 134/492, MAC(51)141, 21 September 1951, Korea: Dollar Cost of Maintenance of Commonwealth Forces; Note by the Treasury; and Annexe A: Draft Agreement Between the Government of the United States of America and the Government of the United Kingdom Concerning Participation of the United Kingdom Forces in United Nations Operations in Korea. See especially Article 7.
114. CAB 134/492, MAC(51)141, 21 September 1951, para. 7(a).
115. Ibid., para. 8.
116. Ibid., para. 11.
117. Ibid., para. 11.
118. CAB 134/492, MAC(51)144, 27 September 1951, Possible United States Measures in Relief of the United Kingdom Trade Gap.
119. CAB 134/492, MAC(51)151, 20 October 1951, Offshore Purchases; Note by the Ministry of Supply.
120. Ibid., para. 4.
121. Ibid., para. 5.
122. The gold and dollar reserves were draining away at the rate of $300 million a month; cf. T 236/3240, The Balance of Payments; Memor-

andum by the Paymaster-General, undated but February 1952. Cf. also
T 236/3070, memorandum of 15 December 1951 on The Sterling
Area by R. W. B. Clarke, Under-Secretary in the Treasury, para. 11:

> despite the devaluation of 1949 and despite the injection of a very
> considerable dollar aid since 1948, we are in a third crisis which is
> the worst of the lot and in which the U.K. and the whole sterling
> area are in a serious balance-of-payments deficit with the whole
> world outside the Sterling Area.

3. 'Trying To Do Too Many Things at Once'

1. CAB 134/856, EA(E)(51)1, 30 November 1951, Economic Policy Committee; Sub-Committee on the Economic Situation. Our Economic Prospects and Objectives. Memorandum by the Chancellor of the Exchequer.
2. Ibid., para. 1.
3. Ibid., para. 2(a).
4. Ibid., para. 3.
5. Ibid., para. 3.
6. Ibid., para. 4.
7. Ibid., para. 4.
8. Ibid., para. 5.
9. T 236/3240, 9 February 1952, Emergency Action; paper prepared in the Overseas Finance Division of the Treasury, para. 46.
10. CAB 134/856, EA(E)(51)1.
11. Ibid., para. 6.
12. CAB 134/856, EA(E)(51)1, para. 7.
13. Ibid., para. 8.
14. Population: America, 149,215,000; Britain, 50,363,000. GNP: America, £79.1 billion; Britain, £10.2 billion. See CAB 134/488, MAC(50)49, 28 November 1950, Comparative Defence Expenditure; tables prepared by the Joint Intelligence Bureau of the Ministry of Defence, p. 3.
15. CAB 134/856, EA(E)(51)1, para. 10.
16. Ibid., para. 11(i).
17. Ibid., para. 11(ii).

18. Ibid.
19. See Correlli Barnett, *The Lost Victory: British Dreams, British Realities 1945–1950* (London, Macmillan, 1996, and Pan Books, 1997), passim, but especially chs 13–16.
20. CAB 134/856, EA(E)(51)1, para. 12.
21. CAB 134/856, EA(E)(51)2, Government Expenditure; Memorandum by the Chancellor of the Exchequer, Appendix I.
22. CAB 134/856, EA(E)51 and 52 series.
23. See Barnett, *Lost Victory*, pp. 86–98, 256, 262, 265, 269, 353–4, 356, 394.
24. D. E. Butler, *The British General Election of 1951* (London, Macmillan, 1952), p. 45.
25. For a critique of inter-war 'moralizing internationalism', its misplaced faith in the League of Nations, and the dire consequences, see Correlli Barnett, *The Collapse of British Power* (London, Eyre Methuen, 1972; paperback: Stroud, Alan Sutton, 1984), pp. 237–48, 274–5, 282–7, 291–305, 328–33.
26. Butler, *British General Election*, p. 55.
27. Ibid., p. 46.
28. See Barnett, *Lost Victory*, ch. 18.
29. Butler, *British General Election*, pp. 55, 59, 105 and 406.
30. Ibid., p. 46.
31. Ibid., pp. 45–6, 55–6.
32. Correlli Barnett, *The Audit of War* (London, Macmillan, 1986, and Pan Books, 1997), p. 47, citing PREM 4 89/2.
33. CAB134/856, EA(E)(51)10, 6 December 1951, Economies in the National Health Service; Memorandum by the Chancellor of the Exchequer, para. 2.
34. Barnett, *Lost Victory*, p. 143.
35. CAB 134/856, EA(E)(51)10, para. 2.
36. Ibid., para. 3. All these figures are for Great Britain only.
37. Though correctly transcribed, there is a mistake in the hotel charge figures; the total saved should be in the proportion 36:30. If the lower total is correct the higher should be £17.10 million; if the higher total is correct the lower should be £14.375 million. These charges include mental patients and mental defectives; oddly the proportions are correct when these patients are excluded (£7.5 million and £9 million).
38. Ibid., para. 4(b).

39. CAB 134/856, EA(E)(51)4th, 7 December 1951, item 2.
40. Ibid.
41. CAB 134/856, EA(E)(51)6th, 12 December 1951, item 1.
42. Ibid.
43. Ibid.
44. Ibid.
45. CC(51)19th, Conclusions, Minute 3, cited in CAB 134/856, EA(E)(52)4.
46. CAB 134/856, EA(E)(52)4, 8 January 1952; National Health Service: Economy Measures. Progress Report by the Minister of Health and the Secretary of State for Scotland, para. 15.
47. CAB 134/856, EA(E)(52)1st, item 1, 10th January 1952.
48. CAB 134/856, EA(E)(51)3, 4 December 1951. Economies in Education. Memorandum by the Chancellor of the Exchequer.
49. CAB 134/856, EA(E)(51)2nd, 5 December 1951, item 1.
50. Ibid., 11 December 1951.
51. CAB 134/856, EA(E)(51)5th meeting, item 5.
52. Ibid.
53. Ibid.
54. CAB 134/856, EA(E)(51)20, 13 December 1951. Sub-Committee on the Economic Situation: Draft Report, paras 27 and 44. The future level of food subsidies was left for consideration in the context of the next Budget.
55. CAB 134/856, EA(E)(51)11, 7 December 1951. Estimates 1952–53 – Ministry of Civil Aviation. For a survey of disastrously misconceived British aviation policy (another manifestation of the 'world power' illusion) see Barnett, *Lost Victory*, ch. 12.
56. CAB 134/856, ES(E)(51)12, 10 December 1951. Magnitude of Expenditure. Memorandum by the President of the Board of Trade.
57. CAB 134/856, EA(E)(51)20, 13 December 1951. Sub-Committtee on the Economic Situation; Draft report to the Cabinet, paras 43–44.
58. CAB 134/856, EA(E)(51)4, 4 December 1951. Civil Service numbers; Memorandum by the Chancellor of the Exchequer, para. 12.
59. CAB 134/856, EA(E)(51)20, para. 47.
60. Ibid., paras 44–45.
61. Ibid., para. 45.
62. Butler, *British General Election*, pp. 101–104, and ch. VII. Cf. p. 102: 'Both sides admitted that times were difficult, said that there was no

easy solution of the nation's problems, announced that the way ahead was hard, and gave due notice that sacrifices would be required from everyone . . . But on neither side were these solemn words followed up with any examples of the specific hardships to come, and each side encouraged the impression that things would get better if only they were returned. It is absurd to claim that by expressing a few forebodings the parties were facing up to the national crisis.'

63. CAB 134/856, EA(E)(51)23, re-draft of Draft Report, para. 5.

64. Ibid.

65. CAB 134/856, EA(E)(51)23, Draft Report, para. 12(a).

66. Ibid., para. 4. Overall deficit: £450 million instead of £350 million; gold-and-dollar deficit: £350 million instead of £250 million. In the event the deficit turned out to be £385 million.

67. Ibid., para. 4.

68. Ibid., para. 11.

69. Ibid., para. 22.

70. Ibid., para. 23.

71. Ibid., para. 22.

72. Ibid., para. 13.

73. Ibid., para. 16.

74. CAB 134/856, EA(E)(51)13, 10 December 1951, para. 9. Butler's analysis of the pernicous side-effects of full employment echo that of his Labour predecessor Gaitskell in December 1950. See Barnett, *Lost Victory*, pp. 350–51.

75. Ibid., para. 12.

76. Ibid., para. 9.

77. Butler had supported Chamberlain's misguided attempt to 'appease' Hitler in 1938 and had been one of those members of Churchill's Government in summer 1940 in favour of finding out through Mussolini what Hitler's peace terms might be.

78. CAB 134/856, EA(E)(51)13, para. 12.

79. Ibid., para. 16.

80. Ibid., para. 7.

81. Cf. Richard Hoggart, *The Uses of Literacy: Aspects of Working Class Life, With Special References to Publications and Entertainments* (London, Chatto and Windus, 1971), p. 110.

82. CAB 134/856, EA(E)(51)13, para. 7.

83. Cf. CAB 134/856, EA(E)(51)17, 11 December 1951, The Investment

Programme. Memorandum by the Chancellor of the Exchequer. NB: these minutes speak of calendar years, not financial years.

84. CAB 134/442, IPC(51)7, Civil Investment in 1952.
85. Ibid., Table II. *Manufacturing Industry*: 1950: £421 million; 1952 existing programme: £357 million; recommendation for 1952: £293 million. *Transport and Communications*: 1950: £365 million; 1952 existing programme: £372 million; recommendation for 1952: £347 million.
86. Ibid. £71 million in 1950; £263 million for 1952 under the existing programme; £231 million under the revised programme. The £231 million compares with £293 million to be spent on Britain's out-of-date and decayed transport and communications network.
87. Ibid., para. 9.
88. Ibid., para. 12.
89. Ibid., para. 14.
90. Ibid., para. 2.
91. Ibid., para. 22.
92. CAB 134/842, EA(52)1st, 2 January 1952, Economic Policy Committee, item 6.
93. All quotes from CAB 134/842, EA(52)1st, 2 January 1952, item 6.
94. CAB 134/843, EA(52)2, 1 January 1952. Board of Trade Investment Programme, 1952.
95. CAB 134/982, IPC(52)3, 8 February 1952, Capital Investment in 1952, para. 2. The British Electricity Authority got £153m instead of £152m; the gas industry £50m instead of £48m; ports £13.6m instead of £12.6m; the Post Office £38.7m instead of £38.4m; iron and steel £63m instead of £55; education (England, Wales and Scotland) £61.9m instead of £59.1m. The discrepancies between these figures and those in n85 above are in the documents.
96. Ibid. All at end-1951 prices.

4. 'A Choice of the Utmost Difficulty'

1. CAB 129/53, C(52)202, 18 June 1952, British Overseas Obligations: Memorandum by the Secretary of State for Foreign Affairs.
2. Ibid., para. 3(a). Eden's history is suspect. Britain as a great power only dates from Marlborough's wars, a matter of some 250 years rather than 'several hundred years'.

3. Ibid., para. 3(b) and (c).

4. Ibid., para. 4.

5. Ibid., para. 5.

6. Commenting on the Harwood Report on 'the Size and Shape of the Armed Forces'. See Correlli Barnett, *The Lost Victory: British Dreams, British Realities 1945–1950* (London, Macmillan, 1996, and Pan Books, 1997), pp. 88–95, and cited sources.

7. CAB 133/131, PEC(52)1st, 30 July 1952.

8. Cited in Michael Carver, *Tightrope Walking: British Defence Policy Since 1945* (London, Hutchinson, 1992), p. 34. After a further half-century of remorseless British economic and political shrinkage relative to the rest of the world, a Labour Prime Minister would still be spouting the same kind of gush. In a millennial message to his constituents, Tony Blair proclaimed that 'there is still something called the British genius, a collection of qualities deep in our character. We will always stand out as a nation.'

9. CAB 131/12, D(52)26, 17 June 1952. Defence Policy and Global Strategy.

10. Ibid., paras 4 and 5.

11. It did not occur to the Chiefs that it might be advantageous to transfer this double liability to Russia and China by allowing selected backward countries to fall under Communist domination.

12. CAB 129/053, C(52)202.

13. Ibid., para. 4.

14. Ibid., para. 5.

15. Ibid., para. 28.

16. Ibid., para. 7.

17. Ibid., para. 7.

18. Ibid., para. 9.

19. Ibid., Annexe.

20. £385 million. Cmd. 9108, p. 9, Table 2.

21. Nor the broader costs to the national economy in terms of defence production, R&D, and withdawal of National Servicemen from productive labour entailed by a defence policy embracing not only the security of Britain-in-Europe but also the world role.

22. CAB 131/12, D(52)8th, item 3: British Overseas Obligations, consideration of memorandum C(52)202 by the Foreign Secretary.

23. Ibid.

24. CAB 131/12, D(52)26, 17 July 1952, Defence Policy and Global Strategy, para. 140.
25. Ibid. See also CAB 131/12, D(52)41, 29 September 1952, The Defence Programme. Report by the Chiefs of Staff: annexed report by the Committee on the Defence Programme, which offered two alternative programmes: the first at a total of £5,000 million over the three years 1953–56, and the second at £4,800 million. These compared with a total of £5,483 million in an earlier 'Global Strategy Costing' (cited in D(52) 41 as GEN 411/19).
26. CAB 131/12, D(52)41, Annex, para. 14.
27. Ibid., paras 14–15.
28. Ibid., Table VIII. Europe: 4 divisions plus 3 brigades. Middle East: 2 divisions plus 2 brigades; Far East (incuding Korea) 1 division plus 5 brigades. The table reckons 13 brigades to be the equivalent of 4.33 divisions.
29. Ibid., para. 33.
30. Ibid., para. 46.
31. CAB 131/12, D(52)46, 31 October 1952, citing his memorandum of 3 October, C(52)316.
32. Ibid., para. 2.
33. Ibid., para. 4.
34. CAB 131/12, D(52)45, 31 October 1952, Defence Programme; Report by the Chiefs of Staff, Annexe I, para. (a)(ii).
35. Ibid., para. (xi).
36. Ibid., paras (xix) and (xx). The arguments employed against the proposed shrinkage in defence expenditure are highly reminiscent of those used by the Minister of Defence and Chiefs of Staff against the Harwood Committee Report in 1949. See Barnett, *Lost Victory*, pp. 88–97.
37. Ibid., para. (xi).
38. CAB 131/12, D(52)45, para. 13. The Central African Federation was outstanding among British political fantasies for the future of British possessions in Africa whereby native peoples mostly still living (literally) in the Stone Age and tiny minorities of white settlers were to be magically evolved in short order into viable Western constitutional democracies.
39. Ibid., para. 3.

40. CAB 131/12, D(52)47, 3 November 1952, Research and Development; memorandum by the Minister of Supply, para. 3.
41. Ibid., para. 4.
42. CAB 131/12, D(52)11th. This meeting discussed D(52)45 and D(52)46.
43. CAB 128/25, CC(52)94th.
44. Ibid.
45. Ibid.
46. According to the President of the Board of Trade in the same Cabinet meeting.
47. £1,010 million according to Cmd. 8800, p. 35, Table 24. See also CAB 134/877, EPB(52)4, 10 May 1952. Defence and the Balance of Payments; report by officials.
48. CAB 128/25, CC(52)94th.
49. CAB 131/12, D(52)48, 3 December 1952, The Future of ANZAM; Memorandum by the Chiefs of Staff.
50. Ibid., para. 8.
51. See Barnett, *Lost Victory*, pp. 55–60, and cited sources.
52. DEFE 4/41, 30 March 1951, annexe to COS minutes: Basic Assumptions for a re-examination of Middle East Strategy. See also CAB 131/12, D(52)26 of 17 June 1952, para. 59: 'Whereas in the past our views on the strategic importance of the Middle East have arisen largely from its position as the gateway to Asia, we must emphasise that South-East Asia is equally the key to the Middle East from the other side of the door.' According to para. 78 of this report the Middle East 'lies at the centre of Britain's sea and air communications to Australasia, India and Pakistan'.
53. CAB 131/12, D(52)50, 6 December 1952, Defence Negotiations with Egypt; Memorandum by the Chiefs of Staff, para. 3.
54. Cmd. 8800, Table 14; the total spent was £245 million (see p. 00).
55. CAB 131/12, D(52)26, para. 54.
56. Ibid.
57. Ibid., para. 79.
58. That is to say, you must hold on to some region, whatever its intrinsic economic or strategic value, for fear that your evacuation will be followed by occupation by another power, such as the Soviet Union – even though that occupation is likely to impose heavy economic

strain on your enemy. The American war in Vietnam and its long Communist aftermath stands as a supreme example of the vacuum theory in action. In the case of the Middle East in 1952, the Chiefs of Staff in D(52)26 acknowledged the region's poverty, while Asia and Africa, the continents linked by the Middle Eastern land-bridge so prized by the Chiefs, were also backward and desperately poor, and hence greedy suckers at the teat of Western aid.

59. CAB 131/9, DO(50)60, 24 July 1950, The Importance of Persian Oil; Memorandum by the Minister of Fuel and Power, and Annexe. See also S. H. Longrigg, *Oil in the Middle East; Its Discovery and Development* (London, Oxford University Press, second edition, 1961), p. 150. On the question of Middle East oil in general, see Benjamin Shwadran, *Middle East Oil and the Great Powers* (New York, John Wiley and Sons, 1973).

60. CAB 131/9, DO(50)60, para. 4.

5. 'An Area of Vital Importance'

1. DEFE 4/41, Annexe to JP(51)58(F), Implications of Military Action against Persia, para. 5(a). This report was considered by the COS at their meeting COS(51)52nd on 22 March 1951.

2. Ibid., para. 5(c).

3. Ibid., para. 7.

4. Confidential Annexe to COS(51)52nd.

5. Cf. DEFE 4/45, COS(51)115th, 13 July 1951, item 6, Confidential Annexe.

6. CAB 128/19, CM(51)48th.

7. CAB 129/46, CP(51)200, 11 July 1951. Persia: Memorandum by the Foreign Secretary.

8. CAB 128/20, CM(51)51st, Minute 2, 12 July 1951.

9. DEFE 4/45, COS(51)117th, 17 July 1951, Confidential Annex.

10. CAB 128/20, CM(51)60th, Minute 6, 27 September 1951.

11. Ibid.

12. Ibid.

13. Ibid.

14. S. H. Longrigg, *Oil in the Middle East; Its Discovery and Development* (London, Oxford University Press, second edition, 1961), pp. 168–70.

In 1953 Mossadeq was overthrown by a coup engineered by British and American intelligence agencies, and in 1954 a deal was struck whereby profits from Iranian oil sales were to be divided 50/50 between the National Iranian Oil Corporation and consortia of Western oil companies. Within these consortia the Anglo-Iranian Oil Company itself saw its old monopoly reduced to 40 per cent, while American oil companies muscled in to the extent of another 40 per cent. Royal-Dutch Shell and the Compagnie Francaise accounted for the remaining 20 per cent. See Longrigg, *Oil in the Middle East*, pp. 276–9.

15. Ibid., p. 171, FN. 1. Figure of dollar balance-of-payments deficit in 1952 from Cmd. 9108, para. 5.

16. The Suez Canal was a convenience rather than a vital communications link. For three years during the Second World War all sea traffic between Britain and regions east of Suez had passed via the Cape, at a cost of a few days' extra steaming and a marginal increase in shipping tonnage employed.

17. PREM 8/1388, pt. III, Morrison to Attlee, 12 October 1951.

18. Ibid., Memorandum, 19 October 1951.

19. See Michael Carver, *Tightrope Walking: British Defence Policy Since 1945* (London, Hutchinson, 1992), pp. 28–9.

20. David Carlton, *Anthony Eden: A Biography* (London, Allen Lane, 1981), pp. 299–300, 305–6, 314–15, 325–7, 340–41.

21. CAB 131/12, D(52)1st, 12 March 1952, item 5.

22. CAB 131/12, D(52)50, 6 December 1952, Defence Negotiations with Egypt; Memorandum by the Chiefs of Staff, para. 2.

23. CAB 131/12, DO(52)50, Annexe, Case A.

24. Ibid., Case D.

25. Ibid.

26. Ibid.

27. Ibid., para 23.

28. Carver, *Tightrope Walking*, p. 29.

29. Ibid.

30. CAB 131/14, D(54)37, 17 November 1954, Annexe: Copy of a Minute dated 10 November 1954 from the Minister of Defence to the Prime Minister.

31. Ibid.: Middle East Joint Headquarters; Memorandum by the Chiefs of Staff, para. 1.

32. Ibid., para. 3.
33. DEFE 4/69, COS(54)22nd, 3 March 1954, Annex to JP(54)24(Final).
34. Ibid.
35. CAB 128/27, Pt 1, CC(54)7th, Minute 2, 7 July 1954. The fantasy had been burgeoning for several months. On 7 January 1954 (CAB 128/27, CC(54)1st, Minute 2) Churchill had speculated to his Cabinet:

> If some military association were eventually to be built up between Turkey and Pakistan, this might turn out to our advantage. If we failed to reach a defence agreement with Egypt and disengaged our forces from the Canal Zone, the general direction of our re-deployment in the Middle East would be to the northward. The creation of a new defensive grouping in the northern part of this area would fit within that movement.

36. Chiefs of Staff briefing in DEFE 4/69, COS(54)42nd.
37. Ibid.
38. Carver, *Tightrope Walking*, p. 31.
39. Ibid., pp. 31–2.
40. Ibid. Askaris were African soldiers.
41. CAB 131/17, DO(56)17, 3 July 1956, United Kingdom Requirements in the Middle East; Report by the Chiefs of Staff. The annexe lists in detail all the setbacks and withdrawals since 1945. However, the COS forbore to mention that the pre-war British commitment to the Middle East had led to the cost-*in*effective wartime campaigns in the theatre, where, after a huge investment in military forces, regional military infrastructure and shipping, British and Commonwealth forces engaged a peak of three and a half German divisions at the Second Battle of Alamein in October–November 1942.
42. All from DO(56)17.
43. CAB 131/17, DO(56)19, 4 July 1956.
44. Ibid. Gan is in the Maldives and Coëtivy is in the Seychelles.
45. CAB 131/15, D(55)14, 11 March 1955, South African Defence and Simonstown: Memorandum by the Minister of Defence, the Secretary of State for Commonwealth Relations and the First Lord of the Admiralty.
46. CAB 131/15, D(55)1, 7 January 1955, Defence Policy – Heavy Aircraft Carriers: memorandum by the Minister of Defence.
47. Ibid.

48. Ibid. The use of 'prestige' in this context only echoes Admiral Lord Mountbatten's complaint in becoming C.-in-C., Mediterranean in 1952 that he had no battleship, only a cruiser, in which to fly his flag: 'We in the Mediterranean are being shown up the whole time by the [U.S.] Sixth Fleet who send their colossal ships following largely in our wake, with powerful press propaganda to show how much superior they are to us.' – letter to Admiral Sir Guy Grantham, 23 August 1852, cited in Philip Ziegler, *Mountbatten: the Official Biography* (London, Collins, 1985), p. 508.

    Yet only two years earlier Mountbatten as commander of the First Cruiser Squadron in the Mediterranean had recognized that navally Britain 'was trying to do too much with too little', and that she was 'developing a Navy which we cannot afford to maintain and which is out of harmony with the requirements of modern war' (Ziegler, *Mountbatten*, p. 496).

49. CAB 131/15, D(55)14.

50. CAB 131/14, D(54)1st, 20 January 1954, item 2.

51. Ibid. Not until March 1955 did the Chiefs of Staff feel able to recommend reducing British land forces in Korea to the 'token force' (of one battalion) which they had originally recommended in 1950 as the maximum British contribution. Cf. CAB 131/14, D(55)15, 17 March 1955: Reduction of Commonwealth Forces in Korea; memorandum by the Chiefs of Staff.

52. CAB 131/16, DC(55)15th, Minute 5, 18 November 1955. The Americans had been told that the British contingent would be reduced to a token force in spring 1956. Winter conditions made it logistically inconvenient to remove the troops earlier.

53. Of course, Communist China was and is a gruesome tyranny, as we today – post-'Cultural Revolution' and post-Tyananmen Square – know even better than Dulles in 1954. But unless such a regime demonstrates by its actions that it is bent on expansionism (like Nazi Germany or pre-war Japan), its domestic character is irrelevant to international relations or to the conduct of other states' foreign policies. China had by 1954 displayed no such aggressive intent, intervening in Korea only in response to MacArthur's foolish advance to her borders, and forbearing to occupy either Hong Kong or the Portuguese colony of Macao, though both were incapable of being successfully defended. The Chinese Government could justifiably

regard Formosa, where the rump of Chiang Kai-shek's Nationalist regime had taken refuge after defeat on the mainland in the civil war, as Chinese territory in rebel hands.

54. The following summary of events leading up to and including the Geneva Conference of May–July 1954 is based on David Carlton, *Anthony Eden: A Biography* (London, Allen Lane, 1981), pp. 338–56; Robert Rhodes James, *Anthony Eden* (London, Weidenfeld and Nicolson, 1986), pp. 375–82.

55. Rhodes James, *Eden*, pp. 376–7.

56. Cited in ibid., p. 377.

57. For the year 1954–55 US defence aid amounted to £61 million, as against Britain's own defence expenditure of £1,519 million. Cf. CAB 131/16, DC(55)43, 14 October 1955, para. 1.

58. H.M. Treasury, *United Kingdom Balance of Payments, 1946–1957* (London, HMSO, 1959), Table 10.

59. To use the technical historiographical term.

60. Carlton, *Eden*, pp. 365–6; Rhodes James, *Eden*, pp. 377, 380.

61. Cf. CAB 131/16, DC(55)43, 14 October 1955, United Kingdom Defence Programe; Memorandum by the Minister of Defence (Duncan Sandys). See also CAB 131/16, DC(55)48, 31 October 1955; The Level of Defence Expenditure; Memorandum by the Chancellor of the Exchequer (R. A. Butler), and CAB 131/16, DC(55)13th, 4 November 1955.

6. 'To Know When to Retreat'

1. Even the author of the Schlieffen Plan recognized that the margin of German numerical superiority over the French might not be sufficient to enable the plan's great outflanking movement to succeed. A sure prior knowledge that the French left flank would be extended by a British Expeditionary Force would have rendered the plan evidently unfeasible. It was the Schlieffen Plan and the urgency of its military timetable that turned a quarrel between Austria-Hungary and Russia into pan-European conflict. See Correlli Barnett, *The Swordbearers; Studies in Supreme Command in the First World War* (London, Eyre and Spottiswoode, 1964; paperback, London, Hodder and Stoughton, 1986), part 1.

2. For British grand strategy in Europe between 1929 and 1939, see Correlli Barnett, *The Collapse of British Power* (London, Eyre Methuen, 1972; paperback: Stroud, Alan Sutton, 1984), pp. 334–45, 382–476, 494–575; Brian Bond, *British Military Policy Between the Two World Wars* (Oxford, the Clarendon Press, 1980), chs 3, 7, 8, 9, 10 and 11.

3. The French army on the Western Front on 10 May 1940 totalled 94 field divisions of mixed quality, with many middle-aged veterans of the Great War, as against the German Army's 136, all youthful first-class troops (Alastair Horne, *To Lose a Battle* (London, Macmillan, 1969), p. 156). In the call-up classes of nineteen- and twenty-year-olds France was outnumbered two to one by Germany (Henri Amouroux, *Le Peuple du Désastre, 1939–1940* (Paris, Editions Robert Laffont, 1976), pp. 115–16).

4. See Correlli Barnett, *The Lost Victory: British Dreams, British Realities 1945–1950* (London, Macmillan, 1996, and Pan Books, 1997), pp. 94–5.

5. Ibid., pp. 99–100.

6. See ibid., ch. 6, for an account of British policy towards the proposed Coal and Steel Authority in 1948–50.

7. The following summary account of negotiations in 1952–4 over the proposed EDC and of the subsequent London Conference of September 1954 is based on David Carlton, *Anthony Eden: A Biography* (London, Allen Lane, 1981), pp. 309–13, 335–6, 360–63; Robert Rhodes James, *Anthony Eden* (London, Weidenfeld and Nicolson, 1986), pp. 349–51, 361, 365, 374, 386–7; Anthony Eden, *Full Circle* (London, Cassell, 1960), pp. 29–47, 146–74.

8. Eden, *Full Circle*, pp. 36–7.

9. Cited in Carlton, *Eden*, p. 336.

10. There were escape clauses, such as military emergencies elsewhere, or financial stringency.

11. True, there was an escape clause in the Paris Treaty: Britain could renege on the promise either in the event of financial stringency or of an 'out-of-Europe' emergency.

12. Cmd. 9728, para. 44.

13. Ibid., para. 68.

14. Cmd. 9108, Table 2.

15. Excluding American defence aid. Cmd. 9412, Table 2.

16. Ibid.

17. Cmnd.113, Table 19.

18. Ibid.

19. Ibid.

20. Cmd. 9728, para. 66.

21. CAB 131/16, DC(55)43. United Kingdom Defence Programme.

22. Cited in Barnett, *Lost Victory*, p. 3.

23. CAB 131/16, DC(55)10th, 29 September 1955, item 2.

24. CAB 131/16, DC(55)43, 14 October 1955, United Kingdom Defence Programme. Memorandum by the Minister of Defence, para. 2. The peak of 10.5 per cent of GNP in 1952–53, compared with the Labour Government's projected peak of 12 per cent, represents the effect of the Conservative Government's decision to spread the rearmament programme over four years instead of three.

25. See Barnett, *Lost Victory*, p. 101 and cited documents.

26. CAB 131/16, DC(55)43, para. 4. If GNP rose by 3.5 per cent annually, it would amount to £19 billion in 1959. Nine per cent of GNP would give a defence budget of £1.71 billion – £202 million short of the total of £1,912 million currently projected by the three service departments and the Ministry of Supply.

27. Ibid., para. 5.

28. Ibid., para. 6.

29. For a guesstimate of the proportion of GNP taken up by extra-European defence commitments, see Barnett, *Lost Victory*, pp. 101–2.

30. CAB 131/16, DC(55)43, para. 9.

31. Ibid.

32. Ibid.

33. Ibid., paras 7 and 8.

34. Ibid., para. 14. This would be an increase of 4 per cent over 1954–55, but still less than the 1953–54 budget.

35. Ibid., para. 16, *Navy*, (i), (iv), and (v), and para. 26.

36. Ibid., para. 16, *Army*, paras (i) to (ix).

37. Ibid., *Air Force*, paras (i) to (vi).

38. Ibid., para. 17. In the 1960s and 1970s just these kinds of shrinkages in the size and deployment of the armed forces, just these kinds of cancellations of advanced but expensive technologies, would gradually take place – never because of far-sighted reappraisal of total-strategy, always because of immediate financial force majeure. See, for example,

Michael Carver, *Tightrope Walking: British Defence Policy Since 1945* (London, Hutchinson, 1992), chs 4–7.

39. The Harwood Committee. It rendered its report, *The Size and Shape of the Armed Forces*, on 28 February 1949. See Barnett, *Lost Victory*, pp. 88–95, and cited documents.

40. See Barnett, *Lost Victory*, pp. 92–5.

41. CAB 131/16, DC(55)43, para. 27.

42. Ibid., para. 38: money at August 1955 prices.

43. £370 million instead of £323 million for the navy, and £600 million instead of £527 million for the air force. Ibid., para. 28.

44. Ibid., para. 31.

45. Ibid., para. 31.

46. Ibid., para. 33, (i).

47. CAB131/16, DC(55)11th, item 3.

48. Ibid.

49. Ibid.

50. CAB 129/78, CP(55)184, 29 November 1955. Overseas Expenditure; Memorandum by the Chancellor of the Exchequer.

51. Diary, February 1950, cited in Barnett, *Lost Victory*, p. 103.

52. CAB 129/78, CP(55)184.

53. All in ibid.

54. Since the outbreak of the Korean War, Germany's world market share in manufacturing exports had risen from 10 per cent to over 15 per cent: Britain's share had dropped from 22 per cent to 20 per cent. See Cmd. 9728, graph on p. 27.

55. CAB 131/16, DC(55)48, 31 October 1955. The Level of Defence Expenditure. Memorandum by the Chancellor of the Exchequer.

56. CAB 131/16, DC(55)48, para. 2(b). The increase of £163 million was based on present costs and prices. See also CAB 129/29, CM(55)45th, Minute 1, 6 December 1955, when Butler pointed out that between the current financial year and 1960–61 the cost to the taxpayer of National Insurance would rise by £131 million and of the National Health Service by £72 million, even without any 'substantial improvements'. However, in discussion it was remarked that although the cost of the welfare state was rising faster than the increase in GNP, the actual proportion of GNP swallowed by the welfare state had been falling year by year.

57. Or, by Butler's calculation, about 2.5 per cent per annum at present costs and prices.
58. CAB 131/16, DC(55)48, para. 5(a).
59. Ibid., para. 5(b).
60. Ibid., para. 6.
61. Ibid., para. 7(a).
62. Ibid., para. 7(b).
63. Cf. CAB 131/16, DC(55)13th, 4 November 1955, which only agreed on inviting further examination of expenditure in 1958–59 by officials of the Ministry of Defence, the Treasury, the service departments and the Ministry of Supply, as a preliminary to further discussion between the Chancellor and the Minister of Defence.
64. Lloyd later upped his bid to £5,031 million: cf. CAB 129/78, CP(55)316: The Defence Programme, para. 18.
65. Cited in Christopher Hibbert, *Wellington: A Personal History* (London, HarperCollins, 1997), p. 301.
66. CAB 129/79, CP(56)30, 8 February 1956. Statement on Defence. Note by the Minister of Defence circulating a proof copy of the 1956 defence White Paper (published as Cmd. 9691).
67. Statement on Defence, para. 8.
68. Ibid., paras 21 and 23.
69. Ibid., para. 34.
70. Ibid., para. 48.
71. Ibid., para. 50.
72. CAB 131/16, DC(55)43, 14 October 1955. United Kingdom Defence Programme – Memorandum by the Minister of Defence.
73. *The Influence of Seapower Upon History 1660–1783* (London, University Paperbacks, 1965; first published in 1890 by Little, Brown & Co., Boston, Mass.).
74. Ibid., p. 30.

7. The Starving of Productive Investment

1. Harold Macmillan, *Tides of Fortune* (London, Macmillan, 1969), p. 364, citing his own diary for 28 October 1951.
2. His wife Dorothy's longterm lover was the bisexual political failure Robert (later Lord) Boothby. See Alistair Horne, *Macmillan 1894–1956*

(London, Macmillan, 1988), pp. 85–90, 98, 115, 178, 296, and 341, and Robert Rhodes James, *Bob Boothby; A Portrait* (London, Hodder and Stoughton, 1991), pp. 113–23, 126–9, 147, and 306–7.

3. Cf. Robert Blake, *The Conservative Party from Peel to Churchill* (London, Eyre & Spottiswoode, 1970), pp. 170–71; T. F. Lindsay, and Michael Harrington, *The Conservative Party 1918–1979* (London, Macmillan, 1979), pp. 267–8.

4. CAB 134/884, ES(52)9, also IPC(53)47, 17 March 1952, Investment in 1953, Note on the Interim Report on the 1953 Investment Programme.

5. Cf. CAB 134/844, EA(52)64, 16 May 1952, Economic Policy Committee. Housing – Steel and Timber Requirements; Memorandum by the Minister of Housing and Local Government, para. 1.

6. CAB 134/856, EA(E)(51)22, 13 December 1951; Sub-Committee on the Economic Situation; Investment in Housing. Memorandum by the Minister of Housing and Local Government.

7. Ibid.

8. Ibid.

9. CAB 134/843, EA(52)2, 21 January 1952, Economic Policy Committee; Housing Programme.

10. CAB 134/842, EA(52)10th, Economic Policy Committee, 2 April 1952, Minute 1.

11. See Correlli Barnett, *The Lost Victory: British Dreams, British Realities 1945–1950* (London, Macmillan, 1996, and Pan Books, 1997), ch. 8.

12. CAB 134/850, EA(54)25th, 25 November 1954, Economic Policy Committee, Minute 1, Capital Investment.

13. Ibid.

14. CAB 134/850, EA(54)25th, 25 November 1954.

15. Ibid.

16. Cmd. 9728, Economic Survey for 1956, p. 9, para. 14.

17. Ibid., p. 8, Table 3. Total gross fixed investment (at 1948 prices) in 1952 was £1,560 million and in 1954 was £1,881 million. Investment in manufacturing rose from £428 million in 1952 to £443 million in 1954; in transport and communications it rose from £158 million to £198 million; and in new dwellings it rose from £388 million to £519 million.

18. Ibid.

19. See Correlli Barnett, *The Audit of War* (London, Macmillan, 1986, and

Pan Books, 1997), ch. 5, for a survey of the British steel industry from the 1890s to 1945, with special reference to the two world wars and pre-1939 rearmament.

20. CAB 87/10, R(45)36, cited in ibid., p. 105.
21. See Barnett, *Lost Victory*, pp. 314–21, for a summary of British steel production and development 1945–52.
22. Cf. CAB 134/847, EA(53)4, 13 January 1953. Steel Supply and Demand in the Future; Memorandum by the Chancellor of the Exchequer and the Minister of Supply. There were political considerations too: since steel was denationalized in 1953, the Government would not wish the industry publicly to fail to produce the steel the nation needed. Cf. CAB 134/437, EA(53)12, 23 January 1953. Steel Supply and Demand in the Future; Memorandum by the Paymaster General (Lord Cherwell), para. 13.
23. Speech on 9 July 1952, quoted in CAB 134/848, EA(53)70, 18 May 1953, Maintenance and Improvement of Roads. Memorandum by the Minister for the Coordination of Transport, Fuel and Power and the Minister of Transport.
24. CAB 134/848, EA(53)70, para. 1.
25. Ibid., para. 7.
26. Ibid.
27. CAB 134/846, EA(53)25th, 28 October 1953.
28. CAB 134/636, PC(48)12th, item 4, 4 June 1948, Speed limit for Heavy Goods Vehicles, re. Memorandum by the Minister of Transport, PC(48)73.
29. CAB 134/645, PC(50)5, 19 January 1950, Production Committee. Length of Public Service Vehicles. Memorandum by the Minister of Transport.
30. Churchill Archives Centre, CLRK 1/3/11.
31. CAB 129/78, CP(55)184.
32. CAB 134/846, EA(53)30th, 2 December 1953, Minute 2. See also CAB 134/849, EA(53)144, 30 November 1953, Roads: Major Improvements and New Construction. Memorandum by the Minister of Transport and Civil Aviation.
33. CAB 134/846, EA(55)30th, Minute 2.
34. CAB 134/982, IPC(53)1, also ES(53)6, 5 February 1953, Investment Programmes Committee; Report on Investment in 1953 and 1954, para. 22.

35. CAB 134/852, EA(54)77, 12 July 1954. Roads; Memorandum by the Lord President of the Council.
36. CAB 134/852, EA(54)16th, Minute 1, 13 July 1954.
37. CAB 134/855, EA(55)8, 14 January 1955. Modernisation and Re-equipment of British Railways. Memorandum by the Minister of Transport and Civil Aviation. This circulated the British Transport Commission report of the same title to members of the Cabinet Economic Policy Committee.
38. Ibid. See also T 234/96, for Treasury discussions with the Board of Trade about the plan from March to October 1955, as also discussions with the BTC.
39. See the pitiless critique of the plan by E. P. Wright of the Treasury on 20 April 1955 in T 234/96.
40. Cf. CAB 134/855, EA(55)8, and Appendix B, Draft Statement to Parliament. See also CAB 129/082, CP(56)210, 20 September 1956, Note by the Lord Chancellor and draft White Paper, para. 19.
41. Cf. CAB 129/78, CP(55)184.
42. As I remember well.
43. See the correspondence in T 234/96.
44. CAB 129/082, CP(56)210, 20 September 1956, The British Transport Commission; Note by the Lord Chancellor.
45. Entitled 'Review of Financial Situation', and included in CAB 129/082, CP(56)210.
46. This report was included in the White Paper. See ibid.
47. Ibid., BTC report 'Review of the Financial Situation'.
48. See Barnett, *Lost Victory*, pp. 278–9.
49. CAB 134/982, IPC(52)9th, 27 November 1952, item 1.
50. Ibid.
51. CAB 134/847, EA(53)31, 23 February 1953. Post Office Investment Programme; Memorandum by the Postmaster General, para. 2.
52. CAB 134/846, EA(53)9th, 11 March 1953, item 2.
53. £120 million. Cf. T 230/403, Final Communique of the Sydney Conference, para. 22.
54. CAB 134/846, EA(53)9th, Minute 2.
55. CAB 134/847, EA(53)31, 23 February 1953. Post Office Investment Programme; Memorandum by the Postmaster General, para. 3.
56. CAB 132/107, SP(53)1, 7 February 1953, Advisory Council on Scientific Policy. Research, Development and Investment. Redraft of

report by the Deputy Chairman, Table 1. British expenditure per person employed: 1948: £50; 1949: £54; 1950: £60; 1951: £70. American: 1948: £195; 1949: £183; 1950: £180; 1951: £250. Sources of Data: Survey of Current Business (USA); Statistical Abstract of the United States, 1951; National Income and Expenditure 1946–51 (GB); Monthly Digest of Statistics (GB).

57. Ibid., Table 3. France: 1948: £59; 1949: £97; 1950: £82. Sweden: 1948: £157; 1949: £146; 1950: £146. Britain:1948: £61; 1949: £66; 1950: £69. Figures based on United Nations Economic Survey of Europe 1950; ECA Recovery Guide, February 1951; and Statistical Abstract of Sweden, 1952.

58. Ibid. The Economic Steering Committee agreed with this diagnosis: cf. CAB 134/843, ES(52)27, 27 March 1952, para. 6.

59. CAB 134/843, EA(52)2, 1 January 1952. Board of Trade Investment Programme; Memorandum by the President of the Board of Trade.

60. Ibid., Appendix A.

61. CAB 134/844, EA(52)67, 17 May 1952. Investment in Productive Industry, para. 1.

62. Ibid.

63. Actually 54 per cent. See ibid., paras 2–3.

64. Ibid., para. 4.

65. CAB 134/842, EA(52)16th, 21 May 1952, Minute 4. See also his memorandum on Investment in Productive Industry in 1953: CAB 134/844, EA(52)83, 13 June 1952.

66. CAB 134/842, EA(52)19th, 18 June 1952, Minute 2; CAB 134/844, EA(52)79, 9 June 1952. Investment in Productive Industry in 1953. Note by the Secretary of State for the Co-ordination of Transport, Fuel and Power.

67. CAB 134/847, E(53)29, 21 February 1953. Investment Programme; Memorandum by the President of the Board of Trade.

68. Ibid.

69. CAB 134/847, EA(53)54, 27 March 1953. Investment in Manufacturing Industry; Memorandum by the Chancellor of the Exchequer, para. 4.

70. CAB 134/847, EA(53)26, 16 February 1953. Investment Programme; Memorandum by the Chancellor of the Exchequer, para. 4. The

Economic Policy Commitee agreed to this on 25 February 1953: CAB 134/846, EA(53)5th, Minute 1.

71. Needed according to EA(52)67: £70 million worth; permitted in 1952: £37.5 million worth. Add the £10 million: £47.5 million or 67.86 per cent.

72. What follows in the present chapter merely summarizes effects of the Conservative Governments' restrictions on capital investment in education and training. The entire field of education and training, from primary schools to universities, between 1945 and 1956 is examined below in ch. 22.

73. Report by the Special Committee on Higher Technological Education (London, HMSO, August 1945).

74. In CAB 132/120, SP(MP)(53)5, 14 September 1953, Advisory Council on Scientific Policy: Sub-Committee on Scientific Manpower.

75. Ibid., para. 10.

76. In Norwich. Ibid., para. 13.

77. Referred to in ED 46/1000, 12 December 1955, draft memorandum to the Cabinet.

78. Ibid.

79. Cmd. 9703.

80. Cf. ED 46/1003, letter from F. F. Turnbull, Under-Secretary at the Treasury, to A. A. Part, Under-Secretary, Ministry of Education, 9 February 1956.

81. An International Comparison of National Products and the Purchasing Power of Currencies, cited in T 230/403.

82. Cf. Statistisches Bundesamt, *Volkswirtschaftliche Gesamtrechnungen* (Stuttgart und Mainz, W. Kohlhammer GmbH, 1985), table 7.1, p. 77, *Fachserie* 18, Reihe 5.7, *Lange Reihen 1950 bis 1984*. In regard to British gross fixed investment, Cmd. 9728, Economic Survey for 1956, table 1, gives an average for the three years 1953–55 of 16 per cent of GNP.

83. T 230/284, 12 November 1954, Central Statistical Office: Investment and The Growth of the Economy 1955–60 ('a first draft of a paper on general problems of investment policy over the next five years'), para. 3. (ii).

84. CAB 134/1230, EP(56)23, 20 February 1956. Note by Economic Steering Committee on reports of the Balance of Payments Prospects

Committee (EP(56)21) and Working Party on World Trade and Economic Conditions (EP(56)22).

8. Operation ROBOT and the Burden of Sterling

1. See Correlli Barnett, *The Lost Victory: British Dreams, British Realities 1945–1950* (London, Macmillan, 1996, and Pan Books, 1997), ch. 6 and cited sources.
2. CAB 134/1231, EP(56)72, 31 August 1956. The Probable Development of the Commonwealth over the Next Ten or Fifteen Years, and the General Political and Economic World Pattern into which the Commonwealth Would Most Satisfactorily Fit (Appreciation prepared in the Commonwealth Relations Office as requested at the Chancellor of the Exchequer's meeting on 31 May), para. 9.
3. CAB 133/131, PEC(52)3, 22 July 1952. Committee on Preparations for Commonwealth Economic Conference. External Economic Policy: Appreciation of the Attitude of Commonwealth Governments; Memorandum by a Group of Officials, para. 7.
4. Ibid., table I. United Kingdom: £229; India £22; West Africa £11; West Indies £13. Malaya's trade per head: £204; the United Kingdom's: £131.
5. Ibid., para. 10, and Annex B.
6. Ibid., para. 35.
7. Ibid.
8. Ibid., para. 36.
9. Ibid., para. 15.
10. Ibid., table I. Only 42 per cent of the UK's imports came from the Commonwealth.
11. Ibid., paras 19, 21, 22, 23.
12. Ibid., paras 12 (a) and 17 (v).
13. Ibid., para. 22.
14. Ibid., para. 27.
15. Cf. CAB 134/887 ES(53)34, 16 September 1953, United Kingdom Export Trends, Appendix, table 5, Total World Exports by Destination. Between 1950 and 1952 exports to the sterling area (excluding the United Kingdom) rose by 11.25 per cent; to Western Europe by 36.5 per cent; to North America by 42 per cent; to Latin America by 17 per

cent. As an export market in 1952 the sterling area was worth less than half Western Europe. See also Alan S. Milward, *The Reconstruction of Western Europe 1945–1951* (London, Routledge, 1984), pp. 488–9.

16. CAB 133/131, PEC(52)20, 1 September 1952. Commonwealth Development; Memorandum by a Group of Officials, para. 5, summarizing paras 21–24, and para. 10. See also para. 22(a)(i).

17. Ibid., para. 9, summarizing para. 39.

18. Ibid.

19. Ibid., para. 40.

20. Ibid.

21. Ibid., para. 45.

22. Ibid., paras 42(a) and 43(a). See also T 236/3070, RWBC/47888, 15 December 1951, The Sterling Area. This is an excellent brief for the Chancellor on the entire question by R. W. B. Clarke, then Under-Secretary at the Treasury, bearing annotations in Butler's own hand.

23. In fact, the problems of sterling and the domestic economy were intimately linked. Cf. T 236/3070, Sir George Bolton, Deputy Governor of the Bank of England, in a letter of 2 January 1952 to Sir Herbert Brittain pronouncing that the fact that British export prices were relatively too high 'was directly due to our unwillingness to introduce any domestic remedies. In other words, whether we admitted it or not, our only solution for domestic inflation was successive devaluations of sterling . . .'

24. Even in the 1960s a British citizen had to obtain Bank of England permission if he wished to buy a humble cottage in Europe, a process which naturally led to much ingenious evasion, such as swap arrangements with Continental friends.

25. Cf. Bolton's letter cited in Note 23.

26. As suggested in a paper of 8 February 1952 on 'Emergency Action' by the Overseas Finance Division of the Treasury in consultation with Sir George Bolton (Deputy Governor of the Bank of England) and Robert Hall (Director of the Economic Section of the Cabinet Office). The covering note was annotated by the Chancellor of the Exchequer: 'Thank you. Keep available.' See T 236/3240. The paper rejected such drastic remedies as another devaluation, disruption of the sterling area, restriction of transferability and import cuts.

27. T 236/3240–3245.

28. T 236/3240, RWBC/4872, para. 1.

29. Ibid., paras 3 and 5.
30. Ibid., para. 5.
31. Ibid.
32. Ibid., para. 7.
33. Ibid., para. 14.
34. Ibid., para. 16.
35. See Barnett, *Lost Victory*, pp. 41–45, 132, 157–8, and ch. 19; Milward, *Reconstruction of Western Europe*, pp. 37–8 and table 11.
36. T 236/3240, RWBC/4872, para. 23(i).
37. Ibid., para. 23(ii).
38. Ibid., para. 25.
39. Ibid.
40. Ibid., para. 29.
41. Ibid.
42. Ibid., para. 31.
43. Ibid., para. 32.
44. Ibid., para. 33. See also T 236/3240, RWBC/4905, 12 February 1952, *Septuagesima Plus*, being a further exposition of his plan by Clarke.
45. T 236/3240, 13 February 1952, *Septuagesima Plus – or Greek Kalends*; note from Copleston to Sir Leslie Rowan, para. 1(i).
46. Ibid., para. 1(ii).
47. Ibid., para. 1(iii).
48. Ibid., para. 3.
49. Ibid., para. 4.
50. T 236/3240, memorandum by Cobbold on 13 February 1952, para. 2.
51. Ibid.
52. Ibid., para. 5(a).
53. Ibid., para. 5(b).
54. Ibid., para. 5(c).
55. Ibid., para. 6.
56. Ibid., para. 7(a).
57. Ibid., para. 7(b).
58. Ibid., para. 7(c).
59. Ibid.
60. Ibid. Cobbold's comment about not using credits or drawing rights to shore up the reserves stands in direct contrast to the decision made under the Labour Government in 1948 to make maintenance of the reserves 'an overriding need' during the receipt of Marshall Aid. See

Barnett, *Lost Victory*, pp. 367–8, citing CAB 124/217, EPC(48)19, 19 March 1948, and EPC(48)24, 25 March 1948.

61. T 236/3240, memorandum of 12 February 1952 from the Governor of the Bank of England to the Chancellor of the Exchequer, para. 8. See also the appendix by Sir George Bolton, Deputy Governor of the Bank, on the technical reasons why 'inconvertibility of sterling in non-resident hands is not a policy which can long be sustained'. Bolton also remarked that Exchange Control 'no longer has public support. It is observed mainly because of fear of being found out . . .'

The present author recalls that as late as 1967 a friend, wishing to purchase a French cottage for a pittance, had to apply to the Bank of England for kind permission, and later had to smuggle out pounds (codenamed 'Apples' in correspondence!) via a professional colleague who was allowed to have a Swiss bank account for research purposes. Such was the privilege of being a citizen of a 'world power' twenty-two years after the Second World War.

62. T 236/3240, 16 February 1952.

63. Ibid., para. 11.

64. As would be expected since he and Bolton were confederates.

65. T 236/3240, RWBC/4915, para. 2.

66. The Prime Minister, Lord Cherwell (Paymaster General), Harry Crookshank (Minister of Health and Leader of the House of Commons), Lord Woolton (Lord President of the Council), Sir David Maxwell Fyfe (Home Secretary), and James Stuart (Secretary of State for Scotland).

67. T 236/3240, External Action; Draft Memorandum by the Chancellor of the Exchequer.

68. Ibid., para. 5. This ministerial get-together had been preceded by a flurry of meetings of senior departmental bureaucrats, at which the unconverted took great alarm at the ROBOT proposals. For the ins-and-outs of the Whitehall battle over ROBOT, see Edwin Plowden, *An Industrialist in the Treasury: The Post-war Years* (London, Andre Deutsch, 1989), ch. 14; and for an exciting day by day account, see Sir Donald MacDougall, then the Chief Adviser to the Prime Minister's Statistical Office, in *Don and Mandarin; Memoirs of an Economist* (London, John Murray, 1987), pp. 85–99.

69. T 236/3240, External Action; Draft Memorandum by the Chancellor of the Exchequer, para. 9(iv).

70. Ibid., para. 20.
71. Ibid.
72. Ibid., para. 21.
73. Ibid., para. 22.
74. Ibid.
75. Ibid., para. 47.
76. Whether or not 'Keynesianism' as practised in the United Kingdom after the Second World War was a caricature of Keynes's own thought is outside the scope of this book. In regard to German policies, see the essay by Ernst Helmstadter, 'The Irrelevance of Keynes to German Economic Policy and to International Economic Co-operation in the 1980s' in Walter Eltis and Peter Sinclair (eds), *Keynes and Economic Policy; The Relevance of The General Theory after Fifty Years* (London, Macmillan Press in association with the National Economic Development Office, 1988), especially pp. 413–15.
77. I am indebted to Dr Walter Eltis, who read this chapter in its first draft, for pointing out in letters of 1 and 12 December 1997 the potential consequences of combining a floating exchange rate with continued 'full-employment' demand management.
78. T 236/3240, External Action, Memorandum by the Chancellor of the Exchequer, para. 51.
79. Plowden, *Industrialist in the Treasury*, p. 146. Cherwell kept his copy, the better to rebut its contents.
80. Ibid.
81. T 236/3240, External Action; memorandum dated 23 February 1952.
82. Ibid., para. 2.
83. Ibid., para. 13.
84. Ibid., para. 14.
85. Ibid., para. 17.
86. Ibid.
87. Ibid., para. 19(1) and (6).
88. Ibid., para. 26.
89. Ibid., para. 27.
90. Cf. R. E. Osgood, *NATO: The Entangling Alliance* (Chicago and London, the University of Chicago Press, 1962), p. 87. The crisis over German rearmament and the European Defence Community was also boiling up.

91. Although Plowden's direct industrial experience was limited to junior posts before the war with the International Standard Electric Corporation and their British subsidiary Standard Telephone and Cables, he pretentiously entitled his post-war memoirs *An Industrialist in the Treasury*. By that token the present author, on the basis of his five years in the Public Relations department of the North Thames Gas Board, could describe himself as 'an industrialist in academe'!

92. T 236/3240, Hall to Plowden, 22 February 1952. Plowden also received a letter of report on the ministerial meeting from the Cabinet Secretary, Sir Edward Bridges, who wrote: 'For my part, my chief feeling is one of relief at some scheme which gives us a chance of retaining control over our affairs, notwithstanding all the difficulties and risks involved.' See T 236/3240, Bridges to Plowden, 22 February 1952.

93. PREM 11/138, Eden to Churchill, 23 February 1952, cited in Plowden, *Industrialist in the Treasury*, pp. 147–8.

94. Ibid., p. 148.

95. He was referring not to the sterling balances accumulated in wartime, but 'new' balances 'accumulated in the belief that no blocking was contemplated . . .' Cf. his letter to Plowden long after, quoted in ibid., p. 148.

96. Ibid. On 1 July 1952, when the idea of ROBOT had been for the moment revived, Robbins wrote after a meeting with Rowan and Bridges: 'In the end, I believe what worries me most about all this is the question of honour . . .' See T 236/3244, Supplementary Notes, para. 14. Concern for honour is of course much to be admired, especially if 'honour' in a particular case serves the national interest. But if it does not, which should come first?

97. T 236/3240, 21/22 February 1952, External Action; minute by Minister of State for Economic Affairs to the Chancellor of the Exchequer, para. 5.

98. Ibid., para. 6.

99. Ibid., paras 8–9.

100. Ibid., para. 10.

101. Ibid., para. 12.

102. Ibid., para. 13.

103. Ibid.

104. Ibid., para. 16.

105. T 236/3240, The Balance of Payments; memorandum by the Paymaster General, 25 February 1952.

106. Ibid.

107. Ibid.

108. Ibid.

109. T 236/3240, 25 February, to the Chancellor of the Exchequer. File copy initialled by Plowden.

110. Ibid., Exchange Rate, etc., 25 February 1952.

111. Ibid., para. 3.

112. T 236/3240, Bolton to the Chancellor (copy to Sir Edward Bridges), 24 February 1952.

113. CAB 128/40, CC(52)23rd, 24th and 25th Conclusions, 28 and 29 February 1952. These supply the provenance for the quotes below from Butler, Cherwell and Salisbury, and from unidentified members of the Cabinet.

114. This 1952 debate about the merits of a fixed or floating pound anticipates the 1990s arguments over British membership of the European Exchange Rate Mechanism.

115. For the details, see especially CAB 128/40, CC(52), 23rd, 24th and 25th Conclusions, paras (a)–(o).

116. Ibid., para. (o).

117. Cf. T 236/3241–5, and Plowden, *Industrialist in the Treasury*, pp. 153–6. When mooted by Butler in July 1952, it never reached the Cabinet. For the fresh discussion, prior to the Commonwealth Economic Conference, of a floating rate, convertibility and blocking (or funding) the sterling balances, see CAB 133/131, 29 August 1952, Committee on Preparations for Commonwealth Economic Conference; Commonwealth Sterling Balances; memorandum by a Group of Officials; and also PEC(52)44, 24 October 1952, Note on 'the Collective Approach to Convertibility'; Memorandum by the Paymaster General.

Needless to say, and in the Paymaster General's own words, 'the proposed "collective approach to convertibility" raised serious difficulties for many of the Commonwealth countries . . .'; and not only serious difficulties but also the usual deep differences of national interest that rendered the very term '*Common*wealth' so meaningless.

118. Butler's phrase; see p. 162, above.

9. 'The Leaders of the Agitation': Motor Vehicles

1. Cf. article headed 'United Action in South Essex' in the Communist publication *World News and Views*, issue of 4 July 1952, which openly proclaimed that the stoppages at Fords and Briggs were giving 'a lead to the country for the wage demands of millions and the anti-Tory fight', as part of 'the development of a mass movement to bring down the Tories and force a general election'.
2. Issue of 18 June 1952.
3. LAB 10/1157, 'Motor Car Manufacturers, *Ford Motor Company Ltd, Dagenham*. Token Strike of one hour each day and complete ban on overtime in protest against rejection of wage increase claim.' IR(Lo)15/1, Regional Industrial Relations Officer (R.I.R.O.) London, to Industrial Relations Department, Headquarters, Ministry of Labour and National Service, 21 June 1952.
4. Ibid., 12 August 1952.
5. Quoted in the *Daily Worker*, 21 June 1952.
6. Issue of 26 June 1952.
7. LAB 10/1157, IR(Lo)15/1, R.I.R.O. London to Industrial Relations Department Headquarters, Ministry of Labour, 25 June 1952.
8. Issue of 4 July 1952.
9. Ostensibly to compel the management immediately to reinstate the handful of workers laid off because of the Briggs strike. This the management refused to do until that strike was over and the flow resumed of car bodies for the laid-off men to work on.
10. Reports in the *Manchester Guardian*, the *News Chronicle* and the *Daily Telegraph*, 5 July 1952. See also LAB 10/1157, IR(Lo) 15/1, R.I.R.O. London to Industrial Relations Department Headquarters, Ministry of Labour and National Service, 5 July 1952.
11. LAB 10/1157, R.I.R.O. to Industrial Relations Department Headquarters, Ministry of Labour, 5 July 1952.
12. *Manchester Guardian*, 8 July 1952.
13. H. A. Turner, Garfield Clack and Geoffrey Roberts, *Labour Relations in the Motor Industry; A Study of Industrial Unrest and an International Comparison* (London, George Allen & Unwin, 1967), p. 275.
14. See LAB 10/613, 'Ford Motor Co. Ltd. Dagenham: Wage dispute, stoppage of work', for documentation relating to this strike.

15. Cf. Francis Beckett, *Enemy Within; The Rise and Fall of the British Communist Party* (London, John Murray, 1995), pp. 109 and 149–52.

16. LAB 10/613. Handwritten letter of 14 March 1946 from J. Wilson to the Minister of Labour.

17. LAB 10/613, announcement dated 1 May 1946.

18. See Turner, Clack and Roberts, *Labour Relations*, passim, but especially chs VIII and IX, for comparisons of the liability to strikes of all the major motor-vehicle firms from 1946 to 1961.

19. The following short account of this strike is based on the correspondence, reports, press cuttings and pamphlet material in LAB 10/1160, 'Vehicle Building. Park Royal Vehicles Ltd, Willedsen and the N.U.V.B. Strike in progress. Dispute over certain piece work prices.' A full objective analysis of the dispute and the factors involved is provided by the Report (published on 3 September 1952) of the Committee of Investigation appointed by the Minister of Labour on 26 August 1952.

20. Letter of 25 August 1952 from A. Johnson & Co. (London) Ltd, export agents, in LAB 10/1160.

21. Ibid.

22. LAB 10/1160, *Report of a Committee of Investigation into a Difference between Park Royal Vehicles Limited and Certain of Their Employees, Members of the National Union of Vehicle Builders or of the Amalgamated Society of Woodcutting Machinists.*

23. The following brief account is based on LAB 10/1168, 'Austin Motor Co Ltd, Longbridge, and the National Union of Vehicle Builders: strike in protest against refusal to re-engage redundant shop steward J. McHugh' (this file on the problems caused by the case of just one worker is about three inches thick in documentation!). See also Cmd. 8839, 'Report of Court of Inquiry into the Dispute between the Austin Motor Co Ltd and certain workpeople, members of the National Union of Vehicle Builders', May 1953; and Turner, Clack and Roberts, *Labour Relations*, pp. 271–5.

24. Since being first employed 'at the Austin' in 1928, McHugh had been fired five times, had left of his own accord twice, and been re-hired seven times. See Cmd. 8839, para. 17.

25. Cmd. 8839, para. 85 (2), (3) and (4).

26. Ibid., para. 85 (5).

27. Turner, Clack and Roberts, *Labour Relations*, p. 275.

28. LAB 10/757, 'Vehicle Building Industry. Differences arising out of the wage claim by the Trade Unions, 1947–1948'.

29. Cited in LAB 10/757.

30. See LAB 10/850, 'Engineering – Motor Car Manufacture. Daimler Motor Co. Ltd., Body Department, Redford, Coventry and N.U.V.B., A.E.U. and A.W.C. M.'

31. Ibid., letter of 1 December.

32. Ibid., National Arbitration Tribunal. Award No. 1489, 17 July 1950.

33. For the relevant correspondence and reports, see LAB 10/1106, Engineering. E.N.V. Engineering Co Ltd, London, N.W.10, and A.E.U. and T.&G.W.U. Stoppage arising out of a foreman's conduct.

34. Ibid., *E.N.V. Engineering Co. Ltd. Strike of Workpeople.* Particulars of effect of strike on firm's customers, 13 December 1951.

35. Ibid., IR(Lo)338, 5 December 1951.

36. Ibid.

37. Ibid.

38. Ibid.

39. Strike Committee's manifesto asking for support from other workers, in LAB 10/1106.

40. Ibid., letters of 9 November from H. Gray and W. A. Roy.

41. According to a handwritten note in LAB 10/1106.

42. *Daily Worker*, 1 and 2 January 1952.

43. LAB 10/1106, Letter from the Director, Engineering and Allied Employers' London and District Association.

44. Ibid., resolution of the A.E.U. Executive Council, 8 January 1952.

45. LAB 10/1106, Report of the Committee of Investigation appointed by the Minister of Labour and National Service to inquire into a difference at the E.N.V. Engineering Co. Ltd., London, 31 January 1952.

46. Turner, Clack and Roberts, *Labour Relations*, p. 242.

47. Ibid., p. 240.

48. Report in *The Times*, 2 May 1955. The report referred to '220' transfer machines. This was an error: the actual number was 22, plus 220 new machine tools. See note of telephone call from Standard's production engineer to the Ministry of Labour in LAB 10/1445. The following account of the strike at Standard is based on the documents in LAB

10/1445, 'Engineering. Standard Motor Car Co Ltd., Coventry, and the Confederation of Shipbuilding and Engineering Unions. Strikes over Redundancy [1956].'

49. Back in 1948 there had been a strike at Austin because the company wished to introduce a new spindle cutter capable of increasing productivity in this process by 140 per cent. Apart from removing the pieceworker's control over his rate of output, it meant a complex business of setting new wage rates for work with the spindle, and then accordingly adjusting the rates for other functions in the factory ('relativity' and all that) – no easy task with twenty separate unions with which to negotiate. See Peter J. S. Dunnett, *The Decline of the British Motor Industry; The Effects of Government Policy, 1945–1979* (London, Croom Helm, 1980), p. 34.

50. Producing the Phase III Vanguard, and the Standard Eight and Ten.

51. See Dunnett, *Decline of the British Motor Industry*, table 2.2., p. 20. In 1954 Standard produced 22,515 Vanguards; in 1955 only 13,080. See Christopher Balfour, *Roads to Oblivion; Triumphs & Tragedies of British Car Makers 1946–56* (Bideford, Bay View Books, 1996), p. 170.

52. Cf. LAB 10/1445, Background Note for PQ [Parliamentary Question] 130/53/56, dated 4 May 1956; also the summary of developments in the strike in LAB 10/1445, IR 266/3/56, Motor-Car Manufacturing. Standard Motor-Car Company Limited, Coventry (Non Federated). Strike in Protest against Dismissals for Redundancy.

53. Issue of 28 April 1956.

54. Ibid.

55. LAB 10/1445, as reported in a telex at 1159 on 1 May 1956 to Ministry of Labour headquarters.

56. See LAB 10/1445.

57. LAB 10/1445, letter from H. S. Weale, Production Director, to the Coventry district secretary, Confederation of Shipbuilding and Engineering Unions, 27 April 1956.

58. As reported in the *Manchester Guardian*, 1 May 1956. The *Daily Telegraph* gives a slightly different version, but the import is the same.

59. As reported in the *Daily Herald*, 4 May 1956.

60. As quoted in the *Coventry Evening Telegraph*, 4 May 1956.

61. LAB 10/1445, The Standard Motor Company, Ltd. Personal Message from the Managing Director to all hourly paid Employees.

62. Ibid.

63. Leader of 7 July 1952, commenting on the current strike at Ford of Dagenham.
64. LAB 10/1445, IR(bi)1997/3/4, 5 June 1956, Report by Regional Office to Headquarters, Ministry of Labour.
65. LAB 10/1445. Standard Motor Company – Redundancies. Notes of a Meeting at 8 St. James's Square on 7th June, 1956.
66. Article by Stephen Parkinson in issue of 8 June 1956.
67. LAB 10/1445, IR.266/3/1956, Standard Motor Company – Redundancies. Notes of a Meeting Held at 8 St James's Square on 11th June, 1956.
68. Ibid. In point of fact, Standard's financial weakness led to its takeover by Massey-Harris-Ferguson in 1957 – the first of the 'Big Five' British motor-car manufacturers to lose its independence (the British Motor Corporation being a merger between Austin and Morris, not a takeover).
69. LAB 10/1445, Dick to Macleod, 13 June 1956.
70. LAB 10/1445, note of a telephone call, 27 June 1956.
71. LAB 10/1445.
72. See report in the *Manchester Guardian*, 30 June 1956.
73. Turner, Clack and Roberts, *Labour Relations*, table VIII/1, p. 232. This gives 37 strikes and 227,700 'striker-days' for the nine calendar years 1931–39; 137 strikes and 986,000 'striker-days' for the ten calendar years 1945–54.
74. Ibid.
75. Ibid., pp. 300–306.
76. Ibid.
77. Ibid., pp. 306–311.
78. Despite the handicaps of defeat, destruction and a three-year time-lag behind Britain in restarting large-scale car production, West Germany had nearly equalled British productivity by 1955–3.9 'equivalent' vehicles per employee to Britain's 4.1. See Dunnett, *Decline of the British Motor Industry*, table 6.6., p. 131, citing D. T. Jones and S. J. Prais, 'Plant Size and Productivity in the Motor Industry: Some International Comparisons', *Oxford Bulletin of Economics and Statistics*, vol. 40 (May 1978), p. 142.

10. 'Actual or Imagined Grievances':
Aircraft and Much Else

1. See Correlli Barnett, *The Audit of War* (London, Macmillan, 1986, and Pan Books, 1997), passim, but especially pp. 67–8, 74, 80, 113, 121 and 154–6.
2. John Stevenson, *British Society 1914–1945* (Harmondsworth, Pelican Books, 1984), p. 197, table 14.
3. See Barnett, *Audit of War*, chs 4, 5, and 8, passim. Along with many other employees of the North Thames Gas Board in the early 1950s, I was myself adept at these skills.
4. See LAB 10/568 for the weekly 'strike charts' which the Ministry of Labour and National Service continued to keep until June 1947.
5. For the full tally, see LAB 10/568.
6. Ibid.
7. The Restoration of Pre-War Practices Act, 1942, provided for the post-war reinstatement of pre-war trade practices departed from during the war for the sake of greater and more efficient output. The 'trade practices' were defined as rules, practices or customs with respect to 'the classes of persons to be or not to be employed' and 'the conditions of employment, hours of work and working conditions'. See LAB 10/604, letter from George Isaacs, Minister of Labour and National Service, on 26 June 1946 to Ernest Bevin, Foreign Secretary, and his reply of 2 July 1946.
8. LAB 10/612, 'Engineering: The Midlands Regional Industrial Relations Officer reports a dispute between Messrs. Fisher and Ludlow Limited Birmingham and Birmingham and Midland Sheet Metal Workers Society; sit-down strike on 4 January 1946 over wages and conditions.'
9. LAB 10/568, 'strike chart' for week ended 6 November 1946.
10. See correspondence and report of the Court of Inquiry in LAB 10/710.
11. Cf. ibid., Award of the Industrial Court, 10 September 1947; letter of 23 April 1947 from H. J. Comber, the L.M.S.'s Chief Officer for Labour and Establishment, to the Secretary, Ministry of Labour and National Service.

12. LAB 10/710, Railway Shopmen. Award of the Industrial Court, 23 October 1946.

13. In 1937. See LAB 10/615, 'Printing Industry: dispute between the British Federation of Master Printers, Newspaper Society and the Printing and Kindred Trades Federation over 40 hour week and 2 weeks' annual holiday.'

14. Ibid., especially Note of a meeting held on 29 July 1946 attended by representatives of the B.F.M.P., the Newspaper Society and the Printing and Kindred Trades Federation.

15. Ibid., Joint Press Statement issued by the British Federation of Master Printers and the Printing and Kindred Trades Federation, 2 October 1946. Earlier, in a classic British labour relations bind, the employers had refused to negotiate while under the duress of the overtime ban, and the unions had refused to lift the ban until the employers agreed to negotiate.

16. LAB 10/568, strike chart for week ending 13 June 1945.

17. Ibid., strike chart for week ending 9 October 1946.

18. Ibid.

19. Ibid.

20. See LAB 10, index to files, for the gamut of disputes in all their rich variety.

21. T 234/74, RLP(56)3, 7 May 1956, Committee on Restrictive Labour Practices: The Ministry of Supply's Experience of Restrictive Labour Practices, para. 9. The memoranda of this Committee in T 234/74, RLP(56)series, especially the Committee's final report, and the minutes of meetings in T234/75 provide a fascinating dossier on the British labour scene in all its petty jealousies, fears and demarcations.

22. See Correlli Barnett, *The Lost Victory: British Dreams, British Realities 1945–1950* (London, Macmillan, 1996, and Pan Books, 1997), chapter 12, and cited documentation.

23. Lab 10/568, the weekly 'strike charts', 1945–47.

24. See LAB 10/1023, 'Engineering Industry. ROLLS ROYCE, Hillington, and A.E.U., General Ironfounders Association, Glasgow, and T.&G.W.U. Stoppage of work arising out of dismissal of two shop stewards, alleged victimisation.'

25. Ibid., report to Ministry of Labour headquarters by the Industrial Relations Officer, Scotland, 15 February 1951. The shop stewards had

imposed an overtime and piece-work ban because of stalled negotiations. The company sought to maintain production by switching
workers as required between the military and civil sides of the factory.
The shop stewards raised the cry that the transferred men had been
put on to work that had been 'blacked'.

26. Ibid.
27. Issue of 16 February 1951.
28. LAB 10/1023, report by I.R.O. (Scotland), 1 March 1951.
29. Ibid., report of I.R.O. (Scotland), 2 April 1951.
30. Ibid., report by I.R.O. (Scotland), 12 June 1951.
31. Barnett, *Audit of War*, p. 157, and cited documentation.
32. The following brief account is based on LAB 10/1030, 'Aircraft
    Production, SHORT BROTHERS and HARLAND Ltd, Belfast,
    and Confederation of Shipbuilding and Engineering Unions. Report
    from Ministry of Supply regarding strike in progress. Dispute concern-
    ing dismissal of shop stewards.'
33. LAB 10/1030, Interim Report of the Court of Inquiry into the causes
    and circumstances of the trade dispute at the Belfast and Newtownards
    factories of Messrs. Short Brothers and Harland Ltd, para. I(a).
34. 'Glassing', or ramming a broken bottle or tankard into someone's face,
    was (and is) a renowned form of argument in the bars of Glasgow.
35. See correspondence in LAB 10/780, and especially the report of the
    Court of Inquiry, dated 18 May 1948.
36. LAB 10/780, report of 29 September 1949.
37. See LAB 10/1043, 'Civil Engineering. R. Costain Ltd., Concrete
    Piling Ltd., Matthew Hall & Co Ltd. and others at Capenhurst Atomic
    Site and A.S.W. Demarcation Dispute regarding the erection of
    Plymax Interior partitions. [1951].' The plant comprised thirty miles
    of main piping and 700 process units.
38. In LAB 10/780.
39. LAB 10/780, R.I.R.O.'s report to Ministry of Labour on a meeting
    between the parties on 30 April 1951.
40. LAB 10/780, report of R.I.R.O. of 5 July 1951.
41. LAB 10/780, report of R.I.R.O., 14 July 1951.
42. A useful if depressing survey is provided by the draft report on
    Restrictive Practices in the Shipbuilding and Ship-repairing Industries,
    16 January 1950, in LAB 10/932.
43. LAB 10/561, 'Shipbuilding and Ship-repairing – AJRO Bristol.

Reports of Dispute between Charles Hill & Sons Ltd., and Boilermakers', Iron & Steel Shipbuilders' Society and Ship constructors & Shipwrights' Association. Stoppage of work: Demarcation. About 100 Riveters stopped work because an acetylene lamp had been issued to shipwrights. The Shipwrights contend that the lamp is common to all grades & they claim the right to use it whenever necessary on their work. Work resumed but discussions still proceeding.'

44. LAB 10/561, report from Industrial Relations Department, Bristol, to Ministry of Labour, London, 5 February 1946.

45. LAB 10/561, award dated 19 March 1946.

46. LAB 10/679, Shipbuilding. Palmers Shipbuilding Company Limited, Hebburn, and Boilermakers' Society: apprehended dispute over firm's intention to have a new flame cutting machine operated by an 'unskilled' worker.

47. LAB 10/679, 'Industrial Courts Act, 1919. Interim Report of a Court of Inquiry into a Dispute at the Naval Yard of Vickers-Armstrongs Ltd, Walker-on-Tyne. Presented by the Minister of Labour and National Service to Parliament by Command of His Majesty, December 1944', part II, para. 5.

48. LAB 10/679, ibid., part II, para. 19.

49. LAB 10/679, Apprehended Dispute: report by Conciliation Officer and R.I.R.O., Newcastle, 4 June 1947.

50. LAB 10/679, ibid.

51. CAB 87/7, R(44)53, Memorandum by the First Lord of the Admiralty to the Cabinet Reconstruction Committee, 16 March 1944.

52. For the course of events and arguments in this dispute see the fat file of papers in LAB 10/806, 'Shipbuilding Industry. R.S. Hayes Ltd, Pembroke Dock, 1948–1952. Demarcation Dispute between the Boilermakers' Society and the Shipconstructors & Shipwrights Association.'

53. LAB 10/806, 10 September 1948.

54. Cited in LAB 10/806, ibid.

55. LAB 10/806, ibid.

56. LAB 10/806, ibid., letter to W. S. Reed, Ministry of Labour and National Service, Cardiff, from R. S. Hayes, 18 December 1948.

57. LAB 10/806, report of the Conciliation Officer, Wales, 15 November 1948.

58. LAB 10/806, TUC award of 21 December 1949, para. 4.

59. LAB 10/929, 'Shipbuilding and Engineering, Vickers–Armstrong Ltd., Barrow in Furness, and Boiler Makers Society. Strike in progress. Demarcation dispute.' Report of 21 September 1949.
60. Ibid., report dated 29 September.
61. Ibid.
62. Ibid., handwritten internal Ministry of Labour paper dated 29 September 1949.
63. Ibid., memorandum dated 4 October 1949.
64. Ibid., report dated 17 October 1949.
65. Ibid.
66. The first local Shipwrights' friendly society dates from 1784, with the amalgamation of several such venerable societies into the Shipconstructors' and Shipwrights' Association dating from 1919. The Order of Friendly Boilermakers was founded in 1834.
67. LAB 10/929, report of R.I.R.O., Manchester, 17 October 1949.
68. Ibid., report of 22 October 1949.
69. Ibid., R.I.R.O.'s report of 28 October 1949.
70. Ibid., note from R.I.R.O. to London, 31 October 1949, and enclosed copy of the Award.
71. LAB 10/1197, Shipbuilding. John Brown & Co Ltd, Clydebank – sub-contractors: J. & C. McEwan Ltd – and the Boilermakers Society and the Shipconstructors and Shipwrights Assocn: Demarcation Dispute.
72. Ibid., handwritten minute of 24 March 1953.
73. In 10/1197.
74. Report of 7 March 1953, in LAB 10/1197.
75. In report by IRO, Scotland, dated 28 November 1955, in LAB 10/1411. 'Shipbuilding. Alex Stephen & Sons Ltd (Sub-Contractors – McEwan Insulators Ltd) and the Boilermakers Society, N.U. of S.M.W. & B [sic], Shipconstructors & Shipwrights Association. Demarcation Dispute on Insulation Work. Correspondence between the Shipbuilders Association and the Shipbuilding Employers Federation.'
76. LAB 10/1452, N.J.A.C. enquiry into efficient use of Manpower – correspondence arising from the decision of the N.J.A.C. to seek information from industry: 'Extracts from Print of Shorthand Notes of Resumed General Wages Conference between the Shipbuilding Employers Federation and the Confederation of Shipbuilding and

Engineering Unions held on 15 March 1955. References to Interferences with Production, Restrictive Practices, Demarcation Disputes, etc.'

77. LAB 10/1411, Report by IRO Scotland dated 20 September 1955.
78. LAB 10/1411, Report by IRO Scotland dated 21 December 1955 entitled 'Demarcation Dispute on Insulation Work at Stephen's Yard, Linthouse'.
79. LAB 10/1411, report dated 14 April 1956.
80. LAB 10/1399, letter cited in report of Wales Office of the Ministry of Labour to London headquarters, 19 August 1955.
81. LAB 10/1371. 'Shipbuilding, Cammell Laird & Co., Birkenhead and the A.S.W., N.U.S.M.W. & B., Boilermakers' Society – Demarcation.
    (1) Strike by Sheet Metal Workers Union in support of a Claim to the work (3″ insulation in aluminium) on Refrigerator Ships.
    (2) Demarcation dispute over air ducting.'

11. 'This Long and Bitter Dispute': the Shipyards

1. For blow by blow documentation, see LAB 10/1371.
2. Ibid., Note (of 22 November 1955 by the R.I.R.O) giving additional information about the dispute affecting joiners at Cammell Laird's yard, Birkenhead, obtained during the course of a visit to the yard on Monday, 21st November, 1955.
3. LAB 10/1371.
4. Ibid.
5. Ibid., I.R.567/3/55.
6. LAB 10/1371.
7. In ibid.
8. Copy letter in ibid.
9. Ibid.
10. Copy letter from George Weir, Agencia Maritima Hondurena S.A., in LAB 10/1371.
11. LAB 10/1371, letter of 27 February from Robert Johnson of Cammell Laird to C. J. Maston CBE, Industrial Relations Department, Ministry of Labour, London.
12. LAB 10/1371.
13. Ibid., Difficulties in the Shipyard of Cammell Laird & Co. Ltd.

REPORT to The Right Honourable the Minister of Labour and National Service, paras 40–41.

14. *Sunday Graphic*, 1 April 1956.
15. Ibid.
16. LAB 10/1371, letter of 7 May 1956 from I. P. Garran to J. F. Hewitt, copied to Sir Wilfred Neden, Chief Industrial Commissioner, Ministry of Labour.
17. Ibid.
18. Ibid., scribbled on the cover sheet to the copy letter from Washington.
19. Report in the *Morning Advertiser*, 14 June 1956.
20. As reported in the *Daily Telegraph*, 9 August 1956. Up till January 1956 British shipowners had been forbidden to buy from Japanese yards by the Import, Export and Customs Powers (Defence) Act of 1939, which, as the President of the Board of Trade and the Minister of Transport and Civil Aviation pointed out in a joint memorandum on 19 January 1956, was intended 'to protect our balance of payments – not to protect the United Kingdom shipbuilding industry'. (See CAB 134/1230, EP(56)7, Imports of Merchant Ships from Japan.) Despite opposition from the First Lord of the Admiralty (see CAB 134/1230, EP(56)8 of 20 January 1956), the Cabinet Economic Policy Committee agreed on 25 January to lift the embargo on imports of Japanese ships, leaving them subject only to the general system of import licensing still in force (CAB 134/656, EP(56)2nd, 25 January 1956, item 1).

    Since the Labour Government had lifted the embargo on British imports of ships from European yards in 1951, this decision meant that the British shipbuilding industry had now had its feather bed removed as well as its eiderdown.
21. Ibid.
22. LAB 10/1282, 'Industrial Courts Act 1919. Report of a Court of Inquiry between employers who are members of the Shipbuilding Employers' Federation and workmen who are members of Trade Unions affiliated to the Confederation of Shipbuilding and Engineering Unions. Presented by the Minister of Labour and National Service to Parliament by Command of Her Majesty, February 1954' (published as Cmd. 9085), para. 13.
23. Ibid., para. 14.

24. Ibid., para. 49, citing a speech by the Chancellor of the Exchequer in the House of Commons on 6 November 1953.

25. See Correlli Barnett, *The Audit of War* (London, Macmillan, 1986, and Pan Books, 1997), chapter 6, for the technical performance of British shipbuilding during the Second World War, and Correlli Barnett, *The Lost Victory: British Dreams, British Realities 1945–1950* (London, Macmillan, 1996, and Pan Books, 1997), pp. 299–303, for its record between 1945 and 1950.

26. See evidence and final report in LAB 10/1282.

27. Ministry of Labour press release of 31 December 1953, in LAB 10/ 1273, 'Engineering and Shipbuilding Industries. Appointment of Courts of Inquiry into Trade Dispute in Engineering and Shipbuilding Industries. [1954]'

28. See LAB 10/1273 for the correspondence, evidence submitted, and Court's report in respect of general engineering (published in 1954 as Cmd. 9084: Industrial Courts Act, 1919. Report of a Court of Enquiry into a Dispute between employers who are members of the Engineering and Allied Employers' National Federation and workmen who are members of Trade Unions affiliated to the Confederation of Shipbuilding and Engineering Trade Unions). See LAB 10/1282 for correspondence, evidence submitted, and Court's report in respect of shipbuilding (published in 1954 as Cmd. 9085: Industrial Courts Act, 1919. Report of a Court of Enquiry into a dispute betwen employers who are members of The Shipbuilding Employers' Federation and workmen who are members of Trade Unions affiliated to the Confederation of Shipbuilding and Engineering Unions).

29. LAB 10/1282, Report, paras 48 and 49.

30. Andrew Shonfield, *British Economic Policy Since the War* (Harmondsworth, Penguin Books, 1958), p. 42.

31. LAB 10/1282, Report, para. 51.

32. Ibid., para. 52.

33. LAB 10/1166, reports by R.I.R.O., Northern Regional Office, to Dame Mary Smieton, Ministry of Labour, 31 March and 29 April 1953, the latter enclosing a copy of an article by Ted Hill in *The United Society of Boilermakers, Shipbuilders and Structural Workers' Report* for April 1953. The National Executive Member was F. A. Stamp.

34. Ibid., letter to Dame Mary Smieton of 29 April 1953.

35. LAB 10/1282, Report, para. 49.

36. Shonfield, *British Economic Policy*, p. 43.

37. LAB 10/1282, Report, para. 62.

38. Ibid., para. 63.

39. Ibid., para. 113.

40. Ibid., paras 117–20.

41. LAB 10/1282, letter of 5 February 1954, from the Shipbuilding Employers' Federation to the Secretary of the Court of Inquiry, reporting the results of detailed investigations on costs within the industry, and estimating that granting the full claim of 15 per cent would add on average 9–10 per cent to costs in British shipbuilding and ship-repairing yards.

42. Sidney Pollard, *The Wasting of the British Economy; British Economic Policy 1945 to the Present* (London and Canberra, Croom Helm, 1982), p. 80.

43. In the period 1946–59 shipbuilding had the worst record of any single industry, accounting for 11.3 per cent of all major strikes in 1946–52, and 16.3 per cent in 1953–9, so narrowly beating the motor-vehicle industry. See J. Durcan, E. McCarthy, and G. Redman, *Strikes in Post-war Britain: study of stoppages of work due to industrial disputes 1946–1973* (London, George Allen & Unwin, 1983), tables 2.14 and 3.14.

44. Ibid.

45. LAB 10/1273, Industrial Courts Act, 1919. Report of a Court of Enquiry into a Dispute between employers who are members of the Engineering and Allied Employers' Federation and workmen who are members of Trade Unions affiliated to the Confederation of Shipbuilding and Engineering Unions, para. 103. The Report was published as Cmd. 9084.

46. Report, para. 5. The higher percentage is partly accounted for by the drop in the contribution of other exports, such as coal.

47. Ibid., paras 6–9.

48. Ibid., para. 12.

49. Ibid.

50. Ibid., para. 17.

51. See LAB 10/1273, letter of 6 January 1954 to the Secretary of the Court of Inquiry from Gavin Martin, General Secretary of the CSEU, and enclosures.

52. Barnett, *Audit of War*, p. 156, quoting from AVIA 15/2536, Training of Labour for the Aircraft Industry.
53. LAB 10/1273, Report of Court of Inquiry, para. 38.
54. Report, para. 39.
55. Ibid., para. 41, citing 'National Income and Expenditure – 1946–1952' to show that gross profits in engineering, shipbuilding and electrical goods rose from £152 million in 1947 to £305 million in 1951.
56. Report, para. 63.
57. Ibid., paras 81–2.
58. Ibid., para. 32.
59. Ibid., para. 33. See also the Court's comments on the pitfalls of interpreting cost-of-living indexes in paras 18–24.
60. T 230/300, Railway Dispute, minute by S. C. Leslie, Head of Information Division, Treasury, 3 January 1955.
61. LAB 10/1273, Report of Court of Enquiry, para. 44.
62. Ibid., para. 43.
63. Ibid., para. 44.
64. Ibid.
65. See correspondence in LAB 10/1273 between the Secretary of the Court of Inquiry and A. C. Happold, Secretary of the Engineering and Allied Employers' National Federation, especially letters from Happold of 28 January and 8 February 1954.
66. Report, para. 58.
67. Ibid., para. 100.
68. Ibid., paras 129 and 130.
69. Ibid., para. 138.
70. Ibid., para. 139.
71. Ibid.
72. Ibid., para. 111.
73. Ibid.
74. Ibid., para. 143.
75. LAB 10/1273, letter of 3 March 1954 from Sir Harold Howitt to Sir Robert J. Sinclair.
76. Three per cent in relation to retail prices in 1952–53, according to Cmd. 9108, Economic Survey, 1954, p. 30.
77. Cf. LAB 10/1273, report of Court of Inquiry, para. 95.
78. Cf. ibid., para. 129.

79. Ibid., para. 146. In this report, as in the report on the shipbuilding dispute, the Court floated the idea of some kind of impartial body which in the national interest would oversee increases of wages and prices. This idea was eventually to be embodied in various futile 'prices and incomes boards' in the 1960s and 1970s, the equivalent of applying feeble brakes in the hope of slowing a powerfully engined car with the accelerator pressed to the floor.

12. 'Custom Versus Development': Coalfields and the Docks

1. After all, it was not until October 1950 that the NCB was even ready to submit a fifteen-year plan of development (*Plan for Coal*) for the approval of the Minister of Fuel and Power, which was granted in 1951. Cf. CAB 134/651, PC(51)86, 12 July 1951, Production Committee. National Plan for Coal. Memorandum by the Minister of Fuel and Power, para. 2. From 1947 through 1951, capital investment averaged only £27.2 million annually. See William Ashworth, with the assistance of Mark Pegg, *The History of the British Coal Industry, Volume 5, 1946–1982: The Nationalized Industry* (Oxford, the Clarendon Press, 1986), table 5.2., p. 203. This curb on investment partly reflects the Labour Government's use of nationalization as a means directly to restrict capital expenditure in industry in order to offset general inflationary pressures and also accommodate the burdens of 'New Jerusalem' and the world role within the limited resources of the economy. See Correlli Barnett, *The Lost Victory: British Dreams, British Realities 1945–1950* (London, Macmillan, 1996, and Pan Books, 1997), chs 8 and 11.

   Although annual investment in colliery development increased from £50 million in 1952 to £95 million in 1955 (Ashworth, *British Coal Industry*, vol. 5, table 5.2), only 20 out of 281 major schemes of development in *Plan for Coal* had yet been completed by the end of the first post-war decade. See below, ch. 14.

2. Coal Mining; Report of the Technical Advisory Committee, Cmd. 6610. It was chaired by Sir Charles Reid, who was to resign from the Board of the National Coal Board in 1948 because of disillusion with the quality of senior management.

3. For an account of the coal industry during the Second World War and a summary of the industry's history from the Great War onwards, see Correlli Barnett, *The Audit of War* (London, Macmillan, 1986, and Pan Books, 1997), ch. 4. For an account of its post-war history under nationalization to 1950, see Barnett, *Lost Victory*, ch. 11. For terse description of the quality of pit managers at the time of nationalization, see Ashworth, *British Coal Industry*, vol. 5, pp. 170–71. For the quality of management up to 1955, see below, ch. 14.

4. Ashworth, *British Coal Industry*, vol. 5, pp. 167–8.

5. Ibid.

6. Ibid., and footnote 1 on p. 168.

7. Ibid., pp. 169–170, and table A.2, pp. 677–8.

8. J. Durcan, E. McCarthy, and G. Redman, *Strikes in Post-war Britain: study of stoppages of work due to industrial disputes 1946–1973* (London, George Allen & Unwin, 1983), table 8.3, p. 245.

9. Ibid., table 8.2, p. 243.

10. Ashworth, *British Coal Industry*, vol. 5, p. 166.

11. See Barnett, *Audit of War*, ch. 4.

12. Ashworth, *British Coal Industry*, vol. 5, pp. 165–6.

13. CAB 134/648, PC(50)99, 27 October 1950. Production Committee. Coal Supplies: Methods of Increasing Production and Reducing Consumption. Memorandum by the Minister of Fuel and Power, para. A1(d).

14. Barnett, *Audit of War*, p. 65, citing Cmd. 6538, *Ministry of Fuel and Power: Statistical Digest for 1938*, table X.

15. CAB 134/648, PC(50)99, part II, para. 11 (iv).

16. CAB 134/648, PC(50)100, Production Committee. Outlook for Coal Supplies and Particularly for Coal Exports during the Five Years 1951–1955. Memorandum by the Minister of Fuel and Power, para. 2(c).

17. CAB 134/648, PC(50)99, II, 2.

18. CAB 134/843, EA(52)1, 1 January 1952, Economic Policy Committee. Coal Output for 1952, para. 3.

19. Ibid., paras 1 and 2.

20. According to the Cabinet Economic Policy Committee. See CAB 134/841, EA(51)1st, 30 November 1951.

21. CAB 134/843, EA(52)44, 10 April 1952. Revision of Coal Budget for 1952 – Memorandum by the Secretary of State for the Co-ordination of Transport, Fuel and Power.

22. CAB 134/846, EA(53)10th, 18 March 1953.

23. Ashworth, *British Coal Industry*, vol. 5, p. 166.

24. Ibid.

25. Reported in the *Daily Express*, 9 January 1956.

26. Deep-mined output in 1955 stood at 211.3 million tons; in 1951 at 212.9 million tons. See Ashworth, *British Coal Industry*, vol. 5, table A.1., p. 672.

27. Ibid., p. 169.

28. Durcan et al., *Strikes in Post-war Britain*, table 8.1, p. 241, shows that days lost through strikes each year in the period 1947–55 only amounted to small percentages of potential working time. Ashworth, *British Coal Industry*, vol. 5, ch. 5 and table A.1., shows that over this period stoppages and go-slows accounted for a total loss of output of less than 1 per cent of actual production. However, if the impact of disaffection in the coal industry was thus quantitatively marginal, it was nevertheless at the same time crucial, because the national problem over coal supplies during the post-war decade also lay at the margin, turning on a few million tons annually even though total production ranged between 200 million tons in 1947 and 225 million tons in 1955.

29. Just over 13 million tons compared with 38 million in 1938 and 29 million in 1889. Cf. Ashworth, *British Coal Industry*, vol. 5, table A.1., p. 672; CAB 134/843, EPB(53)5th; R. C. K. Ensor, *England 1870–1914* (Oxford, the Clarendon Press, 1966), p. 109.

30. CAB 134/853, EA(54)145, 20 December 1954. Economic Policy Committee. The Coal Position. Memorandum by the Minister of Fuel and Power, para. 5. See also CAB 134/853, EA(54)122, 23 November 1954: Coal Imports. Memorandum by the Minister of Fuel and Power, and EA(54)125, 24 November 1954: Coal. Memorandum by the Economic Secretary to the Treasury.

31. CAB 134/652, PC(51)99, 30 July 1951, para. 2.

32. Durcan et al., *Strikes in Post-war Britain*, p. 272.

33. LAB 10/580, 'Report of a Strike at the London Docks over alleged harshness of method of dealing with absenteeism involving the T. & G.W. and the Stevedores Union', letter of 25 October 1945 from F. P. Hogger, London Dock Labour Board, to S. C. Parkin, National Dock Labour Corporation.

34. Kenneth O. Morgan, *Labour in Power, 1945–1951* (Oxford, the Clarendon Press, 1984), p. 373.

35. CAB 134/175, CP(47)138, 28 April 1947, in pursuance of the Cabinet's decision on 17 April, CM(47)37th, Minute 5.

36. See Barnett, *Lost Victory*, pp. 77–8, 198–200.

37. For documentation on this dispute, see LAB 10/735, 'Transport (Docks). Ministry of Transport, Glasgow Docks, and Scottish T.&G.W.U. Strike commenced March 24th, over proposed redundancy of dockers.'

38. LAB 10/735, report of 5 April 1947. The R.I.R.O. (Scotland) was the Regional Industrial Relations Officer.

39. As reported by the R.I.R.O. (Scotland) on 8 April 1947. See LAB 10/735.

40. Ibid., report of 9 April.

41. CAB 134/175, EC(47)1, 30 April 1947, Glasgow and London Dock Workers' disputes. Memorandum by the Minister of Transport, para. 3.

42. LAB 10/665, S&T(CC)(47)5th, 30 April 1947, Supply and Transport Organisation, Co-ordinating Committee.

43. CAB 134/175, EC(47)1, para. 10.

44. Ibid., para. 11.

45. As reported in the *Glasgow Herald* on 28 April 1947.

46. In LAB 10/735.

47. LAB 10/735, report of R.I.R.O. (Scotland), 1 May 1947.

48. Ibid., handwritten note of 2 May 1947.

49. Ibid., report of R.I.R.O. (Scotland) on 5 May 1947.

50. CAB 134/175, EC(47)1st, 1 May 1947, item 2.

51. See copy of the report, dated 13 June 1947, in LAB 10/735.

52. Ibid., para. 2.

53. Ibid., Appendix 'B'.

54. Ibid., para. 3.

55. Ibid., para. 7.

56. LAB 10/735, report of R.I.R.O. (Scotland), 2 April 1948.

57. As reported in ibid.

58. LAB 10/735, report of R.I.R.O. (Scotland), 31 May 1948.

59. Morgan, *Labour in Power*, Appendix IV, citing Annual Statements on United Kingdom Balance of Payments.

60. See Barnett, *Lost Victory*, ch. 19, and the Economic Survey for 1948, Cmd. 7344, ch. I.
61. Report of R.I.R.O. (London) of 6 April 1948, in LAB 10/779, 'Port Transport Industry: Webber, Cook and Palmer (Maconochie's Wharf) & T.G.W.U. and National Amalgamated Stevedores and Dockers. Strike now terminated. Dispute over down-grading of two N.A.S.D. gangers, because of local friction with the T.G.W.U.'
62. LAB 10/779, note of 6 April 1948.
63. LAB 10/783, 'Dock Industry. London Dockers and T.G.W.U. Strike in progress. Dispute over disciplining action against 11 men who refused to load zinc oxide.' Letter to the Sector Manager, National Dock Labour Board, from W. Lessiter, Managing Director, Grand Union (Stevedoring & Wharfage) Co. Ltd, 29 May 1948.
64. LAB 10/783, report of the R.I.R.O. (London), 23 June 1948, entitled 'Strike in the Port of London over disciplinary action by the Dock Labour Board', on which the following summary account of the course of the strike is based.
65. Ibid.
66. LAB 10/783, 'Strictly Confidential' letter of 23 June 1948 from R.I.R.O. (London), W. J. Hull, to A. E. Stillwell, Industrial Relations Department, Ministry of Labour and National Service.
67. As reported in the issue of 21 June 1948.
68. Ibid.
69. LAB 10/783, Draft article for the *Ministry of Labour Gazette*.
70. In LAB 10/783.
71. CAB 134/175, EC(48)1st, 21 June 1948.
72. As suggested in an unsigned ministerial paper in LAB 10/783.
73. CAB 134/175, EC(48)1st.
74. Letter of 22 June 1948 to Sir Cyril L. M. Langham, in LAB 10/783.
75. Ibid., letter of 24 June 1948.
76. CAB 134/175, EC(48)2nd.
77. LAB 10/783, 23 June 1948, Copy of Statement Made by the Prime Minister Today.
78. See newspaper photographs.
79. LAB 10/783, Report of R.I.R.O. (London), 28 June 1948.
80. CAB 134/175, EC(48)3rd.
81. Ibid.
82. Ibid.

83. Ibid.
84. In the words of Ness Edwards, Parliamentary Secretary to the Ministry of Labour and National Service. See LAB 10/783, memorandum of meeting between the Parliamentary Secretary, MLNS, and NJC for the Port Transport Industry, on 28 June 1948 at 4 p.m.
85. LAB 10/783, as reported by R.I.R.O. (London), 30 June 1948.
86. See Morgan, *Labour in Power*, pp. 375–7.
87. In March 1949.
88. Durcan et al., *Strikes in Post-war Britain*, tables 9.2 and 9.3, pp. 275 and 277.
89. The year 1950 had not been free of trouble in the docks. In the Port of London the lads were out in March and April on this or that pretext, and discontent grumbled on thereafter. The biggest ruction resulted from a stoppage by the self-appointed Port Workers Defence Committee in support of three men expelled by the T&GWU for their role in the 1949 London strike. See Laybourn, *A History of British Trade Unionism c. 1770–1990* (Stroud, Sutton Publishing, 1997), pp. 165–6.
90. See LAB 10/1019, 'Dock Industry: All docks in Great Britain implicated – Strike in protest against the wage increase of 11/- recently granted.'
91. Morgan, *Labour in Power*, p. 437.
92. Copy of resolution in LAB 10/1019. 'The Dockers' Charter' signified a claim for 25s. a day minimum as against 21s. under the new national agreement.
93. LAB 10/1019, Notes on Dock Strike; Draft 13.2.1951.
94. Ibid., cover sheet to file.
95. Durcan et al., *Strikes in Post-war Britain*, tables 9.1–3.
96. Ibid., table 9.1. For the effect of the 1955 strikes on sterling, see Cmd. 9728, Economic Survey 1956, para. 62.
97. Cmd. 9728, para. 49. Deficit in 1954: £599m; in 1955: £862m.
98. See Laybourn, *A History*, p. 171.
99. See correspondence and other papers in LAB 10/1277, 'Dock Industry. National Dock Labour Board and the Amalgamated Stevedores and Dockers: refusal of dockers to work overtime until it is agreed that overtime is voluntary not compulsory.'
100. Ibid., letter from the Shipping Secretary of the Society of Motor Manufacturers and Traders, 12 July 1954.

101. Durcan et al., *Strikes in Post-war Britain*, table 9.3., p. 277.

102. Ibid., tables 9.2. and 9.3.

103. Ibid., table 9.3.

104. Durcan, McCarthy and Redman point out that in 1946–52, for example, the workers involved in strikes averaged 1.3 per cent of the national workforce, while the total working days lost through strikes averaged 0.03 per cent of potential working time. Cf. Durcan et al., *Strikes in Post-war Britain*, table 2.2. But such statistics cannot do justice to the commercial damage done to individual industries and companies, nor to the national economy as a whole at a period of great precariousness.

105. CAB 132/34, CIP(HF)(50)11, 31 May 1950, 'The London Docks: a Framework for Study', by R. P. Lynton and S. D. M. King for the British Institute of Management.

106. CAB 132/34, CIP(HF)(50)12, 1 June 1950, Research in the Liverpool Docks (by the Department of Social Studies at Liverpool University), note by Miss J. Woodward.

107. CAB 132/34, CIP(HF)(50)11, para. 4.

108. Ibid., para. 53.1.

109. CAB 132/34, CIP(HF)(50)12, para. 32.

110. CAB 132/34, CIP(HF)(50)11, para. 104.

111. Ibid., para. 101 and 102.1.

112. Ibid., para. 5.

113. Cf. ibid., paras 6–9, and CAB 132/34, CIP(HF)(50)12, paras 11, 29 and 33.

114. CAB 132/34, CIP(HF)(50)12, para. 33.

115. CAB 132/34, CIP(HF)(50)11, para. 15.

116. Ibid., para. 65.

117. Ibid., para. 65.3. Cf. also para. 74.2.

118. Ibid., para. 65.4.

119. See LAB 10/1019, letter from a Mr J. M. MacDonald, former stevedores' supervisor, to magistrates at the Bow Street Police Court, 23 February 1951, during the prosecution of seven strike leaders for alleged conspiracy. The letter is also revealing on the topics of pilferage and resistance to new technology.

120. Ibid., para. 9. Cf. also T 234/74 and 75, passim.

121. Ibid., cross-head to part III.

13. The Psychology of the Underdog

1. T. Single in the *Trades Newspaper*, 13 November 1825, cited in Patricia Hollis (ed.), *Class and Conflict in Nineteenth Century England 1815–1850* (London and Boston, Routledge and Kegan Paul, 1973), p. 45.
2. Ibid.
3. For a brief summary of the evolution of the nature of the British proletariat before 1850, see Correlli Barnett, *The Audit of War* (London, Macmillan, 1986, and Pan Books, 1997), pp. 188–91. For a convincing general history, see E. P. Thompson, *The Making of the English Working Class* (Harmondsworth, Penguin Books, 1968). For selected documents, see Hollis, *Class and Conflict*. For the rise of trade unionism, see Keith Laybourn, *A History of British Trade Unionism c. 1770–1990* (Stroud, Sutton Publishing, 1997), which also summarizes differing interpretations of the evidence by historians.
4. See Keith Laybourn, *A History*, ch. 1; and *British Trade Unionism c. 1770–1990; A Reader in History* (Stroud, Sutton Publishing, 1991), 'Early Trade Unionism c. 1770–1850'.
5. See Laybourn, both cited works, p. 15 in each case.
6. Cited in Laybourn, *British Trade Unionism*, p. 15.
7. Such was the resonance of 'Luddism' in British industrial history that as late as the 1970s and 1980s the term would be still applied to cases of diehard opposition to new technologies and new working practices.
8. Cited in Laybourn, *British Trade Unionism*, p. 24.
9. Cited in ibid., p. 19.
10. Cited in ibid., p. 21.
11. See Barnett, *Audit of War*, ch. 10, 'The Legacy of the Industrial Revolution', and cited sources.
12. 'Concord' in the issue of 12 October 1833, cited in Hollis, op. cit., p. 55.
13. Article in the *Advocate*, 16 February 1833, cited in ibid., p. 62.
14. Laybourn, *A History*, p. 31.
15. Cited in Laybourn, *British Trade Unionism*, p. 54.
16. Laybourn, *A History*, pp. 50–53.
17. See ibid., ch. 2, and John Lovell, *British Trade Unions 1875–1933* (London and Basingstoke, Macmillan Press, 1977), ch. 1.
18. Cited in H. Pelling, *A History of British Trade Unionism* (Harmondsworth, Pelican Books, 1971), p. 104.

19. Laybourn, *A History*, p. 79. On the topic of resistance to new technology, see also Lovell, *British Trade Unions*, pp. 27–9 and 42.

20. Ibid., pp. 71–80; Pelling, *A History*, ch. 6; Lovell, *British Trade Unions*, chs 1 and 2.

21. Laybourn, *British Trade Unionism*, p. 53; and *A History*, p. 76.

22. Pelling, *A History*, p. 112.

23. See R. H. Heindel, *The American Impact on Great Britain 1891–1914* (New York, Octagon Books, 1968), chs VIII–XII. See also Pelling, *A History*, p. 125.

24. See Pelling, *A History*, ch. 6.

25. C. 5809, cited in Laybourn, *British Trade Unionism*, pp. 85–6.

26. See Barnett, *Collapse of British Power*, pp. 43–6 and cited sources.

27. One variant took the form of the syndicalist movement, by which the workers in particular industries were to seize control and run them themselves. Another, a general strike to win control of the state, was proposed by the Frenchman Georges Sorel. See Pelling, *A History*, ch. 7; Laybourn, *A History*, pp. 99–106.

28. Cited in ibid., p. 57.

29. Ibid., p. 59.

30. Pelling, *A History*, pp. 135–7; Laybourn, *A History*, pp. 102–5.

31. Such as aero-engines, magnetos, spark plugs, scientific instruments, drugs and dyes, and sophisticated machine tools. See Barnett, *Collapse of British Power*, pp. 84–8 and cited sources.

32. Cited in Barnett, *Collapse of British Power*, p. 114.

33. *History of the Ministry of Munitions* (London, HMSO, 1922), vol. IV, pt. IV, pp. 74–5.

34. See Barnett, *Collapse of British Power*, pp. 114–17, and cited volumes and parts of the *History of the Ministry of Munitions*.

35. Laybourn, *A History*, p. 109.

36. For accounts of the trade unions and workforce during the Great War, see Laybourn, *A History*, pp. 109–19; Lovell, *British Trade Unions*, ch. 5; Pelling, *A History*, pp. 149–57.

37. Laybourn, *A History*, p. 114.

38. Ibid., p. 118.

39. Cited in ibid., p. 118.

40. Cmd. 3282, p. 361.

41. See Barnett, *Audit of War*, passim, but especially chs 4, 6 and 7.

42. For a survey of labour restrictive practices, especially rigid demarca-

tions, in 1945–56, see T 234/74, RLP(56)2, 24 April 1956, Committee on Restrictive Labour Practices. Terms and Conditions of Employment – Restrictive Labour Practices. Note by the Ministry of Labour. See also T 234/74, Report by the Committee on Restrictive Labour Practices, 1956.

43. Cf. J. Durcan, E. McCarthy, and G. Redman, *Strikes in Post-war Britain: study of stoppages of work due to industrial disputes 1946–1973* (London, George Allen & Unwin, 1983), pp. 403–4. Or as a handwritten amendment to the brief (in LAB 10/1469) prepared for the Parliamentary Secretary to the Ministry of Labour in October 1957 put it:

> When a big strike is in progress too many people are inclined to forget the fact ... that concurrently with the strike the normal processes of collective bargaining are going on quite peacefully in other industries and that over most of our economy agreements are being reached and disagreements are being resolved in one way or another quite amicably without any question of recourse to strike action.

44. Cf. LAB 10/1452, report by the British Railways Productivity Council of March 1957, which listed fourteen main items 'which might be regarded as impediments to production and to the full and efficient use of manpower...' See also T 234/74 and 75 for an across-the-board picture of restrictive practices.

45. Their relative industrial peace concealed mutual acceptance of gross over-manning and elaborate 'who does what' union demarcations, with all the consequent rigidities and inefficiencies in operating plants.

46. Cf. BT 64/4896, United Kingdom Productivity: Report on Productivity prepared by officials at ministerial request, October 1954, Appendix II, para. 10:

> Restrictive practices are not normally adopted for the deliberate purpose of restricting output. The motive behind them is usually the worker's desire to safeguard his relative status, his conditions of work, or – perhaps the most important – his security of employment. The fear of 'working oneself out of a job' is still very real.

47. In LAB 10/1469.

48. Cf. the Standard Motor Company in 1954–56. See pp. 182–9, above.

On the correlation between strike waves and the pace of attempted technological change, see James E. Cronin, *Industrial Conflict in Modern Britain* (London, Croom Helm, and Totowa, NJ, Rowman and Littlefield, 1979), pp. 177–9.

49. CAB 134/849, EA(53)148, 3 December 1953, Efficiency and Output, para. 5. Monckton was referring to the nation as a whole in this industrial context.

50. CAB 134/851, EA(54)25, 6 March 1954, Report of the Productivity and Conditional Aid Committee on 'The Role of Government in Promoting Higher Industrial Productivity', para. 1. See also covering note, EA(54)24, by the President of the Board of Trade, Peter Thorneycroft.

51. David Edgerton, *Science, Technology, and the British Industrial 'Decline', 1870–1970* (Cambridge, Cambridge University Press, 1996), table 5.2, p. 49.

52. 'Productivity in 1953' by Dr. L. Rostas in the *Financial Times*, 14 January 1954, citing estimates by Mr A. A. Adams of the Cambridge University Department of Applied Economics. These are confirmed by Cmd. 9108, para. 55.

53. CAB 134/851, EA(54)25, para. 2.

54. CAB 129/79, CP(56)30, 8 February 1956. Statement on Defence. Note by the Minister of Defence circulating a proof copy of the 1956 defence White Paper (published as Cmd. 9691), para. 68.

55. CAB 134/879, EPB(53)29, 16 September 1953, para. 6.

56. Cmd. 9412, para. 19.

57. Cmd. 9728, Economic Survey 1956, para. 44.

58. Ibid., para. 59.

14. 'Good Management is a Fundamental Requirement'

1. Set up in autumn 1948 on the initiative of Sir Stafford Cripps, Chancellor of the Exchequer, and Paul Hoffman, the Economic Cooperation Administrator in the USA.

2. *Internal Combustion Engines*, Report of a visit to the USA in 1949 of a Productivity Team representing the Internal Combustion Engine Industry (London, Anglo-American Council on Productivity, June 1950). This report covered stationary industrial diesel and petrol

engines of all sizes; marine auxiliary engines of all sizes; diesel engines for rail traction; and diesel and petrol engines for marine propulsion.

3. *Management Accounting*, Report of a Specialist Team which visited the United States of America in 1950 (London, Anglo-American Council on Productivity, November 1950).

4. *Management Accounting*, p. 64.

5. p. 6.

6. p. 51, cited in *Management Accounting*, p. 6.

7. Report, p. 9. The team on 'Cotton Spinning' was also struck by the 'productivity-mindedness of management, supervisory staff and operatives' in America (*Cotton Spinning*, March 1950), p. 5.

8. *Internal Combustion Engines*, p. 7.

9. *Packaging*: Report of a Specialist Team which visited the United States of America in 1950 (London, Anglo-American Productivity Council, September 1950), p. 3.

10. *Internal Combustion Engines*, p. 13.

11. See CAB 132/33, CIP(HF)(49)24, Report on Progress of the Foremanship Research Project for the Medical Research Council and the Human Factors Panel of the Committee on Industrial Productivity, 1 August 1948–15 May 1949, part II. This also reckoned that the 'older' foreman might not know how to handle young workers brought up in an age of radio and films.

12. Ibid., para. 59.

13. According to the productivity team investigating *Internal Combustion Engines*, p. 9. In 1954 a two-man team from the British steel industry found the same pattern in the American steel industry; see Gavin Smellie and Campbell Adamson, *A Study of Steel Productivity in Great Britain and U.S.A.* (Redbourn, R.T.B. Ltd, 1955).

14. *Combustion Engines*, p. 9.

15. *Management Accounting*, p. 14.

16. Smellie and Adamson, *A Study of Steel Productivity*.

17. LAB 10/1360, 'P.M.A.S. British Transport Commission. Factors affecting Human Relations in the Railway Organisation.' Impressions gained by PMAs at courses at the BTC Training Centre, Watford, 1954/55.

18. Ibid.

19. The Report upon a Study of Colliery Management Structure, commissioned in February 1954 by the National Coal Board. The team

leader was Professor R. W. Revans. The team examined the working of twenty-two pits, reporting in November 1956. Cf. R. W. Revans, *The Origins and Growth of Action Learning* (Bromley, Chartwell-Bratt, 1982), pp. 48–55, and interview with Revans in the *Financial Times*, 12 April 1996.

20. This was partly on account of long-standing agreements with unions. See ibid., but see also CAB 134/692, SI(M)(51)7, 30 January 1951, Socialisation of Industries Committee. Training for Leadership in the Socialised Industries. Memorandum by the Minister of Labour and National Service, Appendix A, para. 7.
21. LAB 10/1453, June 1959. Draft report by Working Party of Officials on Shipbuilding Prospects and Remedies.
22. H. Turner, G. Clack and R. Roberts, *Labour Relations in the Motor Industry; A Study of Industrial Unrest and International Comparison* (London, George Allen & Unwin, 1967), pp. 146–7.
23. Smellie and Adamson, *A Study of Steel Productivity*, p. 16.
24. Of the 140,000 manufacturing establishments in the United Kingdom, 82,000 employed no more than ten men. Almost a quarter of the labour force in British manufacturing were in establishments employing fifty men or fewer. Cf. CAB 132/107, SP(53)5, 27 March 1953, Advisory Council on Scientific Policy; Report on the Exploitation of Science by Industry, para. 3 and footnote. See also SUPP 14/140 EAC(49)60, 26 January 1949, 'Engineering Advisory Council'. Memorandum on the Proposals of the Institution of Production Engineers for Increasing Productivity, para. 4, which referred to the production methods of the managements of such small firms as 'often crude and out-of-date, devised out of their own limited experience . . .'
25. *Cotton Spinning*, p. 5.
26. It further helped that close and good relations usually existed between the accountants and the works managers. *Management Accounting*, p. 14.
27. *Internal Combustion Engines*, p. 43.
28. Ibid., p. 11.
29. *Electric Motor Control Gear* (London, September 1950), p. 35.
30. *Management Accounting*, p. 11.
31. Ibid.
32. As those of us who were doing time in British business in the 1950s well remember.

33. Ibid., p. 53.

34. *Electric Motor Control Gear*, p. 31. See also *Internal Combustion Engines*, p. 31.

35. See Correlli Barnett, *The Audit of War* (London, Macmillan, 1986, and Pan Books, 1997), pp. 148–53, citing AVIA 10/104, 'Report of British Mission to United States of America to Study Production Methods, Sept.–Oct. 1942', and AVIA 10/106, 'Sir Roy Fedden's visit to USA: Terms of Reference; Report – Programme of Meetings (including Précis on the Work of the Fedden Mission, or Preliminary Report, circulated on 22 April 1943)'.

36. *Management Accounting*, p. 7.

37. *Internal Combustion Engines*, p. 45.

38. Ibid., p. 7.

39. Ingot tons are a measure of basic production (not of finished output). Smellie and Adamson, *A Study of Steel Productivity*, p. 5. Tons are of 2,000lb in both cases.

40. Cf. Central Policy Review Staff, *The Future of the British Car Industry* (London, HMSO, 1975). This demonstrated that the basic weaknesses in the industry identified by the 1945 Official Sub-Committee on Post-War Re-settlement of the Motor Industry (CAB 87/15, R(I)(45)9, 21 March 1945) – 'too many, often small-scale units, each producing too many models' – remained far from remedied even after a lapse of thirty years.

41. Cf. *Internal Combustion Engines*, p. 45; *Steel Founding* (London, September 1949), p. 37; *Simplification in Industry; Report of an investigation in the United States of America by a group appointed by the Council* (London, October 1949).

42. *Electric Motor Control Gear*, p. 36.

43. *Simplification in Industry*, pp. 6–8.

44. Second Report, *Simplification in British Industry: Report of an inquiry in Britain by the Group, appointed by the Council, which made an investigation of simplification in the United States of America* (London, HMSO, August 1950).

45. Ibid., p. 5.

46. Ibid., p. 10.

47. CAB 134/9, DO(50)7, 28 June 1950, Size and Shape of the Aircraft Industry – Need for Planning to Preserve War Potential. Memor-

andum by the Minister of Supply, Appendices A and B. The Minister recommended reducing the number of firms on government contracts to thirteen, hardly a radical proposal.

48. See SUPP 14/141 and /333, and BT 64/1177 for the relevant documentation.
49. CAB 134/690, SEP/49/29(final), 6 May 1949, Ministry of Supply, Committee for Standardization of Engineering Products, Second Report, Annex 1, para. 24.
50. Ibid., para. 6.
51. (London, HMSO). See also CAB 134/643, PC(49)117, 25 October 1949, memorandum by the Minister of Supply (George Strauss) circulating the report to the Cabinet Production Committee; and the Engineering Advisory Council papers in SUPP 14/141, EAC(49)series.
52. The Lemon Report, p. 9.
53. Ibid., p. 7. For study and debate within the Ministry of Supply in 1949–51 on standardization, see SUPP 14/333; within the Board of Trade in 1949–54, see BT 64/4896.
54. The Lemon Report, pp. 9 and 11.
55. SUPP 14/141, EAC(49)14th, Ministry of Supply. Engineering Advisory Council, 3 March 1949, minutes of meeting on the First Report of the Committee for the Standardisation of Engineering Products – EAC(49)61.
56. SUPP 14/333, Ministry of Supply, minute from A.S./E.2 to E.1(d)., 12 January 1951.
57. Ibid.
58. SUPP 14/333, Ministry of Supply, minute from E.(a) to A.S./E.3., 5 May 1951.
59. Cf. the voluminous material in BT 64/4740 and 4896.
60. BT 64/4896, 25 March 1954. Notes for Minister of State's Speech: General Productivity Points.
61. Smellie and Adamson, *A Study of Steel Productivity*, p. 16.
62. The following discussion of class and education in British management is based on the 1950s studies summarized in *The Background of British Managers: A Review of the Evidence*, unpublished research in 1974 by Dr Ian Glover of the Manpower Studies Research Unit, Heriot-Watt University, Edinburgh. This invaluable compilation, covering the literature from 1955 to 1974, has the one drawback that page references for material cited are not given.

The evocations of different class manners, mannerisms and ways of life are based on my personal observation while in industry during the 1950s.

63. Cf. sources summarized in Glover, *Background of British Managers*. See also D. H. Aldcroft, *Education, Training and Economic Performance 1944 to 1990* (Manchester, Manchester University Press, 1992) and 'The Missing Dimension: Management Education and Training in Post-war Britain' in D. H. Aldcroft and A. Slaven (eds), *Enterprise and Management, Essays in Honour of Peter L. Payne* (London, 1992); and M. Sanderson, *Education and Economic Decline in Britain, 1870 to the 1990s* (Cambridge, Cambridge University Press, 1999), pp. 100–102.

64. Cf. CAB 132/107, SP(53)5, para. 3, footnote.

65. Especially the Reports of the Endowed Schools (Schools Enquiry) Royal Commission of 1867–8 (C. 3966), and the Second Report of the Royal Commission on Technical Instruction of 1884 (C. 3981).

66. Cf. ED 46/739, T757(19)48, National Advisory Council on Education for Industry and Commerce: Sub-Committee on Management Education, October 1952. British Institute of Management: 'Facilities for Management Education in the United Kingdom'. This is a sixty-page survey covering 26 universities, 227 technical colleges and schools, and 31 centres for adult education, and ranging from degree courses to short courses for foremen.

67. Acton Society Trust, *Management Succession* (London, Acton Society Trust, 1956), summarized in Glover, *Background of British Managers*.

68. Ibid., confirmed by G. H. Copeman, *Leaders of British Industry* (London, Gee, 1955), also as summarized in Glover, *Background of British Managers*.

69. Figures in 1969: cf. the INSEAD report summarized in Glover, *Background of British Managers*. The figures would not have been significantly different in 1950–56, and certainly the comparison would not have been any more favourable to Britain.

70. Acording to research carried out in 1961. See P. W. Musgrave, 'The Educational Profiles of Management in Two British Iron & Steel Companies with Some Comparisons, National and International', *British Journal of Industrial Relations*, 4, 2, July 1966, pp. 201–10, summarized in Glover, *Background of British Managers*. In gruesome contrast almost all the foremen in the two British steel companies in the same survey lacked any kind of qualification, however mean.

71. ED 46/739, October 1952, B.I.M. survey 'Facilities for Management Education'.

72. ED 46/739, NAC/SC/52/65, four reports by the Anglo-American Council on Productivity on 'Education for Management', 'The Universities and Industry', 'Training for Supervisors', and 'Training of Operatives'. The British sources typically give no figures for output, so it is not possible to compare the number of degrees offered by the UK institutions and the number of courses offered by the US institutions, but even if each of the 617 US institutions only offered one course, that would still shame the 35 British courses.

73. *Management Education in the 1970s* (London, HMSO, 1970).

74. Chart in ED 46/739, National Advisory Council on Education for Industry and Commerce, 1955.

75. ED 46/739, October 1952, B.I.M. survey 'Facilities for Management Education', October 1952, Appendix III; B.I.M. Information Summary NO. 39, 'Establishments Providing Instruction in Work Study', October 1952.

76. LAB 10/1193, Notes of Talk given by Mr D. R. O. Thomas, Chief Education Officer, United Steel Company, Sheffield, on Executive Training.

77. Cf. Copeman, cited in Glover, *Background of British Managers*, part 2, section 2. Copeman's research covered public companies with net shareholders' assets worth £1 million or more. Responses to questionnaires amounted to over 1,200 directors, or a response rate of 38 per cent.

    Copeman's evidence is supported by the Acton Society Trust report on *Management Succession* in 1956, summarized in Glover, section 4. The Trust found that out of 3,327 managers above the rank of foreman, 19 per cent had been to public school and were degree-holders. It judged that public-school boys enjoyed ten times the chance of being recruited as managers than the average member of the national population.

    Yet further evidence is supplied by R. V. Clements, *Managers: A Study of Their Careers in Industry* (London, Allen & Unwin, 1958), also summarized in Glover, section 4. Clements interviewed 670 managers of various kinds in Lancashire and north-eastern Cheshire, and found that, as paraphrased by Glover, 'those who had higher social origins tended to be those who were most educationally advantaged and also to be those who had progressed farthest in their careers'.

78. D. Granick, *The European Executive* (London, Weidenfeld and Nicolson, 1962), cited in Glover, *Background of British Managers*. The British figure of 1 per cent of managers who had attended Britain's 'elite' institutions compares with the 15 per cent of French managers who had attended the Grandes Écoles.

79. Acton Society Trust, *Management Succession*, summarized in Glover, *Background of British Managers*.

80. My personal knowledge and observation in the early 1950s.

81. See Correlli Barnett, *The Collapse of British Power* (London, Eyre Methuen, 1972; paperback: Stroud, Alan Sutton, 1984), pp. 20–38, and *The Audit of War*, ch. 11, and cited sources.

82. Acton Society Trust, cited in Glover, *Background of British Managers*.

83. I speak from personal experience. In 1951 I sat the civil service examination, failed to win a place in the administrative class, and was offered, of all ludicrous things to a man who cannot count, a post as trainee tax inspector. Hence followed five years in the North Thames Gas Board, where the Chairman was an Old Etonian and the Deputy Chairman an Old Harrovian.

　　See also D. Granick, *The European Executive*, summarized in Glover, *Background of British Managers*, on the way the civil service, with its ethos of job security and social responsibility, and its emphasis on recruiting Oxbridge arts graduates, provided the model for large British businesses.

84. Copeman, summarized in Glover, *Background of British Managers*.

85. Clements as summarized by Glover in his section 4, p. 8. Clements investigated twenty-eight firms ranging in size from 32 employees to 6–10,000.

86. Report from the Select Committee on Scientific Instruction (House of Commons, 15 July 1868), vol. XV, p. iii.

87. A study of the boards of publicly quoted engineering firms in 1952 found that even here only 21.5 per cent of directors had technical qualifications, such as being chartered engineers: cf. Bosworth Monck, 'The Eclipse of the Engineer', *Engineering*, 10 September 1954, pp. 329–34, cited in David Edgerton, *Science, Technology and British Decline 1870–1970* (Cambridge, Cambridge University Press, 1996), p. 26.

88. Cf. Clements, Copeman and the Acton Society Trust, cited in Glover, *Background of British Managers*. Their conclusions were confirmed by the findings of D. G. Clark in *The Industrial Manager; His Background and Career Pattern* (London, Business Publications, 1966). The 'old school tie' may be a cliché, but it also happens to be true.

89. The frequent isolation of technologists and scientists in specialized functions is noted by Clements, Copeman and Clark, op. cit.

    Anecdote: a friend of mine running a printing works in the 1960s wished to buy a major item of modern machinery. Visiting a British manufacturer, he was first entertained to a lavish lunch by a director, who then handed him over to a man in a white coat who actually knew about the kit. When he visited a German manufacturer, he was briefed in detail by the managing director himself, a fully qualified engineer intimately associated with the design of the machine.

90. Copeman, cited in Glover, *Background of British Managers*.

91. Ibid.

92. Ibid.

93. Ibid. See corroborating evidence in Barnett, *Audit of War*, pp. 201–5, summarizing British schools output in 1937–8, when many of the managers of the early 1950s would have been receiving their education.

94. Personal observation by me when in industry in 1952–7.

95. Cf. Glover, *Background of British Managers*, section 5.3.

15. 'Inward-looking Traditionalism': Old Technologies

1. For a summary account of how since the 1920s the coal industry had step by step come to this position of commercial and technological fossilization, see Correlli Barnett, *The Audit of War* (London, Macmillan, 1986, and Pan Books, 1997), ch. 4.

2. Cf. CAB 134/852, EA(54)86, 26 July 1954, Economic Policy Committee, Fuel Policy: Note by the Chancellor of the Duchy of Lancaster and Minister of Materials (Lord Woolton), para. 2.

3. For an account of the commercially soporific effects of the post-war Labour Government's nationalization of the industry, see Correlli Barnett, *The Lost Victory: British Dreams, British Realities 1945–1950* (London, Macmillan, 1996, and Pan Books, 1997), ch. 15. See also

this present book, ch. 12. See also W. Ashworth, *The History of the British Coal Industry*, vol. 5, *1946–1982: The Nationalized Industry* (Oxford, the Clarendon Press, 1986), ch. 5, which documents the double concentration of the nationalized industry in the period 1947–57 on its own internal bureaucratic structure and on boosting production from existing pits, however uneconomic.

4. Cf. CAB 134/854, EA(55)8th, 3 March 1955, minute 2, Coal Prices. According to the Minister of Pensions, the NCB had made an average loss of £2 million a year over the 'nine years' (sic) of its existence.

5. Report of the Advisory Committee on Organisation (NCB, 1955), pp. 23–5.

6. R. Revans, *The Origins and Growth of Action Learning* (Bromley, Chartwell-Bratt, 1982), p. 49, citing 'The Report upon a Study of Colliery Management Structure' commissioned by the NCB and carried out in 1954–6. I am grateful to Mr Alan Smith, former mining engineer with the NCB, for drawing my attention to the relevant pages of Revans' book.

7. See Ashworth, *British Coal Industry*, vol. 5, p. 201, on the retarding of a planned rundown of high-cost production in Cumberland and West Durham because of the 'social damage' it would cause. See ch. 5 for an account of the NCB's centralized bureaucratic structures.

8. Cmd. 6610. For the performance of the industry in the Second World War, and a summary of its history since the late nineteenth century, see Barnett, *Audit of War*, ch. 4.

9. Letter to me, 15 March 1997, from David Clement CBE, formerly Deputy-Director-General of Finance, NCB, 1955–61, and Director-General of Finance, 1961–9.

10. Cf. CAB 134/651, PC(51)86, 12 July 1951, National Plan for Coal: Memorandum by the Minister of Fuel and Power, asking for the Cabinet Production Committee's endorsement. See Ashworth, *British Coal Industry*, vol. 5, ch. 5.

11. Ibid., p. 202 and table 5.2.

12. Ibid.

13. Revans, *Action Learning*, p. 53.

14. See Ashworth, *British Coal Industry*, vol. 5, pp. 77–8 for a full description.

15. Named after J. Anderton, the exceptional General Manager who authorized the work. For an account of the ASL and its role in

mechanizing production, see Joe Townsend, 'Innovation in Coal-mining Machinery: the Case of the Anderton Shearer Loader', in Keith Pavitt (ed.), *Technical Innovation and British Economic Performance: Science Policy Research Unit, Sussex* (London and Basingstoke, Macmillan Press, 1980). See also Ashworth, *British Coal Industry*, vol. 5, ch. 3, which also covers other, less important, innovations.

16. See Pavitt (ed.), *Technical Innovation*,pp. 149–50, and table 8.1. In the next twenty years Eickhoff were to patent more innovative improvements to the ASL than any British rival.

17. I am indebted to Messrs David Clement, Alan Smith and Ronald Hindson for their enlightening correspondence and advice about the coal industry in the post-war era. I apologize to them for not having the space in a book of this scope to discuss in detail all the relevant technical questions (such as 'long wall advancing' versus 'long wall retreating'). The historical interpretation in this chapter is entirely my own.

18. Rates were regulated by the Railway Rates Tribunal, set up under the 1921 Railways Act.

19. 1952 figures, in CAB 134/1180, T(52)37, 12 March 1952, Committee on Road and Rail Transport; Reorganisation of the B.T.C. and its Executives. Note by the Minister of Transport, Appendix IV.

20. See Derek H. Aldcroft, *Studies in Transport History, 1870–1970* (Newton Abbott, and North Pomfret, Vermont, David and Charles, 1974), ch. 11. The one exception to this picture of stasis was the Southern Railway, which electrified its short-haul network (longest route eighty miles: London–Portsmouth) on the third-rail system. The investment gave a return on capital of 8.8 per cent.

21. The Coronation's average speed for the 188 miles London–York was 71.9 m.p.h.; the Fliegender Hamburger's over the 178 miles Berlin–Hamburg was 77 m.p.h. See R. B. Whitehouse (ed.), *Great Trains of the World* (London, New English Library/Hamlyn Books, 1975), pp. 105 and 16. The Germans realigned and relaid track to permit these speeds, an expedient quite out of the question for British management.

22. For restrictions under the Labour Government, see Barnett, *Lost Victory*, ch. 14.

23. Aldcroft, *Studies in Transport History*, pp. 249–52.

24. LAB 10/1360, 'Human Relations in the Railway Industry':

Impressions gained by P.M.A.'s at Courses on Joint Consultation at the B.T.C. Training Centre, Watford, 1954/55.

25. Ibid.
26. Ibid.
27. G. F. Allen, *British Rail After Beeching* (London, Allan, 1966), p. 6, cited in Aldcroft, *Studies in Transport History*, p. 257.
28. Ibid.
29. I am indebted to Mr Alan Smith for pointing out Armand's formidable qualifications and abilities.
30. 'Counter-part' funds. See Barnett, *Lost Victory*, ch. 19 and cited sources. When it came to 'mutual aid' under the post-Korea rearmament programme, the Americans refused to let Britain get away with a similar waste of counter-part funds, and insisted that they be spent on agreed projects like raising productivity. See above, pp. 405–6.
31. W. A. Robson, *Nationalized Industry and Public Ownership* (London, George Allen & Unwin, 1960), p. 96, cited in Aldcroft, *Studies in Transport History*, p. 252.
32. T 234/96, Minute from E. P. Wright to Burke Trend, Under-Secretary at the Treasury, 20 April 1955.
33. *Modernisation and Re-equipment of British Railways* (London, British Transport Commission, December 1954).
34. CAB 134/855, EA(55)8, 14 January 1955, Economic Policy Committee, Modernisation and Re-equipment of British Railways. Memorandum by the Minister of Transport and Civil Aviation. For a discussion by the Committee on this memorandum, see CAB 134/854, EA(55)3rd, item 6, 18 January 1955.
35. T 234/96, minute from Wright to Trend, 20 April 1955.
36. Ibid.
37. T 234/96, Investment Programme, British Transport Commission. Note of a Meeting held in the Treasury, 19 April 1955, between representatives of the Treasury, the Ministry of Transport and Civil Aviation, and the British Transport Commission, para. 3(b).
38. T 234/96, letter of 16 March 1955 from J. R. Willis, Under-Secretary, Ministry of Transport, to G. H. Andrews, Second Secretary at the Board of Trade.
39. T 234/96, Wright to Trend, 20 April 1955.
40. Ibid.
41. See CAB 129/81, CP(56)139, 8 June 1956, The British Transport

Commission, Memorandum by the Minister of Transport and Civil Aviation; CAB 129/082, CP(56)210, 20 September 1956, The British Transport Commission – Note by the Chancellor of the Exchequer, asking for the Cabinet's authority to publish the BTC's proposals as a White Paper.

See this book, above pp. 134–6, for a summary of Whitehall wheel-slipping 1955–6 over approval of the Plan.

42. See the correspondence in March–November 1955 between the Ministry of Transport, the Board of Trade and the Treasury in T 234/96.

43. Ibid.

44. T 234/96, Report by Miss Lupton, Board of Trade, December 1955.

45. Interview in the *Daily Mail*, 22 November 1955.

46. T 234/96, A. T. K. Grant to Burke Trend, 1 June 1955.

47. Ibid., scribbled comment.

48. T 234/96, Paper for the President [of the Board of Trade] on the relationship between British Railways and the Private Locomotive and Railway Rolling Stock Builders, in the context of the export prospects of the British Industry, Appendix D.

49. T 234/96, Capacity in Private Industry for Mainline Diesel Locomotive Production. Note by the Ministry of Supply, 20 May 1955.

50. Ibid. The Ministry of Supply memo does not always distinguish between diesel-electric and diesel (which could mean diesel-hydraulic or diesel-mechanical), or between diesels and mainline diesels.

51. T 234/96, Paper for the President, Appendix D.

52. Ibid.

53. Ibid.

54. Hansard, 9 June 1955, Col. 122–124.

55. T 234/96, Paper for the President, Appendix D.

56. See correspondence in October–November 1955 between the Treasury and the Board of Trade in T 234/96.

57. Cf. T 234/96, letter from J. R. Willis, Ministry of Transport, to J. B. L. Munro, Ministry of Supply, 11 August 1955.

58. This is what ARC (Amey Roadstone Company) bought in the 1980s to haul their heavy freight of quarried stone on what was then still British Rail. These locomotives were more sophisticated in design and much more efficient than their British-built British Rail equivalents.

59. Some of these firms were link-ups between electrical engineering companies and traditional manufacturers of steam engines, such as English-Electric with Vulcan (later taken over), and Robert Stephenson and Hawthorne. In the field of mainline diesel-electric and diesel-hydraulic traction, British manufacturers had to start from scratch making designs licensed from their European rivals, such as MAN, Maybach and Sulzer.

60. It took from 1959 to 1963 even to design the mainline electric locomotives, even though the French, Swiss, Germans and Dutch had already long had in operation tried and tested designs. But not invented here, of course. The 100 mainline electric locomotives for the Euston–Manchester line were divided into as many as five different classes. Diesel motive power in particular suffered from a multiplicity of types, thanks to the sharing out of orders between manufacturers; and some types proved notoriously unreliable, as might have been expected from the steam-age companies that made them. Moreover, the new passenger rolling stock was fitted with more primitive and rougher-riding suspensions than their European equivalents. New suburban carriages were still fitted with traditional slam-doors instead of automatic sliding doors: another mark of the limited fabricating capabilities of the workshops. Cf. Colin Garratt and Max Wade-Matthews, *The Ultimate Encyclopedia of Steam and Rail* (London, Hermes House, 1998), pp. 134–45; Whitehouse (ed.), *Great Trains of the World*, pp. 45–6, 189–94.

61. See Barnett, *Audit of War*, ch. 6, and *Engage the Enemy More Closely; the Royal Navy in the Second World War* (London, Hodder and Stoughton, 1991), pp. 429 and 475; Austen Albu, 'Merchant Shipbuilding and Marine Engineering', in Pavitt (ed.), *Technical Innovation*, pp. 168–9.

62. Albu in Pavitt (ed.), *Technical Innovation*, p. 177.

63. Ibid., p. 175; Barnett, *Engage the Enemy More Closely*, p. 481.

64. Albu in Pavitt (ed.), *Technical Innovation*, pp. 175 and 177.

65. Ibid.

66. Cited in CAB 132/107, SP(53)1, 7 February 1953. Advisory Council on Scientific Policy. Report on Scientific Research and Development in British Industry.

67. Obituary of Symons in the *Daily Telegraph*, 27 November 1995.

68. See the fat file in Lab 10/1353.

69. Colonel R. H. Grierson, formerly Griessman, of S. G. Warburg & Co., quoted in BT 64/4740, Note of a Meeting in Mr. Hill's Room at the Board of Trade, between Mr. Hill and Mr. Francis Rogers, F.O.A.

70. See Roy Rothwell, 'Innovation in Textile Machinery', in Pavitt (ed.), *Technical Innovation*, pp. 125–41, but especially pp. 127–9, and Fig. 7.1; and CAB 134/647, PC(50)82 25 July 1950, Working Party on Research and Development in the Textile Machinery Industry. Joint Memorandum by the President of the Board of Trade and the Minister of Supply, covering the 57-paragraph report of an Official Working Party.

71. Rothwell, in Pavitt (ed.), *Technical Innovation*, p. 129, table 7.1.

72. Cmd. 9412, paras 118–120; J. C. Carr and W. Taplin, *History of the British Steel Industry* (Oxford, Basil Blackwell, and Cambridge, Mass., Harvard University Press, 1962), pp. 595–7.

73. Howard G. Roepke, *Movements of the British Iron and Steel Industry – 1720 to 1951* (Urbana, University of Illinois Press, 1956), pp. 178–9.

74. Cf. CAB 87/10, R(45)36, April 1945. Cabinet Reconstruction Committee. Joint report on the future of the iron and steel industry by officials of the Ministry of Supply and the Board of Trade; and R(45)17th, 30 April 1945.

75. See Barnett, *Audit of War*, ch. 5, for a summary account of the industry's history from 1870 to 1945.

76. The last handmills were closed in 1958. As for the foundries, in December 1981 the journal *Management Today* ran an article on 'Britain's Floundering Foundries' which described a post-war 'declining spiral in which failure became self-generating' despite £38 million in state aid. *Plus ça change* . . .

77. Article by Geoffrey Tweedale, Leverhulme Research Fellow in the History Department, Sheffield University, in the *Independent*, 13 January 1992.

78. In the LD process, a lance (or tube) shoots a jet of oxygen from above at high speed into molten iron held in a vessel similar to a Bessemer converter. This basic oxygen process (BOC) is fast, and produces steel similar to that from the open-hearth process.

79. BT 213/91, Long-term Investment Review: Working party No. 2 (The Pattern of Private Sector Investment). Minutes of a meeting held

in Treasury Chambers, at 3.00 p. m. on Tuesday, 23rd July, 1957, minute 1(b).

80. Ibid., minute 1(c).

16. The 'Practical Man', Science and *Technik*

1. Cited by Professor Peter Doyle in his paper 'Marketing and the Competitive Performance of British Industry: Areas for Research', prepared for the SSRC workshop on the Competitiveness and Regeneration of British Industry, 18–19 November 1983.

2. See Terence Kealey, *The Economic Laws of Scientific Research* (Basingstoke, Macmillan Press, 1996), passim, but especially ch. 9, on the delusion that there is a linear sequence from basic (especially academic) science to market success. As will be seen below, I am persuaded that Kealey's analysis is correct.

3. I am indebted to Mr Alan Smith for pointing this out to me in a letter of 22 January 1996. In the 1960s Sir William Penney (then Chairman of UKAEA) in conversation with Smith justified the decision to persist with gas-cooled, graphite-moderated reactors in preference to the American system by remarking: 'Y'know, I think the Americans could still fall fla-a-at on their faces.' Smith comments: 'I have had many technical discussions with Japanese scientists and engineers. I cannot recall an instance where one of them has erected his own judgement against that of the "market".'

4. W. J. Reader, *Imperial Chemical Industries: A History*, vol. II: *The First Quarter-Century, 1925–1952* (London, Oxford University Press, 1975).

5. CAB 132/108, SP(54)10, 16 July 1954, Seventh Annual Report, as submitted to the Lord President of the Council.

6. Ibid., para. 1.

7. Cf. CAB 132/107, SP(53)5, 27 March 1953. Advisory Council on Scientific Policy. Report on the Exploitation of Science by Industry.

8. Cmd. 6824.

9. CAB 132/108, SP(54)10, para. 6., citing Cmd. 8561.

10. CAB 132/108, SP(54)10, p. 2, footnote.

11. Ibid., Appendix II.

12. CAB 132/108, SP(54)10, table.

13. Ibid.
14. D. Edgerton, *Science, technology and British industrial 'decline' 1870–1990* (Cambridge, Cambridge University Press, 1996), table 5.4, p. 55. Edgerton himself lumps science and technology graduates together in order to reach a combined British total of 8,332 to the German 6,005. But whereas 54 per cent of the German total were technologists, only 32 per cent of the British total were.
15. Cf. ibid., pp. 52–69; Kealey, *Economic Laws*, pp. 186–7, 216–19.
16. Cf. Kealey, *Economic Laws*, pp. 60–70.
17. Paul Benoist, 'Itineraire de mon Voyage en Angleterre', September 1842, cited in Correlli Barnett, *The Audit of War* (London, Macmillan, 1986, and Pan Books, 1997), p. 98.
18. Marconi was inspired by the work of the German physicist Heinrich Herz on electric waves. After coming to London because of failure to find financial backing in Italy, he took out a patent in 1896.
19. Information drawn from *The Oxford Illustrated Encyclopedia of Invention and Technology* (London, B.C.A., 1992). For Britain's general world market performance in new technologies in 1870–1914, see James Foreman-Peck, 'The Balance of Technology Transfers 1870–1914', in Jean-Pierre Dormois and Michael Dintenfass (eds), *The British Industrial Decline* (London, Routledge, 1999).

    Further examples of venerated British scientists or inventors insufficiently aware of market potential are Sir Oliver Lodge, who developed the first radio receiver as a fascinating device, leaving it to Marconi to make a commercial success of radio; and, in the twentieth century, John Logie Baird, with his dead-end invention in 1926 of an electro-mechanical television, and Sir John Cockerell, inventor of the hovercraft in the 1950s, again a man more fascinated by his invention in itself than by its possible commercial exploitation. There is a wonderful photograph of him with his miniature hovering prototype, he in a cloth cap and a fag in his mouth, and the prototype looking like something cobbled together in a garden shed. Who can wonder that he failed to convince British boardrooms?
20. Kealey, *Economic Laws*, pp. 91–2. He points out that the small number of British prizes reflected the small number of British exhibitors. But this hardly redounds to the credit of British commercial enterprise.
21. *Report of the Endowed Schools Commission* (House of Commons, 1867–8), vol. XXXVIII, pt. I, p. 72.

22. C. 1279, *Report of the Royal Commission on Scientific Instruction and the Advancement of Science*, 6th Report; and C. 3981, *Second Report of the Royal Commission on Technical Instruction*. vol. I. Report.

23. See summary of the Report and quotations from it in Correlli Barnett, *The Collapse of British Power* (London, Eyre Methuen, 1972; paperback: Stroud, Alan Sutton, 1984), pp. 100–101.

24. See Kealey, *Economic Laws*, pp. 165–8.

25. See M. Sanderson, *The Universities and British Industry 1850–1970* (London, Routledge and Kegan Paul, 1972), chs 3 and 4; and his masterful summary of conflicting interpretations of the evidence by historians in *Education and Economic Decline in Britain, 1870 to the 1990s* (Cambridge, Cambridge University Press, 1999), ch. 2; Barnett, *Collapse of British Power*, pp. 104–6, and *Audit of War*, pp. 211–12.

26. Sanderson, *Education and economic decline*, pp. 40–45 and cited sources.

27. Cf. Sir James Dewar and the invention of the vacuum flask for storing liquid gas, quinoline for combating malaria, as well as research for such firms as Gilbey's port and Edison's light filaments. See Sanderson, *Education and economic decline*, pp. 50–51.

28. M. Sanderson, *The Universities in the Nineteenth Century* (London, Routledge and Kegan Paul, 1975), pp. 243–4.

29. Robert J. Locke, *The End of the Practical Man: Entrepreneurship and Higher Education in Germany, France and Great Britain, 1880–1940* (Greenwich, Conn., and London, Jai Press, 1984), table II.I, p. 34; Sanderson, *The Universities in the Nineteenth Century*, p. 243.

30. C. A. N. Lowndes, *The Silent Revolution* (London, Oxford University Press, 1937), p. 190.

31. Cd. 5130, p. 90.

32. The following summary of British technological deficiencies in the opening years of the Great War is based on Barnett, *Collapse of British Power* pp. 84–8 (citing the *History of the Ministry of Munitions*) and 'The Audit of the Great War on British Technology' in Dormois and Dintenfass (eds), *The British Industrial Decline*; and Sanderson, *The Universities and British Industry*, ch. 8.

33. Ibid.

34. The following summary of the wartime technological revolution is based on Sanderson, *The Universities and British Industry*, ch. 8; and Barnett, *Collapse of British Power*, pp. 113–17, citing various volumes of the *History of the Ministry of Munitions*.

35. Cd. 8594 (London, HMSO, 1917), p. 70, 'University Institutions in Relation to Industry and Commerce', cited in Sanderson, *The Universities and British Industry*, p. 214.

36. See Barnett, *Collapse of British Power*, pp. 117–20, and part IV.

37. The necessarily brief survey of British performance in *Technik* in 1918–39 that follows is based on Sanderson, *Education and economic decline*, pp. 67–71, Edgerton, *British industrial 'decline'*, pp. 22–6, 32–5, 40–41, 45–6, 53, 58–60; K. Pavitt (ed.), *Technical Innovation and British Economic Performance* (London, Macmillan, 1980), passim, but especially ch. 4; Kealey, *Economic Laws*, pp. 120–21, 133, 181, 186–7, 213–18, 226–7; Barnett, *Collapse of British Power*, pp. 476–93.

38. Cf. N. K. Buxton and D. H. Aldcroft (eds), *British Industry Between the Wars: Instability and Industrial Development, 1919–1939* (London, Scolar Press, 1979).

39. This would be still be true in the mid-1950s. Cf. CAB 132/108, SP(54)10, 16 July 1954, Seventh Annual Report of the Scientific Advisory Council, para. 34.

40. For instance, even in 1939 Austin and Morris cars were still fitted with cart springs at the front rather than independent front suspension.

41. Sanderson, *Education and economic decline in Britain, 1870 to the 1990s*, pp. 70–71. The subjects not specifically listed include medicine, social science, etc.

42. Ibid., p. 65.

43. Barnett, *Audit of War*, p. 204, citing German official statistics.

44. CAB 117/109, Committee on Reconstruction Problems – Policy with regard to Education (1940–43): Education after the War (the 'Green Book'), June, 1943, p. 23. In 1938–9 there was a last-minute spurt in building new technical colleges, thanks to panic about the possibility of another total war.

45. See Edgerton, *British industrial 'decline'*, table 4.1.

46. For the HACS (High-Angle Control System), see Barnett, *Engage the Enemy More Closely: the Royal Navy in the Second World War* (London, Hodder and Stoughton, 1991; paperback, Harmondsworth, Penguin Books, 2000), citing the Clausen Papers in the Churchill Archives Centre, CLSN 1/2.

47. Barnett, *Audit of War*, p. 136.

48. Ibid.

49. Ibid., pp. 139–42.

50. Ibid.
51. Ibid., p. 138.
52. The thermionic valve, the basis of all electronic apparatus until the coming of the transistor, was a British invention – not by a scientist, but by an engineer, Sir John Fleming, in 1904. Fleming was Professor of Electrical Engineering at University College, London from 1885 to 1926.
53. Barnett, *Audit of War*, pp. 178–80.
54. Ibid.
55. Churchill Archives Centre, ROBN4/1/2, Memorandum on the position of the German Firm of Siemens & Halske A.G. and subsidiaries throughout Europe and the World, by T. A. Eades, Managing Director, Auomatic Telephone and Electric Co. Ltd, 20 September 1944.
56. Ibid.
57. Ibid. See also ROBN 4/1/2, Memorandum by J. F. Ford and M. Goodfellow, 27 February 1945, warning that the Post Office Engineering Department 'can hardly fail to fall further behind the U.S.A. in technical progress if Siemens & Halske passes into American hands'.
58. CAB 102/393, Development of Jet Propulsion and Gas Turbine Engines in the United Kingdom, revised draft by Miss Keppel; CAB 102/394, Comments on the above draft by Air Commodore F. Whittle, 13 August 1947.
59. Quotes cited in Barnett, *Audit of War*, pp. 3–5.
60. Cf. David Edgerton, 'Science in the United Kingdom of Great Britain and (Northern) Ireland: a Study in the Nationalisation of Science', in D. Pestre and J. Krige (eds), *Science in the Twentieth Century* (Amsterdam, Harwood Academic, 1997).
61. Cf. David Edgerton, 'Whatever happened to the British Warfare State? The Ministry of Supply, 1945–51', in Helen Mercer et al. (eds), *The Labour Government 1945–51 and Private Industry: the experience of 1945–51* (Edinburgh, Edinburgh University Press, 1992). As he points out, first the Victorian Admiralty and Ordnance Department and later the Air Ministry had their close links with certain firms. But as he also points out, the role of the post-war Ministry of Supply was far wider in scope: virtually a ministry for state-sponsored industrial development.

17. 'Not Wholly Unsuccessful': the Aircraft Industry

1. See Correlli Barnett, *The Lost Victory: British Dreams, British Realities 1945–1950* (London, Macmillan, 1996, and Pan Books, 1997), pp. 228–9, and cited Whitehall records. See the same work, ch. 12, for an account of British civil aviation policy between 1945 and 1950, and its resulting commercial and technical disasters, largely based on the meetings and memoranda of the Cabinet Civil Aviation Committee (CAB 134/57–60, CAC series). See also David Edgerton, *England and the Aeroplane; An Essay on a Militant and Technological Nation* (Basingstoke, Macmillan, 1991), pp. 85–8.
2. It never carried a paying passenger.
3. CAB 134/59, CAC(50)2nd, 5 December 1950. See also CAB 134/59, CAC(50)6, 27 November 1950, The Future of the Brabazon and SR-45: joint memorandum by the Minister of Supply and the Minister of Civil Aviation. Both aircraft were finally broken up in 1953.
4. Barnett, *Lost Victory*, ch. 12. Between 1948–49 and 1950–51 BOAC and BEA turned in combined losses of £25 million. See CAB 134/1204, CAP(56)3, 23 July 1956, Committee on Civil Aviation Policy. Report by the Official Committee, para. 5.
5. CAB 134/138, EA(54)138, Annex A.
6. CAB 134/844, EA(52)69, 23 May 1952. Economic Policy Committee. Expansion of Aircraft Exports. Memorandum by the Minister of Supply and the Secretary of State for Air, para. 1.
7. Ibid., para. 2.
8. Ibid., para. 6.
9. Ibid., para. 8.
10. Ibid., para. 10.
11. Ibid., para. 7.
12. Ibid., para. 11.
13. CAB 131/9, DO(50)47, 28 June 1950, Appendices A and B. The guided weapons and/or missiles under development in the early 1950s included Blue Sky, Sea Slug, Red Shoes, Red Duster, Blue Jay and Red Dean. Cf. CAB 131/15, D(55)4, 10 January 1955, Defence Committee. The Supply of Aircraft and Guided Missiles: Report by the Minister of Supply to the Prime Minister.
14. CAB 134/845, EA(52)111, 29 July 1952, paras 4–6.

15. CAB 124/842, EA(52)17th, 29 May 1952, item 5: Expansion of Aircraft Exports.
16. CAB 134/845, EA(55)111, paras 6–8.
17. Edgerton, *England and the Aeroplane*, p. 95.
18. See R. Locke, *The End of the Practical Man: Entrepreneurship and and Higher Education in Germany, France and Great Britain, 1880–1940* (Greenwich, Conn., and London, Jai Press, 1984), especially chs III–VI.
19. CAB 131/15, DO(55)4, 10 January 1955. The Supply of Aircraft and Guided Missiles. Minister of Supply to the Prime Minister.
20. CAB 131/9, DO(50)47, 28 June 1950.
21. CAB 131/15, DO(55)4, Appendix A, 2(a)(i).
22. Ibid., Appendix A, 2(a)(ii).
23. Ibid., Appendix A, 2(a)(iii).
24. Ibid., Appendix A, 2(c)(i).
25. Ibid., Appendix A, 2(c)(ii).
26. Ibid. The Hunter eventually proved a success, in production until 1959, with a total of 1,972 built. Cf. William Green and Gordon Swanborough, *The Complete Book of Fighters: An Illustrated Encyclopaedia of Every Fighter Aircraft Ever Flown* (London, Salamander Books, 1994), pp. 565–6.
27. Ibid., Appendix A, 2(c)(iv).
28. See the *Daily Telegraph*, 14 August 1999, obituary of the test pilot, Air Vice-Marshal David Dick.
29. CAB 131/15, DO(55)4, para. 7.
30. Ibid.
31. Ibid., 2(c)(iii). See also Green and Swanborough, p. 291.
32. CAB 131/15, DO(55)4, Appendix A, 3(a)(i).
33. Ibid.
34. Ibid., Appendix A, 3(a)(i)(b).
35. Ibid., Appendix A, 3(c)(i).
36. This is not a joke: Blue Cheese was a guided bomb intended for use by the Fleet Air Arm.
37. CAB 131/15, DO(55)2, para. 12.
38. Ibid., section 4.
39. CAB 131/15, DO(55)4, para. 2.
40. Ibid., para. 2(b).
41. See the present work, chs 1 and 2; and Barnett, *Lost Victory*.

42. CAB 131/15, DO(55)4, para. 3 (c).
43. Ibid., para. 3(e).
44. Ibid., para. 3(f).
45. Ibid., para. 3(g).
46. CAB 131/16, DO(55)10, 8 July 1955. Supply of Military Aircraft. Memorandum by the Secretary of State for Air, para. 3.
47. Dennis Baldry (ed.), *The Hamlyn History of Aviation* (London, Hamlyn Books, 1996), p. 123.
48. CAB 134/853, EA(54)138, 12 December 1954. British Civil Aircraft and World Markets. Memorandum by the Minister of Supply, para. 10.
49. CAB 134/855, EA(55)38, 21 February 1955. Proposed Purchase of DC7C Aircraft by BOAC, para. 7.
50. A total of 74 Comet IVs were built in various versions, compared with a total of 1,010 Boeing 707s in all versions. Even the French out-built the Comet with their Sud-Aviation Caravelle, of which a total of 280 were produced. Cf. Baldry (ed.), *Hamlyn History of Aviation*, p. 124; Mark Wagner and Guy Norris, *Classic Jetliners* (London, Osprey Aerospace, 1994), p. 120.
51. CAB 134/855, EA(55)38, 21 February 1955. Proposed Purchase of DC7C Aircraft by B.O.A.C. Memorandum by the Minister of Transport and Civil Aviation, para. 7.
52. Ibid., para. 9.
53. CAB 134/853, EA(54)138, 14 December 1954. British Civil Aircraft and World Markets. Memorandum by the Minister of Supply, para. 1.
54. See Barnett, *Lost Victory*, ch. 12.
55. CAB 134/844, EA(52)69, 28 May 1952.
56. CAB 134/850, EA(54)26th, item 2.
57. See CAB 134/853, EA(54)130–132.
58. CAB 134/853, EA(54)132, 7 December 1954. Import of U.S. Aircraft by Private Operator.
59. CAB 134/850, EA(54)26th, item 2.
60. CAB 134/853, EA(54)138, para. 23(b)(iv).
61. Ibid., para. 13.
62. Ibid., para. 14.
63. Ibid., Annexe A.
64. Ibid., para. 4.

65. Ibid., para. 10.
66. CAB 134/853, EA(54)144, 20 December 1954. British Civil Aircraft. Memorandum by the Minister of Transport and Civil Aviation, para. 5.
67. CAB 134/850, EA(54)28th, 22 December 1954, item 2.
68. CAB 134/855, EA(55)34, 18 February 1955. American Aircraft for British Overseas Airways Corporation. Memorandum by the Minister of Supply and the Minister of Transport and Civil Aviation. See also CAB 134/855, EA(55)38, 21 February 1955. Proposed Purchase of DC7C Aircraft by B.O.A.C. Memorandum by the Minister of Transport and Civil Aviation.
69. CAB 134/855, EA(55)38, para. 3.
70. Cf. CAB 134/854, EA(55)7th, item 1.
71. Ibid., item 3.
72. The long-range Britannia 312 was introduced on the London–New York route in December 1957.
73. Edgerton, *England and the Aeroplane*, pp. 91–2.
74. CAB 131/17, DO(56)9, 26 July 1956. Military Aircraft Programme. Memorandum by the Minister of Defence.
75. Between 1945 and 1974, Labour and Conservative Governments milked the taxpayer of £1,505 million (at 1974 prices) for support of airframe and aero-engine projects, of which Concorde and its Olympus engines (at £703.8 million) accounted for nearly half. Governmental receipts in return amounted to a mere £141.9 million, of which Brabazon and Princess represented nil, and Concorde just £5.8 million. Cf. N. K. Gardner, 'The Economics of Launching Aid', in A. Whiting (ed.), *The Economics of Industrial Subsidies* (London, HMSO, 1976), table I, p. 153, cited in Edgerton, *Science, technology and British industrial 'decline'*, p. 45. It would have been more profitable for the taxpayer to invest in the manufacture and export of plastic garden gnomes.
76. Cf. such technically superb commercial failures of the 1960s as the Vickers VC10, with only 54 produced, and the Hawker-Siddeley Trident, of which 117 were built, compared with the 1,831 built of various versions of its American rival, the Boeing 727. Baldry (ed.), *Hamlyn History of Aviation*, pp. 128–31.
77. See Peter Hall, *Great Planning Disasters* (London, George Weidenfeld and Nicolson, 1980), pp. 88–90. His chapter on 'The Anglo-French

Concorde' is a devastating analysis of how step by insidious step Macmillan's Conservative Government and then Harold Wilson's Labour Government led themselves ever deeper into the grand non-adjustable financial and commercial mess that was the Concorde project.

78. Cmnd. 113, Economic Survey 1957, table 7.

18. Dependence on America: Business Systems and More Besides

1. As a part-time courier in the early 1950s I saw these things for myself. On walking down the quayside at Boulogne to board the ferry for England, couriers suffered from 'the Boulogne crouch', so called because they were weighed down by bags now stuffed with all kinds of consumer goods still not obtainable at home.

2. D. Edgerton, *Science, technology and British industrial 'decline' 1870–1970* (Cambridge, Cambridge University Press, 1996), table 5.1.

3. R. C. O. Matthews, C. H. Feinstein and J. C. Odling-Smee, *British Economic Growth, 1856–1973* (Oxford, Oxford University Press, 1982), p. 435.

4. In 1952 only £34 million of exports out of a total of £2,500 million were represented by goods unknown before the war, such as penicillin, nylon and radar kit. Even if such things as newer types of aircraft were included, the total only amounted to some £200 million, or 8 per cent of total exports. See CAB 132/107, SP(53)5, 27 March 1953. Advisory Council on Scientific Policy: Report on the Exploitation of Science by Industry, para. 8. In the opinion of the authors of this report (para. 5.), large sections of industry were 'conservative and complacent'.

5. See ch. 7 above, and Barnett, *Lost Victory*, ch. 14.

6. SUPP 14/80, PS(CS)(53)12, August 1953, Appendices I and II.

7. SUPP 14/91, Ball and Bearings. N.P.A.C. I. and other reports on Ball and Roller Bearing Industry. Memorandum on The Ball Bearing Industry, Addition to E.C. (B)(48)319, 22 March 1948, para. 8; see also Ball and Roller Bearings – U.K. Supply Position, 9 November 1951. For a general survey of the British bearings industry in the early

1950s, see 'Defence Runs on Bearings' in *The Economist*, 6 September 1952.

8. SUPP 14/91, Addition to E.C. (B)(48)319, 22 March 1948, para. 1; see also Regional Report – N.P.A.C. I (51)393, 6 June 1951.

9. SUPP 14/80, 'Ball and Roller Bearings: Defence Requirements' [1851–53]. Summary, 16 October 1953.

10. See ibid.; also SUPP 14/80, 'Ball and Roller Bearings – Defence Requirements'; SUPP 14/81, 'Ball and Roller Bearings – Forward Ordering' [1950–51]; SUPP 14/82, 'Ball and Roller Bearings – Quality and Inspection'; SUPP 14/86, 'Ball and Roller Bearings – Admiralty Requirements for Expediting Deliveries' [1951–52]; SUPP 14/87, 'Heavy Taper Roller Bearings'; SUPP 14/88, 'Ball and Roller Bearings: German Production' [1946–53]; SUPP 14/89, 'British Timken Ltd: Capital Assistance Scheme, Ball and Roller Bearings'; SUPP 14/91, 'Ball and Roller Bearings: National Production Advisory Council on Industry (NPACI) and other Reports on the Ball and Roller Bearing Industry'; SUPP 14/92, 'Ball and Roller Bearings: Research and Development'; SUPP 14/93 and 94, 'Ball and Roller Bearings – Strategic Reserve of Machine Tools', Parts I and II [1948–52 and 1953–55].

11. Cf. for instance, SUPP 14/80, minutes of meeting at Shell Mex House, 18 May 1951, and extract from 5th meeting of the Defence Programmes Problems Committee, 13 June 1951, item 4. Bearings.

12. SUPP 14/87, Tapered Roller Bearings. Timken Expansion Proposals. Notes for Dep. Sec. (A)'s Meeting at 3.30 p.m. on Monday, July 30th 1951, para. 3. SUPP 14/87 contains the voluminous correspondence relating to this dispute between July 1951 and December 1952.

13. SUPP 14/87, letter to F. J. Pascoe (British Timken) from H. S. Humphreys, Director of Contracts at the Ministry of Supply, 12 December 1952.

14. See SUPP 14/88, Extract from JIB/2/150, 1 July 1953, The Development of West German Industry Since 1945: Ball Bearings.

15. Cf. SUPP 14/88, memorandum of 10 November 1951 by G. H. Singleton.

16. BT 213/91, LIR(WP No 2)(57)7, 4 June 1957, Long Term Investment Review: Working Party No. 2. Investment in the Machine Tool Industry. Note by the Board of trade, paras 3 and 8.

17. The delightfully archaic term used in the annual Economic Surveys.
18. Cf. SUPP 14/88, memorandum of 10 November 1951, by G. H. Singleton.
19. Another quaint description from the Economic Surveys of the period.
20. BT 213/91, LIR(WP No 2)(57)24, 16 August 1957, Long-Term Investment review: Working Party No. 2 (the Pattern of Private Sector Investment); the Electronics Industry, para. 1. British exports of domestic radios and televisions only crept up from 327,000 in 1953 to 344,000 in 1956. Cf. Cmd. 9728, table 27; Cmnd. 113, table 25 and appendix, para. 22; see also BT 213/91, LIR(WP No 2)(57)17, letter of 4 July 1957 from Minister of Supply to Chairman of Long-Term Investment Review: Working Party No. 2 (the Pattern of Private Sector Investment); the Aircraft and the Radio and Telecommunications Industries, para. 3.
21. See the comment of the Conservative Minister of Defence in May 1956, cited on pp. 342–3 above.
22. The summary account of computer development in the 1940s and 1950s which follows is largely based on Martin Campbell-Kelly, *ICL: A Business and Technical History* (Oxford, Clarendon Press, 1989), and Martin Campbell-Kelly and William Aspray, *Computer: A History of the Information Machine* (New York, Basic Books, 1996), both volumes being invaluable in their comprehensive coverage of the primary and secondary sources.

   For a comprehensive survey of the literature on the history of computing, see William Aspray, 'The History of Computing within the History of Information Technology', in *History and Technology*, 1994, vol. II, pp. 7–19.

   I am grateful to Martin Campbell-Kelly for his kindness in reading this section on computers and business systems in draft, and by his comments and criticisms saving me from error. I have also much profited from the advice of Dr Doron Swade, Senior Curator, Computing and Information Technology, the Science Museum. The historical interpretation that follows in the present book is entirely mine, remaining errors and all.
23. Kilburn was twenty-six, Williams thirty-six.
24. Campbell-Kelly, *ICL*, p. 163. See Peter J. Bird, *The First Business Computer* (Wokingham, Hasler Publishing Company, 1994), and 'A

brief history of Computing' by Bill Thompson in *CAM; the Cambridge Alumni Magazine*, Lent Term, 1998, pp. 27–30.

25. So, in the jargon, constituting a 'Kondratiev cycle', after the Russian economist, and signifying a technological development so revolutionary and pervasive in effect as to create a paradigm change in human life. If the steam engine was one such invention, the electric dynamo was a second, and the computer a third.

26. Professor Douglas Hartree, as remembered by Vivian (later Lord) Bowden. Cf. B. V. Bowden, 'The Language of Computers', First Richard Goodman Memorial Lecture, unpublished ts, May 1969, cited in Campbell-Kelly, *ICL*, pp. 163–4.

27. By Harold Wilson, then President of the Board of Trade.

28. Campbell-Kelly, *ICL*, p. 166.

29. H. J. Crawley, 'NRDC Computer Project'. February 1957, NRDC Paper 132, p. 4, cited in ibid., pp. 166–7. See also J. Hendry, *Innovating for Failure* (Boston, M.I.T. Press, 1989).

30. Campbell-Kelly, *ICL*, table 10.4.

31. For the development of LEO, see Peter J. Bird, *LEO – The First Business Computer* (London, Hasler Publishing Company, 1994), chs 2 and 3; and D. Caminer et al., *User-Driven Innovation: The World's First Business Computer* (New York, McGraw-Hill, 1996).

32. Bird, op. cit., p. 87–8.

33. Ibid., p. 106.

34. Ibid., p. 113. It makes a remarkable comment on the wonders of university computer expertise that Lyons' original collaborator, Cambridge University, chose in 1958 to power its new EDSAC 2 with serried banks of unreliable thermionic valves – ten years after William Shockley and his team at Bell Laboratories had invented the transistor, and even though some thirty million transistors were by 1958 being manufactured annually.

35. Ibid., p. 185.

36. Campbell-Kelly, *ICL*, p. 181.

37. For scientific research a computer needed the capacity for high-speed arithmetical processing, but relatively little input–output, and often no magnetic tape storage; for a data-processing computer, card-based peripherals and magnetic tape storage were essential. This note is paraphrased from ibid., p. 181, footnote.

38. Letter of 14 December 1999 to the author from Dr B. M. M. Hardisty, to whom I am obliged for a briefing on the ATLAS project, although the account which follows below is entirely my own responsibility, errors and all.

39. Letter from B. M. M. Hardisty, 14 December 1999.

40. Ibid.

41. Cf. Campbell-Kelly, *ICL*, table 7.3, and p. 219.

42. Campbell-Kelly, *ICL*, p. 181.

43. J. Presper Eckert and John W. Mauchly, who led the research team at the Moore School of Electrical Engineering at the University of Pennsylvania from 1943 to 1946. See ibid., pp. 162–3.

44. Campbell-Kelly, *ICL*, p. 5. The following summary account of the development of the business-systems industry from the 1880s to the mid-1950s is drawn from this work unless otherwise cited.

45. S. G. Koon, 'Hollerith Tabulating Machinery in the Business Office', *Machinery*, 20, 1913, pp. 25–6, cited in ibid., p. 31.

46. R.W. Barnard, *A Century of Service: The Story of the Prudential, 1848–1948* (London, Prudential Assurance Co., 1949), p. 82, cited in ibid., p. 6.

47. As quoted in L. Hannah, *The Rise of the Corporate Economy* (2nd edn. London, Methuen, 1983), p. 86, and cited in ibid.

48. Ibid., p. 7.

49. Ibid., p. 70.

50. Ibid., p. 50.

51. Ibid., p. 52.

52. Ibid.

53. Ibid., p. 67.

54. Such as Burroughs, Comptometer, Elliot-Fisher, National Cash Register, etc., etc. Cf. ibid., p. 61.

55. Ibid., p. 61.

56. Ibid., p. 59.

57. Ibid., pp. 100 and 125.

58. Ibid., ch. 5.

59. The availability and delivery times for all types of office equipment, from the simple, like addressing machines, to the complex, like accounting machines, are listed in SUPP 14/150, Availabilities and Survey of the Supply Position in the United Kingdom, June 1950, Office Machinery.

60. Cited in Campbell-Kelly, *ICL*, p. 144.
61. A. T. Maxwell, transcript of interview with A. L. C. Humphreys, 9 January 1980 (Charles Babbage Institute Archives), cited in ibid., p. 148.
62. In 1949 Powers-Samas spent about 2 per cent of revenue on R&D and BTM probably less; IBM spent 3 per cent of its revenues on R&D: some £3 million, equal to half BTM's total assets that year and 14 times BTM's pre-tax profits. See ibid., pp. 127, 135–6, and 155.
63. Arthur Impey, as reported by A. T. Maxwell, and cited in ibid., p. 135.
64. The Samastronic. Ibid., pp. 158–9.
65. Ibid., p. 169.
66. Cited in ibid., p. 143.
67. Ibid., pp. 153–4.
68. In British industry and commerce in the 1950s salesmanship was an alien skill half-heartedly learned from the Americans. All the textbooks used on British salesmen's courses were American, as I recall from my time on such a course in 1952 with the North Thames Gas Board.
69. Campbell-Kelly, *ICL*, pp. 174–5.
70. For development of the HEC, see ibid., pp. 168–9.
71. M for 'marketable'.
72. Campbell-Kelly, *ICL*, pp. 179–80.
73. Ibid., p. 184–5.
74. Lord Halsbury, 'Ten Years of Computer Development', *Computer Journal*, 1959, pp. 153–9, cited in ibid., p. 186.
75. Ibid., p. 195. To be fair to BTM/ICT, American rivals of IBM were short-circuited by the same problem of swift adaptation. Cf. ibid., pp. 210–12.
76. Ibid., p. 196.
77. Cited in ibid.
78. Table 10.3. in ibid., p. 215.
79. Ibid., pp. 193 and 204.
80. BT 64/4801, 'Automation – Replies from Industries Canvassed by the Board of Trade Enquiry into Automation, 1956–57.' The question-naire was sent to over forty addressees – manufacturers and trade associations in rich variety, nationalized industries, central and local government, even the National Health Service – to find out how far they had got with adopting 'automation'. The term was taken to

embrace automatic measurement, process control, manufacturing operations and handling of materials; it applied equally to plant and offices, and so included computers and business machines.

81. Ibid., Automation in the Rubber Industry.
82. Ibid., reply of Esso Petroleum Company, 15 November 1956. Cf. also British Iron & Steel Federation, 26 October 1956; Gas Council, 26 November 1956; the Treasury on behalf of the non-industrial side of the Civil Service, 9 January 1957.
83. Ibid., undated reply.
84. Ibid., reply of January 1957.
85. Ibid., Central Electricity Authority. Government Automation Enquiry, 29 October 1956.
86. Ibid., Ministry of Health, 7 November 1956, Notes on techniques in office work involving the use of electronic data processing equipment in the hospital service in England and Wales: Accounting Machinery. Equipment in use or proposed by Regional Hospital Boards.
87. Ibid.
88. Campbell-Kelly, *ICL*, p. 209 and Bird, op. cit., p. 169.
89. CAB 134/376, IO(45)2, 20 July 1945, The Future of the Scientific Instrument Industry, para. 10 (ii). The report took the term 'scientific instrument' to cover the fields of research, light industry, electronics, aircraft instrumentation and medicine.
90. Ibid., para. 11 (i) and (ii).
91. Ibid., part VIII.
92. ED 46/547, December 1953. Research and Development in Control Engineering, paper by J. F. Coales of the Engineering Department, Cambridge University.
93. ED 46/547, letter of 25 January 1954 from H. V. Lupton to S. A. ff. Dakin.
94. Ibid.
95. ED 46/547. Control Engineering, Note of a Meeting held on April 30th 1954 at the Board of Trade (Corrected Version). See also the long correspondence in 1954 on these topics in ibid. The 'certain criticisms' must surely include the chronic shortage of trained personnel commonly suffered by advanced technologies, this being a penalty of the neglect of education and training by Labour and Conservative governments in 1945–55. See below, part VI.
96. Minutes IV, 1 and 4 of meeting held on 17 November 1947 in CAB

132/47, CIP(TR)(48)6, Committee on Industrial Productivity. Panel on Technology and Operational Research. Automatic Control and Instrumentation. Methods of Control in Industry.

97. Ibid., para. III. 3.

98. CAB 132/47, CIP(TR)(48)6, Interim Report of the Industrial Electronics Panel. See same file for minutes of the Second Meeting of the Panel on Methods of Control in Industry, 9 February 1948 (NPL paper 7/7/2), and subsequent comments by Sir Charles Darwin.

99. NPL 7/7/2, para. (1.3) (a).

100. Ibid., para. (1.1).

101. Ibid., para. (2.1).

102. Ibid., para. (1.3) (e) and (g).

103. Ibid., para. (1.3) (e) and (f).

104. Ibid., para. (3.1) (a) and (b).

105. Bristol's Instruments, Honeywell-Brown, Foxboro-Yoxall, and Integra, Leeds and Northrup.

106. SUPP 14/184, cited in letter of 9 November 1951 from J. F. Wright, Director & General Manager, Bristol's Instrument Co. Ltd, to R. L. Armstrong, Ministry of Supply.

107. Ibid.

108. BT 213/91, LIR(WP No 2)(57)22, Long-Term Investment Review – Working Party No. 2. The Oil Plant Industry, paras 3 and 4(b).

109. ED 46/547, letter of 14 January 1954 to S. A. ff. Dakin, Board of Trade.

110. ED 46/547, 23 June 1954. For that matter, British suppliers of all sorts of components to the oil industry also failed to match their American, German and Dutch rivals either in price or speed of delivery. See BT 213/91, LIR(WP No 2) 22.

111. BT 64/4801.

112. Cf. ibid., replies of the British Iron & Steel Federation, 6 October 1956, a member of the Sheet and Plate Glass Association, 10 October 1956, the Mobil Oil Company, 15 February 1957, and undated summary of replies from manufacturers of rubber tyres. On the letter (13 November 1956) from The British Plaster Board (Holdings) Ltd., one civil servant had justifiably scribbled that it was 'Wordy but inconclusive', and another had added: 'I doubt if we shall get anything better.' However, a further scribble revealed that its author did not know what a transfer machine was!

113. Ibid., letter of 7 November 1956. See also the undated letter in similar terms from Turners Asbestos Cement Co. Ltd.
114. Ibid., letter to Ministry of Works, 7 November 1956.
115. Ibid., letter from D. W. Morphy, Managing Director, 9 November 1956.
116. In another technology, forklift trucks, a similarly dynamic individual, Emmanuel (later Sir Emmanuel) Kaye, was in the process of turning the previously moribund company of Lansing-Bagnall into a world leader.

19. The Drive-train of Industrial Growth

1. See above, p. 80.
2. *Mediterranean Food* (Harmondsworth, Penguin Books, 1950).
3. The 1950s were my twenties, when I was living in the Surrey suburbs of London, and working in London. The résumé that follows on British-versus-foreign products at that time is based on personal experience and observation.
4. I commuted from Weybridge to London on a Lambretta scooter in 1953–8. I would not have done so on my army Matchless.
5. Such as Walton, Hassell and Port Co. Ltd, or the Home & Colonial Stores. Of such old-fashioned retail operations, only Cullens long survived, purveying groceries to the mid-century equivalent of the carriage trade.
6. David Hillman and David Gibbs, *CENTURY MAKERS: One hundred clever things we take for granted which have changed our lives over the last one hundred years* (London, Weidenfeld and Nicolson, 1998).
7. Kellogg's main British rivals were Force, a breakfast cereal which to my recollection was more suitable for a horse's nosebag, and the ever-favourite Quaker Oats.
8. Hillman and Gibbs, *CENTURY MAKERS*, passim.
9. Penny Sparke, *A Century of Design: Design Pioneers of the Twentieth Century* (London, Mitchell Beazley, 1998), p. 124. Out of 206 personal names cited in this book, only ten are British. See also entry 'British Design' in Stephen Bayley (ed.), *The Conran Directory of Design* (London, Octopus-Conran, 1985), p. 98.
10. See Bayley, *Conran Directory*, ch. 6. Furniture designers like Ernest

Race and Robin and Lucienne Day, talented though they were, could not be said to equal in originality or influence the likes of Aalto or Jacobsen.

11. Cf. the radio company of E. K. Cole, who in 1934 commissioned Wells Coates to design a highly unconventional Bakelite radio set, or the family firm of Donald Gomme, who in 1953 introduced the 'G-Plan' range of furniture in a watered-down 'contemporary' style.

12. Kenneth Grange, who brilliantly designed London Transport's Routemaster buses in the 1950s, had never been trained as an industrial designer but as a fine artist/illustrator who happened to see his future in 'commercial art'. His most relevant training lay in technical illustration while serving in the Royal Engineers. See Sparke, *A Century of Design*, p. 188, and Bayley, *Conran Directory*, p. 140.

13. See Bayley, *Conran Directory*, p. 216.

14. Society of Motor Traders, *The Motor Industry of Great Britain*, 1965, cited in Geoffrey Owen, *From Empire to Europe: The Decline and Revival of British Industry Since the Second World War* (London, HarperCollins, 1999), p. 222.

15. CAB 87/15, R(IO)(459), 21 March 1945. See summary in Correlli Barnett, *The Audit of War* (London, Macmillan, 1986, and Pan Books, 1997), pp. 58–9.

16. Both France and Germany had rationalized mass production, with each main category of car in the hands of a single manufacturer, so achieving maximum economies of scale and tightest focus of marketing effort.

17. For details of British and foreign car models in the 1950s, see Christopher Balfour, *Roads to Oblivion: Triumphs & Tragedies of British Car Makers 1946–56* (Bideford, Bay View Books, 1996); John Wintle, *Car Wars: The International Giants and the world they made* (London, Macmillan, 1995); Michael Allen, *British Saloon Cars of the Fifties* (Leicester, The Promotional Reprint Company, 1995); and Martin Adeney, *The Motor Makers; The Turbulent History of Britain's Car Industry* (London, Collins, 1988).

18. See Correlli Barnett, *The Lost Victory: British Dreams, British Realities 1945–1950* (London, Macmillan, 1996, and Pan Books, 1997), pp. 387–95.

19. 19,980 to the USA; 19,723 to New Zealand; 64,882 to Europe. Balfour, *Roads to Oblivion*, tables pp. 16 and 21.

20. Balfour, *Roads to Oblivion*, p. 21. Exports to the rest of the Common-
    wealth in 1950: India, 10,390; Canada, 76,278; South Africa, 19,532;
    the African colonies, 6,650. Exports of cars to the whole of South
    America only amounted to 19,166.
21. Only sales to the United States accelerated that year in comparison
    with 1950, from 19,980 to 31,328: a short-lived spurt. All figures from
    Balfour, *Roads to Oblivion*, pp. 16 and 21.
22. Cf. SUPP 14/398, 'Motor Industry: Level of Production and Supply
    to the Home Market in 1952 and 1953', Minute of 28 July 1951 citing
    predictions in EPC(DP)(51)2, Conclusion 5, of the impact of rearma-
    ment on civilian car production for home and exports.
23. Balfour, *Roads to Oblivion*, p. 16.
24. Ibid., p. 21.
25. Ibid.
26. CAB 134/1231, German Competition with particular reference to the
    Engineering Industries; A Further Report by the Working Party on
    United Kingdom Export Trends, May 1956, para. 17.
27. The following critical account of the British motor-car industry
    between 1950 and 1956 is *not* an exercise in hindsight, for the mise en
    scène of my first book, a satirical novel called *The Hump Organisation*,
    written in 1955–6 and published in 1957 (London, Alan Wingate),
    was the bungled launching of a botched-up new car, the Hump
    Grosvenor.
28. Lesser takeovers were those of car-body firms by mass car manufactur-
    ers: Briggs by Ford, and Fisher and Ludlow by BMC in 1953.
29. Balfour, *Roads to Oblivion*, pp. 102–5.
30. Ibid.
31. See ibid., passim for a comprehensive survey of all such specialist
    marques and their output, including the one-off Daimler Specials (all
    gold one year, all ivory or lizardskin the next) constructed for the
    London Motor Show in order to gratify at the shareholders' expense
    the vanity of Daimler's Chairman, Sir Bernard Docker, and his tarty
    wife Nora.
32. Sports cars such as Bristol and Frazer-Nash especially attracted roman-
    tic admiration. In the particular case of these two firms, their products
    were derived from pre-war BMW technology and, in the case of
    Frazer-Nash, freshly developed in the late 1940s thanks to the help of
    former staff of the temporarily defunct German company. See SUPP

14/328, letter from H. J. Aldington, Director of AFN Ltd (makers of Frazer-Nash cars) to Sir Stafford Cripps, 12 November 1948.

33. Balfour, *Roads to Oblivion*, pp. 135, 42, 36, 111. According to a retrospective *Daily Telegraph* item on 15 April 1995 on the Invicta Black Prince, its complicated automatic transmission made it almost impossible to reverse.

34. Balfour, *Roads to Oblivion*, pp. 156–62.

35. Ibid., pp. 50–1. The Triumph Motor Company (a wholly owned subsidiary of Standard from 1944) offers a comparable history: annual production of its Renown and Mayflower saloons with 'knife-edge' styling, though well received by the British motoring press, peaked (in 1951) at 3,338 and 13,313. Ibid., pp. 186 and 190. The company's much-admired TR2 and TR3 sports cars each reached a peak production of some 5,000 (in 1954 and 1956 respectively). Triumph thus also offers a further example of wastefully split production runs.

36. Ibid., pp. 114–16. *Autocar* quote as cited in article on the Javelin by Giles Chapman in the *Daily Telegraph* 'Motoring' section of 14 June 1997. The car's designer, Gerald Palmer, later recalled that few designers in the industry at that time 'ever worked to a budget'. Cf. *Daily Telegraph* obituary of Palmer, 20 July 1999.

37. 'Portrait Gallery' in the *Sunday Times* for 21 June 1953.

38. Phil Llewellin in the 'Motoring' section of the *Sunday Telegraph*, 29 November 1997.

39. See table in SUPP 14/395, Jaguar Car Co., Coventry.

40. SUPP 14/395, Lyons to Sir Godfrey Ince, 9 April 1951.

41. SUPP 14/395, copy of article sent on 18 November 1954 by S. Masterman of (E.4(b)), Ministry of Supply, to A.S./E.4. for the Permanent Secretary to read, which he duly did.

42. Ibid. The report also reckoned that the Mercedes 180 was 'far superior . . . in body, chassis, riding and handling . . .' to the British Rover, the nearest equivalent imported car. The Rover was esteemed in Britain as a high-quality motor, fit to carry a bank manager and his bag of clubs to the golf course.

43. Cf. J. Mantle, *Car Wars: The International Giants and the World They Made* (London, Macmillan, 1995), pp. 65–7, 123.

44. This was about 11,500 cars. Dunnett, *Decline of the British Motor Industry*, table 2.2.

45. Adeney, *The Motor Makers*, p. 230.

46. Actual figure was 42,222, according to SUPP 14/400, 'Trade with Western Germany (including the French zone): export of motor vehicles and spares [1953–54]', Production of Cars in Germany During 1951 & 1952.
47. Cf. Giles Chapman in the *Daily Telegraph* 'Motoring' section, 31 August 1996.
48. SUPP 14/395, 1 November 1954, minute from N. Statham to Messrs Laing and Boyd in the Ministry of Supply. According to this minute, some American dealers at the Jaguar launch party said that they were impressed by the engineering of the Volkswagen!
49. Cf. text, photographs and drawings in Michael Allen, *British Saloon Cars*, passim, and Balfour, *Roads to Oblivion*, passim. The prevailing characteristic of sober but imposing 'respectability' is emphasized by the artists' renderings of the cars in contemporary advertisements.
50. Cited in Dunnett, *Decline of the British Motor Industry*, p. 66.
51. Allen, *British Saloon Cars*, pp. 226–33.
52. The Morris Oxford and the Hillman Minx first got OHV engines in 1954. See Allen, *British Saloon Cars*, pp. 86 and 116. Austin adopted the OHV as early as 1947.
53. Cited in Balfour, *Roads to Oblivion*, p. 147.
54. Ibid.
55. Allen, *British Saloon Cars*, pp. 99–106.
56. Ray Newell, *The Morris Minor* (Princes Risborough, Shire Publications, 1998), p. 7.
57. Cf. extract from *Automobilia*, No. 507, September 1948, in SUPP 14/329, 'Motor Industry: Assembly of Foreign Cars in the U.K. [1948]'.
58. Ibid.
59. Allen, *British Saloon Cars*, p. 35, and Balfour, *Roads to Oblivion*, p. 69.
60. Balfour, *Roads to Oblivion*, p. 69.
61. Ibid., pp. 143–5.
62. Ibid., p. 143; Jonathan Wood, *The Volkswagen Beetle* (Princes Risborough, Shire Publications, 1989), p. 18. The Minor's final lifetime total production only came to one and half million, as against the Volkswagen's twenty million.
63. Balfour, *Roads to Oblivion*, p. 143; 'Challenge of the Volkswagen', in *The Economist* for 21 February 1953.
64. Cf. *The Economist*, 21 February 1953.

65. Balfour, *Roads to Oblivion*, p. 143.

66. Cf. articles by Ray Massey in the *Daily Mail*, 21 August 1999, and Peter Waymark in *The Times*, 2 August 1999. See also Jon Pressnell, *The Mini* (Princes Risborough, Shire Publications, 1997).

67. Wood, *Volkswagen Beetle*, p. 20. Total production of the Mini by the end of the century came to some 5 million; total production of the Volkswagen Beetle to some 20 million; total production of the Citroën 2CV and its variants came to nearly 7 million.

68. Ibid., p. 63. Total A30 production in 1952–5 amounted to 159,136; total A70 production in 1948–54 to 93,286 (see ibid., pp. 68 and 65). Rootes and Standards similarly dispersed their much smaller efforts over more than one model, so that production in 1949–55 of Rootes's main seller, the Minx, only reached a total of 391,491, while the Standard Vanguard in 1948–55 only got as far as 214,768. See ibid., pp. 100 and 170.

69. Between 1948 and 1986, according to Rover's Archives Centre.

70. From its launch date in 1961 to 1994. Cf. the *Renault Magazine*, Issue No. 144, Autumn, 1998, p. 39.

71. Adeney, *The Motor Makers*, pp. 66–7.

72. The *Daily Telegraph*, 6 October 1951. In the case of Belgium, British exports dropped from 13,083 in 1949 to 12,034 in 1953, while German exports rose from 5,439 to 20,090. In the case of Switzerland, British exports dropped from 5,468 in 1949 to 2,719 in 1953, while German exports rose from 3,601 to 11,746. Cf. Balfour, *Roads to Oblivion*, table on p. 28.

73. SUPP 14/397, 'Volkswagen Cars: Post-War [1945–53]'. Minute by W. J. Castle enclosed with letter from Roger Jackling to R. Burns in the Board of Trade, 20 November 1953.

74. Ibid.

75. Ibid. See also the *Motor Trader*, 10 June 1953, 'Current German Cars Reviewed' by A. J. K. Moss. For details of the Standard Eight and Ten, complete with worm-and-peg steering and rear cart-springs, see Balfour, *Roads to Oblivion*, pp. 170–72, and Allen, *British Saloon Cars*, pp. 134–9.

76. SUPP 14/395, minutes of meeting on 22 July 1953. The meeting was one long moan about all the difficulties faced by the industry, none of course of their own making.

77. SUPP 14/400, handwritten note of telephone call, 18 December 1953.

78. The only possible British rival was the Bedford-Utilecon Dormobile, a hand-built conversion of the standard Bedford van by the specialist firm of Martin Walker Ltd, Folkestone.

79. SUPP 14/400, note of telephone call, 18 December 1953.

80. SUPP 14/400, letter from A. E. Grant-Crofton to F. F. D. Ward, Ministry of Supply, Engineering Division, 10 December 1953.

81. SUPP 14/400, Quota for Import for German Commercial Vehicles; minute by J. B. Cullen.

82. SUPP 14/173, 'Effects of Ending Dollar Discrimination: Engineering Industries [1955]'. Estimate of the Effects on Imports of Liberalisation: Passenger Cars, Commercial Vehicles and Parts. Minute by J. B. Cullen, A.S./E.4., Ministry of Supply, 21 May 1955, and further minute of 25 May 1955.

83. SUPP 14/400, Report on 'The German Market for United Kingdom Passenger Cars', by the Commercial Counsellor at the British Embassy in Bonn, para. 4(d).

84. Ibid., appendix A.

85. Ibid.

86. Ibid., para. 10.

87. Ibid., para. 11.

88. Ibid., appendix F.

89. SUPP 14/400, Letter from T. Bailey, for Regional Manager, to A. E. Grant-Crofton of the SMMT, 13 August 1954.

90. Ibid., letter from F. E. James, Assistant Sales Manager, to Grant-Crofton, 30 August 1954.

91. Ibid. H. A. Denne, General Export Manager of the Ford Motor Company, noted in his letter of 11 August 1954 to Grant-Crofton that Ford's interests in Germany were looked after by Ford of Germany, but he finished with what reads like a back-handed slap for the native British exporter: '. . . to improve penetration in Western Germany, in addition to effective advertising and Sales effort, the product must be good in finish and performance, Service and parts supply must be of high standard and retail prices must be reduced.'

92. SUPP 14/400, A. E. Grant-Crofton to Dr S. Masterman, Ministry of Supply, 2 September 1954.

93. Ibid.

94. SUPP 14/330, 'P.E.P. (Political and Economic Planning) Report on Motor Industry [1947–49]'.

95. SUPP 14/330, Note [dated 8 June 1948] on the 18th meeting of the P.E.P. Engineering Group on the 31st May, 1948.

96. In retirement he was to become a director of the Goodyear Tyre and Rubber Company (Great Britain) Ltd.

97. SUPP 14/330, letter of 8 June 1948.

98. SUPP 14/173, 21 May 1955, Estimate of the Effects on Imports of Liberalisation: Passenger Cars, Commercial Vehicles and Parts. Minute by J. B. Cullen, A.S./E.4., Ministry of Supply.

99. Owen, table 9.6.

100. CAB 134/1231, Economic Policy Committee memoranda. Report circulated under covering note EP(56)58, 5 July 1956.

101. Ibid., paras 1 and 9.

102. Ibid., para. 33.

103. Ibid., para. 1.

104. Ibid., para. 4.

105. CAB 134/1230, EP(56)21, 18 February 1956, Balance of Payments Prospects Committee; Report – February 1956.

106. T 230/406, draft statement to Cabinet by the Chancellor, February 1956.

107. T 230/406, Memorandum to Sir Edward Bridges, 6 February 1956.

20. 'This Pressing Problem' – Productivity

1. BT 64/4717, Letter dated 7 August 1952 from Minister of Labour – Proposed Productivity Campaign, 1952.

2. This is not to argue that detailed intervention in industry by the state could have solved Britain's problems; it is merely to point out that the Labour Government failed to use the lever of state compulsion available to it.

3. See Correlli Barnett, *The Lost Victory: British Dreams, British Illusions, 1945–1950* (London, Macmillan, 1986; Papermac, 1987), pp. 205–10 and ch. 11.

4. Ibid., pp. 205–11.

5. BT 64/4717, minute by S. A. ff. Dakin, 12 August 1952.

6. Ibid.

7. See Barnett, *Lost Victory*, ch. 19.

8. BT 64/4717, minute of 12 August 1952.

9. Ibid.

10. See BT 64/4717; BT 64/4720, 'Campaign for Productivity: Working Group on Departmental Responsibility for Production [1952–54], Chairman Mr T. Padmore'; and LAB 10/1138, Industrial Productivity. Responsibility of Govt. Departments. Treasury and Board of Trade [1952].

11. BT 64/4717, minute by Ian Gray, Private Secretary to the Parliamentary Secretary at the Board of Trade, 11 September 1952.

12. LAB 10/1138, PWG(52)1st. Working Group on Departmental Responsibility for Productivity.

13. Ibid., PWG(52)1, 11 October 1952, Memorandum by the Ministry of Labour and National Service on its General Productivity Functions; PWG(52)2, 11 October 1952, Memorandum by the Board of Trade on its General Productivity Functions; PWG(52)3, 15 October 1952, Memorandum by the Treasury Information Division on its General Productivity Functions.

14. Ibid., PWG(52)9, circulated on 20 December 1952.

15. Ibid., paras 3 and 22 (a).

16. Ibid., paras 4 and 22 (b).

17. Ibid., paras 16–20 and 22 (h).

18. See the correspondence between Harold Watkinson, Walter Monckton and R. A. Butler in LAB 10/1138.

19. Ibid., Notes of a meeting of Ministers on 23 February 1953.

20. BT 64/4720, Campaign for Productivity: Working Group on Departmental Responsibility for Production. Minute by D. H. Lyal to Sir Maurice Dean, 16 March 1953.

21. Ibid., minute by Sir Maurice Dean, Second Secretary at the Board of Trade, 17 March 1953.

22. Cf. CAB 134/1012, MAC(52)162, 27 August 1952, Mutual Aid Committee, 13th meeting, Minute 2. The American spokesman was the Hon. W. L. Batt. Cotton was one favoured case for treatment.

23. S. A. ff. Dakin, Board of Trade, in ibid.

24. CAB 134/1012, MAC(52)162, minute 2.

25. CAB 134/1012, MAC(52)159, Appendix I, para. 4.

26. A. L. Batt in the meeting of 27 August 1952. Cf. ibid., MAC(52)159.

27. BT 64/4896, U.K. Productivity – report on Productivity prepared by officials at ministerial request: briefing for President of the B.O.T. [sic] and ministers on U.K. productivity, 1953. Final Version of Agreement on Conditional Aid.

28. BT 64/4720, draft of 16 March 1953 of letter to Sir Godfrey Ince, Ministry of Labour and National Service from Sir Frank Lee, Board of Trade.

29. Cf. ROBN 5/8, PCA(53) 2nd and 3rd meetings, 22 June and 30 July 1953.

30. BT 64/4720, Provisional Chart of Committees on Conditional Aid.

31. CAB 134/1012, minute by D. H. Lyal, 14 March 1953. Bodies ranging from the University Grants Committee and the DSIR to the British Institute of Management were all helping to formulate projects in the field of economic and social research. Cf. ROBN 5/8, CA(DWP)(53)1, 29 April 1953, Conditional Aid: Dean [after Sir Maurice Dean, the chairman] Working Party: Programme for Expenditure of the Counterpart of the Conditional Aid Designed for Promoting Productivity of Industry and Stimulating Competition.

32. ROBN 5/8, PCA(53)1, Productivity and Conditional Aid Committee. Terms of Reference and Membership.

33. BT 64/4720, Conditional Aid: Progress Report.

34. Cmd. 8918. Programme of Expenditure of Counterpart Funds derived from United States Economic Aid under section 9(c) of the Mutual Security Act of 1952. Presented by the President of the Board of Trade to Parliament by Command of Her Majesty.

35. Ibid., para. 7.

36. Ibid., para. 3.

37. Ibid., para. 4.

38. Ibid.

39. Ibid., para. 5.

40. The rest of the money was accounted for by a reserve of £201,600, publicity at £188,000, and a contribution to the European Productivity Agency of £257,143 insisted on by the MSA.

41. See ROBN 5/8, PCA (53)series, especially PCA(53)12, and PCA(53)4th.

42. ROBIN 5/8, PCA(53)12, 26 October 1953, Progress Report.

43. BT 64/4740, 'British Productivity Council: liaison with government departments and industry', Organisation and Programme, Note of

Conversation with Mr Francis Rogers, by S. A. ff. Dakin of the Board of Trade, 16 July 1954.

44. LAB 10/1166, 1953 report of the British Productivity Council.

45. LAB 10/1166, letter of 20 October to E. W. Playfair, the Treasury.

46. Sir Ewart Smith, Technical Director of ICI and member of the Council, as cited in *The British Productivity Council*, a 1953 booklet the Council published on its aims and strategies. In LAB 10/1166.

47. LAB 10/1166, *The British Productivity Council*, para. 2.

48. Ibid.

49. Ibid.

50. The BPC's general approach was shared by the Productivity and Conditional Aid Committee's Productivity Working Group, whose interim report of 22 July 1953 (ROBN 5/8, PCA(53)9) opined that the main cause of British productivity being lower than American lay in 'the atmosphere of industry and the attitudes of the parties engaged in it'.

> While there are profound historical and social reasons for the comparative lack of interest in the objective of higher productivity, and the mutual suspicions and hesitations surrounding the subject, the Working Group feel that the simple and direct way to better this state of affairs is for industry itself to set about developing among those concerned a sharper realisation of what is at stake for their industry, their firm and themselves.

The Working Group, like the BPC, saw the means to this realization as lying in 'full and frank discussion' and a 'frank review' of the problems of a particular industry or section of industry. Salvation through seminars!

51. See LAB 10/1166 and BT 64/4740 for detailed documentation of the BPC's Somme-like progress between 1953 and 1956.

52. LAB 10/1166, unsigned Ministry of Labour minute to the Chief Industrial Commissioner, 22 June 1953.

53. Ibid.

54. BT 64/4740, handwritten minute by Miss A. D. Stevens, 8 April 1954.

55. Ibid., minute by S. A. ff. Dakin, 17 March 1954.

56. Ibid.

57. Ibid.

58. Ibid. See also in BT 64/4740 'Notes of an Interview' with the Chairman of the BPC, General Sir Thomas Hutton, made by Dakin on 24 April 1954.

59. Ibid., 'Notes of an Interview' by Dakin, 16 March 1954.

60. Ibid.

61. Ibid., Board of Trade minutes and briefings prior to the meeting, and PL(54)First, the minutes of the first meeting of the Productivity Liaison Committee.

62. Cf. BT 64/4740, PL(54) series.

63. LAB 10/1166, letter of 20 August 1954 from Miss A. D. Stevens in the Board of Trade to S. C. Leslie in the Treasury.

64. Ibid., enclosed note of comments by Regional Commissioners on L.P.C.s in their regions.

65. BPC Bulletin No. 11, included in LAB 10/1166.

66. BT 64/4740, Note of meeting with Mr Preston, Mr Francis Rogers, Mr A. H. Warner and Miss Stevens on Monday, 18 October 1954.

67. See correspondence and minutes in LAB 10/1166, and article in *The Times* of 27 February 1956 on how indifference, not to say local apathy and suspicion, was slowing the work of the Productivity Council.

68. Ibid.

69. A selection, rich in period flavour, is to be found in LAB 10/1166.

70. Supplement to the BPC Bulletin, July 1954.

71. Article by Graham Hutton on 'Productivity for Prosperity' in supplement to BPC *Bulletin*, March 1955. Copy in LAB 10/1166.

72. Cf. the list of guests and the texts of speeches at the luncheon on 14 September 1954, in BT 64/4740.

73. Cf. letter of 28 September 1955 from Peter Thorneycroft to R. A. Butler.

74. Cf. CAB 134/848–55, Economic Policy Committee, Minutes and Memoranda 1953–55, passim, but especially CAB 134/849, EA(53)140, EA(53)148; CAB 134/850, EA(54)6th; CAB 134/851, EA(54)24, 25, and 31.

75. CAB 134/849, EA(53)148, 3 December 1953. Economic Policy Committee. Efficiency and Output. Memorandum by the Minister of Labour and National Service, para. 1.

76. Ibid., para. 7.

77. Ibid., para. 8.
78. CAB 134/851, EA(54)25, The Role of Government in Promoting Higher Productivity, para. 1.
79. CAB 134/851, EA(53)24, 6 March 1954, Economic Policy Committee. Industrial Productivity. Note by the President of the Board of Trade.
80. CAB 134/851, EA(54)31, 12 March 1954. Industrial Productivity. Note by the Minister of Labour and National Service.
81. Ibid.
82. CAB 134/850, EA(54)6th, item 4.
83. CAB 134/851, EA(54)25. See also BT 64/4896, 17 March 1954, internal Board of Trade summary of the Report and comments on it.
84. Harold Watkinson, Parliamentary Secretary, Ministry of Labour and National Service.
85. BT 64/4896, Brief for Ministerial Meeting of 1 April 1954, on Industrial Productivity.
86. See the survey in CAB 134/1227, EP(55)1, 12 April 1955. The Role of Government in Promoting Higher Industrial Productivity. Second Report by the Productivity and Conditional Aid Committee.
87. See correspondence between the Ministry of Labour and the Board of Trade, and BOT internal minutes, in November 1952 in BT 64/4717. See also T 230/284, LTS (55)5, 9 February 1955, Long Term Economic Survey. The Rate of Expansion of Output 1954–1960.
88. Cf. CAB 134/1231, EP(56)58, table 6.
89. T 230/284, LTS(55)5, table 3, handwritten additions.
90. CAB 134/1231, EP(56)58, 5 July 1956.
91. Ibid., para. 30.

21. 'No Fear of Unemployment'

1. Cf. CAB 134/1231, EP(56)58, para. 27 and Cmd. 9728, para. 26.
2. CAB 134/227, EPC(50)124, 1 December 1950. Wages and Prices and Full Employment: memorandum by the Chancellor of the Exchequer. Full extracts are cited in Correlli Barnett, *The Lost Victory: British Dreams, British Realities 1945–1950* (London, Macmillan, 1996, and Pan Books, 1997), p. 350.
3. Ibid.

4. Ibid.

5. CAB 134/856, EA(E)(51)13, 10 December 1951.

6. Ibid.

7. T 230/404. Industrial Relations, Minute of 7 July 1955 to the Economic Secretary at the Treasury from Sir Herbert Brittain.

8. CAB 134/1230, EP(56)18, 10 February 1956. Economic Policy Committee. Restrictive Labour Practices. Memorandum by the Minister of Labour and National Service, paras 3–4.

9. Ibid.

10. CAB 134/1229, EP(56)4th, 13 February 1956, item 2.

11. T 234/74, RLP(56)series: Committee on Restrictive Labour Practices.

12. Cf. summary in para. 10 of the Report of the Committee on Restrictive Labour Practices, September 1956, in T 234/74. The Act prohibited *collective* enforcement of resale price maintenance (but not by individual manufacturers or suppliers); and provided 'for the registration ... of certain restrictive trade agreements and ... the prohibition of such agreements when found contrary to the public interest.' The Act thus fell far short of the outright prohibitions under American legislation.

13. T 234/74, RLP(56)2, 24 April 1956, Committee on Restrictive Labour Practices, Terms and Conditions of Employment – Restrictive Labour Practices. Note by the Ministry of Labour. The papers of the Committee on Restrictive Labour Practices provides an invaluable dossier about these practices and the human attitudes underlying them.

14. Ibid.

15. T 234/74, Report by the Committee on Restrictive Labour Practices, para. 10.

16. Ibid., para. 38.

17. Ibid.

18. Cited in Robert Shepherd, *Iain Macleod* (London, Hutchinson, 1994), p. 113.

19. T 234/74, Report by the Committee on Restrictive Labour Practices, para. 53.

20. Ibid., para. 16.

21. CAB 134/1273, IR(55)1, 17 June 1955, Committee on Industrial Relations. Terms of Reference and Composition. Note by the Secretary of the Cabinet.

22. Ibid., IR(55)1st, 22 June 1955.

23. Ibid.

24. Ibid.

25. CAB 134/1273, IR(55)3, 22 July 1955, The Possibility of Introducing a Legal Requirement for a Period of Reflection before the Taking of Strike Action. Memorandum by the Ministers of Labour and National Service, para. 5.

26. Ibid., para. 8.

27. CAB 134/1273, IR(55)2nd, 28 July 1955, as reported by Monckton.

28. Ibid.

29. CAB 134/1273, IR(55)5, 22 July 1955. Extension of the Liability of Strikers to Legal Proceedings. Memorandum by the Minister of Labour and National Service, para. 7.

30. All ibid., paras 6 and 7. Monckton also advised his colleagues in July 1955 that he saw 'no possibility of extending the present legal provisions for compulsory arbitration, and no need to extend those for voluntary arbitration'. See ibid., IR(55)4, 22 July 1955. Extension of the Principle of Arbitration. Memorandum by the Minister of Labour and National Service, para. 11.

31. Ibid., IR(55)5, para. 5.

32. Certainly they were sensitive, even oversensitive, to the limits of what was politically possible or impossible, but governments of conviction breach such limits.

33. See the lengthy exchange of minutes in LAB 10/1461, especially the seven-page 'Note on Pre-strike Ballots' by G. E. Slater [IR 1328/56], 31 August 1956.

34. CAB 134/1273, IR(55)7, 22 July 1955, The Education of Public Opinion on Industrial Relations. Memorandum by the Minister of Labour and National Service.

35. See Correlli Barnett, *The Collapse of British Power* (London, Eyre Methuen, 1972; paperback editions: Stroud, Alan Sutton, 1984, 1987, 1991, 1993, 1997), part I.

36. CAB 134/1273, IR(55)7.

37. Cf. in particular, T 230/293–301, (1) National Wages Policy. (2) Full Employment Policy, 1946–1957; T 234/51, Economic Situation, 1956. Discussions between the Prime Minister, the Chancellor of the Exchequer and Industrial Bodies. Trades Union Congress; T 234/91–5, A Study by the Committee on Industrial Relations on the Implications of Full Employment, 1955–56 [papers relating to the

production of Cmd. 9725]; T 234/672–5, Stabilisation of Wages and Prices – Policy Files 1956.

38. T 230/299, minute on Draft White Paper on Full Employment, 6 July 1954.

39. Ibid.

40. Ibid.

41. T 230/300, draft letter of 11 March 1955 to the Prime Minister in regard to a paper on wage and price problems by the Parliamentary Secretary to the Ministry of Labour (Harold Watkinson) which had been sent to the Prime Minister for possible circulation to the Cabinet.

42. T 234/51, Talk with Trade Union Council (Meeting of Prime Minister, Chancellor of the Exchequer and Minister of Labour and National Service with T.U.C.), (Monday, 5 March), para. 3.

43. T 234/51, minute of 2 March 1956.

44. T 234/672, section of Prime Minister's draft speech for Perth, 3rd revise.

45. Ibid.

46. T 234/672, Meeting with Heads of Nationalised Industries, 26th June 1956, para. 3.

47. Butler reintroduced the pre-war variable bank rate as a means of mild monetary 'disinflation'.

48. Cf. T 234/51, minute on Short-time Working and Redundancy, March 1956.

49. Ibid. See also T 230/404, CM(55)25th Conclusions, 21 July 1955, item 6.

50. Minimum deposit of 33.33 per cent, and repayment over eighteen months. See Martin Adeney, *The Motor Makers; The Turbulent History of Britain's Car Industry* (London, Collins, 1988), p. 211.

51. Deposit of 15 per cent and twenty-four months' repayment. Cf. ibid.

52. Cf. T 230/404 for the Cabinet's anxious debate on the 'Economic Situation' in CM(55)25th Conclusions, item 6, and the related background discussions of civil servants.

53. Ibid.

54. Cf., apart from such general economic forums as the Cabinet and the Cabinet Economic Policy Committee, the sources cited in endnote 37 above.

55. T 230/298. Record of a Meeting between the Chancellor of the Exchequer and the T.U.C. Economic Committee, 24 June 1952.

56. Cf. minute by S. C. Leslie, 23 March 1955, in T 230/300.
57. T 230/299, Minute on Draft White Paper on Full Employment, 6 July 1954.
58. Cmd. 9725, The Economic Implications of Full Employment.
59. Cf. the sources cited in endnote 37 above.
60. T 234/51, Record of Meeting with TUC, 1st November 1955.
61. Ibid.
62. H. Macmillan, *Riding the Storm* (London, Macmillan, 1971), p. 29.
63. See ibid., ch. II.
64. Ibid. p. 16.
65. Ibid., p. 2.
66. Cf. T 234/51, Prime Minister's personal minute to the Chancellor of the Exchequer, 28 February 1956.
67. Ibid., folio 78.
68. T 234/672, letter of 27 March 1956.
69. Ibid.
70. T 234/672, Prime Minister's Personal Minute to the Chancellor of the Exchequer, 11 April 1956.
71. Ibid.
72. T 234/672, Wages and Prices. Talks with the T.U.C., F.B.I., etc. 26 April, 1956. Memorandum by Robert Hall. He wanted the Government to mount 'a concerted attack . . . for an experimental period', by telling employers that 'it is the wish of the Government that prices should be held steady or reduced wherever possible'; and the TUC that on this basis the future of prices would lie 'in the hands of the workers themselves', depending on whether or not they obtained wages increases 'beyond the capacity of industry'. See also strenuous internal Treasury discussions during March and April in same file.
73. T 234/672, as described to the Prime Minister in a minute by F. A. Bishop, Assistant Secretary, the Cabinet Office, 9 May 1956.
74. T 230/309, copy of CP(56)118, 8 May 1956, Statement on Prices, Appendix I.
75. T 230/309, copy of CM(56)36th Conclusions, 15 May 1956, item 1.
76. Ibid.
77. T 234/672 (also in T 230/309), minutes of Meeting with Trade Union Council Representatives, 10 May 1956, para. 4.
78. Mr H. Douglass, in ibid., para. 7.
79. Ibid.

80. See drafts in T 234/672.

81. T 234/672, minute by Robert Hall reporting on meeting of the Advisory Group on Economic Publicity on 14 May 1956 about the 'Statement on Price Policy' issued after the Prime Minister's speech and of the most recent meeting with the TUC.

82. Quoted in Macmillan, vol. cit., pp. 56–7.

83. Leading article in issue of 26 May 1956.

84. Issue of 26 May 1956.

85. See T 230/310, Economic Situation – Discussions between the Prime Minister, Chancellor of the Exchequer, and Bodies representing both sides of Industry [1956]; and T 234/672. See especially the suggested timetable submitted to the Prime Minister on 29 June 1956 in T 234/672.

86. T 234/672, minutes of meeting with National Union of Manufacturers, 13 June 1956.

87. Ibid.

88. T 234/674, Draft for address by Chancellor to Press Conference week beginning 27 August 1956.

89. Ibid.

90. Cf. T 234/674, correspondence between Macmillan and the Prime Minister, and Macmillan and Macleod in September 1956. See also ibid. and T 230/309 for the voluminous agonizing of civil servants as to what to do next: their solution being the usual one of 'the pre-emptive cringe'.

91. T 234/674, minute of 20 September 1956.

92. Cmnd. 113, para. 49 and table 12.

93. Cmnd. 394. paras 44 and 48.

94. Ibid., para. 38.

95. Ibid., Appendix B, para. 2.

96. I.e., the 'post-war consensus' or 'New Jerusalem', as created in the latter years of the Second World War by the likes of Sir William Beveridge. See Barnett, *Audit of War*, part I.

22. Education for Industrial Defeat

1. See Correlli Barnett, *The Audit of War: The Illusion and Reality of Britain as a Great Nation* (London, Macmillan, 1986; Papermac, 1987).

2. Ibid., ch. 9 and cited official files.

3. Ibid., p. 205 and cited sources.

4. Ibid., part III, passim.

5. There follows a summary version of the detailed account of British education and training in its historical context given in ibid., ch. 11.

6. 1934 figures in ED 46/296, 1944, First Report of the Interdepartmental Standing committee on Further Education and Training, para. 39.

7. Barnett, *Audit of War*, p. 203 and cited sources.

8. Trustees of the Carnegie United Kingdom Trust, *Disinherited Youth: A Report on the 18-plus Age Group; Enquiry Prepared for the Trustees of the Carnegie United Kingdom Trust*, cited in Barnett, *Audit of War*, p. 201.

9. Committee appointed by the President of the Board of Education to consider the Supply, Recruitment and Training of Teachers and Youth Leaders, or McNair Committee (HMSO, 1944).

10. For all the figures in this paragraph, see Barnett, *Audit of War*, pp. 202–3, and cited sources.

11. Ibid.

12. All in ibid., p. 204 and cited sources.

13. Cf. ED 46/296. HTE Committee Paper No. 2, Technical Colleges: Statistics of Higher Technical Education, July 1944; HTE Paper No. 5, An outline of the arrangements in force for the award of National Certificates and Diplomas to students of Colleges and Schools for Further Education in England and Wales, July, 1944.

14. Cmd. 6458.

15. Report on Visits Made by a Deputation to Continental Technical Colleges and Educational Institutions, April 3rd to April 17th, 1935, published by the City of Birmingham Education Committee, July 1935, in ED 46/295.

16. ED 46/295, Interdepartmental Standing Committee on Further Education and Training. Second Report, December 1944. Yet what could be achieved once war freed the British mind from its inhibitions is shown by the 1941 scheme of State Bursaries in Science at universities, starting at Higher Schools Certificate level, in the fields of radio, engineering and chemistry; and extended in 1942 to metallurgy, fuel technology, and chemical engineering. A total of 2,531 State Bursaries were awarded. In 1942 there followed a scheme of Engineering

Cadetships for the age-group sixteen to nineteen who had already left school: 3,020 were awarded in 1942 and 771 in 1943. See CAB 102/239, *History of Education*, Early draft, chs iv–vi, by Dr S. Weitzman, pp. 685–8.

17. Cf. ED 46/295, Special Committee on Higher Technological Education, 5th meeting, 31 August and 1 September 1944, and 10th Meeting, 4–5 January 1945, para. 9.

18. ED 46/295, evidence of Sir Charles Darwin, Director of the National Physical Laboratory, to the Special Committee on Higher Technological Education, minutes of 10th meeting, 4 January 1945, para. 10.

19. Evidence of the Director of LSE, Mr A. M. Carr-Saunders, to the Special Committee on Higher Technological Education, ED 46/295, minutes of 8th meeting, 23–24 November 1944, para. 29.

20. Michael Sanderson, *The Universities and British Industry, 1850–1970* (London, Routledge & Kegan Paul, 1972), p. 271. Similar figures in this chapter are for academic years. Other than low-grade 'commercial courses' in technical institutions, there only existed ill-coordinated propagandist bodies such as the Institute of Personnel Management (founded 1913), the British Council for Commercial and Management Education (1919), and the Institute of Public Administration (1922).

21. Cd. 3966. Report of the Endowed Schools (Schools Enquiry) Royal Commission, vol. I. (1867–8).

22. See Correlli Barnett, *The Collapse of British Power* (London, Eyre Methuen, 1972; paperback editions: Stroud, Alan Sutton, 1984, 1987, 1991, 1993, 1997).

23. The following summary of British developments in education and training from the 1870s to the Second World War is based on the author's full accounts in *The Collapse of British Power*, part I, and *The Audit of War*, ch. 11. See also Michael Sanderson's excellent *Education and economic decline in Britain, 1870 to the 1990s* (Cambridge, Cambridge University Press, 1999), chs 1 to 4.

24. Sir Robert Morant, Permanent Secretary at the Board of Education, 1903–11; J. W. Headlam (later Sir James Headlam-Morley), son of a canon, educated at Eton and King's College, Cambridge, once Professor of Greek and Ancient History at Queen's College, London: J. W. Mackail, who drafted the new regulations for state secondary schools, a Balliol man whose father-in-law was Sir Edward Burne-Jones, and

who was later to be Professor of Poetry at Oxford, and finish up as President of the British Academy in 1932–6. His 1894 book *The Sayings of Christ* was to be republished in 1938.

25. Report of the Royal Commission on Secondary Education, C. 7862, vol. I: *Report*.
26. ED 46/296, H.T.E. Paper No. 3.
27. See Barnett, *Audit of War*, ch. 11, and cited primary and secondary sources.
28. See Barnett, *Collapse of British Power*, pp. 38–42, 96, 98, 100, 103–6, 487–9; and *Audit of War*, ch. 11, and cited sources. See also Sanderson, *Education and economic decline in Britain, 1870s to the 1990s*, chs 1–5.
29. Barnett, *Audit of War*, p. 233.
30. The Interdepartmental Committeee on Further Education and Training, chaired by Lord Hankey (appointed March 1943: first report, April 1944, in ED 46/296; and second report, December 1944, in ED 46/295).
31. ED 46/296, First Report, para. 38.
32. Cmd. 6458. See also files relating to the Board of Education's preceding outline plan, the 'Green book' of June 1941, in ED 136/212, 215 and 218.
33. ED 138/16, meeting on 31 July 1941.
34. *Curriculum and Examinations in Secondary Schools: Report of the Committee of the Secondary School Examination Council Appointed by the President of the Board of Education in 1941* (HMSO, 1943).
35. Ibid., pp. 56–8.
36. Ibid., p. 116.
37. Heads of leading grammar schools, chief education officers and secretaries to university examination boards. Cf. ED 138/16, ED 136/681.
38. CAB 102/238–9, Dr S. Weitzman, *History of Education*, p. 708.
39. ED 46/295, the Special Committee on Higher Technological Education, fourth meeting, 27–28 July 1944, para. 5. The Report of the Committee, chaired by Lord Eustace Percy, was published by HMSO in August 1945.
40. ED 46/295, minutes of meeting of 24 November 1944, para. 32. The so-called 'technical high school' of the 1944 Education Act is not to be confused with a *technische Hochschule* for young people of university age.
41. ED 46/296, First Report, para. 8.

42. Ibid., paras 11–13.

43. Or Percy Committee, after its Chairman, Lord Eustace Percy.

44. The terms were: 'Having regard to the requirements of industry, to consider the needs of higher technological education in England and Wales and the respective contributions to be made thereto by Universities and Technical Colleges, and to make recommendations, among other things, as to the means for maintaining appropriate collaboration between Universities and Technical Colleges in this field.' ED 46/295, Minute to the President from Sir Robert Wood, Deputy Secretary, 1 January 1944.

45. Sir Hector Hetherington, Chairman of the Committee of Vice-Chancellors, and former Professor of Moral Philosophy, and Mr Mouat Jones, Vice-Chancellor of Leeds University. The principal civil servant was Sir Robert Wood, Deputy Secretary of the Board of Education (son of a Baptist minister, City of London School, and a first in part I of the Classics tripos at Jesus College, Cambridge). See ibid.

46. Lord Eustace Percy, *Some Memories*, p. 209, quoted in Sanderson, *Education and economic decline*, p. 349, Note 3.

47. ED 46/295, 28 April 1944.

48. The Principal of the South-West Essex Technical College, Dr H. Lowery.

49. Ibid.

50. Cf. Percy's own paper 'Principles' (ED 46/396, H.T.E. Paper 11); evidence of the Institutions of Mechanical Engineers and of Electrical Engineers (ED 46/295, minutes of second meeting, 25–26 May 1944, paras 24 and 34).

51. ED 46/295, meeting of 28 April 1944.

52. ED 46/296, HTE Paper 69, and ED 46/295, minutes of 10th meeting, 4–5 January 1945; and Report, section III, paras 11–12.

53. Report, section III, paras 11–12.

54. Report, section IV.

55. ED 46/295, meeting of 28 April 1944. Bragg had much more to say in this meeting on such topics as the need for an army of 'scientific workers' (sic) to help the scientists produced by the universities, 'but the way to do this was not to dilute the universities with men of lower calibre nor to turn the Engineering Schools of the Universities into Technische Hochschule.' The function of the existing technical

college, opined Bragg, was 'to produce what might be called the N.C.O. – and higher – of industry . . .'

56. Ibid.
57. Minutes of seventh meeting, 26–27 October 1944.
58. Ibid.
59. Personal note in section VI of the Report.
60. Ibid.
61. Ibid.
62. Cmd. 6824. Report of the Committee appointed by the Lord President of the Council entitled 'Scientific Manpower'.
63. Ibid.
64. Ibid., para. 29.
65. Ibid., para. 303.
66. Ibid., para. 34.
67. Ibid., para. 32.
68. The Weir Committee (Chairman, Sir Cecil Weir; reporting in February 1944) and the Baillieu Committee (Chairman, Sir Clive Baillieu; reporting in February 1946). Both chairmen were prominent industrialists. Both committees were appointed by the Board of Trade. See summaries of, and extracts from, their reports in ED 46/739, Seminar on Problems in Industrial Administration, 1951–2, Paper No. 18.
69. The Weir Report, cited in ibid.
70. Ibid., para. 63(h).
71. The following section on education at all levels in the period 1945–55/6 is an abridgement of a report by me commissioned by the Economic and Social Research Council under contract no. R000221390, *The Relationship Between Education, Training and R&D to Britain's Competitive Efficiency as an Industrial Society 1945–55*. This is now available for consultation in the British Library. See also M. Sanderson, *Education and economic decline*, chs 6–7; *The Missing Stratum: Technical Education 1900–1990s* (London, Athlone Press, 1994); and article 'Social Equity and Industrial Need: a Dilemma of English Education since 1945' in Terry Gourvish and Alan O'Day (eds), *Britain since 1945* (Basingstoke, Macmillan Press, 1991).
72. ED 46/1002, Note dated 9 January 1956.
73. Even by 1955 the raising of the minimum school-leaving age to sixteen (when the new GCSE 'O' Level examination, introduced in 1951, was taken) still remained a deferred hope for the future.

74. The Crowther Committee was a committee of the Central Advisory Council for Education (England).
75. See ED 146/33, EL 5/13, undated.
76. The Albemarle Committee on the Youth Service, ED 124/210, YSC 7/59, table A.
77. Ibid.
78. Calculated from ED 124/210, YSC 7/59, table A.
79. All 1937 English figures from Report of Board of Education, Cmd. 5776, table 7; German 1937 figures from Barnett, *Audit of War*, p. 330, Note 22, and cited German official source. All 1955–7 British figures from ED 124/210, YSC 7/59, table A.
80. ED 146/25, *Early Leaving*: Report of the Central Advisory Council for Education (England).
81. Ibid.
82. Ibid., para. 92.
83. Ibid., paras 98–99.
84. Publications of the Scottish Council for Research in Education, vol. XXXV, 'Social Implications of the 1947 Mental Survey (1953)', pp. 190–91, cited in ED 146/34, CAC 1/4, 9 May 1956. The Scottish findings are supported by computer-based research by the University of Manchester School of Education on statistical samples of fourteen-year-old children in the Greater Manchester area that also found correlations between 'socio-economic status', 'social disorganisation' (sic), quality of parental care, and the scholastic performance of children. See ED 146/33, EL 5/11.
85. ED 146/34, CAC 1/4. The figures correlate with the figures for 1955 school-leavers cited above.
86. £190,440 as against £272,291. See ED 124/210, Youth Service (Albemarle Committee) – Agendas, minutes and working papers, 1958–59, YSC Paper No. 1, September 1958, para. 9.
87. Ibid.
88. Report of the Departmental Committee on the Youth Service in England and Wales, p. 29. See ED 124/209–212 for the Albemarle Committee's minutes and papers.
89. ED 124/210, YSC 7/59, table C; or a total of 59,000 for all age-groups, according to ED 46/1000, Draft Cabinet paper: Technical College Development Plan, 21 November 1955.
90. See Barnett, *Audit of War*, p. 204 and cited German official source.

91. Cf. ED 146/29, CAC 98.
92. ED 46/1000, Draft Cabinet Paper: Technical College Development Plan, 21 November 1955.
93. 43,000 part-time day-students in 1937–38. See ED 136/296, 'Education after the War'; Technical Education: Memorandum by H. B. Wallis, 5 September 1941, summarizing existing provision for further education.
94. Statistisches Bundesamt, *Statistik der Bundesrepublik Deutschland*, Band 214: *Die Berufsbildenden Schulen in den Jahren 1955 und 1956*, p. 10, table 2. Verlag W. Kohlhammer GmbH/Stuttgart und Mainz. It is true that England and Wales also had 383,600 students in the age-group attending part-time evening classes (ED 46/1000, Draft Cabinet Paper; Technical College Development Plan, 21 November 1955). Nonetheless, even if these students are added to the figure for part-time day-students, it still leaves England and Wales some 500,000 short of the German total.
95. ED 124/210, YSC 7/59, table B; Barnett, *Audit of War*, p. 202 and cited source.
96. Killed by economy cuts in 1922.
97. ED 146/29, CAC 102, 17–18 September 1958.
98. ED 46/1000, Draft Cabinet Paper: Technical College Development Plan, 21 November 1955; ED 146/34, K., L. and M. 3/17. Central Council for Education (England), Non-Vocational F. E. including Day Continuation Schools.
99. ED 146/29, Central Advisory Council for Education (England and Wales), 85th Meeting, 22 March 1956.
100. Figures from ED 146/34, CAC 1/4, table 1.
101. Cf. the 1956 sub-committee of the Ministry of Labour's National Joint Advisory Council, chaired by Robert Carr MP, with the task of reporting on the adequacy of intake into apprenticeship and other forms of training in industry. See ED 146/36, pt. 4/15; the influential article, 'Is Apprenticeship Out of Date?' in the *New Scientist* for 24 October 1957 by Professor Lady Williams; article on the 'Weaknesses of Part-time Technical Education' (sic) in the *New Scientist* for 20 November 1958 by Dr Stephen Cotgrove.

    Cotgrove saw apprenticeship as a historical legacy originating in the need for 'craftsmen' with manual skills, whereas today the need was for 'technicians' requiring 'a far greater knowledge of science and technology'. He advocated full-time training in technical colleges – essentially the German system. Both his and Lady Williams's articles appear among the papers of the Crowther '15 to 18' Committee.

See also paper to the Committee by Mr H. A. Warren, 'Full-time Courses in Junior F.E. Colleges', in which he recommended replacing apprenticeship by full-time vocational training over a wide range of occupations, as in the German *Berufsfachschulen* and the French *Centres d'apprentissage*. See ED 146/33, EL 5/10.

102. ED 46/1000, Draft Cabinet Paper: Technical College Development Plan.

103. Cmd. 9703.

104. Ibid., p. 4.

105. ED 46/757, Memorandum on Higher Technological Education, with the Chairman's covering letter of 23 July to the Minister of Education.

106. Figures for 1954. See ED 46/1000, Draft Cabinet Paper: Technical College Development Plan, 21 November 1955, Appendix A, para. 3. The 'tecs' had to provide the part-time courses leading to the Higher National Certificate (HNC) and the full-time courses leading to the Higher National Diploma (HND), plus courses leading to the comparable qualifications of the City and Guilds of London Institute, and to the new Intermediate Certificates and Diplomas in management. The 'tecs' also had to cope with 192,000 eighteen-plus part-time day students.

107. Figure for 1955. See *Die Berufsbildenden Schulen in den Jahren 1955 und 1956*, p. 10, table 2; *Der Hochschulbesuch in Bundesgebiet und Berlin (West) im Sommersemester 1955*, table 2.

108. 9,906 in October 1953; 11,349 in 1955–6. See CAB 132/120, SP(MP)(53)9, Full-Time Students at the Universities 1948/53, 18 November 1953, tables 1 and 2; and ED 46/1002, November 1955; draft passage on the Universities by the Secretary of the University Grants Council for the White Paper on Technical Education.

109. ED 46/1002, table enclosed with letter of 23 January 1956 from the Office of the Lord President of the Council to the Ministry of Education.

110. Estimated figure. Actual figure for 1952–53 was 219. See CAB 132/121, SP(MP)(54)10. All German figures from: Statistische Berichte, *Der Hochschulbesuch in Bundesgebiet und Berlin (West) im Wintersemester 1955/56*, tables 2–4 and 6; *Bestandene Prüfungen an wissenschaftlichen Hochschulen von Sommersemester 1952 bis Sommersemester 1972*, pp. 7 and

28. British figures from ED 46/1002, Draft Passage [for the White Paper on Technical Education] by the Secretary of the University Grants Council, and CAB 132/121, SP(MP)(54)10, 15 October, 1954.

111. ED 46/1002, 23 January 1956, Estimated Output of Scientists and Technologists in Great Britain in 1953/4.

112. Barnett, *Audit of War*, p. 204 and cited German official source.

113. ED 46/756, letter and memorandum of 12 July 1952 from the Head of the Department of Civil and Mechanical Engineering at the University of Nottingham to the Ministry of Education (with his Vice-Chancellor's concurrence), with reference to the Anglo-American Productivity Team's report on the Universities and Industry.

114. ED 46/1002, Draft Passage [for the White Paper on Technical Education] by the Secretary of the University Grants Council.

115. 1953 figures. Cf. CAB 132/108, SP(54)19, 26 November 1954, The Balance of Employment of Scientists: Background Material, tables I and II.

116. ED 46/745, 'National Advisory Council on Education for Industry and Commerce – Higher Technological Education [1953–55]', Minutes, February 1953, NAC/SC/53/78, NAC/SC/53/51, T757(21)/11. The NACEIC then commissioned a report on the topic, which took until December 1953 to complete, enabling the Council in January 1954 to hold fresh discussions on what to do. See ED 46/745, NAC/SC/54/114, report by Sir Arthur Smout and Mr J. Wilson dated 9 December 1953.

117. CAB 132/121, SP(MP)(54)10, 15 October 1954, report of the Committee on Scientific Manpower to the Advisory Council on Scientific Policy, and appendix.

118. ED 46/739, 'National Advisory Council on Education for Industry and Commerce: Joint Educational Committee for Wales; Sub-Committee on Management Education [1952–55]', NAC/SC/52/65, May 1952: discussion on the reports of the Anglo-American Council on Productivity on 'Education for Management', 'The Universities and Industry', 'Training of Supervisors', and 'Training of Operatives'.

119. Cited in ED 46/739, T 757(19)48.

120. Plus four on work study, three on factory planning and layout, two on industrial measurement, and one on production control. See ibid., Appendix I.

121. ED 46/739, Seminar on Problems in Industrial Administration 1951–52, Paper No. 18.
122. ED 46/701, 'National Advisory Council on Education for Industry and Commerce – Standing Committeee [1952–55]', NAC/SC/53/76, and NAC/SC/53/49.
123. Cmnd. 534 (HMSO, September 1958), para. 121.
124. Cmnd. 2267 (HMSO, 1963), para. 502.
125. Ibid., para. 505.
126. Ibid., para. 506.
127. Ibid.
128. A departmental committee of the Ministry of Education chaired by Lt-Col. L. Urwick (then Chairman of the Education Committee of the Institute of Industrial Administration) in 1947. It recommended a 'common intermediate' examination in management studies after three years' evening study in a technical college, and a final diploma examination to be taken at age twenty-five. For summary of the Urwick Report, see ED 46/739, NACEIC, 22 May 1952.

    In 1949 a fresh committee, chaired by A. M. Carr-Saunders, Director of the London School of Economics, reporting on the whole field of commercial education, had recommended creating National Certificates and Diplomas in the field. See ED 46/701, NAC/SC/53/ 82 and NAC/C/53/55.
129. Peter Spooner, 'Schools for Executives', in *Business*, Journal of Management, February 1956.
130. LAB 10/1193, table attached to pamphlet on Management Training issued by The British Engineers' Association and The British Electrical & Allied Manufacturers' Association, arising from the reports of the Anglo-American Productivity Teams on management training.
131. Epithet used by the Director of the BIM in 1952.
132. ED 46/739, NAC/SC/52/65, citing reports of Anglo-American Productivity teams on 'Education for Management' and 'Relations between the Universities and Industry'.
133. 35,926, of which 16,494 in universities, to Britain's 34,338 humanities students (October 1953 figure). German figures from Statistische Berichte, *Der Hochschulbesuch in Bundesgebiet und Berlin (West) im Wintersemester 1955/56*, table 2–4 and 6; *Bestandene Prüfungen an wissenschaftlichen Hochschulen von Sommersemester 1952 bis Sommersemester 1972*,

pp. 7 and 26. British figures from CAB 132/120, SP(MP)(53)9, 18 November 1953. Full-Time Students at the Universities 1948–1953, tables 1 and 2.

134. Ibid.

135. CAB 134/1230, EP(56)34, Economic Policy Committee, 16 March 1956.

136. Ibid.

137. Ardwick Higher Elementary Grade School in Manchester; Professor T. F. Tout, educated at Balliol College, Oxford.

138. Cited in Kenneth Harris, *Attlee* (London, Weidenfeld and Nicolson, 1995), p. 406.

139. See correspondence in ED 46/753, National Advisory Council on Education for Industry and Commerce. Higher Technological Education. Policy arising from Report, 1950–1.

140. From 1948 onwards, the National Advisory Council for Education in Industry and Commerce was the major forum for circular argument about the roles and status of universities and technical colleges, about the distinction between degrees and diplomas, and even possible cooperative linkages between the two types of institution. See ED 46/700–1, 'National Advisory Council on Education for Industry and Commerce – Standing Committee [1948–55]'.

In September 1948 a Joint Committee of this Council and the University Grants Committee was set up as a further debating society for these questions. See ED 46/737, 'National Advisory Committee on Education for Industry and Commerce – Joint Committee with the University Grants Committee' [1948]. See also ED 46/740, 'National Advisory Council on Education for Industry and Commerce: University Education [1948–49]'; and ED 46/741–745, 'National Advisory Council on Education for Industry and Commerce: Higher Technological Education' [1948–55].

141. Cf. LAB 19/323, 'Recruiting and Training of Young Workers for Industry, National Youth Employment Council'. Memoranda, minutes and correspondence, 1949–58.

142. ED 124/201, Memorandum for Submission to the Central Advisory Council for Education, 14 January 1958.

143. Cf. ED 146/34, Central Advisory Council for Education (England) – 'K.L.M. Groups', minutes and papers, 1956, and ED 146/37, 'Sixth

Form Group' papers, 1957–8, and ED 146/38, 'Sixth Form Group', minutes 1957–8.

144. See ED 146/34, KLM 5/25, *Specialisation in Schools. The effects of university requirements on general education in schools, and on the quality and quantity of science students*, by N. F. Mott; and ED 146/37–38, Central Advisory Council for Education (England), 'Sixth Form Group' papers, 1957–8, especially ED 146/37, S.9/28, 10 December 1957, *The Pressure of University Entrance upon the Maintained Grammar Schools*, by M. H. Brown; *Secondary Education* by Br Dr Dennis Gabor, 26 March 1957; paper S.4/14, *General Studies* (summary of papers and discussions); S.9/26, Sixth Form Group, Note by the Chairman (13 December 1957); S.9/27, *Comments on the Science Masters' Association's 'Science and Education'*, written by HM Staff Inspector Mr R. A. R. Tricker; S.2/5, *Specialisation at school – Comparison England / Germany*, 27 March 1957.

145. CAB 134/437, IPC(47)9, 8th October 1947, Appendix 5, para. 2.

146. CAB 134/438, IPC(47)5th, 17 August 1947.

147. In accordance with the terms of the 1945 American loan of $3.75 billion the pound was made freely convertible into any currency. When massed holders of sterling hastened to avail themselves of the opportunity and the gold and dollar reserves evaporated, the old protective corset of exchange control had to be strapped on again. But at home the Labour Government had to slash expenditure across the board, though still maintaining 'imperial' fleets, garrison and air squadrons from the Mediterranean, Palestine, Egypt, Libya and Iraq to South-East Asia and even Japan. See Barnett, *Lost Victory*, part 1.

148. CAB 134/439, IPC(48)8, 16 July 1948, Report on Investment in 1949, and table 54.

149. Ibid., paras 304–6.

150. £4.3 million to £3.9 million. See CAB 134/440, IPC(49)3, 12 May 1949, tables 76 and 77.

151. CAB 134/440, IPC(49)5th, 11 January 1949, item 2.

152. Ibid., para. 270.

153. CAB 134/642, PC(49)61, 27 May 1949, Production Committee, Educational Building Programme 1950–52. Memorandum by the Minister of Education, paras. 2–4.

154. CAB 134/440, IPC(49)75th, 7 November 1949.

155. See Barnett, *Lost Victory*, pp. 255–6 and 296–7.

156. See ibid., pp. 87–99.

157. Ibid., p. 95.

158. CAB 134/441, IPC(50)3rd, 10 January 1950.

159. Ibid.; see also CAB 134/441, IPC(50)2, 25 April 1950, Report on Capital Investment in 1951 and 1952, pars. 239–240.

160. See Cmd. 8195, Economic Survey for 1951, ch. I, *The Impact of Rearmament*. Defence expenditure was to rise to a peak of 10.5 per cent in 1952–53, and then to steady at 9.8 per cent in 1953–54 and 9.0 per cent in 1954–55. See CAB 131/16, DC(55)43, United Kingdom Defence Programme. Memorandum by the Minister of Defence, 14 October 1955, para. 2.

161. CAB 134/651, PC(51)50, 23 April 1951, Production Committee: Educational Investment in 1953.

162. CAB 134/649, PC(51)11th, 2 May 1951.

163. CAB 134/442, IPC(51)2, 5th September 1951, Capital Investment in 1951, 1952 and 1953.

164. Cmd. 8357.

165. CAB 134/856, EA(E)(51)1, 'Economic Policy Committee. Sub-Committee on the Economic Situation': Our Economic Prospects and Objectives. Memorandum by the Chancellor of the Exchequer. See above, ch. 3.

166. CAB 134/856, EA(E)(51)3, 4 December 1951, Economies in Education: Memorandum by the Chancellor of the Exchequer; EA(E)(51)2nd, 5 December 1951, item 1; EA(E)(51)14, 10 December 1951, Economies in Education: Memorandum by the Chancellor of the Exchequer; EA(E)(51)5th, 11 December 1951, item 5.

167. ED 46/754, letter of 1 April 1952 to R. A. Butler. See this file for an eight-page draft memorandum on Higher Technological Education by Butler as Chancellor of the Exchequer, 8 January 1952, and the relevant correspondence between Butler, Lord Woolton, Florence Horsbrugh, and the related civil servants' minute sheets.

168. ED 46/754, letter from Butler to Woolton, 27 March 1952.

169. CAB 134/982, IPC(52)8th, 25 November 1952, item 1, re IPC(WP)(52)54 and 72. In February 1952 educational investment (England and Wales) for 1953 and 1954 was fixed at £60.5 million in each year, and for 1955 a drop to £59 million. See CAB 134/856, EPC(WP)(52)16.

170. CAB 132/120, 'Advisory Council on Scientific Policy: Committee on

Scientific Manpower', SP(MP)(53)5, 14 September 1953. Technical Education – Report by the Select Comittee on Estimates.

171. CAB 132/120, SP(MP)(53)5, para. 8.

172. Ibid., para. 9.

173. Ibid., para. 10.

174. Ibid., para. 11.

175. Ibid., para. 13.

176. Ibid., para. 12.

177. £1–1.25 million out of the existing provision for 1955–56 of £2,450,000. CAB 134/783, 'Committee on Public Expenditure', CCE(54)6th, 21 June, item 5.

178. See CAB 134/783, CCE(54) series, Committee on Civil Expenditure, especially CCE(54)1st, 13 April 1954; CCE(54)2nd, 20 May 1954, item 3; and CCE(54)6th, 21 June 1954, item 5. See also CAB 134/785, CCE(54)30, 9 July 1954. Committee on Public Expenditure; Draft Report of the Committee, para. 7.

179. The references to 1954 are from CAB 46/1000, draft memorandum by the Minister of Education, David Eccles, to the Cabinet, 16 September 1955.

180. CAB 134/1327, SS(56)8, 8 March 1956, Social Services Committee. Prospective Expenditure in the Next Five Years: Memorandum by the Minister of Education.

181. Ibid., para. 10.

182. For the sake of simplicity, England and Wales have been used throughout this chapter as a convenient benchmark for Britain in terms of state-funded educational expenditure. It is legitimate to do so because expenditure in Scotland was fixed by statute at a mere eleven-eightieths (13.75 per cent) of that for England and Wales, and conformed pari passu with changes in English expenditure. In fact, Whitehall documents at the time sometimes wrote of 'Britain' when they specifically meant 'England (and Wales)'; an English tendency then and now irritating to the Scottish.

183. ED 46/1000, 21 November 1955, covering note to draft proposals for reform of higher technological education. The Secretary of the University Grants Council for one was not at all keen on 'rational groups', deleting a sentence from Eccles's draft White Paper which he thought 'a little dangerous because it may lead people to argue that all your

plans and ours ought to be co-ordinated with each other in detail'. Cf. ED 46/1002, letter of 23 January 1956 to A. A. Part from E. Hale, enclosing re-drafted passage.

184. Ibid.
185. Ibid.
186. ED 46/1000, draft Cabinet paper of 12 December 1955.
187. Cmd. 9703. At a total of £100 million, including the cost of extra teaching staff.
188. Even now his plan was far from safe. The Treasury insisted that a cavil be inserted in the White Paper that the capital costs in the initial years of 1957–58 and 1957–59 'will, in common with all other programmes, be subject to review if economic conditions require . . .' See ED 46/1003, letter from F. F. Turnbull, Under-Secretary at the Treasury, to A. A. Part, Under-Secretary, Ministry of Education, 9 February 1956.
189. The first 'C.A.T.' was opened in 1965.

23. The Reckoning

1. In the context of the present narrative the Suez crisis and the Seven Day War are relevant only as an audit on British post-war power and total strategy. For a masterly account of the crisis and the war, see Keith Kyle, *Suez* (New York, St Martin's Press, 1991). For an excellent military analysis, see A. J. Barker, *Suez: The Seven Day War* (London, Faber and Faber, 1964).
2. Kyle, *Suez*, p. 14.
3. A younger son of a baronet, a Durham landowner, Etonian, a First at Oxford in Oriental Languages, and through his mother a descendant of the Greys, including Earl Grey, the Whig Prime Minister who passed the Reform Act of 1832. See Kyle, *Suez*, p. 10; Robert Rhodes James, *Anthony Eden* (London, Weidenfeld and Nicolson, 1986), ch. 1.
4. Cited in Kyle, *Suez*, p. 139, and Richard Lamb, *The Failure of the Eden Government* (London, Sidgwick and Jackson, 1987), p. 201.
5. See CAB 134/228, Economic Policy Committee, EP(55)series, especially memoranda EP(55)53, 54, and 55; and CAB 134/1226, EP(55)11th, 11 November 1955, 'Brussels Conference: Proposals for a European Common Market', a meeting of eleven ministers chaired by R. A. Butler as Chancellor. See also CAB 134/889, Economic Steering

Committee, ES(55)17, 28 October 1955, Report by the Mutual Aid Committee on 'The Political Implications of the Common Market'.

6. A hopeful thought canvassed at the meeting of the Cabinet Economic Policy Committee on 11 November 1955 (CAB 134/1226, EP(55)1th). Nearly half a century later Euro-sceptics were to be comforting themselves with similar thoughts in regard to the single European currency.

7. In the characteristic phrase used to me by Field Marshal Viscount Montgomery of Alamein when recounting a conversation with Eden before Suez.

8. Kyle, *Suez*, p. 171.

9. Barker, *Suez*, pp. 48–9.

10. Barker, *Suez*, pp. 48–9. See also the whole of his ch. 2 for a full description of all the extraordinary shortages and inadequacies of every kind of equipment for Musketeer in all three armed services.

11. These details of deployable army and Royal Air Force strength in the United Kingdom are drawn from Kyle, *Suez*, p. 167–8.

12. Barker, *Suez*, pp. 51–2.

13. As I was told in 1958 by Field Marshal Sir Claude Auchinleck, C-in-C, Middle East in 1941–2.

14. Ibid., p. 169.

15. See Correlli Barnett, *The Lost Victory: British Dreams, British Realities 1945–1950* (London, Macmillan, 1996, and Pan Books, 1997), chs 3–5, and the present book, chs 3–6.

16. Barker, *Suez*, pp. 31–2.

17. Kyle, *Suez*, p. 156–7.

18. Ibid., p. 158, citing James Eayrs, *The Commonwealth and Suez* (Oxford, Oxford University Press, 1964), pp. 15–16, 60.

19. Ibid., p. 159, citing ADM 116/6097, 14 August 1956.

20. Ibid., p. 246.

21. Cited in ibid., p. 243.

22. Ibid., pp. 243–4.

23. The epithet is justifed by the tone and some specifc comments in ministerial and bureaucratic papers and discussions in 1955 on the proposed common market.

24. See Barnett, *Collapse of British Power*, part I, 'All That Is Noble and Good'. Cf. also Noel Annan, *Our Age: the Generation That Made Post-War Britain* (London, Fontana, 1991).

25. Cited in Kyle, *Suez*, p. 358.
26. Ibid., p. 359.
27. A detailed account of the ensuing manoeuvres in the Security Council and exchanges between London and Washington is given in ibid., ch. 19.
28. To be fair, the Defence Minister, Walter Monckton, no doubt well briefed by the Chiefs of Staff, drew the Cabinet's attention to these considerations at a meeting on 28 August. See ibid., p. 213.
29. Cited in ibid., p. 335.
30. Ibid.
31. Cited in ibid.
32. Ibid., p. 226.
33. Ibid.
34. Ibid.
35. Ibid.
36. Cited in ibid., p. 406.
37. All quotes as cited in ibid., pp. 404–5.
38. Cf. the reprint of the editorial in the *Observer Magazine* for 29 December 1999, p. 39.
39. It should be noted that this editorial appeared the day after Eden's television address on 3 November 1956.
40. Cited in Kyle, *Suez*, p. 432.
41. Cited in ibid., p. 433.
42. Anthony Howard's eyewitness account on BBC television twenty years later, cited in ibid., pp. 433–4.
43. Before the politically correct suffer a seizure, they should recall that this was the common term for the inhabitants of the Middle East used by the British armed forces at that time. It is therefore legitimate to employ it in the present narrative context.
44. A Gallup poll on 10–11 November (after the allied landings) found that 53 per cent of respondents approved of the Government's action, and 32 per cent disapproved. However, 68 per cent of Conservatives approved, as against 16 per cent Labour and 24 per cent Liberal. Cited in Rhodes James, p. 557.
45. See BT 213/20 series, '[Quarterly] Reviews on the Relative Competitive Power of U.K. Exports [1954–5]'; T 230/403–406, 'General Economic Situation [1954 to February–March 1956]'.

46. CAB 134/889, ES(55)19, 29 October 1955, Fifth Report of the Working Party on United Kingdom Export Trends.

47. CAB 134/1230, EP(56)21, 18 February 1956, Balance of Payments Prospects Committee. Report – February 1956.

48. CAB 134/1230, EP(56)23. The note was commenting on the February 1956 Report of the Balance of Payments Prospects Committee [EP(56)21] and the Report of the Working Party on World Trade and Economic Conditions [EP(56)22].

49. CAB 134/1230, EP(56)23, 20 February 1956.

50. CAB 129/78, CP(55)184, 29 November 1955. Overseas Expenditure. Memorandum by the Chancellor of the Exchequer. Grants for colonial development and assistance accounted for £27 million; 'other political expenditure' (sic) for £20 million; releases from the sterling balances for £27 million; loans for colonial capital development for £18 million; special Export Guarantee Department credits to Persia and Pakistan to £17 million. Cf. also CP(55)184.

51. CAB 134/1227, EP(55)38, 29 August 1955, para. 57; CAB 133/139, CBP(55)3, 2 December 1955.

52. Ibid.

53. Ibid.

54. T 230/406, draft letter from the Chancellor to the Prime Minister.

55. Ibid., minute to the Prime Minister, 8 February 1956.

56. CAB 134/1231, EP(56)58, para. 2.

57. CAB 134/1231, EP(56)61, Committee on Balance of Payments Prospects. Report on Balance of Payments Prospects for 1956.

58. Ibid., para. 42.

59. See Lamb, pp. 280–82.

60. T 236/4188, cited in Lamb, p. 481.

61. Summary in Kyle, *Suez*, p. 213.

62. Ibid.

63. Lamb, p. 282.

64. Ibid., p. 243.

65. PREM 11/1103, CM(56)74th, cited in Kyle, *Suez*, p. 334. The Cabinet was naturally not told about the Anglo-French-Israeli plot for a joint onslaught on Egypt.

66. Kyle, *Suez*, p. 335.

67. Ibid.

68. Lamb, p. 283.

69. Ibid., p. 253.

70. Kyle, *Suez*, p. 464.

71. Ibid., p. 501.

72. Ibid.

73. As reported by Sir Harold Caccia, British Ambassador in Washington, and cited in Kyle, *Suez*, p. 510.

74. Rhodes James, pp. 583–4.

75. Cited in ibid., p. 584.

76. Ibid.

77. Michael Shanks, 'Suicide of a Nation', article in a special issue of *Encounter* edited by Arthur Koestler (vol. XXI, no.1, July 1963).

78. See Barnett, *Collapse of British Power*, part I, and *The Lost Victory*, ch. 9.

79. T 230/408, Skeleton for Policy. The Past, the Present, the Future, 16 January 1957, notes by the Chancellor of the Exchequer, Peter Thorneycroft, para. 6.

80. Ibid., para. 13.

81. Ibid., para. 17.

82. £163 million, either grants in aid, or capital investment to present or former British colonies and other backward countries, all undertaken out of a sense of imperial responsibility and unlikely ever to show a profit. See T 230/305, The United Kingdom Economy and Defence. Draft Brief for N.A.T.O. Delegation, 27 November 1958, para. 29.

83. £248 million in 1957. See ibid.

84. Cmnd. 124.

85. CAB 131/18, D(57)7th, item 2, 2 August 1957.

86. CAB 131/18, D(57)6th, item 3, 31 July 1957.

87. Ibid.

88. Ibid.

89. DC(57)2nd, 27 February 1957.

90. Ibid.

91. Ibid., DC(57)6th, item 3.

92. See especially the detailed analysis in T 230/305, PR(CS)(57)10, The Impact of the Defence Programme on the National Economy, 19 November 1957.

93. Ibid., para. 56.

94. T 230/305, The United Kingdom Economy and Defence, November 1958, para. 61, 'Conclusion'.

95. 4.96 per cent to 3.24 per cent. With a GDP now fallen to below two-thirds of Germany's ($121 billion to $185 billion), Britain had to spend a higher percentage of it on defence in order to keep her traditional rank within NATO – quite apart from the still continuing, albeit slowly shrinking, costs of the world role. Thus in 1970 Britain's defence budget stood at $5,961 million, virtually level-pegging with Germany's $6,108 million. See *The Military Balance 1971–2* (London, International Institute for Strategic Studies, 1971–2), table 4.

96. The European Free Trade Area (EFTA) consisted of the United Kingdom, Denmark, Portugal, Switzerland, Norway, Austria, and Sweden.

97. See Macmillan's self-congratulatory account of how successfully he crept to Washington and the President in 1957 in *Riding the Storm: 1956–1959* (London, Macmillan, 1971), ch. VII.

98. T 230/408, Skeleton for Policy, para. 21.

99. See Carver, op. cit., pp. 55–61.

100. See Barnett, *Collapse of British Power*, part VI, 'Victory at All Costs'.

101. By 1960 West Germany's GDP would be equal to Britain's, a remarkable achievement from a virtually standing start in 1949; and by 1970 it would be half as big again as Britain's (see note 95 above). Cf. *The Military Balance, 1971–2*, table 4. By 1983 Britain would have fallen to fourteenth place in the non-Communist world in terms of GDP per head. Cf. *World Bank Development Report 1985* (London and New York, Oxford University Press, 1985), tables 1 and 3, pp. 175 and 179.

102. Such as shipbuilding; the native motor-vehicle industry; coal; household 'white' goods; televisions, radios and recording kit; machine tools. New technologies of great promise but stunted in growth included computers and electronic control equipment. Even in chemicals, ICI was to be overtaken in world markets by Germany's revived industry.

103. In spite of the Thatcherite revolution of the 1980s, which destroyed the enervating economic and social environment of the 'postwar consensus', Great Britain in 1999 would rank a mere twenty-seventh in the world for GDP per head, behind (inter alia) France, Germany, Japan, Denmark, Belgium, Norway, Switzerland, and the USA. *World Bank Development Report 2000/2001* (New York, Oxford University Press, 2000), Table 2, pp. 274–5.

Bibliography

UNPUBLISHED SOURCES

Public Record Office

NB: Public Record Office file titles are cited as on the original file covers, not necessarily as on the PRO's descriptive on-line catalogue.

Board of Trade (BT series)

BT 64 series

BT 64/730 O.E.E.C. documents Exchange Scheme. Inclusion of Unofficial Documents on Productivity Issues. [1950]

BT 64/1177 British, Commonwealth, U.S.A., and other Foreign Competitive Powers: Memoranda. [1947–9]

BT 64/1234 Productivity Campaign. [1949]

BT 64/2189 Working Parties. Double Day Shift Working. [1945–7]

BT 64/2230 Productivity. Proposed Memorandum for Steering Committee. [1946]

BT 64/2264 Future Scientific Policy. [1947]

BT 64/2472 Technical Assistance from The U.S.A. (The Nine Points and Discussions at the O.E.E.C. Working Party on Scientific and Technical Information). [1949]

BT 64/4717 Proposed Productivity Campaign, 1952.

BT 64/4720 Campaign for Productivity: Working Group on Departmental Responsibility for Production (Chairman: Mr. T. Padmore). [1952]

BT 64/4740 British Productivity Council. Liaison with Government Departments and Industry. Organisation and Programme. [1952–4]

BT 64/4801 Automation – Replies from Industries Canvassed by the Board of Trade Enquiry into Automation. [1956–7]

BT 64/4896 U.K. Productivity – Report on Productivity prepared by officials at ministerial request: briefing for President of the B.O.T. [sic] and ministers on U.K. productivity. [1953]

BT 195 series

BT 195/23 Productivity in France 1950–51.

BT 195/24 Productivity in Australia 1950–51.

BT 213 series

BT 213/16 The Economic Consequences of the Korean War. [1956]

BT 213/20 Reviews on the Relative Competitive Power of U.K. Exports. [1954–5]

BT 213/39 British Standards Institution – Standing Committee to consider how B.S.I. can assist exports. [1955]

BT 213/78 The Long-Term Outlook for the Engineering Industries. [1957]

BT 213/79 Statistics for Economic Policy. [1956–7]

BT 213/90 Long-Term Investment Reviews – General Papers. [1957]

BT 213/91–2 Long-Term Investment Reviews – Working Party No.2 (on shortage of skilled draftsmen and technicians).

BT 213/93 Long-Term Investment Reviews – Working party No.3 (on techniques for influencing investment).

Cabinet and Cabinet Committees: Minutes and Memoranda (CAB series)

CAB 16 series

CAB 16/209 Strategic Appreciation Committee of the Comittee of Imperial Defence 1939.

CAB 21 series

CAB 21/1985 The Situation in Korea, 1950–1951.

CAB 21/1988 Korea: assistance of U.K. and Commonwealth Forces, 1950.

CAB 21/1991 Korea: implications of participation by U.K. in an international police action, 1950–1951.

CAB 21/2102 The war in Korea: the implications of, on our policy in other parts of the world: co-operation, 1950–1951.

CAB 21/2247 Miscellaneous Briefs Prepared for the Prime Minister, January 1950–June 1950.

CAB 21/2248 Miscellaneous Briefs Prepared for the Prime Minister, July 1950–December 1950.

CAB 29 series
CAB 29/159 Anglo-French Staff Conversations, London, 1939.

CAB 124 series
CAB 124/535 [Barlow] Committee on Scientific Manpower, 1946.
CAB 124/538 British Commonwealth Scientific Committee.
CAB 124/1171–4 Conditional Aid. Working Group re social research. [1952–5]
CAB 124/1176–7 Productivity and Conditional Aid Committee – Anglo-American Consultative Group. [1952–5]
CAB 124/1178 Role of Government in Promoting Higher Productivity

CAB 128–9 series (Conclusions and Memoranda of the Cabinet, 1950–1956)
CAB 128/17– Conclusions of the Cabinet 1950–56
CAB 129/41– Memoranda of the Cabinet 1950–56

CAB 131 series (Meetings and Memoranda of the Cabinet Defence Committee)
CAB 131/1–19 Meetings and Memoranda of the Cabinet Defence Committee 1946–57.

CAB 132 series
CAB 132/106–8 Advisory Council on Scientific Policy. [1952–4]
CAB 132/119–122 Advisory Council on Scientific Policy – Committee on Scientific Manpower, 1952–55.

CAB 134 series
CAB 134/114, CPC(51). Committee on Productive Capacity [1951].
CAB 134/224–5 Economic Policy Committee: Minutes and Memoranda, 1950.
CAB 134/488–492 Mutual Aid Committee: Minutes and Memoranda, 1950–1.
CAB 134/640 Production Committee, 1949.
CAB 134/848–855 Economic Policy Committee, Minutes and Memoranda, 1953–1955.
CAB 134/856 Economic Policy Committee, Sub-Committee on the Economic Situation, Minutes and Memoranda, 1951–52.

CAB 134/869 Committee on External Economic Policy, 1954.

CAB 134/877–881 Economic Planning Board, Minutes and memoranda, 1952–1956.

CAB 134/884–889 Economic Steering Committee, Minutes and Memoranda, 1952–1955.

CAB 134/890 Economic Steering Committee, Working Group on Employment Policy, 1952–53.

CAB 134/935 Home Affairs Committee – Sub-Committee on the Supply of Scientists, 1955.

CAB 134/982 Investment Programmes Committee [official], 1952.

CAB 134/1009 Mutual Assistance Committee, 1952.

CAB 134/1010–1030, 1228, 1231 Mutual Aid Committee, Meetings and Memoranda 1952–1955.

CAB 134/1185 Committee on Trade and Employment, 1953.

CAB 134/1204 Committee on Civil Aviation Policy. [1956]

CAB 134/1226–1231 Economic Policy Committee, Minutes and Memoranda 1955–1956.

CAB 134/1232 Economic Policy Committee: Sub-Committee on Economic Measures, 1956.

CAB 134/1273 Committee on Industrial Relations: Minutes and Memoranda, 1955.

Chiefs of Staff Committee (DEFE series)

DEFE 4/45–70 Minutes, 1950–55.
DEFE 5/40–70 Memoranda, 1950–55.

Ministry of Education (ED series)

ED 46 series

ED 46/295 Special Committee on Higher Technological Education, 1945.

ED 46/537 Technical Education – Committee on Scientific Research and Industrial Productivity 1948–1950.

ED 46/547 Technical Education – Industrial Instrument and Control Engineering, 1954–55.

ED 46/550 Further Education – General, 1945–47.

ED 46/692 Schemes of Further Education, 1946–48.

ED 46/699 National Advisory Council on Education for Industry and Commerce, 1947.

ED 46/700–701 National Advisory Council on Education for Industry and Commerce – Standing Committee, 1948–1955.

ED 46/737 National Advisory Council on Education for Industry and Commerce – Joint Committee with the University Grants Committee, 1948.

ED 46/738–9 National Advisory Council on Education for Industry and Commerce: Sub-Committee on Management Education, 1948–55.

ED 46/740 National Advisory Council on Education for Industry and Commerce – Minutes – University Education, 1948–49.

ED 46/741–745 National Advisory Council on Education for Industry and Commerce – Minutes – Higher Technological Education, 1948–55.

ED 46/752 National Council on Education for Industry and Commerce – Higher Technological Education – Observations on Report on Higher Technological Education, 1950–51.

ED 46/753 National Council on Education for Industry and Commerce – Policy Arising from Report, 1950–51.

ED 46/754 National Advisory Council on Education for Industry and Commerce – Policy Arising from Report, 1952.

ED 46/755 National Advisory Council on Education for Industry and Commerce – Policy Arising out of Report, 1954–55.

ED 46/756–7 Advanced Technological Education 1952–55.

ED 46/1000 Further Education: General Files: Technical Education: Draft White Paper on Technical Education, 1956–57.

ED 46/1001 Further Education: General File: Technical Education: Draft White Paper: Folder I, 1955.

ED 46/1002 and 1003 Drafts leading up to the issue of the White Paper 'Technical Education', Cmd 9703, published in February, 1956. Folder II, January 1956; Folder III, February 1956.

ED 124 series

ED 124/201 King George's Jubilee Trust: Youth Service Committee (Departmental) 1958–1960.

ED 124/209 Youth Service (Albemarle Committee) – Setting up, 1958.

ED 124/210 Youth Service (Albemarle Committee) – Agendas, minutes, papers and working papers, 1958–59.

ED 124/211 Youth Service (Albemarle Committee) – correspondence with persons invited to give oral evidence, 1958–1959.

ED 124/212 Youth Service (Albemarle Committee) – Report, 1959–1960.

ED 146 series

ED 146/29 Central Advisory Council for Education (England). Signed Minutes and Agenda of the Council, 1956–1960 [papers leading to the Crowther Report].

ED 146/31 Central Advisory Council for Education (England) – Written Evidence submitted by various Associations and summaries of oral evidence.

ED 146/32–33 Central Advisory Council for Education (England) – 'Early Leaving Group', Minutes and Memoranda.

ED 146/34 Central Advisory Council for Education (England) – 'KLM Groups', Minutes and Papers, 1956.

ED 146/35 Central Advisory Council for Education (England) – 'Middle Group' (Pre-Technical), Minutes.

ED 146/36 Central Advisory Council for Education (England) – PT (Pre-Technical) Papers.

ED 146/37–38 Central Advisory Council for Education (England) – 'Sixth Form Group' Papers and Minutes 1957–58.

ED 146/39 First Draft Report, Pts 1–7, Vol I, 1959.

ED 146/40 Final report as published.

ED 146/41 Crowther Report, Volume II, correspondence with the Central Office of Information, 1956–59, re a social survey into young people.

ED 146/43 Crowther Report, Volume III: Social Survey – Final Draft Report, 1957.

Foreign Office (FO series)

FO 371/84053–84195 [1950].
FO 371/92721–92853 [1951].

Ministry of Labour and National Service (LAB series)

LAB 10 series

LAB 10/37 Stoppage of Work in protest against dismissals due to shortage of parts made by firms involved in B.M.C. strike (Fisher and Ludlow).

LAB 10/536 Report of an Inquiry by Sir John Foster under the Conciliation Acts 1896 into a dispute between certain Trade Unions and certain omnibus undertakings. Members of the National Council for the *Omnibus Industry*. [1945]

LAB 10/561 Shipbuilding and Shiprepairing – R.J.R.O., Bristol, Reports on Dispute between Charles Hill & Sons and Boilermakers and Iron and Steel Shipbuilders Society and Ship Constructors and Shipwrights Assoc. Stoppage of work: Demarcation. About 100 Riveters stopped work because an acetylene lamp had been issued to shipwrights. The Shipwrights contend that the lamp is common to all grades & they claim the right to use it wherever necessary on this work. Work resumed but discussions are still continuing. [1945]

LAB 10/566 Working Parties in Industry. General I.R. Questions. [1945–46]

LAB 10/567 Report of Committee of Enquiry into London Dock Strike of March 1945 (The Ammon Report).

LAB 10/568 Trade Stoppages: Weekly Return to the Minister, 1945–47.

LAB 10/580 Report of a Strike at the London Docks over alleged harshness of method of dealing with absenteeism involving the T.& G.W. and the Stevedores Union.

LAB 10/588 Report of the Evershed Commission on the Cotton Industry, 1945–46.

LAB 10/594 Reduction in work hours and the effect in industries. [1946]

LAB 10/604 Restoration of Pre-War Trade Practices Act 1942. Fixing of Appointed Day. [1946]

LAB 10/612 Engineering. The Midlands Regional Industrial Relations Officer reports a dispute between Messrs Fisher & Ludlow Ltd., Birmingham, and Birimingham & Midland Sheet Metal Workers Society. Sit down strike on 4/1/46 over wages and conditions.

LAB 10/613 Ford Motor Co. Ltd., Dagenham – Wage Dispute. Stoppage of Work. [1946]

LAB 10/615 Printing Industry. Dispute between the British Federation of Master Printers, Newspaper Society and the Printing & Kindred Trades Federation over 40 hour week and 2 weeks' annual holiday. [1946]

LAB 10/663 Wages Information Board. *Working Party on the Stabilisation of Wages.* Correspondence with various Government Departments concerning draft statement to National Joint Advisory Council on subsidies, grants and price fixing arrangements. [1947]

LAB 10/664 Compulsory pre-strike ballot. Minister's request for note. [1956]

LAB 10/664 Stabilisation of Wages. Official Working Party to implement the decisions announced by the Prime Minister on 6 August 1947.

LAB 10/665 Port Transport Industry. London Dockers Strike – lighterage section – River Thames – Strike by 400 Lightermen, Stevedores & Dockers, April 22–May 4, 1947. In sympathy with Glasgow Dockers.

LAB 10/679 Shipbuilding. Palmer's Shipbuilding Co Ltd, Hebburn, and Boilermakers' Society. Apprehended Dispute over firm's intention to have a new flame cutting machine operated by 'unskilled' worker. [1944]

LAB 10/698 Meat Distribution: Meat Transport Pool and T. & G.W.U., 1947: Strike at Smithfield Market: 1700 drivers involved, over the discharge of two drivers for refusing to obey orders in connection with the staggering of vehicles at the docks.

LAB 10/710 Railways: London, Midland and Scottish Railway and A.E.U. Dispute regarding the manning of mechanical press at Crewe Works, 1947.

LAB 10/735 Transport (Docks). Ministry of Transport, Glasgow Docks, and Scottish T.& G.W.U. Strike commenced March 24th, over proposed redundancy of dockers. [1947]

LAB 10/757 Vehicle Building Industry. Differences arising out of the wage claim by the Trade Unions, 1947–48.

LAB 10/759 Restoration of Pre-War Trade Practices Act 1942 – Restrictive Practices – General File.

LAB 10/779 Port Transport Industry: Webber, Cook and Palmer (Maconochie's Wharf) and T.G.W.U. and National Amalgamated Stevedores and Dockers. Strike now terminated. Dispute over down-grading of two N.A.S.D. gangers, because of friction with the T. and G.W.U., 1948.

LAB 10/780 Dispute between Glasgow Herald and Scottish Typographical Association, 1948. Committee of Investigation under section 2(i)(a) of Conciliation Act 1896.

LAB 10/783 Dock Industry. London Docks and T.G.W.U. Strike in Progress. Dispute over disciplinary action against 11 men who refused to load zinc oxide. [1948]

LAB 10/806 Shipbuilding Industry. R.S. Hayes Ltd., Pembroke Dock, 1948–1952. Demarcation Dispute between the Boilermakers' Society and the Shipconstructors & Shipwrights Assoc.

LAB 10/821 Wages Information Branch: Engineering Industry, including Govt. Industries. Claim for increase in wages. Report of Court of Enquiry (1948–50).

LAB 10/850 Engineering – Motor Car Manufacture. Daimler Motor Car Ltd., Body Dept, Redford, Coventry and N.U.V.B., A.E.U., and A.W.C.M. Strike now terminated. Dispute over method of selection of 240 workers for discharge. Further R.I.R.O. report of 27/10/49 of dispute between above firm and N.U.V.B. over piecework rates. Strike in progress (1949–50).

LAB 10/929 Shipbuilding and Engineering. VICKERS ARMSTRONG Ltd, Barrow in Furness, and Boiler Makers Society. Strike in progress. Demarcation Dispute.

LAB 10/932 Shipbuilding and Shiprepairing Industry. Restrictive Practices impeding production (1949–50).

LAB 10/982 Dutch Industrial Organisations Act.

LAB 10/1019 Dock Industry: All docks in Great Britain implicated in strike in protest against the wage increase of 11/- recently granted. [1951]

LAB 10/1023 Engineering Industry. ROLLS ROYCE Hillington and A.E.U., General Ironfounders Association, Glasgow, and T. and G.W.U. Stoppage of work arising out of dismissal of two shop stewards, alleged victimisation. [1951]

LAB 10/1030 Aircraft Production. SHORT BROTHERS and HARLAND Ltd., Belfast, and Confederation of Shipbuilding and Engineering Unions. Report from Ministry of Supply regarding strike in progress. Dispute concerning dismissal of shop stewards.

LAB 10/1043 Civil Engineering. R. Costain Ltd., Concrete Piling Ltd., Matthew Hall & Co Ltd. and others at Capenhurst Atomic Site and A.S.W. Demarcation Dispute regarding the erection of Plymax Interior partitions. [1951]

LAB 10/1106 Engineering. E.N.V. Engineering Co Ltd., London, N.W.10., and A.E.U. and T.G.W.U. Stoppage of work arising out of a foreman's conduct. [1951–52]

LAB 10/1138 Industrial Productivity. Responsibility of Govt. Departments. Treasury and Board of Trade. [1952]

LAB 10/1157 Motor Car Manufacturers. Ford Motor Company Ltd., Dagenham. Token Strike of one hour each day and complete ban on overtime in protest against rejection of wage increase claim. [1952]

LAB 10/1160 Vehicle Building. Park Royal Vehicles Ltd., Willesden, and the N.U.V.B. Strike in progress. Dispute over certain piece work rates.

LAB 10/1166 Industrial Productivity. Formation of the British Productivity Council. [1953]

LAB 10/1168 Engineering. Austin Motor Co. Ltd., Longbridge, and the N.U.V.B. – Strike in Protest against firm's refusal to re-engage redundant shop steward J. McHugh. [1953]

LAB 10/1206 Austin Motor CO. Ltd, Report of Court of Enquiry, 1953. [published as Cmd. 8839]

LAB 10/1215 Human Relations in Industry in Relation to Increased Productivity. Proposal to set up Sub-Committee of National Joint Advisory Councils to consider action to promote still higher standards of human relations. [1953–54]

LAB 10/1216 Human Relations in Industry to increase Productivity. Proposal for Booklet to be issued by M.L.N.S. [1954]

LAB 10/1217 Human Relations in Industry to increase Productivity – N.J.A.C. Sub-Committee on Human Relations. Useful Re-actions to leaflets I.R.L.4 (Human Relations In Industry). [1954]

LAB 10/1253 Engineering. WAR OFFICE (P.P. Staffordshire Territorial and Auxiliary Forces Assoc) and the C.E.U. Objection by union to the proposed construction by Army Personnel of Bailey Bridge in Training Area. [1953]

LAB 10/1272 Joint Co-Ordinating Committee for Government Industrial Establishments. Question of Policy when strikes occur in Government Industrial Establishments. [1953]

LAB 10/1273 Engineering and Shipbuilding Industries. Appointment of Courts of Enquiry into Trade Dispute in Engineering and Shipbuilding Industries. [1954]

LAB 10/1277 *Dock Industry*. National Dock Labour Board and the Amalgamated Stevedores & Dockers. Refusal of Dockers to work overtime until it is agreed that overtime is voluntary, not compulsory. [1954]

LAB 10/1279 Appointment of Court of Enquiry. Difference between Employers' and Workers' Sides of National Council for the Omnibus Industry. Report. [1954: published as Cmd. 9093]

LAB 10/1292 Wages Information Branch. Letter from Mr C. E. Pitman of Sir Isaac Pitman & Sons Ltd., to Sir Godfrey Ince, requesting an interview, for discussion of proposal for a supplementary unemployment scheme for the PRINTING INDUSTRY. [1954]

LAB 10/1353 United Thread Mills Ltd, Glasgow, and the National Union of Dyers, Bleachers, and Textile Workers. Protest against the allocation of work to spinners on new types of machine. [1954]

LAB 10/1360 P.M.A.S. British Transport Commission. Factors affecting Human Relations in the Railways Organisation. [1955–59]

LAB 10/1378 Iron & Steel. The Steel Company of Wales, Port Talbot, and the Iron & Steel Confederation. Request for Appointment of a Single Arbitrator to determine the manning of newly introduced machinery. [1955]

LAB 10/1391 Request from Mr Le Harivel of E.P.A. (via B.O.T.) for case histories giving U.K. examples of welfare and human relations in industry (I.R. 'E' to name the firms. C.O.I. to write case histories). [1955]

LAB 10/1399 Shipbuilding. R.S. Hayes (Pembroke Dock) Ltd., and the Boilermakers Society, Shop-Constructors and Shipwrights Association. Demarcation Dispute. [1954–55]

LAB 10/1432 Proposed White Paper on Full Employment and Price Stability. [1954–61]

LAB 10/1445 Engineering. Standard Motor Co Ltd., Coventry, and the Confederation of Shipbuilding and Engineering Unions. Strikes over Redundancy. [1956]

LAB 10/1461 Compulsory Strike Ballot: Briefing for Minister. [1956–57]

LAB 10/1583 Industrial Relations in the Motor Industry: Background Paper. [1961]

LAB 19 series

LAB 19/323 Recruitment and Training of Young Persons in Industry – National Youth Employment Council Paper No 24. Action by Y.E.S. – Pamphlet for Industry 'Training and Employment of Young Persons in Industry'. Memoranda, Minutes and Correspondence. [1949–58]

LAB 43 series

LAB 43/33 National Joint Advisory Council Sub-Committee re Restrictive Labour Practices: H. S. Morrison; Rt. Hon. J. M. Wilson, O.B.E., M.P., Board of Trade; Sir Vincent Tewson C.B.E., M.C., Trade Union Congress; Sir John Forbes-Robertson, K.C.M.G., British Employers Federation; J. Benstead C.B.E., British Transport Commission; Viscount Hyndley, C.B.E., National Coal Board. [1950–51]

LAB 43/38 Captain Peter Thorneycroft, M.P., Board of Trade: Minister asked to speak about Restrictive Labour Practices, should this question be asked in connection with proposed legislation to amend Monopolies Act 1948 and to enlarge the scope of the Monopolies and Restrictive Practices Commission? [1951]

LAB 43/40 Lord Woolton, C.H. suggests that a meeting should be held between the T.U.C., and the Employers' Organisation [sic] to discuss the removal of restrictive practices from both sides of industry. [1956]

LAB 43/271 Restrictive Labour Practices: statements and articles. [1956]

Ministry of Supply (SUPP series)

SUPP 14 series

SUPP 14/1–2 Steel Economy Sub-Committee 1952–1953.

SUPP 14/80 Ball and Roller Bearings: Defence Requirements. [1951–53]

SUPP 14/81 Ball and Roller Bearings – Forward Ordering. [1950–51]

SUPP 14/82 Ball and Roller Bearings – Quality and Inspection.

SUPP 14/86 Ball and Roller Bearings – Admiralty Requirements for Expediting Deliveries. [1951–52]

SUPP 14/87 British Timken Ltd., Duston, Northampton, Expansion of capacity for heavy taper bearings.

SUPP 14/88 German Ball and Roller Bearing Production. [1946–51]

SUPP 14/89 British Timken Ltd., Capital Assistance Scheme, Ball and Roller Bearings.

SUPP 14/91 Ball and Roller Bearings. NPACI and other reports on Ball and Roller Bearing Industry.

SUPP 14/92 Ball and Roller Bearings – Research and Development.

SUPP 14/93–94 Ball and Roller Bearings – Strategic Reserve of Machine Tools, Parts I and II. [1954–55]

SUPP 14/140 Engineering Advisory Council – Memorandum on Proposals of the Institution of Production Engineers for Increasing Productivity. [1949]

SUPP 14/141 Engineering Advisory Council – Memorandum on Steel Economy.

SUPP 14/142 Engineering Advisory Council – Memorandum on Report of the Committee for Standardization of Engineering Products.

SUPP 14/150 Board of Trade Survey of the Supply Position in the United Kingdom. Ministry of Supply Contribution to June 1950 Edition.

SUPP 14/151 National Advisory Council for the Motor Industry –
General.
SUPP 14/168 Sparking Plugs – Insulators: Question of Importation from
U.S.A.
SUPP 14/169 Part I, Market Investigation Committee: Digests on
Engineering Exports.
SUPP 14/171 Sir George Nelson: Memorandum on Exporters' Problems.
SUPP 14/173 Effects of Ending Dollar Discrimination: Engineering
Industries.
SUPP 14/174 U.S. Foreign Operations Administration – Comparative
prices of U.K. Engineering Products.
SUPP 14/176 Instruments for Atomic Energy (Security Control).
SUPP 14/184 General Production Matters on Manufacturing Schemes,
Bristols' Instrument Co. Ltd. [1947]
SUPP 14/186 Machine Tools – General Policy. [1951]
SUPP 14/312 Machine Tools Supply for the Motor Industry (Policy).
[1946]
SUPP 14/326 Motor Cars Production Policy. [1949]
SUPP 14/327 Motor Cars Design Policy. [1949]
SUPP 14/328 Purchase Tax on Motor Vehicles. [1948]
SUPP 14/329 Motor Industry. Assembly of Foreign Cars in the U.K.
[1948]
SUPP 14/330 P.E.P. (Political and Economic Planning) Report on the
Motor Industry. [1947]
SUPP 14/333 Standardisation of Engineering Products. Main Report –
Publication and consideration.
SUPP 14/395 Jaguar Car Co., Coventry.
SUPP 14/396 Importation of Foreign Cars. [1946–49]
SUPP 14/397 Volkswagen Cars – Post-War. [1945–53]
SUPP 14/398 Motor Industry. Level of Production and Supply to the
Home Market 1952 and 1953.
SUPP 14/399 Trade with Western Germany – including the French Zone.
Export of Motor Vehicles and Spares.
SUPP 14/400 Trade with Western Germany (including French Zone).
Export of Motor Vehicles and Spares. [1952–54]
SUPP 14/401 Restrictive Practices in the Motor Industry. [1949]

Treasury (T series)

T 228 series

T 228/322 Scientific Research and Development: Civil Research Priorities.

T 228/611–12 Sub-Committee on Technical Assistance: United Kingdom/ European Programmes Administration general policy. [1954–56]

T 230 series

T 230/284 Long-Term Survey of the Income of the United Kingdom. [1955–56]

T 230/293–4 1. National Wages Policy 2. Full Employment Policy. [1948–50]. N.B: these files were re-studied by civil servants in 1955–6.

T 230/295–301 1. National Wages Policy. 2. Full Employment Policy. 1950–57.

T 230/305 Economic Policy, 1956–58.

T 230/309–11 Economic Situation – Discussions between the Prime Minister, Chancellor of the Exchequer, and Bodies representing both sides of Industry. [1956–58]

T 230/403–8 The General Economic Situation 1952–7.

T 234 series

T 234/51 Economic Situation, 1956. Discussions between the Prime Minister, the Chancellor of the Exchequer and Industrial Bodies. Trades Union Congress.

T 234/74 Committee on Restrictive Labour Practices, memoranda, 1956.

T 234/75 Committee on Restrictive Labour Practices, minutes, 1956.

T 234/91–4 A Study by the Committee on Industrial Relations on the Implications of Full Employment, 1955–56. [Papers relating to production of Cmd. 9725]

T 234/96 British Transport Commission Railway Modernisation Plan – Effect on Private Locomotive and Wagon Building Industry. [1955]

T 234/156 Strikes: possible measures to lessen effect on the Economy. [1957–58]

T 234/636–7 Effect of Industrial Disputes on the National Economy. [1956–60]

T 234/672–5 Stabilisation of Wages and Prices – Policy Files. [1956]

Bibliography

Churchill Archives Centre, Churchill College, Cambridge

CLRK: Sir Richard Clarke
CLSN: Hugh Clausen
ROBN: Sir Austin Robinson
TODD: Lord Todd

COMMAND PAPERS AND
OFFICIAL PUBLICATIONS

Command Papers

C. 3966 *Endowed Schools (Schools Enquiry) Commission, Report of*, Vol I
(1867–8)

C. 3981 *Second Report of the Royal Commissioners on Technical Instruction*, Vol
I, *Report* (1884)

C. 7862 *Report of the Royal Commission on Secondary Education*, Vol I: *Report*
(1895)

Cd. 5130 *Report of the Board of Education, 1908–9* (1910)

Cd. 8594 *University Institutions in Relation to Industry and Commerce* (1917)

Cmd. 3282 *Final Report of the Committee on Trade and Industry* (1928–29)

Cmd. 5776 *Report of the Board of Education* (1937)

Cmd. 6153 *Report of the Royal Commission on the Distribution of the Industrial
Population* (1940)

Cmd. 6404 *Social Insurance and Allied Services* (1942)

Cmd. 6458 *Educational Reconstruction* (1943)

Cmd. 6502 *A National Health Service* (1944)

Cmd. 6527 *Employment Policy* (1944)

Cmd. 6528 *Ministry of Fuel and Power: Statistical Digest for 1938*

Cmd. 6550–1 *Social Insurance*, Parts I and II (1944)

Cmd. 6564 *Statistics Relating to the War Effort of the United Kingdom* (1944)

Cmd. 6610 *Coal Mining: Report of the Technical Advisory Committee* (1945)

Cmd. 6824 *Report of the Committee appointed by the Lord President of the
Council entitled 'Scientific Manpower'* (1946)

Cmd. 8195 *Economic Survey for 1951* (1951)

Cmd. 8357 *Statement of Economic Policy for the Development of Higher
Technological Education in Great Britain* (1951)

Cmd. 8509 *Economic Survey for 1952* (1952)

Cmd. 8800 *Economic Survey for 1953* (1953)

Cmd. 8875 *University Development: Report by the University Grants Council on the Years 1947–52* (1958)

Cmd. 8918 *Programme of Expenditure of Counterpart Funds derived from United States Economic Aid under Section 9(c) of the Mutual Security Act of 1952. Presented by the President of the Board of Trade to Parliament by Command of Her Majesty*

Cmd. 9084 *Industrial Courts Act, 1919. Report of a Court of Enquiry into a Dispute between Employers who are members of the Engineering and Allied Employers' Federation and workmen who are members of Trade Unions affiliated to the Confederation of Shipbuilding and Engineering Unions* (1954)

Cmd. 9085 *Industrial Courts Act. Report of a Court of Enquiry into a Dispute between employers who are members of the Shipbuilding Employers' Federation and workmen who are members of Trade Unions affiliated to the Confederation of Shipbuilding and Engineering Unions* (1954)

Cmd. 9108 *Economic Survey for 1954* (1954)

Cmd. 9412 *Economic Survey 1955* (1955)

Cmd. 9691 *Statement on Defence* (1956)

Cmd. 9703 *Technical Education* (1956)

Cmd. 9728 *Economic Survey 1956* (1956)

Cmnd. 113 *Economic Survey 1957* (1957)

Cmnd. 394 *Economic Survey 1958* (1958)

Cmnd. 534 *University Development: Report by the University Grants Council for the Years 1952–57* (1958)

Cmnd. 2267 *University Development: Report by the University Grants Council for the Years 1957–62* (1963)

OFFICIAL PUBLICATIONS

British

Census of Production, 1951 (London, HMSO, 1955)

Central Policy Review Staff, The Future of the British Car Industry (London, HMSO, 1945)

Committee appointed by the President of the Board of Education to consider the Supply, Recruitment and Training of Teachers and Youth Leaders [the McNair Committee] (HMSO, 1944)

Committee of Investigation into the Cotton Textile Machinery Industry, Report (London, HMSO, 1947)

Curriculum and Examinations in Secondary Schools: Report of the Committee of the Secondary School Examination Council Appointed by the President of the Board of Education in 1941 (HMSO, 1943)

General Report of the Select Committee on Estimates, Session 1955/56, *The Development Areas* (London, HMSO, 1956)

Historical Record of the Census of Production 1907 to 1970 (London, Government Statistical Service, ND)

History of the Ministry of Munitions, 12 vols. (London, HMSO, 1922)

Report by the Special Committee on Higher Technological Education (London, HMSO, 1945)

Second Report of the Select Committee on Estimates, Session 1955/56, *The Development Areas* (London, HMSO, 1956)

Social Trends (London, Central Statistical Office, 1991)

United Kingdom Balance of Payments, 1946–1957 (London, H.M. Treasury, 1959)

German

Statistisches Bundesamt, Volkswirtschaftliche Gesamtrechnungen, Fachserie 18, Reihe 7, Lange Reihen 1950 bis 1984

– Statistik der Bundesrepublik Deutschland, Band 214: *Die Berufsbildenden Schulen in den Jahren 1955 und 1956*

– *Statistische Berichte. Der Hochschulbesuch in Bundesgebiet und Berlin (West) im Wintersemester 1955–56*

– *Bestandene Prüfungen an Wissenshaftlichen Hochschulen von Sommersemester 1952 bis Sommersemester 1972*
 (all Stuttgart und Mainz, Verlag W. Kohlhammer GmbH)

SECONDARY SOURCES

Acton Society Trust, *Management Succession* (London, Acton Society Trust, 1956)

Adeney, M., *The Motor Makers: The Turbulent History of Britain's Car Industry* (London, Collins, 1988)

Aldcroft, D., *Education, Training and Economic Performance 1944 to 1990* (Manchester, Manchester University Press, 1992)

- 'Government Control and the Origin of Restrictive Trade Practices in Great Britain', *Accounts Magazine*, vol. 66 no. 675, September 1962, pp. 671–87
- 'The Missing Dimension: Management Education and Training in Postwar Britain', in Aldcroft, D., and Slaven, A. (eds), *Enterprise and Management: Essays in Honour of Peter L. Payne* (Aldershot, Scolar Press, 1992)
- *Studies in Transport History, 1870–1970* (Newton Abbott, London, Vancouver and North Pomfret, David and Charles, 1974)
- and Richardson, H., *The British Economy, 1870–1939* (London, Macmillan, 1969)

Allen, G. Freeman, *British Rail After Beeching* (London, W. H. Allan, 1966)

Allen, M., *British Saloon Cars of the Fifties* (Leicester, The Promotional Reprint Company, 1995)

Amouroux, H., *Le Peuple du Desastre, 1939–1940* (Paris, Editions Robert Laffont, 1976)

Andrew, C., *For the President's Eyes Only: Secret Intelligence and the American Presidency from Washington to Bush* (London, HarperCollins, 1995)

Anglo-American Council on Productivity (reports cited):
- *Cotton Spinning* (March 1950)
- *Education for Management*
- *Electric Motor Control Gear* (September 1950)
- *Internal Combustion Engines* (June 1950)
- *Management Accounting* (November 1950)
- *Packaging* (September 1950)
- *Relations Between the Universities and Industry*
- *Simplification in Industry* (October 1949)
- *Simplification in British Industry* (August 1950)
- *Steel Founding* (September 1949)
- *Training of Operatives* (1951)
- *Training of Supervisors* (1951)
- *The Universities and Industry* (1951)

Annan, N., *Our Age: The Generation That Made Post-War Britain* (London, Fontana, 1991)

Anon, 'Old runabout reborn as the new rickshaw', article on the Citroën 'Deux Chevaux' in the *Observer*, 27 October 1996

Argles, M., *South Kensington to Robbins: An Account of English Technical Education since 1851* (London, Longman, 1964)

Ashworth, W., with the assistance of Pegg, M., *The History of the British*

Coal Industry, Vol. 5, *1946–1982: The Nationalized Industry* (Oxford, the Clarendon Press, 1986)

Aspray, W., 'The History of Computing within the History of Information Technology', in *History and Technology*, 1994, Vol. II pp. 7–19.

Bacon, R. and Eltis, W., *Britain's Economic Problem: Too Few Producers*, 2nd edition (London, Macmillan, 1978)

Baldry, D. (ed.), *The Hamlyn History of Aviation* (London, Hamlyn Books, 1996)

Balfour, C., *Roads to Oblivion: Triumphs and Tragedies of British Car Makers 1946–56* (Bideford, Bay View Books, 1996)

Balfour, M., *West Germany* (London, Ernest Benn, 1968)

Barber, J., *The Prime Minister since 1945* (Oxford, Blackwell, for the Institute for Contemporary British History, 1991)

Barker, A., *Suez: The Seven Day War* (London, Faber and Faber, 1964)

Barnett, Correlli, *The Audit of War: The Illusion and Reality of Britain as a Great Nation* (London, Macmillan, 1986; Papermac, 1987)

– *The Collapse of British Power* (London, Eyre Methuen, 1972; paperback editions: Stroud, Alan Sutton, 1984, 1987, 1991, 1993, 1997)

– *The Desert Generals* (London, Peter Kimber, 1960; revised edition, London, Cassell Military Paperbacks, 1999)

– *Engage the Enemy More Closely: the Royal Navy in the Second World War* (London, Hodder and Stoughton, 1991; paperback, Penguin Books, 2000)

– *The Hump Organisation* (London, Alan Wingate, 1957)

– *The Lost Victory: British Dreams, British Illusions, 1945–1950* (London, Macmillan, 1986; Papermac, 1987)

– *The Swordbearers: Studies in Supreme Command in the First World War* (London, Eyre and Spottiswoode, 1964; London, Cassell Military Paperbacks, 2000)

Bayley, S. (ed.), *The Conran Directory of Design* (London, Octopus Conran, 1985)

Baylis, J., *Anglo-American Defence Relations 1939–80: The Special Relationship* (London, Macmillan, 1982)

Beckett, F., *Enemy Within: The Rise and Fall of the British Communist Party* (London, John Murray, 1995)

Bird, P., *The First Business Computer* (Wokingham, Hasler Publishing Company, 1994)

Bibliography

Blake, Robert, *The Conservative Party from Peel to Churchill* (London, Eyre & Spottiswoode, 1970)

Bond, B., *British Military Policy Between the Two World Wars* (Oxford, Clarendon Press, 1980)

Bond, R., 'A heritage of achievement; The Rover story', in the *Eastern Daily Press*, issue of 1 February 1994

Bowden, B., 'The Language of Computers', First Richard Goodman Memorial Lecture, May 1969

Boyle, P., *Marketing and the Competitive Performance of British Industry: Areas for Research* (paper prepared for the Social Science Research Council workshop on the Competitiveness and Regeneration of British Industry, 18–19 November 1983)

British Transport Commission, *Modernisation and Re-equipment of British Railways* (London, British Transport Commission, 1954)

Broadbent, Sir E., *The Military and Government: From Macmillan to Heseltine* (London, RUSI-Macmillan, 1990)

Brown, W. A. and Opie, R., *American Foreign Assistance* (Washington, Brookings Institution, 1953)

Bullock, A., *Ernest Bevin: Foreign Secretary 1945–1951* (London, Heinemann, 1984)

Bullock, J., *The Rootes Brothers: Story of a Motoring Empire* (Yeovil, Patrick Stephens, 1993)

Bulmer, M. (ed.), *Mining and Social Change: Durham County in the Twentieth Century* (London, Croom Helm, 1978)

Burgess-White, D., 'The Secret History of the British Motor Car' (parts 1–6), *Daily Telegraph*, January–February 1996

Butler, D., *British General Elections since 1945* (Oxford, Blackwell, for the Institute for Contemporary British History, 1989)

– *The British General Election of 1951* (London, Macmillan, 1952)

Buxton, N., and Aldcroft, D. (eds), *British Industry Between the Wars: Instability and Industrial Development, 1919–1939* (London, Scolar Press, 1979)

Cairncross, A. and Watts, Nina, *The Economic Section 1939–1961: a study in economic advising* (London, Routledge and Kegan Paul, 1989)

Caminer, D., et al., *User-Driven Innovation: The World's First Business Computer* (New York, McGraw-Hill, 1996)

Campbell-Kelly, M., *ICL: A Business and Technical History* (Oxford, Clarendon Press, 1989)

– and Aspray, W., *Computer: A History of the Information Machine* (London, Basic Books, 1996)

Cannadine, D. and Price, S. (eds), *Rituals of Royalty: Power and Ceremonial in Traditional Societies* (Cambridge, Cambridge University Press, 1987)

Carlton, D., *Anthony Eden: a Biography* (London, Allen Lane, 1981)

– *Britain and the Suez Crisis* (Oxford, Blackwell, for the Institute for Contemporary British History, 1988)

Carr, J. C. and Taplin, W., assisted by Wright, A. E. G., *History of the British Steel Industry* (Oxford, Basil Blackwell, and Cambridge, Mass., Harvard University Press, 1962)

Carver, M., *Tightrope Walking: British Defence Policy Since 1945* (London, Hutchinson, 1992)

Castle, H. G., *Britain's Motor Industry* (London, Clerke and Cocheran, 1950)

Central Statistical Office, *Social Trends*, 21st Edition (London, HMSO, 1991)

Chapman, G., 'The legend that may yet Triumph', in the *Daily Telegraph*, issue of 23 November 1996

– 'Cars That Time Forgot' (all in the *Daily Telegraph*): 'The Lea-Francis Lynx,' issue of 4 February 1995; 'The Standard Vanguard Sportsman', issue of 10 June 1995; 'The Tornado Typhoon Sportsbrake', issue of 24 June 1995; 'The Vauxhall Victor F-Type Estate', issue of 14 December 1996

– 'Here they are – the best and the worst of British', in the *Daily Telegraph*, issue of 20 January 1996

Charmley, J., *Churchill: The End of Glory; a Political Biography* (London, Hodder and Stoughton, 1993)

– *Splendid Isolation? Britain, the Balance of Power, and the Origins of the First World War, 1874–1914* (London, Hodder and Stoughton, 1999)

Checkland, S., *The Rise of Industrial Society in England* (London, Longman, 1964)

Chester, N., *The Nationalisation of British Industry 1945–51* (London, HMSO, 1975)

Church, R. A., *Herbert Austin; The British Motor Car to 1941* (London, Europa Press, 1979)

– *The rise and decline of the British motor industry* (Cambridge, Cambridge University Press, 1995)

Cipolla, C. (ed.), *The Fontana Economic History of Europe*, vol. 6, *Contemporary Economies – 1* (London, Collins/Fontana Books, 1976)

Clarke, D., *The Industrial Manager: His Background and Career Pattern* (London, Business Publications, 1966)

Clarke, P., *Hope and Glory: Britain 1900–1990* (London, Allen Lane, 1996)

– 'Keynes, New Jerusalem, and British Decline', in Clarke, P., and Trebilcock, C. (eds), *Understanding Decline: Perceptions and Realities of British Economic Performance* (Cambridge, Cambridge University Press, 1997)

Clements, R., *Managers: A Study of Their Careers in Industry* (London, Allen and Unwin, 1958)

Coates, D., and Hillard, J. (eds), *UK Economic Decline: Key Texts* (Hemel Hempstead, Prentice Hall/Harvester Wheatsheaf, 1995)

Coates, K., and Silburn, R., *Poverty, Deprivation and Morale in a Nottingham Community: St Ann's* (Nottingham, Nottingham University Department of Adult Education, 1967)

Conrad, J., *The Nigger of the 'Narcissus': A Tale of the Sea* (London, The Gresham Publishing Company, 1925)

Copeman, G., *Leaders of British Industry* (London, Gee, 1956)

Court, W. H. B., *Coal* (London, HMSO and Longmans, Green, 1951)

Cox, J., with Kriegbaum, H., *Growth, Innovation and Employment: An Anglo-German Comparison* (London, Anglo-German Foundation for the Study of Industrial Society, 1980)

Crawley, H., 'NRDC Computer Project', NRDC Paper 132, February, 1957

Cronin, J., *Industrial Conflict in Modern Britain* (London, Croom Helm, and Totowa, New Jersey, Roman and Littlefield, 1979)

Cross, J., *Whitehall and the Commonwealth* (London, Routledge and Kegan Paul, 1967)

Cross, R., *The Silver Lining: Britain in Colour 1945–1952* (London, Sidgwick and Jackson, 1985)

Dahrendorf, R., *On Britain* (London, British Broadcasting Corporation, 1982)

Dale, H., *The Higher Civil Service of Great Britain* (London, Oxford University Press, 1941)

Darby, P., *British Defence Policy East of Suez, 1947–1968* (Oxford, Oxford University Press, for the Royal Institute of International Affairs, 1973)

Darwin, J., *Britain and Decolonization* (Basingstoke, Macmillan Education, 1988)

Bibliography

- *The End of the British Empire* (Oxford, Blackwell, for the Insitute for
  Contemporary British History, 1991)
David, E., *Mediterranean Food* (Harmondsworth, Penguin Books, 1950)
Denton, G., Forsyth, M. and MacLennan, M., *Economic Planning and
  Policies in Britain, France and Germany* (London, George Allen and
  Unwin, 1968)
Design Council, *Industrial Design in the United Kingdom* (London, Design
  Council, 1977)
Dilnot, A. W., Kay, J. A. and Morris, J. N., *The Reform of Social Security*
  (London, Institute of Fiscal Studies and Oxford University Press, 1984)
Dormois, J.-P., and Dintenfass, M. (eds), *The British Industrial Decline*
  (London, Routledge, 1999)
Dow, J. C. R., *The Management of the British Economy 1945–60* (Cambridge,
  Cambridge University Press: National Institute for Economic and Social
  Research, Students' Edition 3, 1970)
Dunleavy, P., *The Politics of Mass Housing in Britain, 1945–1975: A Study of
  Corporate Power and Professional Influence in the Welfare State* (Oxford,
  Clarendon Press, 1981)
Dunnett, P. J. S., *The Decline of the British Motor Industry: The Effects of
  Government Policy 1945–1979* (London, Croom Helm, 1980)
Durcan, J., McCarthy, E., and Redman, G., *Strikes in Post-war Britain: a
  study of stoppages of work due to industrial disputes* (London, George Allen
  and Unwin, 1983)
Dutton, D., *Anthony Eden: A Life and Reputation* (London, Arnold, 1996)

Eayrs, J., *The Commonwealth and Suez* (Oxford, Oxford University Press, 1964)
Eden, A., *The Memoirs of the Rt. Hon. Sir Anthony Eden, K.G., P.C.,
  M.C.: Full Circle* (London, Cassell, 1960)
Edgerton, D., *England and the Aeroplane: An Essay on a Militant and
  Technological Nation* (Basingstoke, Macmillan, 1991)
- 'The Prophet Militant and Industrial: The Peculiarities of Correlli
  Barnett', *Twentieth Century British History*, 1991, vol. 2, no. 3
- *Science, technology and the British industrial 'decline' 1870–1970* (Cambridge,
  Cambridge University Press, 1996)
- 'Science in the United Kingdom of Great Britain and (Northern
  Ireland): a Study in the Nationalisation of Science', in Pestre, D., and
  Krige, J. (eds), *Science in the Twentieth Century* (Amsterdam, Harwood
  Academic, 1997)

678

– 'Whatever happened to the British Warfare State? The Ministry of Supply, 1945–51', in Mercer, H., et al., *The Labour Government 1945–51 and Private Industry: the experience of 1945–51* (Edinburgh, Edinburgh University Press, 1992)

Eltis, W., and Sinclair, P. (eds), *Keynes and Economic Policy: The Relevance of The General Theory after Fifty Years* (London, Macmillan Press, in association with the National Economic Development Office, 1988)

Ensor, R., *England 1870–1914* (Oxford, the Clarendon Press, 1966)

Feinstein, C., *Statistical Tables of National Income, Expenditure and Output of the United Kingdom, 1855–1965* (Cambridge, Cambridge University Press, 1972)

Ferguson, T., and Cunnison, J., *In Their Early Twenties: A Study of Glasgow Youth* (London, Oxford University Press for the Nuffield Foundation, 1956)

– *The Young Wage-Earner: A Study of Glasgow Boys* (London, Oxford University Press, for the Nuffield Foundation, 1951)

Foot, M., *Aneurin Bevan, A Biography*, Vol. Two: *1945–1960* (London, Davis-Poynter, 1973)

Foreman-Peck, J., 'The Balance of Technology Transfers 1870–1914', in Dormois, J.-P., and Dintenfass, M. (eds), *The British Industrial Decline* (London, Routledge, 1999)

Gaddis, J., *We Now Know: Rethinking Cold War History* (Oxford, Clarendon Press, 1997)

Gallagher, J., *The Decline, Revival and Fall of the British Empire* (Cambridge, Cambridge University Press, 1982)

Gallup, G. (general editor), *The Gallup International Opinion Polls: Great Britain 1937–1975*, Vol. I, *1937–1964* (New York, Random House, 1977)

Gann, L. and Duignan, P. (eds), *Colonialism and Africa 1870–1960* (Cambridge, Cambridge University Press, 1969)

Gardner, N., 'The Economics of Launching Aid', in Whiting, A. (ed.), *The Economics of Industrial Subsidies* (London, 1976)

George, S., *Britain and European Integration since 1945* (Oxford, Blackwell, for the Institute of Contemporary British History, 1991)

Glass, D. (ed.), *Social Mobility in Britain* (London, Routledge and Kegan Paul, 1954)

Glennerster, H., *British Social Policy since 1945* (Oxford, Blackwell, for the Institute for Contemporary British History, 1995)

Glover, I., *The Background of British Managers: A Review of the Evidence* (unpublished monograph, 1974)

– and Kelly, M., *Engineers in Britain: A Sociological Study of the Engineering Dimension* (London, Allen and Unwin, 1987)

Goldthorpe, J., *Social Mobility and Class Structure in Modern Britain* (London, Clarendon Press, 1979)

– and Lockwood, D., Bechhofer, F. and Platt, J., *The Affluent Worker* (Cambridge, Cambridge University Press, 1968)

Goncharov, S., Lewis, J., and Lutai, X., *Uncertain Partners: Stalin, Mao, and the Korean War* (Stanford, Stanford University Press, 1993)

Gourvish, T., and O'Day, A. (eds), *Britain since 1945* (Basingstoke, Macmillan Press, 1991)

Gowing, M., *Independence and Deterrence: Britain and Atomic Energy, 1945–1952*, Vol. I: *Policy Making* (London, Macmillan, 1982)

Graham, A. and Seldon, A. (eds), *Government and Economies in the Post-war World; economic policies and comparative performance, 1945–85* (London, Routledge, for the Institute for Contemporary British History, 1990)

Granick, D., *The European Executive* (London, Weidenfeld and Nicolson, 1962)

Green, W., and Swanborough, G., *The Complete Book of Fighters: An Illustrated Encyclopaedia of every fighter ever flown* (London, Salamander Books, 1994)

Grove, E., *Vanguard to Trident: British Naval Policy Since World War Two* (London, The Bodley Head, 1987)

Gummett, P., *Scientists in Whitehall* (Manchester, Manchester University Press, 1980)

Guttsman, W. L., *The British Political Elite* (London, MacGibbon and Kee, 1963)

Hall, P., *Great Planning Disasters* (London, Weidenfeld and Nicolson, 1980)

Halsey, A., Heath, A., and Ridge, J., *Origins and Destinations: Family, Class and Education in Modern Britain* (Oxford, Clarendon Press, 1979)

Handy, C., Gordon, C., Gow, I., and Randlesome, C., *Making Managers* (London, Pitman, 1988)

Harris, K., *Attlee* (London, Weidenfeld and Nicolson, 1995)

Harrison, P., *The Inner City* (Harmondsworth, Penguin Books, 1983)

Hastings, M., *The Korean War* (London, Michael Joseph, 1987)

Heindel, R. H., *The American Impact on Britain 1891–1914* (New York, Octagon Books, 1968)

Hendry, J., *Innovating for Failure* (Boston, M.I.T. Press, 1989)

Hennessy, P., *Never Again: Britain 1945–1951* (London, Jonathan Cape, 1992)

– *Whitehall* (London, Secker, 1986)

– and Arends, A., *Mr Attlee's Engine Room: Cabinet Committee Structure and the Labour Governments 1945–51*, Strathclyde Papers on Government and Politics No. 26 (Glasgow, Strathclyde University, 1983)

Hewison, R., *Culture and Consensus; England, art and politics since 1940* (London, Methuen, 1995)

Hibbert, C., *Wellington: a Personal History* (London, HarperCollins, 1997)

Hickey, M., *Korean War: The West Confronts Communism 1950–1953* (London, John Murray, 1999; paperback edition, 2000)

Hilken, T., *Engineering at Cambridge University, 1783–1965* (Cambridge, Cambridge University Press,1967)

Hillman, D., and Gibbs, D., *CENTURY MAKERS: One hundred clever things we take for granted which have changed our lives over the last one hundred years* (London, Weidenfeld and Nicolson, 1998)

Hobsbawm, E. J., *Industry and Empire* (Harmondsworth, Pelican Books, 1969)

Hoggart, R., *The Uses of Literacy: Aspects of Working Class Life With Special Reference to Publications and Entertainments* (London, Chatto and Windus, 1971)

Holland, R., *The Pursuit of Greatness: Britain and the World Role 1900–1970* (London, Fontana, 1991)

Hollis, P. (ed.), *Class and Conflict in Nineteenth Century England 1815–1850* (London and Boston, Routledge and Kegan Paul, 1973)

Horne, A., *To Lose a Battle* (London, Macmillan, 1969)

– *Macmillan 1894–1956, Vol. I of the Official Biography* (London, Macmillan, 1988)

Hovey, J., *A Tale of Two Ports: London and Southampton* (London, The Industrial Society, 1990)

Hyam, R., *Britain's Imperial Century 1815–1914* (2nd edition, Basingstoke, Macmillan Press, 1993)

Institute of Manpower Studies, *Competence and Competition: Training and Education in the Federal Republic of Germany, the United States and Japan* (London, NEDO Books, 1984)

International Institute of Strategic Studies, *The Military Balance 1971–2*
(London, 1971)

Jackson, M. P., *The Price of Coal* (London, Croom Helm, 1974)

Jacobs, E., and Worcester, R., *Typically British? The Prudential MORI Guide*
(London, Bloomsbury, 1991)

Jones, L., *Shipbuilding in Britain Mainly Between the World Wars* (Cardiff,
University of Wales Press, 1957)

Kahn, A. E., *Britain in the World Economy* (London, Pitman, 1946)

Kavanagh, D. and P., *Consensus Politics from Attlee to Thatcher* (Oxford,
Blackwell, for the Institute for Contemporary British History, 1989)

Kealey, T., *The Economic Laws of Scientific Research* (Basingstoke, Macmillan
Press, 1996)

Keeling, B. S. and Wright, A. E. G., *The Development of the Modern British
Steel Industry* (London, Longmans, 1964)

Kelly, S., and Gorst, A. (eds), *Whitehall and the Suez Crisis* (London, Frank
Cass, 2000)

Kemp, M., 'The great British car catastrophe', in the *Daily Mail*, issue of 3
July 1980

Knaplund, P., *Britain, Commonwealth and Empire* (London, Hamish
Hamilton, 1956)

Kyle, K., *Suez* (New York, St Martin's Press, 1991)

Lamb, R., *The Failure of the Eden Government* (London, Sidgwick and
Jackson,1987)

Lawrence, P., *Invitation to Management* (Oxford, Blackwell, 1986)

Laybourn, K., *British Trade Unionism c. 1770–1990: A Reader in History*
(Stroud, Alan Sutton, 1991)

– *A History of British Trade Unionism c. 1770–1990* (Stroud, Sutton,
1997)

Lindsay, T. F., and Harrington, Michael, *The Conservative Party 1918–1979*
(London, Macmillan, 1979)

Locke, R., *The End of the Practical Man: Entrepreneurship and Higher
Education in Germany, France and Great Britain, 1880–1940* (Greenwich,
Conn., and London, Jai Press, 1984)

Longrigg, S., *Oil in the Middle East; Its Discovery and Development* (London,
Oxford University Press, 1961)

Bibliography

Louis, R., *The British Empire in the Middle East 1945–1951* (Oxford, Oxford University Press, 1984)

Lovell, J., *British Trade Unions, 1875–1933* (London, Pelican Books, 1971)

Lowndes, C., *The Silent Social Revolution* (London, Oxford University Press, 1937)

Lynton, R. P., and King, S. D. M., *The London Docks: A Framework for Study* (London, British Institute of Management,

McCrone, G., *Regional Policy in Britain* (London, Allen and Unwin, 1969)

MacDougall, D., *Don and Mandarin; Memoirs of an Economist* (London, John Murray, 1987)

Macmillan, H., *Riding the Storm, 1956–59* (London, Macmillan, 1971)

Mahan, A., *The Influence of Seapower Upon History, 1660–1783* (London, University Paperbacks, 1965; first edition, Boston, Mass., Little, Brown and Co., 1890)

Mansergh, N., *The Commonwealth Experience* (London, Weidenfeld and Nicolson, 1969)

– *Survey of British Commonwealth Affairs: Problems of Wartime Co-operation and Post-war Change, 1939–1952* (Oxford, Oxford University Press, 1958)

Mantle, J., *Car Wars: The International Giants and the World They Made* (London, Macmillan, 1995)

Marquand, D., *Welfare or Welfare State? Contradictions and Dilemmas in Social Policy* (Basingstoke, Macmillan Press, 1996)

– and Seldon, A, *The Ideas That Shaped Post-War Britain* (London, Fontana Press, 1996)

Martin, L.W., *British Defence Policy: The Long Recessional* (London, IISS, 1969)

Marwick, A., *British Society Since 1945* (London, Allen Lane, 1982)

Mathias, P., *The First Industrial Nation* (London, Methuen, 1969)

Matthews, R., Feinstein, C., and Odling-Smee, J., *British Economic Growth, 1856–1973* (Oxford, Oxford University Press, 1982)

Maxey, G. and Silberston, A., *The Motor Industry* (London, Allen and Unwin, 1959)

May, E. (ed.), *American Cold War Strategy; Interpreting NSC-68* (Boston, Mass., St Martin's Press, 1993)

Mercer, H., Rollings, N. and Tomlinson, J. (eds), *The Labour Government and Private Industry: The Experience of 1945–1951* (Edinburgh, Edinburgh University Press, 1992)

683

Bibliography

Middlemass, K., *Power, Competition and the State*, Vol. I, *Britain in Search of Balance 1940–1961* (London, Macmillan, 1986)

Middleton, R., *The British Economy Since 1945: Engaging With the Debate* (Basingstoke, Macmillan, 2000)

Miller, J. D. B., *Britain and the Old Dominions* (London, Chatto and Windus, 1966)

Millward, A., *The Reconstruction of Western Europe 1945–1951* (London, Routledge, 1984)

Monck, B., 'The Eclipse of the Engineer', in *Engineering*, 10 September 1954, pp. 329–34

Morgan, K. O., *Labour in Power 1945–1951* (Oxford, the Clarendon Press, 1984)

Morris, D. (ed.), *The Economic System in the UK* (3rd edition, Oxford, Oxford University Press, 1985)

Musgrave, P., 'The Educational Profiles of Management in Two British Iron and Steel Companies with Some Comparisons, National and International', in *The British Journal of Industrial Relations*, vol. 4, issue 2, July 1966, pp. 201–10

Nelson, W. H., *Small Wonder: The amazing story of the Volkswagen* (London, Hutchinson, 1967)

Newell, R., *The Morris Minor* (Princes Risborough, Shire Publications, 1998)

Osgood, R., *NATO: The Entangling Alliance* (Chicago, University of Chicago Press, 1962)

Overy, R. J., *William Morris, Viscount Nuffield* (London, Europa Press, 1976)

Owen, G., *From Empire to Europe: The Decline and Revival of British Industry Since the Second World War* (London, HarperCollins, 1999)

Oxford Illustrated Encyclopedia of Invention and Technology (London, BCA, 1992)

Pavitt, K. (ed.), *Technical Innovation and British Economic Performance* (London, Macmillan, 1980)

Peden, G., *British Rearmament and the Treasury 1932–1939* (Edinburgh, Scottish Academic Press, 1979)

Pelling, H., *A History of British Trade Unionism* (Harmondsworth, Pelican Books, 1971)

P.E.P., *Growth in the British economy: a study of economic problems and policies in contemporary Britain* (London, Allen and Unwin for Political and Economic Planning, 1960)

Percy, E., *Some Memories* (London, Eyre and Spottiswoode, 1958)

Perry, P., *The Evolution of British Manpower Policy from the Statute of Artificers 1563 to the Industrial Training Act 1964* (published by the author, 1976)

Pestre, D., and Krige, J. (eds), *Science in the Twentieth Century* (Amsterdam, Harwood Academic, 1997)

Pliatzky, L., *Getting and Spending: Public Expenditure, Employment and Inflation* (Oxford, Basil Blackwell, 1982)

Plowden, E., *An Industrialist in the Treasury: The Post-War Years* (London, Andre Deutsch, 1989)

Pollard, S., *Britain's Prime and Britain's Decline* (London, Edward Arnold, 1989)

– *The Wasting of the British Economy: British Economic Policy from 1945 to the Present* (London, Croom Helm, 1982)

Prais, S., *Vocational Qualifications of the Labour Force in Britain and Germany* (London, National Institute of Economic Research, 1981)

– and Wagner, K., *Schooling Standards in Britain and Germany: Some Summary Comparisons Bearing on Economic Efficiency* (London, National Institute of Economic Research, 1983)

Pressnell, J., *The Mini* (Princes Risborough, Shire Publications, 1997)

Reader, W., *Imperial Chemical Industries: A History*, Vol. II: *The First Quarter-Century, 1925–1952* (London, Oxford University Press, 1975)

Revans, R., *The Origins and Growth of Action Learning* (Bromley, Chartwell-Bratt, 1982)

Reynolds, D., *Britannia Overruled* (London, Longman, 1991)

Rhodes James, R., *Anthony Eden* (London, Weidenfeld and Nicolson, 1986)

Robbins, K., *The Eclipse of a Great Power: Modern Britain, 1870–1975* (London, Longman, 1983)

Robson, W., *Nationalized Industry and Public Ownership* (2nd edition, London, Allen and Unwin, 1962)

Roepke, H., *Movements of the British Iron and Steel Industry – 1720 to 1951* (Urbana, University of Illinois Press, 1956)

Roskamp, K., *Capital Formation in West Germany* (Detroit, Wayne University Press, 1965)

Sanders, D., *Losing an Empire, Finding a Role* (Basingstoke, Macmillan Education, 1990)

Sanderson, M., *Education and economic decline in Brtain, 1870 to the 1990s* (Cambridge, Cambridge University Press, 1999)

– *The Missing Stratum: Technical School Education 1900- 1990s* (London, Athlone Press, 1994)

– *The Universities and British Industry, 1850–1970* (London, Routledge and Kegan Paul, 1972)

Shanks, M., article in *'Suicide of a Nation'*: special issue of *Encounter* edited by Koestler, A. (vol. xxi. no. 1, July 1963)

– *The Stagnant Society* (revised edition, Harmondsworth, 1972)

Shay, P. Jr., *British Rearmament in the Thirties: Politics and Profits* (Princeton, Princeton University Press, 1977)

Shaw, E., *The Labour Party since 1945* (Oxford, Blackwell, for the Institute for Contemporary History, 1996)

Shaw, T., *Eden, Suez and the Mass Media: Propaganda and Persuasion during the Suez Crisis* (London, I. B. Tauris, 1996)

Shepherd, R., *Iain Macleod* (London, Hutchinson, 1994)

Shonfield, A., *British Economic Policy Since the War* (Harmondsworth, Penguin Books, 1958)

Shwadran, B., *Middle East Oil and the Great Powers* (New York, 1973)

Skidelsky, R., *John Maynard Keynes: Fighting for Britain Vol. 3: 1937–1946* (London, Macmillan, 2000)

Smellie, G., and Adamson, C., *A Study of Steel Productivity in Great Britain and U.S.A.* (Redbourn, R.T.B. Ltd, 1955)

Snyder, W. P., *Politics of British Defence Policy 1945–1962* (Columbus, Ohio, Ohio State University Press, 1964)

Social and Community Planning Research, *British Social Attitudes Survey* (Aldershot, Gower Publishing, 1988)

Sparke, P., *A Century of Design: Design Pioneers of the Twentieth Century* (London, Mitchell Beazley, 1998)

Stevenson, J., *British Society 1914–1945* (Harmondsworth, Pelican Books, 1984)

Theakston, K., *The Civil Service since 1945* (Oxford, Blackwell, for the Institute for Contemporary British History, 1995)

Thompson, B., 'A Brief History of Computing', in *CAM: the Cambridge Alumni Magazine*, Lent term, 1998

Thompson, E. P., *The Making of the English Working Class* (Harmondsworth, Pelican Books, 1974)

Townsend, J., 'Innovation in Coal-mining Machinery: the Case of the Anderton Shearer Loader', in Pavitt, K. (ed.), *Technical Innovation and British Economic Performance* (Macmillan Press, London and Basingstoke, for the Science Policy Research Unit, University of Sussex, 1980)

Trustees of the Carnegie United Kingdom Trust, *Disinherited Youth: A Report on the 18-plus Age Group: Enquiry Prepared for the Trustees of the Carnegie United Kingdom Trust* (Edinburgh, 1943)

Turner, G., *The Car Makers* (Harmondsworth, Penguin Books, 1964)

Turner, H., Clack, G., and Roberts, R., *Labour Relations in the Motor Industry; A Study of Industrial Unrest and International Comparison* (London, George Allen and Unwin, 1967)

Wagner, M., and Norris, G., *Classic Jetliners* (London, Osprey Aerospace, 1994)

Webster, C., *The Health Services Since the War*, Vol. I: *Problems of Health Care: the National Health Service Before 1957* (London, HMSO, 1988)

Wettern, D., *The Decline of British Seapower* (London, Jane's Publishing, 1982)

Whitehouse, R. (ed.), *Great Trains of the World* (London, New English Library/Hamlyn Books, 1975)

Wintle, J., *Car Wars: The International Giants and the world they made* (London, Macmillan, 1995)

Wood, J., *The Volkswagen Beetle* (Princes Risborough, Shire Publications, 1989)

– *Wheels of Misfortune* (London, Sidgwick and Jackson,)

World Bank Development Report 2000/2001 (New York, Oxford University Press, 2000)

Worswick, G., and Ady, P. (eds), *The British Economy in the 1950s* (Oxford, Clarendon Press, 1962)

Wyatt, R., *The Austin, 1906–1952* (Newton Abbott and London, David and Charles, 1981)

Ziegler, P., *Mountbatten; the Official Biography* (London, Collins, 1985)

Index

Index

Labour policy, 45, 73, 139, 419;
neglect, 138–9
industry, directors, 285–8
industry, managers, 284–5, 288–9
industry, productivity, 269–70,
278–9, 403, 406–9, 564
inflation: Conservative policy
(1955–56), 428–33; full
employment policy, 63, 71–2,
428–33; Labour policy, 45;
ROBOT, 162, 163
Information, Ministry of, 493
Inland Steel Company, Chicago, 279
instruments industry, 366–7
International Computers and
Tabulators Ltd (ICT), 362, 364,
365
International Court, 95
International Harvester, 189
International Monetary Fund (IMF),
151, 170, 500, 501–2, 503
investment, industrial, *see* industry
(capital investment)
Investment Programmes Committee
(IPC), 73, 137, 139, 474–6, 478
Invicta, 380; Black Prince, 621
Iran, 91, 93–6, 118
Iraq, 91, 483
iron and steel, 4, 304–5, 484, *see also*
steel industry
Iron and Steel Shipbuilders' Society,
208
Iron and Steel Trades Confederation,
431
Isaacs, George, 183, 188
Isetta, 374
Israel, Suez crisis, 490–1, 501
Issigonis, Alec, 387
Italy: consumer boom, 346; GDP
(1950), 346; invasion of Abyssinia,
7, 14, 483; motor industry, 380;
navy, 9; railways, 135, 136
ITT, 323

Jack, D. T., 214, 221
Jaguar Cars, 381–5
Japan: exports, 112, 270; GDP (1950),
346; industry, 41, 43, 507;
occupation of Manchuria, 5, 7,
14; productivity, 269;
shipbuilding, 227, 572; threat to
Australia and New Zealand, 6, 9,
10
Johnson, Robert, 220
Joint Intelligence Bureau, 36
Joint Planning Staff, 93
Jones, Mouat, 639
Jowett Javelin, 381

Kariba Dam, 118
Kaye, Emmanuel, 618
Keightley, Sir Charles, 493, 495
Kellogg Company, 375
Kelly, Sir David, 17, 22
Kennan, George, 1, 13, 17
Kenya: British forces, 102; Mau Mau,
101
Keynes, John Maynard, 1st Baron
Keynes, 34, 113, 117, 163, 175
Kilburn, Tom, 350
Kim Il Sung, 521
King George's Jubilee Trust, 473
King's Shipyard, Deptford, 259
Kodak, 352
Korean War: British forces, 31, 104,
273; economic effects, 75, 85, 104;
invasion of South Korea, 1, 3–4,
12, 106, 345; retreat, 28, 326, 420

Labour, Ministry of: Barker dispute,
188–9; Cammell Laird dispute,
219; conciliation pressures, 268;
defence programme, 48; ENV
dispute, 191–2; LMS dispute, 202;
productivity policy, 406; Regional
Industrial Relations Officer
(RIRO), 180, 188–9, 190, 207,

Index

209, 212–14; restrictive practices dossier, 422; strike charts, 201, 203; Timken bearings factory, 348; vocational training, 450

labour, skilled, 46, 47–8

Labour Government (1945–51): aircraft industry, 325–6; devaluation (1949), 188; education policy, 67, 142; exports, 203; foreign policy, 10–11, 85, 333; industrial investment policy, 138; industrial relations, 183, 240, 426; Korean War, 75; NRDC, 351, 404; productivity, 403–4; railways, 295; rearmament programme, 419; scientific policy, 308

Lancashire, cotton mills, 302, 303

Land Rover, 389

Lansing-Bagnall, 618

Laos, 106

LARC computer, 354

Lea-Francis, 380

Leader, SS, 218, 220–3

League of Nations: creation, 490, 506; Eden's position, 63, 483, 490–1; faith in, 321; Iraq mandate, 100; role, 7; Labour policy, 35

Leathers, Frederick James, 1st Viscount Leathers, 131, 141, 238

Lee, Frank, 166

Lemon, Sir Ernest, 281–2

Lemon Report, 281

Lend-Lease Act, 10, 11

Lennox-Boyd, Alan, 131–2

LEO (Lyons Electronic Office), 352–3

Leo Computers Ltd, 353

Leslie, S. C., 429

Leyland Motors, 189, 392

Liberal Government (1914), 4–5, 8

Libya, 90, 96, 102, 483, 486–7

Linjebuss, Sweden, 185

Liverpool: dockers, 241, 249, 251, 252, 254–5; shipbuilding, 219; strike (1911), 264; university, 315

living standards, 77, 181, 372

Lloyd, Selwyn: on aircraft investment, 339–40; on BOAC aircraft purchase, 337–8, 341; on British overseas role, 84; on Comet, 336, 338; defence programme, 112–17; military aircraft report, 330–4; Suez, 491, 502, 504

Lloyd George, David, 317

Lloyds of London, 139

Local Productivity Committees, 412, 414–15

Locarno Treaty, 7, 107

Location of Industry Informal Committee, 348

Lockheed Constellation, 325, 335

Lodge, Henry Cabot, 492

Lodge, Sir Oliver, 602

Loewy, Raymond, 376, 385

London, City of, 5, 139

London, Midland and Scottish Railway (LMS), 202

London Motor Show, 620

London School of Economics, 448

London Transport, 184, 296

London University: computer, 354; external degrees, 467; Imperial College, 330, 410; Queen Mary College, 319; University College, 318

Lord, Leonard, 386, 389

Loughborough College of Technology, 410

Lowery, H., 639

Lucas, Joseph, 194, 395

Luddism, 258

Lyons, J., Ltd, 351, 352–3

Lyons, Sir William, 381–5

productivity, 269, 279;
shipbuilding industry, 302; 'special
relationship', 21, 24, 58, 109–10,
488, 500, 502, 514–15; steel
industry, 283, 305–6, 316; Suez,
488, 492, 500, 502, 503–4; UN
resolution on China, 51; wages,
439; WWII, 507
United Steel Company, 271, 305
UNIVAC computer, 355
University Grants Committee
(Council): Conditional Aid
Programme, 407, 408, 410;
management education, 469–70;
role, 450; technology degrees,
472, 650
Urwick Report, 645
Urwin, Harry, 195

Valiant bomber, Vickers, 328, 329,
330–1, 485
Van Loo (dock strike organizer), 247
Vauxhall, 380, 386, 396
VC10, Vickers, 609
Venom fighter, Vickers, 331
Versailles Treaty, 7, 108, 506
Vespa scooters, 373
Vice-Chancellors, Committee of,
450, 456–7
Vickers: anti-aircraft guns, 321;
military aircraft, 330–1; Powers-
Samas takeover, 360: *see also*
individual aircraft
Vickers-Armstrong, 209, 212, 214,
223
Victor bomber, 330, 331
Victoria, Queen, 262
Victoria Park, dock strike meetings,
246, 249, 250
Vietminh, 105
Vietnam, 106
Viscount aircraft, Vickers, 328, 334,
340, 342

Volkswagen: after-sales service, 378;
factories, 179; industrial relations,
200; mass production, 379, 380,
389, 390; Microbus, 391;
production, 181–2, 388, 433;
reliability, 378
Volvo, 189, 191
von Neumann, John, 350
Vulcan bomber, 330, 331

wage levels: engineering industries,
228; full employment effects, 164;
Macmillan's policy, 434–40;
shipbuilding industry, 224, 227;
wage-price spiral, 421
Warman (strike-leader), 195–6, 197
Watermen, Lightermen, Tugmen and
Bargemen's Union, 241, 247, 249,
253
Watkinson, Harold, 630, 633
Watson, Thomas, 359
Watson, Thomas Jr., 364
Watson-Watt, Sir Robert, 307, 322
Weale, H. S., 199
Wedgwood, Josiah, 304, 311
Weeks, Sir Ronald, 360–1
Weir Committee, 468, 640
Weizmann, Chaim, 318
Wellington, Arthur Wellesley, Duke
of, 120, 513
West India Docks, 246
Western European Union (WEU),
111
Westinghouse, 319
Westland Aircraft, 189
White, William, 222–3
Whittle, Sir Frank, 307
Wilkes, Maurice, 350
Wilkinson, Ellen, 471–2, 474
Williams, Freddie, 350
Wilson, Harold, 52, 515
Wilson, Woodrow, 524
Wimpey, 484

Index